COMPUTERISED ACCOUNTING

USING MYOB® ACCOUNTRIGHT 2016.2

MELLIDA FROST
EUAN SUTHERLAND

COMPUTERISED ACCOUNTING

USING MYOB® ACCOUNTRIGHT 2016.2

MELLIDA FROST
EUAN SUTHERLAND

Computerised Accounting: Using MYOB AccountRight 2016.2
1st Edition
Mellida Frost
Euan Sutherland

Publishing manager: Dorothy Chiu
Publishing editor: Chee Ng
Developmental editor: Gregory Hazelwood
Senior project editor: Nathan Katz
Cover designer: Emilie Pfitzner
Text designer: Norma Van Rees
Editor: Judith Bamber
Proofreader: Jade Jakovcic
Indexer: Julie King
Permissions research: Miriam Allen
Art direction: Danielle Maccarone
Typeset by MPS Limited

Any URLs contained in this publication were checked for currency during the production process. Note, however, that the publisher cannot vouch for the ongoing currency of URLs.

Previous editions of this title published by Pearson Australia (a division of Pearson Australia Group Pty Ltd).

This first Cengage edition published in 2018.

Disclaimer:

This material is designed to provide general information on how to use MYOB® AccountRight 2016.2. The information provided may not apply to earlier or later versions of the program. This material is not designed to provide specific business, accounting or legal advice for particular circumstances. Business circumstances vary greatly, so before you rely on this material for any important matter for your business, you should make your own enquiries about whether the material is relevant, current, and sufficiently comprehensive. We recommend you seek your own professional advice in this regard. Legislation, regulations and tax rulings are complex and detailed, and are subject to change. Cengage Learning Australia Pty Ltd and the authors specifically disclaim any liability for any claim arising out of or in any way connected with access to, use of or reliance on these materials.

For product information and technology assistance,
in Australia call **1300 790 853**;
in New Zealand call **0800 449 725**

For permission to use material from this text or product, please email **aust.permissions@cengage.com**

National Library of Australia Cataloguing-in-Publication Data
Creator: Frost, Mellida, author.
Title: Computerised accounting : using MYOB accountright 2016.2 / Mellida Frost; Euan Sutherland.
ISBN: 9780170371650 (paperback)
Notes: Includes index.
Subjects: MYOB (Computer program) Accounting--Computer programs--Problems, exercises, etc. Small business--Accounting--Computer programs--Problems, exercises, etc.
Other Creators/Contributors: Sutherland, Euan, author.

Cengage Learning Australia
Level 7, 80 Dorcas Street
South Melbourne, Victoria Australia 3205

Cengage Learning New Zealand
Unit 4B Rosedale Office Park
331 Rosedale Road, Albany, North Shore 0632, NZ

For learning solutions, visit **cengage.com.au**

Printed in China by 1010 Printing International Limited.
1 2 3 4 5 6 7 21 20 19 18 17

BRIEF CONTENTS

CONTENTS

PART A

PART B

Contents

PART C

Guide to the text

As you read this text you will find a number of features in every chapter to enhance your study of Computerised Accounting and help you understand how the theory is applied in the real world.

CHAPTER OPENING FEATURES

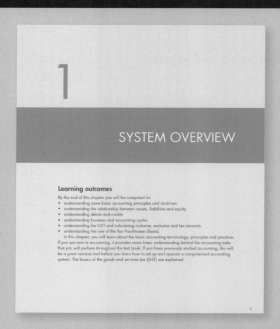

Identify the key concepts that the chapter will cover with the **Learning objectives** at the start of each chapter.

FEATURES WITHIN CHAPTERS

CLICK PATHS

Recipe-style **click paths** in bullet form are provided to help learners understand the logic behind every 'click' of a mouse, and connect with the MYOB software.

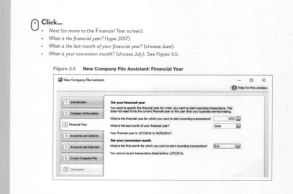

PRACTICE

Analyse simulated scenarios and perform practical tasks on MYOB AccountRight 2016.2 through formative **Practice** sections.

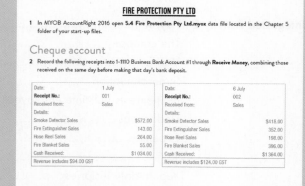

THIS IS WHY

Understand the reasoning behind why certain actions are performed with the **This is why** boxes

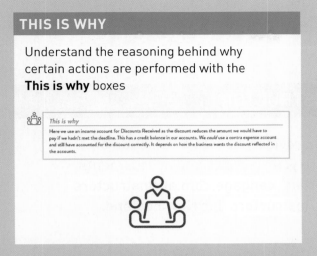

REMEMBER THIS

Remember This boxes highlight key ideas and concepts that are important to completing workbooks accurately.

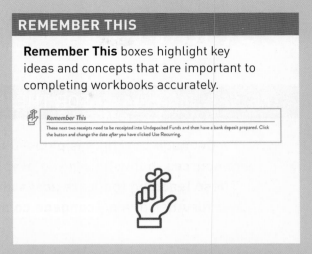

TIP

Tip boxes provide hints and shortcuts for working with MYOB software.

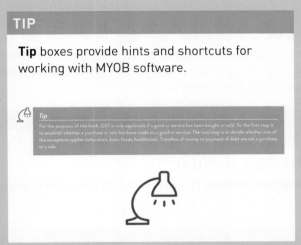

END-OF-CHAPTER FEATURES

The **Summary** section helps learners revise and recall key concepts learnt in the chapter.

The **Assessment** section provides opportunities for learners to test their knowledge and skills. Instructors may utilise the questions as assessment tools.

Guide to the online resources

FOR THE INSTRUCTOR

Cengage Learning is pleased to provide you with a selection of resources that will help you prepare your lessons and assessments. These teaching tools are accessible via cengage.com.au/instructors for Australia or cengage.co.nz/instructors for New Zealand.

INTERMEDIATE MAPPING GRID

The **Intermediate Mapping Grid** is a mapping document that shows how the content of this book relates to the **FNSACC406 Set up and operate a computerised accounting system** unit.

SOLUTIONS MANUAL

The **Solutions Manual** provides detailed solutions to every question in the text.

WORD-BASED TEST BANK

This bank of questions has been developed in conjunction with the text for creating quizzes, tests and exams for your students. Deliver these though your LMS and in your classroom.

POWERPOINT™ PRESENTATIONS

Use the chapter-by-chapter **PowerPoint** slides to enhance your lecture presentations and handouts by reinforcing the key principles of your subject.

ARTWORK FROM THE TEXT

Add the digital screenshot files into your course management system, use them in student handouts, or copy them into your lecture presentations.

FOR THE STUDENT

Visit http://www.cengagebrain.com to access the
Computerised Accounting companion website. You'll find:

CENGAGE**brain**

- MYOB start-up files
- A link to download AccountRight MYOB 2016.2 from the MYOB website.

Maximise your revision opportunities with the AccountRight MYOB 2016.2
Accounting Practice Set, available as a separate eBook.

ABOUT THE AUTHORS

Mellida Frost

Mellida has over 20 years' experience in account keeping; including preparing the payroll for over 200 employees, maintaining accounting systems and preparing monthly financial and management reports. The combination of high grades at University (including Commendations from the Board of Examiners) and varied practical accounting experience has resulted in a thorough understanding of the financial accounting process. She has completed her Masters of Professional Accounting and several advanced taxation courses through the Tax Institute.

Her flair for systemising and simplifying administrative and accounting processes has led to a successful boutique business, specialising in troubleshooting and teaching employees to streamline business processes. Her teaching responsibilities at Curtin University have included teaching MYOB, Quickbooks, MBA Global Accounting for Managers and Accounting Technologies, as well as preparing tests and administration. Mellida's ability to teach accounting subjects with zeal has led to student-voted faculty awards for teaching. She is a regular Tax Help volunteer and enjoys embroidery and growing carnivorous plants.

Euan Sutherland

Euan Sutherland combines his training in Accounting with his many years' experience in adult education in Australia and overseas. This has resulted in the careful structure of his textbooks, where basic concepts are explained, demonstrated, practised and learned in a realistic and logical manner.

Sutherland has been an accredited MYOB author for many years. His acclaimed publications demonstrate his expertise in accounting, MYOB Business Management Software and the principles of learning.

ACKNOWLEDGMENTS

The authors and Cengage would like to thank the following reviewers for their incisive and helpful feedback:

- Linda Lamb – Technical reviewer
- Antonia Wood – TAFE NSW, North Coast Institute (Macksville campus)
- Liz Sahin – TAFE NSW, Northern Sydney Institute
- Chris Fergus – TAFE NSW, Western Sydney Institute
- Brian Marshall – TAFE NSW, North Coast Institute
- Joe Bagnato – VECCI, CAE and Lonsdale Institute
- Richard Korn – TasTAFE
- John Davison – Nelson Marlborough Institute of Technology, New Zealand.

Cengage would also like to thank the MYOB team, particularly David Wilson and Justin Scholten for their support.

PREFACE

Welcome to the first edition of *Computerised Accounting, Using MYOB AccountRight 2016.2*. The text is fully aligned with the aims and content of the updated Vocational Education and Training packages.

Students will find the instructions and the exercises clear and easy to follow, while the skill-building approach adopted ensures that new material is introduced at a pace that keeps their interest alive. The exercises and multiple practice companies ensure students are exposed to different businesses. Some practice companies extend over several chapters in the book so that students will benefit from an ongoing scenario.

This book has been designed to build the participant's skills and confidence in their bookkeeping ability in ways that have been described as both interesting and practical. Some prior knowledge of bookkeeping and computers is presumed, however, everything else is explained in detail. Computerised bookkeeping is a skill. Skills are developed by practice.

MYOB software has been written with the average business owner in mind, assuming there is little accounting knowledge. The instructions and examples given in this book are equally valid for students using AccountRight Enterprise software and very similar to AccountRight desktop version. Having completed all the activities suggested in *Computerised Accounting, Using MYOB AccountRight 2016.2*, 1st edition, you will have confidence in your ability to handle the challenges of bookkeeping in a commercial environment, including preparation of the Business Activity Statement (BAS).

There is a dedicated website for students using this textbook, which is described in detail later.

Good luck with your study and your career.

Mellida Frost and Euan Sutherland

DOWNLOADING MYOB SOFTWARE

MYOB AccountRight can be downloaded from a link on the companion website and is to be used with the start-up files to complete the exercises. For ease of reference, the link is: http://download.myob.com/au/Compliance_2016-2/AccountRight/MYOB_AccountRight_Setup_2016.2.2.exe.

Using the start-up files

The start-up files are to be used in conjunction with the exercises for use on a PC (they do not work on a Mac). The start-up files are contained in folders that have the same names as the chapters where they will be used: Chapter 2, Chapter 3, etc. They must be downloaded from the website to your hard drive before they can be used. To do this you proceed as follows:

Click...

- MYOB Resources.
- *Start-up Files*. A new window opens.
- *Save File* and *OK*. All MYOB files are automatically saved to *Downloads* in a zip file on your C: Drive. Open Windows Explorer and ...
- Locate the folder called *all start up* with a type of Compressed (zipped) Folder. See Figure P1. Right-click on this folder to open a menu.

Figure P1   Windows Explorer: Compressed (zipped) folder

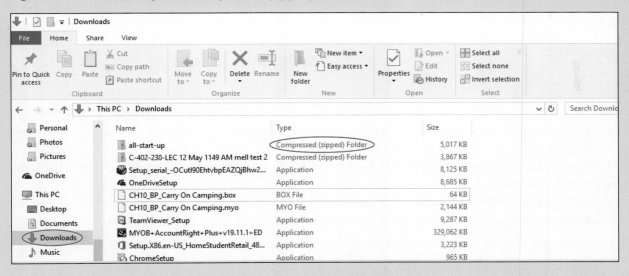

- Click on *Extract* All.
- Make note of where the folder is being saved or follow the instructions of your tutor, who may ask you to change your folder by clicking the *Browse* button. See Figure P2.
- Click *Extract*. A new folder called *all-start-up* will have been created containing the MYOB files for each chapter.

Figure P2   Extraction box

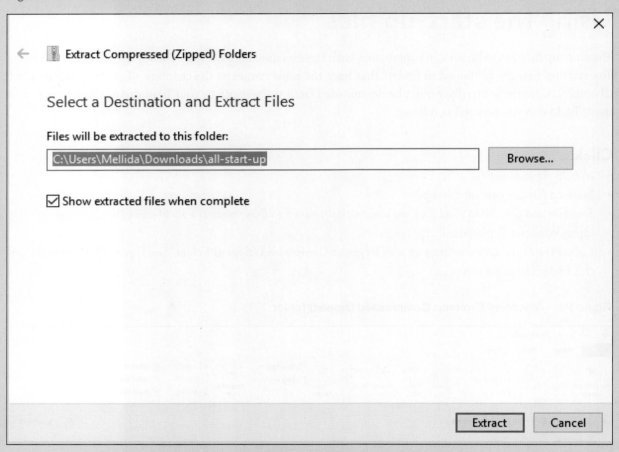

The next step may be very important as the downloaded files can sometimes be *read-only* (that is, they can't be changed in any way).

As MYOB changes your files with each transaction, this *read-only* property (if it is present) must be removed. To achieve this, each of the folders must be treated on its own. For example, in Chapter 3:

1 Double click Chapter 3 in your *start-up files* folder until you come across the list of MYOB files.

2 Select the top file with a mouse click.

3 Hold down the *Shift* key and click the last file. This selects all the files in the folder.

4 Right-click anywhere in your selection. A menu appears.

5 Click *Properties* from the options given. A dialogue box appears. See Figure P3.

6 Check *Read-only* in *Attributes*. If there is a tick there, remove it by clicking in the box.

7 Click *Apply* (if active), then *OK*. If there is no tick, just click *OK*. The files with the *Read-only* tick removed are ready for use by MYOB.

Figure P3   Properties dialogue box

8   Follow steps 2 and 3 again to select all the files.

9   Right click anywhere in the selection. A menu appears.

10 Click *Copy* from the options given.

11 Find the folder called *My AccountRight Files* under Documents/MYOB.

12 Right click on the file, then click *Paste*. All of the MYOB files are now available to be opened by the
    MYOB software.

    Exit Windows Explorer.

USING THIS BOOK

The directions in this book are designed to enable students to complete the activities in *Computerised Accounting, Using MYOB AccountRight 2016.2*, 1st edition, using the MYOB AccountRight Live accounting package:

- In the classroom with a minimum of teacher support, or

- At their own pace in a home environment.

  All the textbook exercises and scenarios have:

- start-up files supplied

- plain English directions

- suggested solutions to all exercises and scenarios.

The exercises in each chapter of the textbook are carefully graded, with each activity being slightly longer or slightly more complicated than the preceding one.

Each of the chapters has been addressed independently of the others and contains full instructions on the topic being covered. They can, therefore, be studied in any order.

1

SYSTEM OVERVIEW

Learning outcomes

By the end of this chapter you will be competent in:
- understanding some basic accounting principles and doctrines
- understanding the relationship between assets, liabilities and equity
- understanding debits and credits
- understanding business and accounting cycles
- understanding the GST and calculating inclusive, exclusive and tax amounts
- understanding the role of the Tax Practitioners Board.

In this chapter, you will learn about the basic accounting terminology, principles and practices. If you are new to accounting, it provides some basic understanding behind the accounting tasks that you will perform throughout the text book. If you have previously studied accounting, this will be a great revision tool before you learn how to set up and operate a computerised accounting system. The basics of the goods and services tax (GST) are explained.

Accounting basics

Accounting is the process of analysing, classifying, recording and summarising the financial transactions of an enterprise into journals and ledgers. From these journals and ledgers, the financial statements are prepared. The financial statements are then analysed and the results communicated to interested parties of the enterprise and regulatory bodies. By preparing financial statements, the management and stakeholders of the enterprise can make informed decisions about the future of the business.

Conventions

Fundamental accounting conventions set out the basic concepts that govern the way the accounting profession operates. They provide guides to procedures based on established custom and general acceptance in accounting. They set the standard for accounting practices.

The accounting entity convention stipulates that, for accounting purposes, the proprietor of an enterprise is always considered to be distinct and separate from the business itself. This applies regardless of what form of enterprise it is. Further, all transactions are recorded from the perspective of the enterprise. For example, if Mr Chen starts a small business with $50 000, then from the perspective of the business the $50 000 is a liability that the enterprise owes to Mr Chen. From Mr Chen's perspective, however, his investment in the business would be considered an asset. But Mr Chen might have innumerable other assets that have nothing to do with the current enterprise, so it can be seen that the only satisfactory way for an accountant to keep the financial records of the enterprise is on the understanding that the affairs of the accounting entity are separate from those of the proprietor.

The *monetary convention* makes the rather obvious stipulation that all transactions must be expressed in dollars and cents before they can be entered in an accounting record. In Australia, they would be recorded in Australian dollars and cents.

The *historical record* convention stipulates that the monetary values used in accounting should be derived only from actual events. Assets, expenses and liabilities are recorded at the actual amounts at which they have been incurred.

The *accounting period convention* assumes that accounting records will be segmented into fixed periods of time (month, quarter, year, etc.). It is particularly important with regard to the calculation of profit to know the length of time it took to generate that profit. For example, if the Mr Chen mentioned above showed a profit of $1000, he might be delighted if it took only a day to earn it, but less so if it took a year or longer.

The *going concern convention* assumes that the life of a business enterprise is expected to be ongoing: that continued existence rather than liquidation is the normal business process.

Doctrines

Accounting doctrines are policies that are not as widely accepted as the conventions described above.

The *doctrine of conservatism* can carry the idea of *playing safe* to extreme lengths, often by undervaluing assets, creating excessive provision for doubtful debts, or by charging the cost of the purchase of a fixed asset to an expense account (which will be written off against profits). Thus, conservatism can be seen to imply the creation of secret or undisclosed reserves, which is in direct conflict with the next doctrine.

The *doctrine of disclosure* is the general requirement that all accounting statements should be scrupulously honest, with full and complete disclosure of all pertinent information. *The Corporations Act 2001* in Australia provides some framework and regulation covering disclosure.

The *doctrine of consistency* requires that an enterprise keeps its accounting practices unchanged from one accounting period to the next so that accurate comparisons can be made. However, if changes must be made to take in changes in circumstances, then full disclosure in the accounts is appropriate.

The *doctrine of materiality* concerns the degree of detail and accuracy contained in financial reports and records. For example, it is usual for the published annual financial reports to contain only dollar amounts, with the cents omitted to make them easier to read; however, the actual accounts in the enterprise would be exact.

Assets, liabilities and proprietorship

Assets of an enterprise comprise all the properties possessed (e.g. cash, inventory, vehicles, etc.), plus money owed by debtors for goods or services, or for money loaned to others. Realisable assets can be defined as all property that can be used to discharge liabilities.

Liabilities are amounts owing to creditors for goods or services received or for money borrowed. Usually they are claims by others against the business as a whole rather than against a particular asset.

Proprietorship (or equity) is the excess of assets over liabilities and represents the interest of the owners in the enterprise.

The *accounting equation* is an explanation of the relationship between assets, liabilities and proprietorship:

$$\text{e.g. Assets} = \text{Liabilities} + \text{Proprietorship}$$
$$\text{or Liabilities} = \text{Assets} - \text{Proprietorship}$$
$$\text{or Proprietorship (and thus Net Assets)} = \text{Assets} - \text{Liabilities}$$

It will be understood from the above that any increase in assets without a corresponding increase in liabilities (by prudent management or good fortune) must represent an increase in proprietorship, while an increase in liabilities without a corresponding increase in assets (by poor management or ill fortune) must represent a decrease in proprietorship.

Debits and credits are the terms used in accounting to determine the column in the ledger that should receive an entry and are abbreviated *Dr* and *Cr*.

The rules covering the recording of increases and decreases in assets and liabilities are:

- *Debit* increases assets and decreases liabilities.
- *Credit* increases liabilities and decreases assets.

Double-entry accounting is the term used to describe the system of accounting that uses debits and credits to record transactions. It is based on the belief that each transaction has a twofold effect, and by recording the debit effect in one account and the credit effect in another account an accurate and complete record is achieved. It follows that the total of the debit entries and the total of the credit entries must be equal, since each transaction gives rise to equal debits and credits.

A *trial balance* is a check on the arithmetical accuracy of the ledger, and is a listing of all the accounts and their balances. If debit account balances are put in one column and credit account balances in another, the sum total of each column should be equal. If all the balances are put in the same column, and credit balances subtracted from debit ones, the result should be zero.

To get a clearer understanding of debits and credits, look at the following business transactions and the accounts affected. (GST will be ignored at this stage.)

Example:

1　Bob's Car Hire purchased a new motor vehicle on credit for $32 000.
  - The accounts affected are the Motor Vehicle and Creditors (purchased on credit). The Motor Vehicle account (an asset to the enterprise) will increase by $32 000 and will be debited. The Creditors account (a liability to the enterprise) will also increase by $32 000 and will be credited.
2　John Brown invested an additional $10 000 capital into his business.
  - The accounts affected are Bank and Capital. The Bank account (an asset to the enterprise) will increase by $10 000 and will be debited. The Capital account of John Brown (recorded under proprietorship) will also increase by $10 000 and will be credited.

3 Bob's Car Hire paid $5000 off a Creditor's account.
 - The accounts affected are Bank and Creditors. The Bank account (an asset to the enterprise) will decrease by $5000 and so will be credited (a reduction to an asset). The Creditor's account will decrease by $5000 and will be debited (a reduction to a liability).

Remember This

The principle of accounting states that for every debit entry there is a corresponding credit entry of an equal amount.

Business and accounting cycles

The *business* or *operating cycle* relates to the repetitive nature of business activity, and can be illustrated thus:

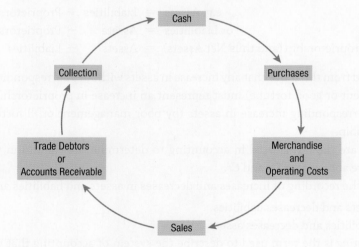

It will be the aim of management to keep the time taken to complete the operating cycle as short as possible so that funds are turning over quickly and profits are accumulating.

The *accounting cycle* relates to the sequence of accounting events that take place in an accounting period, and can be illustrated thus:

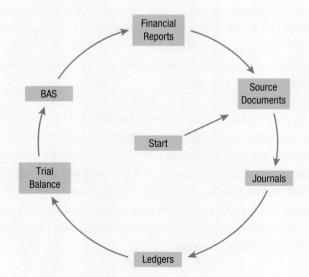

All business transactions are recorded on source documents (invoices, adjustment notes, cash receipts, cheque butts, etc.) at the time of the transaction. At a convenient time, the information is transferred to journals and then to ledgers, followed by a trial balance. An integrated computer accounting system records the transactions and immediately creates journal and ledger entries, making it possible for financial reports to be produced at any time.

Business classifications

Regulatory authorities, such as the Australian Securities and Investments Commission (ASIC http://asic.gov.au) and the Australian Taxation Office (ATO https://www.ato.gov.au), have set definitions in relation to the sizes of business enterprises, setting their financial reporting requirements. As a bookkeeper or accountant you must comply with government and other regulatory bodies. To ensure you are up to date with current requirements you should refer to the websites of these regulatory bodies, as requirements can change over time.

The reporting requirements of the enterprise will depend on how the enterprise is classified.

ASIC defines a business as a small business if they satisfy two of the following three criteria:

- an annual revenue of less than $25 million
- fewer than 50 employees at the end of the financial year
- consolidated gross assets of less than $12.5 million at the end of the financial year.

The ATO defines a small business as one that has annual turnover (excluding GST) of less than $2 million. A small business can elect to use either the cash or accrual method of accounting and to report and pay their GST annually.

Enterprises with an annual turnover of less than $20 million can elect to report and pay their GST quarterly.

ASIC defines a business as a large business if they satisfy two of the following three criteria:

- an annual revenue of $25 million or more
- controls 50 or more employees at the end of the financial year
- consolidated gross assets is $12.5 million or more at the end of the financial year.

The ATO defines a large business (for the purpose of market segmentation) as being an enterprise or group with an annual turnover or $20 million or more. Such enterprises must report to the ATO on a monthly basis (electronically).

Income tax basics

The income tax rate for all Australian companies was 30% for many years. This rate was reduced to 28.5% for small business entities only (companies with less than a $2 million aggregated turnover) for income years starting on or after 1 July 2015. *Income tax* is calculated on the 'profit' of the business. Profit is calculated as the total value of revenue (before GST) less the value of expenses for the period (before GST). If the total of the revenue exceeds the total expenses, then a profit is deemed to have been made. If the total of the expenses exceeds the revenue then a loss is deemed to have been made. The Statement of Income (Profit & Loss Statement) will identify the value of any profit or loss for the period.

Calculating income tax goes beyond the scope of this text and will not be discussed any further.

GST basics

The goods and services tax (GST) is a system of taxation where the tax amount is added to the final sales price being paid by the customer for most commercial transactions in Australia. So, effectively, the business collects the tax on top of its usual sales and remits it to the Australian Taxation Office (ATO).

Since its introduction in July 2000, the amount of the GST for most transactions has been set at 10%, a low figure by international standards. Although the Commonwealth is responsible for the collection of the tax (through the ATO), all the monies collected go to the states to finance their ongoing expenditure. However, not all the tax collected in each state is returned to that state; rather, the money is pooled by the ATO and then sent to the states according to a formula agreed upon prior to the introduction of the GST, with some states getting more than was collected and others less. Predictably, this causes some friction between states, with those receiving less than they contribute feeling hard done by.

The standard GST rate can be changed only by unanimous agreement between all the state governments and the Commonwealth.

The operation of the GST proceeds along the following lines:

- Each business operating in Australia with an annual turnover of $75 000 or more is required to register with the ATO to collect the GST. A business with an annual turnover of less than $75 000 or a non-profit body with a turnover of less than $150 000 has the option of registering or not, as they see fit.
- Registering is simply a matter of contacting the ATO (via their website, or other means) and completing a form detailing their business information. The advantage (for the business) of being registered is that it can then claim back from the ATO all of the GST it pays in operating the business. The main disadvantage lies in the time lost in collecting, recording, reporting and remitting GST collected to the ATO.
- Cancellation of GST registration can occur by applying to the ATO using the relevant form if the business ceases operation in its current form or if the enterprise is no longer required to be registered (because the annual turnover falls below the threshold for compulsory registration).
- Having registered to collect the GST, retailers add the 10% tax to the normal sales price of their goods. The price displayed to customers must include the GST. Each sale that includes GST is accompanied by a tax invoice that documents the sale and the amount of tax that is included.
- Suppliers of services (rather than goods) often quote a GST-exclusive figure, then add the tax at the foot of the tax invoice.
- GST collected from customers (also known as clients, patients or passengers depending on the enterprise) is collected and banked along with other receipts in the normal course of business.
- Business expenses (purchases of goods to be resold and operating costs) often contain a GST element. Known by the ATO as *input tax credits*, this GST paid is subject to refund from the ATO.
- Each business keeps a record of the tax invoices it receives (and pays), and of the tax invoices it issues (and receives payment for).
- The Business Activity Statement (BAS) is the method by which a business calculates and reports the amount of GST it is liable to remit to the ATO (or the size of any refund). This is covered in Chapters 14 and 15.
- Most registered businesses complete their activity statement each quarter, either electronically or on a customised paper form. The form is received from the ATO towards the end of each quarter and the enterprise has until the 21st (or 28th) of the following month to return the form (and payment).
- Enterprises are required to have evidence of all the transactions (above $75) they report, but no evidence is submitted accompanying the BAS. The ATO uses statistics from similar enterprises to provide a benchmark to help in identifying unusual activities for possible further investigation or audit.

Most, but not all, sales and other income (also known as supply) is subject to the GST, and the legislation provides for three main classifications:

- *Taxable*: GST is collected on sales and other income, and GST paid out in relation to the income can be reclaimed as input tax credits. This section covers most goods and services, including prepared food, confectionery, snacks, many bakery products, ice cream and biscuit goods.

- *GST-free*: This is a limited section covering most basic food for human consumption, including fresh fruit and vegetables, meat, eggs, bread, cheese, milk, tea and coffee. Also GST-free is the supply of education (but not textbooks) and health and accommodation for the aged. GST paid (for example in paying for freight inwards on GST-free items, or for electricity) in the supply of items in this section *can* be claimed as input tax credits.
- *Input-taxed*: The significance of this classification is that while no GST is added to the sales price, no GST paid out can be claimed as input tax credits. The supply of domestic rental accommodation is an example here, where the landlord does not charge GST to the tenant, and cannot claim input tax credits for any costs involved.

The GST is a *consumer* tax so ultimately is paid by the end user of the product. A GST-registered business will pay the GST on a supplier invoice, then claim the GST portion back as a credit.

> ### Tip
>
> For the purposes of this book, GST is only applicable if a good or service has been bought or sold. So the first step is to establish whether a purchase or sale has been made on a good or service. The next step is to decide whether one of the exceptions applies (education, basic foods, healthcare). Transfers of money or payment of debt are *not* a purchase or a sale.

GST Collected is the liability account where the GST portion of the invoice is posted. This will be given to the ATO and does not form any part of the profit and loss.

GST Paid is the contra liability account where the GST paid to suppliers is posted. It effectively reduces the amount of GST that needs to be forwarded to the ATO.

Let's be very clear on this: GST collected is *never* income belonging to the business. If a business owner complains about how much GST they have to pay to the ATO, gently remind them that it was never actually their money in the first place. The business has collected it *from* the customer for the sole purpose of passing it on to the ATO.

Calculating GST

There are some terms that you need to become familiar with regarding the GST:

- *GST Exclusive* is the price *before* GST is added on. This is the amount that belongs to the business.
- *GST Inclusive* is the price with the GST already *included*.

For instance, a GST-registered business wants to sell a product for $100. It is required to add on the 10% GST by the ATO, so it has to charge its customers $110. See Figure 1.1.

Figure 1.1   GST example

$100.00	GST Exclusive	Income
$10.00	GST	Liability
$110.00	GST Inclusive	Bank or Accounts Receivable

Figure 1.2 shows some quick formulas that will help you calculate the different components of the GST.

Figure 1.2   GST formulas

Calculate From	To	Equation	Example
GST Inclusive	GST Exclusive	GST Inclusive/1.1	$110/1.1 = 100$
GST Exclusive	GST Inclusive	GST Exclusive $\times$ 1.1	$100 \times 1.1 = 110$
GST Inclusive	GST Component	GST Inclusive/11	$110/11 = 10$
GST Exclusive	GST Component	GST Exclusive $\times$ 0.1	$100 \times 0.1 = 10$

MYOB will do the calculations for you, of course, but it is useful to understand what the totals should be for when you check your invoices.

Tax Practitioners Board

The *Tax Agent Services Act 2009* established the Tax Practitioners Board (TPB) to provide for the registration of tax agents and BAS agents. The aim is to:

- ensure that agents maintain appropriate skills and knowledge
- investigate complaints against agents
- ensure that unregistered agents do not purport to be registered agents.

BAS agents are governed in the same way as tax agents, but are only able to provide a limited range of services relating to the taxation laws relevant to provision of BAS services.

A Code of Professional Conduct for tax agents and BAS agents has been enshrined in legislation, and passing the 'Fit and Proper Person' test is an important registration requirement. In deciding whether an individual is a fit and proper person, the TPB has regard to whether:

- the individual is of good fame, integrity and character
- one of the following events has occurred to the individual in the last five years:
  - convicted of a serious taxation offence
  - convicted of an offence involving fraud or dishonesty
  - penalised for being a promoter of a tax exploitation scheme
  - penalised for implementing a scheme that has been promoted on the basis of conformity with a product ruling in a way that is materially different from that described in the product ruling
  - became an undischarged bankrupt or go into external administration
  - sentenced to a term of imprisonment.
- the individual had the status of an undischarged bankrupt in the last five years
- the individual served a term of imprisonment, in whole or in part, at any time during the previous five years.

The TPB has the power to impose penalties for breach of the code that vary from a caution, through suspension or termination of registration, to action in the Federal Court.

Registration requirements for a BAS agent include 'Relevant Experience', which means work by the individual:

- as a tax agent or BAS agent registered under the new law
- as a tax agent registered under the old law
- under the supervision and control of a BAS agent or a tax agent registered under the new law
- under the supervision and control of a tax agent under the old law
- of another kind approved by the board in the course of which the individual's work has included substantial involvement in one or more types of BAS services. (This means more than just being involved from time to time in the provision of BAS services.)

Application for registration as a BAS agent can be done online at http://www.tpb.gov.au where full information concerning all aspects of the TPB is available.

Summary

◆ Accounting is the process of analysing, classifying, recording and summarising financial transactions to ultimately produce financial statements for stakeholders.

◆ For accounting purposes, the business is considered completely separate from its proprietor or owner.

◆ Assets are owned by the business and include cash, accounts receivable and fixed assets such as equipment and motor vehicles.

◆ Liabilities are owed by the business and include credit cards, loans and accounts payable.

◆ The difference between the assets and liabilities is known as equity and is the owners stake in the company.

◆ Goods and services tax (GST) is currently 10% and is basically charged on any goods or services provided or used by a GST-registered entity (with some exceptions).

◆ An enterprise must register for GST if its annual turnover surpasses the threshold (currently $75 000 for businesses and $150 000 for non-profit bodies).

◆ GST-free means the good or service has been specifically excluded from being subject to GST through legislation. This includes basic foods, education and healthcare services.

◆ GST is a consumer tax and so is ultimately paid by the end user.

Assessments

Activity (debits and credits)

From the following unrelated transactions, you are required to analyse the information, identify and classify the accounts affected, determine if the account affected has increased or decreased and whether the account would be debited or credited. (Ignore any GST.)

Transaction	Accounts affected	Increased or decreased	Debit or credit
Example: Proprietor introduced $25 000 cash as capital on commencement of business.	Asset Equity	Increased Increased	Debit Credit
The enterprise purchased an item of machinery from Toshiba Ltd for $28 000 cash.			
The enterprise purchased stock/inventory worth $500 on credit.			
The enterprise took out a loan from the ABC bank for $120 000.			

Activity (calculating GST)

Using the equations in Figure 1.2.

Calculate...	Formula	Answer
Example: ...the tax component of a GST inclusive invoice of $121.00.	GST Inclusive/11	121/11 = $11.00
...the GST Exclusive component of a $145.20 GST Inclusive invoice.		
...the GST inclusive amount of a $80.50 GST Exclusive invoice.		
...the tax component on a $84.70 GST Inclusive invoice.		

2

INTRODUCTION TO MYOB

Learning outcomes

By the end of this chapter you will be competent in:
- working your way around the modules
- understanding the top menu bar
- backing up a company file
- restoring a company file from a backup
- importing and exporting information to and from text files.

This will be only a brief introduction to the MYOB software, as each subsequent chapter will teach you a separate module. This chapter walks you through how to open, close, backup and restore a company file, as well as navigating various tool bars. We learn how to change preferences and access the sample company Clearwater.

MYOB overview

MYOB has specifically been written so that business owners with little or no bookkeeping experience could still perform the basic functions, such as creating invoices and receiving payments from customers. In most cases, transactions are easy to edit, so if the business owner makes a mistake a bookkeeper or accountant can fix it.

There are several different versions of MYOB, targeted to different business needs. Small businesses who don't need payroll or sophisticated inventory management can use AccountRight Basics. If your business needs slightly more advanced inventory management, then AccountRight Standard might be a better option. If your business has slightly more advanced needs or needs to pay employees, AccountRight Plus and AccountRight Premiere would be suitable.

Your instructor will provide you with a link to download MYOB or perhaps you will be using a computer which already has the software set up. The four different versions of MYOB can all be accessed using the one software. There is also the option of upgrading to a higher level version as circumstances change.

Like the Microsoft suite of products (such as Word and Excel) you need to create a file first, which can then be opened, updated and closed repeatedly. The file extension or suffix for this file is .myox.

With Word or Excel, you can open the documents from anywhere on your computer or from a USB drive. However, with MYOB, you can only access these .myox files when they are in the folder specifically created by the MYOB software. The pathway is:

Documents/MYOB/MyAccountRight Files. You can create subfolders in this file if you wish.

Dashboard

To open MYOB, click on the MYOB shortcut on the Desktop. See Figure 2.1.

Figure 2.1   MYOB AccountRight program shortcut

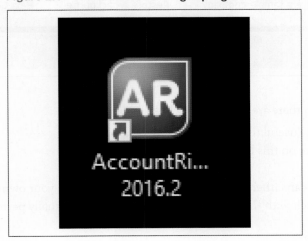

This opens a Dashboard (Figure 2.2) with a variety of options, all of which are quite self-explanatory:

- *Open a company file*: opens an existing MYOB company file to be updated or reviewed.
- *Create a company file*: the initial set-up of the company file is done here through an interview process.
- *Upgrade a company file*: upgrades the company file from a previous version of MYOB.

Figure 2.2   **MYOB Dashboard**

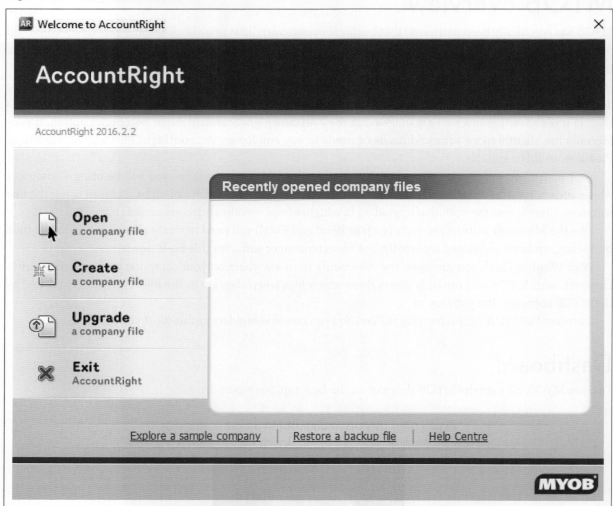

At the base of the screen there are the following links:

- *Explore a sample company* (useful to practise in)
- *Restore a backup file* (more on this later in this chapter)
- *Help Centre*.

From this point on, you can either follow the instructions through on your own MYOB or read this chapter – this is to familiarise yourself with the software, so you don't need to actually perform these tasks.

Click...

- *Explore a Sample Company* (in the Dashboard).
- + button next to 2016.2.
- *Clearwater_Plus_AU.myox* See **Figure 2.3**.
- *Open*. The sign-on screen appears. You don't need to enter a password.
- *OK*. The MYOB Command Centre opens. See **Figure 2.4**.

Figure 2.3   **MYOB Library Browser**

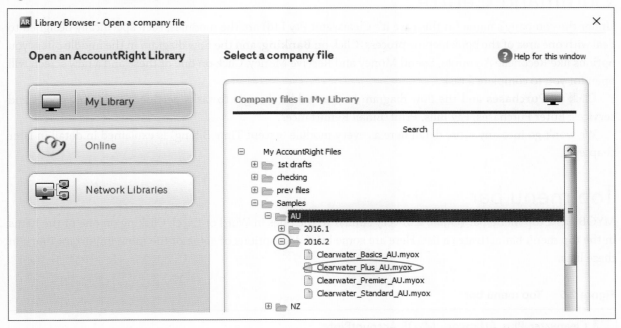

Figure 2.4   **MYOB Command Centre**

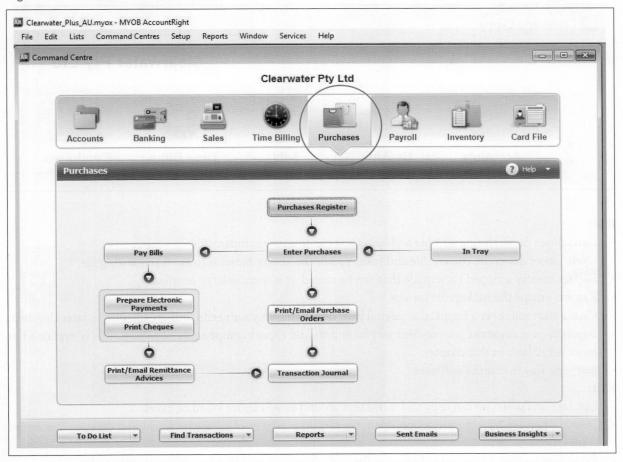

Command Centre

Under the company's name (in this case it's Clearwater Pty Ltd) are the modules, each specifically designed to deal with one area of the bookkeeping process. Click on **Banking**, and the flow diagram in the middle offers you options like Reconcile Accounts, Spend Money and Receive Money. Click on one of these and a new screen will open for you to complete a task.

Click on **Purchases** and the flow diagram in the middle changes to tasks pertinent to buying goods and services: Enter Purchases, Pay Bills, Print/Email Remittances.

We won't go into any more detail here as every module (except Time Billing) is explained in detail in later chapters.

Top menu bar

MYOB has a top menu bar (Figure 2.5) very similar to the ones in Word or Excel. Clicking on one of the items in the top menu bar activates a list. Here are some brief descriptions of some of the more important items in these lists.

Figure 2.5   Top menu bar

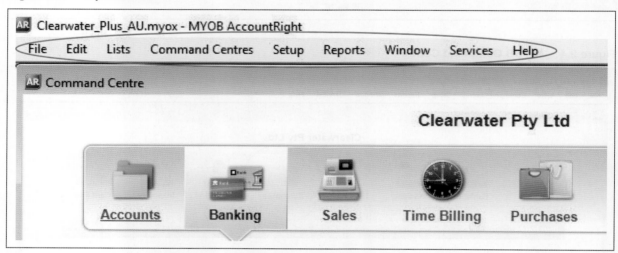

File:
- *New*: closes down the current file and helps you create a new company file.
- *Open*: closes down the current file and takes you to the library browser to open an existing file.
- *Backup*: creates a zipped backup file that can be stored on a thumbnail or emailed.
- *Restore*: unzips the backup file for use.
- *Close a Year*: rolls over a financial or payroll year, depending on your needs. This is explained in later chapters.
- *Import/Export Assistant*: an excellent way to import and export components of MYOB. This is explained in more detail later in this chapter.
- *Exit*: one way to exit the software.

Edit:
- *Cut, copy and paste*: we can copy and move text around as we can for Word or Excel.
- *Delete*: when we have a transaction open, we can do a variety of deletions (including deleting the entire transaction).
- *Recap Transaction*: a great way of viewing the underlying journals that go with your transaction.

Lists:
- *Jobs*: a great way of tracking which income and expenses belong to a particular project. The setup can be done here.
- *Recurring Transactions*: where to find, edit and delete any recurring transactions (explained in Chapter 5).

Setup:
- *Easy Setup Assistant*: helps us set up our important modules such as purchases, sales and payroll.
- *Balances*: opening balances for a variety of ledgers.
- *Linked Accounts*: automatically links certain fields to specified general ledger accounts. These are explained in more detail in later chapters.
- *User Access*: where you can designate who can access which parts of MYOB. For instance, an accounts clerk probably wouldn't have access to the sensitive payroll information.
- *Preferences*: a further way of customising your company file to your needs. Explained in more detail later this chapter.
- *Customise Forms*: to personalise your forms such as purchase orders and sales invoices with your logo, other fields or text.
- *Company Information*: details about your company, which can be edited.
- *Load Tax Tables*: to check which tax tables you have loaded for your payroll.

Reports:
- One of the ways to access to your Reports Index. The other way is to click Reports at the bottom of the screen.

Window:
- The bottom portion of this menu will show you all the windows that you have open. This is especially useful as you may accidentally open up, for instance, several Spend Money windows and one may get hidden behind the other. See Figure 2.6. Click on the window you wish to bring to the front of the screen.

Help:
- This has a variety of help options. You need to be connected to the Internet.

Figure 2.6   **Top menu bar: Window**

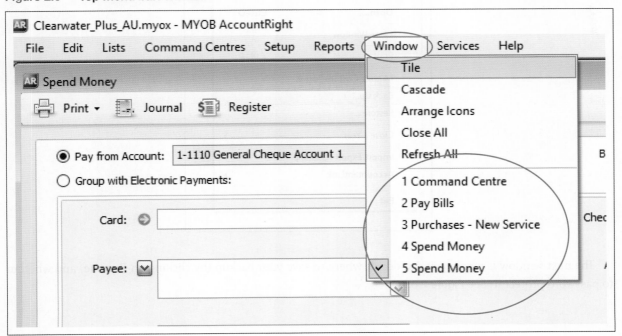

Backup

Backing up company files is very important in business. Even the most reliable computer system cannot guarantee everlasting trouble-free operation. While not of great use in the student environment, where start-up files and short exercises are the norm, regular backup of company data is a normal activity in the commercial world.

In order to safeguard company information, it is recommended that the backup copies are kept in a location away from the computer. The time spent in making backups pales to insignificance when compared to the time that would be required to enter lost data in the event of a computer malfunction. In business, backups should be completed on a regular basis, and stored off site. Most companies will run a backup at the end of each day. Some companies will set the backup to run automatically at around midnight each night and check that it ran successfully first thing the following morning. In this day and age, the backups can be stored in the cloud rather than running the backup to a disk or drive and physically storing this off site.

MYOB will give several warnings about making a backup of the company data prior to starting a new financial year and prior to starting a new payroll year.

Click...

- *File* (in the top menu bar).
- *Back Up*. See Figure 2.7. If you get a message asking you to close all your windows first, click *OK* then *Window* (in the top menu bar) to find and close all your windows.
- *Next*. Read the warning screen.
- *OK*.

Figure 2.7   **File menu: Back Up**

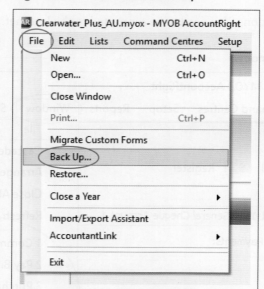

The next window is where you can decide where to save your backup (by clicking on **Browse**) and whether to password protect it. See Figure 2.8.

Figure 2.8   Back Up

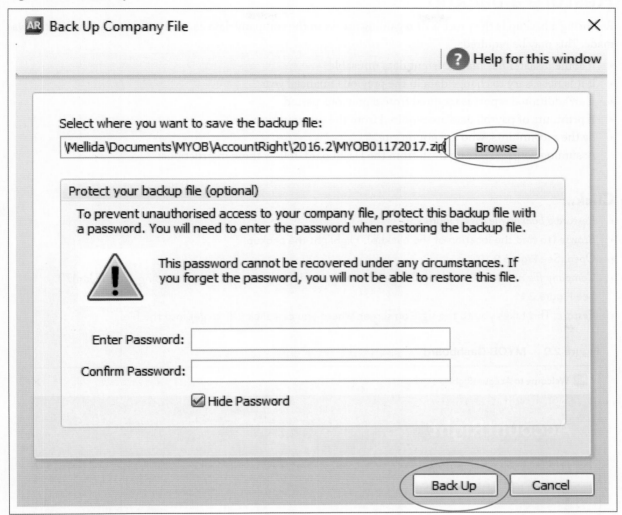

The naming protocol of backups may be stipulated by the company or business you are employed by. MYOB's naming protocol in the screenshot – MYOB01172017.zip – consists of MYOB (the program), 01172017 (the date the backup was made, in this case 17 January 2017), and .zip (the file extension, a compressed file backup). As I have many clients (a couple of whom I might see on the same day) I will add a meaningful suffix after the date, such as DC or PXRFS.

Once you have chosen where to save the file and the naming protocol, click **Back Up** at the base of the screen.

Once the backup has run, you will be taken back to the Command Centre. MYOB often prompts you to make a backup before exiting the company file.

Tip

If the backup file isn't too big, you can email it to the business owner. That way the backup will be easily accessible. If you use Dropbox or one of the other free online storage facilities, remember to password-protect the backup.

Restore a backup

Restoring a backup is the process of regaining access to the company data as it was at the time the backup was made. This may be required:

- if some disaster has made current data unusable
- if it is necessary to change data in the previous financial year
- if an additional report is required from a previous period
- if printouts of payroll data are required from the previous year
- by the accountants, who are not on site.
  Assuming you are starting fresh from the Dashboard, follow these instructions:

Click...

- *Restore a backup file.* See **Figure 2.9.**
- *Browse* (to find the location of the backup). Highlight the backup.
- *Open.* See **Figure 2.10.**
- *Company file name* (choose something different from the original – perhaps including 'from17Jan17'). See **Figure 2.11.**
- *Restore.* This takes you to the sign-on screen where you can click OK to get into the file.

Figure 2.9   MYOB Dashboard

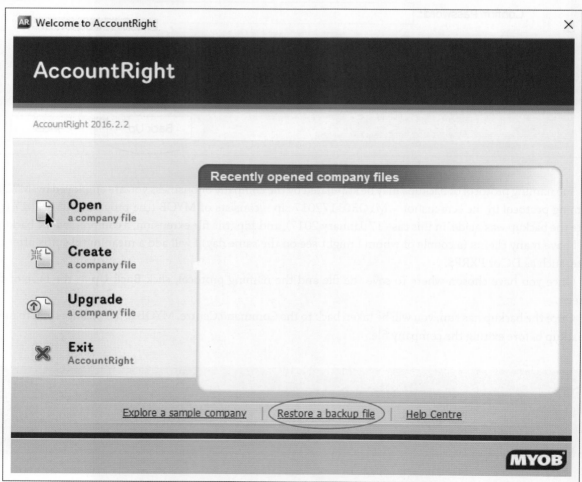

Figure 2.10   **Restoring file screens**

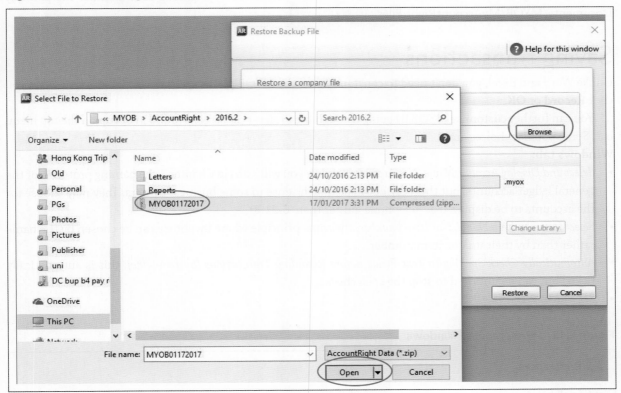

Figure 2.11   **Final restoring file screen**

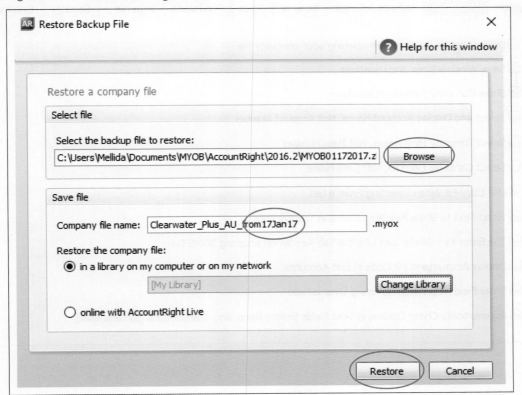

Alternatively, you can restore it to another subfolder in your library: as long as it is under the pathway Documents/MYOB/MyAccountRight Files.

Saving transactions

Unlike Word and Excel, you don't need to constantly save the MYOB file, as each transaction is saved when you click **Record** or **OK**.

You can further customise MYOB by going through the Preferences screens found in **Setup** on the top menu bar. Some popular choices are:

Windows tab:

- *Select and Display Account Name, Not Account Number*: you will learn in Chapter 3 the naming protocols of the general ledger accounts, but this may not make much sense to some business owners. They may choose for the accounts to be displayed as 'telephone' rather than '6-2190'
- *Select Items by Item Name, Not Item Number*: the same principle where inventory can be chosen by the name rather than by their unique item number.
- *Automatically Check Spelling In Text Fields Before Recording Transactions [System-wide]*: this is automatically ticked but can be unticked to stop the spell checks.
- See Figure 2.12.

Figure 2.12   **Preferences: Windows**

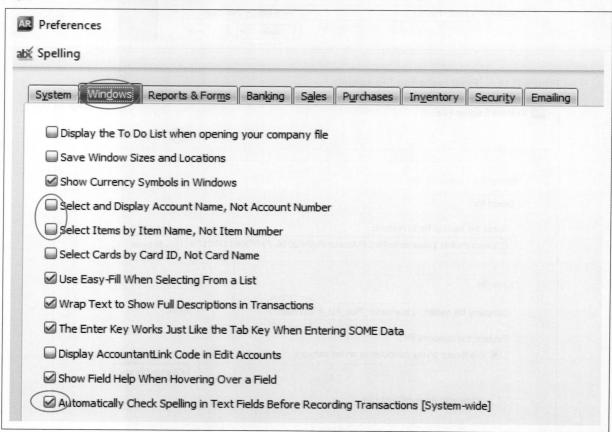

Sales Tab:

- *Automatically Print Sales When They Are Recorded*: useful if you print a copy for your own records or if you send invoices through the post.
- *Delete Quotes upon Changing to and Recording as an Order or Invoice*: helps get rid of superfluous records in the Sales Register.
- *If Credit Limit is Exceeded on Sale Warn And Continue*: this helps the sales clerk or cashier know if a customer has overshot their credit limit.
- See Figure 2.13.

Figure 2.13   Preferences: Sales

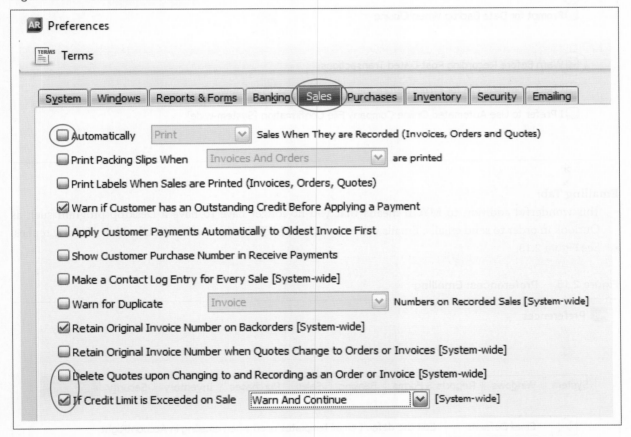

Security Tab:

- *Transactions CAN'T be Changed; They Must be Reversed [System-wide]*: this is a common feature to ensure that bogus invoices cannot be entered and then deleted. This feature is most commonly turned off because this would prevent simple edits being made if the business owner has made a mistake.
- *Lock Periods: Disallow Entries Prior to . . .*: this feature is commonly used once a financial year has been completed by the accountant so that no transactions can accidentally be processed in the previous financial year.
- *Warn Before Recording Post-Dated Transactions*: a handy feature to ensure that transactions aren't processed with a forward date. It is just a warning so if you actually *do* intend the transaction to have a date later than today's date, you can just override it.
- See Figure 2.14.

Figure 2.14   Preferences: Security

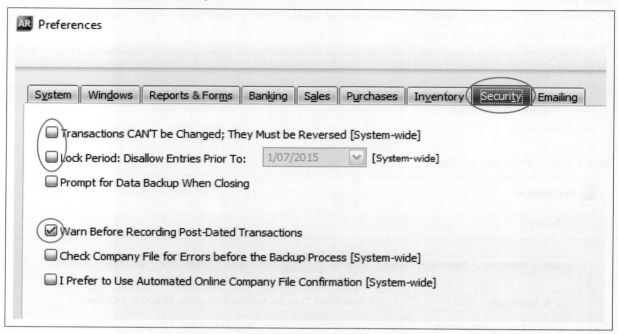

Emailing Tab:
- This wonderful addition to MYOB means that you no longer have to have a Desktop program such as Outlook in order to send emails. Emails will be sent from MYOB with a return email address for any replies.
- See Figure 2.15.

Figure 2.15   Preferences: Emailing

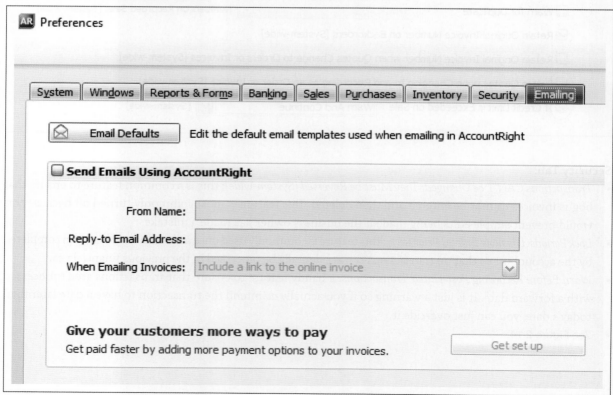

Exporting and importing data

A popular way of moving data from one software package to another is exporting and importing the data. The sort of data that can be exported and imported includes accounts, customer/supplier/employee cards, sale/purchase/payment/receipt transactions.

It can get a bit technical, so this demonstration only shows an export of supplier from a MYOB data file and the subsequent import into a different MYOB file. You are *not* expected to do any of this in the rest of the book.

If you need more instruction than this, go to the Help Centre for videos and step-by-step instructions.

Click...

- *File* (in the menu bar line).
- *Import/Export Assistant*. See Figure 2.16.
- *Export Data* (in the Data Type screen).
- *Next*.
- *Export* (select *Cards*).
- *Select Cards type* (select *Supplier Cards*). See Figure 2.17.
- *Next*.
- *Format* (leave Tabs selected).
- *Next*.

Figure 2.16   **File: Import/Export Assistant**

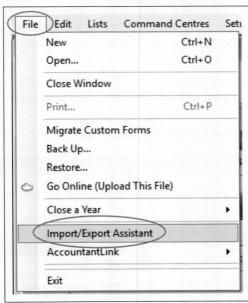

Figure 2.17   **Import and Export Assistant: Data Type**

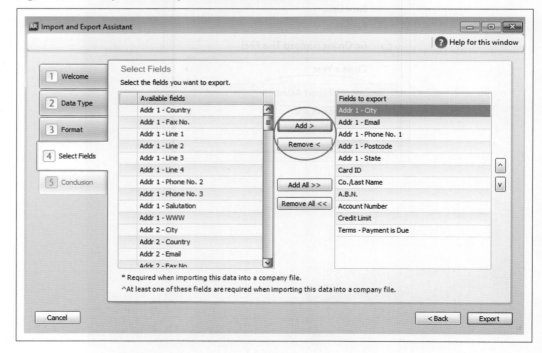

The **Select Fields** screen is where you would choose all of the fields you wish to export. The list of **Available fields** on the left side is in alphabetical order so you may need to scroll up and down to find the fields you wish to export. Once you have located a field, highlight it by clicking on it then click the **Add** button in the centre. It will be moved to the list on the right.

If you accidentally tick a field you don't want, highlight it on the list on the right side then click the **Remove** button in the centre. It doesn't matter what order the list is in. See **Figure 2.18**.

Figure 2.18   **Import and Export Assistant: Select Fields**

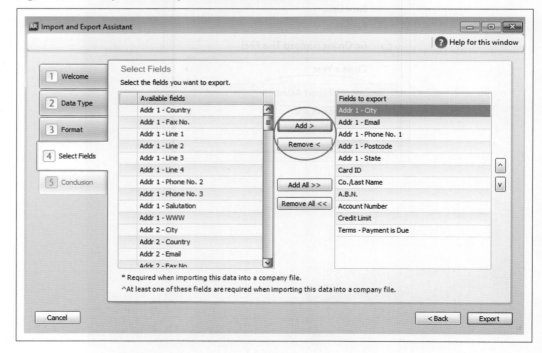

Click...

- *Export* (choose a place to save the file so you can retrieve it later).
- *Close.*
- *Open* the MYOB file you wish to Import into.
- *File* (in the top menu line).
- *Import/Export Assistant.*
- *Import data* (in the Welcome screen).
- *Import* (select *Cards*).
- *Browse* (find the place where the list was exported – in this case it will be a text file called Suppliers). See **Figure** 2.19.
- *Next.* Read the Format screen. There are some extra importing options including what to do with 'excess' data. We won't make any changes to the fields. See Figure 2.20.

Figure 2.19   Import File Type

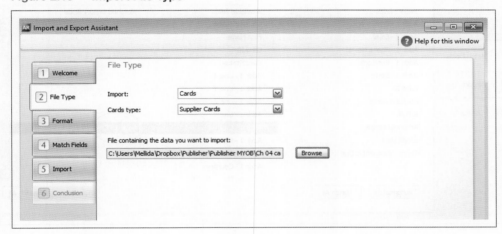

As you can see, the Import and Export screens look very similar. In this import function we need to link the fields in the left list called **Import Fields** to the fields in the list on the right. Again, the order doesn't matter as long as you match the fields correctly to each other.

Figure 2.20   Import Format screen

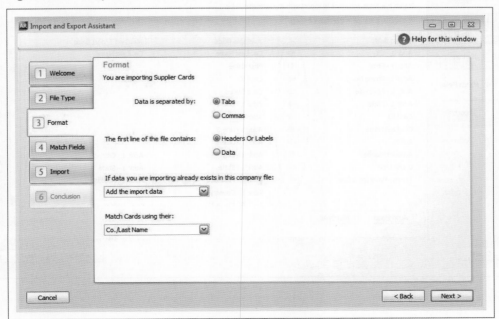

Click...

- *Next*. We are now in the Match Fields screen.
- the field you wish to link in the left list (to highlight it).
- the field you wish to link it to in the right list. See Figure 2.21. to scroll up and down the list, working your way through it and ensuring you link to the appropriate accounts. See Figure 2.22.
- *Next*.
- *Import*. The message will explain to you what has been imported and how to solve any errors.

Figure 2.21   **Import function: Match Fields**

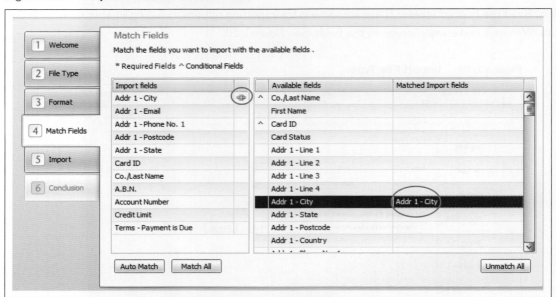

Figure 2.22   **Import function: Match Fields completed**

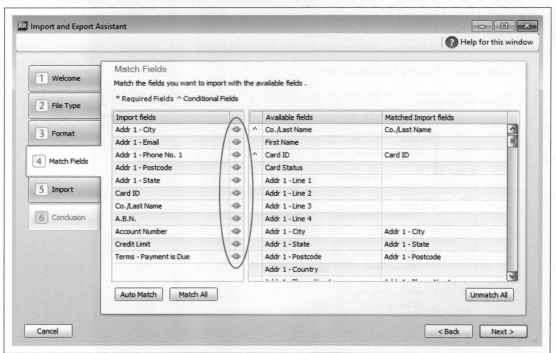

Summary

◆ MYOB is written for business owners with little or no bookkeeping experience.
◆ MYOB can only be opened if the company file is in a designated folder under Documents/MYOB/ AccountRight Files.
◆ Each module has a different flow diagram specific to that range of tasks.
◆ It is important to backup the company file regularly and remove the backup from site.
◆ The business can further customise MYOB through the Preferences in the Setup to reflect the business preferences.
◆ Data can be imported and exported using an Import/Export Assistant.

3

CREATING A NEW COMPANY FILE

Learning outcomes

By the end of this chapter you will be competent in:

• accessing MYOB
• creating and activating a new company file
• understanding the chart of accounts
• adding, editing and deleting accounts
• entering account opening balances.

Setting up a company file in MYOB is relatively straight forward if you have some basic information. MYOB has been specifically written for non-accountants and uses an interview system to help guide the user through the setup process. Opening balances are generally produced by an accountant, but once it has all been set up in MYOB the business owner can often perform many of the bookkeeping functions.

Company file setup

Before being able to create a new data file, you will need to have some details on hand about the company. The details required to create the file (and cannot be changed) include:

- the version of MYOB you have purchased/will be using
- a valid serial number (provided when the package was purchased)
- the company name (other company details can be added or changed later)
- the current financial year for the data (the year for the year end, e.g. year ending June 2018 would be shown as 2018) including the last month of the financial year
- the conversion month (the month that you will start entering information for; e.g. if you changed your system over in October 2017 and plan to enter opening balances from 30 September 2017, your conversion month will be October)
- if you intend to use a pre-existing MYOB chart of accounts list, you will need to know what industry your company is in so that the relevant accounts will be added to your file.

1 Double click the shortcut to the MYOB program on your Desktop (Figure 3.1) to create a new company file or to access a data file that has already been set up.

Figure 3.1   **MYOB AccountRight program shortcut**

The Welcome screen opens. If company files had already been set up, they would be opened from this screen by clicking Open. However, as we are setting up a company file we need to click **Create** (Figure 3.2).

Figure 3.2   **MYOB AccountRight welcome screen**

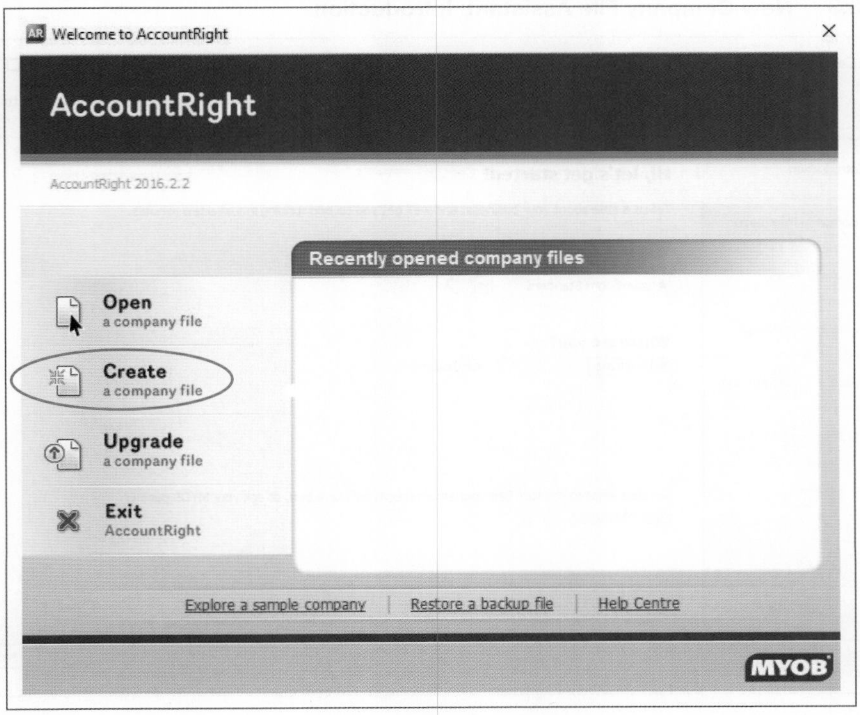

COZY DRY CLEANERS PTY LTD

2 Create a new company file.

The following demonstration walks you through MYOB's interview system (called the New Company File Assistant).

> **Cozy Dry Cleaners Pty Ltd**
> Cozy Corner Beach
> Albany WA 6330
> ABN 62 266 506 622
>
> **Phone:** 0413 202 020
> **Email:** cozycleaners@bigpond.com
> **Financial Year:** 2017
> **Last Month of Financial Year:** June
> **Conversion Month:** July
> **Industry Classification:** Service
> **Type of Business:** Dry cleaners

Click...

- *Which AccountRight are you using?* (choose *AccountRight Standard*).
- *Where are you?* (choose *Australia*). See Figure 3.3.
- *Serial Number* (insert one if you have been given one, otherwise leave blank).
- *Company Name* (type *Cozy Dry Cleaners Pty Ltd* – and add your student ID; this is so you can locate your own report when printed out with the other students).
- *ABN* (insert the company's ABN, as provided above, without the spaces). Press the Tab key and the spaces insert automatically.
- *Address* (type in the company address, as provided above). Press *Enter* to get to the next line of the address.
- *Phone Number* (type the phone number, as provided above).
- *Email Address* (type in the address, as provided above). Compare with Figure 3.4.

Figure 3.3   New Company File Assistant: Introduction

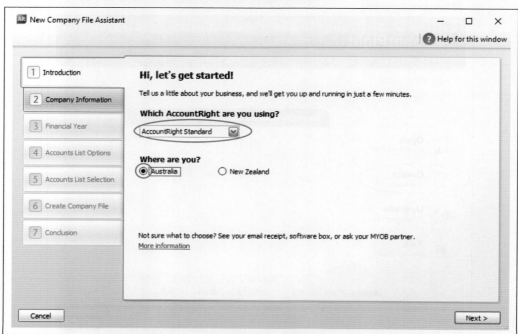

Figure 3.4　**New Company File Assistant: Company Information**

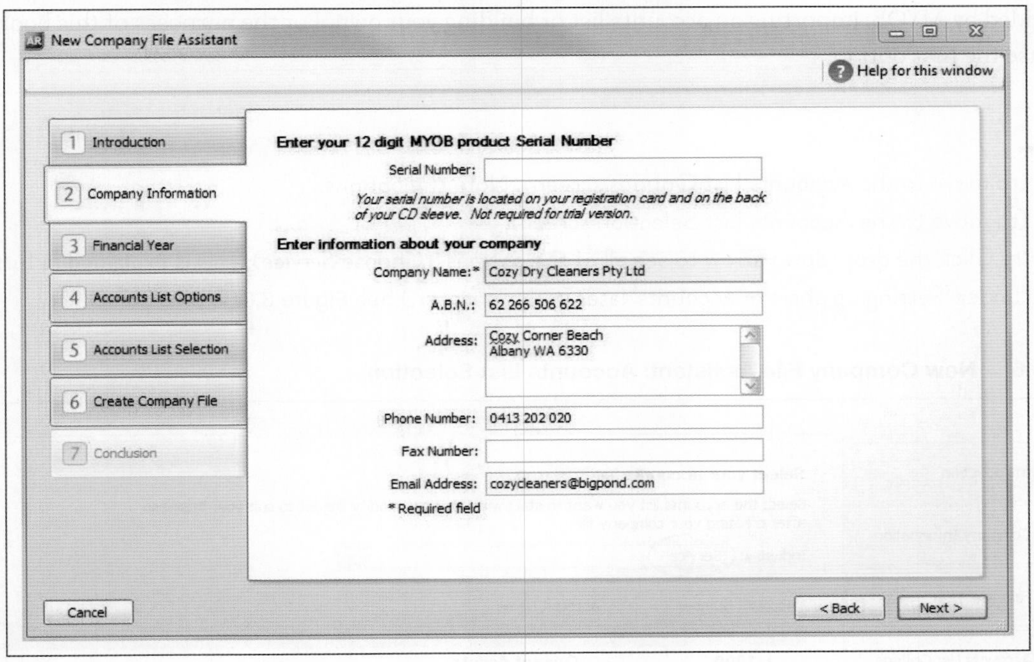

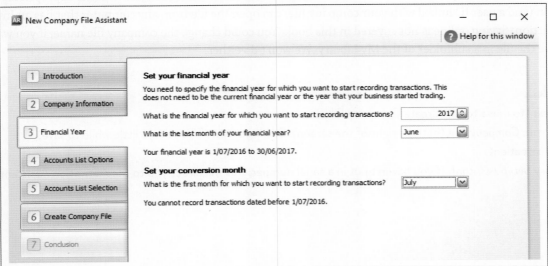

Next we need to set up the financial year. Be careful with the conversion month! This is the first month in which you can record your transactions. Choose the wrong month and it may not work in with your opening balances (explained later in this chapter). None of this information can be changed after the company file has been created.

Click...

- *Next* (to move to the Financial Year screen).
- *What is the financial year?* (type *2017*).
- *What is the last month of your financial year?* (choose *June*).
- *What is your conversion month?* (choose *July*). See Figure 3.5.

Figure 3.5　**New Company File Assistant: Financial Year**

The next step involves setting up the accounts list. You have a choice here of starting with a chart of accounts list provided by MYOB, importing an accounts list or building your own. For the purposes of this book, we will always use the first option.

Click...

- *Next* (to move to the Accounts List Options screen). Note the options.
- *Next* (to move to the Accounts List Selection screen).
- *Industry* Click the drop-down arrow to see all of the options. (Choose *Service*). This is explained in further detail under 'Setting up chart of accounts' later in this chapter.) See Figure 3.6.

Figure 3.6   New Company File Assistant: Accounts List Selection

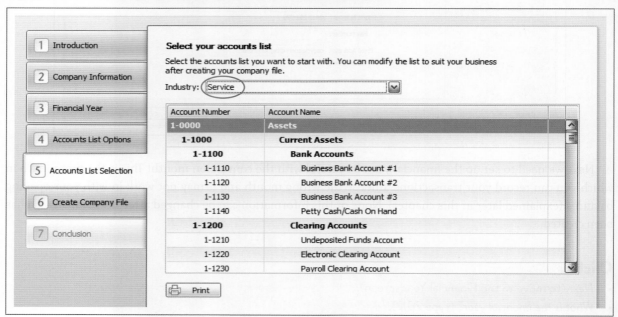

The final step is to save your company file. All company files saved locally are saved into a file located in your Documents folder. This means that only the people who have access to your computer can access the company file. MYOB also gives you the alternative to save your file online, meaning anyone with the appropriate MYOB version (and a user ID linked with your company file) can open the file from any computer that has an Internet connection. Saving online is not covered in this book. You could change the company file name, if you wanted, or save the file in a subfolder of the My Library. We won't do either.

Click...

- *Next* (to move to the Create Company File screen).
- *Create Company File* (bottom right of the screen). See Figure 3.7. This takes a little while to save, so be patient.
- *Easy Setup Assistant*. If you haven't put in a serial number, this will direct you to the Activation Assistant.

Figure 3.7   **New Company File Assistant: Create Company File**

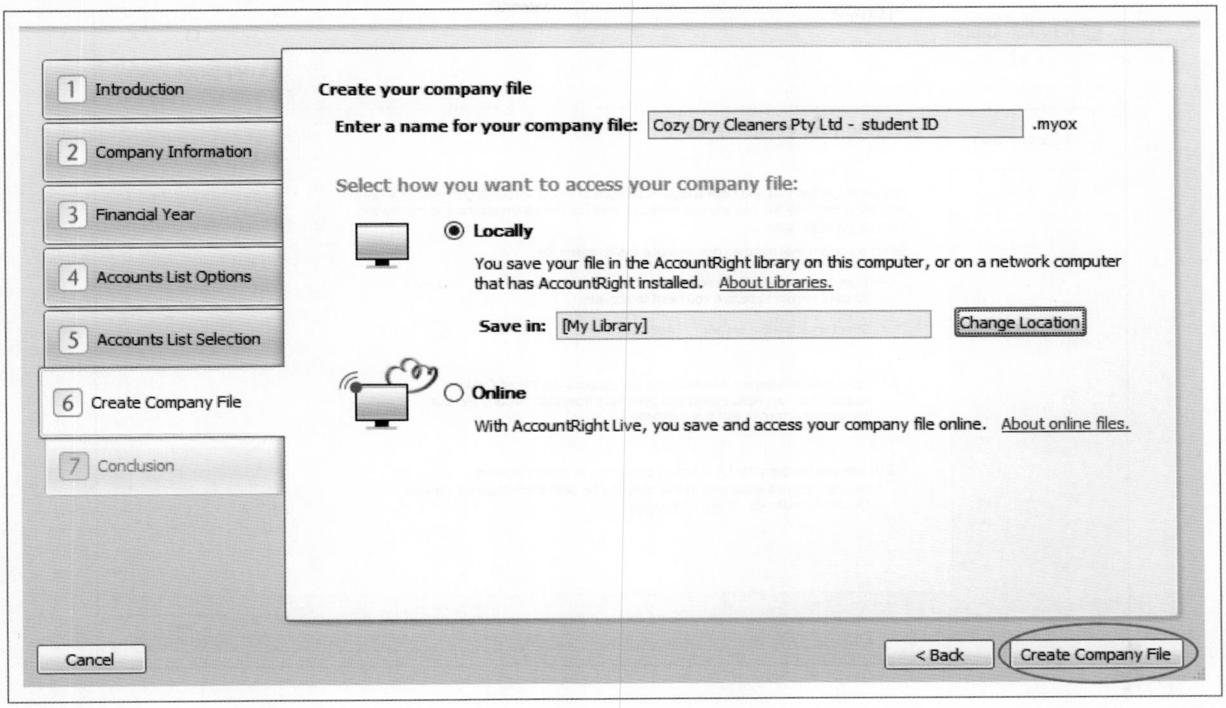

The Activation Assistant has three options, as shown in **Figure 3.8**:

- *I use this company file to record and edit my business transactions.* The first two choices in the drop-down menu (Activate Online or Activate by Phone) require you to have the serial number for your purchased MYOB software. You can choose the third option, Activate Later, if you are setting up a company file for a trial or if you (or your client) intend to purchase the software soon.
- *I only need to view my information in this company file.* This can be used if you only require read-only access, such as if you are going back to old financial years for information.
- *I use the company file for practice, evaluation or study purposes.* This provides a 30-day trial, which may be used so that you (or you client) can evaluate whether MYOB works for you. This is the option that we will be using throughout the book.

Click...

- *I use this company file for practice, evaluation or study purposes* (third option) or follow your instructor's instructions. Compare with Figure 3.8.
- *Next.* Read the warning screen.
- *OK.*

Figure 3.8   **MYOB Activation Assistant**

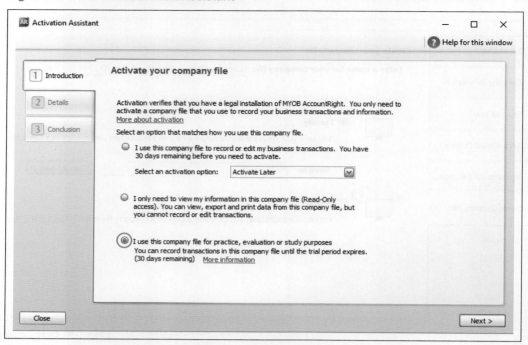

Nice work! You have set up your first company file.

Setting up chart of accounts

Easy Setup Assistant

The Easy Setup Assistant screen should be open. If not, click on **Setup** in the top menu bar and then click on **Easy Setup Assistant**. We will be setting up the Accounts. See Figure 3.9.

Figure 3.9   **Easy Setup Assistant**

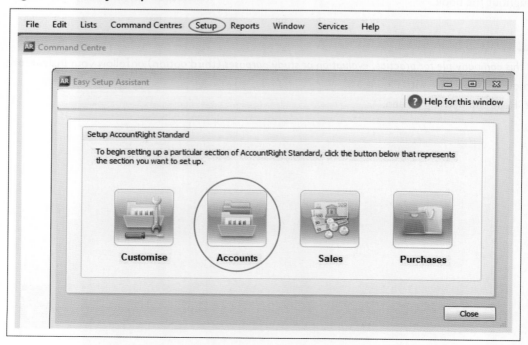

Read the Introduction screen and then click **Next** to get to the Accounts List screen. The five major classifications of general ledger accounts that make up the financial reports have been broken into eight groups, each beginning with a specific prefix. (The basic account groups and their prefixes are shown in Figure 3.11.) MYOB also has two basic levels of accounts:

- *Detail* accounts are the accounts that can have transactions posted against them.
- *Header* accounts (which are in bold) demarcate the detail accounts and help put them into useful groups.

So, for example, if you scroll down to 1-2200 Office Equipment (a bolded header account), you will see that the two detail accounts are in normal writing and indented. Office Equipment At Cost accounts and Accum. Depr. Office Equipment accounts are grouped together by the header account and indented. See Figure 3.10.

Figure 3.10   **Office Equipment header and detail accounts**

⊙	**1-2200**	**Office Equipment**
⊙	1-2210	Office Equipment At Cost
⊙	1-2220	Accum. Depr. Office Equipment

Figure 3.11   **MYOB account list examples**

Prefix	Basic Type	Header	Detail Example
1	Asset	Bank Accounts	1-1110 Business bank account #1 1-1120 Business bank account #2
		Other Current Assets	1-1310 Trade Debtors
		Non-Current Assets	Assets at cost and Accumulated depreciation such as 1-2110 Furniture at Cost 1-2120 Accum. Depr. Furniture
2	Liabilities	Current Liabilities	2-1110 Visa #1 2-1210 GST Collected 2-1220 GST Paid
		Non-Current Liabilities	2-2100 Business Loan # 1
3	Equity	Equity	3-1000 Owners/shareholders Capital
4	Income	Income	4-1000 Services Income
5	Cost of Sales	Cost of Sales	5-1000 Purchases
6	Expenses	Expenses	6-1300 Bank Fees 6-1900 legal Fees
7			Unavailable to users – this account subset is used by the MYOB program in the background when processing closing journals
8	Other Income	Other Income	8-1000 Interest Income
9	Other Expense	Other Expense	9-1000 Interest Expense

We have been given an opening trial balance for Cozy Dry Cleaners Pty Ltd (see Figure 3.12), so we need to:

1 adjust the MYOB chart of accounts to mirror the trial balance
2 add, edit and delete accounts as instructed
3 enter opening account balances.

Figure 3.12   **Cozy Dry Cleaners Pty Ltd Trial Balance**

Cozy Dry Cleaners Pty Ltd
Trial Balance
as at 30/06/20CY

Account No.	Account Name	Debit	Credit
1-1110	Cheque Account	30 900.00	
1-1310	Accounts Receivable	110.00	
1-1320	Inventory	2 500.00	
1-2110	Furniture at cost	10 000.00	
1-2120	Accum. Depr. Furniture		600.00
1-2210	Office Equipment at cost	3 600.00	
1-2220	Accum. Depr. Office Equipment		200.00
1-2410	Motor Vehicles at cost	8 000.00	
1-2420	Accum. Depr. Motor Vehicles		1 200.00
1-2510	Plant & Equip at cost	30 000.00	
1-2520	Accum. Depr. Plant & Equip		1 000.00
2-1510	Accounts Payable		283.80
2-2100	Business Loan #1		42 000.00
3-1000	Laurel Healey Capital		44 000.00
3-2000	Laurel Healey Drawings	4 173.80	
	TOTALS	**89 283.80**	**89 283.80**

You will notice the four buttons at the bottom of the Accounts List screen: **New**, **Edit**, **Delete** and **Import**. See Figure 3.13.

Figure 3.13   **Accounts list modification buttons**

Editing accounts

The first account in the trial balance is 1-1110 Cheque Account, but the corresponding account in MYOB AccountRight is 1-1110 Business Bank Account #1. So, we need to edit the MYOB account to fit with our trial balance.

Click...

- *1-1110* once to highlight it.
- *Edit*. This opens the general ledger account card.
- *Account Name* (delete the words in there and type *Cheque Account*). Compare with Figure 3.14. Note this is a detail account.
- *Details* tab at the top of the screen. The tax code is N-T and is correct.
- *OK*.

Figure 3.14   **Editing a general ledger account**

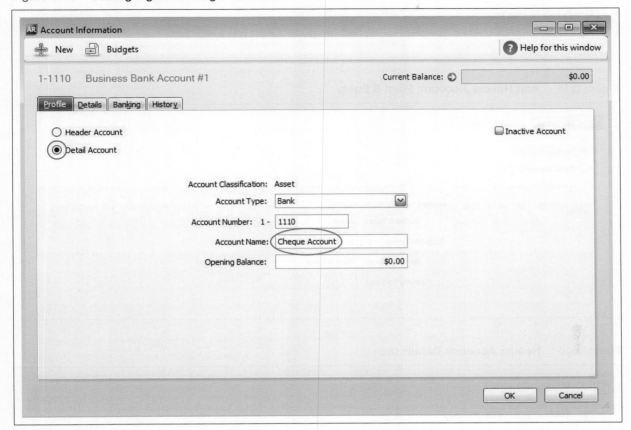

Edit the following accounts:

Account No.	New Account Name	Tax Code
1-1310	Accounts Receivable	N-T
2-1510	Accounts Payable	N-T
3-1000	Laurel Healey Capital	N-T
3-2000	Laurel Healey Drawings	N-T
4-1000	Dry Cleaning Income	GST
4-2000	Shirt Laundering Income	GST
6-6000	Motor Vehicle Expense (*change to a detail account*)	GST

Adding accounts

We don't have the Plant & Equip account codes in our MYOB file. They can be added as follows:

Click...

- *New* button (in the Accounts List screen) at the bottom of the screen.
- *Header Account* (top left of the screen).
- *Account Type* (choose *Asset*).
- *Account Number* (type *2600*). Press the Tab key to move to the next field.

- *Account Name* (type *Plant & Equip*). See Figure 3.15.
- *Details* tab at the top.
- *When Reporting, Generate a Subtotal for This Section* (make sure it is ticked). See Figure 3.16.
- *OK*.

Figure 3.15   **Add Header Account: Plant & Equip**

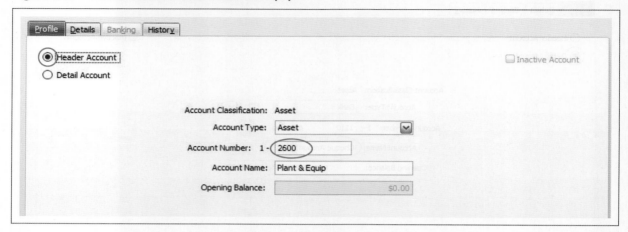

Figure 3.16   **Header Account: Details tab**

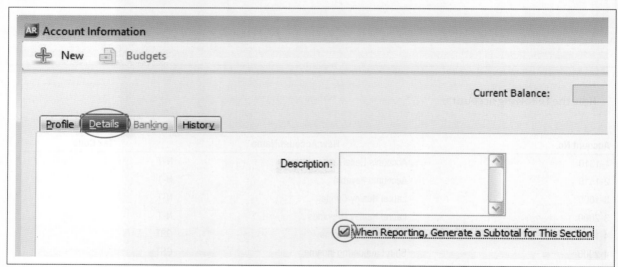

Add some more accounts. They are all *Detail* accounts.

Account Type	Account No.	Account Name	Tax Code
Fixed Asset	1-2610	Plant & Equip at cost	CAP
Fixed Asset	1-2620	Accum. Depr. Plant & Equip	N-T
Income	4-2500	Fur & Leather Cleaning Income	GST
Income	4-9000	Discounts Received	GST
Cost of Sales	5-1000	Supply Purchases	GST
Cost of Sales	5-9000	Discounts Given	GST

Remember This

Check the tax codes in the Details tab as you go.

Deleting accounts

There are a lot of extra accounts, but deleting all the extra accounts would take a long time, so we will just delete a few.

Click...

- *6-6100 Motor Vehicle Registration* (in the Accounts List screen) to highlight it.
- *Delete* (button at the bottom of the screen). See Figure 3.17.

Figure 3.17 **Deleting accounts**

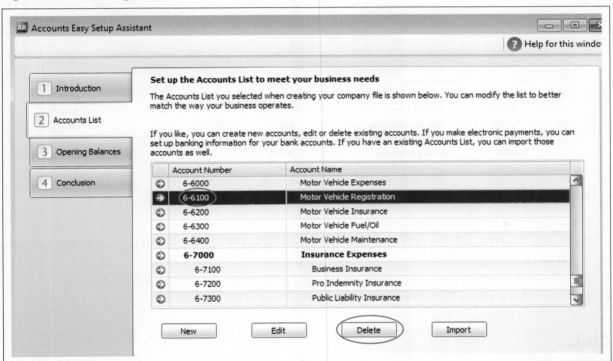

Also delete the following accounts:

Account No.	Account Name
1-1130	Business Bank Account #3
2-1140	Visa #2
6-6200	Motor Vehicle Insurance
6-6300	Motor Vehicle Fuel/Oil

There are several other general ledger accounts we need to delete but it can be annoying having to scroll down to the account, so we will use an alternative deletion method.

Click...

- *Cancel* (bottom left hand side) to return to the Command Centre. Close or minimise the Easy Setup Assistant.
- *Accounts* module.
- *Accounts List*. See Figure 3.18.

Figure 3.18   **Accounts module: Accounts List**

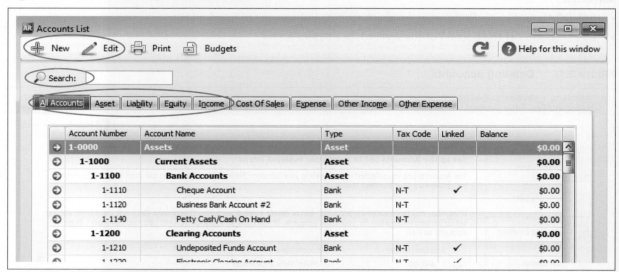

You can see that in the Accounts List:

- There are several tabs near the top (All accounts, Asset, Liability etc) that separate the general ledger accounts into their categories.
- At the top left there are icons for adding new accounts and editing accounts (as well as searching).
- The right column shows the balance of the accounts (all zero at the moment).

Click...

- *Expense* tab.
- *Search* field (type *motor*). A list appears of all expenses with the word motor in it. See Figure 3.19.
- *Zoom arrow* next to Motor Vehicle Maintenance. This opens the card.
- *Edit* on the top menu bar.
- *Delete Account*. See Figure 3.20.

Figure 3.19   Accounts List: Search in Expense tab

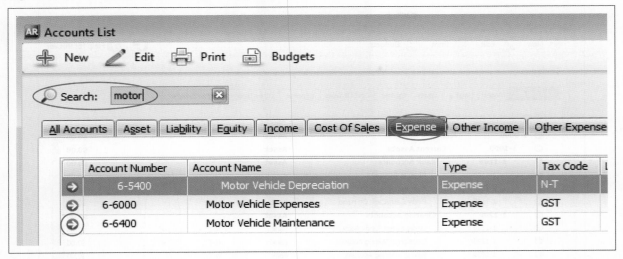

Figure 3.20   Accounts List: deleting an account

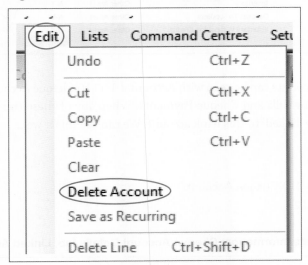

Delete the following accounts by typing **insurance** in the Search field:

Account No.	Account Name
6-7100	Business Insurance
6-7200	Pro Indemnity Insurance
6-7300	Public Liability Insurance

Linked accounts

Click on the **All Accounts** tab and delete the writing from the Search field. You will notice that some accounts in the account list show a tick in the column labelled Linked. See **Figure 3.21**. Accounts with this tick are 'linked' to services or transactions.

Figure 3.21 **Accounts List: All Accounts tab, linked accounts**

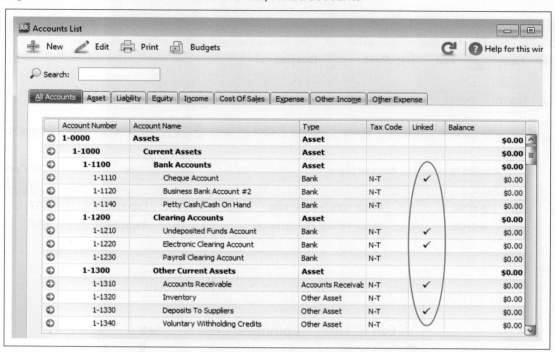

An example of linked accounts can be seen with Account # 1-1110 Cheque Account – this account is 'linked' to Customer Receipts, Paying Bills and Cheque Payments. When any of these transactions are processed, the transaction is automatically 'linked' to this bank account. We can see this if we...

Click...

- *The zoom arrow next to 1-1110 Cheque Account.*
- *Details* tab. See Figure 3.22.

Figure 3.22 **Accounts information: Cheque Account Details tab, Linked Accounts**

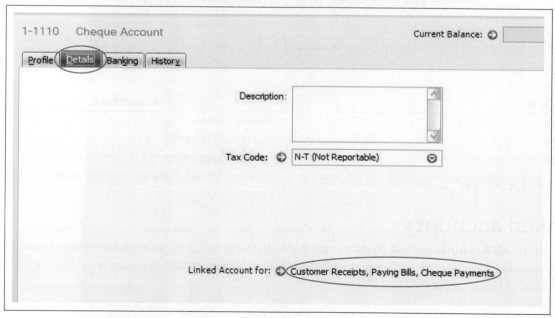

There are some fields in various MYOB screens where you don't physically need to enter an account code, as anything put in these fields will automatically go to the accounts that we specify in this Linked Fields section. We change the linked accounts like this:

Click...

- *Setup* on the top menu line.
- *Linked Accounts*.
- *OK* (to close the other windows).
- *Sales Accounts*. See Figure 3.23.
- *I give discounts for early payment* (type 5-9000). See Figure 3.24.
- OK

Figure 3.23   **Setup: Linked Accounts**

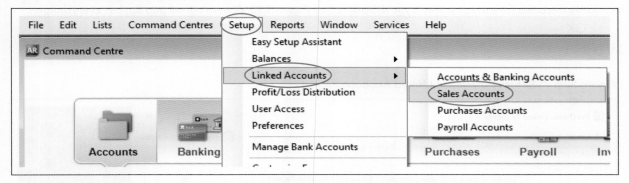

Figure 3.24   **Setup: Sales Linked Accounts**

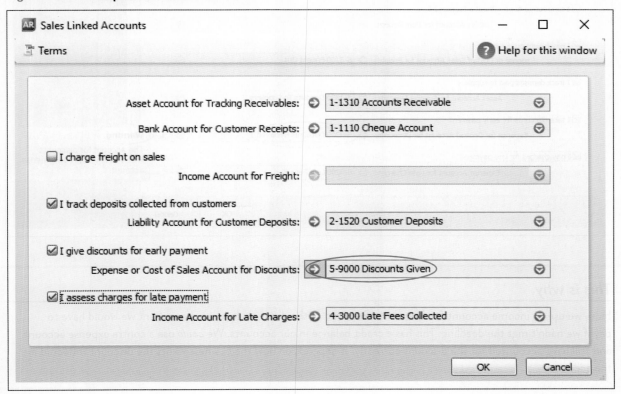

So now every time a **prompt payment discount** is calculated for a customer by MYOB, it will automatically be posted to account 5-9000.

Look at the other fields in Figure 3.24. If you charged freight on any of your sales, you would tick the top box and allocate an income account to go with it. Then every time you entered an amount into the freight field in the customer invoice (dealt with in Chapter 8), that amount would automatically get posted to the Freight Income Account.

The next step is to do the same for the Linked Purchase Accounts.

> **Prompt payment discount**
> Occurs when the entity paying the invoice pays within a stipulated time and is rewarded for the early payment with a discount.

Click...

- *Setup* on the top menu line.
- *Linked Accounts.*
- *Purchases Accounts.*
- *I take discounts for early payment* (type *4-9000*). See Figure 3.25. A warning will pop up, but everything is OK.
- *OK.*

Figure 3.25   Setup: Purchases Linked Accounts

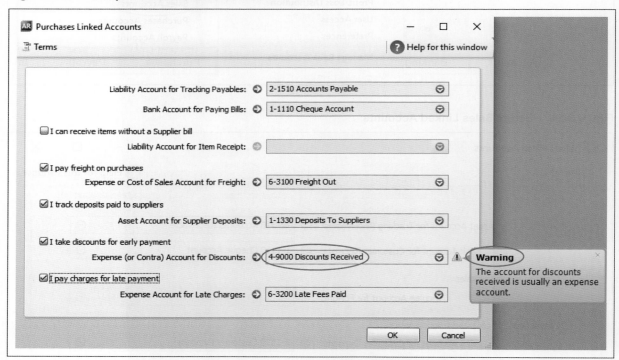

This is why

Here we use an income account for Discounts Received as the discount reduces the amount we would have to pay if we hadn't met the deadline. This has a credit balance in our accounts. We *could* use a contra expense account and still have accounted for the discount correctly. It depends on how the business wants the discount reflected in the accounts.

Entering account opening balances

So we have now created a new company file and amended the chart of accounts to suit the business' needs. The company may also have account opening balances that need to be entered. Assets, liabilities and equity will already exist whether it is a brand-new business or a continuing business changing their accounting system. We were given a trial balance for Cozy Dry Cleaners Pty Ltd as at 30 June 2017 in **Figure 3.12**, which needs to be entered into our new company.

Click...

- *Setup* on the top menu line.
- *Easy Setup Assistant.*
- *Accounts.*
- *Opening Balances* (left menu) to take you straight to the correct window. See **Figure 3.26**.

Figure 3.26   Accounts Easy Setup Assistant: Opening Balances

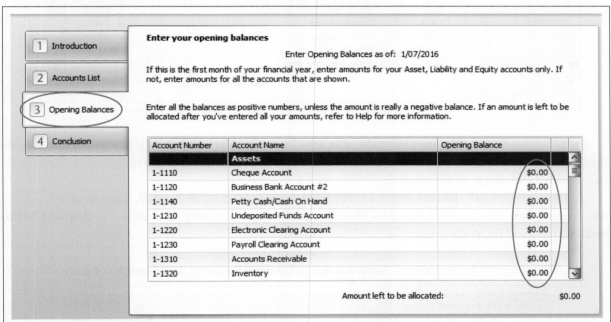

You will immediately notice that the trial balance in **Figure 3.12** (page 36) has two columns of numbers and the MYOB opening balances in **Figure 3.26** have only one column. We will enter *most* of the account balances as a positive number. MYOB will recognise the account by the account prefix and register the entry as either a debit (for an asset) or a credit (for a liability or equity).

A negative value will need to be entered for the accounts that seem to have the *opposite* balance from the normal. These contra accounts are easy to spot as they are in the credit column for assets and debit column for the liability and equity accounts. Accounts such as accumulated depreciation reduce the overall value of the asset; GST paid reduces the amount of the GST liability and owner/shareholder drawings reduce the equity in the business. Using the trial balance in **Figure 3.12**, enter the opening balances into MYOB.

Click...

- the right-hand column next to Cheque Account (insert *30 900*).
- the right-hand column next to *Inventory* (insert *2500*).

- the right-hand column next to Furniture At Cost (insert *10 000*).
- the right-hand column next to Accum. Depr. Furniture (insert *–$600*). To continue adding in the positive debit balances and negative credit balances for the assets. See Figure 3.27.

Figure 3.27   Accounts Easy Setup Assistant: Opening Balances, Assets

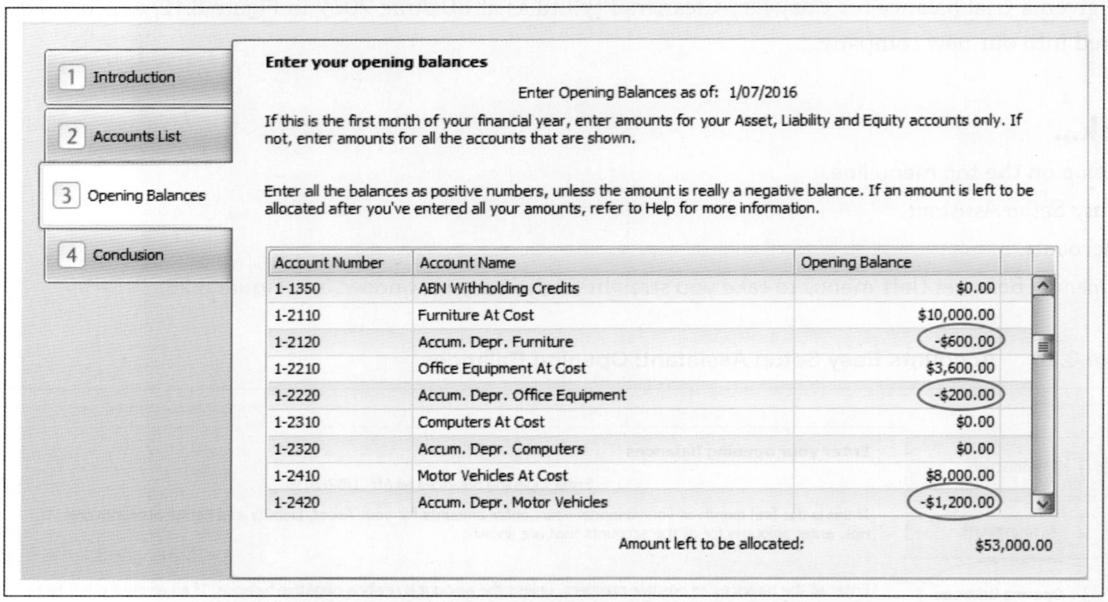

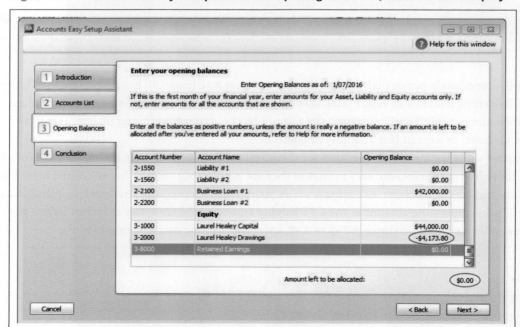

You will notice that the **Amount left to be allocated** (bottom right hand corner) is $53 000 by the time you have entered balances up to the **Accum. Depr. Motor Vehicles**. This amount needs to be zero by the time we have finished entering in all the balances.

Continue adding in the balances for the liabilities and equity (prefixes of 2 and 3), using negatives *only* for the accounts that are in the *debit* side of the trial balance. See Figure 3.28 which also shows the **Amount left to be allocated** as $0.00. We balance.

Figure 3.28   Accounts Easy Setup Assistant: Opening Balances, Liabilities And Equity

Click...

- *Next* (only if you balance).
- *Close* (to close the Accounts Assistant).
- *Close* (to close the Easy Setup Assistant).

Congratulations! You have now finished one entire setup of a company file. Now for some practice...

Practice

THE BLINDS MAN

1   In MYOB AccountRight 2016, create a new data file based on the following information, using the *AccountRight Standard Australian* version:

> **The Blinds Man**
> 21 Penola Rd
> Mount Gambier SA 5290
> ABN 78 303 458 861
>
> **Phone:** (08) 8725 5122
> **Financial Year:** 2017
> **Last month of financial year:** June
> **Conversion Month:** July
> **Industry Classification:** Service
> **Main Business Activity:** Installation of custom-made blinds.

Click the **Easy Setup Assistant** once you have finished the company file setup. Use the third activation option – **I use this file for evaluation purposes**.

2   Click **Accounts** in the Easy Setup Assistant and make the following changes in the Accounts List:

	Account Type	Account No.	New Account Name	Tax Code
Edit	Bank	1-1110	Cheque Account	N-T
Edit	Acc. Receivable	1-1310	Accounts Receivable	N-T
Edit	Acc. Payable	2-1510	Accounts Payable	N-T
Edit	Income	4-1000	Sale of Blinds	GST
Edit	Income	4-2000	Installation Income	GST
Add	Income	4-9000	Discounts Received	GST
Add	Cost of Sales	5-1000	Purchase of Blinds	GST
Add	Cost of Sales	5-2000	Sub Contractors	GST
Add	Cost of Sales	5-9000	Discounts Given	GST

Change the linked accounts:

Type	Terms	From	To
Sales	I give discounts for early payment	6-3300 Discounts Given	5-9000 Discounts Given
Purchases	I take discounts for early payment		4-9000 Discounts Received

Then make the following changes:

	Account Type	Account No.	New Account Name
Delete	Expense	6-3300	Discounts Given
Delete	Expense	6-7100	Public Liability Insurance

3 Insert the following account opening balances:

Account No.	Account Name	Debit	Credit
1-1110	Cheque Account	10594.00	
1-1310	Accounts Receivable	4400.00	
1-2210	Office Equip at cost	1800.00	
1-2220	Accum. Depr. Office Equip		100.00
2-1510	Accounts Payable		594.00
2-2100	Business Loan #1		10000.00
3-1000	Owners Capital		6500.00
3-2000	Owners Drawings	400.00	
	TOTALS	**17194.00**	**17194.00**

Remember This

The amount left to be allocated needs to be zero. Some of the accounts are contra accounts so they need to be added in as a *negative*.

Summary

◆ Once the company file has been saved, the conversion date and financial year can't be changed.

◆ In order to access the company file, it must be saved either online or under Documents/MYOB/My AccountRight Files.

◆ You can use Easy Setup Assistant to add, edit and delete accounts when customising the chart of accounts or you can use the Accounts List in the Accounts module.

◆ Account Opening Balances should be entered in Easy Setup Assistant.

◆ The opening balances must come to zero at the end, so some opening balances need to be entered as negatives (contra accounts).

◆ Certain fields in the MYOB forms are linked to specific general ledger accounts and these can be customised through Setup on the top menu bar.

Assessment

The Ice Cream Parlour

1   Create a new data file (AccountRight Standard, Australian version) based on the following information using an account list provided by MYOB:

> **The Ice Cream Parlour Pty Ltd**
> Darlinghurst Road
> KINGS CROSS NSW 2011
> ABN 58 101 277 285
>
> **Phone:** (02) 9358 1999
> **Email:** icparlour@bigpond.com
> **Financial Year:** 2017
> **Last month of financial year:** June
> **Conversion Month:** July
> **Industry Classification:** Retail
> **Core Business:** Sell ice cream to the public (cash) and other small businesses (credit).

Click the **Easy Setup Assistant** once you have finished the company file setup. Use the third activation option – **I use this file for evaluation purposes**.

2   Open the **Accounts** Easy Setup Assistant and make the following changes in the Accounts List:

	Account Type	Account No.	New Account Name	Tax Code
Edit	Bank	1-1110	Cheque Account	N-T
Edit	Acc. Payable	2-1510	Accounts Payable	N-T
Edit	Income	4-1000	Sales	GST
Add	Income	4-9000	Discounts Received	GST
Edit	Cost of Sales	5-1000	Purchases	GST
Edit	Cost of Sales	5-9000	Discounts Given	GST

Change the linked accounts:

Type	Terms	From	To
Sales	I give discounts for early payment	6-3300 Discounts Given	5-9000 Discounts Given
Purchases	I take discounts for early payment		4-9000 Discounts Received

Then make the following changes:

	Account Type	Account No.	New Account Name
Delete	Expense	6-3500	Discounts Given
Delete	Expense	6-7200	Public Liability Insurance

3   Insert the following account opening balances:

Account No.	Account Name	Debit	Credit
1-1110	Cheque Account	8920.00	
1-2210	Office Equip at cost	12500.00	
1-2210	Store Fittings at cost	16800.00	
1-2220	Accum. Depr. Store Fittings		1800.00
2-1510	Accounts Payable		2420.00
2-2100	Business Loan #1		25000.00
3-1000	Owners Capital		10000.00
3-2000	Owners Drawings	1000.00	
	TOTALS	40220.00	40220.00

Backup the company file and submit it to your instructor using the protocol they give you.

4

CREATING CARDS AND PRODUCING REPORTS

Learning outcomes

By the end of this chapter you will be competent in:
- creating customer and supplier cards
- specifying customer and supplier credit terms
- producing reports for a number of modules
- customising reports to meet the business requirements
- exporting reports in a variety of formats.

This chapter explains the card system and how to create new customer and supplier cards. The Reports Index is explained, as well as how to customise and format reports. In some reports, MYOB allows for the 'drilling down' of information so the user can see what transactions make up the report numbers.

Background information

In a manual account-keeping system, information about various components of the business are often kept on a card:

- An *entity* card contains information about a particular entity that has dealings with the business. Entities can be companies, individuals and government departments. Examples of an entity card are customers, suppliers and employees. The type of information commonly kept in these cards includes names, addresses, contact numbers, terms of trade for the customers and suppliers or hourly rate and entitlements for employees.
- An *inventory* card contains information about products that the business sells. The information kept on these cards may include sale price, stock levels, preferred supplier, as well as components or part numbers if it is a manufacturing business.
- An *asset* card contains information about a single asset or a group of assets including date of purchase, cost, serial numbers or identification numbers and service history.

MYOB uses the same system electronically.

Creating a card

Electronic cards enable the company to keep track of, or a record of, all transactions associated with a particular customer, supplier or employee. It also allows the business to process transactions more efficiently as the relevant card can be accessed quickly and all associated details will be carried across into the transaction file – a customer's address, contact details, selling information, delivery address, credit terms, discounts, etc.

Employee cards will be set up in Chapter 11, so we will only set up the customer and supplier cards in this chapter. The information required will generally be provided on the invoices themselves, but for simplicity's sake we will use as the source document a reference card that would be used in a manual bookkeeping system. See Figure 4.1.

Figure 4.1   **Customer card information**

Name:	Cozy Corner Hilton P/L
Card ID:	CUS 001
Address:	Cozy Corner Beach
	Albany WA 6330
Phone:	(08) 9748 2155
Email:	housekeeper@cchilton.com.au
Website:	www.cchilton.com.au
Contact:	June Budd
Terms:	10%/10, net 30
Income Account:	4-1000
Credit Limit:	$2000.00

1 Create a customer card

Click **Card List** (in the Card File module). See Figure 4.2. A window opens that looks vaguely like the Account List in that it has New and Edit buttons along the top of the screen, a Search field and tabs underneath which group cards together in categories. See Figure 4.3.

Figure 4.2   **Card File module**

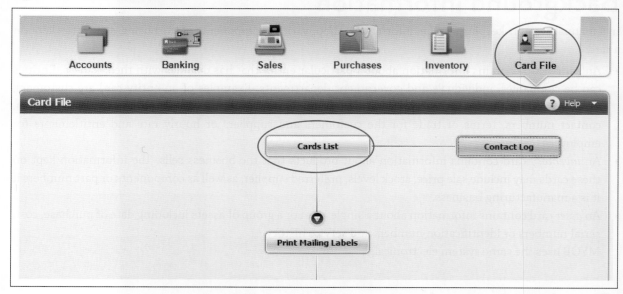

Figure 4.3   **Cards List**

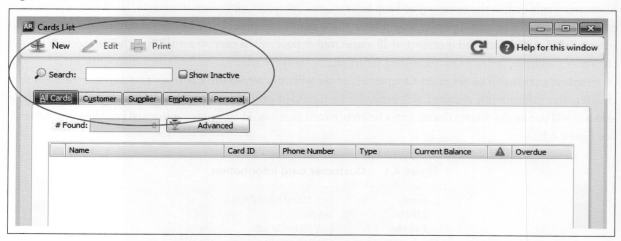

Click...

- *New* (top left side of the screen).
- *Card type* (select *Customer*).
- *Card ID* (type *CUS 001*). Fill out all of the contact details up to and including the contact name. Compare with Figure 4.4.
- *Selling Details* tab.
- *Income Account* (type *4-1000*).
- *Payment is Due* (in the Customer Terms Information at the bottom part of the screen). Select *In a Given No. of Days*.
- *Discount Days* (type *10*).
- *Balance Due Days* (type *30*).
- *% Discount for Early Payment*: (type *10*). See Figure 4.5.

Figure 4.4   Card Information: Profile

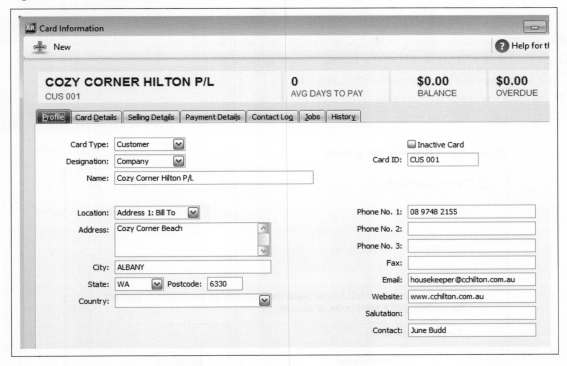

Figure 4.5   Card Information: Selling Details

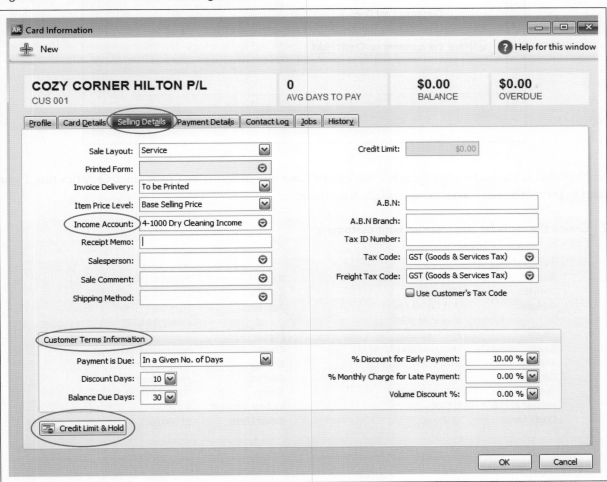

Put in the credit limit you have granted this customer.

Click...

- *Credit Limit & Hold* (bottom left of the screen). A new screen opens.
- *Credit Limit* (type *2000*). Compare with Figure 4.6.
- *OK* (to close the credit limit screen).
- *OK* (to close the customer card).

Figure 4.6   **Credit Limit & Hold**

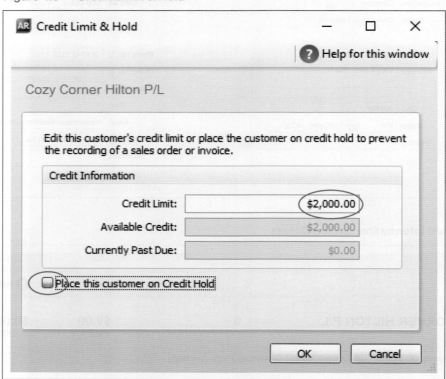

Note that at the bottom left there is a box named Place this customer on Credit Hold. *Only* tick this if you want to prevent any new sales being made to this customer.

2   Create the cards for two more account customers:

Name:	Cozy Corner Novotel P/L	Name:	Regent of Cozy Corner P/L
Card ID:	CUS 002	Card ID:	CUS 003
Address:	Cozy Corner Beach Albany WA 6330	Address:	Cozy Corner Beach Albany WA 6330
Phone:	(08) 9748 3907	Phone:	(08) 9748 9105
Email:	hk@ccnovatel.com.au	Email:	housekeeper@ccregent.com.au
Website:	www.ccnovatel.com.au	Website:	www.ccregent.com.au
Contact:	Dora Chen	Contact:	Helen Dravich
Terms:	10%/10, net 30	Terms:	10%/10, net 30
Income Account:	4-1000	Income Account:	4-2000
Credit Limit:	$1 000.00	Credit Limit:	$1 000.00

We follow the same process for the supplier invoices. The only difference is this time we add an ABN in the details tab and type in the credit limit straight into the field. Figure 4.7 shows the profile card for Tulloch Pty Ltd.

Figure 4.7   Tulloch Pty Ltd Supplier Card: Buying Details tab

TULLOCH PTY LTD	0	$0.00	$0.00
SUP 001	AVG DAYS TO PAY	BALANCE	OVERDUE

Profile | Card Details | **Buying Details** | Payment Details | Contact Log | History

Purchase Layout:	Service		Credit Limit:	$10,000.00
Printed Form:			Available Credit:	$10,000.00
Purchase Order Delivery:	To be Printed		Currently Past Due:	$0.00
			A.B.N:	53 153 355 133
Expense Account:	5-1000 Supply Purchases		A.B.N Branch:	
Payment Memo:			Tax ID Number:	
Purchase Comment:			Tax Code:	GST (Goods & Services Tax)
Shipping Method:			Freight Tax Code:	GST (Goods & Services Tax)
				☐ Use Supplier's Tax Code

Supplier Terms Information

Payment is Due:	In a Given No. of Days		% Discount for Early Payment:	10.00 %
Discount Days:	7		Volume Discount %:	0.00 %
Balance Due Days:	30			

3 Create the following cards for Cozy Dry Cleaners' account suppliers:

Remember This

Remember to change the Card Type to Supplier.

Name:	Tulloch Pty Ltd
Card ID:	SUP 001
Address:	52 Hay Street
	Perth WA 6000
Phone:	(08) 9748 2155
Email:	orders@tulloch.com.au
Website:	www.tulloch.com.au
Contact:	John Doran
Terms:	10%/7, net 30
Expense Account:	5-1000
Credit Limit:	$10 000.00
ABN:	53 153 355 133

Name:	Klenasol Care P/L
Card ID:	SUP 002
Address:	77 Bassett Street
	Mona Vale NSW 2103
Phone:	(02) 9979 6866
Fax:	(02) 9979 6864
Email:	klenasol@bigpond.com.au
Contact:	Thomas Kenny
Terms:	10%/10, net 30
Expense Account:	5-1000
Credit Limit:	$10 000.00
ABN:	09 597 454 908

Name:	Miller Systems P/L
Card ID:	SUP 003
Address:	2 Railway Parade
	Lidcombe NSW 2141
Phone:	(02) 9643 2772
Email:	milsys@nlc.net.au
Contact:	Martin Lindley
Terms:	10%/10, net 30
Expense Account:	5-1000
Credit Limit:	$15 000.00
ABN:	39 093 338 193

Searching for a card

Some businesses will set up their cards with a specific card identifier which could be in a numerical format, an alphabetical format or a combination of both. The identifier may not be relevant to the customer or supplier name. Within MYOB there are various search options. To look for a card, you will need to go into the Card File Command Centre, and into the Card List.

If you know you are looking for a particular supplier, you can refine your search to only suppliers by clicking the Supplier tab. If you click on the title bar label of Name, you can sort the data into alphabetical order and search for your supplier alphabetically. If you click on Card ID, it can be sorted in ID number. Another method is to simply use the Search function. See **Figure 4.8**.

Figure 4.8   **Cards List: Supplier tab**

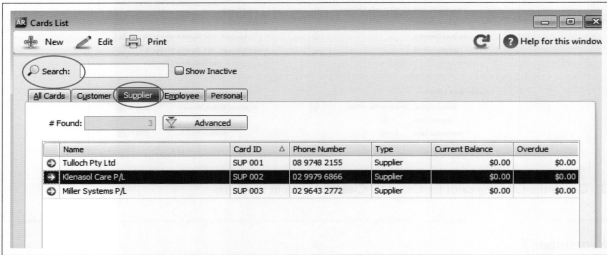

Supplier and customer cards can also be created when recording transactions in the Banking, Sales and Purchases modules.

Practice

THE BLINDS MAN

1   In MYOB AccountRight 2016 open **4.2 The Blinds Man.myox** from Chapter 4 of your start-up files in your online resources or use the data file that you created in Chapter 3.

2   Create cards for the following suppliers:

Name:	Apollo Blinds P/L		**Name:**	Luxaflex P/L
Card ID:	SUP 001		**Card ID:**	SUP 002
Address:	44 Barton Terrace		**Address:**	85 Hindley Street
	Adelaide SA 5000			Adelaide SA 5000
Phone:	(08) 9267 3222		**Phone:**	(08) 9516 6371
Email:	sales@apollo.net.au		**Email:**	sales@luxaflex.com.au
Contact:	Dave Kenny		**Contact:**	Franco Tosoni
Terms:	10%/10, net 30		**Terms:**	10%/10, net 30
Expense Account:	5-1000		**Expense Account:**	5-1000
Credit Limit:	$5 000.00		**Credit Limit:**	$5 000.00
ABN:	91 091 228 676		**ABN:**	52 901 298 023

Name:	Litemaster Blinds P/L
Card ID:	SUP 003
Address:	158 Gawler Place
	Adelaide SA 5000
Phone:	(08) 9223 5500
Email:	sales@litemaster.com.au
Contact:	Harry Freeman
Terms:	10%/10, net 30
Expense Account:	5-1000
Credit Limit:	$3 000.00
ABN:	23 223 978 633

Name:	Wynstan Blinds P/L
Card ID:	SUP 004
Address:	11 East Terrace
	Adelaide SA 5000
Phone:	(08) 9643 2772
Email:	sales@wynstan.com.au
Website:	wynstan.com.au
Contact:	Martin Lindley
Terms:	10%/10, net 30
Expense Account:	5-1000
Credit Limit:	$5 000.00
ABN:	13 213 675 567

Name:	Energy Plus
Card ID:	SUP 005
Address:	PO BOX 2065
	Adelaide SA 5000
Phone:	13 13 13
Email:	info@energyplus.com.au
Terms:	Net 15
Expense Account:	6-1700
ABN:	18 675 213 567

3 Create cards for the following customers:

Name:	East Motor Inn P/L
Card ID:	CUS 001
Address:	Grouch Street
	Mount Gambier SA 5290
Phone:	(08) 8725 2354
Email:	steve@emi.com.au
Contact:	Steve Streeter
Terms:	10%/10, net 30
Expense Account:	4-1000
Credit Limit:	$5 000.00

Name:	Grandview Hotel P/L
Card ID:	CUS 002
Address:	Lake Terrace
	Mount Gambier SA 5290
Phone:	(08) 8725 5755
Email:	john@grandview.com.au
Contact:	John Worth
Terms:	10%/10, net 30
Expense Account:	4-1000
Credit Limit:	$10 000.00

Name:	Lakeview Apartments P/L
Card ID:	CUS 003
Address:	6 Helen Street
	Mount Gambier SA 5290
Phone:	(08) 8725 3141
Email:	manager@lakeview.com.au
Contact:	Angelo Falls
Terms:	10%/10, net 30
Expense Account:	4-1000
Credit Limit:	$10 000.00

Name:	Meriton Holdings P/L
Card ID:	CUS 004
Address:	Jubilee Highway
	Mount Gambier SA 5290
Phone:	(08) 8725 4311
Email:	manager@mhold.com.au
Contact:	Dario Lennon
Terms:	10%/10, net 30
Expense Account:	4-1000
Credit Limit:	$5 000.00

THE ICE CREAM PARLOUR

1 In MYOB AccountRight 2016 open **4.3 The Ice Cream Parlour.myox** from Chapter 4 of your start-up files in your online resources or use the data file that you created in Chapter 3.

2 Create cards for the following suppliers:

Name:	Alpino Gelato P/L
Card ID:	SUP 001
Address:	90 Addison Road
	Marrickville NSW 2204
Phone:	(02) 9569 3667
Email:	sales@alpino.net.au
Contact:	Maria Palmer
Terms:	10% 7 days/Net 15
Expense Account:	5-1000
Credit Limit:	$5 000.00
ABN:	76 485 221 761

Name:	Peters Ice Creams P/L
Card ID:	SUP 002
Address:	1 Maitland Place
	Baulkham Hills NSW 2153
Phone:	(02) 9659 0699
Email:	sales@peters.com.au
Website:	petersice.com.au
Contact:	Lisa Woods
Terms:	10% 10 days/Net 30
Expense Account:	5-1000
Credit Limit:	$5 000.00
ABN:	22 695 191 494

Name:	Streets Ice Creams P/L
Card ID:	SUP 003
Address:	7 Alan Street
	Fairfield NSW 2165
Phone:	(02) 9755 7899
Email:	sales@sweetevents.com.au
Contact:	Angela Morosi
Terms:	10% 10 days/Net 30
Expense Account:	5-1000
Credit Limit:	$5 000.00
ABN:	44 939 622 109

Name:	Norgen-Vaaz P/L
Card ID:	SUP 004
Address:	66 Dublin Street
	Smithfield NSW 2164
Phone:	(02) 9756 2283
Email:	sales@norgenvaas.com.au
Contact:	Dora Norgen
Terms:	10% 7 days/Net 15
Expense Account:	5-1000
Credit Limit:	$5 000.00
ABN:	27 132 645 102

3 Create cards for the following customers:

Name:	Mary's Ice Creamery
Card ID:	CUS 001
Address:	126 Felton Road
	Carlingford NSW 2118
Phone:	(02) 9762 2800
Email:	mary@marys.com.au
Contact:	Mary Martin
Terms:	5%/10, Net 30
Expense Account:	4-1000
Credit Limit:	$4 000.00

Name:	Corner Store
Card ID:	CUS 002
Address:	24a Redfern Road
	Alexandria NSW 2130
Phone:	(02) 9246 3888
Email:	paul@cornerstore.com.au
Contact:	Paul Jones
Terms:	5%/10, Net 30
Expense Account:	4-1000
Credit Limit:	$2 000.00

Name:	Kent Road School
Card ID:	CUS 003
Address:	6 Kent Road
	Epping NSW 21321
Phone:	(02) 8725 3141
Email:	principal@kentroad.edu.au
Contact:	Eliza Jane
Terms:	5%/10, Net 30
Expense Account:	4-1000
Credit Limit:	$2 000.00

Reports

Throughout this book you will be producing reports to verify your work. These are the sort of reports that are also used for management purposes.

1 In MYOB AccountRight 2016 open **4.4 Fire Protection Pty Ltd.myox** from Chapter 4 of your start-up files in your online resources. This has a month's worth of transactions in it.

Like most lists in MYOB, the Reports Centre is broken into tabs or sections. Click on **Reports** at the bottom of the Command Centre or **Reports** on the top menu line to access the **Reports** index. See Figure 4.9.

Figure 4.9   Command Centre: Fire Protection Pty Ltd

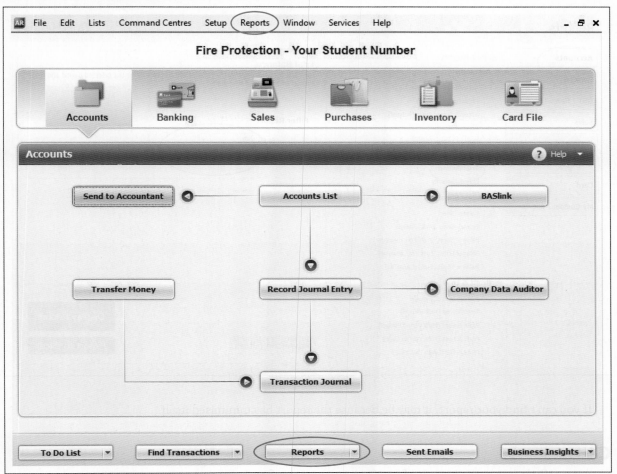

The left column is a menu of all the modules available in this particular version of MYOB.

As you click on the individual tabs in the left column, the reports change in the middle column to reflect the module chosen. These are further split up into groups with bolded headings.

The right column contains the filters, where the reports can be customised by (mostly) dates. It also offers you more advanced filters, which will take you straight to the report before it is populated.

2 Open up the trial balance dated 30 June 2018:

Click...

- *Accounts* from the left menu.
- *Trial Balance* from the middle menu.
- *Filter Report/As of* (select July).
- *Financial Year* (choose *This Year (FY 2018)*). See Figure 4.10.
- *Display Report*.

Figure 4.10 **Reports Index: Trial Balance**

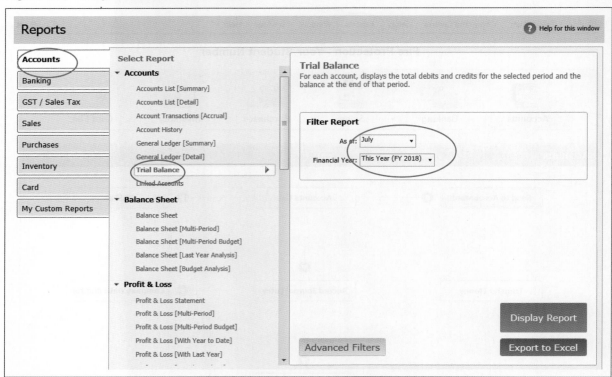

If you can't find your report, it may be because the report has minimised itself.

Click...

- *AccountRight icon* at the bottom of your computer screen. See Figure 4.11.
- *Trial Balance Report* to maximise it. It should look like Figure 4.12.

Figure 4.11 **Computer task bar**

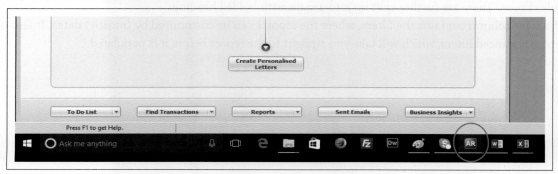

Figure 4.12   Trial Balance for Fire Protection Pty Ltd

Account Name	Debit	Credit	YTD Debit	YTD Credit
	Fire Protection Pty Ltd **44 Boorea Street** **Lidcombe NSW 2141** **Trial Balance** **July 2017**			
Business Bank Account #1		$3 202.50	$24 297.50	
Provision for Doubtful Debts		$200.00		$200.00
Inventory	$5 000.00		$35 000.00	
Prepayments		$160.00	$740.00	
Accrued Revenue	$750.00		$750.00	
Furniture At Cost	$0.00		$2 700.00	
Accum. Depr. Furniture		$22.50		$247.50
Office Equipment At Cost	$0.00		$6 000.00	
Accum. Depr. Office Equipment		$61.33		$1 155.13
Motor Vehicles At Cost	$12 000.00		$12 000.00	
Visa #1		$0.00		$1 281.20
GST Collected		$1 088.00		$1 088.00
GST Paid	$2 245.00		$2 245.00	
Accrued Expenses		$600.00		$600.00
Business Loan #1		$13 200.00		$13 200.00
Shari Offen Capital		$0.00		$64 500.00
Smoke Detector Sales		$3 940.00		$3 940.00
Fire Extinguisher Sales		$3 320.00		$3 320.00
Hose Reel Sales		$1 800.00		$1 800.00
Fire Blanket Sales		$1 820.00		$1 820.00
Service and Installation		$750.00		$750.00
Opening Stock	$30 000.00		$30 000.00	
Smoke Detector Purchase	$2 000.00		$2 000.00	
Fire Extinguisher Purchases	$4 400.00		$4 400.00	
Hose Reel Purchases	$1 750.00		$1 750.00	
Fire Blanket Purchases	$1 700.00		$1 700.00	
Closing Stock		$35 000.00		$35 000.00
Advertising & Marketing	$600.00		$600.00	
Bank Fees	$75.00		$75.00	
Bad and Doubtful Debts	$200.00		$200.00	
General Repairs & Maintenance	$50.00		$50.00	
Council Rates	$1 650.00		$1 650.00	
Wages & Salaries Expenses	$2 600.00		$2 600.00	
Office Equipment Depreciation	$83.83		$83.83	
Business Insurance	$110.00		$110.00	
Interest Income		$49.50		$49.50
Total:	**$65 213.83**	**$65 213.83**	**$128 951.33**	**$128 951.33**

Formatting reports

Have a look at the three tabs on the tool bar at the top of the page (shown in Figure 4.13).

Figure 4.13 **Reports tool bar**

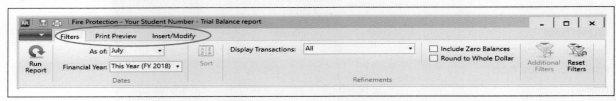

The first one is **Filters** and, as the name suggests, this is where you can change the filters used on your report. We want the report to be for July 2017 so we need to choose *July* in the month field and then *This Year (FY 2018)*. This is because the financial year is from July 2017 to June 2018. Click *Display* and the report opens.

If you wanted to change the date while in the report, you just need to use the drop-down arrows next to the *As of* field in the top left corner and then click the green *Run Report* arrow to refresh the screen.

The *Display Transactions* field gives you the options of which transactions you would like to show. Year-end adjustments are generally done by the accountant to update the accounts so they are a true reflection of the business operations. These are explained in more detail in Chapter 10. Removing them from the report means that you can see the actual transactions that went through the company for that month.

Further along the tool bar are two boxes where you can decide whether to *Include Zero Balances* or *Round to Whole Dollars*.

The **Print Preview** tab allows you to change the way the report is printed. Click on the arrows underneath *Margin*, *Orientation* and *Size* to see what changes can be made. You don't need to refresh the report – once the change is made, it will be reflected in the print preview.

The **Insert/Modify** tab is probably the most fun tab:

- The *Fields* button allows you to choose what fields to include in the report. Click on it to see which fields you can remove or include.
- *Picture* allows you to put, for instance, your company logo into the report before PDFing it. Once you have inserted the picture, you can drag it to wherever you would like it to sit in the report.
- *Text Box* can be used to insert comments or extra information in the header or the footer of the report.
- *Shapes/Line* can be used in the header and footer as well.
- If you wanted to change the look of your header or footer, you could use the *Field Properties* to change the fonts, colour and sizes, just like a Microsoft Word document.
- *Page numbering* and *Row shading* are both self-explanatory. If you are unsure, hover your mouse over one of them and an explanation will come up.
- *Show/Hide* allows you to put in extra columns if you wish. For the trial balance, the only available field is the *Account No*. You would insert it in the report like this:

Click...

- *Show/Hide*. Another window opens. See Figure 4.14.
- *Account No.* in the left column (to highlight it).
- *Show* (in between the two columns). This moves the Account No. over to the right column.
- *OK*. It automatically updates your report with the Account Numbers. If you wish to remove it, just click *Show/Hide* again, highlight the Account No. and click *Hide*.

Figure 4.14   **Show/Hide**

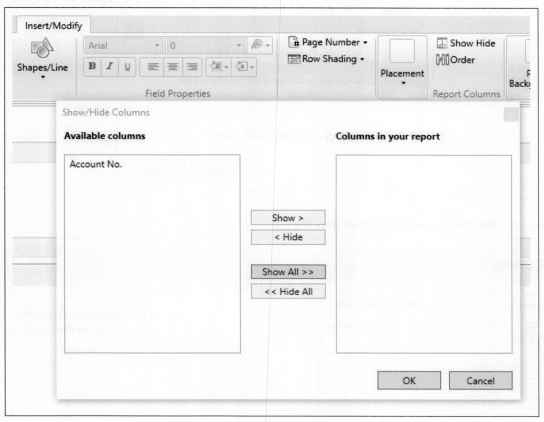

If we wanted to save this report with a logo and changes to the header and footer, we can click at any stage on the down arrow button to the left of the Filters tab. This gives you some more option. See Figure 4.15. Choose **Save as** and a window pops up asking where you can change the name and you can write a description (Figure 4.16) and it will then save it under **My Custom Reports** in the Reports Index. See Figure 4.17.

Figure 4.15   **Report output arrow: options**

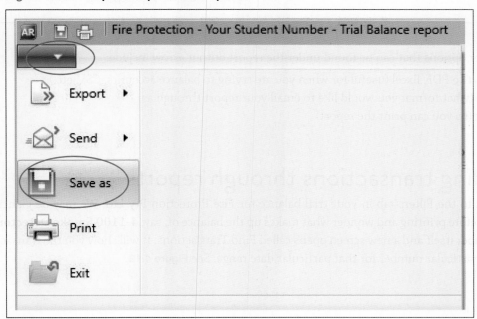

Figure 4.16   **Report output arrow: Save As**

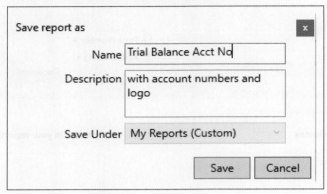

Figure 4.17   **Reports Index: My Custom Reports**

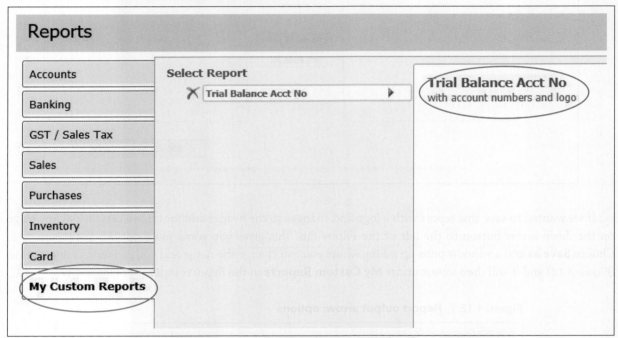

Other options that can be found under the report output arrow include:

- *Export* to PDF, Excel (useful for when you are trying to balance accounts, CSV, etc.)
- *Send* (what format you would like to email your report through as)
- *Print* (so you can print the report)
- *Exit*.

Finding transactions through reports

Go back to the Filters tab in your trial balance for Fire Protection Pty Ltd. We may be glancing through the report before printing and wonder what makes up the balance of, say, **4-1100 Smoke Detector Sales**. Click on the number itself and a new screen opens called Find Transactions. It will show you the transactions that make up this particular number for that particular date range. See **Figure 4.18**.

Figure 4.18   Find Transactions: 4-1100 Smoke Detector Sales

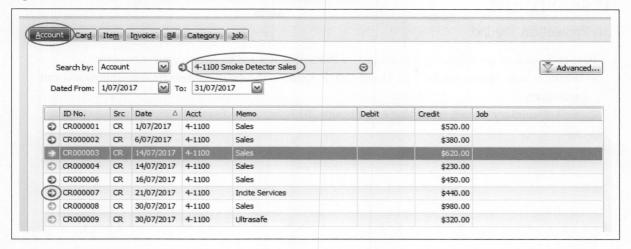

Here, we can click on the white zoom arrows to drill down (open up) that particular transaction. If the zoom arrow is in a blue background, as circled in Figure 4.18, we can edit or delete the transaction; if the zoom arrow is in a grey background, as per the transaction below the one circled in the same figure, we can't edit or delete unless we delete another linked transaction (we won't go into that process here).

As this is a completely separate screen, we can change any filter we want here – dates, accounts, tabs – without affecting the original trial balance.

We are now finished with the trial balance, so close down the report and the Find Transaction screen.

Remember This

If you can't find a screen you know you have open, click on Window in the top menu bar. You can then click on the list below it. If that screen doesn't show up in the list, click on the AccountRight icon on the bottom of your tool bar and it may show up there.

This completes the instruction for this chapter.

Summary

♦ MYOB uses electronic cards to store customer, supplier and employee information.
♦ This information will flow through to the transactions in the appropriate module. Customer information appears in the Sales module. Supplier information appears in the Purchases module.
♦ The card list can be sorted according to any of the column headings by clicking on that heading.
♦ The left column of the Reports Index has the individual modules found in that version of MYOB as well as a couple of additional headings.
♦ The middle column of the Reports Index has the actual reports for each module, which can be filtered or modified as needed.

Assessment

Fire Protection Pty Ltd

1   Find and produce the following reports in Fire Protection Pty Ltd to give to your instructor:
- Profit & Loss Statement for 1 to 31 July 2017. Remove the email address field and show account numbers.
- GST [Summary – cash] report for 1 to 31 July 2017. Export to Excel.

5

CASH ACCOUNTING

Learning outcomes

By the end of this chapter you will be competent in:
- using the MYOB banking module
- entering receipts and payment from source documents
- creating and using recurring transactions
- extracting and recording information from bank statements
- performing bank reconciliations
- processing petty cash transactions
- processing and reconciling credit card transactions
- producing relevant reports.

The Banking module is used to record Money Spent (for the purchase of trading stock, expenses, or other purposes) and Money Received (from sales or other income). Though this chapter specifically deals with cash Accounting, the Banking module can be used in conjunction with accrual accounting as well. You cannot access the individual accounts in any of the subsidiary ledgers from the Banking module, so all payment for transactions recorded in the Sales or Purchases modules must be completed within those modules (i.e. Pay Bills in the Purchases module and Receive Payments in Sales).

Basic accounting background

There are two accounting systems that are acceptable to the Australian Taxation Office (ATO) for use in preparation of the Business Activity Statement (BAS; explained in detail in Chapters 14 and 15). The first is *accrual accounting*, whereby business transactions are recorded at the time a purchase or sale takes place, *regardless of when payment occurs*. This system is used by many business operations, and Accounts Payable and Accounts Receivable are created to help track the invoices and payments/receipts. Prompt payment discounts (given or taken) must be recorded to keep an accurate record of debtor and creditor accounts, as must any finance charges or account-keeping fees for late payment.

MYOB uses the Purchases and Sales modules to access creditors' and debtors' individual accounts in the respective subsidiary ledgers. The Inventory module may be used if the business buys and sells inventory items or has standard rates for services. These are explained in later chapters.

The second system, *cash accounting*, records transactions *when payment is made*. Only the net cash received or paid out (after any discounts or other charges) is recorded, so it is less complicated and less time-consuming for small businesses. Also, because GST liability arises on transactions only after payment has been received from customers, the probability of a cashflow problem is reduced.

Using the Banking module

MYOB uses the Banking module to record Money Spent (for the purchase of trading stock, expenses, or other purposes) and Money Received (from sales or other income). You cannot access invoices listed in the subsidiary ledgers for individual customer or supplier accounts from the Banking module, so all payment for transactions recorded in the Sales or Purchases modules *must* be completed within those modules (i.e. Pay Bills in the Purchases module and Receive Payments in Sales). Purchases and Sales are discussed in detail in Chapters 6, 7 and 8.

Recording transactions

- Use Spend Money for all purchases and expenses.
- Use Receive Money for all sales and other income.

Many of the activities in cash accounting are repetitive, with only minor changes from one activity to the next. MYOB's *Recurring Transactions* feature can be very useful in increasing speed and accuracy, and will be used frequently.

Bank reconciliation

Bank reconciliation (that is, the comparison of your records with those of the bank) is also a very important business activity and must be undertaken regularly so that any differences can be quickly resolved. The bank statement is a *true* reflection of money that has gone in and out of your bank account(s). Your MYOB file must contain *at least* the transactions that are in the bank statement.

Undeposited funds

In order to keep MYOB's record of receipts as close as possible to the bank's record of deposits, we will be grouping receipts received on the same day in an *Undeposited Funds* account. We then *Prepare a Bank Deposit* when the cash is taken to the bank. You will see how important this is when you come to do your first bank reconciliation.

Each cheque paid by the bank is recorded separately on the bank statement, so no grouping of payments occurs. However, if the business pays several suppliers in the one electronic funds transfer (EFT) transaction through the bank, this gets grouped together into an electronic clearing account or a separate creditor clearing account, depending on organisational policy.

There are two ways in which MYOB can record accounting data:

- In a 'live' situation, where income and expenditure are recorded as they occur on the actual date of each transaction.
- In a retrospective manner, where income and expenses are recorded in batches at the end of the month. If the correct transaction dates are used, MYOB will sort the items into date order, so there will be no difference in the end-of-month reports.

We will be using the second of these methods.

Receive money

MAGNETIC BOATS

1 In MYOB AccountRight 2016, open **5.1 Magnetic Boats.myox** data file located in the Chapter 5 folder of your start-up files.
2 Record the following cash receipt, which is GST *Inclusive*:

Date:	3 June 2017
Receipt no.:	001
Received from:	Cash Sales
Details:	
Hire of Boats	$517.00
Fishing Tackle Sales	82.50
Confectionery Sales	48.40
GST-Free Sales	37.00
Cash Received:	$684.90
Revenue includes $58.90 GST	

Click...
- *Banking* module (in the Command Centre).
- *Receive Money* (in the accounting area). See **Figure 5.1**. This opens a new window.

Figure 5.1   Banking module: Receive Money

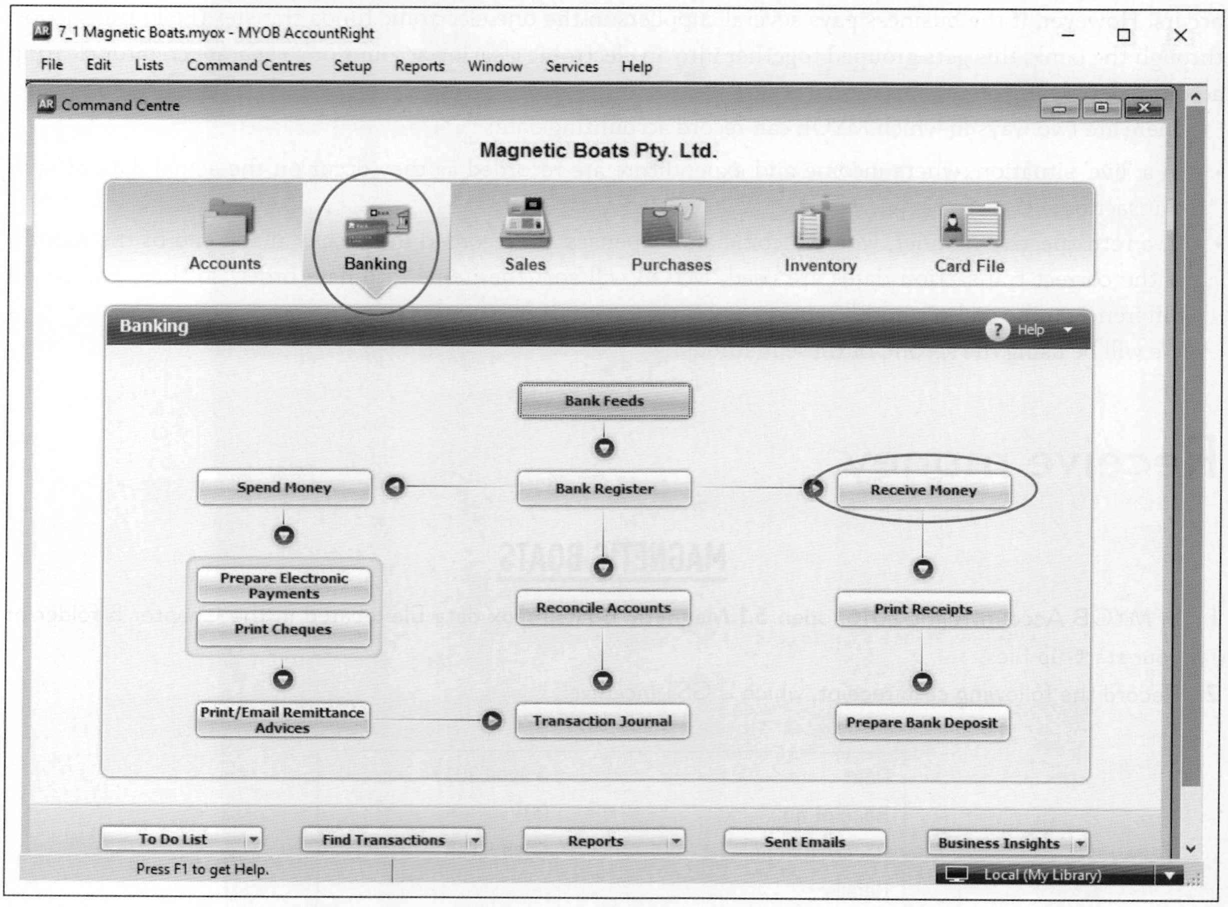

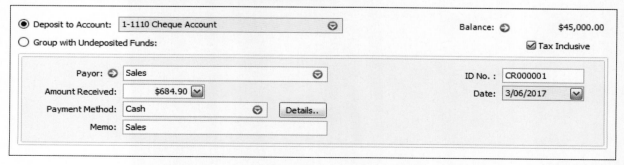

We complete the top half of the window first with the basic information we have. This is what shows in the Bank Register or reconciliation.

Click...

- *Tax Inclusive* (if check-box is not already ticked) as the amounts shown are the actual amounts of the cheques and therefore are GST *Inclusive*.
- *Date* (insert *3/06/17* and press the Tab key).
- *Payor* (type *Sales*). Press Enter.
- *Amount Received* (insert *684.90* and press the Tab key).
- *Payment Method* (select *Cash*).
- *Memo* (insert *Sales* if not already there). Compare with Figure 5.2.

Figure 5.2   Banking module: Receive Money (top half)

Now we complete the bottom half of the window, which is where we allocate the Money Received to the general ledger accounts.

Click...

- *Account No.* (select *4-1000 Hire of Boats*).
- *Amount* (insert *517.00*).
- *Account No.* (select *4-2000 Fishing Tackle Sales*).
- *Amount* (insert *82.50*).
- *Account No.* (select *4-3000 Confectionery Sales*).
- *Amount* (insert *48.40*).
- *Account No.* (select *4-4000 GST Free Sales*).
- *Amount* (insert or accept *37.00*). Check that all the figures agree with your source document, the receipt, including the tax amount. See Figure 5.3.
- *Save as Recurring* (button at base of the window). See Figure 5.3. This opens another window. See Figure 5.4.
- *Frequency* (change this to *Never*).
- *OK*. This transaction is now available to 'copy' so next time you have a similar transaction, you can use this template and just change the numbers. More information on this later in the chapter.

Figure 5.3   **Receive Money**

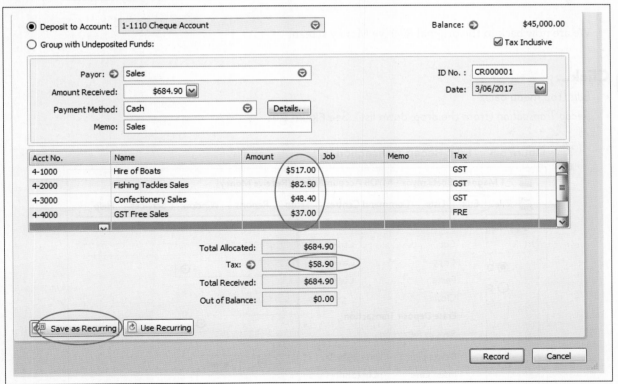

Figure 5.4 **Recurring Transaction screen**

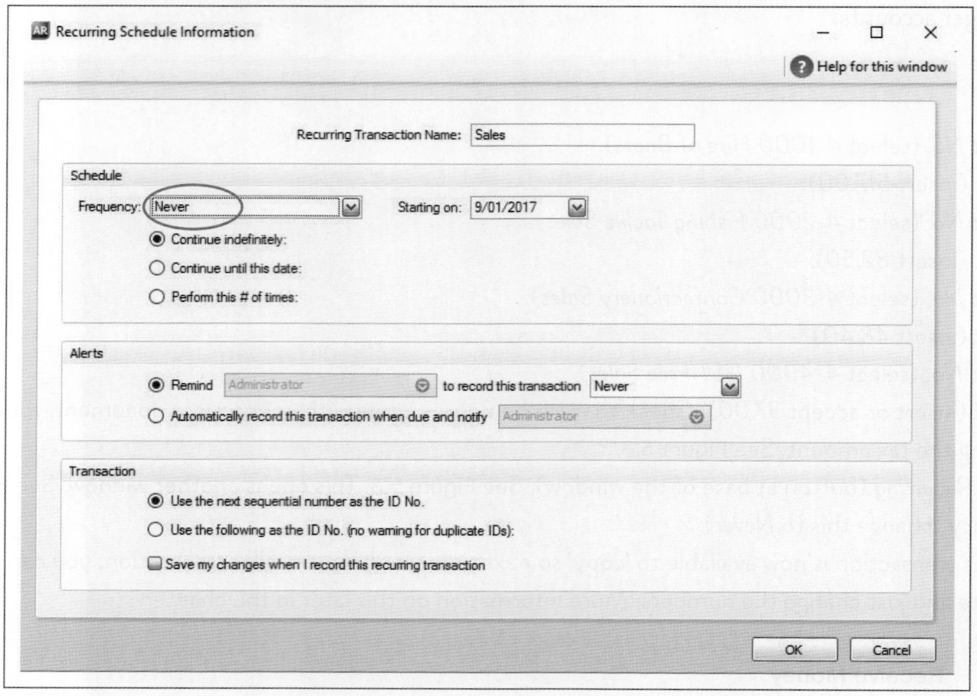

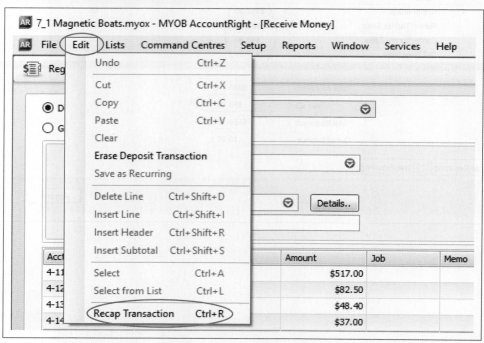

We are now back to the original Receive Money screen.

Click...

- *Edit* (top menu bar).
- *Recap Transaction* (from the drop-down list). See Figure 5.5.

Figure 5.5 **Edit: Recap Transaction**

Figure 5.6   **Receive Money: Recap Transaction window**

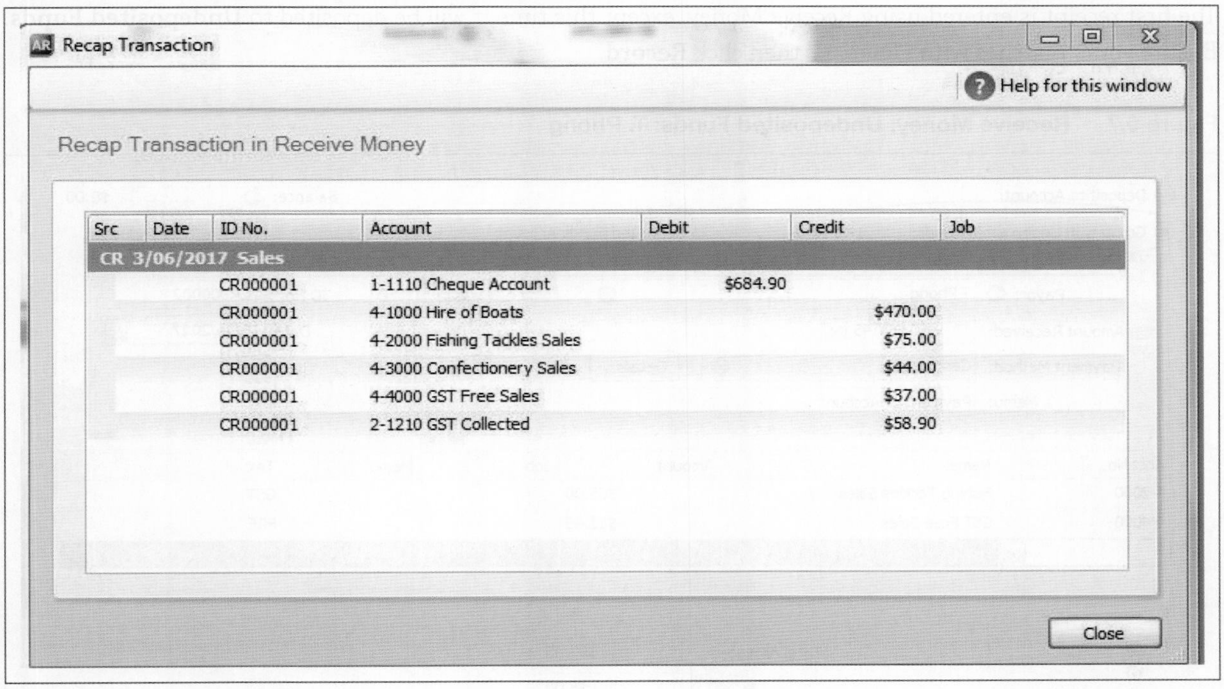

It can be seen from **Figure 5.6** that:

- Cheque Account (an asset) will be debited with the total cash received.
- The four sales accounts (revenue) will be credited with the GST Exclusive amount.
- GST Collected (a liability) will be credited with the total tax collected.

Click...

- *Close* (after understanding the debits and credits shown).
- *Record* (to register the income).

3 Receipts from different sources on the same day are grouped and banked as one amount to keep MYOB's records in line with those of the bank.

Date:	6 June	
Receipt No.	002	
Received from:	T. Phong	
Details:		
Payment of Account		
Fishing Tackle Sales		$55.00
GST-Free Sales		12.45
Cheque Received:		$67.45
Revenue includes $5.00 GST		

Date:	6 June	
Receipt No.	003	
Received from:	Sales	
Details:		
Hire of Boats		$352.00
Fishing Tackle Sales		70.40
Confectionery Sales		58.30
GST-Free Sales		41.00
Cash Received:		$521.70
Revenue includes $43.70 GST		

Step 1: Enter receipts with the same date into Undeposited Funds.
The first receipt is entered using Receive Money, except this time it will be deposited to **Undeposited Funds**. Ensure yours matches with Figure 5.7 then click **Record**.

Figure 5.7   **Receive Money: Undeposited Funds: T. Phong**

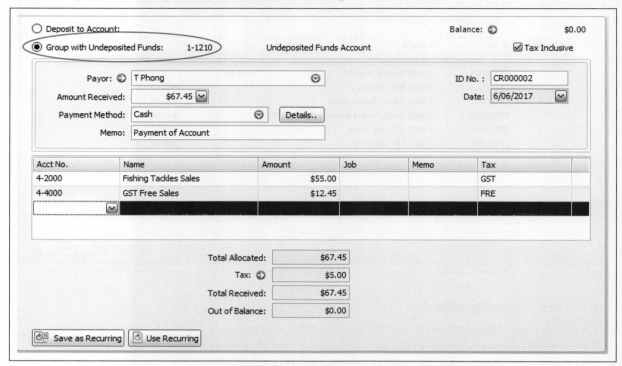

The second receipt is entered using Receive Money Recurring Transaction, as it is similar to the very first receipt we entered for 3 June.

Click...

- *Use Recurring* (button at base of the window).
- *Select* (to activate the Sales template).
- *Group with Undeposited Funds* (click this button again).
- *Amount Received* (type 521.70). Change all the Amounts Received in the second half of the screen and make sure it balances with your source document, the receipt. See Figure 5.8.

Figure 5.8   **Receive Money: Undeposited Funds: Sales**

		Balance: ⊙	$67.45
○ Deposit to Account:			
◉ Group with Undeposited Funds:	1-1210 Undeposited Funds Account	☑ Tax Inclusive	

				ID No. :	CR000003
Payor: ⊙	Sales ⊙				
Amount Received:	$521.70 ⊡			Date:	6/06/2017 ⊡
Payment Method:	Cash ⊙	Details..			
Memo:	Sales				

Acct No.	Name	Amount	Job	Memo	Tax	
4-1000	Hire of Boats	$352.00			GST	
4-2000	Fishing Tackles Sales	$70.40			GST	
4-3000	Confectionery Sales	$58.30			GST	
4-4000	GST Free Sales	$41.00			FRE	

Total Allocated:	$521.70
Tax: ⊙	$43.70
Total Received:	$521.70
Out of Balance:	$0.00

[⊞ Save as Recurring] [⊡ Use Recurring]

[Record]   [Cancel]

Click...

- *Record*.
- *Cancel* (to return to the Command Centre).

Tip

If you deposited this receipt directly into the Cheque Account by mistake, you can fix it with the following process:

Click...

- *Transaction Journal* (in a Command Centre).
- *Dated From* (change to the first day of the month of your transaction) and *To* (change to the last day of the month of your transaction). See **Figure 5.9**.
- *Identify the transaction* (you may need to scroll down).
- *Zoom arrow* (at the left of the transaction). Make your correction.
- *OK* (to register the change).
- *Close* (to exit the journal).

Figure 5.9 **Transaction Journal: Receipts**

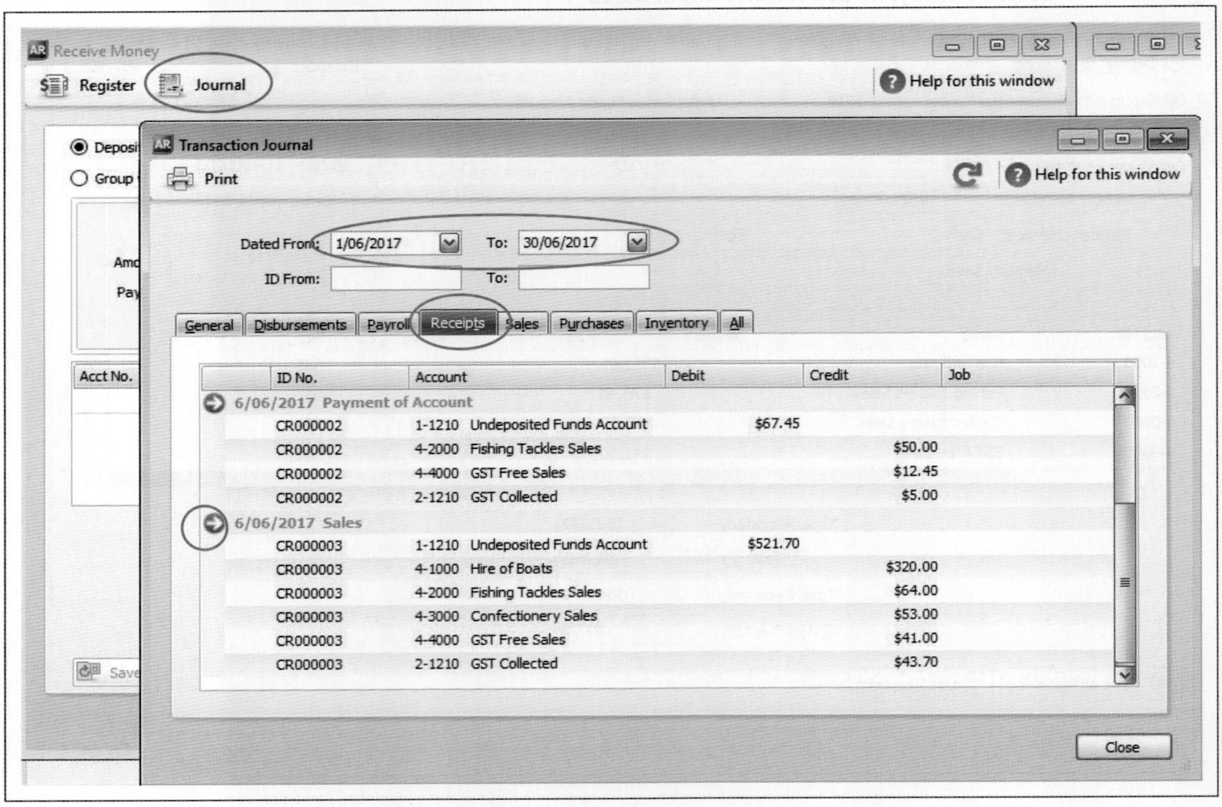

Step 2: Prepare the bank deposit.

Click...

- *Prepare Bank Deposit* (bottom right in the Banking module).
- *Date* (insert *6/06/17*).
- *Tick box* (above the Deposit column). This ticks the two deposits available. Make sure it balances with Figure 5.10.
- *Record* (to register the bank deposit).

The two receipts are grouped as one bank deposit.

Figure 5.10   **Banking: Prepare Bank Deposit**

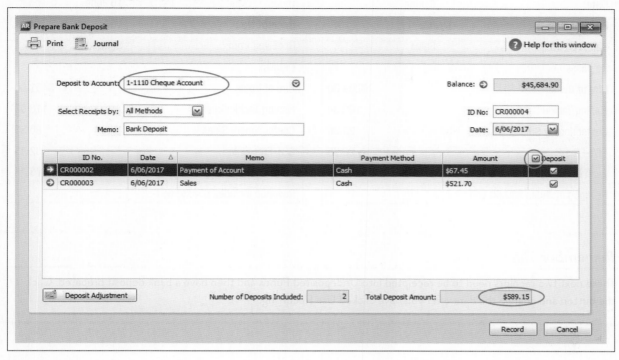

Tip

To change entries that form part of a bank deposit, first delete the transaction that deposits the full amount into the bank (by clicking the zoom arrow, *Edit* in the top menu bar, then *Delete*). Make whatever change you need to do in the individual receipts. Then record a new deposit when you are done.

4   Continue recording receipts, grouping those received on the same day before making that day's bank deposit.

Tip

Check every transaction after you have finished entering in the details to ensure they are correct. Common mistakes include wrong date, transposed amounts and deposited into the incorrect account. It is easier to do a quick check before recording than having to swim through many transactions to find the mistake!

Remember This

These next two receipts are on different dates so need to go directly into the Cheque Account. Remember to change the top button back to Deposit to Account if necessary.

Date:	8 June
Receipt No.:	005
Received from:	Sales
Details:	
Hire of Boats	$209.00
Fishing Tackle Sales	102.30
Confectionery Sales	25.30
GST-Free Sales	26.25
Cash Received:	$362.85
Revenue includes $30.60 GST	

Date:	10 June
Receipt No.:	006
Received from:	Sales
Details:	
Hire of Boats	$451.00
Fishing Tackle Sales	110.00
Confectionery Sales	80.30
GST-Free Sales	32.45
Cash Received:	$673.75
Revenue includes $58.30 GST	

Remember This

These next two receipts need to be receipted into Undeposited Funds and then have a bank deposit prepared. Click the button and change the date *after* you have clicked Use Recurring.

Date:	16 June
Receipt No.:	007
Received from:	Sales
Details:	
Hire of Boats	$396.00
Fishing Tackle Sales	81.40
Confectionery Sales	39.60
GST-Free Sales	42.85
Cash Received:	$559.85
Revenue includes $47.00 GST	

Date:	16 June
Receipt No.:	008
Received from:	A. Kitamura
Details:	
Hire of Boats	$88.00
Fishing Tackle Sales	11.00
Confectionery Sales	13.20
GST-Free Sales	9.60
Cheque Received:	$121.80
Revenue includes $10.20 GST	

Date:	20 June
Receipt No.:	010
Received from:	Sales
Details:	
Hire of Boats	$462.00
Fishing Tackle Sales	217.80
Confectionery Sales	113.30
GST-Free Sales	51.85
Cash Received:	$844.95
Revenue includes $72.10 GST	

Date:	22 June
Receipt No.	011
Received from:	Sales
Details:	
Hire of Boats	$231.00
Fishing Tackle Sales	84.70
Confectionery Sales	36.30
GST-Free Sales	39.20
Cash Received:	$391.20
Revenue includes $32.00 GST	

Date:	27 June		Date:	27 June
Receipt No.:	012		**Receipt No.:**	013
Received from:	Sales		Received from:	P. Blossom
Details:			Details:	
Hire of Boats	$1 078.00		Hire of Boats	$44.00
Fishing Tackle Sales	411.40		Fishing Tackle Sales	13.20
Confectionery Sales	94.05		Confectionery Sales	42.90
GST-Free Sales	56.25		GST-Free Sales	8.50
Cash Received:	$1639.70		Cheque Received:	$108.60
Revenue includes $143.95 GST			Revenue includes $9.10 GST	

Date:	30 June		Date:	30 June
Receipt No.:	015		**Receipt No.:**	016
Received from:	Sales		Received from:	P. Blossom
Details:			Details:	
Hire of Boats	$440.00		Hire of Boats	$66.00
Fishing Tackle Sales	77.00		Fishing Tackle Sales	8.80
Confectionery Sales	82.50		Confectionery Sales	15.40
GST-Free Sales	12.95		GST-Free Sales	13.60
Cash Received:	$612.45		Cheque Received:	$103.80
Revenue includes $54.50 GST			Revenue includes $8.20 GST	

Spend Money

Cheque or EFT payments are also made from the Banking module.

1 Record the following payment:

Date:	1 June
Cheque No.:	005104
Payee:	Island Real Estate P/L
Details: Rent	
Monthly Shop Rent	$1 100.00
Payment includes $100.00 GST	

Click...

- *Spend Money* (in the Banking module).
- *Tax Inclusive* (if check-box is not already ticked) as the amounts shown are the actual amounts of the cheques and therefore are GST *Inclusive*.
- *Cheque No.* (insert *005104*). Press the Tab key.
- *Date* (insert *1/06/17*). Press the Tab key.
- *Amount* (insert *1100*). Press the Tab key.
- *Card* (select *Island Real Estate*).

- *Memo* (insert *Monthly Shop Rent*). Press the Tab key.
- *Account No.* Press the Tab key. (This calls up a list of account codes. Select *6-2300 Rent.*)
- *Amount* (the *$1100.00* will appear).
- *Tax* (this should read *GST*).
- *Cheque Already Printed* (tick the check-box).
- *Remittance Advice Delivery Status* (select *Already Printed or Sent*). This is because we are not printing cheques. We are recording cheques we have already written.
- *Save as Recurring* (change the frequency to *Never* and leave all other fields as they are).
- *Save* (after checking the details). Compare with **Figure 5.11**.
- *Record* (to register this payment).

Figure 5.11   **Banking: Spend Money**

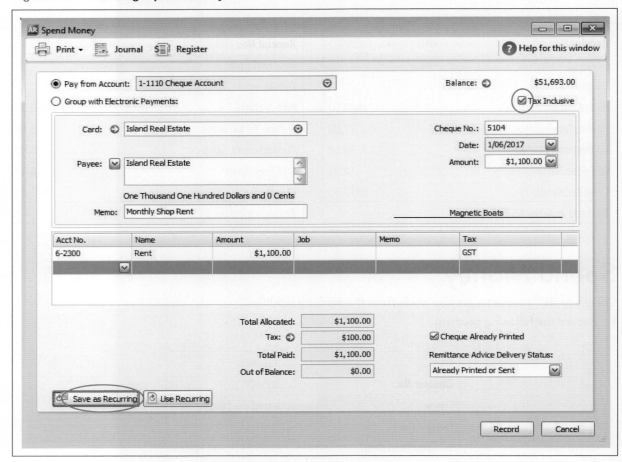

Now enter in the rest of the cheques. Change the memo to reflect the purchase type (e.g. the memo on cheque 5105 is Purchase of Confectionery). Save as Recurring according to the note under each of the following cheques.

Tip

When you purchase something that you will sell later (as with cheque 5105) then the MYOB general ledger code begins with 5. So scroll up and choose the correct code to match the description.

Date:	1 June
Cheque No.:	005105
Payee:	Cash Payment
Details: Purchases	
Purchase of confectionery	$88.00
Payment includes $8.00 GST	

Save as Recurring: Never. Name: Purchases Confectionery.

Date:	2 June
Cheque No.:	005106
Payee:	Cash Payment
Details: Wages	
Fortnightly Wages	$800.00
Payment includes $0.00 GST (Tax code is N-T)	

Save as Recurring: Fortnightly. Name: Fortnightly Wages.

This is why

Fortnightly wages do not incur GST as they are covered under the Income Tax regime. The Tax Code N-T stands for Not Reportable. They are still a tax deduction.

Date:	5 June
Cheque No.:	005107
Payee:	Cash Payment
Details: Purchases	
GST-Free Purchase	$50.00
Tax Code: FRE	

Save as Recurring: Never. Name: Purchases GST Free.

Date:	5 June
Cheque No.:	005108
Payee:	The Advertiser P/L
Details: Advertising	
Monthly Advertisement:	$165.00
Payment includes $15.00 GST	

Save as Recurring: Monthly. Name: The Advertiser.

Date:	12 June
Cheque No.:	005109
Payee:	Cash Payment
Details: Purchases	
Purchase of Fishing Tackle	$352.00
Payment includes $32.00 GST	

Save as Recurring: Monthly. Name: Purchase of Fishing Tackle.

Date:	12 June
Cheque No.:	005110
Payee:	Ampol
Details: Hire Boat Operating Costs	
Fuel for boats	$220.00
Payment includes $20.00 GST	

Save as Recurring: Monthly. Name: Fuel for Boats.
Hint: boat fuel is a cost of goods sold.

You can click the **Use Recurring** button to record most of the following transactions. Or you can use the shortcut keys **Alt + U**.

Date:	16 June
Cheque No.:	005111
Payee:	Cash Payment
Details: Purchases	
GST-Free Purchase	$35.00
Tax Code: FRE	

Date:	16 June
Cheque No.:	005112
Payee:	Cash Payment
Details: Wages	
Fortnightly Wages	$800.00
Tax Code: N-T	

Date:	20 June	Date:	21 June
Cheque No.:	005113	**Cheque No.:**	005114
Payee:	Cash Payment	Payee:	Cash Payment
Details: Purchases		Details: Purchases	
Purchase of Fishing Tackle	$132.00	GST-Free Purchase	$40.00
Payment includes $12.00 GST		Tax Code: FRE	

Date:	30 June	Date:	30 June
Cheque No.:	005115	**Cheque No.:**	005116
Payee:	Tieppo	Payee:	Cash Payment
Details: Hire Boat Operating Costs		Details: Wages	
Payment of Account	$792.00	Fortnightly Wages	$800.00
Payment includes $72.00 GST		Tax Code: N-T	

After completing all the cheques, click **Cancel** to close the window down.

Produce reports

Now we can have a look at some reports.

Bank Register report

1 Produce Bank Register.

Click...

- *Reports* at the bottom of the Command Centre.
- *Banking* in the left menu.
- *Bank Register* in the middle menu (under the Cheques and Deposits bolded heading).
- *Dated From* (type *01/06/2017*) and *To* (type *30/06/2017*).
- *Display Report*. See **Figure 5.12** and **5.13**.

Figure 5.12   Reports Index: Banking

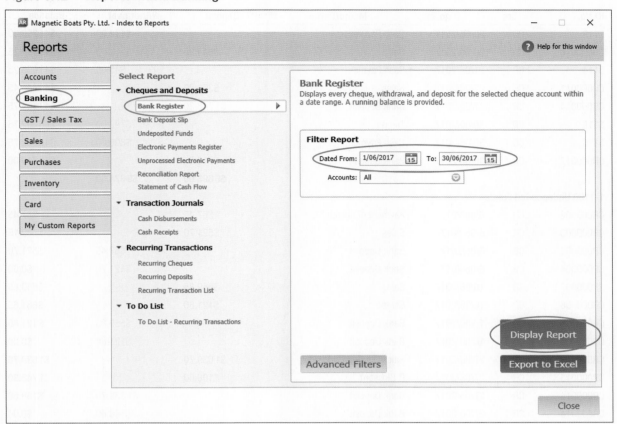

Figure 5.13   Bank Register: Magnetic Boats

Magnetic Boats Pty Ltd
Arcadia
Magnetic Island Qld 4819
Bank Register
June 2017

ID No.	Src	Date	Memo/Payee	Deposit	Withdrawal	Balance
1-1110 Cheque Account						
5104	CD	1/06/2017	Island Real Estate		$1 100.00	$43 900.00
5105	CD	1/06/2017	Cash Payment		$88.00	$43 812.00
5106	CD	2/06/2017	Cash Payment		$800.00	$43 012.00
CR000001	CR	3/06/2017	Sales	$684.90		$43 696.90
5107	CD	2/06/2017	Cash Payment		$50.00	$43 646.90
5108	CD	5/06/2017	The Advertiser		$165.00	$43 481.90
CR000004	CR	6/06/2017	Bank Deposit	$589.15		$44 071.05
CR000005	CR	8/06/2017	Sales	$362.85		$44 433.90
CR000006	CR	10/06/2017	Sales	$673.75		$45 107.65
5109	CD	12/06/2017	Cash Payment		$352.00	$44 755.65
5110	CD	12/06/2017	Ampol		$220.00	$44 535.65
5111	CD	16/06/2017	Cash Payment		$35.00	$44 500.65
5112	CD	16/06/2017	Cash Payment		$800.00	$43 700.65
CR000009	CR	16/06/2017	Bank Deposit	$681.65		$44 382.30

ID No.	Src	Date	Memo/Payee	Deposit	Withdrawal	Balance
5113	CD	20/06/2017	Cash Payment		$132.00	$44 250.30
CR000010	CR	20/06/2017	Sales	$844.95		$45 095.25
5114	CD	21/06/2017	Cash Payment		$40.00	$45 055.25
CR000011	CR	22/06/2017	Sales	$391.20		$45 446.45
CR000014	CR	27/06/2017	Bank Deposit	$1 748.30		$47 194.75
5115	CD	30/06/2017	Tieppo		$792.00	$46 402.75
5116	CD	30/06/2017	Cash Payment		$800.00	$45 602.75
CR000017	CR	30/06/2017	Bank Deposit	$716.25		$46 319.00
				$6 693.00	**$5 374.00**	

1-1180 Undeposited Funds

ID No.	Src	Date	Memo/Payee	Deposit	Withdrawal	Balance
CR000002	CR	6/06/2017	Payment of Account	$67.45		$67.45
CR000003	CR	6/06/2017	Sales	$521.70		$589.15
CR000004	CR	6/06/2017	Bank Deposit		$67.45	$521.70
CR000004	CR	6/06/2017	Bank Deposit		$521.70	$0.00
CR000007	CR	16/06/2017	Sales	$559.85		$559.85
CR000008	CR	16/06/2017	Sales	$121.80		$681.65
CR000009	CR	16/06/2017	Bank Deposit		$559.85	$121.80
CR000009	CR	16/06/2017	Bank Deposit		$121.80	$0.00
CR000012	CR	27/06/2017	Sales	$1 639.70		$1 639.70
CR000013	CR	27/06/2017	P. Blossom	$108.60		$1 748.30
CR000014	CR	27/06/2017	Bank Deposit		$1 639.70	$108.60
CR000014	CR	27/06/2017	Bank Deposit		$108.60	$0.00
CR000015	CR	30/06/2017	P. Blossom	$612.45		$612.45
CR000016	CR	30/06/2017	Sales	$103.80		$716.25
CR000017	CR	30/06/2017	Bank Deposit		$612.45	$103.80
CR000017	CR	30/06/2017	Bank Deposit		$103.80	$0.00
				$3 735.35	**$3 735.35**	

Check your own Bank Register against the example above. Particularly note that the balance shown at the bottom of the Undeposited Funds account is zero. Any balance there should be removed by making the appropriate bank deposits before proceeding.

Reconcile bank account

2 The following bank statement has been received from the Townsville branch of the *Which?* Bank and must be reconciled with your records.

Which? Bank
101 Sturt Street
Townsville Qld 4810
Statement of Account for Magnetic Boats Pty Ltd
June

Date	Details	Withdrawals	Deposits	Balance
01	Balance b/f			$45 000.00 Cr
02	Cheque 5105	88.00		44 912.00 Cr
02	Cheque 5106	800.00		44 112.00 Cr
03	Cheque 5107	50.00		44 062.00 Cr
03	Deposit		684.90	44 746.90 Cr
06	Cheque 5104	1 100.00		43 646.90 Cr
07	Cheque 5109	352.00		43 294.90 Cr
07	Deposit		589.15	43 884.05 Cr
07	Cheque 5108	165.00		43 719.05 Cr
09	Cheque 5112	800.00		42 919.05 Cr
09	Deposit		362.85	43 281.90 Cr
10	Cheque 5110	220.00		43 061.90 Cr
10	Deposit		673.75	43 735.65 Cr
16	Cheque 5111	35.00		43 700.65 Cr
16	Deposit		681.65	44 382.30 Cr
20	Deposit		844.95	45 227.25 Cr
20	Cheque 5113	132.00		45 095.25 Cr
22	Deposit		391.20	45 446.45 Cr
27	Deposit		1 748.30	47 194.75 Cr
28	Interest on account		183.35	47 378.10 Cr
30	Bank Fees	35.00		47 343.10 Cr
30	Statement Closing Balance			47 343.10 Cr

Your MYOB records show that there is a balance of $46 319.00 in the Cheque Account. See Figure 5.14. The bank statement above says there is $47 343.10.

The two sets of figures must be *reconciled* to show that they are both correct.

Figure 5.14   **Accounts module: Accounts List extract**

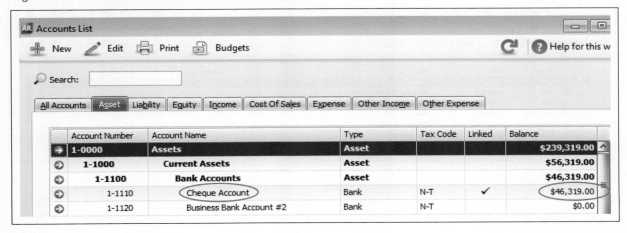

To do the bank reconciliation, you proceed as follows:

Click...

- *Reconcile Accounts* (in the Banking module). See **Figure 5.15**. A new window opens.
- *Account* (select *1-1110 Cheque Account*).
- *Closing Statement Balance* (type *47 343.10*).
- *Bank Statement Date* (type *30/06/17*). See **Figure 5.16**. Press the Tab key.

Figure 5.15   Command Centre: Banking module

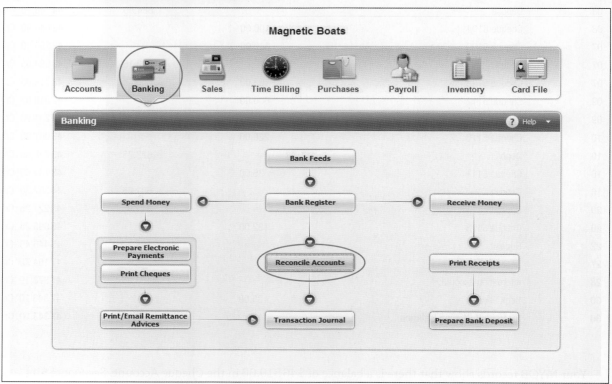

Figure 5.16   Banking: Reconcile Accounts

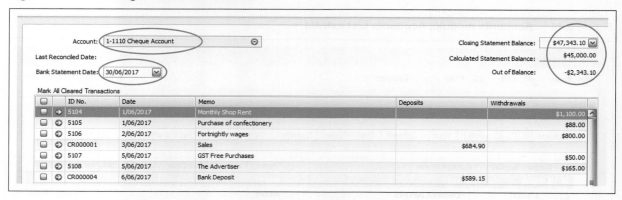

The *Closing Statement Balance* is the closing balance shown in the bank statement as at a certain date, in this case 30/06/2017.

The *Calculated Statement Balance* is the closing balance in MYOB as at the same date.

The *Out of Balance* will vary as amounts are matched and ticked off between MYOB and the bank statement. It is important to complete the fields in the top section of your bank reconciliation correctly as you want:

$$\text{Closing Statement Balance} = \text{Calculated Statement Balance}$$

Working *from* your bank statement *to* your MYOB:

- Locate the first transaction in your bank statement in the book. In this case, it is Cheque 5105 dated 2 June for $88.00.
- Find the corresponding transaction in MYOB. In this case, it is the second line.
- Tick both the paper bank statement and the MYOB bank statement. You can tick in MYOB by either clicking on the number $88.00 or clicking in the check-box to the left of the window. See Figure 5.17.

Figure 5.17   **Reconciling transactions in MYOB**

Continue this process, matching transactions as you go. If you come across a discrepancy, the bank statement is considered correct and you need to amend the transaction in MYOB. This can be done by clicking on the white zoom arrow next to the transaction.

Tip

After ticking five to eight consecutive transactions, compare your Calculated Statement Balance in MYOB to the balance on the right side of your paper bank statement. If they don't match, you know there is an error in the preceding transactions and it is easier to pick up now than it would be when searching through the entire month of transactions. If they do match, then you know you are correct up to that point. Check the balances again after ticking another five to eight transactions. If there is a discrepancy, then you know it is in the transactions between the time you last balanced and now.

Note that (for this exercise) after you have reconciled all of the deposits and cheques from the bank statement to MYOB, you should:

- be out of balance by $148.35
- have two withdrawals *unticked,* and
- have one deposit *unticked.* See Figure 5.18.

Figure 5.18   Reconciled transactions between MYOB and bank statement

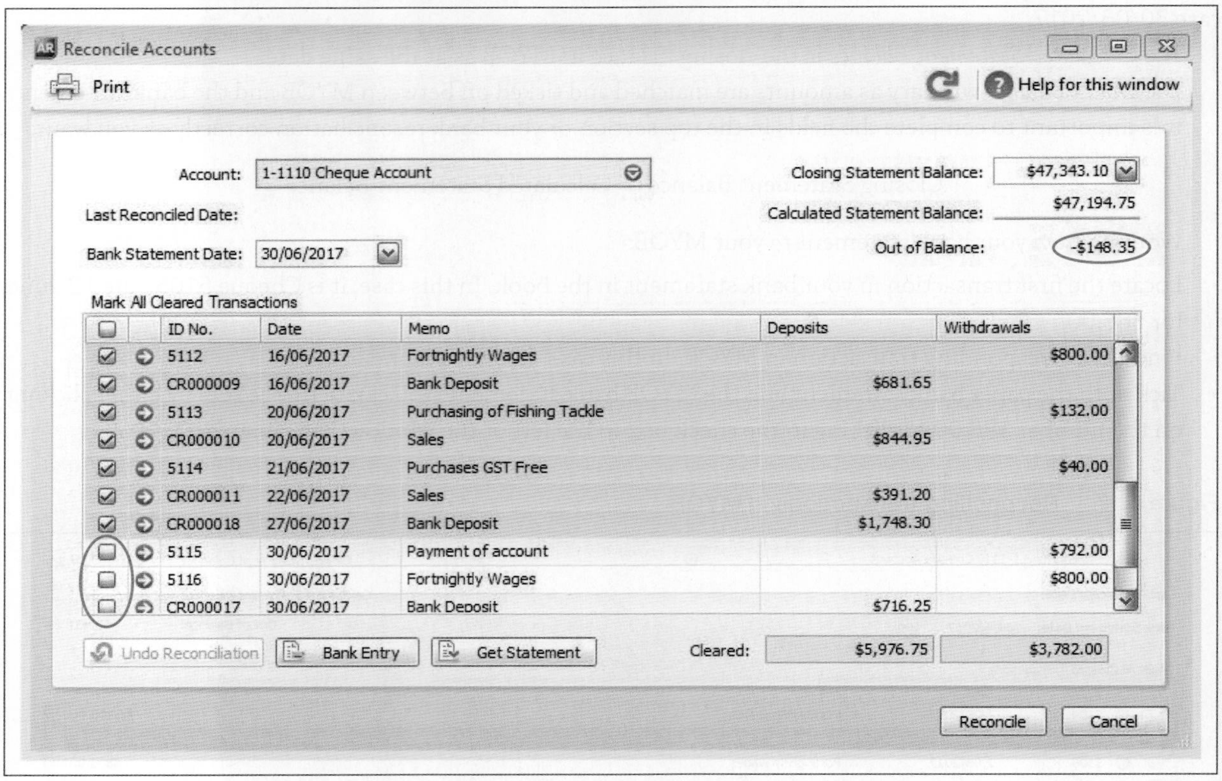

From time to time, you will come across transactions that are in the bank statement, but not in MYOB. These transactions generally don't have a source document and include:

- loan repayments directly debited from the bank account
- bank fees and interest expenses (if the account has an overdraft)
- bank interest income
- direct deposits from customers who may or may not have sent a remittance advice.

Figure 5.19 shows an extract from the bank statement. These transactions can be found in the bank statement but have not been processed in MYOB.

Figure 5.19   Extract from bank statement

28	Interest on account		183.35	47 378.10 Cr
30	Bank Fees	35.00		47 343.10 Cr
30	**Statement Closing Balance**			**47 343.10 Cr**

Any loan repayments and customer deposits can be entered through the Banking module, using Spend Money and Receive Money respectively.

The bank fees, interest expense and interest income can be entered into MYOB thusly:

Click...

- *Bank Entry* (bottom of the window). Another window opens.
- *Amount* in the Service Charges section (type *35.00*).
- *Date* (type *30/06/17* if necessary).
- *Expense Account* (choose *6-1300 Bank Fees*).
- *Memo* (insert *Bank Fees*).

- *Tax Code* (check it is *FRE* as there is no GST on bank fees or interest).
- *Amount* in the Interest Earned section (type *183.35*).
- *Date* (type *30/06/17* if necessary).
- *Income Account* (choose *8-1000 Interest Income*).
- *Memo* (insert *Interest received*).
- *Tax Code* (check it is *ITS* as there is no GST on interest). Compare with Figure 5.20.
- Record.

Figure 5.20   Bank and deposit adjustments

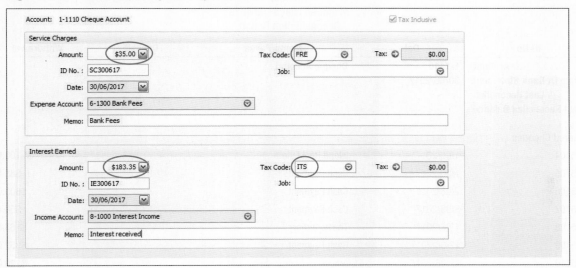

The end result should be:

- *Out of Balance* at the top of the window should be zero.
- The two withdrawals dated 30 June 2017 are still unticked as the cheques haven't been presented to the bank.
- The deposit dated 30 June 2017 is unticked as it hasn't been deposited to the bank. See Figure 5.21.

Figure 5.21   Reconciled transactions where banks statement is the source document

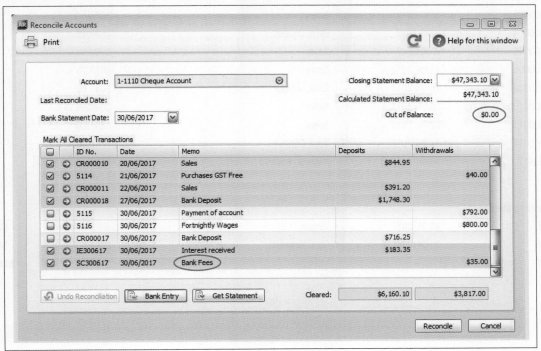

Click...

- *Reconcile* (button at bottom right of the window).
- *Print report* (on the new window that pops up). Compare your report with **Figure** 5.22.
- *Reconcile* (back on the Reconcile Accounts window)
- *Reconcile* (on the new window that pops up).

Figure 5.22   **Bank Reconciliation Report**

ID No	Date	Memo/Payee	Deposit	Withdrawal
Account:	1-1110	Cheque Account		
Date Of Bank Statement:	30/06/2017			
Last Reconciled:				
Last Reconciled Balance:				
Cleared Cheques				
5104	1/06/2017	Island Real Estate		$1 100.00
5105	1/06/2017	Cash Payment		$88.00
5106	2/06/2017	Cash Payment		$800.00
5107	5/06/2017	Cash Payment		$50.00
5108	5/06/2017	The Advertiser		$165.00
5109	12/06/2017	Cash Payment		$352.00
5110	12/06/2017	Ampol		$220.00
5111	16/06/2017	Cash Payment		$35.00
5112	16/06/2017	Cash Payment		$800.00
5113	20/06/2017	Cash Payment		$132.00
5114	21/06/2017	Cash Payment		$40.00
SC300617	30/06/2017	Bank Fees		$35.00
		Total:	**$0.00**	**$3 817.00**
Cleared Deposits				
CR000001	3/06/2017	Sales	$684.90	
CR000004	6/06/2017	Bank Deposit	$589.15	
CR000005	8/06/2017	Sales	$362.85	
CR000006	10/06/2017	Sales	$673.75	
CR000009	16/06/2017	Bank Deposit	$681.65	
CR000010	20/06/2017	Sales	$844.95	
CR000011	22/06/2017	Sales	$391.20	
CR000014	27/06/2017	Bank Deposit	$1 748.30	
IE300617	30/06/2017	Interest received	$183.35	
		Total:	**$6 160.10**	**$0.00**
Outstanding Cheques				
5115	30/06/2017	Tieppo		$792.00
5116	30/06/2017	Cash Payment		$800.00
		Total:	**$0.00**	**$1 592.00**

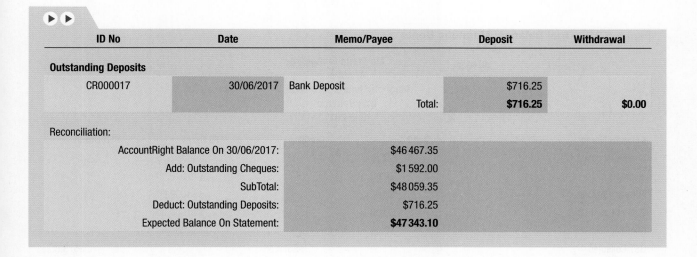

ID No	Date	Memo/Payee	Deposit	Withdrawal
Outstanding Deposits				
CR000017	30/06/2017	Bank Deposit	$716.25	
		Total:	**$716.25**	**$0.00**
Reconciliation:				
AccountRight Balance On 30/06/2017:		$46 467.35		
Add: Outstanding Cheques:		$1 592.00		
SubTotal:		$48 059.35		
Deduct: Outstanding Deposits:		$716.25		
Expected Balance On Statement:		**$47 343.10**		

The ticked (reconciled) transactions are removed as they have been matched with the bank statement. All that is left are the three transactions which may well turn up in the July bank statement. See Figure 5.23.

Figure 5.23 Reconciled accounts after first reconciliation

Click...

- *Cancel* (to exit).

More reports

3 June 30 is the end of the financial year, so the following reports are required:

- Trial Balance (to have a record of the closing balances of each account in the general ledger).
- GST [Summary – Cash] (to have an accurate record of the GST liability).
- Balance Sheet (to see Magnetic Boats' financial position).
- Profit & Loss Statement (to see the profitability of the business).

Trial Balance

Click...

- *Reports* (button at base of the Command Centre).
- *Accounts* (in the left column menu).
- *Trial Balance* (in the middle column menu).
- *As of* (select *June*).
- *Financial Year* (select *This Year (FY2017)*).
- *Display*. Compare with Figure 5.24.

Figure 5.24   **Trial Balance: Magnetic Boats**

Magnetic Boats
Arcadia
Magnetic Island QLD 4819
Trial Balance
June 2017

Account Name	Debit	Credit	YTD Debit	YTD Credit
Cheque Account	$1 467.35		$46 467.35	
Inventory	$0.00		$10 000.00	
Furniture At Cost	$0.00		$8 000.00	
Boat equip At Cost	$0.00		$25 000.00	
Boats At Cost	$0.00		$150 000.00	
GST Collected		$573.55		$573.55
GST Paid	$259.00		$259.00	
Business Loan #1		$0.00		$200 000.00
Owner's/Shareholder's Capital		$0.00		$38 000.00
Hire of Boats		$3 940.00		$3 940.00
Fishing Tackles Sales		$1 205.00		$1 205.00
Confectionery Sales		$590.50		$590.50
GST Free Sales		$383.95		$383.95
Hire Boats Operating Cost	$920.00		$920.00	
Fishing Tackles Purchases	$440.00		$440.00	
Confectionery Purchases	$80.00		$80.00	
GST Free Purchases	$125.00		$125.00	
Advertising & Marketing	$150.00		$150.00	
Bank Fees	$35.00		$35.00	
Rent	$1 000.00		$1 000.00	
Wages & Salaries Expenses	$2 400.00		$2 400.00	
Interest Income		$183.35		$183.35
Total:	**$6 876.35**	**$6 876.35**	**$244 876.35**	**$244 876.35**

The Trial Balance shows the debits and credits to each account for the month of June, and for the Year to Date (YTD).

GST [Summary – Cash]

Click...

- *Reports* (button at base of the Command Centre).
- *GST/Sales Tax* (in the left column menu).
- *GST [Summary – Cash]* (in the middle column menu).
- *Dated From* (type *1/06/17*) and *To* (type *30/06/17*).
- *Display.* Compare with Figure 5.25.

Figure 5.25   GST [Summary – Cash]: Magnetic Boats

	Magnetic Boats Arcadia Magnetic Island QLD 4819 GST [Summary – Cash] June 2017					
Code	Description	Rate	Sale Value	Purchase Value	Tax Collected	Tax Paid
FRE	GST Free	0.00%	$383.95	$160.00		
GST	Goods & Services Tax	10.00%	$6 309.05	$2 849.00	$573.55	$259.00
ITS	Input Taxed Sales	0.00%	$183.35			
N-T	Not Reportable	0.00%		$2 400.00		
				Total:	$573.55	$259.00

- **FRE** items include bank fees and some food items. Though they are technically a good or a service (and they are bought or sold – see Chapter 1) , the tax rate is 0%.
- **GST** items include the 10% tax on income and expenses, for example on goods and services that are bought and sold.
- **ITS** items include bank interest received.
- **N-T** items are not reportable on the BAS and include wages and transfers between bank accounts. These transactions are not bought or sold, so are not under the GST taxation regime.

Balance Sheet

This shows the business' debts and liabilities and ultimately the owner's interest in the business (known as Owners Equity).

Click...
- *Reports Index* screen.
- *Accounts* (in the left column menu).
- *Balance Sheet* (in the middle column menu).
- *As Of* (type *30/06/17*).
- *Display*. Compare with Figure 5.26.

Figure 5.26   Balance Sheet: Magnetic Boats

	Magnetic Boats Arcadia Magnetic Island QLD 4819 Balance Sheet June 2017		
Assets			
Current Assets			
Bank Accounts			
Cheque Account	$46 467.35		
Total Bank Accounts		$46 467.35	
Other Current Assets			
Inventory	$10 000.00		
Total Other Current Assets		$10 000.00	
Total Current Assets			$56 467.35

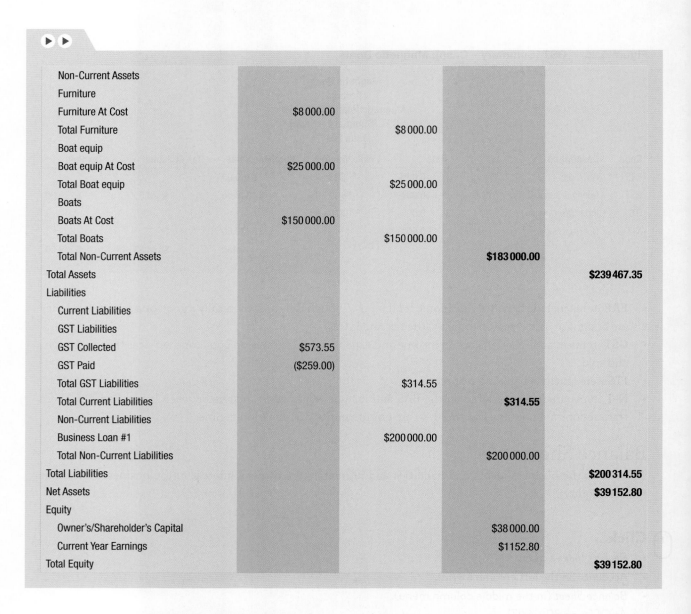

Non-Current Assets			
Furniture			
Furniture At Cost	$8 000.00		
Total Furniture		$8 000.00	
Boat equip			
Boat equip At Cost	$25 000.00		
Total Boat equip		$25 000.00	
Boats			
Boats At Cost	$150 000.00		
Total Boats		$150 000.00	
Total Non-Current Assets			**$183 000.00**
Total Assets				**$239 467.35**
Liabilities			
Current Liabilities			
GST Liabilities			
GST Collected	$573.55		
GST Paid	($259.00)		
Total GST Liabilities		$314.55	
Total Current Liabilities			**$314.55**
Non-Current Liabilities			
Business Loan #1		$200 000.00	
Total Non-Current Liabilities			$200 000.00
Total Liabilities				**$200 314.55**
Net Assets				**$39 152.80**
Equity			
Owner's/Shareholder's Capital			$38 000.00
Current Year Earnings			$1 152.80
Total Equity				**$39 152.80**

The Accounting Equation balances.

$$\text{Assets} = \text{Liabilities} + \text{Equity}$$
$$\$239\,467.35 = \$200\,314.55 + \$39\,152.80$$

Profit & Loss Statement

Also sometimes called a Revenue Statement, this shows details of income and expenditure over a fixed period of time and allows for the calculation of profit or loss for the business over that period.

- Gross Profit is Sales minus Cost of Sales.
- Operating Profit is Gross Profit minus Expenses.
- Net Profit is Operating Profit minus Other Expenses and plus Other Income.

Click...

- *Reports* menu.
- *Accounts* (in the left column menu).
- *Profit & Loss Statement* (in the middle column menu).
- *Dated From* (type *1/06/17*) and *To* (type *30/06/17*).
- *Display*. Compare with Figure 5.27.

Figure 5.27   **Profit & Loss Statement: Magnetic Boats**

Magnetic Boats
Arcadia
Magnetic Island QLD 4819
Profit & Loss Statement
June 2017

Income			
Hire of Boats		$3 940.00	
Fishing Tackles Sales		$1 205.00	
Confectionery Sales		$590.50	
GST Free Sales		$383.95	
Total Income			**$6 119.45**
Cost of Sales			
Hire Boats Operating Cost		$920.00	
Fishing Tackles Purchases		$440.00	
Confectionery Purchases		$80.00	
GST Free Purchases		$125.00	
Total Cost of Sales			**$1 565.00**
Gross Profit			**$4 554.45**
Expenses			
General Expenses			
Advertising & Marketing	$150.00		
Bank Fees	$35.00		
Rent	$1 000.00		
Total General Expenses		**$1 185.00**	
Payroll Expenses			
Wages & Salaries Expenses	$2 400.00		
Total Payroll Expenses		**$2 400.00**	
Total Expenses			**$3 585.00**
Operating Profit			**$969.45**
Other Income			
Interest Income		$183.35	
Total Other Income			$183.35
Total Other Expenses			$0.00
Net Profit/(Loss)			**$1 152.80**

Financial year rollover

After the accountants have done what they need to and adjusting journals are done at the end of the financial year, the financial year needs to be rolled over and locked down. The end results of closing your financial year are:

- The balance of your current year earnings account is transferred to your retained earnings account.
- Your profit and loss accounts of income and expenses (prefixes of 4, 5, 6, 8 and 9) are returned to zero.

1 In MYOB AccountRight 2016 open **5.2 Magnetic Boats.myox data** file located in the Chapter 5 folder of your start-up files, or continue with your own data file from the previous exercise.

2 Start a new financial year.

Click...

- *File* (in the top menu bar).
- *Close a Year* (from the drop-down menu).
- *Close a Financial Year* (from the next menu). See Figure 5.28.

Figure 5.28   Closing a financial year

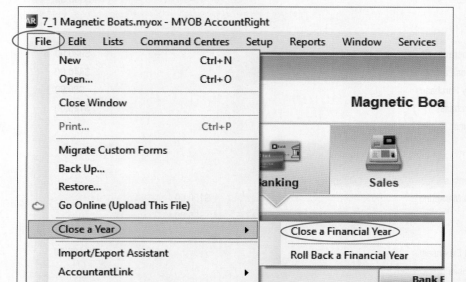

Click...

- *Yes I'm the only user*. Read the screen.
- *Next*. Read the screen.
- *Next*. Read the screen. You only need to do this if you use the Audit Trail feature, which is a way of tracing who has done which transactions or deletions in the MYOB system.
- *Next*. Don't do a backup on this occasion, though you would do a backup in a real-life situation.
- *Close the Financial Year*.
- *Close*.

3 Lock the accounting period to prevent any accidental changes to the records now that the end-of-period reports have been produced.

Click...

- *Setup* (in the top menu bar).
- *Preferences* (from the drop-down menu).
- *Security* (the tab on top right of the window).
- *Lock Period: Disallow Entries Prior To* (type *30/06/17*). See Figure 5.29.
- OK.

Figure 5.29   Locking the period

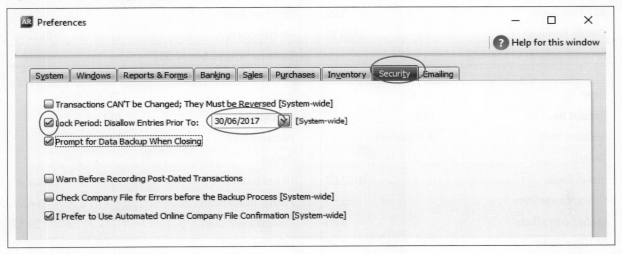

More transactions

1   Record the following receipts for July, combining those received on the same day before making the day's bank deposit.

Remember This
___

First, click *Use Recurring* at the bottom of the window to call up the template. Then change the date and numbers.

Date:	7 July
Receipt No.:	018
Received from:	Sales
Details:	
Hire of Boats	$181.50
Fishing Tackle Sales	38.50
Confectionery Sales	51.70
GST-Free Sales	17.00
Cash Received:	$288.70
Revenue includes $24.70 GST	

Date:	14 July
Receipt No.:	019
Received from:	Sales
Details:	
Hire of Boats	$253.00
Fishing Tackle Sales	71.50
Confectionery Sales	52.80
GST-Free Sales	21.40
Cash Received:	$398.70
Revenue includes $34.30 GST	

Date:	18 July		Date:	18 July
Receipt No.:	020		**Receipt No.:**	021
Received from:	P Blossom		Received from:	Sales
Details:			Details:	
Hire of Boats	$96.80		Hire of Boats	$374.00
Fishing Tackle Sales	14.30		Fishing Tackle Sales	74.80
Confectionery Sales	9.90		Confectionery Sales	58.30
GST-Free Sales	5.20		GST-Free Sales	25.45
Cheque Received:	$126.20		Cash Received:	$532.55
Revenue includes $11.00 GST			Revenue includes $46.10 GST	

Date:	21 July		Date:	21 July
Receipt No.:	023		**Receipt No.:**	024
Received from:	A. Kitamaura		Received from:	Sales
Details:			Details:	
Hire of Boats	$132.00		Hire of Boats	$308.00
Fishing Tackle Sales	5.50		Fishing Tackle Sales	104.50
Confectionery Sales	8.80		Confectionery Sales	59.40
GST-Free Sales	1.25		GST-Free Sales	28.25
Cheque Received:	$147.55		Cash Received:	$500.15
Revenue includes $13.30 GST			Revenue includes $42.90 GST	

Date:	28 July		Date:	31 July
Receipt No.:	026		**Receipt No.:**	027
Received from:	Sales		Received from:	Sales
Details:			Details:	
Hire of Boats	$385.00		Hire of Boats	$385.00
Fishing Tackle Sales	221.10		Fishing Tackle Sales	169.40
Confectionery Sales	214.50		Confectionery Sales	80.85
GST-Free Sales	32.55		GST-Free Sales	41.20
Cash Received:	$853.15		Cash Received:	$676.45
Revenue includes $74.60 GST			Revenue includes $57.75 GST	

2 Record the following payments made during July, using recurring transactions where there is one available:

Date:	1 July
Cheque no.:	5117
Payee:	Island Real Estate
Details: Monthly Shop Rent	
Rent	$1 100.00
Payment includes $100.00 GST	

Date:	1 July
Cheque no.:	5118
Payee:	Ampol
Details: Purchases	
Fuel for Boats	$302.50
Payment includes $27.50 GST	

Date:	5 July
Cheque no.:	5119
Payee:	The Advertiser
Details: Monthly Advertisement	
Advertising	$165.00
Payment includes $15.00 GST	

Date:	7 July
Cheque no.:	5120
Payee:	Cash Payment
Details: Purchases	
Purchase of Fishing Tackle	$387.20
Payment includes $35.20 GST	

Date:	11 July
Cheque no.:	5121
Payee:	Cash Payment
Details: Purchases	
Purchase of Confectionery	$275.00
Payment includes $25.00 GST	

Date:	14 July
Cheque no.:	5122
Payee:	Cash Payment
Details: Fortnightly Wages	
Wages	$800.00
Tax Code: N-T	

Date:	21 July
Cheque no.:	5123
Payee:	Optus
Details: Payment of Phone Account	
Telephone	$165.00
Payment includes $15.00 GST	

Date:	25 July
Cheque no.:	5124
Payee:	Ampol
Details: Purchases	
Fuel for Boats	$132.00
Payment includes $12.00 GST	

Set Optus up as a new supplier card

Date:	28 July
Cheque no.:	5125
Payee:	Cash Payment
Details: Fortnightly Wages	
Wages	$800.00
Tax Code: N-T	

Date:	31 July
Cheque no.:	5126
Payee:	Cash Payment
Details: Purchases	
GST-Free Purchases	$64.00
Tax Code: FRE	

3 Print or display the July Bank Register (Figure 5.30).

Figure 5.30   Bank Register: Magnetic Boats July 17

			Magnetic Boats Arcadia Magnetic Island QLD 4819 Bank Register July 2017			
ID No.	**Src**	**Date**	**Memo/Payee**	**Deposit**	**Withdrawal**	**Balance**
1-1110 Cheque Account						
5117	CD	1/07/2017	Island Real Estate		$1 100.00	$45 367.35
5118	CD	1/07/2017	Ampol		$302.50	$45 064.85
5119	CD	5/07/2017	The Advertiser		$165.00	$44 899.85
5120	CD	7/07/2017	Cash Payment		$387.20	$44 512.65
CR000018	CR	7/07/2017	Sales	$288.70		$44 801.35
5121	CD	11/07/2017	Cash Payment		$275.00	$44 526.35
5122	CD	14/07/2017	Cash Payment		$800.00	$43 726.35
CR000019	CR	14/07/2017	Sales	$398.70		$44 125.05
CR000022	CR	18/07/2017	Bank Deposit	$658.75		$44 783.80
5123	CD	21/07/2017	Optus		$165.00	$44 618.80
CR000028	CR	21/07/2017	Bank Deposit	$647.70		$45 266.50
5124	CD	25/07/2017	Ampol		$132.00	$45 134.50
5125	CD	28/07/2017	Cash Payment		$800.00	$44 334.50
CR000026	CR	28/07/2017	Sales	$853.15		$45 187.65
5126	CD	31/07/2017	Cash Payment		$64.00	$45 123.65
CR000027	CR	31/07/2017	Sales	$676.45		$45 800.10
				$3 523.45	**$4 190.70**	
1-1210 Account Undeposited Funds						
CR000020	CR	18/07/2017	P. Blossom	$126.20		$126.20
CR000021	CR	18/07/2017	Sales	$532.55		$658.75
CR000022	CR	18/07/2017	Bank Deposit		$126.20	$532.55
CR000022	CR	18/07/2017	Bank Deposit		$532.55	$0.00
CR000023	CR	21/07/2017	A. Kitamaura	$147.55		$147.55
CR000024	CR	21/07/2017	Sales	$500.15		$647.70
CR000028	CR	21/07/2017	Bank Deposit		$147.55	$500.15
CR000028	CR	21/07/2017	Bank Deposit		$500.15	$0.00
				$1 306.45	**$1 306.45**	

Check in particular that the closing balance for Undeposited Funds (at the base of the far-right column) is zero. Any remaining balance at this point would mean that one or more bank deposits have not been completed correctly.

4 Reconcile your MYOB records with the following statement received from the *Which?* Bank, updating MYOB with information from the statement.

Which? Bank
101 Sturt Street
Townsville Qld 4819
Statement of Account for Magnetic Boats Pty Ltd
July 2017

Date	Details	Withdrawals	Deposits	Balance	
01	**Balance b/f**			**$47 343.10**	**Cr**
01	Deposit		716.25	48 059.35	Cr
01	Cheque 5115	792.00		47 267.35	Cr
01	Cheque 5116	800.00		46 467.35	Cr
01	Cheque 5117	1 100.00		45 367.35	Cr
04	Cheque 5118	302.50		45 064.85	Cr
04	Cheque 5119	165.00		44 899.85	Cr
07	Deposit		288.70	45 188.55	Cr
09	Cheque 5120	387.20		44 801.35	Cr
11	Cheque 5121	275.00		44 526.35	Cr
14	Cheque 5122	800.00		43 726.35	Cr
14	Deposit		398.70	44 125.05	Cr
18	Deposit		658.75	44 783.80	Cr
18	Cheque Book Fee	35.00		44 748.80	Cr
21	Deposit		647.70	45 396.50	Cr
28	Cheque 5125	800.00		44 596.50	Cr
28	Interest on account		197.20	44 793.70	Cr
28	Deposit		853.15	45 646.85	Cr
31	Bank Fees	35.00		45 611.85	Cr
31	**Statement Closing Balance**			**45 611.85**	**Cr**

5 Print or display a Reconciliation report for Cheque Account 1-1110, statement date 31 July 2017. See Figure 5.31.

Figure 5.31 Cheque Account Reconciliation report July 17

Magnetic Boats
Arcadia
Magnetic Island QLD 4819
Reconciliation Report

ID No.	Date	Memo/Payee	Deposit	Withdrawal
Account: 1-1110		Cheque Account		
Date Of Bank Statement: 31/07/2017				
Last Reconciled: 30/06/2017				
Last Reconciled Balance: $47 343.10				
Cleared Cheques				
5115	30/06/2017	Tieppo		$792.00
5116	30/06/2017	Cash Payment		$800.00
5117	1/07/2017	Island Real Estate		$1 100.00

▶ ▶

▶ ▶

ID No.	Date	Memo/Payee	Deposit	Withdrawal
5118	1/07/2017	Ampol		$302.50
5119	5/07/2017	The Advertiser		$165.00
5120	7/07/2017	Cash Payment		$387.20
5121	11/07/2017	Cash Payment		$275.00
5122	14/07/2017	Cash Payment		$800.00
SC310717	21/07/2017	Cheque Book Fee		$35.00
5125	28/07/2017	Cash Payment		$800.00
SC310717	31/07/2017	Bank Fees		$35.00
		Total:	**$0.00**	**$5 491.70**

Cleared Deposits

CR000017	30/06/2017	Bank Deposit	$716.25	
CR000018	7/07/2017	Sales	$288.70	
CR000019	14/07/2017	Sales	$398.70	
CR000022	18/07/2017	Bank Deposit	$658.75	
CR000028	21/07/2017	Bank Deposit	$647.70	
CR000026	28/07/2017	Sales	$853.15	
IE310717	31/07/2017	Interest Received	$197.20	
		Total:	**$3 760.45**	**$0.00**

Outstanding Cheques

5123	21/07/2017	Optus		$165.00
5124	25/07/2017	Ampol		$132.00
5126	31/07/2017	Cash Payment		$64.00
		Total:	**$0.00**	**$361.00**

Outstanding Deposits

CR000027	31/07/2017	Sales	$676.45	
		Total:	**$676.45**	**$0.00**

Reconciliation:

AccountRight Balance On 31/07/2017:	$45 927.30
Add: Outstanding Cheques:	$361.00
SubTotal:	$46 288.30
Deduct: Outstanding Deposits:	$676.45
Expected Balance On Statement:	$45 611.85

Click *Reconcile.*

Petty cash and credit cards

Many business expenses are too small to justify the use of a separate cheque for each expense. Two common ways to handle these transactions are as follows:

- *Petty Cash Imprest*, in which an advance of cash is obtained by cashing a cheque. The money is kept in a secure place (usually in the office) where it is looked after by an appropriate person who keeps a record of the small payments made. When the petty cash fund is getting low, it is *reimbursed* to its original amount by cashing another cheque.

• *Company Credit Cards* can also be used in many cases, and the credit card monthly statement is the record of expenses. The balance is then paid with one cheque by the due date after reconciling with the company's records.

MAGNETIC BOATS

Petty cash

1   In MYOB AccountRight 2016, open **5.3 Magnetic Boats.myox** located in the Chapter 5 folder of your start-up files or use your own Magnetic Boats data file.

2   To start a Petty Cash Imprest:

Click...

• *Spend Money* (in the Banking Command Centre).
• *Date* (insert *1/08/17*).
• *Amount* (insert *50.00*).
• *Payee* (insert *Cash Payment*).
• *Memo* (insert *Petty Cash Imprest*).
• *Account No.* (select *1-1140 Petty Cash – Tax Code N-T*). Compare with **Figure 5.32**.
• *Record.*

Figure 5.32   Spend Money: begin Petty Cash Imprest

This is why

GST is applicable on sales and purchases. *This* transaction merely moves money from one asset (the bank) to another asset (petty cash), so there is no GST.

3 Use the Petty Cash Imprest to make the following payments. Don't fill out the supplier card name. Just use the memo:

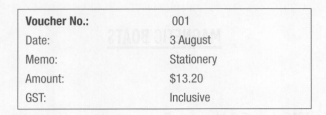

Voucher No.:	001
Date:	3 August
Memo:	Stationery
Amount:	$13.20
GST:	Inclusive

Click...

- *Pay from Account in Spend Money (select 1-1140 Petty Cash).*
- *Date (insert 3/08/17).*
- *Amount (insert 13.20).*
- *Memo (insert Office Supplies).*
- *Account No. (select 6-2800 Stationery – Tax Code GST).* Compare with **Figure 5.33**.
- *Record.*

Figure 5.33   Spend Money: from Petty Cash

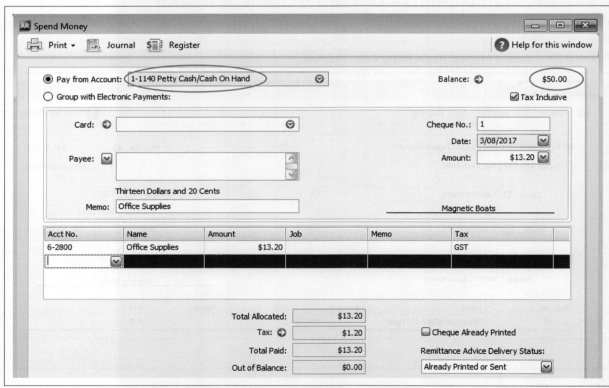

The balance in the top right side updates with the current balance after every transaction is recorded. Keep an eye on it as you do the petty cash payments below.

4 Make more petty cash payments

Voucher No.:	002
Date:	10 August
Memo:	Postage
Amount:	$6.60
GST:	Inclusive

Voucher No.:	003
Date:	17 August
Memo:	Cleaning Expenses
Amount:	$17.00
GST:	Inclusive

Voucher No.:	004
Date:	24 August
Memo:	Parking
Amount:	$11.00
GST:	Inclusive

5 When you have recorded the last payment from the Petty Cash Imprest, note that the balance remaining in the fund is only $2.20. So, you should have $47.80 worth of receipts and $2.20 worth of coins.

The Imprest must now be made back up to its original $50.00; this is known as *reimbursing* petty cash. Some operations reimburse regularly at the end of each month, while others just reimburse as required when the fund gets low.

You are still in the Spend Money window.

 Click...

- *Pay from Account* (select *1-1110 Cheque Account*).
- *Date* (insert *25/08/17*).
- *Amount* (insert *47.80*).
- *Payee* (insert *Cash Payment*).
- *Memo* (insert *reimburse petty cash*).
- *Account No.* (select *1-1140 Petty Cash – Tax Code N-T*). Compare with **Figure 5.34.**
- *Record.*

Figure 5.34   Spend Money: from Petty Cash

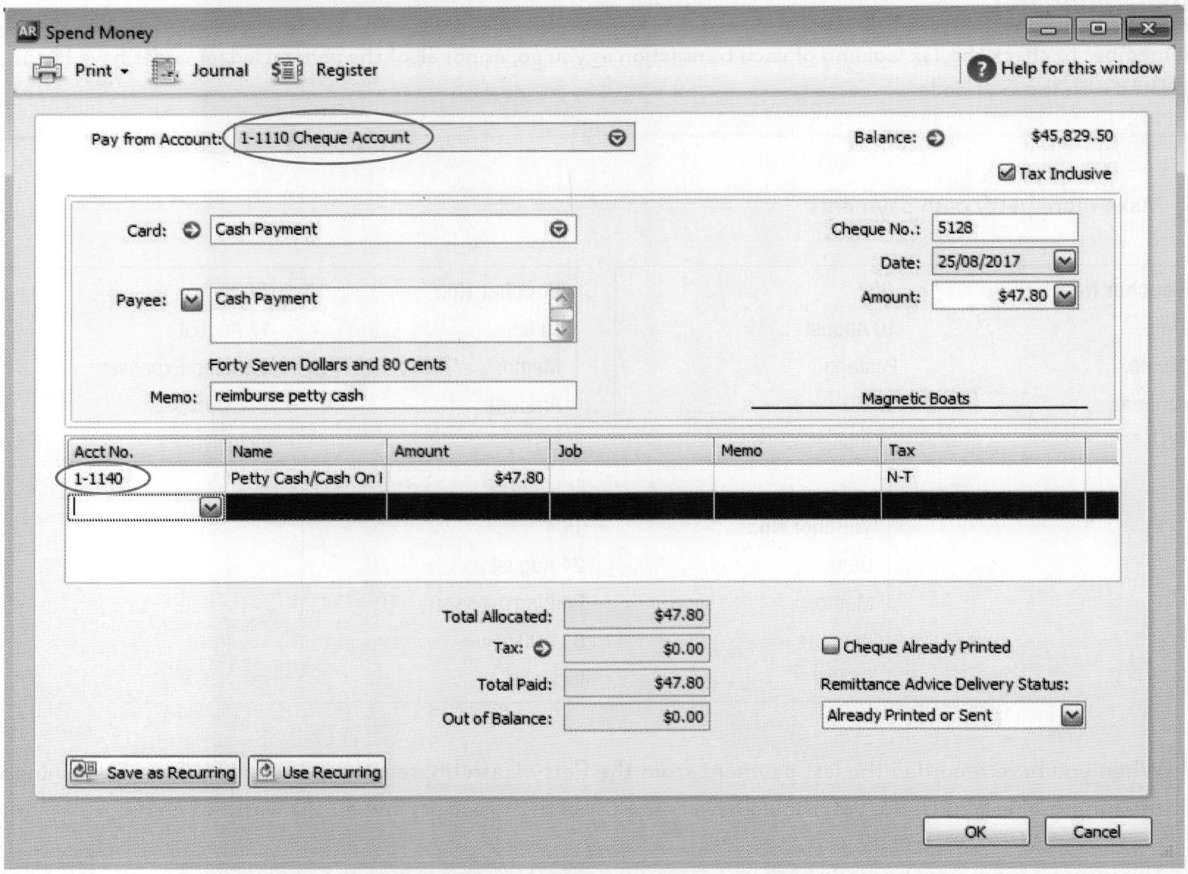

You can find that 1-1140 is now back to $50 by going to the Accounts List in the Accounts module.

Some organisations require a petty cash reconciliation to be done before each cheque reimbursement. This is done the same way as the bank reconciliation for the Cheque Account. However, the closing statement balance is the amount of cash available.

Credit card

Payments from credit cards are also recorded through Spend Money and are reconciled through Reconcile Accounts. The statement date is often not the end of the month, so always use the closing date on the credit card.

6   Process the following payments that were made using the company Visa card.

Reference No.:	001
Date:	4 August
Payee:	The Advertiser
Debit Account:	6-1200
Amount:	$55.00
GST:	Inclusive

Click...

- *Pay from Account* in *Spend Money* (select *2-1110 Visa Card #1*).
- *Date* (insert *4/08/17*).
- *Amount* (insert *55.00*).
- *Card* (select *The Advertiser* from the drop-down menu).
- *Memo* (insert *mid-week advertising*).
- *Account No.* (select *6-1200 Advertising & Marketing – Tax Code GST*). Compare with **Figure 5.35**.
- *Record*.

Figure 5.35 **Spend Money: from Visa card**

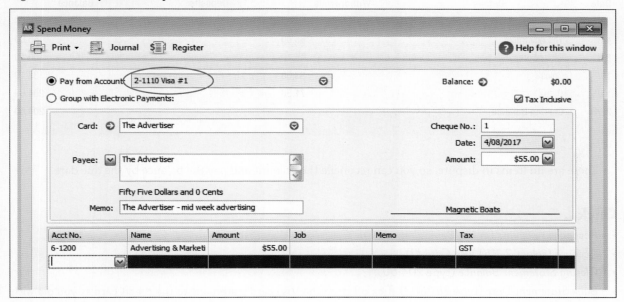

7 Process more Visa card receipts

Reference No.:	002
Date:	8 August
Payee:	Officeworks
Details:	Stationery
Amount:	$45.10
GST:	Inclusive

Reference No.:	003
Date:	10 August
Payee:	Coles
Details:	Cleaning
Amount:	$33.00
GST:	Inclusive

Reference No.:	004
Date:	15 August
Payee:	Optus
Details:	telephone
Amount:	$71.50
GST:	Inclusive

8 When you have recorded the last of the Visa payments you will reconcile against the following credit card statement below with an ending date of 21 August 2017.

| | | | *What?* Visa card | | |
| | | | Magnetic Boats | | |

			From:	22/07/2017	
			To:	21/08/2017	
	Date Payment Due	**Opening Balance**	**Closing Balance**		**Minimum Repayment**
	28 August 2017	$0.00	204.60		$12.00

Date	Details	Withdrawals	Deposits	Balance
22/7	Opening Balance			0.00
4/8	The Advertiser	55.00		55.00
8/8	Officeworks	45.10		100.10
10/8	Coles	33.00		133.10
15/8	Optus	71.50		204.60
21/8	**Closing Balance**			**204.60**

There are no items in dispute, so you can reconcile the account and pay the balance by the due date.

Click...

- *Reconcile Accounts* (in the Banking module).
- *Account* (select *2-1110 Visa Card #1*).
- *Closing Statement Balance* (type *204.60*).
- *Bank Statement Date* (type *21/08/17*). Tick off from the Visa card statement to the credit card as you did with the Cheque Account at the beginning of the chapter. See Figure 5.36.
- *Reconcile*.
- *Reconcile* (in the window that opens – we don't have to print reports every time).
- *Cancel*.

Figure 5.36   **Reconcile Accounts: Visa card**

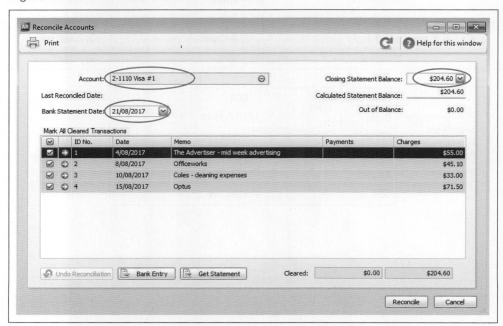

9 Pay the credit card with BPAY through the bank.

Click...

- *Spend Money* (in the Banking module).
- *Pay from Account* (top left of window 1-1110 Cheque Account).
- Date (insert *28/08/17*).
- Amount (insert *$204.60*).
- Memo (insert *Visa account*).
- Account No. (select *2-1110 Visa*).
- Tax Code (*N-T* should be selected).
- *Record*.
- *Cancel* (to return to the Command Centre).

10 Examine the Petty Cash and Visa transactions just completed.

Click...

- *Find Transactions* (at base of the Command Centre, next to Reports).
- *Account* tab.
- *Search by Account* (select *1-1140 Petty Cash*).
- *Dated From* (type *1/08/17*) and To (type *31/08/17*). Press the Tab key. See Figure 5.37.

Figure 5.37   Find Transactions: Accounts tab, Petty Cash

Petty Cash is an asset; therefore cash going into the account is a debit and payments made from the fund (reducing the balance) are credits.

Click...

- *Search by Account* (select *2-1110 Visa #1*).
- *Dated From* (type *1/08/17*) and To (type *31/08/17*). Press the Tab key. See Figure 5.38.

Figure 5.38   **Find Transactions: Accounts tab, Visa Card**

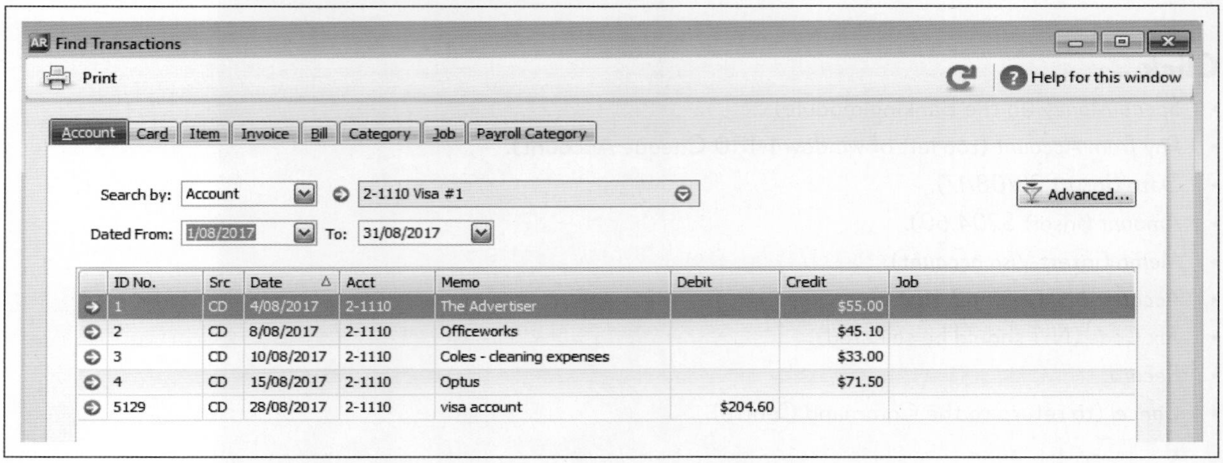

Visa is a liability; therefore amounts charged on the card increase the amount owed and these are credits. The payment that reduces the debt is a debit.

Your instruction for this chapter is now complete.

Practice

FIRE PROTECTION PTY LTD

1   In MYOB AccountRight 2016 open **5.4 Fire Protection Pty Ltd.myox** data file located in the Chapter 5 folder of your start-up files.

Cheque account

2   Record the following receipts into 1-1110 Business Bank Account #1 through **Receive Money**, combining those received on the same day before making that day's bank deposit.

Date:	1 July
Receipt No.:	001
Received from:	Sales
Details:	
Smoke Detector Sales	$572.00
Fire Extinguisher Sales	143.00
Hose Reel Sales	264.00
Fire Blanket Sales	55.00
Cash Received:	$1 034.00
Revenue includes $94.00 GST	

Date:	6 July
Receipt No.:	002
Received from:	Sales
Details:	
Smoke Detector Sales	$418.00
Fire Extinguisher Sales	352.00
Hose Reel Sales	198.00
Fire Blanket Sales	396.00
Cash Received:	$1 364.00
Revenue includes $124.00 GST	

Date:	14 July
Receipt No.:	003
Received from:	Sales
Details:	
Smoke Detector Sales	$682.00
Fire Extinguisher Sales	605.00
Hose Reel Sales	462.00
Fire Blanket Sales	286.00
Cash Received:	$2 035.00
Revenue includes $185.00 GST	

Date:	14 July
Receipt No.:	004
Received from:	Sales
Details:	
Smoke Detector Sales	$253.00
Fire Extinguisher Sales	209.00
Hose Reel Sales	132.00
Fire Blanket Sales	77.00
Cash Received:	$671.00
Revenue includes $61.00 GST	

Date:	16 July
Receipt No.:	006
Received from:	Sales
Details:	
Smoke Detector Sales	$495.00
Fire Extinguisher Sales	583.00
Hose Reel Sales	187.00
Fire Blanket Sales	264.00
Cash Received:	$1 529.00
Revenue includes $139.00 GST	

Date:	21 July
Receipt No.:	007
Received from:	Incite Services
Details:	
Smoke Detector Sales	$484.00
Fire Extinguisher Sales	429.00
Hose Reel Sales	176.00
Fire Blanket Sales	352.00
Cash Received:	$1 441.00
Revenue includes $131.00 GST	

Date:	30 July
Receipt No.:	008
Received from:	Sales
Details:	
Smoke Detector Sales	$1 078.00
Fire Extinguisher Sales	957.00
Hose Reel Sales	220.00
Fire Blanket Sales	352.00
Cash Received:	$2 607.00
Revenue includes $237.00 GST	

Date:	30 July
Receipt No.:	009
Received from:	Ultrasafe
Details:	
Smoke Detector Sales	$352.00
Fire Extinguisher Sales	374.00
Hose Reel Sales	341.00
Fire Blanket Sales	220.00
Cash Received:	$1 287.00
Revenue includes $117.00 GST	

3 Record the following payments through **Spend Money**.

Date:	1 July
Cheque no.:	10231
Payee:	Lidcombe Real Estate
Details: Council rates	
Council rates	$1 650.00
Tax Code: FRE	

Date:	2 July
Cheque no.:	10232
Payee:	Purchases
Details: Purchases	
Purchase of Smoke Detectors	$2 200.00
Payment includes $200.00 GST	

Date:	9 July		Date:	9 July
Cheque no.:	10233		**Cheque no.:**	10234
Payee:	Purchases		Payee:	Purchases
Details: Purchases			Details: Wages	
Purchase of Fire Blankets	$1 870.00		Fortnightly Wages	$1 000.00
Payment includes $170.00 GST			Tax Code: N-T	

Date:	16 July		Date:	22 July
Cheque no.:	10235		**Cheque no.:**	10236
Payee:	The Advertiser		Payee:	Purchases
Details: Advertising			Details: Purchases	
Advertising	$660.00		Fire Extinguisher Purchases	$4 840.00
Payment includes $60.00 GST			Payment includes $440.00 GST	

Date:	23 July		Date:	30 July
Cheque no.:	10237		**Cheque no.:**	10238
Payee:	Wages		Payee:	Purchases
Details: Fortnightly Wages			Details: Purchases	
Wages	$1 000.00		Purchase of Hose Reels	$1 925.00
Tax Code: N-T			Payment includes $175.00 GST	

4 Display or print the Bank Register for your records. Ensure the Undeposited Funds balance is zero.

5 Reconcile your records with the following bank statement.

Which? Bank
10 Olympic Drive
Lidcombe NSW 2141
Statement of Account for Fire Protection Pty Ltd
July 2017

Date	Details	Withdrawals	Deposits	Balance
01	Balance b/f			$27 500.00 Cr
01	Deposit		1 034.00	28 534.00 Cr
01	*Cheque Book fee	45.00		28 489.00 Cr
02	Cheque 10231	1 650.00		26 839.00 Cr
05	Cheque 10232	2 200.00		24 639.00 Cr
07	Deposit		1 364.00	26 003.00 Cr
09	Cheque 10234	1 000.00		25 003.00 Cr
09	Cheque 10233	1 870.00		23 133.00 Cr
14	Deposit		2 706.00	25 839.00 Cr
17	Deposit		1 529.00	27 368.00 Cr
21	Deposit		1 441.00	28 809.00 Cr
25	Cheque 10236	4 840.00		23 969.00 Cr
28	Interest on account		49.50	24 018.50 Cr
28	Cheque 10237	1 000.00		23 018.50 Cr
30	Bank Fees	30.00		22 988.50 Cr
30	**Statement Closing Balance**			**22 988.50 Cr**

* The cheque book fee is a bank fee

6 Display or Print the bank reconciliation report and compare with Figure 5.39.

Figure 5.39   **Cheque Account Reconciliation report: Fire Protection Pty Ltd**

Fire Protection Pty Ltd
44 Boorea Street
Lidcombe NSW 2141

Reconciliation Report

ID No.	Date	Memo/Payee	Deposit	Withdrawal
Account:	1-1110	Business Bank Account #1		
Date Of Bank Statement:	31/07/2017			
Last Reconciled:				
Last Reconciled Balance:				
Cleared Cheques				
10231	1/07/2017	Lidcombe Real Estate		$1 650.00
SC310717	1/07/2017	Cheque Book Fees		$45.00
10232	2/07/2017	Purchases		$2 200.00
10233	9/07/2017	Purchases		$1 870.00
10234	9/07/2017	wages		$1 000.00
10236	22/07/2017	Purchases		$4 840.00
10237	23/07/2017	Wages		$1 000.00
SC310717	30/07/2017	bank fees		$30.00
		Total:	**$0.00**	**$12 635.00**
Cleared Deposits				
CR000001	1/07/2017	Sales	$1 034.00	
CR000002	6/07/2017	Sales	$1 364.00	
CR000005	14/07/2017	Bank Deposit	$2 706.00	
CR000006	16/07/2017	Sales	$1 529.00	
CR000007	21/07/2017	Incite Services	$1 441.00	
IE310717	28/07/2017	interest received	$49.50	
		Total:	**$8 123.50**	**$0.00**
Outstanding Cheques				
10235	16/07/2017	The Advertiser		$660.00
10238	30/07/2017	Purchases		$1 925.00
		Total:	**$0.00**	**$2 585.00**
Outstanding Deposits				
CR000010	30/07/2017	Bank Deposit	$3 894.00	
		Total:	**$3 894.00**	**$0.00**

Reconciliation:

AccountRight Balance On 31/07/2017:	$24 297.50
Add: Outstanding Cheques:	$2 585.00
SubTotal:	$26 882.50
Deduct: Outstanding Deposits:	$3 894.00
Expected Balance On Statement:	$22 988.50

Petty cash

7 Record initial Petty Cash Imprest amount.

Date:	1 August
Cheque no.:	10239
Payee:	Cash
Details: Petty Cash Imprest	
Petty Cash	$50.00
Tax Code: N-T	

8 Use Petty Cash to make the following payments:

Voucher No.:	001		**Voucher No.:**	002
Date:	5 August		Date:	8 August
Memo:	Parking		Memo:	Postage
Amount:	$6.60		Amount:	$16.50
GST:	Inclusive		GST:	Inclusive

Voucher No.:	003		**Voucher No.:**	004
Date:	17 August		Date:	28 August
Memo:	Cleaning Expenses		Memo:	Stationery
Amount:	$20.35		Amount:	$6.05
GST:	Inclusive		GST:	Inclusive

9 Petty cash reimbursement cheque:

Date:	31 August
Cheque no.:	10240
Payee:	Cash
Details: reimb petty cash	
Cash	$49.50
Tax Code: N-T	

10 Produce a Bank Register for petty cash only (by typing 1-1140 in the Accounts Field in the Filter Reports section. See Figure 5.40). Click **Display Report**. Compare with Figure 5.41.

Figure 5.40   **Reports Filters: Bank Register**

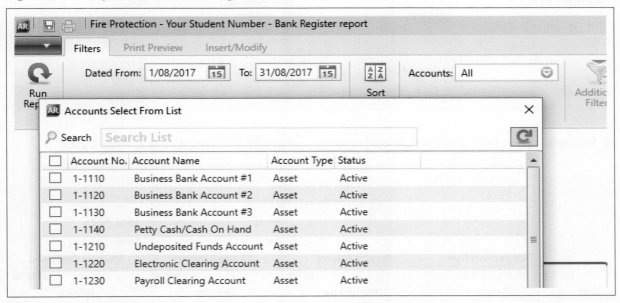

Figure 5.41   **Bank Register: Petty Cash**

Fire Protection Pty Ltd
44 Boorea Street
Lidcombe NSW 2141
Bank Register
August 2017

ID No.	Src	Date	Memo/Payee	Deposit	Withdrawal	Balance
1-1140	Petty Cash/Cash On Hand					
10239	CD	1/08/2017	Petty cash imprest	$50.00		$50.00
1	CD	5/08/2017	Parking		$6.60	$43.40
2	CD	8/08/2017	Postage		$16.50	$26.90
3	CD	17/08/2017	Cleaning expenses		$20.35	$6.55
4	CD	28/08/2017	stationery		$6.05	$0.50
10240	CD	31/08/2017	reimburse petty cash	$49.50		$50.00
				$99.50	**$49.50**	

Credit card

11 Process the following payments that were made using the company Visa card.

Reference No.:	001
Date:	4 August
Payee:	Merli Co
Details:	Smoke Detector Purchases
Amount:	$1 122.00
GST:	Inclusive

Reference No.:	002
Date:	6 August
Payee:	Officeworks
Details:	Printing
Amount:	$77.00
GST:	Inclusive

Reference No.:	003		Reference No.:	004
Date:	8 August		Date:	15 August
Payee:	Merli Co		Payee:	Optus
Details:	Fire Blanket Purchases		Details:	Telephone
Amount:	$1 100.00		Amount:	$61.60
GST:	Inclusive		GST:	Inclusive

12 Reconcile against the following credit card statement below with an ending date of 17 August 2017.

What? Visa Card
Fire Protection Pty Ltd

			From:	18/07/2017	
			To:	17/08/2017	
	Date Payment Due	**Opening Balance**		**Closing Balance**	**Minimum Repayment**
	28 August 2017	**$0.00**		**2 360.60**	**$142.00**
Date	**Details**	**Withdrawals**		**Deposits**	**Balance**
22/7	Opening Balance				0.00
4/8	Merli Co	1 122.00			1 122.00
6/8	Officeworks	77.00			1 199.00
8/8	Merli Co	1 100.00			2 299.00
15/8	Optus	61.60			2 360.60
21/8	**Closing Balance**				2 360.60

Compare against the reconciliation report in Figure 5.42.

Figure 5.42   Visa card Reconciliation Report

Fire Protection Pty Ltd
44 Boorea Street
Lidcombe NSW 2141
Reconciliation Report

ID No.	**Date**	**Memo/Payee**	**Deposit**	**Withdrawal**
Account:	2-1110	Visa #1		
Date Of Bank Statement:	17/08/2017			
Last Reconciled:				
Last Reconciled Balance:				
Cleared Charges				
1	4/08/2017	Merli Co.		$1 122.00
2	6/08/2017	Officeworks		$77.00
3	8/08/2017	Merli Co.		$1 100.00
4	15/08/2017	Optus		$61.60
		Total:	$0.00	$2 360.60

Reconciliation:

AccountRight Balance On 17/08/2017:	$2 360.60
Subtract: Outstanding Charges:	$0.00
SubTotal:	$2 360.60
Add: Outstanding Payment:	$0.00
Expected Balance On Statement:	$2 360.60

Summary

- Cash Accounting records transactions at the time that payment is made, irrespective of when goods changed hands or services were performed.
- Only the net cash received or paid out (after allowing for discounts or other charges) is recorded.
- Spend Money is used in the Banking module to record all payments (for Purchases, Expenses or other purposes).
- Receive Money is used in the Banking module to record all receipts (from Sales or other income).
- The Banking module has no access to any individual accounts in the subsidiary ledgers: it addresses general ledger accounts only.
- MYOB's Recurring Transactions feature is used extensively to increase the speed and accuracy of recording transactions.
- Receipts that come from different sources on the same day are grouped in an Undeposited Funds account prior to taking to the bank.
- Preparing a bank deposit from the Undeposited Funds keeps MYOB's records in line with those of the bank.
- Printing a Bank Register report for the month is a good way to compare your records with those of the bank.
- Bank reconciliation involves adding items of which you had no prior knowledge (called Bank Entries) to your records from the bank statement.
- Your accounts are reconciled with the bank's records when you have all the items ticked in MYOB that appear in the bank statement and the Out of Balance figure is zero.
- Petty Cash can be conveniently accounted for in the Banking module, with small payments being made out of the Petty Cash account, and this account being reimbursed as required with a cheque from the main account.
- Credit card payments can be recorded in MYOB, with your records being reconciled with the monthly credit card statement, and paid by cheque from the main account by the due date.

Assessment

Hobby Co.

1 In MYOB AccountRight 2016, create a new data file based on the following information and using *AccountRight Plus Australian* version:

> **Hobby Co.**
> 197 Pitt Street,
> Sydney NSW 2000
> ABN 51 301 220 115
>
> **Phone:** (02) 9221 0666
> **Email:** sales@hobbyco.com.au
> **Current Financial Year:** 2018
> **Conversion Month:** July
> **Industry Classification:** Retail
> **Main Business Activity:** Sale of hobby supplies

Click the **Easy Setup Assistant** once you have finished the company file setup. Use the third activation option – **I use this file for evaluation purposes**.

2 Change the following names in the list of accounts either through Easy Setup Assistant or the **Accounts List** in the Accounts module:

	Account type	Account number	New account name	Tax code
Edit	Bank	1-1110	Cheque Account	N-T
Edit	Income	4-1000	Arts & Crafts Kit Sales	GST
Edit	Income	4-2000	Model Kit Sales	GST
Edit	Cost of Sales	5-1000	Arts & Crafts Kit purchases	GST
Edit	Cost of Sales	5-2000	Model Kit purchases	GST
Edit	Expense	6-2600	Rent	GST

3 Insert the following account opening balances:

Trial Balance as at 30/06/17			
Account no.	Account name	Debit	Credit
1-1110	Cheque Account	18 000.00	
1-1320	Inventory	35 000.00	
1-2210	Office Equipment At Cost	5 200.00	
1-2410	Store Fittings At Cost	3 800.00	
1-2420	Acc. Depr. Store Fittings		2 000.00
3-1000	Owner Shareholder Capital		60 000.00
	Totals	62 000.00	62 000.00

4 Create brief profile cards for the following customers:

Customer name	Customer ID
Sales	C 01
Bergs Hobbies	C 02
Leeman Hobbies	C 03

5 Create brief profile cards for the following suppliers:

Supplier name	Supplier ID
Purchases	S 01
Sydney Real Estate	S 02
The Advertiser	S 03
Wages	

6 Record the following receipts through **Receive Money**, using Undeposited Funds for those received on the same day before making that day's bank deposit. Make recurring transactions where you feel it is appropriate. Remember to use the correct income accounts.

Date:	3 July 17
Receipt no.:	001
Received from:	Sales
Details:	
Arts & Craft Sales	$495.00
Model Kit Sales	660.00
Cash received:	$1 155.00
Revenue includes $105.00 GST	

Date:	7 July 17
Receipt no.:	002
Received from:	Sales
Details:	
Arts & Craft Sales	$253.00
Model Kit Sales	462.00
Cash received:	$715.00
Revenue includes $65.00 GST	

Date:	10 July 17
Receipt no.:	003
Received from:	Sales
Details:	
Arts & Craft Sales	$682.00
Model Kit Sales	583.00
Cash received:	$1 265.00
Revenue includes $115.00 GST	

Date:	10 July 17
Receipt no.:	004
Received from:	Bergs Hobbies
Details:	
Arts & Craft Sales	$429.00
Model Kit Sales	352.00
Cash received:	$781.00
Revenue includes $71.00 GST	

Date:	24 July
Receipt no.:	006
Received from:	Sales
Details:	
Arts & Craft Sales	$517.00
Model Kit Sales	693.00
Cash received:	$1 210.00
Revenue includes $110.00 GST	

Date:	24 July
Receipt no.:	007
Received from:	Leeman Hobbies
Details:	
Arts & Craft Sales	$451.00
Model Kit Sales	209.00
Cash received:	$660.00
Revenue includes $60.00 GST	

Date:	28 July 17
Receipt no.:	009
Received from:	Sales
Details:	
Arts & Craft Sales	$467.50
Model Kit Sales	418.00
Cash received:	$885.50
Revenue includes $80.50 GST	

Date:	30 July 17
Receipt no.:	010
Received from:	Sales
Details:	
Arts & Craft Sales	$814.00
Model Kit Sales	924.00
Cash received:	$1 738.00
Revenue includes $158.00 GST	

7 Record the following payments made during July, using the correct cost of sales accounts:

Date:	1 July 17
Cheque no.:	23001
Payee:	Purchases
Details: Cash Purchases	
Arts & Craft Kit Purchases	$1 100.00
Payment includes $100.00 GST	

Date:	2 July 17
Cheque no.:	23002
Payee:	Purchases
Details: Cash Purchases	
Model Kit Purchases	$2 200.00
Payment includes $200.00 GST	

Date:	8 July 17
Cheque no.:	23003
Payee:	Wages
Details: Wages	
Fortnightly wages	$1 200.00
Tax Code: N-T	

Date:	12 July 17
Cheque no.:	23004
Payee:	The Advertiser
Details: Advertising	
Monthly advertisements	$550.00
Payment includes $50.00 GST	

Date:	17 July 17
Cheque no.:	23005
Payee:	Purchases
Details: Cash Purchases	
Model Kit Purchases	$990.00
Payment includes $90.00 GST	

Date:	21 July 17
Cheque no.:	23006
Payee:	Purchases
Details: Cash Purchases	
Arts & Craft Kit Purchases	$1 650.00
Payment includes $150.00 GST	

Date:	22 July 17
Cheque no.:	23007
Payee:	Wages
Details: Wages	
Fortnightly wages	$1 200.00
Tax Code: N-T	

Date:	30 July 17
Cheque no.:	23008
Payee:	Sydney Real Estate
Details: Rent	
Monthly shop rent	$3 300.00
Payment includes $300.00 GST	

8   Reconcile your records with the following bank statement:

Which? Bank **356 George Street** **Sydney NSW 2000** **Statement of Account for Hobby Co.** **July 17**					

Date	Details	Withdrawals	Deposits	Balance
01	**Balance b/f**			**$18 000.00 Cr**
01	Cheque Book Fee	50.00		17 950.00 Cr
02	Cheque 23001	1 100.00		16 850.00 Cr
02	Cheque 23002	2 200.00		14 650.00 Cr
03	Deposit		1 155.00	15 805.00 Cr
07	Deposit		715.00	16 520.00 Cr
09	Cheque 23003	1 200.00		15 320.00 Cr
10	Deposit		2 046.00	17 366.00 Cr
17	Cheque 23005	990.00		16 376.00 Cr
21	Cheque 23006	1 650.00		14 726.00 Cr
22	Cheque 23007	1 200.00		13 526.00 Cr
24	Deposit		1 870.00	15 396.00 Cr
28	Deposit		885.50	16 281.50 Cr
28	Interest on account		21.00	16 302.50 Cr
30	Bank Fees	30.00		16 272.50 Cr
31	**Statement Closing Balance**			**16 272.50 Cr**

9   Produce a bank reconciliation report to give to your instructor and finish reconciling.

Petty Cash

1   Record initial Petty Cash Imprest amount.

Date:	1 August
Cheque no.:	23009
Payee:	Cash
Details: Petty Cash Imprest	
Cash	$50.00
Tax Code: N-T	

2   Use Petty Cash to make the following payments. You don't need to use the Supplier, just the memo:

Voucher No.:	001
Date:	5 August
Memo:	Parking
Amount:	$5.50
GST:	Inclusive

Voucher No.:	002
Date:	7 August
Memo:	Postage
Amount:	$8.80
GST:	Inclusive

Voucher No.:	003
Date:	12 August
Memo:	SIM Card (telephone expense)
Amount:	$5.50
GST:	Inclusive

Voucher No.:	004
Date:	16 August
Memo:	Stationery
Amount:	$15.40
GST:	Inclusive

3   Petty cash reimbursement cheque:

Date:	18 August
Cheque no.:	23010
Payee:	Cash
Details: reimb petty cash	
Cash	$35.20
Tax Code: N-T	

4   Produce a Bank Register report for petty cash only (by clicking on the **Accounts** drop down arrow at the **Filter Report** stage. This, too, goes to your instructor.

Credit Card

1   Process the following payments that were made using the company Visa card.

Reference No.:	001
Date:	4 August
Payee:	Sharon Co
Details:	Model Kit purchases
Amount:	$880.00
GST:	Inclusive

Reference No.:	002
Date:	6 August
Payee:	Officeworks
Details:	Printing
Amount:	$54.00
GST:	Inclusive

Reference No.:	003		Reference No.:	004
Date:	11 August		Date:	15 August
Payee:	Sharon Co		Payee:	Energywise
Details:	Arts & Craft Kit purchase		Details:	Electricity
Amount:	$1 650.00		Amount:	$61.60
GST:	Inclusive		GST:	Inclusive

2   Reconcile against the following credit card statement with an ending date of 23 August 2017.

What? Visa Card Hobby Co.				
		From:	24/07/2017	
		To:	23/08/2017	
Date Payment Due	**Opening Balance**	**Closing Balance**	**Minimum Repayment**	
28 August 2017	**$0.00**	**2 650.60**	**$112.00**	

Date	Details	Withdrawals	Deposits	Balance
24/7	Opening Balance			0.00
4/8	Sharon Co	880.00		880.00
6/8	Officeworks	54.00		934.00
11/8	Sharon Co	1 650.00		2 584.00
15/8	Energywise	61.60		2 645.60
18/8	Monthly Bank Fees	5.00		2 650.60
23/8	**Closing Balance**			**2 650.60**

Prepare the credit card reconciliation report to give to your instructor and complete the reconciliation.

6

ACCRUAL ACCOUNTING INTRODUCTION

Learning outcomes

By the end of this chapter you will be competent in:
- understanding the difference between cash and accrual accounting
- understanding various payment terms
- using Easy Setup Assistant for purchases and sales
- recording historical information for suppliers and customers
- producing reports to verify opening Accounts Payable and Accounts Receivable control accounts.

Accrual accounting is technically a more accurate way to record transactions than cash accounting. It produces more meaningful reports as income and expenses are recorded when incurred, rather than when the invoice or bill is paid. This chapter lays the groundwork for Chapters 7 and 8, explaining the principles behind Accounts Payable and Accounts Receivable. We also set up historical transactions for each and use reports to verify the general ledger control account totals.

Basic accounting background

Accrual accounting is the term used when transactions are recorded *at the time the purchase* or *sale takes place*, not when the payment has taken place, as is the case in *cash accounting*. This is the system used in all but the smallest of businesses because it gives a clearer picture of when revenue is earned and when expenses are incurred. This is important when making management decisions, such as when to invest excess funds or employ more casual workers.

Accrual accounting is more complex than cash accounting but, as with cash accounting, each transaction in accrual accounting has a source document (invoice, receipt, etc.) and these are batched into 'like' transactions and entered into MYOB in the respective modules – Sales or Purchases. The underlying journals are shown in Figure 6.1.

Figure 6.1   Underlying journals for Accounts Payable and Accounts Receivable

	Debit	**Prefix**	**Credit**	**Prefix**
Sell Good/service	Accounts Receivable	1	Income Account	4
Receive Payment	Bank Account	1	Accounts Receivable	1
Buy Good/service	Expense Account	5, 6 or 9	Accounts Payable	2
Pay Bill	Accounts Payable	2	Bank Account, loan or credit card	1 or 2

The respective **subsidiary ledgers** are updated with each transaction. The creditor or debtor has their own account that keeps a running balance of what invoices have been recorded, any returns and any payments received or made. This is explained in more detail later in this chapter.

Reports can then be produced which inform the reader either of how much the business owes its creditors (suppliers) or how much its debtors (customers) owe the business at that particular time.

> **Subsidiary ledgers**
> Contains detailed information on the transactions that make up the balance of the control general ledger account in the chart of accounts

Accounts Payable and the MYOB Purchases module

Most of the purchases, as the term is used here, refer to the acquisition of goods or services that *are to be sold* later in the company's normal course of business. We will not be using the *Inventory* module as this is covered in Chapter 9. Some purchases are for general expenses, such as electricity and rent.

A purchase may be paid for at the time the goods or services are obtained (cash purchase) or, by arrangement, at a later date (credit purchase).

When a supplier agrees to give your business credit, they will often require a credit application form to be completed with information about your business and the contact details of suppliers you currently use to act as referees. After all, if they are going to be giving you the goods or services in advance of the payment, they want to know that there is a likelihood that they will be paid!

If the supplier has agreed to grant you credit, they will let you know:

- *your credit limit*: a dollar amount at which they will stop supplying you until you have paid earlier invoices.
- *the credit terms*: within what time period your invoices need to be paid. Some common credit terms include:
  - *COD (Cash on Delivery)*: you have to pay straight away and have no credit terms.
  - *In a given number of days*: invoices are due to be paid a certain number of days after their invoice date. For example, Net 14 means an invoice dated 15 June should be paid before 29 June, an invoice dated 22 of June should be paid before 5 July, etc.
  - *Net after End of Month*: the goods purchased in a particular month are summarised in an account statement at the end of that month, and are due for payment within a certain number of days from the end of that month. For example, Net 15 after **EOM** means that all invoices with a June date need to be paid by the 15 July.

> **EOM**
> The abbreviation for 'End of Month'.

  - *Prompt payment discount*: in order to encourage prompt or early payment of monthly accounts, your supplier may offer this discount. For example, 2%/10, Net 30 means you should pay within 30 days after the invoice date, and if you pay within 10 days of the invoice date, you get a 2% discount.
  - *Finance charge* or *account service fee*: a penalty imposed for late payment.

The credit purchase cycle often works like this:

- A *quote* may be obtained from one or more prospective suppliers for the supply of particular goods or services. This is just the recording of an enquiry, and implies no obligation to purchase.
- An *order* is the next level of activity, and this is a formal request for the supply of specific goods or services. Such an order is often in writing.
- A *bill* (sometimes called an *invoice*) is the top level of purchasing activity, and implies that the goods or services have been received. At this point an accounting transaction is created (a *purchase*) and you assume the liability to pay for it (a *debt*), which is considered a *liability* to the business.
- When you pay the bill, another transaction occurs, in which the business' asset *cash* decreases (or the liability *credit card* increases) and the liability *creditor* (or Account Payable) decreases.

Transition from one level to the next is handled smoothly in MYOB, with the option being available to pay the bill at the time of receipt (*Pay Today*), or to include it with other *Accounts Payable* for payment at a later date.

In *manual bookkeeping*, the purchases of goods are recorded in *journals* on a daily basis, with the monthly totals being transferred to the various general ledger accounts. Payments made to suppliers are recorded in the Cash Payments journal, with the monthly totals also being transferred to the various general ledger accounts.

In *computer accounting*, the journals and general ledgers are updated instantly with each purchase. Payment of all supplier accounts is made in the Pay Bills section of the Purchases module, where each payment is linked directly to the invoices being paid. Other payments (business expenses, etc.) can be made in the Spend Money section in the Banking module. If the invoice is entered in the Purchases module, the payment *must* be entered in the Purchases module.

In both manual and computer accounting, the supplier subsidiary ledgers are updated with every transaction as they occur.

MYOB supplies invoices in five different layouts, or styles, each having a different appearance and each being appropriate to a different type of purchase or sale:

- *Service* layout is used if you want to record the purchase or sale of something that is not in the *Items List*, or if the business is not keeping track of inventory.
- *Item* layout is used to record the sale of inventory items.
- *Professional* layout is used to record services provided to customers.
- *Time Billing* layout is used when a customer is being billed according to the amount of time spent on a job and the expertise of the employee doing the work.
- *Miscellaneous* layout is used to make adjustments and in situations where no printed form is required, for example bad debts.

Historical purchases

When converting from, for instance, a manual accounting system to a computerised accounting system you may find that your opening trial balance for MYOB has an amount in Accounts Payable (a liability). This is the amount that you owe your suppliers. The expense and GST have already been accounted for when the transaction was originally recorded. The underlying journal entry would have been:

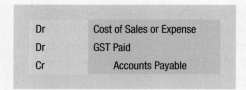

Dr	Cost of Sales or Expense
Dr	GST Paid
Cr	Accounts Payable

We still need the transaction entered into MYOB so we can record the payment against it, but we don't want to enter it through the Purchases module as it means we will be recording the same transaction a second time. This would overstate the expense and GST paid on the one side and either overstate Accounts Payable or understate the bank account on the other. We use the Purchases Easy Setup Assistant to record these historical transactions to prevent this.

1 Open MYOB AccountRight 2016 file called **6.1 Cozy Dry Cleaners.myox** or use the company file that you last updated in Chapter 4.

2 Open up the trial balance and purchases Aged Receivables so we can see the difference after we have entered the historical balances.

Double-click **Reports** at the bottom of the Command Centre.

Click...

- *Accounts* on the left menu.
- *Trial Balance*.
- *Filter Report As of June 2016*. See **Figure 6.2**.
- *Display Report*. This is the same as the trial balance in Chapter 3 where we entered in the opening balances. See **Figure 6.3**.
- The minimise button, top right hand side. It looks like a dash. See **Figure 6.4**. This minimises the report so you should be back at your *Index to Reports* screen. We will come back to this report later.
- *Purchases* (on the left menu).
- *Aged Payables [Detail]* (in the middle menu).
- *Filter Report As of* (type *30/06/2016*). See **Figure 6.5**.
- *Display Report*. It will come up with a screen saying there is no information to display as you haven't entered in the historical transactions yet. See **Figure 6.6**.
- The minimise button (shown in **Figure 6.4**) so we can refresh the reports after entering our historical information.

Figure 6.2   Reports Index: Trial Balance

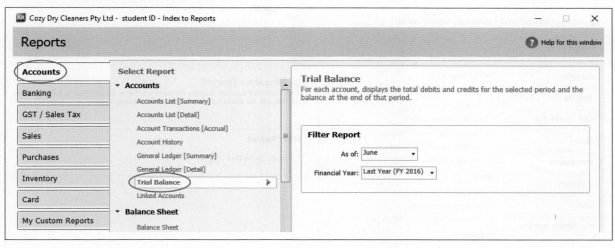

Figure 6.3   Trial Balance as at 30 June 2016

Cozy Dry Cleaners Pty Ltd
Cozy Corner Beach
Albany WA 6330
ABN: 62 266 506 622
Trial Balance
June 2016

Account Name	Debit	Credit	YTD Debit	YTD Credit
Cheque Account	$30 900.00		$30 900.00	
Accounts Receivable	$110.00		$110.00	
Inventory	$2 500.00		$2 500.00	
Furniture At Cost	$10 000.00		$10 000.00	
Accum. Depr. Furniture		$600.00		$600.00
Office Equipment At Cost	$3 600.00		$3 600.00	
Accum. Depr. Office Equipment		$200.00		$200.00
Motor Vehicles At Cost	$8 000.00		$8 000.00	
Accum. Depr. Motor Vehicles		$1 200.00		$1 200.00
Plant & Equip At Cost	$30 000.00		$30 000.00	
Acc Depr Plant & Equip		$1 000.00		$1 000.00
Accounts Payable		$283.80		$283.80
Business Loan #1		$42 000.00		$42 000.00
Lauren Healey Capital		$44 000.00		$44 000.00
Lauren Healey Drawings	$4 173.80		$4 173.80	
Total:	**$89 283.80**	**$89 283.80**	**$89 283.80**	**$89 283.80**

Figure 6.4   Report: Minimise button

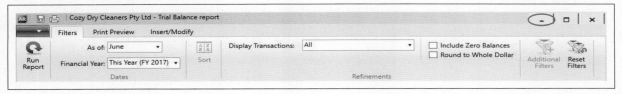

Figure 6.5   Reports: Aged Payables [Detail]

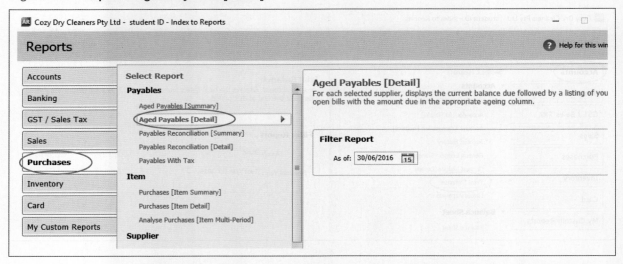

Figure 6.6   Aged Payables [Detail] report: no information

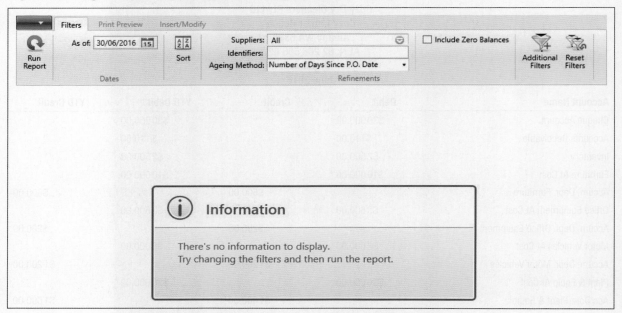

Easy Setup Assistant: Purchases

1   Customise the Purchases module.

 Click...

- *Setup* in the top menu bar.
- *Easy Setup Assistant.*

- *Choose Purchases*. Read the Introduction screen.
- *Next*.
- *Layout* (choose *Service*).
- *Next*.
- *Buying Details*. Here we would put the most commonly used expense account and credit limit from our suppliers or we can leave it blank. Leave it blank.
- *Next*.
- *Tax Codes*. Read the screen.
- *Next*.
- *Payment Information*. Here is where we would put the most commonly used payment method and credit terms. In this case, the most commonly used credit terms are 10% 10 days/Net 30. Change the defaults so your screen matches with Figure 6.7.
- *Next*.
- *Linked Accounts*. Read the screen.
- *Next*.
- *Supplier Cards*. Here is where you can enter your supplier cards, if you hadn't already. As you have already added the supplier cards in Chapter 4.
- *Next*.
- *Historical Purchases* screen. This is where we will enter our outstanding suppliers. Note that the total Linked Payables Account Balance in the bottom right hand side of the screen is $283.80. See Figure 6.8.

Figure 6.7   **Payment Information screen**

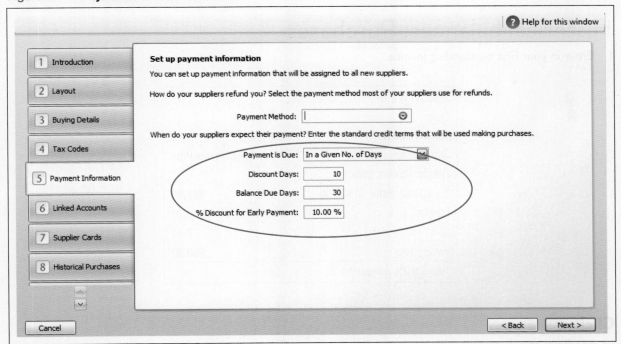

Figure 6.8   **Historical Purchases screen**

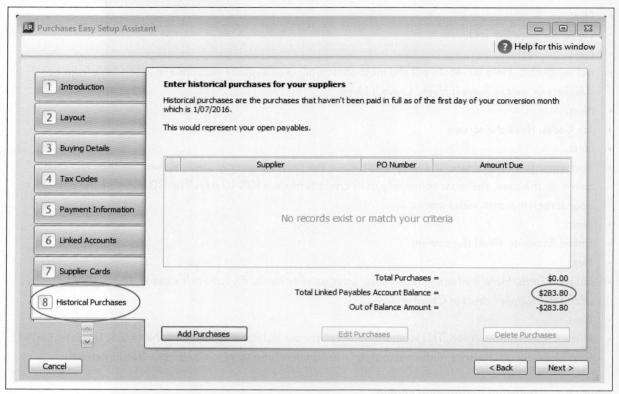

Historical balances: Purchases

1   Enter in your first outstanding invoice.

Tulloch Pty Ltd	
Date:	13 June
Tax Invoice No.	02425
Supplied to:	Cozy Dry Cleaners P/L
Details: Dowper Solvent	
2 x 10 litre cubes @ $31.90	$63.80
Freight	9.20
GST:	7.30
Invoice Total:	$80.30
Terms: 10% 7 days/Net 30	

Click...

- *Add Purchases* (bottom left hand corner of the Historical Purchases window).
- *Supplier Name* (type *Tul* and the autofill should offer you *Tulloch Pty Ltd*).
- *Use Supplier* (at the bottom of that window).
- *Date* (type *13/06/16*).
- *Supplier Invoice* (type *2425*).
- *Total Including Tax* (type *80.30*). Press Tab. The tax should automatically calculate. Compare with Figure 6.9 and ensure we match.
- *Record*. Read the information screen.
- *OK*.

Figure 6.9   Pre-Conversion Purchase

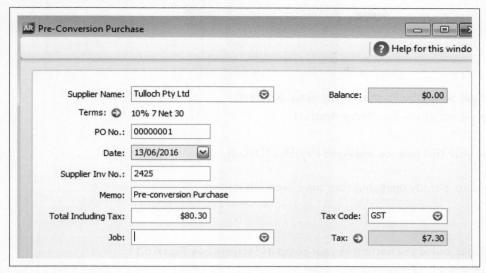

2 Add the following invoice in the same area.

Klenasol Care Pty Ltd	
Date:	15 June
Tax Invoice No.:	11114
Supplied to:	Cozy Dry Cleaners P/L
Details: Long Black Dress Covers	
50 with zip @ $3.50	$175.00
Freight	10.00
GST:	18.50
Invoice Total:	$203.50
Terms: 10%/10/Net 30	

After recording the above invoice, your Historical Purchases screen should look like Figure 6.10.

Figure 6.10   Historical Purchases: Out Of Balance Amount

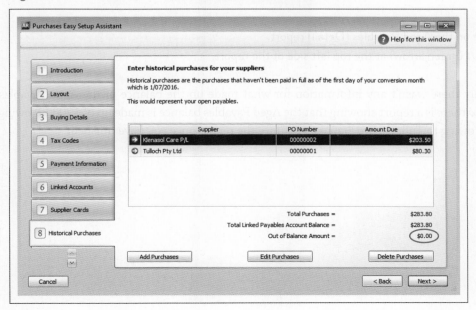

Note that the Total Purchases = Total Linked Payables Account Balance, so the Out of Balance Amount is zero.

Click...

- *Next.*
- *Close* (to get out of the *Purchases Easy Setup Assistant*).
- *Close* (to get out of the *Easy Setup Assistant*).

3 Redisplay your trial balance and Aged Payables [Detail].

These reports are already open, but they have been minimised.

Click...

- *AccountRight icon* at the bottom of your computer screen. See **Figure 6.11**.
- *Trial Balance report* to maximise it.
- *Run report* (green arrow) at the top left side of the report.

Nothing changes. The trial balance has *not* been affected by the processing of the historical purchases. That is what we wanted.

Figure 6.11 Computer task bar

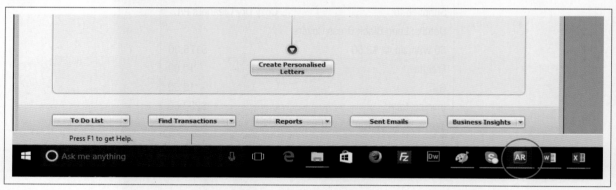

Click...

- *Maximise* on the Aged Payables [Detail] report.
- *Run report* (green arrow) at the top left side of the report.

Previously there wasn't any information for what made up the balance of the Aged Payables in the trial balance. *Now* there is a report showing that the Aged Payables balance is made up of $203.50 owing to Klenasol and $80.30 owing to Tulloch. See **Figure 6.12**. Close the report once you have finished.

Figure 6.12   **Aged Payables [Detail] report**

Cozy Dry Cleaners Pty Ltd
Cozy Corner Beach
Albany WA 6330
ABN: 62 266 506 622
Aged Payables [Detail]
As of 30/06/2016

ID No.	Date	Total Due	0–30	31–60	61–90	90+
Klenasol Care P/L						
SUP 002						
Thomas Kenny						
02 9979 6866						
10% 10 Net 30						
00000002	15/06/2016	$203.50	$203.50	$0.00	$0.00	$0.00
Total:		$203.50	$203.50	$0.00	$0.00	$0.00
Tulloch Pty Ltd						
SUP 001						
John Doran						
08 9748 2155						
10% 7 Net 30						
00000001	13/06/2016	$80.30	$80.30	$0.00	$0.00	$0.00
Total:		$80.30	$80.30	$0.00	$0.00	$0.00
Grand Total:		$283.80	$283.80	$0.00	$0.00	$0.00
Ageing Percent:			100.0%	0.0%	0.0%	0.0%

Accounts Receivable and the MYOB Sales module

A *sale*, as the term is used here, refers to the supply of the goods or services that are the company's normal course of business.

A sale may be paid for at the time the goods or services are supplied (cash sale) or, by an arrangement, at a later date (credit sale).

When a customer asks for your business to give them credit, you should ask them to fill out a credit application form similar to the one you were given yourself from the supplier. And for the same reason: you would like to know there is a likelihood that you will get paid!

If you agree to grant credit to a customer, you will need to let them know their credit limit and the credit terms. You may also decide to encourage the prompt or early payment by customers of their accounts by offering, a *prompt payment discount*. You may also charge a penalty in the form of a *finance charge* or *account service fee* for late payment.

The credit sales cycle often works like this:

- A *quote* may be given in response to an enquiry from a prospective customer for the supply of particular goods or services. This is just the recording of an offer to supply, and implies no obligation on the customer, who might find a better offer elsewhere. A quote does *not* give rise to a transaction in the books of accounts.
- An *order* is the next level of activity, and this is a formal request for the supply of a service, or for specific goods that may not currently be in stock. Such an order may be in writing, but an accounts transaction has not yet been created unless the customer pays a deposit.

- An *invoice* is the top level of activity, and implies that the goods or services have been supplied. At this point an accounting transaction is created (a *sale*) and the customer assumes the liability to pay for it (a *debt*), which is considered an *asset* to your business.
- When the customer pays another transaction occurs, in which the business's asset *cash* increases, and the asset *debtor* (or Account Receivable) decreases.

Transition from one level to the next is handled smoothly in MYOB, with the option being available to receive the payment of the invoice straight away (*Pay Today*) or to include it with other *Accounts Receivable* waiting for the payment at a later date.

Again, in *manual bookkeeping*, sales are recorded in *journals* on a daily basis, with the monthly totals being transferred to the various general ledger accounts. Payments received from customers are recorded in the Cash Receipts Journal, with the monthly totals also being transferred to the various general ledger accounts.

In *computer accounting* the journals, ledgers and customers' accounts are updated instantly with each transaction. Receipt from customer accounts are made in the Receive Payments section of the Sales module, where each receipt is linked directly to the invoice being paid. Other receipts (interest received, proceeds of sale of an asset, etc.) can be made in the Receive Money section in the Banking module. If a sale has been recorded in the Sales module, the money received for that invoice *must* be entered in the Sales module.

In both manual and computer accounting, the customer subsidiary ledgers are updated with every transaction as they occur.

1 Your trial balance should still be open from the previous exercise, so you only need to open up your Aged Receivables [Detail] report. Go back to your Reports Index.

Click...

- *Sales* on the left menu.
- *Aged Receivables [Detail]*.
- *Filter Report As of* (type *30/06/2016*).
- *Display Report*. It will come up with a screen saying there is no information to display as you haven't entered in the historical transactions yet.
- *Minimise* button, so we can refresh the reports after entering our historical information.

Easy Setup Assistant: Sales

Historical sales are handled the same way in sales as they were in purchases. To prevent overstatement of income, GST collected, bank or Accounts Receivable, the historical sales are recorded through the Sales Easy Setup Assistant.

1 Continue with the MYOB AccountRight 2016.1 file you used for Purchases.
2 Open up the Easy Setup Assistant for sales.

Click...

- *Setup* in the top menu bar.
- *Easy Setup Assistant*.
- *Choose Sales*. Read the Introduction screen.
- *Next*.
- *Layout* (choose *Service*).

- *Next.*
- *Selling Details.* Here we would put the most commonly used expense account and credit limit from our customers or we can leave it blank. In the Credit Limit field, type *1000* (as this is this the standard limit that Cozy Dry Cleaners gives to most of its customers) and press the Tab key.
- *Next.*
- *Tax Codes.* Read the screen.
- *Next.*
- *Payment Information.* Here is where we would put the most commonly used payment method and credit terms. In this case, the most commonly used credit terms are 10% 10 days/Net 30. Change the defaults so your screen matches with **Figure 6.13**.
- *Next.*
- *Linked Accounts.* Read the screen
- *Next.*
- *Customer Cards.* Here is where you can enter your customer cards, if you hadn't already. As you have already added the customer cards in the Chapter 4.
- *Next.*
- *Historical Sales* screen. This is where we will enter our outstanding customers. Note that the Total Linked Receivables Account Balance in the bottom right hand side of the screen is $110.00. See **Figure 6.14**.

Figure 6.13   Payment Information screen: Sales

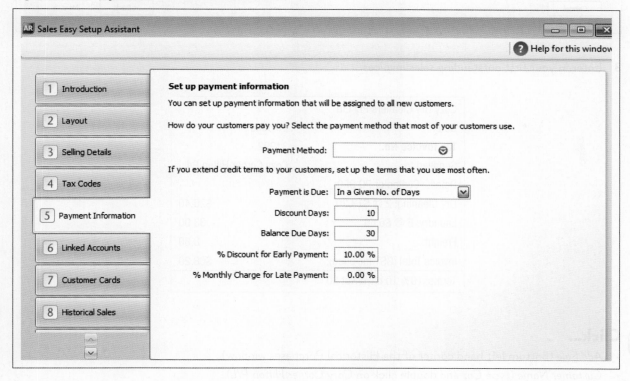

Figure 6.14   **Historical Sales screen**

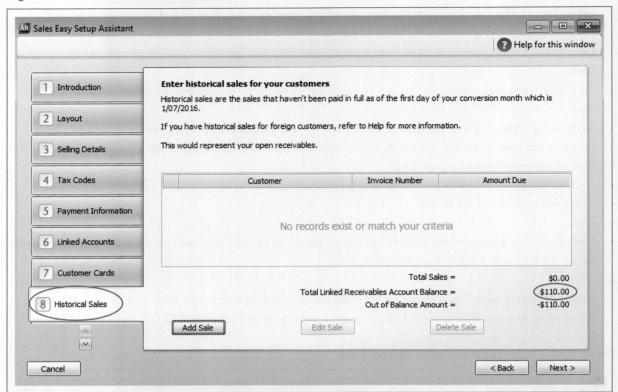

3 Enter in your first outstanding sales invoices.

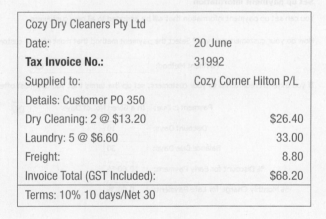

Cozy Dry Cleaners Pty Ltd	
Date:	20 June
Tax Invoice No.:	31992
Supplied to:	Cozy Corner Hilton P/L
Details: Customer PO 350	
Dry Cleaning: 2 @ $13.20	$26.40
Laundry: 5 @ $6.60	33.00
Freight:	8.80
Invoice Total (GST Included):	$68.20
Terms: 10% 10 days/Net 30	

🖱 **Click...**

• *Add Sale* (bottom left hand corner of the Historical Purchases window).
• *Customer Name* (type *Coz* and double click on *Cozy Corner Hilton P/L*).
• *Invoice No.* (type *31992*).
• *Date* (type *20/06/16*).
• *Customer PO No.* (type *350*).
• *Total Including Tax* (type *68.20*). Press Tab. The tax should automatically calculate. Compare with Figure 6.15 and ensure we match.
• *Record.* Read the Information screen.
• *OK.*

Figure 6.15   Pre-Conversion Sale

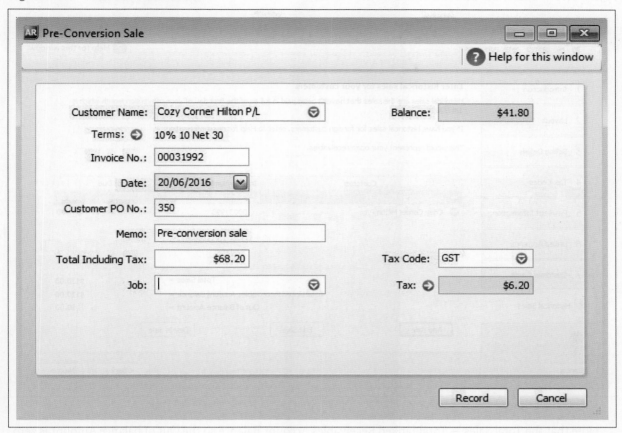

4 Add the following invoice in the same area.

Cozy Dry Cleaners Pty Ltd	
Date:	28 June
Tax Invoice No.:	31998
Supplied to:	Cozy Corner Hilton P/L
Details: Customer PO 351	
Laundry: 5 @ $6.60	33.00
Freight:	8.80
Invoice Total (GST Included):	$41.80
Terms: 10% 10 days/Net 30	

After recording the above invoice, your Historical Sales screen should look like **Figure 6.16**.

Figure 6.16   Historical Sales: Out Of Balance Amount

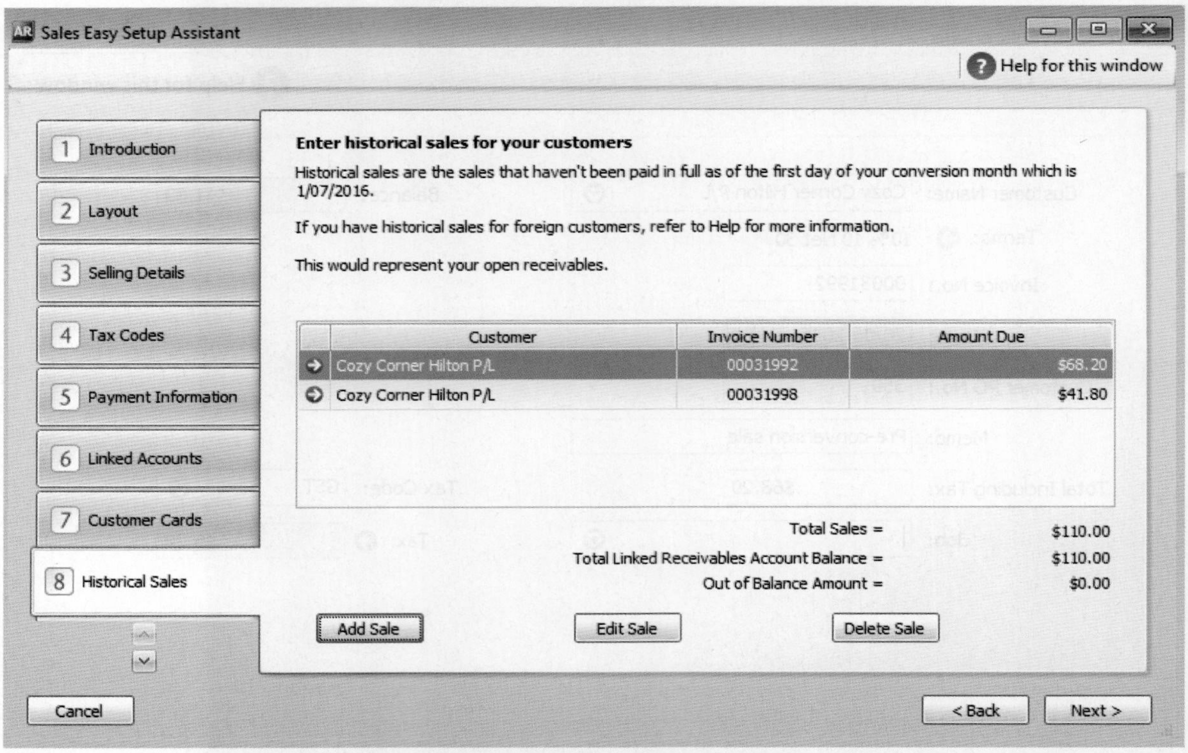

Note that the Total Sales = Total Linked Receivables Account Balance so the Out of balance Amount is zero.

Click...

- *Next.*
- *Close* (to get out of the *Sales Easy Setup Assistant*).
- *Close* (to get out of the *Easy Setup Assistant*).

5 Redisplay your trial balance and Aged Receivables [Detail].

Nothing changes in the trial balance as it has *not* been affected by the processing of the historical statements.

Now there is a report showing that the Accounts Receivable balance is made up of two invoices of $68.20 and $41.80 owing from Cozy Corner Hilton P/L. See **Figure 6.17**.

Figure 6.17   Aged Receivables [Detail] report

Cozy Dry Cleaners Pty Ltd
Cozy Beach Corner
ALBANY WA 6330
ABN: 62 266 506 622
Aged Receivables
As of 30/06/2016

ID No.	Date	Total Due	0–30	31–60	61–90	90+
Cozy Corner Hilton P/L						
CUS 001						
June Budd						
08 9748 2155						
10% 10 Net 30						
00031992	20/06/2016	$68.20	$68.20	$0.00	$0.00	$0.00
00031998	28/06/2016	$41.80	$41.80	$0.00	$0.00	$0.00
Total:		$110.00	$110.00	$0.00	$0.00	$0.00
Grand Total:		$110.00	$110.00	$0.00	$0.00	$0.00
Ageing Percent:			100.0%	0.0%	0.0%	0.0%

Practice

THE BLINDS MAN

1   In MYOB AccountRight 2016, open the **6.2 The Blinds Man.myox** data file from the Chapter 6 folder of your start-up files, or use your own file.

2   Use the Easy Setup Assistant > Purchases to set up the service invoice and enter the following historical balances.

Luxaflex P/L	
Date:	25 June
Tax Invoice No.:	43998
Supplied to:	The Blinds Man
Details: Blinds as per your PO 0580	
1 x units @ $300.00	$300.00
Freight	20.00
GST:	32.00
Invoice Total:	$352.00
Terms: 10% 10 days/Net 30	

Litemaster Blinds P/L	
Date:	28 June
Tax Invoice No.:	80561
Supplied to:	The Blinds Man
Details: Blinds as per your PO 0581	
1 x units @ $200.00	$200.00
Freight	20.00
GST:	22.00
Invoice Total:	$242.00
Terms: 10% 10 days/Net 30	

3   Using Easy Setup Assistant > Sales, set the invoice layout to a service layout and record the outstanding historical sales.

The Blinds Man Pty Ltd	
Date:	28 June
Tax Invoice No.:	33157
Supplied to:	East Motor Inn P/L
Details: Customer PO 432	
Supply of Blinds:	$1 100.00
Installation:	0.00
Freight:	0.00
Invoice Total (GST Included):	$1 100.00
Terms: 10% 10 days /Net 30	

The Blinds Man Pty Ltd	
Date:	29 June
Tax Invoice No.:	33158
Supplied to:	Grandview Hotel P/L
Details: Customer PO 732	
Supply of Blinds:	$300.00
Installation:	150.00
Freight:	45.00
Invoice Total (GST Included):	$495.00
Terms: 10% 10 days /Net 30	

The Blinds Man Pty Ltd	
Date:	30 June
Tax Invoice No.:	33159
Supplied to:	Lakeview Apartments P/L
Details: Customer PO 294	
Supply of Blinds:	$1 100.00
Installation:	495.00
Freight:	55.00
Invoice Total (GST Included):	$1 650.00
Terms: 10% 10 days /Net 30	

The Blinds Man Pty Ltd	
Date:	30 June
Tax Invoice No.:	33160
Supplied to:	Meriton Holdings P/L
Details: Customer PO 522	
Supply of Blinds:	$1 100.00
Installation:	0.00
Freight:	55.00
Invoice Total (GST Included):	$1 155.00
Terms: 10% 10 days /Net 30	

4 Produce two reports:

- Aged Payables [Detail] to 30 June 2016. See Figure 6.18.
- Aged Receivables [Detail] to 30 June 2016. See Figure 6.19.

Figure 6.18   Aged Payables [Detail] report: The Blinds Man

The Blinds Man
21 Penola Road,
Mount Gambier SA 5290
Aged Payables [Detail]
As of 30/06/2016

ID No.		Date	Total Due	0–30	31–60	61–90	90+
Litemaster Blinds P/L							
SUP 003							
Harry Freeman							
08 9223 5500							
10% 10 Net 30							
	00000581	28/06/2016	$242.00	$242.00	$0.00	$0.00	$0.00
		Total:	$242.00	$242.00	$0.00	$0.00	$0.00

ID No.	Date	Total Due	0–30	31–60	61–90	90+
Luxaflex P/L						
SUP 002						
Franco Tosoni						
08 9516 6371						
10% 10 Net 30						
00000580	25/06/2016	$352.00	$352.00	$0.00	$0.00	$0.00
Total:		$352.00	$352.00	$0.00	$0.00	$0.00
Grand Total:		$594.00	$594.00	$0.00	$0.00	$0.00
Ageing Percent:			100.0%	0.0%	0.0%	0.0%

Figure 6.19   Aged Receivables [Detail] report: The Blinds Man

The Blinds Man
21 Penola Road
Mount Gambier SA 5290
Aged Receivables [Detail]
As of 30/06/2016

ID No.	Date	Total Due	0–30	31–60	61–90	90+
East Motor Inn						
CUS 001						
Steve Streeter						
08 8725 2354						
10% 10 Net 30						
00033157	28/06/2016	$1 100.00	$1 100.00	$0.00	$0.00	$0.00
Total:		$1 100.00	$1 100.00	$0.00	$0.00	$0.00
Grandview Hotel						
CUS 002						
John Worth						
08 8725 5755						
10% 10 Net 30						
00033158	29/06/2016	$495.00	$495.00	$0.00	$0.00	$0.00
Total:		$495.00	$495.00	$0.00	$0.00	$0.00
Lakeview Apartments P/L						
CUS 003						
Angelo Falls						
08 8725 3141						
10% 10 Net 30						
00033159	30/06/2016	$1 650.00	$1 650.00	$0.00	$0.00	$0.00
Total:		$1 650.00	$1 650.00	$0.00	$0.00	$0.00

ID No.		Date	Total Due	0–30	31–60	61–90	90+
Meriton Holdings P/L							
CUS 004							
Dario Lennon							
08 8725 4311							
10% 10 Net 30							
	00033160	30/06/2016	$1 155.00	$1 155.00	$0.00	$0.00	$0.00
		Total:	$1 155.00	$1 155.00	$0.00	$0.00	$0.00
		Grand Total:	$4 400.00	$4 400.00	$0.00	$0.00	$0.00
		Ageing Percent:		100.0%	0.0%	0.0%	0.0%

THE ICE CREAM PARLOUR

1 In MYOB AccountRight 2016, open the **6.3 The Ice Cream Parlour.myox** data file from the Chapter 6 folder of your start-up files, or use your own file.

2 Use the Easy Setup Assistant > Purchases to set up the service invoice and enter the following historical balances.

Alpino Gelato P/L	
Date:	30 June
Tax Invoice No.:	00706
Supplied to:	The Ice Cream Parlour
Details: PO 0005	
14 x Ice Cream Cakes @ $40.00	$560.00
Freight	40.00
GST:	60.00
Invoice Total:	$660.00
Terms: 10% 7 days/Net 15	

Norgen-Vaaz P/L	
Date:	30 June
Tax Invoice No.:	89991
Supplied to:	The Ice Cream Parlour
Details: PO 0006	
2 x 25 litre Ice Cream @ $100.00	$200.00
Freight	50.00
GST:	25.00
Invoice Total:	$275.00
Terms: 10% 7 days/Net 15	

Peters Ice Creams P/L	
Date:	30 June
Tax Invoice No.:	9989
Supplied to:	The Ice Cream Parlour
Details: PO 0007	
4 x 25 litre Ice Cream @ $100.00	$400.00
Freight	40.00
GST:	44.00
Invoice Total:	$484.00
Terms: 10% 10 days/Net 30	

Streets Ice Cream P/L	
Date:	30 June
Tax Invoice No.:	20892
Supplied to:	The Ice Cream Parlour
Details: PO 0008	
11 x 25 litre Ice Cream @ $80.00	$880.00
Freight	30.00
GST:	91.00
Invoice Total:	$1 001.00
Terms: 10% 10 days/Net 30	

There are no historical customer sales for this business.

Open up the Aged Payables [Detail] report to 30 June 2016 and compare with **Figure 6.20**.

Figure 6.20   Aged Payables [Detail] report: The Ice Cream Parlour

The Ice Cream Parlour
Darlinghust Road
Kings Cross NSW 2011
Aged Payables [Detail]
As of 30/06/2016

ID No.	Date	Total Due	0–30	31–60	61–90	90+
Alpino Gelato P/L						
SUP 001						
Maria Palmer						
02 9569 3667						
10% 7 Net 15						
00000005	30/06/2016	$660.00	$660.00	$0.00	$0.00	$0.00
Total:		$660.00	$660.00	$0.00	$0.00	$0.00
Norgen-Vaaz P/L						
SUP 004						
Dora Norgen						
02 9756 2283						
10% 7 Net 15						
00000006	30/06/2016	$275.00	$275.00	$0.00	$0.00	$0.00
Total:		$275.00	$275.00	$0.00	$0.00	$0.00
Peters Ice Creams P/L						
SUP 002						
Lisa Woods						
02 9659 0699						
10% 10 Net 30						
00000007	30/06/2016	$484.00	$484.00	$0.00	$0.00	$0.00
Total:		$484.00	$484.00	$0.00	$0.00	$0.00
Streets Ice Cream P/L						
SUP 003						
Angela Morosi						
02 9755 7899						
10% 10 Net 30						
00000008	30/06/2016	$1 001.00	$1 001.00	$0.00	$0.00	$0.00
Total:		$1 001.00	$1 001.00	$0.00	$0.00	$0.00
Grand Total:		$2 420.00	$2 420.00	$0.00	$0.00	$0.00
Ageing Percent:			100.0%	0.0%	0.0%	0.0%

Summary

◆ Accrual accounting records transactions at the date of the invoice, irrespective of when payment is made.

◆ Each supplier (creditor) or customer (debtor) has its own subsidiary ledger which is a running balance of invoices recorded, any returns and payments made or received.

◆ The Accounts Payable control account (a liability) should balance with the creditor subsidiary ledgers.

◆ The Accounts Receivable control account (an asset) should balance with the debtor subsidiary ledgers.

◆ Historical purchases or historical sales need to be entered through the Easy Setup Assistant or the accounts will be overstated.

◆ The purchase cycle is often: a quote is received, then an order placed, the supplier invoice received and then paid.

◆ The sales cycle is often: a quote is given, then an order received, an invoice is sent to the customer and then they pay it.

Assessment

Arkaroola B&B

1   In MYOB AccountRight 2016, create a new data file based on the following information, using the *AccountRight Standard Australian* version:

> **Arkaroola B&B P/L**
> 21 Pirie Street,
> Arkaroola SA 5710
> ABN 21 221 402 201
>
> **Phone:** (08) 9249 2065
> **Fax:** (08) 9249 4715
> **Email:** arkaroolab&b@bigpond.com
> **Current Financial Year:** 2017
> **Conversion Month:** July
> **Type of Business:** Service

The main business activity of Arkaroola B&B is providing casual bed and breakfast accommodation. They use a service layout for their invoices.

2   Make the following changes in the List of Accounts:

	Account type	Account number	New account name	Tax code
Edit	Bank	1-1110	Cheque Account	N-T
Edit	Acc. Receivable	1-1310	Accounts Receivable	N-T
Edit	Acc. Payable	2-1510	Accounts Payable	N-T
Edit	Income	4-1000	B&B Income	GST
Edit	Income	4-2000	Packed Lunch Sales	GST
Add	Cost of Sales	4-9000	Discounts Received	GST
Add	Cost of Sales	5-2000	Purchases	FRE
Add	Cost of Sales	5-9000	Discounts Given	GST

Change the linked accounts:

Type	Terms	From	To
Sales	I give discounts for early payment	6-3300 Discounts given	5-9000 Discounts Given
Purchases	I take discounts for early payment		4-9000 Discounts Received

Then make the following changes:

	Account type	Account number	New account name	Tax Code
Delete	Expense	6-3300	Discounts Given	
Delete	Expense	6-7300	Public Liability Insurance	

3   Insert the following account opening balances:

Account no.	Account name	Debit	Credit
1-1110	Cheque Account	10 400.00	
1-2110	Furniture at cost	20 000.00	
2-1220	GST Paid	40.00	
2-1510	Accounts Payable		440.00
3-1000	Owners Capital		30 000.00
		30 440.00	30 440.00

Remember This

GST Paid is a contra account so it needs to be added in as a *negative*.

4   Create cards for the following suppliers using Easy Setup Assistant > Purchases:

Name:	Arkaroola Supplies P/L
Card ID:	SUP 001
Address:	45 Pirie Street
	Arkaroola SA 5710
Phone:	(08) 9249 2891
Contact:	Dave Mawson
Terms:	10% 10 days/Net 30
Expense Account:	5-2000
Credit Limit:	$1000.00
ABN:	65 145 209 404

Name:	Arkaroola Laundry P/L
Card ID:	SUP 002
Address:	71 Pirie Street
	Arkaroola SA 5710
Phone:	(08) 9249 1893
Contact:	Julia Green
Terms:	10% 10 days/Net 30
Expense Account:	5-2000
Credit Limit:	$1000.00
ABN:	22 001 102 550

5   Record the outstanding supplier balances in MYOB:

Arkaroola Supplies P/L	
Date:	30 June
Tax Invoice No.:	11011
Supplied to:	Arkaroola B&B
Details: PO 0001	
Sundry packaged food items	$280.00
Delivery	20.00
GST:	30.00
Invoice Total:	$330.00
Terms: 10% 10 days/Net 30	

Arkaroola Laundry P/L	
Date:	30 June
Tax Invoice No.:	20442
Supplied to:	Arkaroola B&B
Details: PO 0002	
Laundry Services	$95.00
Delivery	5.00
GST:	10.00
Invoice Total:	$110.00
Terms: 10% 10 days/Net 30	

6 Create cards for the following customers:

Name:	Flinders Exploration		**Name:**	Mount Painter Tours
Card ID:	CUS 001		**Card ID:**	CUS 002
Address:	266 Hindley Street		**Address:**	66 North Terrace
	Adelaide SA 5000			Adelaide SA 5000
Phone:	(08) 9512 6671		**Phone:**	(08) 9514 5336
Email:	martin@flinex.com.au		**Email:**	helen@paintertours.com.au
Contact:	Martin Fletcher		**Contact:**	Helen Clark
Terms:	10% 10 days/Net 30		**Terms:**	10% 10 days/Net 30
Income Account:	4-1000		**Income Account:**	4-1000
Credit Limit:	$10 000.00		**Credit Limit:**	$10 000.00

There are no historical sales for this company.

7 Produce the Aged Payables [Summary] to 30 June 2016.

7

ACCOUNTS PAYABLE

Learning outcomes

By the end of this chapter you will be competent in:

- processing a range of supplier credit transactions in both a service and a trading environment
- entering purchases and payments on account (credit)
- accessing account information using account enquiry procedures
- printing relevant reports including reports to validate accounts payable control account.

Many suppliers will extend credit to some of their repeat customers instead of insisting on payment at the time of the sale. The business receiving these purchases will post the supplier invoices (also known as bills) to Accounts Payable, a liability account. When payment for these credit purchases are made, these figures are removed from Accounts Payable. Thus, the Accounts Payable account has a running balance of how much is owed to suppliers at any given point in time. In this chapter, you will work your way through the purchases process from quote to payment of supplier invoices.

Basic accounting background

The basics of accrual accounting were covered in Chapter 6. In this chapter:

- We will be using the *Purchases* module.
- The quotes, orders and purchases are entered in MYOB on the date of the *source document*.
- The payments are made later in the month and processed on the date that they were paid.
- We will be using *Service* style purchase invoices throughout these exercises.

Purchases and payments

COZY DRY CLEANERS

1 In MYOB AccountRight 2016, open the **7.1 Cozy Dry Cleaners.myox** data file from the Chapter 7 folder of your start-up files, or use the file you completed for this business in Chapter 6.

In this exercise, we will follow a purchase order through its 'life cycle' from the request to the supplier to delivery and then payment.

Record a purchase order

2 Place a purchase order with a supplier for some dry-cleaning solvent.

Cozy Dry Cleaners Pty Ltd	
Cozy Corner Beach	
Albany WA 6330	
ABN 62 266 506 622	
Purchase Order Number:	00003
Date:	1 July
Supplier:	Tulloch Pty Ltd
3 x 10 litre cubes of Dowper Solvent @ $31.90 each plus GST.	
Delivery:	Road Freight

First let's look at the price on your purchase order. As the purchase order says 'plus GST', it means that GST is added on *afterwards*, which means the price quoted there is *GST Exclusive*.

Example

GST Exclusive	100.00	Dr Expense
GST (10%)	+10.00	Dr GST Paid contra liability
GST Inclusive	110.00	Cr Accounts Payable

Remember This

GST Exclusive does *not* mean there isn't any GST. It means it is the price quoted *before* the tax is added on.

Click...

- *Purchases* (in the Command Centre).
- *Enter Purchases*. See Figure 7.1.
- *Purchase Type* (change this to *Order*). The colour of the form will change to yellow.
- To remove the *Tax Inclusive* tick if necessary (as the prices quoted are GST Exclusive).
- The drop-down arrow at Supplier (to activate the list of Suppliers). See Figure 7.2.
- Tulloch Pty Ltd

Figure 7.1   Purchases module: Enter Purchases

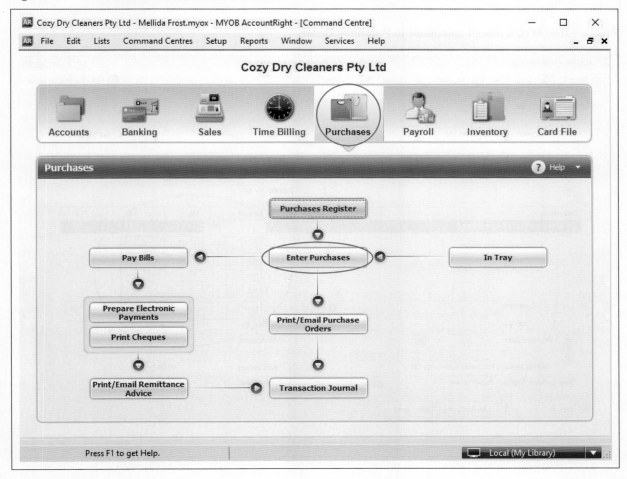

Figure 7.2   Placing an order: first steps

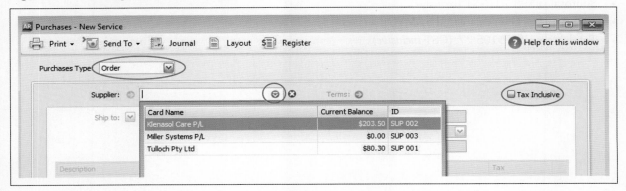

Click...

- *Purchase No.* (it should say *00000003*). Press the Tab key.
- *Date* (type *1/07/16*).
- *Description* (type *3 x 10 litre cubes of Dowper Solvent*). Press the Tab key twice. Note the account number automatically appears. This is because it was entered into Tulloch's card in Chapter 5.
- *Amount* (type *31.9**). The MYOB inbuilt calculator opens. See Figure 7.3. (Type *3*) then press the Enter key. The total cost of the purchase order is calculated. Press the Tab key.
- *Ship Via* (type *Road* and it will autofill to *Road Freight*. Either double-click on *Road Freight* or click *Use Method* button on bottom right hand side of the window).

Figure 7.3   MYOB inbuilt calculator in Purchase Order

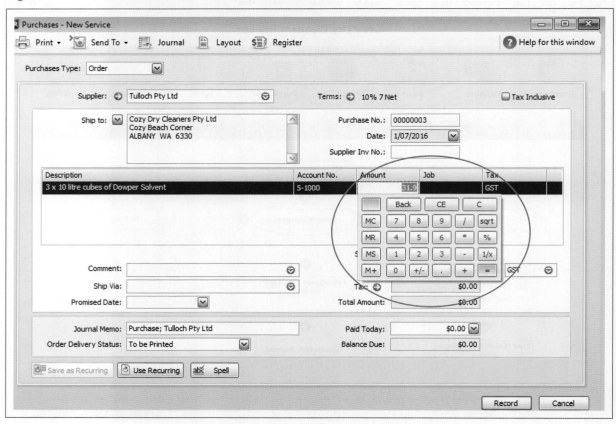

More line items could be added if necessary, but let's have a look at the transaction (Figure 7.4):

- Subtotal is $95.70 (GST *Exclusive*).
- 10% GST has been calculated by MYOB as being $9.57.
- Total Amount is $105.27. (GST *Inclusive*).

Figure 7.4   **Purchase Order: Tulloch Pty Ltd**

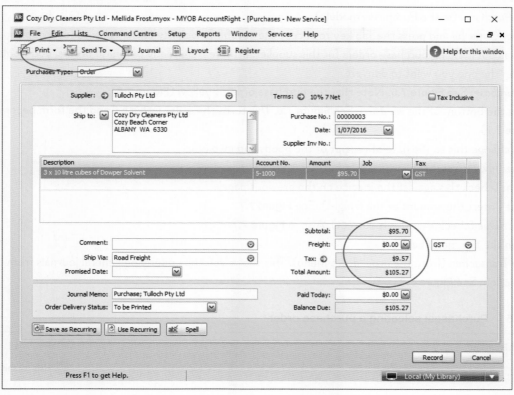

If there is any change in the price of the goods the order will be edited later. The cost of the freight will be added after the supplier's invoice is received. The order can be printed to post or emailed to the supplier by using the buttons on the top left hand side of the screen. See **Figure 7.4** above.

Click...

- *Record.*
- *Cancel* (to return to the Command Centre).

Convert the purchase order to a supplier invoice

3 The order above is delivered on 3 July accompanied by the following invoice:

Tulloch Pty Ltd	
Date:	3 July
Tax Invoice No.:	03925
Supplied to:	Cozy Dry Cleaners P/L
Details: Dowper Solvent	
3 x 10 litre cubes @ $31.90	$95.70
Freight	9.30
GST:	10.50
Invoice Total:	$115.50
Terms: 10% 7 days/Net 30.	

Click...

- *Enter Purchases* (in the Purchases module).
- *Supplier* (type *Tul* and press the Tab key to accept the autofill *Tulloch Pty Ltd*). A new window pops up. This is a list of all outstanding purchase orders for this supplier. If there were many purchase orders, you would have to click on the one you want to convert.
- *Use Purchase*. See Figure 7.5. Note that the purchase order is yellow (Figure 7.6).
- *Bill* (at the bottom of the window). See Figure 7.6. This turns the order into a bill and the form becomes blue (Figure 7.7).
- *Date* (change this to the date of receipt of the goods and invoice).
- *Supplier Inv. #* (insert the invoice number).
- *Amount* (check this against the invoice on the previous page).
- *Freight* (insert the amount of the freight). See Figure 7.7.
- *Balance Due* (check that this is correct). Also in Figure 7.7.
- *Edit* (in the top menu bar).
- *Recap Transaction* (from the drop-down menu). This shows you the underlying general journals from this transaction. See Figure 7.8.

Figure 7.5   **Purchases: selecting a purchase order**

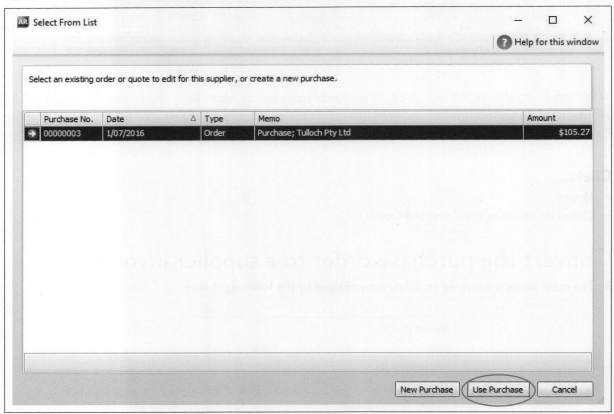

Figure 7.6   Purchase order: Bill button

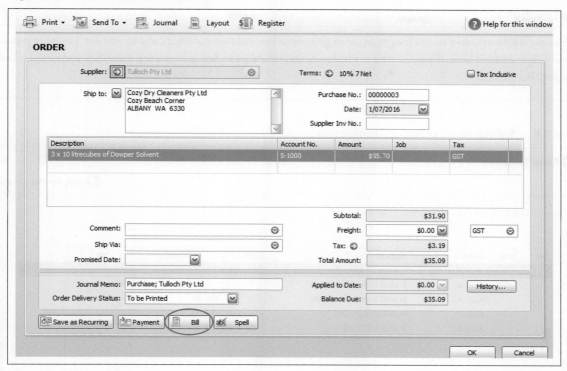

Figure 7.7   Tulloch supplier invoice

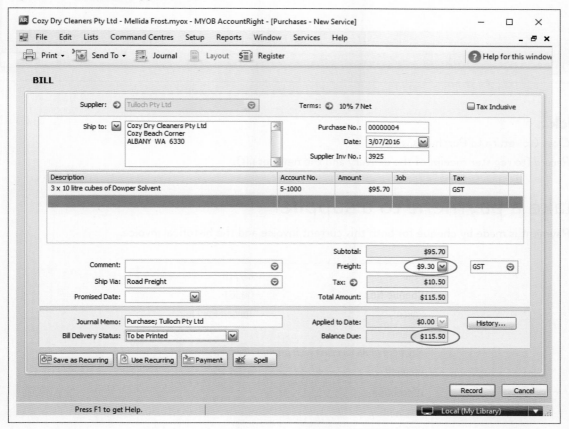

Computerised Accounting A Systematic Approach

This is why

The Freight field was linked to the freight expense general ledger account automatically so you don't need to put a general ledger code in here. If you wanted to change it, you would go to Setup in the top menu bar and click Linked Accounts/Purchases.

Figure 7.8   Tulloch invoice: Recap Transaction

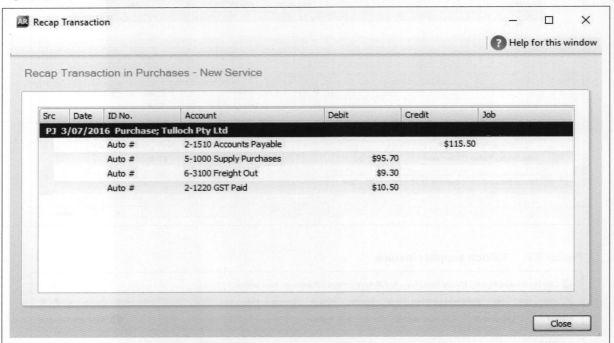

Click...

- *Close* (to return to Purchases window).
- *Record* (to register receipt of the delivery and the new details).

Make a payment to a supplier

4 Payment is made by cheque for both this current invoice and the historical invoice.

Date:	6/7/16
Cheque No.:	00361
Payee:	Tulloch Pty Ltd
Details:	
Payment of all invoices with prompt payment discount	
Amount:	$184.25
Dissection	
Discount:	10.50
GST Component:	1.05
Discount Total:	11.55

Click...

- *Purchases* (in the Command Centre).
- *Pay Bills* (in the accounting area). See Figure 7.9.
- *Supplier List* drop-down arrow (at right of the Supplier text box).
- *Tulloch Pty Ltd* (select this from the list).
- *Cheque No.* (insert *361*).
- *Date* (change to *6/07/16*).
- *Amount* (insert *184.25*: the debt less the calculated discount on the second invoice).
- *Amount Applied* (click at the top of the far-right column). See Figure 7.10.
- *Amount Applied* (second line). Press the Tab key (to apply the payment to the invoice).
- Ensure the *Finance Charge* and *Out of Balance* are zero. See Figure 7.11.
- *Edit* (top menu bar).
- *Recap Transaction* (to check what is about to happen). See Figure 7.12.

Figure 7.9   Purchases module: Pay Bills

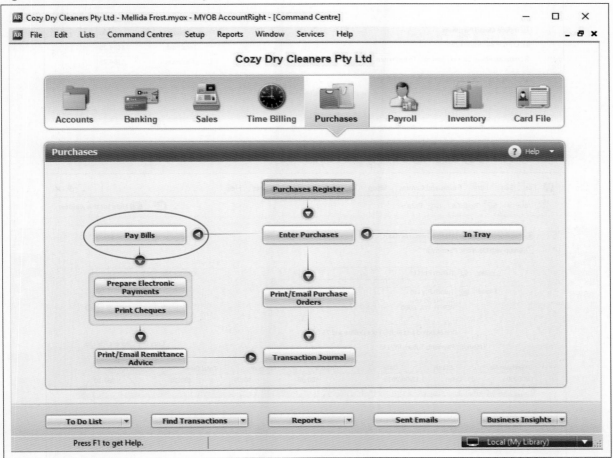

Figure 7.10   Pay Bills: Tulloch Pty Ltd started

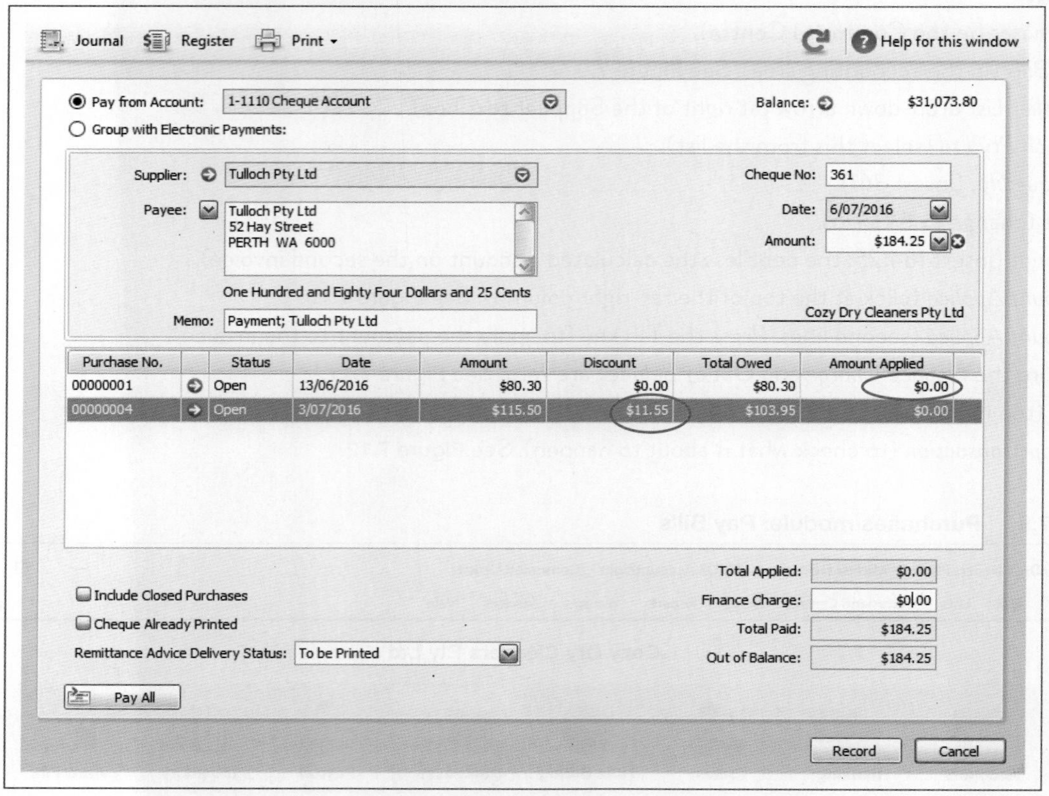

Figure 7.11   Pay Bills: Tulloch Pty Ltd completed

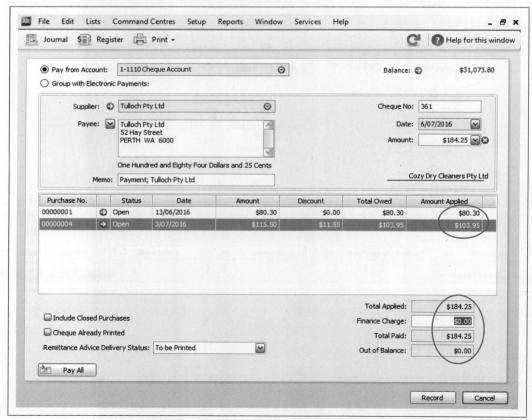

Figure 7.12   **Recap Transaction: Tulloch Pty Ltd**

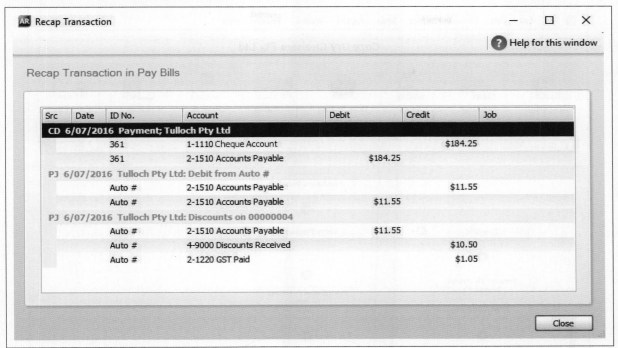

You only have to insert the number of the first cheque. Future cheques will display the correct number automatically.

The following is an explanation of what is shown in the three journal entries in Figure 7.12:

- *First journal*: Cash Disbursements (CD) records that the Cheque Account will be reduced (credited) and the debt owed to the creditor (Accounts Payable) will also be reduced (debited) by the payment.
- *Second journal*: Purchases Journal (PJ) records the two discounts being applied to the appropriate bill.
- *Third journal*: the Purchases Journal's record of the discount of $10.50 that will be taken for prompt payment of the debt, and that because of this the GST Paid for the supplies will be reduced (credited) by $1.05.

Click...

- *Close* (when you have understood the display).
- *Record* (to register the payment).
- *Print Later* (we don't need a record of this).
- *Cancel* (to return to the Command Centre).

The debits and credits involved in the transaction just completed will now be examined in more detail.

Investigate the accounts

5   Another way to check these transactions is to go through the Transaction Journal. This is also the way to locate, open and correct the transaction if you need to.

Click...

- *Transaction Journal* (in the Command Centre). See Figure 7.13.
- *Purchases* tab (at top of the window). See Figure 7.14.
- *Dated From* (change to *1/07/16*) and *To* (change to *31/07/16*). Press the Tab key.

Figure 7.13   Purchases module: Transaction Journal

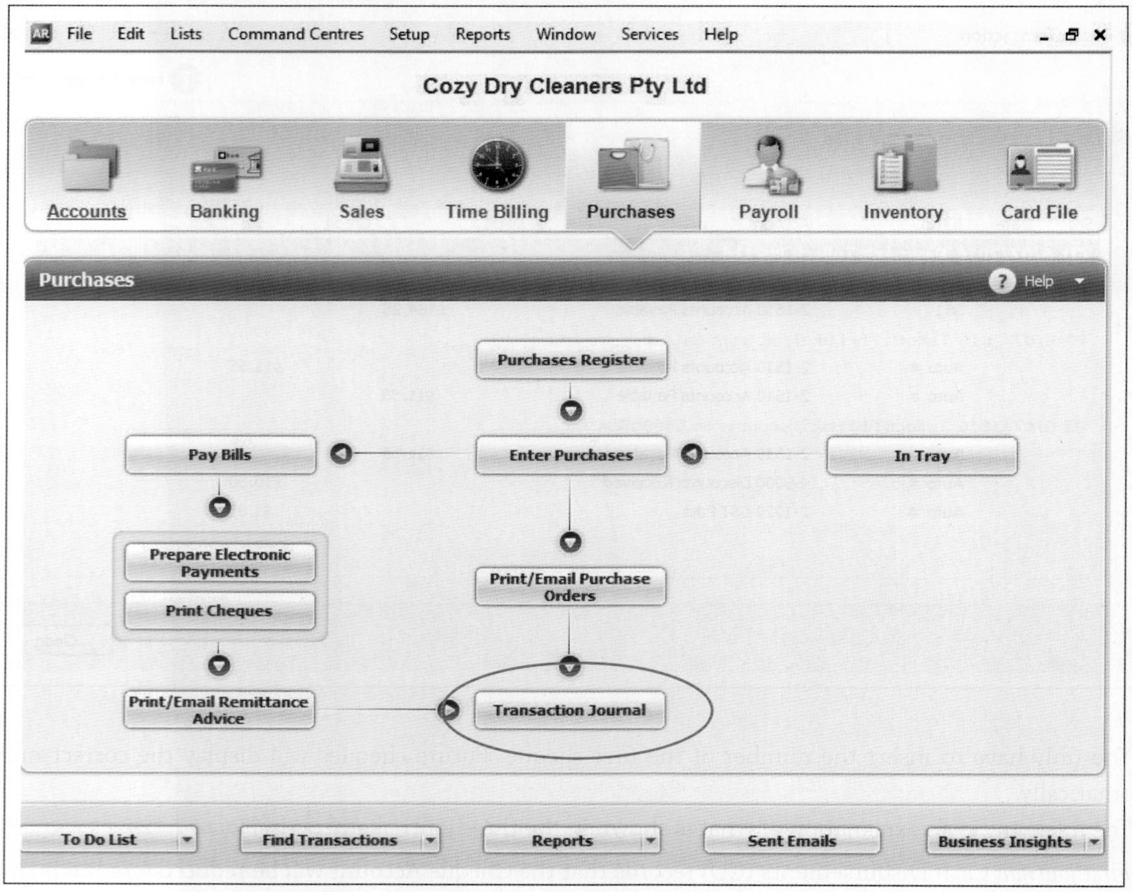

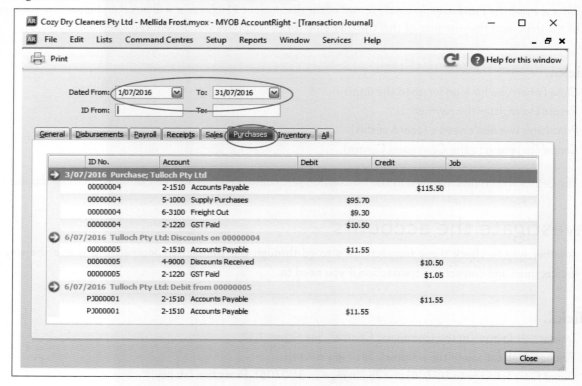

Figure 7.14   Transaction Journal: Purchases tab

The three Purchase transactions are shown in detail from the perspective of the general ledger. To edit or view a transaction, click on the white zoom arrow to the left of the transaction date; here you will see that:

- The original purchase on 3 July for the full amount has gone to Accounts Payable.
- The discount taken for prompt payment has been processed, showing the reduction in GST Paid.
- The total discount taken is applied to Accounts Payable to reduce the debt owed to the supplier.

The cheque payment isn't in there because it is not a purchase – it is a payment. We will have a look at this a little later in the chapter.

Click...
- *Close* (to exit the Transaction Journal).
- *Find Transactions* (in the base of the Command Centre next to Reports).
- *Account* (tab at top of the window).
- *Dated From* (change to *1/07/16*) and *To* (change to *31/07/16*).
- *Account* (type *5-1000*). Press the Tab key. See Figure 7.15.

Figure 7.15   **Find Transactions: Account tab Supply Purchases**

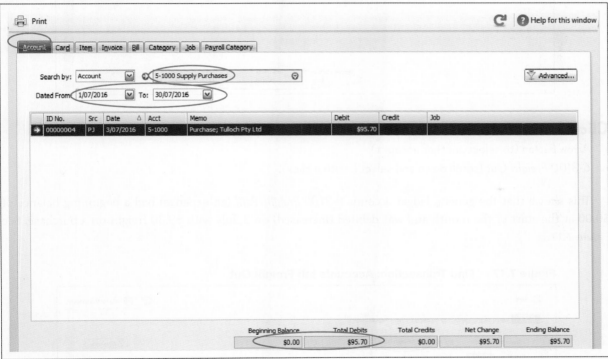

This shows that the general ledger account *5-1000 Supply Purchases* (cost of sales) had a beginning balance of $0.00 at the start of the month and was debited (increased) on 3 July with a $95.70 purchase from Tulloch Pty Ltd.

Click...
- *Arrow button* (to select another account).
- *2-1220 GST Paid* (scroll down and select it with a click).

This shows that the general ledger account *2-1220 GST Paid* (a contra or negative liability which is effectively an asset) had a beginning balance of $0.00 at the start of the month and was debited (increased) on 3 July with $10.50 tax on a purchase from Tulloch Pty Ltd. GST Paid was reduced (credited) on 6 July by $1.05 when the prompt payment discount that lessened the cost of the purchase was applied, to give an Ending Balance of $9.45. See Figure 7.16.

Figure 7.16   **Find Transaction: Accounts tab GST Paid**

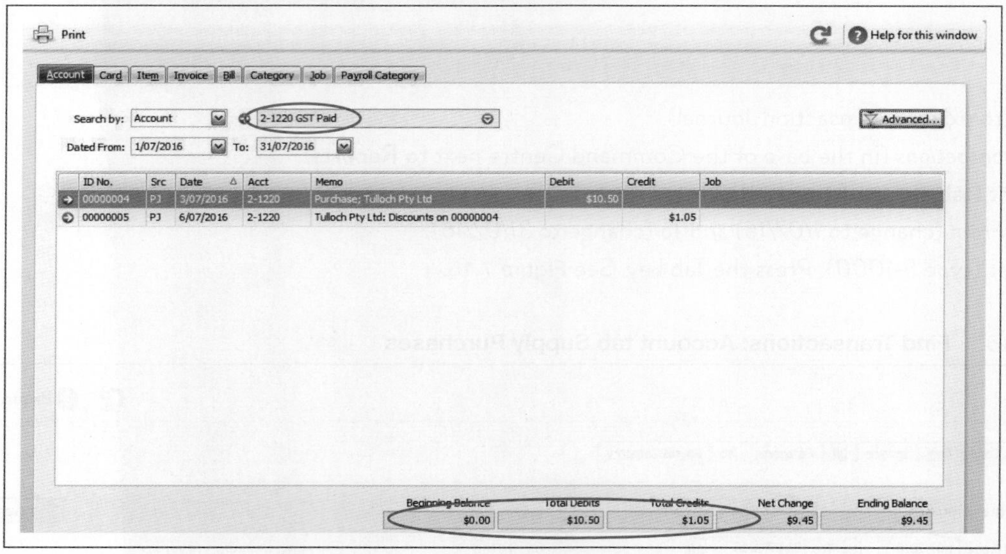

Click...

- *Arrow button* (to select another account).
- *6-3100 Freight Out* (scroll down and select it with a click).

This shows that the general ledger account *6-3100 Freight Paid* (an expense) had a beginning balance of $0.00 at the start of the month and was debited (increased) on 3 July with $9.30 freight on a purchase. See Figure 7.17.

Figure 7.17   **Find Transaction: Accounts tab Freight Out**

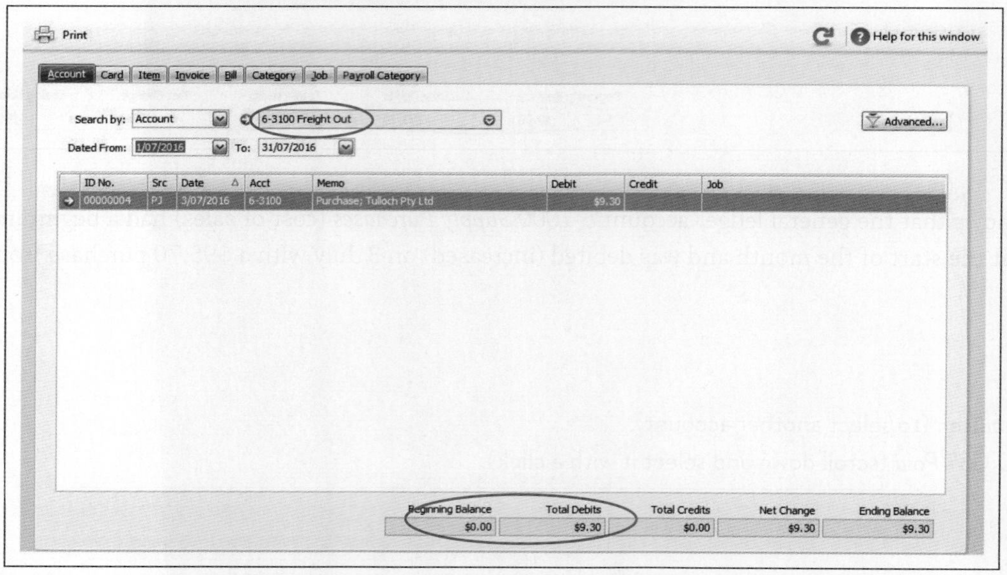

We will now examine the second part of the transaction, the payment.

 Click...

- *Transaction Journal* (in the Command Centre).
- *Disbursements* tab (at top of the window). See Figure 7.18.
- *Dated From* (change to *1/07/16*) and *To* (change to *31/07/16*). Press the Tab key.

Figure 7.18   Transaction Journal: Disbursements tab

The Transaction Journal (above) shows that the Cheque Account (an asset) has been credited (reduced) by the amount of the payment, and the Accounts Payable liability account has been debited (reduced) by the same amount.

 Click...

- *Close* (to exit the Transaction Journal).
- *Find Transactions* (in the base of the Command Centre next to Reports).
- *Account* (tab at top of the window).
- *Dated From* (change to *1/07/16*) and *To* (change to *31/07/16*).
- *Account* (type *1-1110*). Press the Tab key. See Figure 7.19.

Figure 7.19   Find Transaction: Account tab Business Bank Account #1

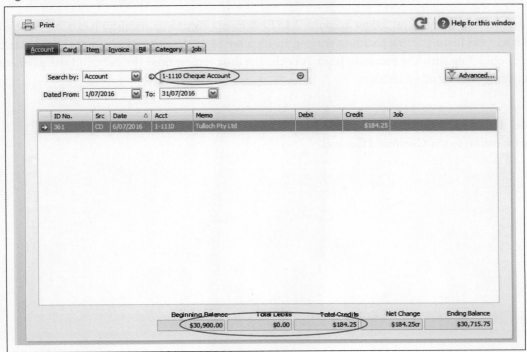

This shows that the general ledger account *1-1110 Business Bank Account #1* (an asset) had a beginning balance of $30 900.00 at the start of the month and was credited (decreased) on 6 July with the $184.25 payment to Tulloch.

Click...

- *Arrow button* (to select another account).
- *2-1510 Accounts Payable* (you will need to scroll down to find it). See Figure 7.20.

Figure 7.20   Find Transaction: Accounts Tab: Accounts Payable

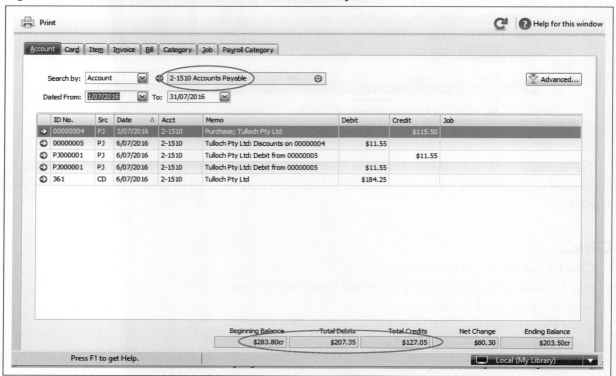

This shows that the general ledger account *2-1510 Accounts Payable* (a liability) had a beginning balance of $283.80cr (the historical transactions entered in Chapter 6) at the start of the month and was credited (increased) on 3 July with the purchase from Tulloch. The discount reduced the debt and the payment in full gives an ending balance of $203.50cr.

Click...

- *Close* (to return to the Command Centre).

More transactions

6 Record the following orders to suppliers:

<table>
<tr><td>
Cozy Dry Cleaners Pty Ltd
Cosy Corner Beach
Albany WA 6330
ABN 62 266 506 622

Purchase Order Number: 00006
Date: 9 July
Supplier: Klenasol Care P/L
100 Long Black Dress Covers (with Zip) at $3.50 each plus GST.
Delivery: Air Freight
</td>
<td>
Cozy Dry Cleaners Pty Ltd
Cosy Corner Beach
Albany WA 6330
ABN 62 266 506 622

Purchase Order Number: 00007
Date: 9 July
Supplier: Miller Systems P/L
1 roll of Repairs Needed Flag Tags at $25.00 plus GST.
Delivery: Kwikasair
</td></tr>
</table>

Cozy Dry Cleaners Pty Ltd
Cosy Corner Beach
Albany WA 6330
ABN 62 266 506 622

Purchase Order Number: 00008
Date: 12 July
Supplier: Tulloch Pty Ltd
1 x 25 litres of Emulsifier & Spotter at $264.00 plus GST.
Delivery: Road Freight

7 Convert your purchase orders to bills as the goods have been received, accompanied by the following invoices:

Klenasol Care Pty Ltd
Date: 15 July
Tax Invoice No.:   11418
Supplied to: Cozy Dry Cleaners P/L
Details: Long Black Dress Covers

100 with zip @ $3.50	$350.00
Freight	35.00
GST:	38.50
Invoice Total:	$423.50

Terms: 10% 10 days/Net 30

Miller Systems Pty Ltd
Date: 15 July
Tax Invoice No.:   33025
Supplied to: Cozy Dry Cleaners P/L
Details: 'Repairs Needed' Flag Tags

1 Roll @ $25.00	$25.00
Freight	5.00
GST:	3.00
Invoice Total:	$33.00

Terms: 10% 10 days/Net 30

Tulloch Pty Ltd
Date: 15 July
Tax Invoice No.:   03957
Supplied to: Cozy Dry Cleaners P/L
Details: Emulsifier & Spotter

1 x 25 litres @ $264.00	$264.00
Freight	6.00
GST:	27.00
Invoice Total:	$297.00

Terms: 10% 7 days/Net 30.

8   Record the following payments to suppliers:

Date:	20/7/16
Cheque No.:	00362
Payee:	Tulloch Pty Ltd
Details:	
Payment of all invoices with prompt payment discount	
Amount:	$267.30

Dissection	
Discount:	27.00
GST Component:	2.70
Discount Total:	29.70

Date:	24/7/16
Cheque No.:	00363
Payee:	Klenasol Care
Details:	
Payment of all invoices with prompt payment discount	
Amount:	$584.65

Dissection	
Discount:	38.50
GST Component:	3.85
Discount Total:	42.35

Date:	24/7/16
Cheque No.:	00364
Payee:	Miller Systems
Details:	
Payment of all invoices with prompt payment discount	
Amount:	$29.70

Dissection	
Discount:	3.00
GST Component:	0.30
Discount Total:	3.30

Produce reports

9   Produce a Purchases & Payables Journal report to check the accuracy of your work.

Click...
- *Reports* (at the bottom of the Command Centre).
- *Purchases* (in the left menu).
- *Purchases & Payables Journal* in the middle menu (under the bolded Transaction Journals heading).
- *Dated From* (type 1/07/16) and *To* (type 31/07/16). See Figure 7.21.
- *Display*. See Figure 7.22.

Figure 7.21   Reports: Purchases

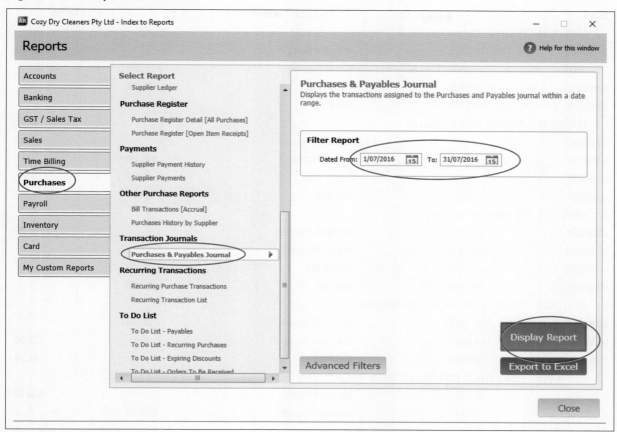

Figure 7.22   Purchases & Payables Journal

COZY DRY CLEANERS PTY LTD
COZY BEACH CORNER
ALBANY WA 6330
PURCHASES & PAYABLES JOURNAL
1/07/2016 TO 31/07/2016

ID No.	Account No.	Account Name	Debit	Credit
PJ 3/07/2016 Purchase; Tulloch Pty Ltd				
00000004	2-1510	Accounts Payable		$115.50
00000004	5-1000	Supply Purchases	$95.70	
00000004	6-3100	Freight Out	$9.30	
00000004	2-1220	GST Paid	$10.50	
PJ 6/07/2016 Tulloch Pty Ltd: Discounts on 00000004				
00000005	2-1510	Accounts Payable	$11.55	
00000005	4-9000	Discounts Received		$10.50
00000005	2-1220	GST Paid		$1.05
PJ 6/07/2016 Tulloch Pty Ltd: Debit from 00000005				
PJ000001	2-1510	Accounts Payable		$11.55
PJ000001	2-1510	Accounts Payable	$11.55	

▶ ▶

ID No.	Account No.	Account Name	Debit	Credit
PJ 15/07/2016 Purchase; Klenasol Care P/L				
00000006	2-1510	Accounts Payable		$423.50
00000006	5-1000	Supply Purchases	$350.00	
00000006	6-3100	Freight Out	$35.00	
00000006	2-1220	GST Paid	$38.50	
PJ 15/07/2016 Purchase; Miller Systems P/L				
00000007	2-1510	Accounts Payable		$33.00
00000007	5-1000	Supply Purchases	$25.00	
00000007	6-3100	Freight Out	$5.00	
00000007	2-1220	GST Paid	$3.00	
PJ 15/07/2016 Purchase; Tulloch Pty Ltd				
00000008	2-1510	Accounts Payable		$297.00
00000008	5-1000	Supply Purchases	$264.00	
00000008	6-3100	Freight Out	$6.00	
00000008	2-1220	GST Paid	$27.00	
PJ 20/07/2016 Tulloch Pty Ltd: Discounts on 00000008				
00000009	2-1510	Accounts Payable	$29.70	
00000009	4-9000	Discounts Received		$27.00
00000009	2-1220	GST Paid		$2.70
PJ 20/07/2016 Tulloch Pty Ltd: Debit from 00000009				
PJ000002	2-1510	Accounts Payable		$29.70
PJ000002	2-1510	Accounts Payable	$29.70	
PJ 24/07/2016 Klenasol Care P/L: Discounts on 00000006				
00000010	2-1510	Accounts Payable	$42.35	
00000010	4-9000	Discounts Received		$38.50
00000010	2-1220	GST Paid		$3.85
PJ 24/07/2016 Miller Systems P/L: Discounts on 00000007				
00000011	2-1510	Accounts Payable	$3.30	
00000011	4-9000	Discounts Received		$3.00
00000011	2-1220	GST Paid		$0.30
PJ 24/07/2016 Klenasol Care P/L: Debit from 00000010				
PJ000003	2-1510	Accounts Payable		$42.35
PJ000003	2-1510	Accounts Payable	$42.35	
PJ 24/07/2016 Miller Systems P/L: Debit from 00000011				
PJ000004	2-1510	Accounts Payable		$3.30
PJ000004	2-1510	Accounts Payable	$3.30	
		Grand Total:	**$1 042.80**	**$1 042.80**

10 Produce a Purchase Register [All Purchases] report and understand the contents. (You are in the Reports menu.)

⊙ Click...

- *Purchases* (in the left menu).
- *Purchases Register Detail [All Purchases]* in the middle menu.
- *Filter Report Dated From* (type *1/07/2016*) and *To* (type *31/07/16*).
- *Display.* See Figure 7.23.

Figure 7.23   **Purchases & Payables Journal report**

Cozy Dry Cleaners Pty Ltd
Cozy Beach Corner
Albany WA 6330
Purchase Register Detail [All Purchases]
July 2016

Date	PO No.	Supplier Inv. No.	Supplier Name	Amount	Amount Due	Status	Received
3/07/2016	00000004	3925	Tulloch Pty Ltd	$115.50	$0.00	Closed	
6/07/2016	00000005		Tulloch Pty Ltd	($11.55)	$0.00	Closed	
15/07/2016	00000006	11418	Klenasol Care P/L	$423.50	$0.00	Closed	
15/07/2016	00000007	33025	Miller Systems P/L	$33.00	$0.00	Closed	
15/07/2016	00000008	3957	Tulloch Pty Ltd	$297.00	$0.00	Closed	
20/07/2016	00000009		Tulloch Pty Ltd	($29.70)	$0.00	Closed	
24/07/2016	00000010		Klenasol Care P/L	($42.35)	$0.00	Closed	
24/07/2016	00000011		Miller Systems P/L	($3.30)	$0.00	Closed	
			Total:	**$782.10**	**$0.00**		

11 Examine your Supplier Ledger. This shows transactions grouped by suppliers for the selected date range. (You are still in the Reports menu.)

Click...

- *Purchases* (in the left menu).
- *Purchases [Supplier Summary]* in the middle menu.
- *Filter Report Dated From* (type *1/07/2016*) and *To* (type *31/07/16*).
- *Display*. See Figure 7.24.

Figure 7.24   **Purchases [Supplier Summary] report**

Cozy Dry Cleaners Pty Ltd
Cozy Beach Corner
Albany WA 6330
Purchases [Supplier Summary]
July 2016

ID No.	Original Date	Purchase Amount	Tax	Current Balance	Status	Due Date
Klenasol Care P/L						
00000006	15/07/2016	$350.00	$38.50	$0.00	Closed	
00000010	24/07/2016	($38.50)	($3.85)	$0.00	Closed	
		$311.50	$34.65	$0.00		
Miller Systems P/L						
00000007	15/07/2016	$25.00	$3.00	$0.00	Closed	
00000011	24/07/2016	($3.00)	($0.30)	$0.00	Closed	
		$22.00	$2.70	$0.00		

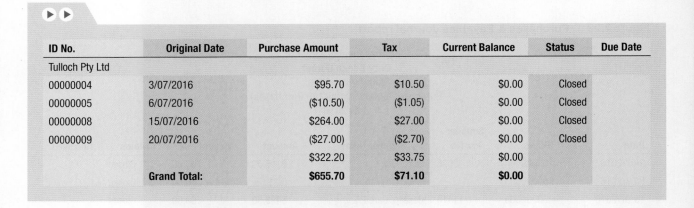

ID No.	Original Date	Purchase Amount	Tax	Current Balance	Status	Due Date
Tulloch Pty Ltd						
00000004	3/07/2016	$95.70	$10.50	$0.00	Closed	
00000005	6/07/2016	($10.50)	($1.05)	$0.00	Closed	
00000008	15/07/2016	$264.00	$27.00	$0.00	Closed	
00000009	20/07/2016	($27.00)	($2.70)	$0.00	Closed	
		$322.20	$33.75	$0.00		
	Grand Total:	**$655.70**	**$71.10**	**$0.00**		

Practice

THE BLINDS MAN

1 In MYOB AccountRight 2016, open the. **7.2 The Blinds Man.myox** data file from the Chapter 7 folder of your start-up files, or use your own file from Chapter 6.

> ### This is why
> You don't need to provide prices in a purchase order as it has no effect on the accounts until it is converted to a bill.

2 Place the following orders with your suppliers in July 2016, clicking **OK** to the window that opens.

The Blinds Man 21 Penola Road, Mount Gambier SA 5290 ABN 78 303 458 861 **Purchase Order Number:** 0581 Date: 6 July Supplier: Apollo Blinds P/L Please supply: 2 x Vertical Drapes type AVB 2600 with fittings. Dimensions: Width: 3000mm; Height 2400mm. Delivery: Road Freight	The Blinds Man 21 Penola Road, Mount Gambier SA 5290 ABN 78 303 458 861 **Purchase Order Number:** 0582 Date: 6 July Supplier: Luxaflex P/L Please supply: 3 x Venetian Blinds type LVB 420 with fittings. Dimensions: Width: 2400mm; Height 1800mm. Delivery: Road Freight
The Blinds Man 21 Penola Road, Mount Gambier SA 5290 ABN 78 303 458 861 **Purchase Order Number:** 0583 Date: 6 July Supplier: Wynstan Blinds P/L Please supply: 5 x Sunscreen Rollers type RB 175 with fittings. Dimensions: Width: 3600mm; Length 2400mm. Delivery: Road Freight	The Blinds Man 21 Penola Road, Mount Gambier SA 5290 ABN 78 303 458 861 **Purchase Order Number:** 0584 Date: 6 July Supplier: Litemaster Blinds P/L Please supply: 3 x Holland Blinds type HB 501 with fittings. Dimensions: Width: 2000mm; Height 3000mm. Delivery: Road Freight

3 Convert your purchase orders to bills as the goods have been received accompanied by the following invoices:

Apollo Blinds P/L	
Date:	15 July
Tax Invoice No.:	19051
Supplied to:	The Blinds Man
Details: Drapes as per your PO 0581	
2 x units @ $500.00	$1 000.00
Freight	50.00
GST:	105.00
Invoice Total:	$1 155.00
Terms: 10% 10 days/Net 30	

Luxaflex P/L	
Date:	15 July
Tax Invoice No.:	44082
Supplied to:	The Blinds Man
Details: Blinds as per your PO 0582	
3 x units @ $300.00	$900.00
Freight	60.00
GST:	96.00
Invoice Total:	$1 056.00
Terms: 10% 10 days/Net 30	

Wynstan Blinds P/L	
Date:	15 July
Tax Invoice No.:	55801
Supplied to:	The Blinds Man
Details: Blinds as per your PO 0583	
5 x units @ $800.00	$4 000.00
Freight	100.00
GST:	410.00
Invoice Total:	$4 510.00
Terms: 10% 10 days/Net 30	

Litemaster Blinds P/L	
Date:	15 July
Tax Invoice No.:	80956
Supplied to:	The Blinds Man
Details: Blinds as per your PO 0584	
3 x units @ $200.00	$600.00
Freight	60.00
GST:	66.00
Invoice Total:	$726.00
Terms: 10% 10 days/Net 30	

4 Enter the following invoice (no purchase order, so use the invoice number 1374-2 in the Purchase number field as well):

Energy Plus	
Date:	15 July
Tax Invoice No.:	1374-2
Supplied to:	The Blinds Man
Details: Electricity to 21 Penola Road, Mount Gambier SA	$142.60
GST:	14.26
Invoice Total:	$156.86
Terms: Net 15	

5 Place the following orders with your suppliers:

The Blinds Man	
21 Penola Road, Mount Gambier SA 5290	
ABN 78 303 458 861	
Purchase Order Number:	0585
Date:	19 July
Supplier:	Apollo Blinds P/L
Please supply:	
5 x Vertical Drapes type AVB 2600 with fittings.	
Dimensions: Width: 3000mm; Height 2400mm.	
Delivery:	Road Freight

The Blinds Man	
21 Penola Road, Mount Gambier SA 5290	
ABN 78 303 458 861	
Purchase Order Number:	0586
Date:	19 July
Supplier:	Luxaflex P/L
Please supply:	
4 x Venetian Blinds type LVB 420 with fittings.	
Dimensions: Width: 2400mm; Height 1800mm.	
Delivery:	Road Freight

The Blinds Man	
21 Penola Road, Mount Gambier, SA 5290	
ABN 78 303 458 861	
Purchase Order Number:	0587
Date:	19 July
Supplier:	Wynstan Blinds P/L
Please supply:	
2 x Sunscreen Rollers type RB 175 with fittings.	
Dimensions: Width: 3600mm; Length 2400mm.	
Delivery:	Road Freight

The Blinds Man	
21 Penola Road, Mount Gambier, SA 5290	
ABN 78 303 458 861	
Purchase Order Number:	0588
Date:	19 July
Supplier:	Litemaster Blinds P/L
Please supply:	
4 x Holland Blinds type HB 501 with fittings.	
Dimensions: Width: 2000mm; Height 3000mm.	
Delivery:	Road Freight

6 Record the following payments to suppliers:

Date:	22/7/16
Cheque No.:	00862
Payee:	Apollo Blinds
Details:	
Payment of all invoices with prompt payment discount	
Amount:	$1 039.50
Dissection	
Discount:	105.00
GST Component:	10.50
Discount Total:	115.50

Date:	22/7/16
Cheque No.:	00863
Payee:	Luxaflex P/L
Details:	
Payment of all invoices with prompt payment discount	
Amount:	$1 302.40
Dissection	
Discount:	96.00
GST Component:	9.60
Discount Total:	105.60

Date:	22/7/16
Cheque No.:	00864
Payee:	Energy Plus
Details:	
Payment of invoice	
Amount:	$156.86
Dissection	
Payment:	
GST Component:	
Payment Total:	

Date:	22/7/16
Cheque No.:	00865
Payee:	Wystan Blinds
Details:	
Payment of all invoices with prompt payment discount	
Amount:	$4 059.00
Dissection	
Discount:	410.00
GST Component:	41.00
Discount Total:	451.00

Date:	22/7/16
Cheque No.:	00866
Payee:	Litemaster Blinds P/L
Details:	
Payment of all invoice with prompt payment discount	
Amount:	$895.40
Dissection	
Discount:	66.00
GST Component:	6.60
Discount Total:	72.60

7 Convert your purchase orders to bills as the goods have been received accompanied by the following invoices:

Apollo Blinds P/L	
Date:	25 July
Tax Invoice No.:	19122
Supplied to:	The Blinds Man
Details:	PO 0585
5 x units @ $500.00	$2 500.00
Freight	100.00
GST:	260.00
Invoice Total:	$2 860.00
Terms: 10% 10 days/Net 30	

Luxaflex P/L	
Date:	25 July
Tax Invoice No.:	44128
Supplied to:	The Blinds Man
Details: Blinds as per your PO 0586	
4 x units @ $300.00	$1 200.00
Freight	80.00
GST:	128.00
Invoice Total:	$1 408.00
Terms: 10% 10 days/Net 30	

Wynstan Blinds P/L	
Date:	25 July
Tax Invoice No.:	56004
Supplied to:	The Blinds Man
Details: Blinds as per your PO 0587	
2 x units @ $800.00	$1 600.00
Freight	40.00
GST:	164.00
Invoice Total:	$1 804.00
Terms: 10% 10 days/Net 30	

Litemaster Blinds P/L	
Date:	25 July
Tax Invoice No.:	80956
Supplied to:	The Blinds Man
Details: Blinds as per your PO 0588	
4 x units @ $200.00	$800.00
Freight	80.00
GST:	88.00
Invoice Total:	$968.00
Terms: 10% 10 days/Net 30	

8 Produce the following reports for your records:

- Purchase Register Detail [All Purchases] for July. See Figure 7.25.
- Aged Payables [Summary] as at 30 July. See Figure 7.26.
- Purchases [Supplier Summary] for June. See Figure 7.27.

Figure 7.25   Purchase Register [All Purchases] report

The Blinds Man
21 Penola Rd
Mount Gambier SA 5290
Purchase Register Detail [All Purchases]
July 16

Date	PO No.	Supplier Inv No.	Supplier Name	Amount	Amount Due	Status	Received
15/07/2016	00000581	19051	Apollo Blinds P/L	$1 155.00	$0.00	Closed	
15/07/2016	00000582	44082	Luxaflex P/L	$1 056.00	$0.00	Closed	
15/07/2016	00000583	55801	Wynstan Blinds P/L	$4 510.00	$0.00	Closed	
15/07/2016	00000584	80956	Litemaster Blinds P/L	$726.00	$0.00	Closed	
25/07/2016	00000585	19122	Apollo Blinds P/L	$2 860.00	$2 860.00	Open	
25/07/2016	00000586	44128	Luxaflex P/L	$1 408.00	$1 408.00	Open	

Date	PO No.	Supplier Inv No.	Supplier Name	Amount	Amount Due	Status	Received
19/07/2016	00000587	56004	Wynstan Blinds P/L	$1 804.00	$1 804.00	Open	
25/07/2016	00000588	80956	Litemaster Blinds P/L	$968.00	$968.00	Open	
22/07/2016	00000589		Apollo Blinds P/L	($115.50)	$0.00	Closed	
22/07/2016	00000590		Luxaflex P/L	($105.60)	$0.00	Closed	
22/07/2016	00000591		Wynstan Blinds P/L	($451.00)	$0.00	Closed	
22/07/2016	00000592		Litemaster Blinds P/L	($72.60)	$0.00	Closed	
15/07/2016	1374-2	1374-2	Energy Plus	$156.86	$0.00	Closed	
			Total:	**$13 899.16**	**$7 040.00**		

Figure 7.26　Aged Payables [Summary] report

The Blinds Man
21 Penola Rd
Mount Gambier SA 5290
Aged Payables [Summary]
As of 31/07/2016

Name	Total Due	0–30	31–60	61–90	90+
Apollo Blinds P/L	$2 860.00	$2 860.00	$0.00	$0.00	$0.00
Litemaster Blinds P/L	$968.00	$968.00	$0.00	$0.00	$0.00
Luxaflex P/L	$1 408.00	$1 408.00	$0.00	$0.00	$0.00
Wynstan Blinds P/L	$1 804.00	$1 804.00	$0.00	$0.00	$0.00
Total:	**$7 040.00**	**$7 040.00**	**$0.00**	**$0.00**	**$0.00**
Ageing Per # cent:		**100.0%**	**0.0%**	**0.0%**	**0.0%**

Figure 7.27　Purchases [Supplier Summary] report

The Blinds Man
21 Penola Rd
Mount Gambier SA 5290
Purchases [Supplier Summary]
July 2016

ID No.	Original Date	Purchase Amount	Tax	Current Balance	Status	Due Date
Apollo Blinds P/L						
00000585	25/07/2016	$2 500.00	$260.00	$2 860.00	Open	24/08/2016
00000581	15/07/2016	$1 000.00	$105.00	$0.00	Closed	
00000589	22/07/2016	($105.00)	($10.50)	$0.00	Closed	
		$3 395.00	$354.50	$2 860.00		
Energy Plus						
1374-2	15/07/2016	$142.60	$14.26	$0.00	Closed	
		$142.60	$14.26	$0.00		
Litemaster Blinds P/L						
00000588	25/07/2016	$800.00	$88.00	$968.00	Open	24/08/2016
00000584	15/07/2016	$600.00	$66.00	$0.00	Closed	
00000592	22/07/2016	($66.00)	($6.60)	$0.00	Closed	
		$1 334.00	$147.40	$968.00		

ID No.	Original Date	Purchase Amount	Tax	Current Balance	Status	Due Date
Luxaflex P/L						
00000586	25/07/2016	$1 200.00	$128.00	$1 408.00	Open	24/08/2016
00000582	15/07/2016	$900.00	$96.00	$0.00	Closed	
00000590	22/07/2016	($96.00)	($9.60)	$0.00	Closed	
		$2 004.00	$214.40	$1 408.00		
Wynstan Blinds P/L						
00000587	25/07/2016	$1 600.00	$164.00	$1 804.00	Open	24/08/2016
00000583	15/07/2016	$4 000.00	$410.00	$0.00	Closed	
00000591	22/07/2016	($410.00)	($41.00)	$0.00	Closed	
		$5 190.00	$533.00	$1 804.00		
	Grand Total:	**$12 065.60**	**$1 263.56**	**$7 040.00**		

Adjustment notes

An *adjustment note* is issued by a supplier when the goods they sold are returned by the customer because they were damaged upon arrival or unsuitable for their purpose. The adjustment note is recorded as a negative invoice (that is, the amount 'received' is recorded as a negative). It is then applied against the invoice on which the damaged goods originated to reduce the amount of that invoice. We never go into the original invoice and change it. We always use an adjustment note.

The following exercise contains practice recording purchase orders, converting them to invoices and applying payments as well as instructions on how to record and apply a supplier adjustment note. In real life, you would generally not receive an adjustment on the freight as it is generally supplied by a third party carrier. However, in these examples we do adjust the freight just in case it is an in-house delivery service and an adjustment allowed.

THE ICE CREAM PARLOUR

1   In MYOB AccountRight 2016.1, open the **7.3 The Ice Cream Parlour.myox** data file from the Chapter 7 folder of your start-up files, or use your own file from Chapter 6.

2   Record the following payments to suppliers:

Date:	2/7/16
Cheque No.:	5001
Payee:	Alpino Gelato
Details:	
Payment of all invoices with prompt payment discount	
Amount:	$594.00
Dissection	
Discount:	60.00
GST Component:	6.00
Discount Total:	66.00

Date:	2/7/16
Cheque No.:	5002
Payee:	Norgen-Vaaz
Details:	
Payment of all invoices with prompt payment discount	
Amount:	$247.50
Dissection	
Discount:	25.00
GST Component:	2.50
Discount Total:	27.50

Date:	2/7/16
Cheque No.:	5003
Payee:	Peters Ice Cream
Details:	
Payment of all invoices with prompt payment discount	
Amount:	$435.60

Dissection	
Discount:	44.00
GST Component:	4.40
Discount Total:	48.40

Date:	2/7/16
Cheque No.:	5004
Payee:	Streets Ice Cream
Details:	
Payment of all invoices with prompt payment discount	
Amount:	$900.90

Dissection	
Discount:	91.00
GST Component:	9.10
Discount Total:	100.10

Tip

If you are paying all of the supplier invoices, you can click on *Pay All* in the bottom left side of the screen. However, you still need to check that the amount of the cheque (and the prompt payment discount) in MYOB matches with your source document.

3 Place the following orders with your suppliers:

The Ice Cream Parlour P/L

Darlinghurst Road, Kings Cross NSW 2011

ABN 58 101 277 285

Purchase Order Number:	013
Date:	10 July
Supplier:	Alpino Gelato P/L
Please supply:	

5 large decorated ice cream cakes at your list price of $40.00 each plus GST.

Delivery:	Courier

The Ice Cream Parlour P/L

Darlinghurst Road, Kings Cross NSW 2011

ABN 58 101 277 285

Purchase Order Number:	014
Date:	10 July
Supplier:	Norgen-Vaaz P/L
Please supply:	

3 x 25 litre containers of liqueur ice cream at your list price of $100.00 each plus GST.

Delivery:	Courier

The Ice Cream Parlour P/L

Darlinghurst Road, Kings Cross NSW 2011

ABN 58 101 277 285

Purchase Order Number:	015
Date:	10 July
Supplier:	Peters Ice Creams P/L
Please supply:	

3 x 25 litre containers of choc-whirl ice cream at your list price of $90.00 each plus GST.

Delivery:	Courier

The Ice Cream Parlour P/L

Darlinghurst Road, Kings Cross NSW 2011

ABN 58 101 277 285

Purchase Order Number:	016
Date:	10 July
Supplier:	Streets Ice Creams P/L
Please supply:	

3 x 25 litre containers of vanilla ice cream at your list price of $80.00 each plus GST.

Delivery:	Courier

4 Convert your purchase orders to bills as the goods have been received accompanied by the following invoices:

Norgen-Vaaz P/L	
Date:	12 July
Tax Invoice No.:	90018
Supplied to:	The Ice Cream Parlour
Details: PO 0014	
3 x 25 litre Ice Cream @ $100.00	$300.00
Freight	20.00
GST:	32.00
Invoice Total:	$352.00
Terms: 10% 7 days/Net 15	

Alpino Gelato P/L	
Date:	12 July
Tax Invoice No.:	00855
Supplied to:	The Ice Cream Parlour
Details: PO 0013	
5 x Ice Cream Cakes @ $40.00	$200.00
Freight	20.00
GST:	22.00
Invoice Total:	$242.00
Terms: 10% 7 days/Net 15	

Peters Ice Creams P/L		
Date:		12 July
Tax Invoice No.:		10035
Supplied to:		The Ice Cream Parlour
Details: PO 0011		
3 x 25 litres Ice Cream @ $90.00	$270.00	$270.00
Freight		20.00
GST:		29.00
Invoice Total:		$319.00
Terms: 10% 10 days/Net 30		

Streets Ice Creams P/L	
Date:	12 July
Tax Invoice No.:	20901
Supplied to:	The Ice Cream Parlour
Details: PO 0012	
3 x 25 litre Ice Cream @ $80.00	$240.00
Freight	20.00
GST:	26.00
Invoice Total:	$286.00
Terms: 10% 10 days/Net 30	

> ### Tip
> If you highlight the date and press the + key, it will add one day to the current date. Press the − key and it will reduce the current date by one day. So instead of typing in the date of 12/07/16, you can just press the + key twice.

Record adjustment note

5 One of the decorated ice cream cakes was found to have been damaged in transit when its container was opened and the following adjustment note must be recorded.

Alpino Gelato P/L	
Date:	12 July
Adjustment Note No.:	054
Allowed to:	The Ice Cream Parlour
Details: PO 0009, Invoice No. 00855	
1 x Ice Cream Cake @ $40.00	−$40.00
Freight	−4.00
GST:	−4.40
Adjustment Total:	−$48.40

Click...

- *Enter Purchases* (in the Purchases module).
- *Supplier* (choose *Alpino Gelato*).
- *Date* (type *12/07/16*) Press the Tab key.
- *Supplier Inv. No.* (type *Adj 054*).
- *Description* (type *Damaged cake on invoice 855*).
- *Amount* (type *−40*).
- *Tax code* should be *GST*.
- *Freight* (type *−4*). See Figure 7.28.
- *Edit* on the top menu bar.
- *Recap Transaction*. A new window opens. See Figure 7.29.

Figure 7.28   Enter Sales: adjustment note

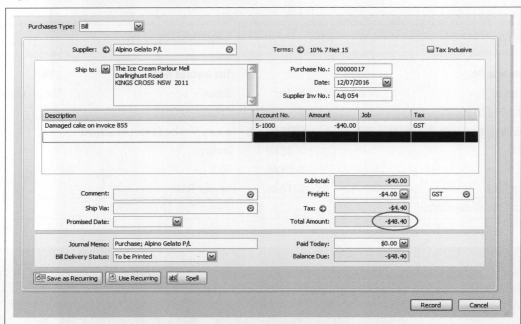

Figure 7.29   Recap Transaction: adjustment note

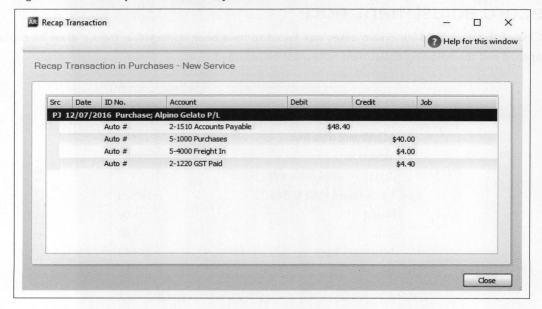

This shows that Alpino Gelato (an Account Payable – a liability) will be debited (reduced) when this adjustment note is recorded. The two cost of sales and one liability accounts will be credited (also reduced).

Click...
- *Close* (when you have understood the display).
- *Record* (to register the payment).
- *Cancel* (to return to the Command Centre).

The next step is to reduce the *appropriate* invoice by the amount of the adjustment.

Click...
- *Purchases Register* (in the Purchases module).
- *Returns & Debits* (tab at top of the window). You will see the only adjustment note there (the one you have just done) highlighted.
- *Apply to Purchase* (button near base of the window).
- *Date* (change to *12/07/16*).
- *Discount* (delete the suggested figure if there is one).
- *Amount Applied* (click in the far-right column). Press the Tab key. Check the *Finance Charge* and *Out of Balance* at the bottom right hand side are zero. See Figure 7.30.
- *Record*.

Figure 7.30   Sales: Settle Returns & Debits

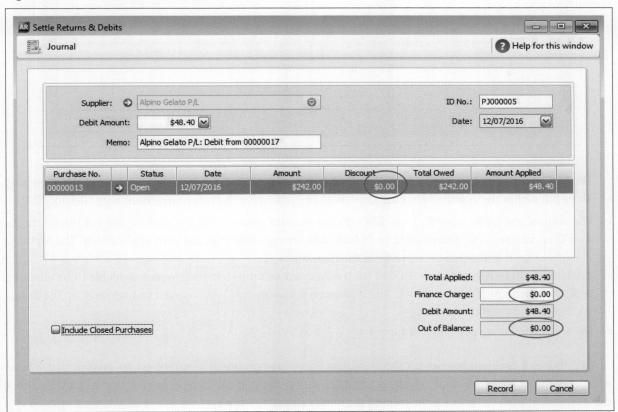

Let us look at the end result of creating and applying the adjustment note.

⊙ **Click...**

- *All Purchases* (tab in the Purchases Register).
- *Search By* (use the drop-down arrow to change to *Supplier* and in the box that appears, type *Alp* and press the Tab key to accept the autofill).
- *Dated From* (change to *1/07/16*) and *To* (change to *31/07/16*).
- Figure 7.31 shows all transactions for Alpino Gelato for that date range.

Figure 7.31 **All Purchases: Alpino Gelato**

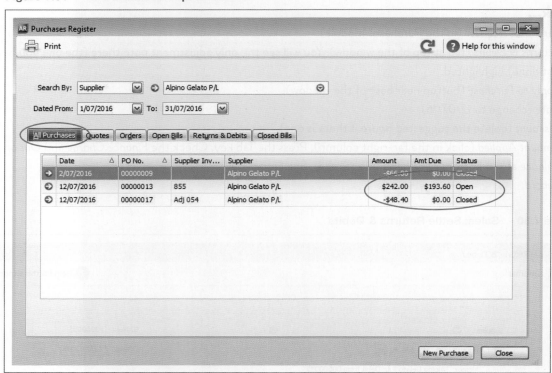

The $66 adjustment note dated 2 July 2016 is the prompt payment discount that we received when we paid our June bill within the specified discount days. We can see that for the two transactions dated 12 July 2016:

- The original invoice number 855 was $242 (in the Amount column) but the amount due is $193.60 (in the Amt Due column). The difference is the $48.40 adjustment note that has been applied to it. The Status is Open because it still needs payment from the customer.
- Adjustment note Adj 054 was −$48.40 (in the Amount column) but the amount available to be allocated is $0.00 (in the Amt Due column). This is because it has already been applied to invoice 855. The Status is Closed.

6 Record the following payments to suppliers:

MYOB has a problem in that it cannot calculate a prompt payment discount on an invoice that has an adjustment note applied to it. It calculates the discount on the original invoice. Ensure that you always check the discount column or calculate the prompt payment discount yourself.

$$\text{Amount of invoice showing in Pay Bills} \times \text{Discount \%} = \text{Discount}$$
$$\$193.60 \qquad \times 10\% \qquad = \$19.36$$

Overwrite the numbers in the Discount column with the amount you have calculated (in this case, $19.36). See Figure 7.32.

Date:	18/7/16
Cheque No.:	5005
Payee:	Alpino Gelato
Details:	
Payment of all invoices with prompt payment discount	
Amount:	$174.24
Dissection	
Discount:	17.60
GST Component:	1.76
Discount Total:	19.36

Date:	18/7/16
Cheque No.:	5006
Payee:	Norgen-Vaaz
Details:	
Payment of all invoices with prompt payment discount	
Amount:	$316.80
Dissection	
Discount:	32.00
GST Component:	3.20
Discount Total:	35.20

Date:	18/7/16
Cheque No.:	5007
Payee:	Peters Ice Cream
Details:	
Payment of all invoices with prompt payment discount	
Amount:	$287.10
Dissection	
Discount:	29.00
GST Component:	2.90
Discount Total:	31.90

Date:	18/7/16
Cheque No.:	5008
Payee:	Streets Ice Cream
Details:	
Payment of all invoices with prompt payment discount	
Amount:	$257.40
Dissection	
Discount:	26.00
GST Component:	2.60
Discount Total:	28.60

Figure 7.32   Pay Bills: Alpino Gelato

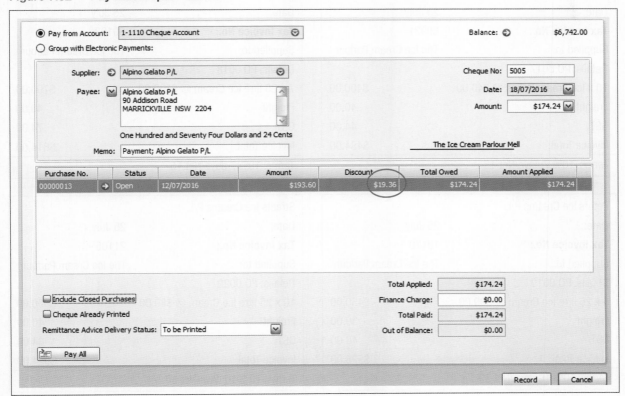

7 Place the following orders with your suppliers:

The Ice Cream Parlour P/L	
Darlinghurst Road, Kings Cross NSW 2011	
ABN 58 101 277 285	
Purchase Order Number:	00000017
Date:	23 July
Supplier:	Alpino Gelato P/L
Please supply:	
10 large decorated ice cream cakes at your list price of $40.00 each plus GST.	
Delivery:	Courier

The Ice Cream Parlour P/L	
Darlinghurst Road, Kings Cross NSW 2011	
ABN 58 101 277 285	
Purchase Order Number:	00000018
Date:	23 July
Supplier:	Norgen-Vaaz P/L
Please supply:	
7 x 25 litre containers of liqueur ice cream at your list price of $100.00 each plus GST.	
Delivery:	Courier

The Ice Cream Parlour P/L	
Darlinghurst Road, Kings Cross NSW 2011	
ABN 58 101 277 285	
Purchase Order Number:	00000019
Date:	23 July
Supplier:	Peters Ice Creams P/L
Please supply:	
5 x 25 litre containers of choc-whirl ice cream at your list price of $90.00 each plus GST.	
Delivery:	Courier

The Ice Cream Parlour P/L	
Darlinghurst Road, Kings Cross NSW 2011	
ABN 58 101 277 285	
Purchase Order Number:	00000020
Date:	23 July
Supplier:	Streets Ice Creams P/L
Please supply:	
10 x 25 litre containers of vanilla ice cream at your list price of $80.00 each plus GST.	
Delivery:	Courier

8 Convert your purchase orders to bills as the goods have been received accompanied by the following invoices:

Alpino Gelato P/L	
Date:	25 July
Tax Invoice No.:	00931
Supplied to:	The Ice Cream Parlour
Details: PO 0017	
10 x Ice Cream Cakes @ $40.00	$400.00
Freight	40.00
GST:	44.00
Invoice Total:	$484.00
Terms: 10% 7 days/Net 15	

Norgen-Vaaz P/L	
Date:	25 July
Tax Invoice No.:	90103
Supplied to:	The Ice Cream Parlour
Details: PO 0018	
7 x 25 litre Ice Cream @ $100.00	$700.00
Freight	40.00
GST:	74.00
Invoice Total:	$814.00
Terms: 10% 7 days/Net 15	

Peters Ice Creams P/L	
Date:	25 July
Tax Invoice No.:	10120
Supplied to:	The Ice Cream Parlour
Details: PO 0019	
5 x 25 litre Ice Cream @ $90.00	$450.00
Freight	30.00
GST:	48.00
Invoice Total:	$528.00
Terms: 10% 10 days/Net 30	

Streets Ice Creams P/L	
Date:	25 July
Tax Invoice No.:	21105
Supplied to:	The Ice Cream Parlour
Details: PO 0020	
10 x 25 litre Ice Cream @ $80.00	$800.00
Freight	40.00
GST:	84.00
Invoice Total:	$924.00
Terms: 10% 10 days/Net 30	

9 Record the following adjustment notes that were received from suppliers for stock damaged in transit and apply to the appropriate invoice.

Alpino Gelato P/L	
Date:	25 July
Adjustment Note No.:	074
Allowed to:	The Ice Cream Parlour
Details: PO 0017, Invoice No. 00931	
2 x Broken Ice Cream Cakes @ $40.00	−$80.00
Freight	−4.00
GST:	−8.40
Adjustment Total:	

Streets Ice Creams P/L	
Date:	25 July
Adjustment Note No.:	1002
Supplied to:	The Ice Cream Parlour
Details: PO 0020, Invoice No. 21105	
1 x leaking 25 litre Ice Cream @ $80.00	−$80.00
Freight	−4.00
GST:	−8.40
Invoice Total:	−$92.40

10 Produce the following reports for your records:
- Purchase Register Detail [All Purchases] for July. **Figure 7.33**.
- Aged Payables [Summary] as at 31 July. **Figure 7.34**.
- Supplier Ledger for 1 July to 31 July. **Figure 7.35**.

Figure 7.33   Purchase Register Detail [All Purchases]: The Ice Cream Parlour

The Ice Cream Parlour
Darlinghust Road
Kings Cross NSW 2011
Purchase Register Detail [All Purchases]
July 2016

Date	PO No.	Supplier Inv No.	Supplier Name	Amount	Amount Due	Status	Received
2/07/2016	00000009		Alpino Gelato P/L	($66.00)	$0.00	Closed	
2/07/2016	00000010		Norgen-Vaaz P/L	($27.50)	$0.00	Closed	
2/07/2016	00000011		Peters Ice Creams P/L	($48.40)	$0.00	Closed	
2/07/2016	00000012		Streets Ice Cream P/L	($100.10)	$0.00	Closed	
12/07/2016	00000017	90018	Norgen-Vaaz P/L	$352.00	$0.00	Closed	
12/07/2016	00000018	855	Alpino Gelato P/L	$242.00	$0.00	Closed	
12/07/2016	00000019	10035	Peters Ice Creams P/L	$319.00	$0.00	Closed	
10/07/2016	00000020	20901	Streets Ice Cream P/L	$286.00	$0.00	Closed	
12/07/2016	00000021	Adj 054	Alpino Gelato P/L	($48.40)	$0.00	Closed	
18/07/2016	00000022		Alpino Gelato P/L	($19.36)	$0.00	Closed	
18/07/2016	00000023		Norgen-Vaaz P/L	($35.20)	$0.00	Closed	
18/07/2016	00000024		Peters Ice Creams P/L	($31.90)	$0.00	Closed	
18/07/2016	00000025		Streets Ice Cream P/L	($28.60)	$0.00	Closed	
25/07/2016	00000030	931	Alpino Gelato P/L	$484.00	$391.60	Open	
23/07/2016	00000031	90103	Norgen-Vaaz P/L	$814.00	$814.00	Open	
25/07/2016	00000032	10120	Peters Ice Creams P/L	$528.00	$528.00	Open	
25/07/2016	00000033	21105	Streets Ice Cream P/L	$924.00	$831.60	Open	
25/07/2016	00000034	Adj 074	Alpino Gelato P/L	($92.40)	$0.00	Closed	
25/07/2016	00000035	Adj 1002	Streets Ice Cream P/L	($92.40)	$0.00	Closed	
			Total:	**$3 358.74**	**$2 565.20**		

Figure 7.34   Aged Payables [Summary]: The Ice Cream Parlour

The Ice Cream Parlour
Darlinghust Road
Kings Cross NSW 2011
Aged Payables [Summary]
As of 31/07/2016

Name	Total Due	0–30	31–60	61–90	90+
Alpino Gelato P/L	$391.60	$391.60	$0.00	$0.00	$0.00
Norgen-Vaaz P/L	$814.00	$814.00	$0.00	$0.00	$0.00
Peters Ice Creams P/L	$528.00	$528.00	$0.00	$0.00	$0.00
Streets Ice Cream P/L	$831.60	$831.60	$0.00	$0.00	$0.00
Total:	**$2 565.20**	**$2 565.20**	**$0.00**	**$0.00**	**$0.00**
Ageing Per cent:		**100.0%**	**0.0%**	**0.0%**	**0.0%**

Figure 7.35   Supplier Ledger: The Ice Cream Parlour

The Ice Cream Parlour
Darlinghust Road
Kings Cross NSW 2011
Supplier Ledger
July 2016

Date	Src	ID No.	Memo	Transaction Amount	Balance
Alpino Gelato P/L	SUP 001				$660.00
2/07/2016	PJ	00000009	Alpino Gelato P/L: Discounts on 00000005	($66.00)	$594.00
2/07/2016	PJ	PJ000001	Alpino Gelato P/L: Debit from 00000009	$0.00	$594.00
2/07/2016	CD	5001	Alpino Gelato P/L MARRICKVILLE NSW 2204	($594.00)	$0.00
12/07/2016	PJ	PJ000005	Alpino Gelato P/L: Debit from 00000021	$0.00	$0.00
12/07/2016	PJ	00000021	Purchase; Alpino Gelato P/L	($48.40)	($48.40)
12/07/2016	PJ	00000018	Purchase; Alpino Gelato P/L	$242.00	$193.60
18/07/2016	CD	5005	Alpino Gelato P/L MARRICKVILLE NSW 2204	($174.24)	$19.36
18/07/2016	PJ	PJ000006	Alpino Gelato P/L: Debit from 00000022	$0.00	$19.36
18/07/2016	PJ	00000022	Alpino Gelato P/L: Discounts on 00000018	($19.36)	$0.00
25/07/2016	PJ	PJ000010	Alpino Gelato P/L: Debit from 00000034	$0.00	$0.00
25/07/2016	PJ	00000030	Purchase; Alpino Gelato P/L	$484.00	$484.00
25/07/2016	PJ	00000034	Purchase; Alpino Gelato P/L	($92.40)	$391.60
			Total:	($268.40)	$391.60
Norgen-Vaaz P/L	SUP 004				$275.00
2/07/2016	PJ	PJ000002	Norgen-Vaaz P/L: Debit from 00000010	$0.00	$275.00
2/07/2016	PJ	00000010	Norgen-Vaaz P/L: Discounts on 00000006	($27.50)	$247.50
2/07/2016	CD	5002	Norgen-Vaaz P/L 66 Dublin Street SMITHFIELD NSW 2164	($247.50)	$0.00
12/07/2016	PJ	00000017	Purchase; Norgen-Vaaz P/L	$352.00	$352.00
18/07/2016	PJ	PJ000007	Norgen-Vaaz P/L: Debit from 00000023	$0.00	$352.00
18/07/2016	PJ	00000023	Norgen-Vaaz P/L: Discounts on 00000017	($35.20)	$316.80

Date	Src	ID No.	Memo	Transaction Amount	Balance
18/07/2016	CD	5006	Norgen-Vaaz P/L 66 Dublin Street SMITHFIELD NSW 2164	($316.80)	$0.00
23/07/2016	PJ	00000031	Purchase; Norgen-Vaaz P/L	$814.00	$814.00
			Total:	$539.00	$814.00
Peters Ice Creams P/L	SUP 002				$484.00
2/07/2016	PJ	00000011	Peters Ice Creams P/L: Discounts on 00000007	($48.40)	$435.60
2/07/2016	PJ	PJ000003	Peters Ice Creams P/L: Debit from 00000011	$0.00	$435.60
2/07/2016	CD	5003	Peters Ice Creams P/L 1 Maitland Place BAULKHAM HILLS NSW 2153	($435.60)	$0.00
12/07/2016	PJ	00000019	Purchase; Peters Ice Creams P/L	$319.00	$319.00
18/07/2016	PJ	00000024	Peters Ice Creams P/L: Discounts on 00000019	($31.90)	$287.10
18/07/2016	PJ	PJ000008	Peters Ice Creams P/L: Debit from 00000024	$0.00	$287.10
18/07/2016	CD	5007	Peters Ice Creams P/L 1 Maitland Place BAULKHAM HILLS NSW 2153	($287.10)	$0.00
25/07/2016	PJ	00000032	Purchase; Peters Ice Creams P/L	$528.00	$528.00
			Total:	$44.00	$528.00
Streets Ice Cream P/L	SUP 003				$1 001.00
2/07/2016	PJ	00000012	Streets Ice Cream P/L: Discounts on 00000008	($100.10)	$900.90
2/07/2016	CD	5004	Streets Ice Cream P/L 7 Alan Street FAIRFIELD NSW 2165	($900.90)	$0.00
2/07/2016	PJ	PJ000004	Streets Ice Cream P/L: Debit from 00000012	$0.00	$0.00
10/07/2016	PJ	00000020	Purchase; Streets Ice Cream P/L	$286.00	$286.00
18/07/2016	CD	5008	Streets Ice Cream P/L 7 Alan Street FAIRFIELD NSW 2165	($257.40)	$28.60
18/07/2016	PJ	00000025	Streets Ice Cream P/L: Discounts on 00000020	($28.60)	$0.00
18/07/2016	PJ	PJ000009	Streets Ice Cream P/L: Debit from 00000025	$0.00	$0.00
25/07/2016	PJ	00000033	Purchase; Streets Ice Cream P/L	$924.00	$924.00
25/07/2016	PJ	00000035	Purchase; Streets Ice Cream P/L	($92.40)	$831.60
25/07/2016	PJ	PJ000011	Streets Ice Cream P/L: Debit from 00000035	$0.00	$831.60
			Total:	($169.40)	$831.60

Practice

ARKAROOLA B&B

1 In MYOB AccountRight 2016, open **7.4 Arakoola B&B.myox** data file from the Chapter 7 folder of your start-up files or use your own file. These transactions are in July 2016.

2 Place the following orders with your suppliers. Create and use recurring transactions to help you.

Arkaroola B&B P/L	Arkaroola B&B P/L
21 Pirie Street, Arkaroola SA 5710	21 Pirie Street, Arkaroola SA 5710
ABN 21 221 402 201	ABN 21 221 402 201
Purchase Order Number: 00000003	**Purchase Order Number:** 00000004
Date: 5 July	Date: 5 July
Supplier: Arkaroola Supplies P/L	Supplier: Arkaroola Laundry P/L
Please supply:	Please supply laundry services:
5 Dozen Eggs @ $4.00 per dozen.	10 Double Sheets @ $2.00 each plus GST.
3 kg Bacon @ $10.00 per kilo.	10 Single Sheets @ $1.00 each plus GST.
4 loaves Sliced Bread @ $2.00 each.	30 Pillow Cases @ $0.50 each plus GST.
4 kg Sugar @ $1.50 per kilo.	30 Towels @ $1.50 each plus GST.
Delivery: Best Way	Delivery: Best Way

3 Record the following payments to suppliers:

Date: 7/7/16	Date: 7/7/16
Cheque No.: 01082	**Cheque No.:** 01083
Payee: Arkaroola Supplies	Payee: Arkaroola Laundry
Details:	Details:
Payment of May invoices with prompt payment discount	*Payment of May invoices with prompt payment discount*
Amount: $297.00	Amount: $99.00
Dissection	**Dissection**
Discount: 30.00	Discount: 10.00
GST Component: 3.00	GST Component: 1.00
Discount Total: 33.00	Discount Total: 11.00

4 Convert your purchase orders to bills as the goods have been received accompanied by the following invoices:

Arkaroola Supplies P/L		Arkaroola Laundry P/L
Date: 8 July		Date: 8 July
Tax Invoice No.: 11211		**Tax Invoice No.:** 20886
Supplied to: Arkaroola B&B		Supplied to: Arkaroola B&B
Details: PO 0003		Details: PO 0004
Sundry food items $64.00		Laundry Services $90.00
Delivery 2.00		Delivery 5.00
GST: 0.20		GST: 9.50
Invoice Total: $66.20		Invoice Total: $104.50
Terms: 10% 10 days/Net 30		Terms: 10% 10 days/Net 30

> ### Remember This
>
> Always check that the Tax and Total Amount fields at the bottom of the MYOB screen match the amount on the invoice.

5 Place the following orders with your suppliers:

Arkaroola B&B P/L	Arkaroola B&B P/L
21 Pirie Street, Arkaroola SA 5710	21 Pirie Street, Arkaroola SA 5710
ABN 21 221 402 201	ABN 21 221 402 201
Purchase Order Number: 00000007	**Purchase Order Number:** 00000008
Date: 12 July	Date: 12 July
Supplier: Arkaroola Supplies P/L	Supplier: Arkaroola Laundry P/L
Please supply:	Please supply laundry services:
10 Dozen Eggs @ $4.00 per dozen.	20 Double Sheets @ $2.00 each plus GST.
5 kg Bacon @ $10.00 per kilo.	10 Single Sheets @ $1.00 each plus GST.
10 loaves Sliced Bread @ $2.00 each.	50 Pillow Cases @ $0.50 each plus GST.
1 kg Coffee @ $20.00 per kilo.	50 Towels @ $1.50 each plus GST
Delivery: Best Way	Delivery: Best Way

6 Record the following payments to suppliers:

Date: 14/7/16	Date: 14/7/16
Cheque No.: 01084	**Cheque No.:** 01085
Payee: Arkaroola Supplies	Payee: Arkaroola Laundry
Details:	Details:
Payment invoices with prompt payment discount	*Payment of invoice with prompt payment discount*
Amount: $59.58	Amount: $94.05
Dissection	**Dissection**
Discount: 6.60	Discount: 9.50
GST Component: 0.02	GST Component: 0.95
Discount Total: 6.62	Discount Total: 10.45

7 Convert your purchase orders to bills as the goods have been received accompanied by the following invoices:

Arkaroola Supplies P/L		Arkaroola Laundry P/L	
Date:	15 July	Date:	15 July
Tax Invoice No.:	11248	**Tax Invoice No.:**	20902
Supplied to:	Arkaroola B&B	Supplied to:	Arkaroola B&B
Details: PO 0007		Details: PO 0008	
Sundry food items	$130.00	Laundry Services	$150.00
Delivery	5.00	Delivery	10.00
GST:	0.50	GST:	16.00
Invoice Total:	$135.50	Invoice Total:	$176.00
Terms: 10% 10 days/Net 30		Terms: 10% 10 days/Net 30.	

8 Record the following adjustment notes that were received from suppliers for faulty work or produce and apply to the appropriate invoice.

Arkaroola Supplies P/L	
Date:	17 July
Adjustment Note No.:	201
Supplied to:	Arkaroola B&B
Details: PO 0007, Invoice 11248	
Faulty food items	−$18.00
Delivery	0.00
GST:	0.00
Invoice Total:	−$18.00

Arkaroola Laundry P/L	
Date:	17 July
Adjustment Note No.:	312
Supplied to:	Arkaroola B&B
Details: PO 0008, Invoice 20902	
Laundry Services unsatisfactory	−$20.00
Delivery	0.00
GST:	−2.00
Invoice Total:	−$22.00

9 Place the following orders with your suppliers:

Arkaroola B&B P/L	
21 Pirie Street, Arkaroola, SA 5710	
ABN 21 221 402 201	
Purchase Order Number:	00000009
Date:	22 July
Supplier:	Arkaroola Supplies P/L
Please supply:	
12 Dozen Eggs @ $4.00 per dozen.	
6 kg Bacon @ $10.00 per kilo.	
10 loaves Sliced Bread @ $2.00 each.	
1 carton Single-Serve Cereal @ $100.00 each.	
Delivery:	Best Way

Arkaroola B&B P/L	
21 Pirie Street, Arkaroola, SA 5710	
ABN 21 221 402 201	
Purchase Order Number:	00000010
Date:	22 July
Supplier:	Arkaroola Laundry P/L
Please supply laundry services:	
20 Double Sheets @ $2.00 each plus GST.	
20 Single Sheets @ $1.00 each plus GST.	
60 Pillow Cases @ $0.50 each plus GST.	
60 Towels @ $1.50 each plus GST.	
Delivery:	Best Way

10 Record the following payments to suppliers:

Date:	24/7/16
Cheque No.:	01086
Payee:	Arkaroola Supplies
Details:	
Payment of invoices with prompt payment discount	
Amount:	$105.75
Dissection	
Discount:	11.71
GST Component:	0.04
Discount Total:	11.75

Date:	24/7/16
Cheque No.:	01087
Payee:	Arkaroola Laundry
Details:	
Payment of all invoices with prompt payment discount	
Amount:	$138.60
Dissection	
Discount:	14.00
GST Component:	1.40
Discount Total:	15.40

11 Convert your purchase orders to bills as the goods have been received accompanied by the following invoices:

Arkaroola Supplies P/L	
Date:	25 July
Tax Invoice No.:	11264
Supplied to:	Arkaroola B&B
Details: PO 00009	
Sundry food items	$228.00
Delivery	15.00
GST:	1.50
Invoice Total:	$244.50
Terms: 10% 10 days/Net 30.	

Arkaroola Laundry P/L	
Date:	25 July
Tax Invoice No.:	20961
Supplied to:	Arkaroola B&B
Details: PO 00010	
Laundry Services	$180.00
Delivery	10.00
GST:	19.00
Invoice Total:	$209.00
Terms: 10% 10 days/Net 30	

12 Produce the following reports for your records:

- Purchase Register Detail [All Purchases] for July. See Figure 7.36.
- Aged Payables [Summary] as at 31 July. See Figure 7.37.

Figure 7.36   Purchase Register Detail [All Purchases]: Arkaroola B&B

Arkaroola B&B P/L
21 Pirie Street
Arkaroola SA 5710
Purchase Register Detail [All Purchases]
July 2016

Date	PO No.	Supplier Inv No.	Supplier Name	Amount	Amount Due	Status	Received
7/07/2016	00000005		Arkaroola Supplies	($33.00)	$0.00	Closed	
7/07/2016	00000006		Arkaroola Laundry	($11.00)	$0.00	Closed	
8/07/2016	00000007	20886	Arkaroola Laundry	$104.50	$0.00	Closed	
8/07/2016	00000008	11211	Arkaroola Supplies	$66.20	$0.00	Closed	
14/07/2016	00000011		Arkaroola Supplies	($6.62)	$0.00	Closed	
14/07/2016	00000012		Arkaroola Laundry	($10.45)	$0.00	Closed	
15/07/2016	00000013	11248	Arkaroola Supplies	$135.50	$0.00	Closed	
24/07/2016	00000013		Arkaroola Supplies	($11.75)	$0.00	Closed	
15/07/2016	00000014		Arkaroola Laundry	$176.00	$0.00	Closed	
24/07/2016	00000014		Arkaroola Laundry	($15.40)	$0.00	Closed	
25/07/2016	00000015	11264	Arkaroola Supplies	$244.50	$244.50	Open	
17/07/2016	00000015	201	Arkaroola Supplies	($18.00)	$0.00	Closed	
25/07/2016	00000016	20961	Arkaroola Laundry	$209.00	$209.00	Open	
17/07/2016	00000016		Arkaroola Laundry	($22.00)	$0.00	Closed	
			Total:	**$807.48**	**$453.50**		

Figure 7.37 **Aged Payables [Summary]: Arkaroola B&B**

Arkaroola B&B P/L 21 Pirie Street Arkaroola SA 5710 Aged Payables [Summary] As of 31/07/2016					
Name	**Total Due**	**0–30**	**31–60**	**61–90**	**90+**
Arkaroola Laundry	$209.00	$209.00	$0.00	$0.00	$0.00
Arkaroola Supplies	$244.50	$244.50	$0.00	$0.00	$0.00
Total:	**$453.50**	**$453.50**	**$0.00**	**$0.00**	**$0.00**
Ageing Per cent:		**100.0%**	**0.0%**	**0.0%**	**0.0%**

Summary

◆ All dealings with Accounts Payable (trade creditors) take place in the Purchases module in MYOB.

◆ The Purchases module is the Subsidiary Accounts Payable Ledger and is linked to the Accounts Payable control account in the general ledger.

◆ Each transaction in the Purchases module automatically updates the general ledger control account.

◆ An order to a supplier is a formal request to supply goods or services, and is the way a successful quote is accepted.

◆ A bill is generated when goods or services have been supplied and, until payment has been made, this bill is an Account Payable.

◆ An adjustment note is generated when goods are returned to a supplier or when a service has been unsatisfactory, and this has the effect of reducing the Accounts Payable.

◆ Errors are located in the Transaction Journals, which are accessed directly from the Command Centre. Here, the zoom arrow brings up the original transaction, which can be deleted or corrected.

◆ A wide variety of reports are available in the Purchases module to give detailed information on the operation of the business.

◆ The Purchases and Payables Journal is a detailed record of each transaction that has taken place within the Purchases module over a specific period of time.

Assessment

Meyers Cakes

1 In MYOB AccountRight 2016, create a new data file based on the following information using *AccountRight Standard Australian* version:

> **Meyer's Cakes Pty Ltd.**
> 147 North Terrace
> Adelaide SA 5000
> ABN 31 233 312 133
>
> **Phone:** (08) 8217 7523
> **Email:** meyerscakes@hotmail.com
> **Current Financial Year:** 2018
> **Conversion Month:** July
> **Industry Classification:** Retail
> **Main Business Activity:** Sale of luxury cakes

Click the **Easy Setup Assistant** once you have finished the company file setup. Use the third activation option – **I use this file for evaluation purposes**.

2   Change the following names in the List of Accounts:

	Account type	Account no.	New account name	Tax code
Edit	Bank	1-1110	Cheque Account	N-T
Edit	Acc Receivable	1-1310	Accounts Receivable	N-T
Edit	Other Current Asset	1-1340	Prepaid Insurance	GST
Edit	Fixed Asset (Header)	1-2300	Delivery Van	
Edit	Fixed Asset	1-2310	Deliver Van at cost	CAP
Edit	Fixed Asset	1-2320	Acc. depr. Delivery Van	N-T
Edit	Acc. Payable	2-1510	Accounts Payable	N-T
Edit	Equity	3-1000	Terry Meyer Capital	N-T
Edit	Equity	3-2000	Terry Meyer Drawings	N-T
Edit	Income	4-1000	Sales	GST
Add	Income	4-9000	Discounts Received	GST
Edit	Cost of Sales	5-1000	Purchases	GST
Edit	Cost of Sales	5-9000	Discounts Given	GST

3   Change the linked accounts:

Type	Terms	From	To
Sales	I give discounts for early payment	6-3500 Discounts given	5-9000 Discounts Given
Purchases	I take discounts for early payment		4-9000 Discounts Received

4   Then make the following changes:

	Account type	Account no.	New account name
Delete	Expense	6-3500	Discounts Given
Delete	Income	4-2000	Sales Income # 2
Delete	Income	4-3000	Sales Income # 3

5   Insert the following account opening balances:

Trial Balance as at 30/06/17			
Account no.	Account name	Debit	Credit
1-1110	Cheque Account	60 340.00	
1-1310	Accounts Receivable	5 830.00	
1-1340	Prepaid Insurance	1 100.00	
1-2210	Office Equipment at cost	3 630.00	
1-2310	Deliver Van At Cost	20 800.00	
1-2320	Acc. Depr. Delivery Van		1 000.00
1-2410	Store Fittings at cost	13 000.00	
1-2420	Acc Depr. Store Fittings		1 450.00
2-1110	Visa Card		330.00
2-1220	GST Paid	302.00	
2-1510	Accounts Payable		3 322.00
2-2100	Business Loan #1		90 000.00
3-1000	Terry Meyer Capital		10 000.00
3-2000	Terry Meyer Drawings	1 100.00	
	Totals	**106 102.00**	**106 102.00**

6   Create cards for the following suppliers using Easy Setup Assistant. Invoices have the service layout:

Name:	Edible Art
Card ID:	SUP 001
Address:	340 Tapley's Hill Road,
	Seaton SA 5023
Phone:	(08) 9356 3111
Email:	easales@telstra.com.au
Contact:	Derek Perkins
Terms:	10% 10 days/Net 30
Expense Account:	5-1000
Credit Limit:	$5 000.00
ABN:	60 106 202 601

Name:	Independent Bakery
Card ID:	SUP 002
Address:	176 Greenhill Road,
	Parkside SA 5063
Phone:	(08) 9271 0444
Email:	indebake@hotmail.com
Contact:	Dianne Hall
Terms:	10% 10 days/net 30
Expense Account:	5-1000
Credit Limit:	$5 000.00
ABN:	55 768 127 675

Name:	Yum Tarts
Card ID:	SUP 003
Address:	13 Colley Terrace,
	Glenelg SA 5045
Phone:	(08) 9294 1555
Email:	yumtarts@telstra.com.au
Contact:	Harry Yum
Terms:	10% 10 day/Net 30
Expense Account:	5-1000
Credit Limit:	$7 500.00
ABN:	60 106 202 601

7   Record the outstanding supplier balances in MYOB using June 2017

Edible Art

Date:	30 June
Tax Invoice No.:	10004
Supplied to:	Meyer's Cakes
Details: PO 0001	
21 decorated cakes @ $70.00	$1 470.00
Freight	30.00
GST:	150.00
Invoice Total:	$1 650.00
Terms: 10%10 days/Net 30.	

Independent Bakery

Date:	30 June
Tax Invoice No.:	30001
Supplied to:	Meyer's Cakes
Details: PO 0002	
6 large cakes @ $60.00	$360.00
Freight	40.00
GST:	40.00
Invoice Total:	$440.00
Terms: 10%10 days/Net 30	

Yum Tarts

Date:	30 June
Tax Invoice No.:	51596
Supplied to:	Meyer's Cakes
Details: PO 0003	
43 fruit tarts @ $25.00	$1 075.00
Freight	45.00
GST:	112.00
Invoice Total:	$1 232.00
Terms: 10%10 days/Net 30.	

8   Place the following orders with your suppliers:

Meyer's Cakes P/L	
147 North Terrace, Adelaide, SA 5000	
ABN 31 233 312 133	
Purchase Order Number:	00000004
Date:	6 July
Supplier:	Edible Art
Please supply:	
10 decorated cakes at your list price of $60.00 each plus GST.	
Delivery:	Best Way

Meyer's Cakes P/L	
147 North Terrace, Adelaide, SA 5000	
ABN 31 233 312 133	
Purchase Order Number:	00000005
Date:	6 July
Supplier:	Independent Bakery
Please supply:	
20 large cakes at your list price of $50.00 each plus GST.	
Delivery:	Best Way

Meyer's Cakes P/L	
147 North Terrace, Adelaide, SA 5000	
ABN 31 233 312 133	
Purchase Order Number:	00000006
Date:	6 July
Supplier:	Yum Tarts
Please supply:	
50 fruit tarts at your list price of $25.00 each plus GST.	
Delivery:	Best Way

9   Record the following payments to suppliers:

Date:	9/7/17
Cheque No.:	06453
Payee:	Edible Art
Details:	
Payment of all invoices with prompt payment discount	
Amount:	$1 485.00

Dissection	
Discount:	150.00
GST Component:	15.00
Discount Total:	165.00

Date:	9/7/17
Cheque No.:	06454
Payee:	Independent Bakery
Details:	
Payment of all invoices with prompt payment discount	
Amount:	$396.00

Dissection	
Discount:	40.00
GST Component:	4.00
Discount Total:	44.00

Date:	9/7/17
Cheque No.:	06455
Payee:	Yum Tarts
Details:	
Payment of all invoices with prompt payment discount	
Amount:	$1 108.80

Dissection	
Discount:	112.00
GST Component:	11.20
Discount Total:	123.20

10 Convert your purchase orders to bills as the goods have been received accompanied by the following invoices:

Edible Art	
Date:	10 July
Tax Invoice No.:	10159
Supplied to:	Meyer's Cakes
Details: PO 0004	
10 decorated cakes @ $60.00	$600.00
Freight	30.00
GST:	63.00
Invoice Total:	$693.00
Terms: 10%10 days/Net 30.	

Independent Bakery	
Date:	10 July
Tax Invoice No.:	30007
Supplied to:	Meyer's Cakes
Details: PO 0005	
20 large cakes @ $50.00	$1 000.00
Freight	40.00
GST:	104.00
Invoice Total:	$1 144.00
Terms: 10%10 days/Net 30.	

Yum Tarts	
Date:	10 July
Tax Invoice No.:	51603
Supplied to:	Meyer's Cakes
Details: PO 0006	
50 fruit tarts @ $25.00	$1 250.00
Freight	50.00
GST:	130.00
Invoice Total:	$1 430.00
Terms: 10%10 days/Net 30.	

11 Record the following adjustment notes that were received from suppliers for stock damaged in transit and apply to the appropriate invoice:

Edible Art	
Date:	10 July
Adjustment Note No.:	304
Supplied to:	Meyer's Cakes
Details: PO 0004, Invoice 10159	
1 decorated cake @ $60.00	−$60.00
Freight	−3.00
GST:	−6.30
Adjustment Total:	−$69.30

Independent Bakery	
Date:	10 July
Adjustment Note No.:	443
Supplied to:	Meyer's Cakes
Details: PO 0005, Invoice 30007	
1 large cake @ $50.00	−$50.00
Freight	−2.00
GST:	−5.20
Adjustment Total:	−$57.20

Yum Tarts	
Date:	10 July
Adjustment Note No.:	399
Supplied to:	Meyer's Cakes
Details: PO 0006, Invoice 51603	
4 fruit tarts @ $25.00	−$100.00
Freight	−4.00
GST:	−10.40
Adjustment Total:	−$114.40

12 Place the following orders with your suppliers:

Meyer's Cakes P/L	Meyer's Cakes P/L
147 North Terrace, Adelaide SA 5000	147 North Terrace, Adelaide, SA 5000
ABN 31 233 312 133	ABN 31 233 312 133
Purchase Order Number: 00000007	**Purchase Order Number:** 00000008
Date: 16 July	Date: 16 July
Supplier: Edible Art	Supplier: Independent Bakery
Please supply:	Please supply:
15 decorated cakes at your list price of $60.00 each plus GST.	25 large cakes at your list price of $50.00 each plus GST.
Delivery: Best Way	Delivery: Best Way

Meyer's Cakes P/L
147 North Terrace, Adelaide, SA 5000
ABN 31 233 312 133
Purchase Order Number: 00000009
Date: 16 July
Supplier: Yum Tarts
Please supply:
100 fruit tarts at your list price of $25.00 each plus GST.
Delivery: Best Way

13 Record the following payments to suppliers:

Date: 17/7/17		Date: 17/7/17	
Cheque No.: 06456		**Cheque No.:** 06457	
Payee: Edible Art		Payee: Independent Bakery	
Details:		Details:	
Payment of all invoices with prompt payment discount		*Payment of all invoices with prompt payment discount*	
Amount: $561.33		Amount: $978.12	
Dissection		**Dissection**	
Discount:	56.70	Discount:	98.80
GST Component:	5.67	GST Component:	9.88
Discount Total:	62.37	Discount Total:	108.68

Date:	17/7/17
Cheque No.:	06458
Payee:	Yum Tarts
Details:	
Payment of all invoices with prompt payment discount	
Amount:	$1 184.04
Dissection	
Discount:	119.60
GST Component:	11.96
Discount Total:	131.56

14 Convert your purchase orders to bills as the goods have been received accompanied by the following invoices:

Edible Art	
Date:	19 July
Tax Invoice No.:	10243
Supplied to:	Meyer's Cakes
Details: PO 0007	
15 decorated cakes @ $60.00	$900.00
Freight	45.00
GST:	94.50
Invoice Total:	$1 039.50
Terms: 10%10 days/Net 30.	

Independent Bakery	
Date:	19 July
Tax Invoice No.:	30078
Supplied to:	Meyer's Cakes
Details: PO 00008	
25 large cakes @ $50.00	$1 250.00
Freight	50.00
GST:	130.00
Invoice Total:	$1 430.00
Terms: 10%10 days/Net 30.	

Yum Tarts	
Date:	19 July
Tax Invoice No.:	51689
Supplied to:	Meyer's Cakes
Details: PO 0009	
100 fruit tarts @ $25.00	$2 500.00
Freight	100.00
GST:	260.00
Invoice Total:	$2 860.00
Terms: 10%10 days/Net 30.	

15 Record the following adjustment notes that were received from suppliers for stock damaged in transit and apply to the appropriate invoice:

Edible Art	
Date:	19 July
Adjustment Note No.:	315
Supplied to:	Meyer's Cakes
Details: PO 0007, Invoice 10243	
2 decorated cakes @ $60.00	−$120.00
Freight	−6.00
GST:	−12.60
Adjustment Total:	−$138.60

Independent Bakery	
Date:	19 July
Adjustment Note No.:	467
Supplied to:	Meyer's Cakes
Details: PO 0008, Invoice 30078	
1 large cake @ $50.00	−$50.00
Freight	−2.00
GST:	−5.20
Adjustment Total:	−$57.20

Yum Tarts	
Date:	19 July
Adjustment Note No.:	411
Supplied to:	Meyer's Cakes
Details: PO 0009, Invoice 51689	
5 fruit tarts @ $25.00	−$125.00
Freight	−5.00
GST:	−13.00
Adjustment Total:	−$143.00

16 Place the following orders with your suppliers:

Meyer's Cakes P/L	Meyer's Cakes P/L
147 North Terrace, Adelaide, SA 5000	147 North Terrace, Adelaide, SA 5000
ABN 31 233 312 133	ABN 31 233 312 133
Purchase Order Number:　00000010	**Purchase Order Number:**　00000011
Date:　25 July	Date:　25 July
Supplier:　Edible Art	Supplier:　Independent Bakery
Please supply:	Please supply:
20 decorated cakes at your list price of $60.00 each plus GST.	30 large cakes at your list price of $50.00 each plus GST.
Delivery:　Best Way	Delivery:　Best Way

Meyer's Cakes P/L

147 North Terrace, Adelaide, SA 5000

ABN 31 233 312 133

Purchase Order Number:　　00000012

Date:　　25 July

Supplier:　　Yum Tarts

Please supply:

100 fruit tarts at your list price of $25.00 each plus GST.

Delivery:　　Best Way

17 Record the following payments to suppliers:

Date:	27/7/17	Date:	27/7/17
Cheque No.:	06459	**Cheque No.:**	06460
Payee:	Edible Art	Payee:	Independent Bakery
Details:		Details:	
Payment of all invoices with prompt payment discount		*Payment of all invoices with prompt payment discount*	
Amount:	$810.81	Amount:	$1 235.52
Dissection		**Dissection**	
Discount:	81.90	Discount:	124.80
GST Component:	8.19	GST Component:	12.48
Discount Total:	90.09	Discount Total:	137.28

Date:	27/7/17
Cheque No.:	06461
Payee:	Yum Tarts
Details:	
Payment of all invoices with prompt payment discount	
Amount:	$2 445.30
Dissection	
Discount:	247.00
GST Component:	24.70
Discount Total:	271.70

18 Convert your purchase orders to bills as the goods have been received accompanied by the following invoices:

Edible Art	
Date:	28 July
Tax Invoice No.:	10302
Supplied to:	Meyer's Cakes
Details: PO 0010	
20 decorated cakes @ $60.00	$1 200.00
Freight	60.00
GST:	126.00
Invoice Total:	$1 386.00
Terms: 10%10 days/Net 30.	

Independent Bakery	
Date:	28 July
Tax Invoice No.:	30101
Supplied to:	Meyer's Cakes
Details: PO 00011	
30 large cakes @ $50.00	$1 500.00
Freight	60.00
GST:	156.00
Invoice Total:	$1 716.00
Terms: 10%10 days/Net 30.	

Yum Tarts	
Date:	28 July
Tax Invoice No.:	51716
Supplied to:	Meyer's Cakes
Details: PO 0012	
100 fruit tarts @ $25.00	$2 500.00
Freight	100.00
GST:	260.00
Invoice Total:	$2 860.00
Terms: 10%10 days/Net 30.	

19 Produce the following reports for your tutor:
  – Purchase Register Detail [All Purchases] for July.
  – Aged Payables [Summary] as at 31 July.

8

ACCOUNTS RECEIVABLE

Learning outcomes

By the end of this chapter you will be competent in:

- processing a range of customer credit transactions in both a service and a trading environment
- entering sales and receipts on account (credit)
- entering cash sales and receipts
- accessing account information using account enquiry procedures
- printing relevant reports to validate Accounts Receivable control account.

Many businesses extend credit to some of their repeat customers instead of insisting on payment at the time of the sale. These sales are posted to Accounts Receivable, an asset account. When payment is received, these figures are removed from Accounts Receivable. Thus, the Accounts Receivable account has a running balance of how much customers (debtors) owe at any given point in time. In this chapter, you will work your way through the sales process from quote to receipt of payment. It will be very straightforward as it is nearly exactly the same as Accounts Payable.

Basic accounting background

The basics of accrual accounting were covered in Chapter 6.

In this chapter:

- We will be using the *Sales* module.
- The quotes, orders and sales are entered in MYOB on the date of the *source document*.
- The payments are sometimes received later in the month and are processed using the date they are received. We will be using *Service* style sales invoices throughout these exercises.

Sales and receipts

COZY DRY CLEANERS

1 In MYOB AccountRight 2016, open the **8.1 Cozy Dry Cleaners.myox** data file from the Chapter 8 folder in your start-up files, or continue with your own file.

Record a sales order

2 A Customer purchase order is received from an account customer together with their guests' laundry and dry cleaning. *Their* purchase order becomes *our* sales order:

Cozy Corner Hilton P/L	
Cozy Corner Beach,	
Albany, WA 6330	
Date:	2 July
Purchase Order Number:	352
Supplier:	Cozy Dry Cleaners P/L
Standard Dry Cleaning:	6 garments @ $13.20
Laundry Service:	10 garments @ $6.60
Ship Via:	Best Way

Click...

- *Enter Sales* (in the Sales module). See **Figure 8.1**.
- *Sales Type* in the top left of the window (change this to *Order*). The colour will change to yellow.
- Ensure the *Tax Inclusive* box is ticked (as the prices quoted are GST *inclusive*).
- *Customer* drop-down arrow (to activate the list of customers). See **Figure 8.2**.

Figure 8.1   **Sales module: Enter Sales**

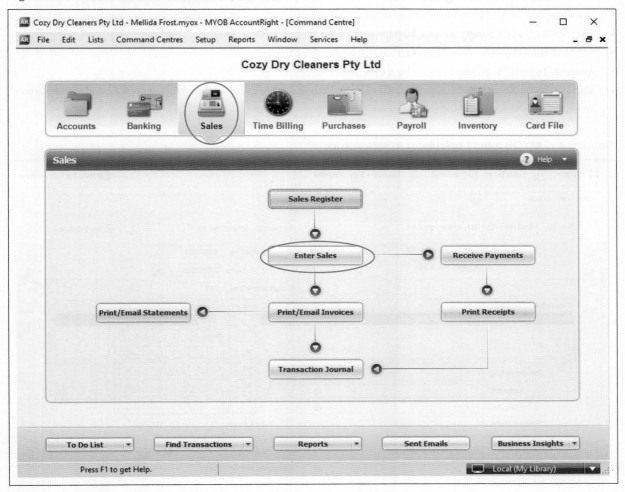

Figure 8.2   **Recording a sales order: first steps**

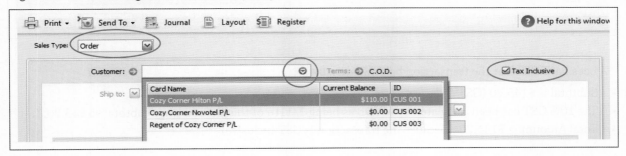

Click...

- *Customer* (choose *Cozy Corner Hilton*).
- *Date* (type 2/07/16).
- *Customer PO No.* (type 352).
- *Description* (type *Standard Dry Cleaning 6 garments (@ $13.20 each*).
- *Account No.* (type or accept *4-1000*). Press the Tab key.

- *Amount* (type *13.2**). The MYOB inbuilt calculator opens. See Figure 8.3. (Type *6*) then press the Enter key. The total cost of the line is calculated. Press the Tab key three times to move onto the next line.
- *Description* (type *Laundry Service 10 garments @ $6.60*). Press the Tab key.
- *Account No.* (click the drop-down arrow and select *4-2000*).
- *Amount* (type *10*6.60*) and press the Enter key.
- *Ship Via* (Type *be* and it will autofill to Best Way. Either double click on *Best Way* or click *Use Method* button on bottom right hand side of the window).

Figure 8.3   MYOB inbuilt calculator in sales order

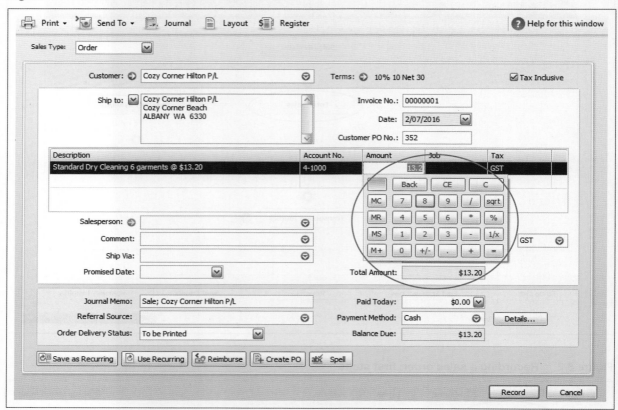

Let's have a look at the transaction below (Figure 8.4):

- Subtotal is $145.20 (GST *Inclusive*).
- The 10% GST has been calculated by MYOB as being 1/11th of this GST *Inclusive* subtotal so $13.20.
- Total Amount is $145.20. (Because the transaction is GST Inclusive).

Figure 8.4   **Sales order: Cozy Corner Hilton**

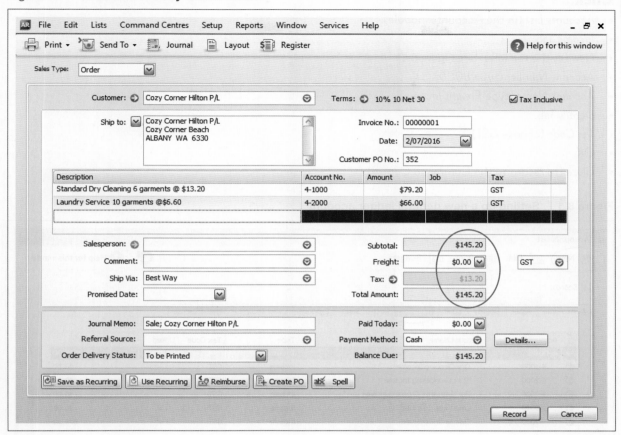

If there is any change in the service provided the order will be edited later. The cost of delivery will be added when the service has been completed.

Remember This
_____

You can use *Recurring Transactions* to save a template of your orders.

Click...

- *Record.*
- *Add* (if the spell check activates).
- *Cancel* (to return to the Command Centre).

Adding Linked Freight account

Because Cozy Dry Cleaners was set up using the MYOB *Service* accounts list, the freight income account wasn't automatically set up. We need to do that now as we charge freight to our customers when returning their dry cleaning.

Click...

- *Accounts List* (in the Accounts module).
- *Income* Tab.
- *New* (at the top left). See **Figure 8.5**.
- *Account Number* (type *8000*).
- *Account Name* (type *Freight Income*).
- *Details* Tab.
- *Tax Code* (choose *GST*).
- *OK*.
- *Close* (to return to the Command Centre).

Figure 8.5   **Setting up a new general ledger account**

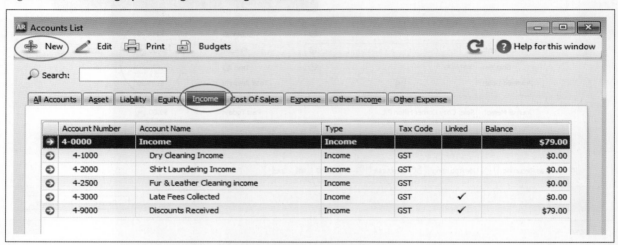

The next step is to link this account so it automatically comes up in the invoices.

Click...

- *Setup* (in the top menu line).
- *Linked Accounts*.
- *Sales Accounts*.
- *I charge freight on sales* (box on left side).
- *Income Account for Freight* (type *4-8000*). Press the Tab key. See **Figure 8.6**.
- *OK*.

Figure 8.6   **Setting up a Linked Freight account**

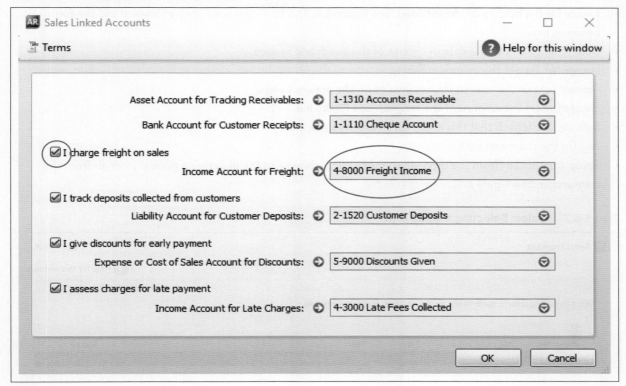

Convert sales order to a customer invoice

3 The cleaning is completed the same day and the goods are returned to the customer accompanied by the following invoice:

Cozy Dry Cleaners Pty Ltd	
Date:	2 July
Tax Invoice No.:	32001
Supplied to:	Cozy Corner Hilton P/L
Details: Customer PO 352	
Dry Cleaning: 6 @ $13.20	$79.20
Laundry: 10 @ $6.60	66.00
Freight:	17.60
Invoice Total (GST Included):	$162.80
Terms: 10% 10 days/Net 30.	

Click...

- *Enter Sales* (still in the Sales module).
- *Customer* (type *Coz* and double click on *Cozy Corner Hilton P/L*). A new window pops up. This is a list of all outstanding sales orders for this customer. If there were many, you would have to click on the one you want to convert.

- *Use Sale*. See Figure 8.7. Note that the sales order is yellow.
- *Invoice* (at the bottom of the window). See Figure 8.8. This turns the order into an invoice and the form becomes blue.
- *Date* (change this to the date of receipt of the goods and invoice).
- *Invoice No.* (insert the invoice number).
- *Amount* (check this against the tax invoice on the previous page).
- *Freight* (insert the amount of the freight). See Figure 8.9.
- *Balance Due* (check that this is correct). Also in Figure 8.9.
- *Edit* (in the top menu bar).
- *Recap Transaction* (from the drop-down menu). This shows you the underlying general journals from this transaction. See Figure 8.10.

Figure 8.7   **Sales: Selecting a sales order**

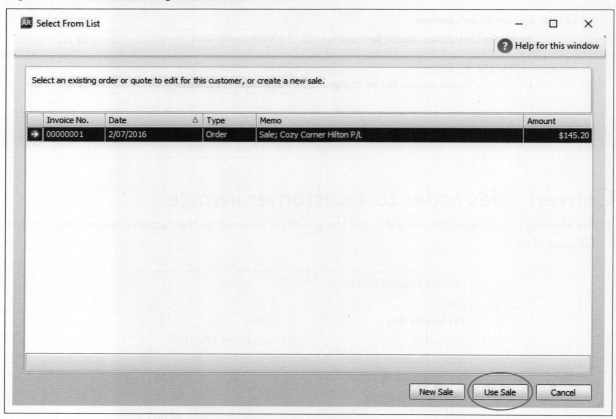

Figure 8.8   Sales order: Invoice button

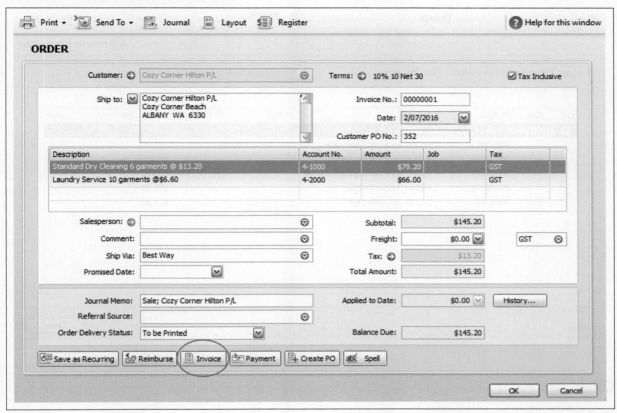

Figure 8.9   Cozy Corner Hilton Customer Invoice

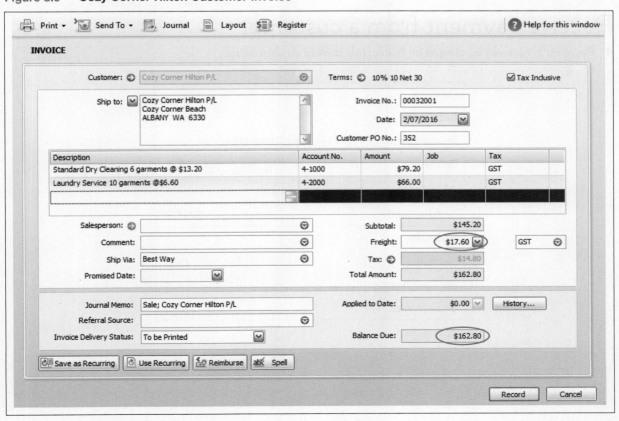

Figure 8.10   Cozy Corner Hilton Invoice: Recap Transaction

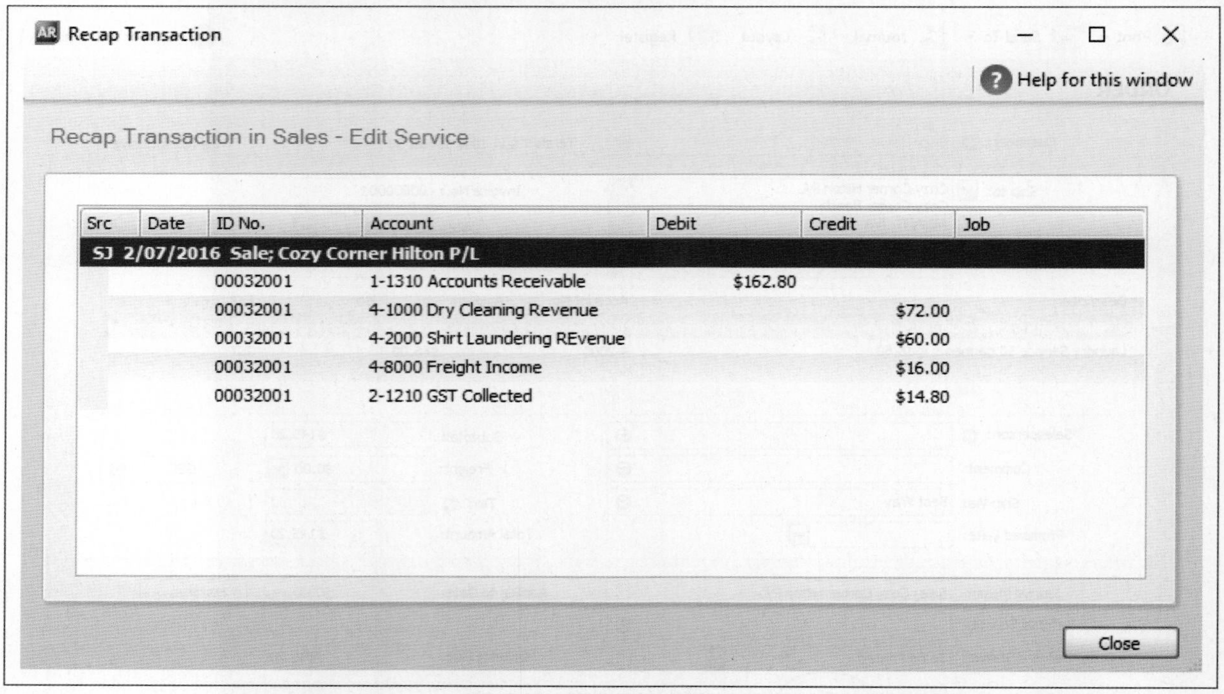

Src	Date	ID No.	Account	Debit	Credit	Job
SJ	**2/07/2016**	**Sale; Cozy Corner Hilton P/L**				
		00032001	1-1310 Accounts Receivable	$162.80		
		00032001	4-1000 Dry Cleaning Revenue		$72.00	
		00032001	4-2000 Shirt Laundering REvenue		$60.00	
		00032001	4-8000 Freight Income		$16.00	
		00032001	2-1210 GST Collected		$14.80	

Click...

- *Close* (to return to Sales window).
- *Record*.

Receive payment from a customer

4   Payment is received by cheque on 6 July. It is banked straight away.

Date:	06/7/16
Receipt No.	054
Received from:	Cozy Corner Hilton
Details:	
All invoices after prompt payment discount	
Cash Received:	$252.34
Dissection	
Discount:	18.60
GST Component:	1.86
Discount Total:	20.46

Click...

- *Sales* (in the Command Centre).
- *Receive Payments* (in the accounting area). See Figure 8.11.
- *Customer List* drop-down arrow (at right of the customer text box).
- *ID No.* (insert *25*).
- *Cozy Corner Hilton* (select this from the list).
- *Date* (change to 6/07/16).
- *Amount Received* (insert *252.34*: the debt less the calculated discount on the second and third invoices).
- *Amount Applied* (click at the top of the far-right column).
- *Amount Applied* (second line). Press the Tab key (to apply the payment to the invoice).
- *Amount Applied* (third line). Press the Tab key (to apply the payment to the invoice). See Figure 8.12.
- Ensure that *Finance Charge* and *Out of Balance* are zero. See Figure 8.13.
- *Edit* (top menu bar).
- *Recap Transaction* (to check what is about to happen). See Figure 8.14.

Tip

If all of the invoices are being paid using the one receipt, you could click the *Receive All* at the bottom left of the window (Figure 8.13) after you have entered the date.

Figure 8.11   **Sales module: Receive Payments**

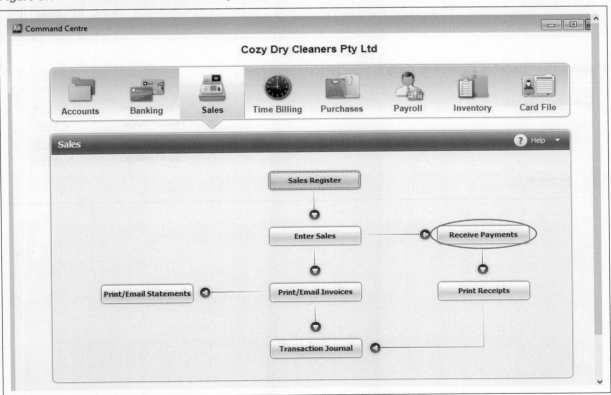

Figure 8.12   **Receive Payments: Cozy Corner Hilton**

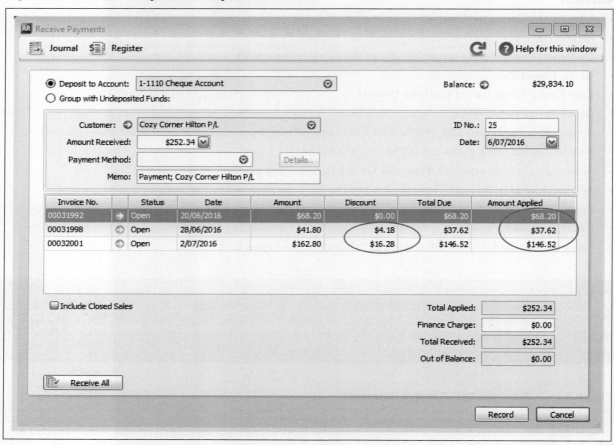

Figure 8.13   **Receive Payments: Cozy Corner Hilton completed**

Figure 8.14   **Recap Transaction: Cozy Corner Hilton**

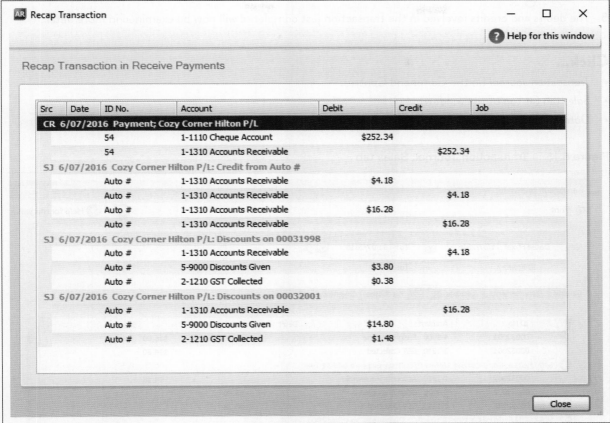

Src	Date	ID No.	Account	Debit	Credit	Job
CR	**6/07/2016**	**Payment; Cozy Corner Hilton P/L**				
		54	1-1110 Cheque Account	$252.34		
		54	1-1310 Accounts Receivable		$252.34	
SJ	**6/07/2016**	**Cozy Corner Hilton P/L: Credit from Auto #**				
		Auto #	1-1310 Accounts Receivable	$4.18		
		Auto #	1-1310 Accounts Receivable		$4.18	
		Auto #	1-1310 Accounts Receivable	$16.28		
		Auto #	1-1310 Accounts Receivable		$16.28	
SJ	**6/07/2016**	**Cozy Corner Hilton P/L: Discounts on 00031998**				
		Auto #	1-1310 Accounts Receivable		$4.18	
		Auto #	5-9000 Discounts Given	$3.80		
		Auto #	2-1210 GST Collected	$0.38		
SJ	**6/07/2016**	**Cozy Corner Hilton P/L: Discounts on 00032001**				
		Auto #	1-1310 Accounts Receivable		$16.28	
		Auto #	5-9000 Discounts Given	$14.80		
		Auto #	2-1210 GST Collected	$1.48		

Close

You only have to insert the number of the first receipt. Future receipts will display the correct number automatically.

The following is an explanation of what is shown in the four journal entries in Figure 8.14:

- *First journal*: Cash Receipts (CR) records that the Cheque Account will be increased (debited) and the debt owed by the customer (Accounts Receivable) will also be reduced (credited) by the deposit.
- *Second journal*: Sales Journal (SJ) records the two prompt payment discounts being applied to the appropriate invoices.
- *Third and fourth journal*: These Sales Journals' record that two discounts were given of $3.80 and $14.80 excluding GST (debited to 5-9000), and that because of this the GST Collected for the invoices will be reduced (debited) by $0.38 and 1.48 respectively.

Click...

- *Close* (when you have understood the display).
- *Record* (to register the payment).
- *Print Later* (we don't need a record of this).
- *Cancel* (to return to the Command Centre).

Investigate the accounts

5   The debits and credits involved in the transaction just completed will now be examined in more detail.

Click...

- *Transaction Journal* (in the Command Centre).
- *Sales* tab (at top of the window).
- *Dated From* (change to 1/07/16) and *Dated To* (change to 31/07/16). Press the Tab key. See Figure 8.15.

Figure 8.15   Transaction Journal: Sales tab

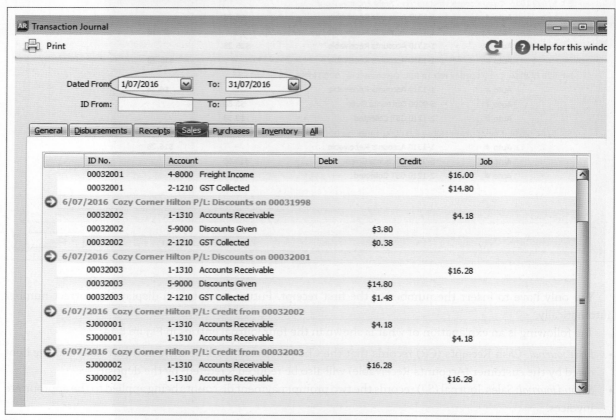

The four transactions are shown in detail from the perspective of the general ledger:

- The original sale processed on 2 July for the full amount goes to Accounts Receivable.
- The two discounts given for prompt payment have been processed, showing the reduction in GST received.
- The total discounts given is applied to Accounts Receivable to reduce the debt owed by the customer.

The deposit isn't in there because it is not a sale – it is a receipt. We will have a look at this a little later in this chapter.

Click...

- *Close* (to exit the Transaction Journal).
- *Find Transactions*.
- *Account* (tab at top of the window).

- *Dated From* (change to 1/07/16) and *Dated To* (change to 31/07/16).
- *Account* (type *4-1000*). Press the Tab key. See Figure 8.16.

Figure 8.16   Find Transaction: Accounts tab Dry Cleaning Revenue

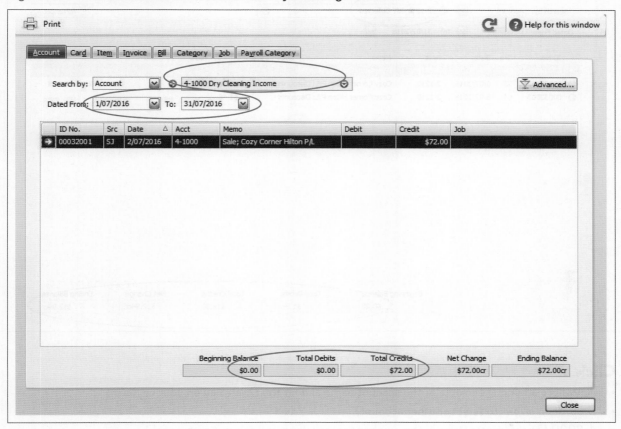

This shows that the general ledger account *4-1000 Dry Cleaning income* (income) had a beginning balance of $0.00 at the start of the month and was credited (increased) on 2 July with a $72.00 sale to Cozy Corner Hilton.

Click...

- Anywhere around the middle of the account name and hit the *Delete* key on your keyboard.
- *Drop-down arrow* (to select another account).
- *2-1210 GST Collected* (type in the number or scroll down and select it with a click).

This shows that the general ledger account *2-1210 GST Collected* (a liability) had a beginning balance of $0.00 at the start of the month and was credited (increased) on 2 July with $14.80 tax collected on a sale to Cozy Corner Hilton. *GST Collected* was reduced (debited) on 6 July by $0.38 and $1.48 when the prompt payment discounts that lessened the sale was applied, to give an ending balance of $12.94. See **Figure 8.17**.

Figure 8.17   Find Transaction: Accounts tab, GST Collected

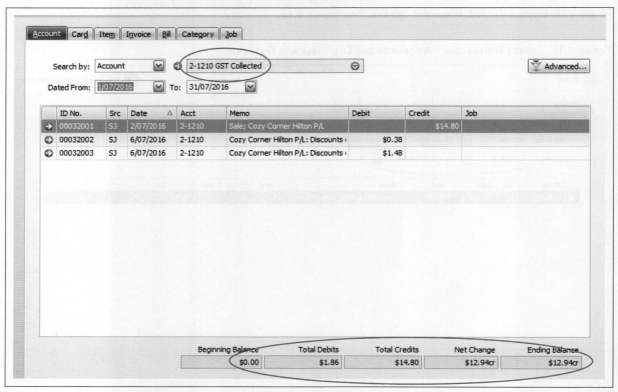

Click...

- Anywhere around the middle of the account name and hit the *Delete* key on your keyboard.
- *Drop-down arrow* (to select another account).
- *4-8000 Freight Income* (type in the number or scroll down and select it with a click).

This shows that the general ledger account *4-8000 Freight Income* (income) had a beginning balance of $0.00 at the start of the month and was credited (increased) on 2 July with $16.00 freight on a sale.

Click...

- Anywhere around the middle of the account name and hit the *Delete* key on your keyboard.
- *Drop-down arrow* (to select another account).
- *4-2000 Shirt Laundering Revenue* (type in the number or scroll down and select it with a click).

This shows that the general ledger account *4-2000 Shirt Laundering Income* (income) had a beginning balance of $0.00 at the start of the month and was credited (increased) on 2 July with $60.00 income on a sale.

Click...

- *Card* tab (top line, next to the *Accounts* tab).
- *Drop-down arrow* (choose *Cozy Corner Hilton*). Press the Tab key.

This shows the customer's account in detail. The sale, the tax and the freight are debits. The payment, the discount given (and its associated reduction in tax) are credits. See **Figure 8.18**.

Figure 8.18   Find Transaction: Card tab, Cozy Corner Hilton

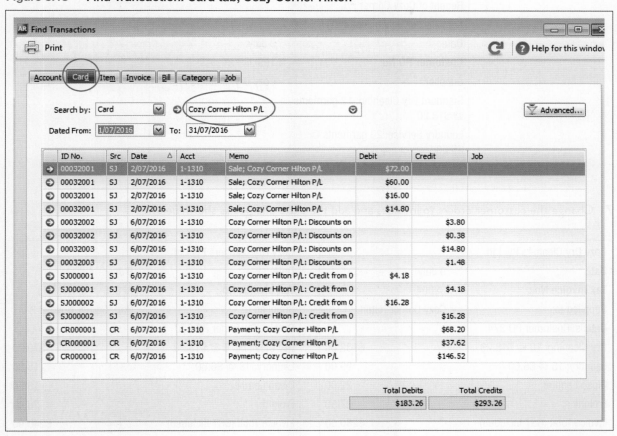

More orders

6 Orders are received from account customers together with their guests' laundry and dry cleaning:

Cozy Corner Hilton P/L
Cozy Corner Beach, Albany, WA 6330

Date:	9 July
Customer PO No:	374
Supplier:	Cozy Dry Cleaners P/L
Standard Dry Cleaning: 10 garments @ $13.20	
Laundry Service: 15 garments @ $6.60	
Ship Via:	Best Way

Cozy Corner Novotel P/L
Cozy Corner Beach, Albany, WA 6330

Date:	9 July
Customer PO No:	650
Supplier:	Cozy Dry Cleaners P/L
Standard Dry Cleaning: 6 garments @ $13.20	
Laundry Service: 18 garments @ $6.60	
Ship Via:	Best Way

```
Regent of Cozy Corner P/L
Cozy Corner Beach, Albany, WA 6330
Date:                              9 July
Customer PO No:                    199
Supplier:                          Cozy Dry Cleaners P/L
Standard Dry Cleaning: 12 garments
@ $13.20
Laundry Service: 20 garments @
$6.60
Ship Via:                          Best Way
```

7 Change the customer orders to invoices and add the extra charges as shown below:

```
Cozy Dry Cleaners Pty Ltd
Date:                    9 July
Tax Invoice No.:         32004
Supplied to:             Cozy Corner Hilton P/L
Details: Customer PO 374
Dry Cleaning: 10 @ $13.20          $132.00
Laundry: 15 @ $6.60                  99.00
Clean Leather:                       22.00
Freight:                             27.50
Invoice Total (GST Included):      $280.50
Terms: 10% 10 days/Net 30.
```

```
Cozy Dry Cleaners Pty Ltd
Date:                    9 July
Tax Invoice No.:         32005
Supplied to:             Cozy Corner Novotel P/L
Details: Customer PO 650
Dry Cleaning: 6 @ $13.20            $79.20
Laundry: 18 @ $6.60                 118.80
Clean Leather:                       16.50
Freight:                             26.40
Invoice Total (GST Included):      $240.90
Terms: 10% 10 days/Net 30.
```

```
Cozy Dry Cleaners Pty Ltd
Date:                    9 July
Tax Invoice No.:         32006
Supplied to:             Regent of Cozy Corner P/L
Details: Customer PO 199
Dry Cleaning: 12 @ $13.20          $158.40
Laundry: 20 @ $6.60                 132.00
Fur Cleaning:                        35.20
Freight:                             24.20
Invoice Total (GST Included):      $349.80
Terms: 10% 10 days/Net 30.
```

8 Orders are received from account customers together with their guests' laundry and dry cleaning:

Cozy Corner Hilton P/L	
Cozy Corner Beach, Albany, WA 6330	
Date:	16 July
Customer PO No.:	392
Supplier:	Cozy Dry Cleaners P/L
Standard Dry Cleaning: 8 garments @ $13.20	
Laundry Service: 18 garments @ $6.60	
Ship Via:	Best Way

Cozy Corner Novotel P/L	
Cozy Corner Beach, Albany, WA 6330	
Date:	16 July
Customer PO No.:	679
Supplier:	Cozy Dry Cleaners P/L
Standard Dry Cleaning: 12 garments @ $13.20	
Laundry Service: 15 garments @ $6.60	
Ship Via:	Best Way

Regent of Cozy Corner P/L	
Cozy Corner Beach, Albany, WA 6330	
Date:	16 July
Customer PO No.:	214
Supplier:	Cozy Dry Cleaners P/L
Standard Dry Cleaning: 16 garments @ $13.20	
Laundry Service: 12 garments @ $6.60	
Ship Via:	Best Way

9 Record receipt of the following payments from customers. You can see that there are orders available for paying in the Receive Payments screen. *Never* apply a payment to an order. Only apply payments to an invoice.

Date:	16/7/16
Receipt No.	026
Received from:	Cozy Corner Hilton
Details:	
All invoices after prompt payment discount	
Cash Received:	$252.45
Dissection	
Discount:	25.50
GST Component:	2.55
Discount Total:	28.05

Date:	16/7/16
Receipt No.	027
Received from:	Cozy Corner Novotel
Details:	
All invoices after prompt payment discount	
Cash Received:	$216.81
Dissection	
Discount:	21.90
GST Component:	2.19
Discount Total:	24.09

Date:	16/7/16
Receipt No.	028
Received from:	Regent of Cozy Corner
Details:	
All invoices after prompt payment discount	
Cash Received:	$314.82
Dissection	
Discount:	31.80
GST Component:	3.18
Discount Total:	34.98

10 Change the customer orders to invoices and add the extra charges as shown below:

Cozy Dry Cleaners Pty Ltd	
Date:	16 July
Tax Invoice No.:	32007
Supplied to:	Cozy Corner Hilton P/L
Details: Customer PO 392	
Dry Cleaning: 8 @ $13.20	$105.60
Laundry: 18 @ $6.60	118.80
Freight:	28.60
Invoice Total (GST Included):	$253.00
Terms: 10% 10 days/Net 30	

Cozy Dry Cleaners Pty Ltd	
Date:	16 July
Tax Invoice No.:	32008
Supplied to:	Cozy Corner Novotel P/L
Details: Customer PO 679	
Dry Cleaning: 12 @ $13.20	$158.40
Laundry: 15 @ $6.60	99.00
Freight:	39.60
Invoice Total (GST Included):	$297.00
Terms: 10% 10 days/Net 30.	

Cozy Dry Cleaners Pty Ltd	
Date:	16 July
Tax Invoice No.:	32009
Supplied to:	Regent of Cozy Corner P/L
Details: Customer PO 214	
Dry Cleaning: 16 @ $13.20	$211.20
Laundry: 12 @ $6.60	79.20
Leather Cleaning:	8.80
Freight:	30.80
Invoice Total (GST Included):	$330.00
Terms: 10% 10 days/Net 30.	

11 The following adjustment note was issued to the Regent of Cozy Corner for unsatisfactory cleaning:

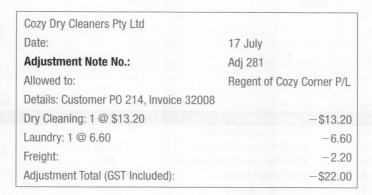

Cozy Dry Cleaners Pty Ltd	
Date:	17 July
Adjustment Note No.:	Adj 281
Allowed to:	Regent of Cozy Corner P/L
Details: Customer PO 214, Invoice 32008	
Dry Cleaning: 1 @ $13.20	−$13.20
Laundry: 1 @ 6.60	−6.60
Freight:	−2.20
Adjustment Total (GST Included):	−$22.00

The adjustment note is recorded as a *negative* invoice (that is, the amount is recorded as a negative).

Click...

- *Enter Sales* (In the *Sales* module).
- *Customer* (choose *Regent of Cozy Corner*).
- *Invoice No.* (type *Adj 281*). Press Tab key.
- *Date* (type 17/07/16) Press the Tab key.
- *Description* (type *Unsatisfactory cleaning on invoice 32008*).
- Complete the rest of the details from the adjustment note above, remembering to allocate the correct negative amounts to the correct accounts. See **Figure 8.19**.
- *Edit* on the top menu bar.
- *Recap Transaction*. A new window opens. See **Figure 8.20**.

Figure 8.19   Enter Sales: adjustment note

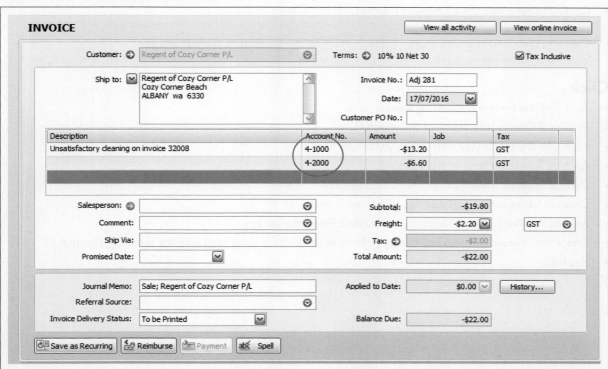

Figure 8.20   **Recap Transaction: adjustment note**

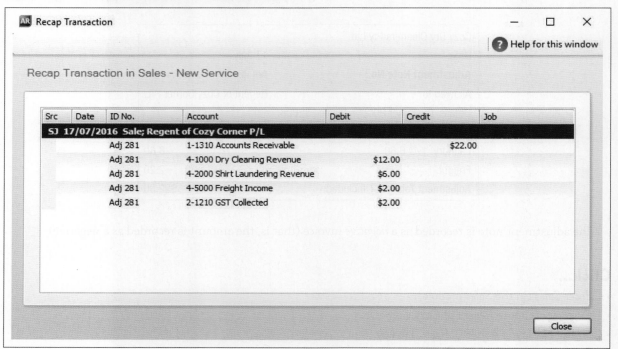

This shows that the Regent of Cozy Corner (an Account Receivable – an asset) will be credited (reduced) when this allowance is recorded. The three income and liability accounts will be debited (also reduced).

Click...

- *Close* (when you have understood the display).
- *Record* (to register the payment).
- *Cancel* (to return to the Command Centre).

The next step is to reduce the *appropriate* invoice by the amount of the adjustment.

Click...

- *Sales Register* (in the accounting area).
- *Returns & Credits* (tab at top of the window).
- Highlight the credit you wish to apply (there is only one).
- *Apply to Sale* (near base of the window).
- *Date* (change to 17/07/16).
- *Discount* (delete the suggested figure if there is one).
- *Amount Applied* (click in the far-right column). Press the Tab key.
- Check that *Finance Charge* and *Out of Balance* at the bottom right hand side are zero. See Figure 8.21.
- Record.

Figure 8.21 **Sales: Settle Returns & Credits**

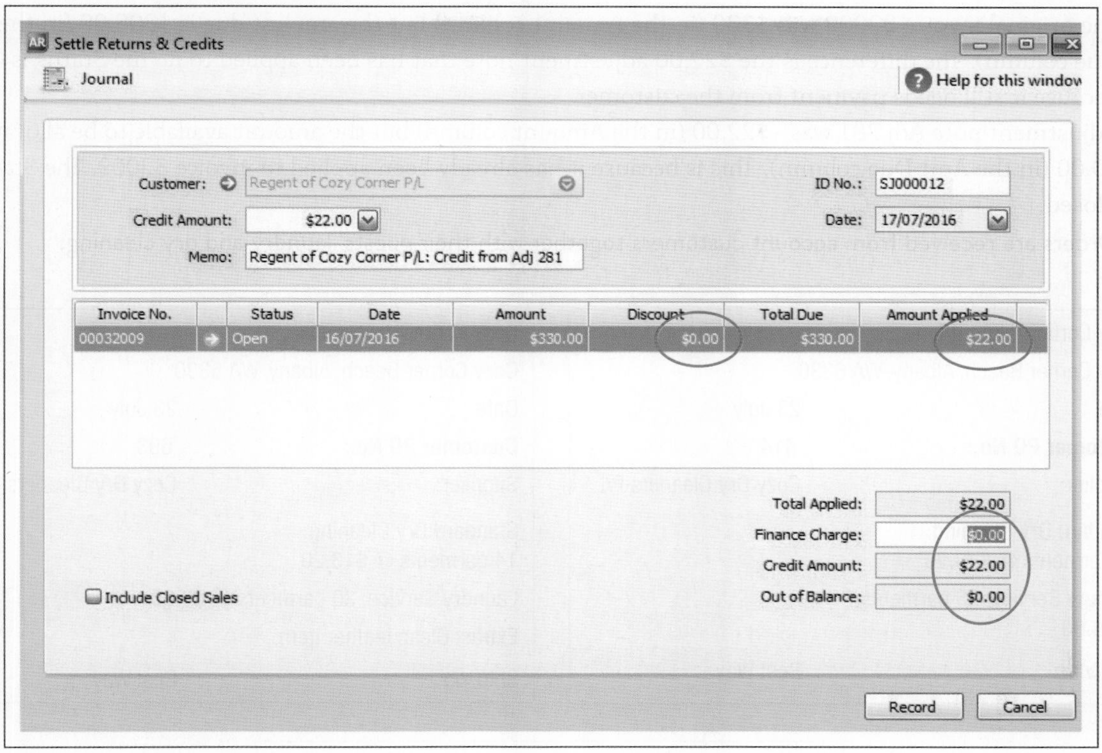

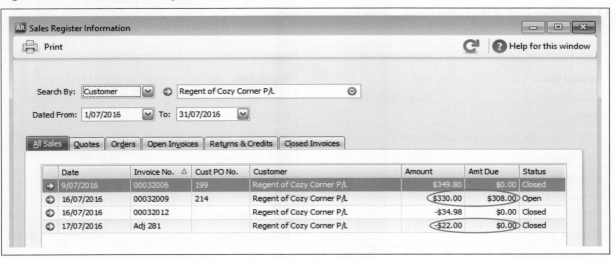

Let us look at the end result of creating and applying the adjustment note.

Click...

- *All Sales* (tab in the Sales Register).
- *Search By* (use the drop-down arrow to change to *Customer* and in the box that appears, type *Regent* and press the Tab key to accept the autofill).
- *Dated From* (change to 1/07/16) and *To* (change to 31/07/16).
- Figure 8.22 shows all transactions for *Regent of Cozy Corner* for that date range.

Figure 8.22 **Sales: Sales Register Information**

We can see that:

- The original invoice 32009 was $330 (in the Amount column) but the amount due is $308.00 (in the Amt Due column). The difference is the $22.00 adjustment note that has been applied to it. The Status is Open because it still needs payment from the customer.
- Adjustment note Adj 281 was −$22.00 (in the Amount column) but the amount available to be allocated is $0.00 (in the Amt Due column). This is because it has already been applied to invoice 32009. The Status is Closed.

12 Orders are received from account customers together with their guests' laundry and dry cleaning:

Cozy Corner Hilton P/L	
Cozy Corner Beach, Albany, WA 6330	
Date:	23 July
Customer PO No.:	414
Supplier:	Cozy Dry Cleaners P/L
Standard Dry Cleaning: 20 garments @ $13.20	
Laundry Service: 25 garments @ $6.60	
Ship Via:	Best Way

Cozy Corner Novotel P/L	
Cozy Corner Beach, Albany, WA 6330	
Date:	23 July
Customer PO No.:	693
Supplier:	Cozy Dry Cleaners P/L
Standard Dry Cleaning: 14 garments @ $13.20	
Laundry Service: 30 garments @ $6.60	
Extras: Clean leather item.	
Ship Via:	Best Way

Regent of Cozy Corner P/L	
Cozy Corner Beach, Albany, WA 6330	
Date:	23 July
Customer PO No.:	228
Supplier:	Cozy Dry Cleaners P/L
Standard Dry Cleaning: 20 garments @ $13.20	
Laundry Service: 20 garments @ $6.60	
Ship Via:	Best Way

13 Record receipt of the following payments from customers:

Date:	23/7/16
Receipt No.	029
Received from:	Cozy Corner Hilton
Details:	
All invoices after prompt payment discount	
Cash Received:	$227.70
Dissection	
Discount:	23.00
GST Component:	2.30
Discount Total:	25.30

Date:	23/7/16
Receipt No.	030
Received from:	Cozy Corner Novotel
Details:	
All invoices after prompt payment discount	
Cash Received:	$267.30
Dissection	
Discount:	27.00
GST Component:	2.70
Discount Total:	29.70

Date:	23/7/16
Receipt No.	031
Received from:	Regent of Cozy Corner
Details:	
All invoices after prompt payment discount	
Cash Received:	$277.20
Dissection	
Discount:	28.00
GST Component:	2.80
Discount Total:	30.80

Tip

Beware: Just like in the Accounts Payable module, MYOB can't calculate the prompt payment discount on an invoice with an adjustment note applied to it. So always calculate the prompt payment discount yourself, just to be sure.

14 Change the customer orders to Invoices and add the extra charges as shown below:

Cozy Dry Cleaners Pty Ltd	
Date:	23 July
Tax Invoice No.:	32012
Supplied to:	Cozy Corner Hilton P/L
Details: Customer PO 414	
Dry Cleaning: 20 @ $13.20	$264.00
Laundry: 25 @ $6.60	165.00
Leather cleaning:	38.50
Freight:	27.50
Invoice Total (GST Included)	$495.00
Terms: 10% 10 days/Net 30.	

Cozy Dry Cleaners Pty Ltd	
Date:	23 July
Tax Invoice No.:	32013
Supplied to:	Cozy Corner Novotel P/L
Details: Customer PO 693	
Dry Cleaning: 14 @ $13.20	$184.80
Laundry: 30 @ $6.60	198.00
Leather Cleaning:	30.80
Freight:	26.40
Invoice Total (GST Included):	$440.00
Terms: 10% 10 days/Net 30.	

Cozy Dry Cleaners Pty Ltd		
Date:	23 July	
Tax Invoice No.:	32014	
Supplied to:	Regent of Cozy Corner P/L	
Details: Customer PO 228		
Dry Cleaning: 20 @ $13.20		$264.00
Laundry: 20 @ $6.60		132.00
Leather cleaning:		16.50
Freight:		44.00
Invoice Total (GST Included):		$456.50
Terms: 10% 10 days/Net 30.		

15 Record the following adjustment notes that were issued to the customers for unsatisfactory cleaning. Apply them to their appropriate invoices:

Cozy Dry Cleaners Pty Ltd		
Date:	23 July	
Adjustment Note No.:	Adj 282	
Allowed to:	Cozy Corner Hilton P/L	
Details: Customer PO 414, Invoice 32012		
Dry Cleaning: 2 @ $13.20		−$26.40
Laundry: 1 @ 6.60		−6.60
Freight:		−3.30
Adjustment Total (GST Included):		−$36.30

Remember This

Ensure you split up the adjustment note into its correct account codes. Dry Cleaning should be allocated to 4-1000, Laundry should be allocated to 4-2000.

Cozy Dry Cleaners Pty Ltd		
Date:	24 July	
Adjustment Note No.:	Adj 283	
Allowed to:	Cozy Corner Novotel P/L	
Details: Customer PO 693, Invoice 32013		
Dry Cleaning: 1 @ $13.20		−$13.20
Laundry: 2 @ 6.60		−13.20
Freight:		−3.30
Adjustment Total (GST Included):		−$29.70

Produce reports

16 Produce an Aged Receivables [Summary] as at 30 July for your records.

Click...

- *Sales* (in the *Reports* Index).
- *Aged Receivables [Summary]*.
- *Filter Report As of* (type *31/07/16*).
- *Display*. See Figure 8.23.

Figure 8.23   **Reports: Aged Receivables [Summary]**

Cozy Dry Cleaners Pty Ltd
Cozy Beach Corner
Albany WA 6330
Aged Receivables [Summary]
As of 31/07/2016

Name	Total Due	0–30	31–60	61–90	90+
Cozy Corner Hilton P/L	$458.70	$458.70	$0.00	$0.00	$0.00
Cozy Corner Novotel P/L	$410.30	$410.30	$0.00	$0.00	$0.00
Regent of Cozy Corner P/L	$456.50	$456.50	$0.00	$0.00	$0.00
Total:	$1 325.50	$1 325.50	$0.00	$0.00	$0.00
Ageing Percent:		100.0%	0.0%	0.0%	0.0%

The Aged Receivables [Summary] report shows you how much money is owed by each customer. If you wanted to know the individual invoices and amounts, you would use the Aged Receivables [Detail] report.

17 Produce a Sales Register [All Sales] report. (You are in the Reports menu.)

Click...

- *Sales* (in the left menu).
- *Sales Register Detail [All Sales]* in the middle menu. You will need to scroll down to find it.
- *Filter Report Dated From* (type *1/07/2016*) and *To* (type *31/07/16*).
- Display. See Figure 8.24.

Figure 8.24   **Sales Register Detail [All Sales] report**

Cozy Dry Cleaners Pty Ltd
Cozy Beach Corner
Albany WA 6330
Sales Register Detail [All Sales]
July 2016

Date	Invoice No.	Customer PO No.	Customer Name	Amount	Amount Due	Status
23/07/2016	00000285		Cozy Corner Hilton P/L	($25.30)	$0.00	Closed
23/07/2016	00000286		Cozy Corner Novotel P/L	($29.70)	$0.00	Closed
23/07/2016	00000287		Regent of Cozy Corner P/L	($30.80)	$0.00	Closed

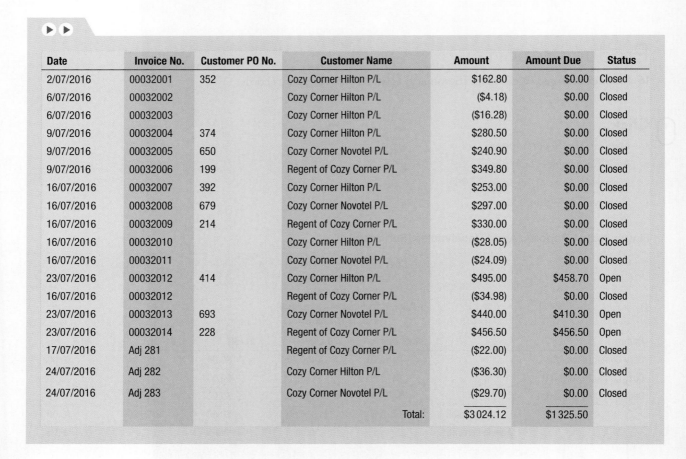

Date	Invoice No.	Customer PO No.	Customer Name	Amount	Amount Due	Status
2/07/2016	00032001	352	Cozy Corner Hilton P/L	$162.80	$0.00	Closed
6/07/2016	00032002		Cozy Corner Hilton P/L	($4.18)	$0.00	Closed
6/07/2016	00032003		Cozy Corner Hilton P/L	($16.28)	$0.00	Closed
9/07/2016	00032004	374	Cozy Corner Hilton P/L	$280.50	$0.00	Closed
9/07/2016	00032005	650	Cozy Corner Novotel P/L	$240.90	$0.00	Closed
9/07/2016	00032006	199	Regent of Cozy Corner P/L	$349.80	$0.00	Closed
16/07/2016	00032007	392	Cozy Corner Hilton P/L	$253.00	$0.00	Closed
16/07/2016	00032008	679	Cozy Corner Novotel P/L	$297.00	$0.00	Closed
16/07/2016	00032009	214	Regent of Cozy Corner P/L	$330.00	$0.00	Closed
16/07/2016	00032010		Cozy Corner Hilton P/L	($28.05)	$0.00	Closed
16/07/2016	00032011		Cozy Corner Novotel P/L	($24.09)	$0.00	Closed
23/07/2016	00032012	414	Cozy Corner Hilton P/L	$495.00	$458.70	Open
16/07/2016	00032012		Regent of Cozy Corner P/L	($34.98)	$0.00	Closed
23/07/2016	00032013	693	Cozy Corner Novotel P/L	$440.00	$410.30	Open
23/07/2016	00032014	228	Regent of Cozy Corner P/L	$456.50	$456.50	Open
17/07/2016	Adj 281		Regent of Cozy Corner P/L	($22.00)	$0.00	Closed
24/07/2016	Adj 282		Cozy Corner Hilton P/L	($36.30)	$0.00	Closed
24/07/2016	Adj 283		Cozy Corner Novotel P/L	($29.70)	$0.00	Closed
			Total:	$3 024.12	$1 325.50	

18 Examine your Customer Ledger. This shows transactions grouped by Customers for the selected date range. (You are still in the Reports menu.)

Click...

- *Sales* (left menu)
- *Customer Ledger* (in the middle menu).
- *Filter Report Dated From* (type *1/07/2016*) and *To* (type *31/07/16*).
- Display. See Figure 8.25.

Figure 8.25   Customer Ledger report

Cozy Dry Cleaners Pty Ltd
Cozy Beach Corner
Albany WA 6330
Customer Ledger
July 2016

Date	Src	ID No.	Memo	Transaction Amount	Balance
Cozy Corner Hilton P/L	CUS 001				$110.00
2/07/2016	SJ	00032001	Sale; Cozy Corner Hilton P/L	$162.80	$272.80
6/07/2016	SJ	00032002	Cozy Corner Hilton P/L: Discounts on 00031998	($4.18)	$268.62
6/07/2016	SJ	SJ000001	Cozy Corner Hilton P/L: Credit from 00032002	$0.00	$268.62

Date	Src	ID No.	Memo	Transaction Amount	Balance
6/07/2016	SJ	00032003	Cozy Corner Hilton P/L: Discounts on 00032001	($16.28)	$252.34
6/07/2016	SJ	SJ000002	Cozy Corner Hilton P/L: Credit from 00032003	$0.00	$252.34
6/07/2016	CR	CR000001	Payment; Cozy Corner Hilton P/L	($252.34)	$0.00
9/07/2016	SJ	00032004	Sale; Cozy Corner Hilton P/L	$280.50	$280.50
16/07/2016	SJ	00032010	Cozy Corner Hilton P/L: Discounts on 00032004	($28.05)	$252.45
16/07/2016	SJ	SJ000003	Cozy Corner Hilton P/L: Credit from 00032010	$0.00	$252.45
16/07/2016	CR	26	Payment; Cozy Corner Hilton P/L	($252.45)	$0.00
16/07/2016	SJ	00032007	Sale; Cozy Corner Hilton P/L	$253.00	$253.00
23/07/2016	SJ	00000285	Cozy Corner Hilton P/L: Discounts on 00032007	($25.30)	$227.70
23/07/2016	SJ	SJ000007	Cozy Corner Hilton P/L: Credit from 00000285	$0.00	$227.70
23/07/2016	CR	29	Payment; Cozy Corner Hilton P/L	($227.70)	$0.00
23/07/2016	SJ	00032012	Sale; Cozy Corner Hilton P/L	$495.00	$495.00
23/07/2016	SJ	SJ000010	Cozy Corner Hilton P/L: Credit from Adj 282	$0.00	$495.00
24/07/2016	SJ	Adj 282	Sale; Cozy Corner Hilton P/L	($36.30)	$458.70
			Total:	$348.70	$458.70
Cozy Corner Novotel P/L	CUS 002				$0.00
9/07/2016	SJ	00032005	Sale; Cozy Corner Novotel P/L	$240.90	$240.90
16/07/2016	SJ	00032011	Cozy Corner Novotel P/L: Discounts on 00032005	($24.09)	$216.81
16/07/2016	SJ	SJ000004	Cozy Corner Novotel P/L: Credit from 00032011	$0.00	$216.81
16/07/2016	CR	CR000002	Payment; Cozy Corner Novotel P/L	($216.81)	$0.00
16/07/2016	SJ	00032008	Sale; Cozy Corner Novotel P/L	$297.00	$297.00
23/07/2016	SJ	00000286	Cozy Corner Novotel P/L: Discounts on 00032008	($29.70)	$267.30
23/07/2016	SJ	SJ000008	Cozy Corner Novotel P/L: Credit from 00000286	$0.00	$267.30
23/07/2016	CR	CR000004	Payment; Cozy Corner Novotel P/L	($267.30)	$0.00
23/07/2016	SJ	00032013	Sale; Cozy Corner Novotel P/L	$440.00	$440.00
24/07/2016	SJ	Adj 283	Sale; Cozy Corner Novotel P/L	($29.70)	$410.30
24/07/2016	SJ	SJ000011	Cozy Corner Novotel P/L: Credit from Adj 283	$0.00	$410.30
			Total:	$410.30	$410.30
Regent of Cozy Corner P/L	CUS 003				$0.00
9/07/2016	SJ	00032006	Sale; Regent of Cozy Corner P/L	$349.80	$349.80
16/07/2016	SJ	00032012	Regent of Cozy Corner P/L: Discounts on 00032006	($34.98)	$314.82
16/07/2016	SJ	SJ000005	Regent of Cozy Corner P/L: Credit from 00032012	$0.00	$314.82
16/07/2016	CR	CR000003	Payment; Regent of Cozy Corner P/L	($314.82)	$0.00

Date	Src	ID No.	Memo	Transaction Amount	Balance
16/07/2016	SJ	00032009	Sale; Regent of Cozy Corner P/L	$330.00	$330.00
17/07/2016	SJ	Adj 281	Sale; Regent of Cozy Corner P/L	($22.00)	$308.00
17/07/2016	SJ	SJ000006	Regent of Cozy Corner P/L: Credit from Adj 281	$0.00	$308.00
23/07/2016	SJ	00000287	Regent of Cozy Corner P/L: Discounts on 00032009	($30.80)	$277.20
23/07/2016	SJ	SJ000009	Regent of Cozy Corner P/L: Credit from 00000287	$0.00	$277.20
23/07/2016	CR	CR000005	Payment; Regent of Cozy Corner P/L	($277.20)	$0.00
23/07/2016	SJ	00032014	Sale; Regent of Cozy Corner P/L	$456.50	$456.50
			Total:	$456.50	$456.50

Sales quotes

A *quote* is a firm offer to supply goods and/or services at a set price. It is normal for customers to obtain quotes from several competing sources and then to accept the one they prefer, using price, quality, speed of delivery, etc. to come to their decision.

THE BLINDS MAN

1 In MYOB AccountRight 2016, open **the 8.2 The Blinds Man.myox** file from the Chapter 8 folder in your start-up files, or use your own file.

2 Record the following quote given to a customer:

```
The Blinds Man
21 Penola Road, Mount Gambier, SA 5290
ABN 78 303 458 861
Quote Number:          33161
Date:                  2 July
Customer:              East Motor Inn P/L
Supply and install:
2 x Vertical Drapes type AVB 2600 with fittings.
Dimensions: Width 3000mm; Height 2400mm.
Price including GST:   $1 705.00
```

Click...

- *Enter Sales* (In the *Sales* module).
- *Sales Type* (in the top left of the window; change this to *Quote*). The colour will change to pink.
- Ensure the *Tax Inclusive* box is ticked (as the prices quoted are GST *Inclusive*).
- *Customer* drop-down arrow (to activate the list of customers) and select *East Motor Inn*.
- *Date* (type 2/07/16).
- *Description* (type *Supply and Install 2 x Vertical drapes type AVB 2600 with fittings. Width 3000mm height 2400mm*).

Chapter 8 Accounts Receivable

- *Account No.* (type or accept *4-1000*). Press the Tab key.
- *Amount* (type *1705.00*). Press the Tab key. See **Figure 8.26**.
- *Save Quote.*
- *Cancel* (to return to the Command Centre).

Figure 8.26   Sales Quote: East Motor Inn

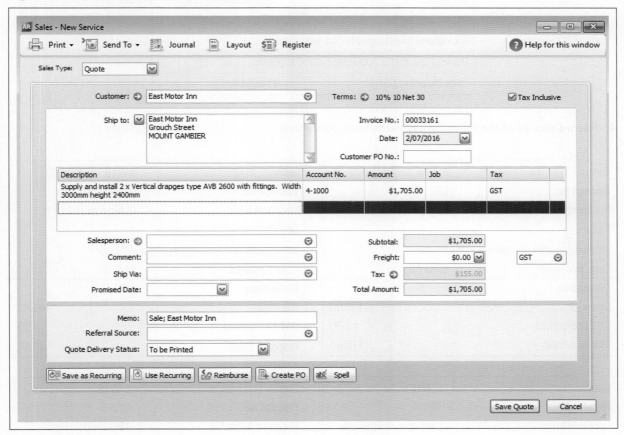

If there is any change in the service provided the quote can be updated and re-sent or the order or invoice can be edited later.

3 Record the following quotes:

The Blinds Man		The Blinds Man	
21 Penola Road, Mount Gambier, SA 5290		21 Penola Road, Mount Gambier, SA 5290	
ABN 78 303 458 861		ABN 78 303 458 861	
Quote Number:	33162	**Quote Number:**	33163
Date:	2 July	Date:	2 July
Customer:	Grandview Hotel P/L	Customer:	Lakeview Apartments P/L
Supply and install:		Supply and install:	
3 x Venetian Blinds type LVB 420 with fittings.		5 x Sunscreen Rollers type RB 175 with fittings.	
Dimensions: Width 2400mm; Height 1800mm.		Dimensions: Width 3600mm; Length 2400mm.	
Price including GST:	$1 386.00	Price including GST:	$5 060.00

```
The Blinds Man
21 Penola Road, Mount Gambier, SA 5290
ABN 78 303 458 861
```

Quote Number:	33164
Date:	2 July
Supplier:	Meriton Holdings P/L
Supply and install:	
3 x Holland Blinds type HB 501 with fittings.	
Dimensions: Width 2000mm; Height 3000mm.	
Price including GST:	$1 056.00

4 Record receipt of the following payments from customers:

Date:	5/7/16
Receipt No.	022
Received from:	East Motor Inn
Details:	
All invoices after prompt payment discount	
Cash Received:	$990.00
Dissection	
Discount:	100.00
GST Component:	10.00
Discount Total:	110.00

Date:	5/7/16
Receipt No.	023
Received from:	Grandview Hotel P/L
Details:	
All invoices after prompt payment discount	
Cash Received:	$445.50
Dissection	
Discount:	45.00
GST Component:	4.50
Discount Total:	49.50

Date:	5/7/16
Receipt No.	024
Received from:	Lakeview Apartments
Details:	
All invoices after prompt payment discount	
Cash Received:	$1 485.00
Dissection	
Discount:	150.00
GST Component:	15.00
Discount Total:	165.00

Date:	5/7/16
Receipt No.	025
Received from:	Meriton Holdings
Details:	
All invoices after prompt payment discount	
Cash Received:	$1 039.50
Dissection	
Discount:	105.00
GST Component:	11.50
Discount Total:	115.50

5 While a *quote* is an offer of supply at a certain price, it is accepted when the customer issues a purchase *order*. The East Motor Inn has issued the following order:

East Motor Inn P/L

Grouch Street, Mount Gambier, SA 5290

Date:	5 July
Customer PO No.:	541
Supplier:	The Blinds Man P/L
Supply and install as per your Quote No. 33161	
2 x Vertical Drapes type AVB 2600 with fittings.	
Dimensions: Width 3000mm; Height 2400mm.	
Quoted Price:	$1 705.00

Remember This

A *customer's* purchase order is *your* sales order.

Click...

- *Enter Sales* (In the *Sales* module).
- *Customer* drop-down arrow (select *East Motor Inn*). Another window opens showing available quotes for this customer.
- *Use Sale* (at the bottom of the window). This prefills the screen for you.
- *Order* (at the base of this window). The window changes colour to yellow.
- *Date* (type 5/07/16).
- *Customer PO. No.* (type 541). See Figure 8.27.
- *Record.*

Figure 8.27   Sales order: East Motor Inn

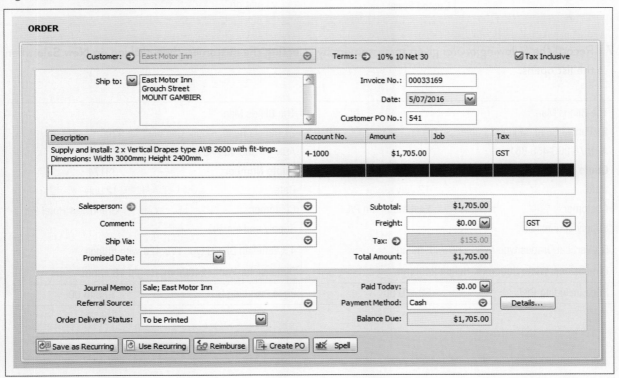

> ### *This is why*
>
> Because quote and orders do *not* affect the accounts at all, MYOB has different colours for different forms. After a while, you subconsciously become aware whether you are working with the correct form or not.

6 Process the following orders accepting quotes:

Grandview Hotel P/L	
Lake Terrace, Mount Gambier, SA 5290	
Date:	5 July
Customer PO No.:	749
Supplier:	The Blinds Man P/L
Supply and install as per your Quote No. 33162	
3 x Venetian Blinds type LVB 420 with fittings.	
Dimensions: Width 2400mm; Height 1800mm.	
Quoted Price:	$1 386.00

Lakeview Apartments P/L	
6 Helen Street, Mount Gambier, SA 5290	
Date:	5 July
Customer PO No.:	306
Supplier:	The Blinds Man P/L
Supply and install as per your Quote No. 33163	
5 x Sunscreen Rollers type RB 175 with fittings.	
Dimensions: Width 3600mm; Length 2400mm.	
Quoted Price:	$5 060.00

Meriton Holdings P/L	
Jubilee Highway, Mount Gambier, SA 5290	
Date:	5 July
Customer PO No.:	559
Supplier:	The Blinds Man P/L
Supply and install as per your Quote No. 33164	
3 x Holland Blinds type HB 501 with fittings.	
Dimensions: Width 2000mm; Height 3000mm.	
Quoted Price:	$1 056.00

7 Record the following *quotes* given to customers by selecting the customer, then clicking on **New Sale** when the list opens.

The Blinds Man	
21 Penola Road, Mount Gambier, SA 5290	
ABN 78 303 458 861	
Quote Number:	33173
Date:	12 July
Customer:	East Motor Inn P/L
Supply and install:	
5 x Vertical Drapes type AVB 2600 with fittings.	
Dimensions: Width 3000mm; Height 2400mm.	
Price including GST:	$3 410.00

The Blinds Man	
21 Penola Road, Mount Gambier, SA 5290	
ABN 78 303 458 861	
Quote Number:	33174
Date:	12 July
Customer:	Grandview Hotel P/L
Supply and install:	
4 x Venetian Blinds type LVB 420 with fittings.	
Dimensions: Width 2400mm; Height 1800mm.	
Price including GST:	$1 848.00

The Blinds Man	
21 Penola Road, Mount Gambier, SA 5290	
ABN 78 303 458 861	
Quote Number:	33175
Date:	12 July
Customer:	Lakeview Apartments P/L
Supply and install:	
2 x Sunscreen Rollers type RB 175 with fittings.	
Dimensions: Width 3600mm; Length 2400mm.	
Price including GST:	$2 024.00

The Blinds Man	
21 Penola Road, Mount Gambier, SA 5290	
ABN 78 303 458 861	
Quote Number:	33176
Date:	12 July
Customer:	Meriton Holdings P/L
Supply and install:	
4 x Holland Blinds type HB 501 with fittings.	
Dimensions: Width 2000mm; Height 3000mm.	
Price including GST:	$1 188.00

8 Set up the Freight Income account (tax code of GST) and link it through Setup/Linked Accounts as we did in Cozy Dry Cleaners on page 202.

9 Change the customer *orders* on the following page to invoices and split the charges between supply and installation. Figure 8.28 shows how the first completed invoice for the East Motor Inn on the following page should look.

Figure 8.28   **Invoice: East Motor Inn**

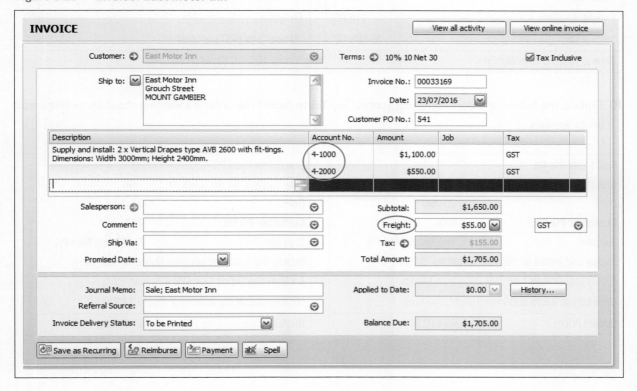

The Blinds Man Pty Ltd		The Blinds Man Pty Ltd	
Date:	23 July	Date:	23 July
Tax Invoice No.:	33169	**Tax Invoice No.:**	33170
Supplied to:	East Motor Inn P/L	Supplied to:	Grandview Hotel P/L
Details: Customer PO 541		Details: Customer PO 749	
Supply of Blinds:	$1 100.00	Supply of Blinds:	$990.00
Installation:	550.00	Installation:	330.00
Freight:	55.00	Freight:	66.00
Invoice Total (GST Included):	$1 705.00	Invoice Total (GST Included):	$1 386.00
Terms: 10% 10 days/Net 30.		Terms: 10% 10 days/Net 30.	

The Blinds Man Pty Ltd		The Blinds Man Pty Ltd	
Date:	23 July	Date:	23 July
Tax Invoice No.:	33171	**Tax Invoice No.:**	33172
Supplied to:	Lakeview Apartments P/L	Supplied to:	Meriton Holdings P/L
Details: Customer PO 306		Details: Customer PO 559	
Supply of Blinds:	$4 400.00	Supply of Blinds:	$660.00
Installation:	550.00	Installation:	330.00
Freight:	110.00	Freight:	66.00
Invoice Total (GST Included):	$5 060.00	Invoice Total (GST Included):	$1 056.00
Terms: 10% 10 days/Net 30.		Terms: 10% 10 days/Net 30.	

10 Process the following orders accepting quotes. Say **Yes** to record the order if a warning about exceeding credit limits appears.

East Motor Inn P/L	
Grouch Street, Mount Gambier, SA 5290	
Date:	23 July
Customer PO No.:	583
Supplier:	The Blinds Man P/L
Supply and install as per your Quote No. 33173	
5 x Vertical Drapes type AVB 2600 with fittings.	
Dimensions: Width 3000mm; Height 2400mm.	
Quoted Price:	$3 410.00

Grandview Hotel P/L	
Lake Terrace, Mount Gambier, SA 5290	
Date:	23 July
Customer PO No.:	768
Supplier:	The Blinds Man P/L
Supply and install as per your Quote No. 33174	
4 x Venetian Blinds type LVB 420 with fittings.	
Dimensions: Width 2400mm; Height 1800mm.	
Quoted Price:	$1 848.00

<table>
<tr><td>Lakeview Apartments P/L</td><td></td></tr>
<tr><td colspan="2">6 Helen Street, Mount Gambier, SA 5290</td></tr>
<tr><td>Date:</td><td>23 July</td></tr>
<tr><td>**Customer PO No.:**</td><td>322</td></tr>
<tr><td>Supplier:</td><td>The Blinds Man P/L</td></tr>
<tr><td colspan="2">Supply and install as per your Quote No. 33175</td></tr>
<tr><td colspan="2">2 x Sunscreen Rollers type RB 175 with fittings.</td></tr>
<tr><td colspan="2">Dimensions: Width 3600mm; Length 2400mm.</td></tr>
<tr><td>Quoted Price:</td><td>$2 024.00</td></tr>
</table>

<table>
<tr><td>Meriton Holdings P/L</td><td></td></tr>
<tr><td colspan="2">Jubilee Highway, Mount Gambier, SA 5290</td></tr>
<tr><td>Date:</td><td>23 July</td></tr>
<tr><td>**Customer PO No.:**</td><td>571</td></tr>
<tr><td>Supplier:</td><td>The Blinds Man P/L</td></tr>
<tr><td colspan="2">Supply and install as per your Quote No. 33176</td></tr>
<tr><td colspan="2">4 x Holland Blinds type HB 501 with fittings.</td></tr>
<tr><td colspan="2">Dimensions: Width 2000mm; Height 3000mm.</td></tr>
<tr><td>Quoted Price:</td><td>$1 188.00</td></tr>
</table>

11 Record receipt of the following payments from customers:

<table>
<tr><td>Date:</td><td>25/7/16</td></tr>
<tr><td>**Receipt No.**</td><td>026</td></tr>
<tr><td>Received from:</td><td>East Motor Inn</td></tr>
<tr><td>Details:</td><td></td></tr>
<tr><td colspan="2">*All invoices after prompt payment discount*</td></tr>
<tr><td>Cash Received:</td><td>$1 534.50</td></tr>
<tr><td>**Dissection**</td><td></td></tr>
<tr><td>Discount:</td><td>155.00</td></tr>
<tr><td>GST Component:</td><td>15.50</td></tr>
<tr><td>Discount Total:</td><td>170.50</td></tr>
</table>

<table>
<tr><td>Date:</td><td>25/7/16</td></tr>
<tr><td>**Receipt No.**</td><td>027</td></tr>
<tr><td>Received from:</td><td>Grandview Hotel P/L</td></tr>
<tr><td>Details:</td><td></td></tr>
<tr><td colspan="2">*All invoices after prompt payment discount*</td></tr>
<tr><td>Cash Received:</td><td>$1 247.40</td></tr>
<tr><td>**Dissection**</td><td></td></tr>
<tr><td>Discount:</td><td>126.00</td></tr>
<tr><td>GST Component:</td><td>12.60</td></tr>
<tr><td>Discount Total:</td><td>138.60</td></tr>
</table>

<table>
<tr><td>Date:</td><td>25/7/16</td></tr>
<tr><td>**Receipt No.**</td><td>028</td></tr>
<tr><td>Received from:</td><td>Lakeview Apartments</td></tr>
<tr><td>Details:</td><td></td></tr>
<tr><td colspan="2">*All invoices after prompt payment discount*</td></tr>
<tr><td>Cash Received:</td><td>$4 554</td></tr>
<tr><td>**Dissection**</td><td></td></tr>
<tr><td>Discount:</td><td>460.00</td></tr>
<tr><td>GST Component:</td><td>40.60</td></tr>
<tr><td>Discount Total:</td><td>500.60</td></tr>
</table>

<table>
<tr><td>Date:</td><td>25/7/16</td></tr>
<tr><td>**Receipt No.**</td><td>029</td></tr>
<tr><td>Received from:</td><td>Meriton Holdings</td></tr>
<tr><td>Details:</td><td></td></tr>
<tr><td colspan="2">*All invoices after prompt payment discount*</td></tr>
<tr><td>Cash Received:</td><td>$950.40</td></tr>
<tr><td>**Dissection**</td><td></td></tr>
<tr><td>Discount:</td><td>96.00</td></tr>
<tr><td>GST Component:</td><td>9.60</td></tr>
<tr><td>DiscountTotal:</td><td>105.60</td></tr>
</table>

12 Change the customer orders to invoices and split up the charges into their appropriate income accounts:

The Blinds Man Pty Ltd	
Date:	30 July
Tax Invoice No.:	33173
Supplied to:	East Motor Inn P/L
Details: Customer PO 583	
Supply of Blinds:	$2 750.00
Installation:	550.00
Freight:	110.00
Invoice Total (GST Included):	$3 410.00
Terms: 10% 10 days/Net 30.	

The Blinds Man Pty Ltd	
Date:	30 July
Tax Invoice No.:	33174
Supplied to:	Grandview Hotel P/L
Details: Customer PO 768	
Supply of Blinds:	$1 320.00
Installation:	440.00
Freight:	88.00
Invoice Total (GST Included):	$1 848.00
Terms: 10% 10 days/Net 30.	

The Blinds Man Pty Ltd	
Date:	30 July
Tax Invoice No.:	33175
Supplied to:	Lakeview Apartments P/L
Details: Customer PO 322	
Supply of Blinds:	$1 760.00
Installation:	220.00
Freight:	44.00
Invoice Total (GST Included):	$2 024.00
Terms: 10% 10 days/Net 30.	

The Blinds Man Pty Ltd	
Date:	30 July
Tax Invoice No.:	33176
Supplied to:	Meriton Holdings P/L
Details: Customer PO 571	
Supply of Blinds:	$880.00
Installation:	220.00
Freight:	88.00
Invoice Total (GST Included):	$1 188.00
Terms: 10% 10 days/Net 30.	

13 Produce the following reports for your records:

• Aged Receivables [Summary] as at 31 July. See Figure 8.29.
• Sales Register Detail [All Sales] for July. See Figure 8.30.
• Sales Register Detail [All Sales] for July *for quotes only*. Use the report you produced above, but change the Sales Status filter to Quotes and refresh by clicking the green arrow. See Figures 8.31 and 8.32.

Figure 8.29   Aged Receivables [Summary]: The Blinds Man

The Blinds Man
21 Penola Rd
Mount Gambier SA 5290
Aged Receivables [Summary]
July 2016

Name	Total Due	0–30	31–60	61–90	90+
East Motor Inn	$3 410.00	$3 410.00	$0.00	$0.00	$0.00
Grandview Hotel P/L	$1 848.00	$1 848.00	$0.00	$0.00	$0.00
Lakeview Apartments P/L	$2 024.00	$2 024.00	$0.00	$0.00	$0.00
Meriton Holdings P/L	$1 188.00	$1 188.00	$0.00	$0.00	$0.00
Total:	$8 470.00	$8 470.00	$0.00	$0.00	$0.00
Ageing Percent:		100.0%	0.0%	0.0%	0.0%

Figure 8.30   Sales Register Detail [All Sales]: The Blinds Man

The Blinds Man
21 Penola Rd
Mount Gambier SA 5290
Sales Register Detail [All Sales]
July 2016

Date	Invoice No.	Customer PO No.	Customer Name	Amount	Amount Due	Status
2/07/2016	00033161		East Motor Inn	$1 705.00		Quote
2/07/2016	00033162		Grandview Hotel P/L	$1 386.00		Quote
2/07/2016	00033163		Lakeview Apartments P/L	$5 060.00		Quote
2/07/2016	00033164		Meriton Holdings P/L	$1 056.00		Quote
5/07/2016	00033165		East Motor Inn	($110.00)	$0.00	Closed
5/07/2016	00033166		Grandview Hotel P/L	($49.50)	$0.00	Closed
5/07/2016	00033167		Lakeview Apartments P/L	($165.00)	$0.00	Closed
5/07/2016	00033168		Meriton Holdings P/L	($115.50)	$0.00	Closed
23/07/2016	00033169	541	East Motor Inn	$1 705.00	$0.00	Closed
23/07/2016	00033170	749	Grandview Hotel P/L	$1 386.00	$0.00	Closed
23/07/2016	00033171	306	Lakeview Apartments P/L	$5 060.00	$0.00	Closed
23/07/2016	00033172	559	Meriton Holdings P/L	$1 056.00	$0.00	Closed
12/07/2016	00033173		East Motor Inn	$3 410.00		Quote
30/07/2016	00033173	583	East Motor Inn	$3 410.00	$3 410.00	Open
12/07/2016	00033174		Grandview Hotel P/L	$1 848.00		Quote
30/07/2016	00033174	768	Grandview Hotel P/L	$1 848.00	$1 848.00	Open
12/07/2016	00033175		Lakeview Apartments P/L	$2 024.00		Quote
30/07/2016	00033175	322	Lakeview Apartments P/L	$2 024.00	$2 024.00	Open
12/07/2016	00033176		Meriton Holdings P/L	$1 188.00		Quote
30/07/2016	00033176	571	Meriton Holdings P/L	$1 188.00	$1 188.00	Open
25/07/2016	00033177		East Motor Inn	($170.50)	$0.00	Closed
25/07/2016	00033178		Grandview Hotel	($138.60)	$0.00	Closed
25/07/2016	00033179		Lakeview Apartments P/L	($506.00)	$0.00	Closed
25/07/2016	00033180		Meriton Holdings P/L	($105.60)	$0.00	Closed
			Total:	**$33 993.30**	**$8 470.00**	

Figure 8.31   Sales Register Detail [All Sales] report: Sales Status Quotes

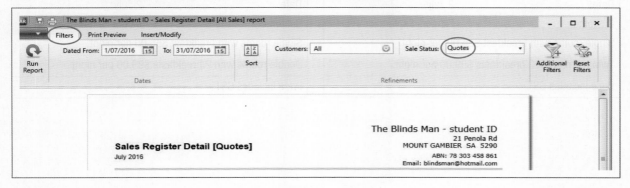

235

Figure 8.32   **Sales Register Detail [Quotes]: The Blinds Man**

The Blinds Man
21 Penola Rd
Mount Gambier SA 5290
Sales Register Detail [Quotes]
July 2016

Date	Invoice No.	Customer PO No.	Customer Name	Amount	Amount Due	Status
2/07/2016	00033161		East Motor Inn	$1 705.00		Quote
2/07/2016	00033162		Grandview Hotel P/L	$1 386.00		Quote
2/07/2016	00033163		Lakeview Apartments P/L	$5 060.00		Quote
2/07/2016	00033164		Meriton Holdings P/L	$1 056.00		Quote
12/07/2016	00033173		East Motor Inn	$3 410.00		Quote
12/07/2016	00033174		Grandview Hotel P/L	$1 848.00		Quote
12/07/2016	00033175		Lakeview Apartments P/L	$2 024.00		Quote
12/07/2016	00033176		Meriton Holdings P/L	$1 188.00		Quote
			Total:	**$17 677.00**	**$0.00**	

Practice

ARKAROOLA B&B

1   In MYOB AccountRight 2016, open the **8.3 Arkaroola B&B.myox** data file from the Chapter 8 folder in your start-up files, or continue with your own Arkaroola B&B data file.

2   Record the following quotes given to customers in July 2016. Enter the nightly cost in the Amount column so you can use the Recurring Transaction feature:

Arkaroola B&B P/L	
21 Pirie Street, Arkaroola, SA 5710	
ABN 21 221 402 201	
Quote Number:	0001
Date:	2 July
Customer:	Flinders Exploration P/L
Single rooms with breakfast $55.00 per night.	
Twin rooms with 2 breakfasts $99.00 per night.	
Price includes GST	

Arkaroola B&B P/L	
21 Pirie Street, Arkaroola, SA 5710	
ABN 21 221 402 201	
Quote Number:	0002
Date:	2 July
Customer:	Mount Painter Tours P/L
Single rooms with breakfast $55.00 per night.	
Double rooms with 2 breakfasts $99.00 per night.	
Price includes GST	

3 Process the following orders accepting quotes:

Flinders Exploration P/L	Mount Painter Tours P/L
266 Hindley Street, Adelaide, SA 5000	66 North Terrrace, Adelaide, SA 5000
Date: 5 July	Date: 5 July
Customer PO No.: 662	**Customer PO No.:** 205
Supplier: Arkaroola B&B P/L	Supplier: Arkaroola B&B P/L
Please supply:	Please supply:
3 single rooms; in 5 July, out 10 July.	1 single room; in 5 July, out 8 July.
3 twin rooms; in 5 July, out 10 July.	5 double rooms; in 5 July, out 8 July.
As per your quote no. 0001	As per your quote no. 0002

Remember This

Not all of the line items get allocated to the same income account.

4 Change the customer orders to invoices and itemise the charges as shown below:

Arkaroola B&B P/L	Arkaroola B&B P/L
Date: 10 July	Date: 10 July
Tax Invoice No.: 00003	**Tax Invoice No.:** 00004
Supplied to: Flinders Exploration P/L	Supplied to: Mount Painter Tours P/L
Details: Customer PO 662 $825.00	Details: Customer PO 205
3 Singles x 5 nights: 1 485.00	1 Single x 3 nights: $165.00
3 Twins x 5 nights: 247.50	5 Doubles x 3 nights: 1 485.00
45 packed lunches @ $5.50: $2 557.50	39 packed lunches @ $5.50: 214.50
Invoice Total (GST Included):	Invoice Total (GST Included): $1 864.50
Terms: 10% 10 days/Net 30..	Terms: 10% 10 days/Net 30.

5 Process the following orders for accommodation:

Flinders Exploration P/L	Mount Painter Tours P/L
266 Hindley Street, Adelaide, SA 5000	66 North Terrace, Adelaide, SA 5000
Date: 12 July	Date: 12 July
Customer PO No.: 680	**Customer PO No.:** 214
Supplier: Arkaroola B&B P/L	Supplier: Arkaroola B&B P/L
Please supply:	Please supply:
3 single rooms; in 12 July, out 17 July.	3 single rooms; in 12 July, out 18 July.
4 twin rooms; in 12 July, out 17 July.	3 double rooms; in 12 July, out 18 July
As per your quote no. 0001	As per your quote no. 0002

6 Record receipt of the following payments from customers:

Date:	15/7/16
Receipt No.	326
Received from:	Flinders Exploration
Details:	
All invoices after prompt payment discount	
Cash Received:	$2 301.75
Dissection	
Discount:	232.50
GST Component:	23.25
Discount Total:	255.75

Date:	15/7/16
Receipt No.	327
Received from:	Mt Painter Tours
Details:	
All invoices after prompt payment discount	
Cash Received:	$1 678.05
Dissection	
Discount:	169.50
GST Component:	16.95
Discount Total:	186.45

7 Change the customer orders to invoices and itemise the charges as shown below:

Arkaroola B&B P/L	
Date:	17 July
Tax Invoice No.:	00005
Supplied to:	Flinders Exploration P/L
Details: Customer PO 680	
3 Singles x 5 nights:	$825.00
4 Twins x 5 nights:	1 980.00
55 packed lunches @ $5.50:	302.50
Invoice Total (GST Included):	$3 107.50
Terms: 10% 10 days/Net 30.	

Arkaroola B&B P/L	
Date:	17 July
Tax Invoice No.:	00006
Supplied to :	Mount Painter Tours P/L
Details: Customer PO 214	
3 Singles x 6 nights:	$990.00
3 Doubles x 6 nights:	1 782.00
40 packed lunches @ $5.50:	220.00
Invoice Total (GST Included):	$2 992.00
Terms: 10% 10 days/Net 30.	

8 Process the following orders for accommodation:

Flinders Exploration P/L	
266 Hindley Street, Adelaide, SA 5000	
Date:	19 July
Customer PO No.:	702
Supplier:	Arkaroola B&B P/L
Please supply:	
1 single room; in 19 July, out 24 July.	
4 twin rooms; in 19 July, out 24 July.	
As per your quote no. 0001	

Mount Painter Tours P/L	
66 North Terrace, Adelaide, SA 5000	
Date:	19 July
Customer PO No.:	226
Supplier:	Arkaroola B&B P/L
Please supply:	
1 single room; in 19 July, out 24 July.	
5 double rooms; in 19 July, out 24 July.	
As per your quote no. 0002	

9 Record receipt of the following payments from customers:

Date:	22/7/16
Receipt No.	328
Received from:	Flinders Exploration
Details:	
All invoices after prompt payment discount	
Cash Received:	$2 796.75
Dissection	
Discount:	282.50
GST Component:	28.25
Discount Total:	310.75

Date:	22/7/16
Receipt No.	329
Received from:	Mt Painter Tours
Details:	
All invoices after prompt payment discount	
Cash Received:	$2 692.80
Dissection	
Discount:	272.00
GST Component:	27.20
Discount Total:	299.20

10 Change the customer orders to invoices and itemise the charges as shown below:

Arkaroola B&B P/L	
Date:	24 July
Tax Invoice No.:	00009
Supplied to:	Flinders Exploration P/L
Details: Customer PO 702	
1 Single x 5 nights:	$275.00
4 Twins x 5 nights:	1 980.00
45 packed lunches @ $5.50:	247.50
Invoice Total (GST Included):	$2 502.50
Terms: 10% 10 days/Net 30.	

Arkaroola B&B P/L	
Date:	24 July
Tax Invoice No.:	00010
Supplied to:	Mount Painter Tours P/L
Details: Customer PO 226	
1 Single x 5 nights:	$275.00
5 Doubles x 5 nights:	2 475.00
55 packed lunches @ $5.50:	302.50
Invoice Total (GST Included):	$3 052.50
Terms: 10% 10 days/Net 30.	

11 Produce the following reports for your records:

- Aged Receivables [Summary] as at 31 July. See Figure 8.33.
- Sales Register Detail [All Sales] for July. See Figure 8.34.

Figure 8.33 **Aged Receivables [Summary]: Arkaroola B&B**

Arkaroola B&B P/L
21 Pirie Street
Arkaroola SA 5710
Aged Receivables [Summary]
As of 31/07/2016

Name	Total Due	0–30	31–60	61–90	90+
Flinders Exploration	$2 502.50	$2 502.50	$0.00	$0.00	$0.00
Mount Painter Tours	$3 052.50	$3 052.50	$0.00	$0.00	$0.00
Total:	**$5 555.00**	**$5 555.00**	**$0.00**	**$0.00**	**$0.00**
Ageing Percent:		**100.00%**	**0.00%**	**0.00%**	**0.00%**

Figure 8.34 **Sales Register Detail [All Sales]: Arkaroola B&B**

Arkaroola B&B P/L
21 Pirie Street
Arkaroola SA 5710
Sales Register Detail [All Sales]
July 2016

Date	Invoice No.	Customer PO No.	Customer Name	Amount	Amount Due	Status
2/07/2016	00000001		Flinders Exploration	$154.00		Quote
2/07/2016	00000002		Mount Painter Tours	$154.00		Quote
10/07/2016	00000003	662	Flinders Exploration	$2 557.50	$0.00	Closed
10/07/2016	00000004	205	Mount Painter Tours	$1 864.50	$0.00	Closed
17/07/2016	00000005	680	Flinders Exploration	$3 107.50	$0.00	Closed
17/07/2016	00000006	214	Mount Painter Tours	$2 992.00	$0.00	Closed
15/07/2016	00000007		Flinders Exploration	($255.75)	$0.00	Closed
15/07/2016	00000008		Mount Painter Tours	($186.45)	$0.00	Closed
24/07/2016	00000009	702	Flinders Exploration	$2 502.50	$2 502.50	Open
22/07/2016	00000009		Flinders Exploration	($310.75)	$0.00	Closed
24/07/2016	00000010	226	Mount Painter Tours	$3 052.50	$3 052.50	Open
22/07/2016	00000010		Mount Painter Tours	($299.20)	$0.00	Closed
			Total:	**$15 332.35**	**$5 555.00**	

Summary

◆ All dealings with Accounts Receivable (trade debtors) take place in the Sales module in MYOB.

◆ The Sales module is the subsidiary Accounts Receivable Ledger and is linked to the Accounts Receivable control account in the general ledger.

◆ Each transaction in the Sales module automatically updates the general ledger control account.

◆ MYOB uses electronic cards to keep details about the customers of the business. These cards can be very brief, containing only the name of the customer, or can be very detailed and contain selling, payment, contact and history information.

◆ A quote is an offer to a customer to supply goods or services at a certain price in response to an invitation from the customer to do so.

◆ An order from a customer is a formal request to supply services or goods, and is the way a successful quote is accepted.

◆ An invoice is generated when goods or services have been supplied and, until payment has been made, this invoice is an Account Receivable.

◆ An adjustment note can be generated when goods are returned by a customer or when a service has been unsatisfactory, and this has the effect of reducing the Accounts Receivable.

◆ Errors are located in the Transaction Journals which are accessed directly from the Command Centre. Here, the zoom arrow brings up the original transaction, which can be deleted or corrected.

◆ A wide variety of reports are available in the Sales module to give detailed information on the operation of the business.

◆ The Sales & Receivables Journal is a detailed record of each transaction that has taken place within the Sales module over a specific period of time.

Assessment

Holmes & Kelly

1 In MYOB AccountRight 2016., create a new company data file based on the following information using *AccountRight Standard Australian* version.

> **Holmes & Kelly Pty Ltd**
> 359 Park Street,
> Brunswick VIC 3056
> ABN 42 233 502 133
>
> **Phone:** (03) 3380 6701
> **Current** Financial **Year:** 2018
> **Conversion Month:** July
> **Industry Classification:** Service
> **Main Business Activity:** Barrister & Solicitor – Civil Court Cases

Click the **Easy Setup Assistant** once you have finished the company file setup. Use the third activation option – **I use this file for evaluation purposes**.

2 Change the following names in the list of accounts:

	Account type	Account no.	New account name	Tax code
Edit	Bank	1-1110	Cheque Account	N-T
Edit	Acc. Receivable	1-1310	Accounts Receivable	N-T
Edit	Acc Payable	2-1510	Accounts Payable	N-T
Edit	Equity	3-1000	Judy Holmes (change to header account)	
Add	Equity	3-1100	Judy Holmes Capital	N-T
Add	Equity	3-1200	Judy Holmes Drawings	N-T
Edit	Equity	3-2000	Josephine Kelly (change to header account)	
Add	Equity	3-2100	Josephine Kelly Capital	N-T
Add	Equity	3-2200	Josephine Kelly Drawings	N-T
Edit	Income	4-1000	Fees Judy Holmes	GST
Edit	Income	4-2000	Fees Josephine Kelly	GST
Add	Income	4-9000	Discounts Received	GST
Add	Cost of Sales	5-1000	Reimbursable Costs	GST
Add	Cost of Sales	5-9000	Discounts Given	GST

3 Change the linked accounts:

Type	Terms	From	To
sales	I give discounts for early payment	6-3300 Discounts Given	5-9000 Discounts Given
Purchases	I take discounts for early payment		4-9000 Discounts Received

4 Then make the following changes:

	Account type	Account no.	New account name	Tax code
Delete	Expense	6-3300	Discounts Given	
Delete	Expense	6-2800	Waste Removal	
Delete	Expense	6-4500	Directors Fees	

5 Insert the following account opening balances:

Trial Balance as at 30/06/17			
Account no.	Account name	Debit	Credit
1-1110	Cheque Account	15 000.00	
1-1310	Accounts Receivable	11 000.00	
1-2210	Office Equipment At Cost	5 000.00	
1-2410	Motor Vehicle At Cost	32 000.00	
1-2420	Acc. Depr. Motor Vehicle		2 000.00
2-1210	GST Collected		1 000.00
3-1100	Judy Holmes Capital		35 000.00
3-1200	Judy Holmes Drawings	5 000.00	
3-2100	Josephine Kelly Capital		35 000.00
3-2200	Josephine Kelly Drawings	5 000.00	
	Totals	87 000.00	87 000.00

6 Create cards for the following customers:

Name:	Baird Investments
Card ID:	CUS 001
Address:	709 High Street, Armadale VIC 3143
Phone:	(03) 9509 3242
Email:	billbaird@telstra.com
Contact:	Bill Baird
Terns:	10% 10 days/Net 30
Income Account:	4-1000
Credit Limit:	$10 000.00

Name:	Mull Holdings
Card ID:	CUS 002
Address:	31 Bodley Street, Beaumaris VIC 3193
Phone:	(03) 9589 3261
Email	david@mullhold.com.au
Contact:	David Haines
Terns:	10% 10 days/Net 30
Income Account:	4-2000
Credit Limit:	$10 000.00

Name:	Sky Investments
Card ID:	CUS 003
Address:	66 Lygon Street, Carlton VIC 3053
Phone:	(03) 9662 1388
Email:	lachlan@aso.net.au
Contact:	Lachlan O'Connor
Terns:	10% 10 days/Net 30
Income Account:	4-1000
Credit Limit:	$10 000.00

Name:	Wild Fitness
Card ID:	CUS 004
Address:	45 Foster Street, Dandenong VIC 3175
Phone:	(03) 9792 9757
Email:	jane@wildfit.com.au
Contact:	Jane Harvey
Terns:	10% 10 days/Net 30
Income Account:	4-2000
Credit Limit:	$10 000.00

7 Record the historical customer balances for June 2017 in MYOB.

Holmes & Kelly Pty Ltd

Date:	30 June
Tax Invoice No.:	30515
Client:	Baird Investments
Details:	
Legal advice	$550.00
Legal investigation	$1 650.00
Invoice Total (including GST):	$2 200.00
Terms: 10% 10/ Net 30	

Holmes & Kelly Pty Ltd

Date :	30 June
Tax Invoice No.:	30516
Client:	Mull Holdings
Details:	
Civil Court appearance	$5 280.00
Invoice Total (including GST):	$5 280.00
Terms: 10% 10/ Net 30	

Holmes & Kelly Pty Ltd

Date:	30 June
Tax Invoice No.:	30517
Client:	Sky Investments
Details:	
Conveyancing	$1 650.00
Invoice Total (including GST:	$1 650.00
Terms: 10% 10 days/Net 30.	

Holmes & Kelly Pty Ltd

Date:	30 June
Tax Invoice No.:	30518
Client:	Wild Fitness
Details:	
Civil Court appearance	$1 870.00
Invoice Total (including GST):	$1 870.00
Terms: 10% 10 days/Net 30.	

8   Record invoices for the following services to clients using the default income accounts:

Holmes & Kelly Pty Ltd	
Date:	8 July
Tax Invoice No.:	30519
Client:	Baird Investments
Details:	
Legal advice	$550.00
Legal investigation	$1 650.00
Invoice Total (including GST):	$2 200.00
Terms: 10% 10/ Net 30	

Holmes & Kelly Pty Ltd	
Date :	8 July
Tax Invoice No.:	30520
Client:	Mull Holdings
Details:	
Civil Court appearance	$4 400.00
Invoice Total (including GST):	$4 400.00
Terms: 10% 10/ Net 30	

Holmes & Kelly Pty Ltd	
Date:	8 July
Tax Invoice No.:	30521
Client:	Sky Investments
Details:	
Conveyancing	$1 650.00
Invoice Total (including GST):	$1 650.00
Terms: 10% 10 days/Net 30.	

Holmes & Kelly Pty Ltd	
Date:	8 July
Tax Invoice No.:	30522
Client:	Wild Fitness
Details:	
Civil Court appearance	$3 300.00
Invoice Total (including GST):	$3 300.00
Terms: 10% 10 days/Net 30.	

9   Record receipt of the following payments from clients:

Date:	9/7/17
Receipt No.	126
Received from:	Baird Investments
Details:	
All invoices after prompt payment discount	
Cash Received:	$3 960.00
Dissection	
Discount:	400.00
GST Component:	40.00
Discount Total:	440.00

Date:	9/7/17
Receipt No.	127
Received from:	Mull Holdings
Details:	
Invoice 30516 after prompt payment discount	
Cash Received:	$4 752.00
Dissection	
Discount:	480.00
GST Component:	48.00
Discount Total:	528.00

Date:	9/7/17
Receipt No.	128
Received from:	Sky Investments
Details:	
All invoices after prompt payment discount	
Cash Received:	$2 970.00
Dissection	
Discount:	300.00
GST Component:	30.00
Discount Total:	330.00

Date:	9/7/17
Receipt No.	129
Received from:	Wild Fitness
Details:	
All invoices after prompt payment discount	
Cash Received:	$4 653.00
Dissection	
Discount:	470.00
GST Component:	47.00
Discount Total:	517.00

10 Record the following adjustment note and apply to the appropriate invoices:

Holmes & Kelly Pty Ltd	
Date:	12 July
Adjustment Note No.	Adj 758
Client:	Mull Holdings
Details:	
Special allowance	
Civil Court appearance discount on invoice 30520	
Adjustment Total (including GST):	−$550.00
	−$550.00

11 Record invoices for the following services to clients:

Holmes & Kelly Pty Ltd	
Date:	16 July
Tax Invoice No.	30530
Client:	Baird Investments
Details:	
Legal representation	$3 080.00
Invoice Total (including GST):	$3 080.00
Terms: 10% 10 days/Net 30.	

Holmes & Kelly Pty Ltd	
Date:	16 July
Tax Invoice No.:	30531
Client:	Mull Holdings
Details:	
Civil Court appearance	$1 320.00
Invoice Total (including GST):	$1 320.00
Terms: 10% 10 days/Net 30.	

Holmes & Kelly Pty Ltd	
Date:	16 July
Tax Invoice No.:	30532
Client:	Sky Investments
Details:	
Conveyancing	$3 300.00
Invoice Total (including GST):	$3 300.00
Terms: 10% 10 days/Net 30.	

Holmes & Kelly Pty Ltd	
Date:	16 July
Tax Invoice No.:	30533
Client:	Wild Fitness
Details:	
Civil Court appearance	$4 180.00
Invoice Total (including GST):	$4 180.00
Terms: 10% 10 days/Net 30.	

12 Record receipt of the following payments from clients. Discounts have not been included so you need to calculate the discounts yourself where appropriate:

Date:	16/7/17
Receipt No.	130
Received from:	Baird Investments
Details:	
All invoices after prompt payment discount where appropriate	
Cash Received:	$2 772.00
Dissection	
Discount:	
GST Component:	
Discount Total:	

Date:	16/7/17
Receipt No.	131
Received from:	Mull Holdings
Details:	
All invoices after prompt payment discount where appropriate	
Cash Received:	$4 653.00
Dissection	
Discount:	
GST Component:	
Discount Total:	

Date:	16/7/17
Receipt No.	132
Received from:	Sky Investments
Details:	
All invoices after prompt payment discount where appropriate	
Cash Received:	$2 970.00
Dissection	
Discount:	
GST Component:	
Discount Total:	

Date:	16/7/17
Receipt No.	133
Received from:	Wild Fitness
Details:	
All invoices after prompt payment discount where appropriate	
Cash Received:	$3 762.00
Dissection	
Discount:	
GST Component:	
Discount Total:	

13 Record invoices for the following services to clients:

Holmes & Kelly Pty Ltd	
Date:	24 July
Tax Invoice No.:	30534
Client:	Baird Investments
Details:	
civil court	$1 100.00
Invoice Total (including GST):	$1 100.00
Terms: 10% 10 days/Net 30.	

Holmes & Kelly Pty Ltd	
Date:	24 July
Tax Invoice No.:	30535
Client:	Mull Holdings
Details:	
Civil Court appearance	$3 135.00
Invoice Total (including GST):	$3 135.00
Terms: 10% 10 days/Net 30.	

Holmes & Kelly Pty Ltd	
Date:	24 July
Tax Invoice No.:	30536
Client:	Sky Investments
Details:	
Legal investigation	$1 375.00
Invoice Total (including GST):	$1 375.00
Terms: 10% 10 days/Net 30.	

Holmes & Kelly Pty Ltd	
Date:	24 July
Tax Invoice No.:	30537
Client:	Wild Fitness
Details:	
Civil Court appearance	$5 225.00
Invoice Total (including GST):	$5 225.00
Terms: 10% 10 days/Net 30.	

14 Record the following adjustments to invoices:

Holmes & Kelly Pty Ltd	
Date:	30 July
Adjustment Note No.	adj 759
Client:	Baird Investments
Details:	
Special allowance	
Assisting in court	−$110.00
Adjustment Total (including GST):	−$110.00

Holmes & Kelly Pty Ltd	
Date:	30 July
Adjustment Note No.:	30550
Client:	Wild Fitness
Details:	
Special allowance	
Civil Court appearance	−$1 045.00
Adjustment Total (including GST):	−$1 045.00

15 Produce the following reports for your records:
   – Aged Receivables [Summary] as at 31 July.
   – Sales Register Detail [All Sales] for July.

INVENTORY

Learning outcomes

By the end of this chapter you will be competent in:

- accessing and operating a computer inventory system linked to a general ledger
- setting up inventory items in accordance with organisational requirements
- setting up opening balances of inventory
- setting minimum quantities to trigger a reordering alert
- processing all inventory and associated transactions
- processing cash sales and cash purchases for inventory through the Sales and Purchases modules
- using the To Do List for reordering inventory when stocks are low
- maintaining the Inventory ledger
- setting up MYOBs inventory Auto-Build feature
- recording stocktakes.

Inventory are goods that have been purchased (or manufactured) for resale. In this chapter, you will learn how MYOB performs all the functions of the periodic and perpetual inventory systems. Purchases and sales of stock can be easily recorded and inventory and cost of sales is accounted for automatically when using the perpetual system.

Basic accounting background

An *inventory* is a list of property that is held for sale in the normal course of business. It can also include items that are in the course of production for sale.

Accounting for inventory is very important in business as the costs associated with inventory relate directly to profit. The total cost of inventory can include the purchase price of the goods, plus expenses relating directly to them, such as freight inwards, import duty and storage.

Profit is measured in segments of time (month, quarter, year, etc.), so inventory and its costs must be similarly measured. In looking at the movement of inventory over a period of time it is the *cost of goods sold* (known in MYOB as *Cost of Sales*) that is important. Two sets of figures are required:

- the cost of goods sold during the current accounting period, which is matched against the income from sales for the same period
- the value of inventory that has not been sold and is to be carried forward to the next accounting period.
  There are two basic ways in which to account for inventory: periodic inventory and perpetual inventory.

Periodic inventory

In a *periodic inventory system*, there are no running balances of the individual inventory items. A physical count of all the items in stock needs to be done (periodically) and the results are noted down. A unit value (or price) is allotted to each item and from this the value of inventory can be ascertained. The cost of goods sold can be obtained from the following formula:

$$\text{Cost of Goods Sold} = (\text{Opening Stock} + \text{Purchases} - \text{Closing Stock})$$

For example:

Opening Stock		$20 000.00
Purchases	+	10 000.00
Subtotal	=	30 000.00
Closing Stock	−	18 000.00
Cost of Goods Sold	=	$12 000.00

To the value of stock on hand at the start of the accounting period (the Opening Stock) we add the cost of goods purchased during the period. A *stocktake* (that is, a physical counting of the stock) at the end of the period gives the value of stock that has not been sold (Closing Stock) and will be carried forward into the next accounting period. This figure is subtracted from the sum of the Opening Stock and Purchases to find the Cost of Goods Sold.

The Closing Stock of one accounting period is the Opening Stock of the next one. Adjusting inventory under a periodic inventory system is explained in Chapter 10.

Perpetual inventory

In the *perpetual inventory system*, an ongoing record is kept in an Inventory ledger of the inward and outward movement of inventory items, with their quantity and book-value both being recorded. The usual form of a manual Inventory ledger is stock cards or loose-leaf sheets in which there is an account for each inventory item. Each receipt of an item would be debited to its account and each issue (or sale) of the item credited, and the balance should reflect the actual quantity and value of the item in inventory.

		IN		OUT		BALANCE	
Date	**Reference (Purchase/Sale No.)**	**Quantity**	**Value**	**Quantity**	**Value**	**Quantity**	**Value**
2016							
June 1	P. 251	15	$300.00			15	$300.00
June 2	S. 310			10	$200.00	5	$100.00
June 4	P. 267	10	$200.00			15	$300.00
June 5	S. 335			4	$80.00	11	$220.00

Inventory Ledger Card
Item: Bomboo Logs
Code: BL500 Australandscapes

A physical stocktake is carried out from time to time and the results compared with the ledger balances, which may need to be adjusted to show the true situation. A particular advantage of the perpetual inventory system is that spot checks can be made of any stock item at any time and comparison with the ledger will reveal discrepancies (from theft, wastage or other causes).

It can be seen from the above that keeping track of inventory can be a very time-consuming activity in a manual accounting system, no matter which method of recording inventory is chosen.

Computers are excellent at keeping track of inventory, as they can automatically increase the quantity and value with each purchase, and decrease these with each sale using the perpetual inventory system.

The steps in creating inventory in MYOB are:

Step 1: Create a Profile for each item that will make up the inventory.
Step 2: Set the Buying and Selling details for each item.
Step 3: Tell MYOB how many of each item are already in stock.
Step 4: Tell MYOB the unit cost of the items already in stock.

Now MYOB will increase inventory with each purchase made using a *Purchase Item Invoice* and decrease it with each sale recorded on a *Sales Item Invoice*, and can be set to give an alert when stocks are low and reordering is required.

A physical stocktake is done periodically (often annually) to keep MYOB's record in line with the actual quantity of items on the ground.

We use the *Item* layout for purchases and sales.

Perpetual inventory

AURORA COFFEE

1   In MYOB AccountRight 2016, open the **9.1 Aurora Coffee.myox** file located in the Chapter 9 folder of your start-up files.

Create an inventory item

2 Create an inventory card for an espresso machine.

Item Number	E-100
Item Name	Espresso Machine
Cost of Sales Account	5-1100
Income Account	4-1100
Inventory Account	1-1320
Tax Code	GST
Minimum Stock Level	20
Primary Supplier	Saeco
Supplier Item No.	ESP072
Default Reorder Quantity	50
Base Selling Price	$22.00
Selling Unit of Measure	Each
Price Includes GST	Yes

Click...

- *Items List* (in the Inventory module). See **Figure 9.1**.
- *New* (at the top left of the Items List screen).
- *Item Number* (type *E-100*). Press the Tab key.
- *Name* (type *Espresso Machine*).
- *I Buy This Item* check-box.
- *I Sell This Item* check-box.
- *I Inventory This Item* check-box.
- *Cost of Sales Account* (select *5-1100*).
- *Income Account for Tracking Sales* (select *4-1100*).
- *Asset Account for Item Inventory* (select *1-1320*). See **Figure 9.2**.

Figure 9.1   Inventory module: Items List

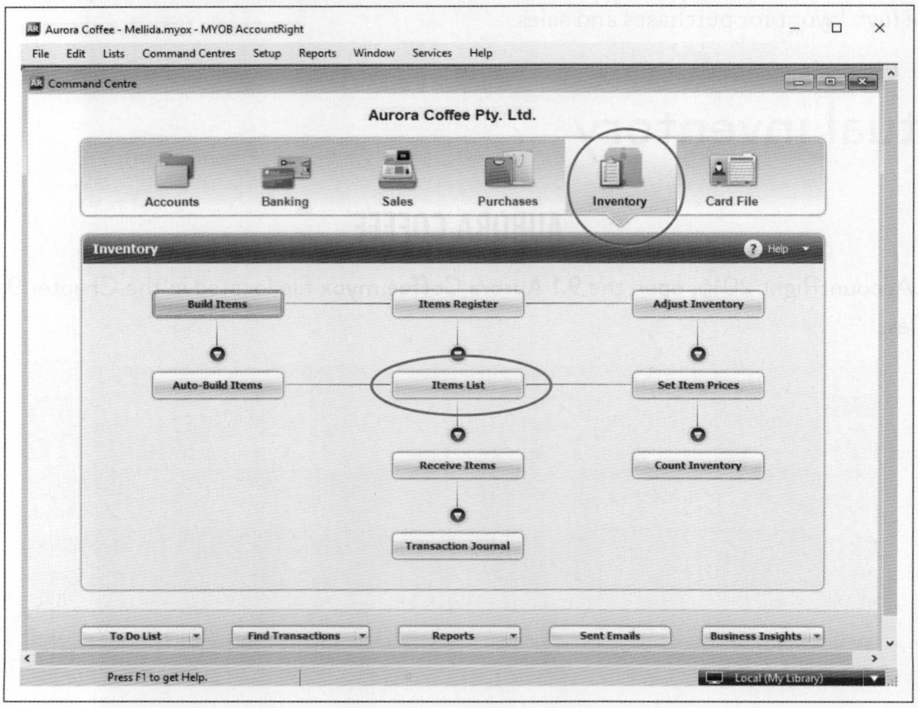

Figure 9.2   **Items List: Profile tab**

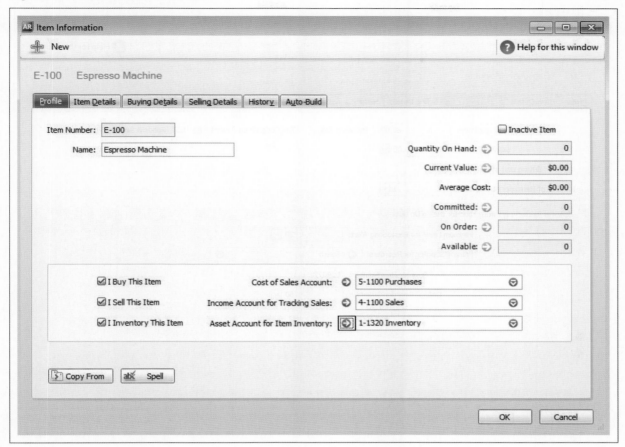

The next step is to set up the buying details, which includes restocking information. This is a useful feature which puts a Stock Alert into your To Do List when MYOB detects that your inventory is getting below a certain point that you have preset. A few mouse clicks and a purchase order is set up to the primary supplier for a predetermined reorder quantity.

Click...

- *Buying Details* tab. See **Figure 9.3.**
- *Buying Unit of Measure* (insert *each*).
- *Number of Items per Buying Unit* (insert *1*).
- *Tax Code When Bought* (select *GST*).
- *Minimum Level for Restocking Alert* (insert *20*).
- *Primary Supplier* (type *Saeco*).
- *Supplier Item Number* (type *ESP072*).
- *Default Reorder Quantity* (insert *50*). See **Figure 9.3.**

Figure 9.3   **Items List: Buying Details tab**

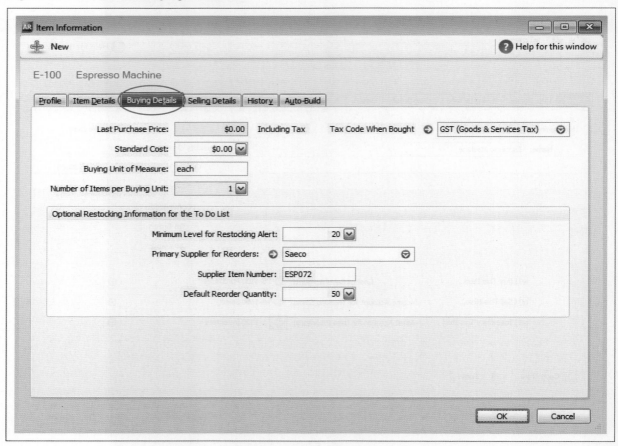

The final step is to set up the selling details.

Click...

- *Selling Details* tab. See Figure 9.4.
- *Base Selling Price* (insert *22.00*).
- *Selling Unit of Measure* (insert *each*).
- *Number of Items per Selling Unit* (insert *1*).
- *Tax Code When Sold* (select *GST*).
- *Inclusive/Exclusive* (select *Prices are Tax Inclusive*). Compare with Figure 9.4.
- *OK*.

Figure 9.4   **Items List: Selling Details tab**

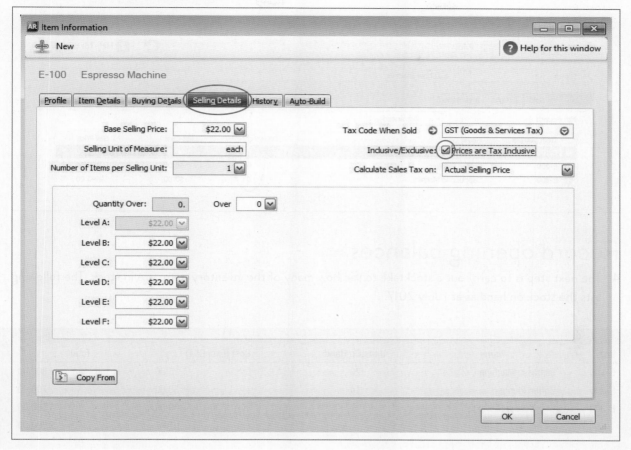

3 Create the following inventory items:

Item Number	E-200		Item Number	E-300
Item Name	Coffee Plunger		Item Name	Cappuccino Machine
Cost of Sales Account	5-1100		Cost of Sales Account	5-1100
Income Account	4-1100		Income Account	4-1100
Inventory Account	1-1320		Inventory Account	1-1320
Tax Code	GST		Tax Code	GST
Minimum Stock Level	10		Minimum Stock Level	5
Primary Supplier	Saeco		Primary Supplier	Saeco
Supplier Item No.	CP242		Supplier Item No.	CAP684
Default Reorder Quantity	30		Default Reorder Quantity	20
Base Selling Price	$66.00		Base Selling Price	$440.00
Selling Unit of Measure	Each		Selling Unit of Measure	Each
Price Includes GST	Yes		Price Includes GST	Yes

Your final items list should look like **Figure 9.5**. Note that there are zero items on hand. Click **Close** to return to the command centre.

Figure 9.5   Items Lists before Opening Balance

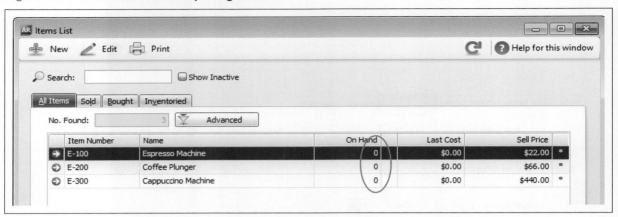

Record opening balances

4 The next step is to carry out a stocktake to see how many of the inventory items are in stock. The following lists the stock on hand as at 1 July 2017.

Item	Name	Units On Hand	Cost (Excl GST)	Total
E-100	Espresso Machine	20	15.00	300.00
E-200	Coffee Plunger	14	50.00	700.00
E-300	Cappuccino Machine	5	300.00	1 500.00
			TOTAL	**2 500.00**

Because you ticked **I Inventory this item** in the Item Cards, the Units on Hand need to be added to MYOB as you cannot record a sale unless MYOB has the item recorded in stock. If you had left the **I Inventory this item** *unticked*, you could record a sale as MYOB is not trying to keep track of the inventory item movement.

Click...

- *Count Inventory* (in the Inventory module).
- Type the *Units on Hand* into the appropriate section in the *Counted* column.
- *Adjust Inventory*. See **Figure 9.6**.
- *Default Adjustment Account* (type *1-1320*). Press *Continue*. See **Figure 9.7**.
- *Continue*. A message comes up saying MYOB thinks you are putting in opening balances.
- *Opening Balances*. The screen that appears explains about Adjusting balances.
- *Continue* (do not click *Adjust Balances*).
- *Date* (type *1/07/17*).
- *Unit Cost* (add each unit cost to the inventory item as per your stocktake list). Compare with **Figure 9.8**.
- *Record*.

Figure 9.6   **Count Inventory window**

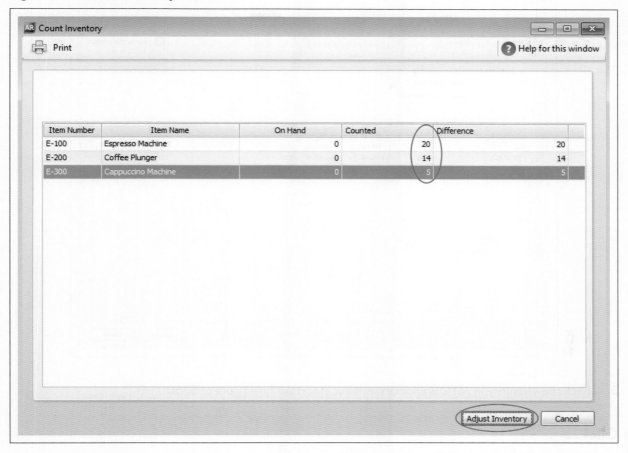

Figure 9.7   **Adjustment Information window**

Figure 9.8   **Adjust Inventory journal**

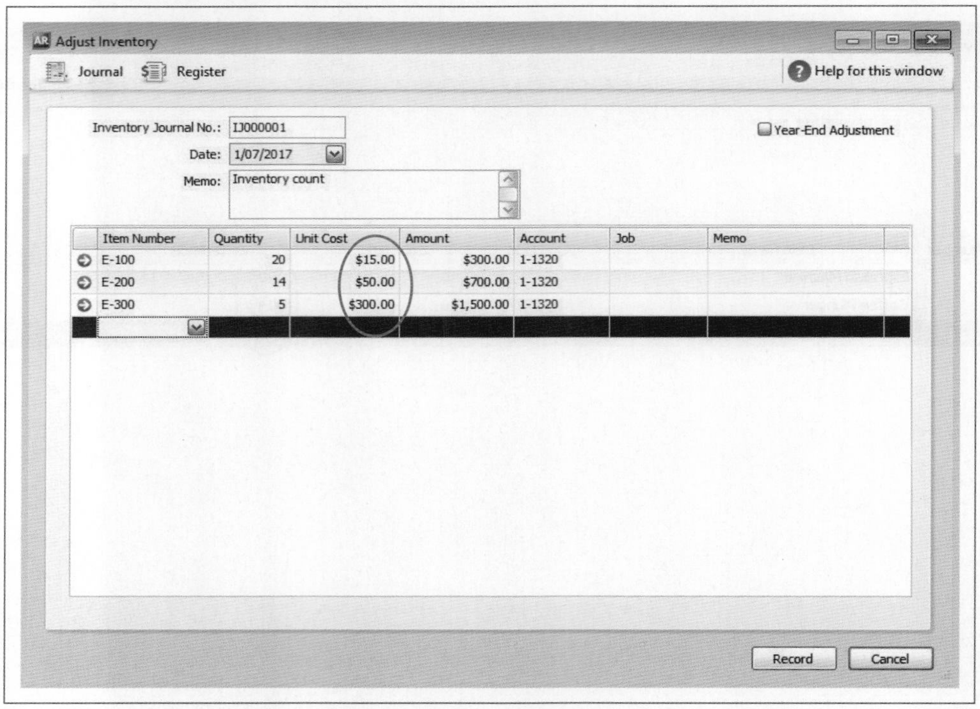

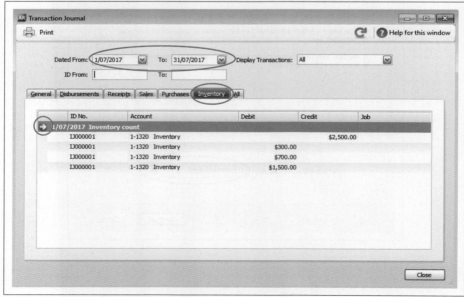

5 Check the inventory in MYOB balances with our stocktake final figure of $2500.00

Click...

- *Transaction Journal* (at the bottom of the Inventory module).
- *Dated from* (type *1/07/17*) and *To* (type *31/07/17*). If you have made any mistakes, you can correct it by clicking the zoom arrow. See Figure 9.9.
- *Close*.

Figure 9.9   **Transaction Journal: Inventory**

Record inventory transactions

6 Sell some inventory items:

Aurora Coffee	
Date:	2 July
Tax Invoice No.:	3310
Supplied to:	Grace Bros
Details: Customer PO 749	
10 x Espresso Machines @ $22.00	$220.00
5 x Coffee Plunber @ $66.00	$330.00
4 x Cappuccino Machines @ $440.00	$880.00
Invoice Total (GST Included):	$1 430.00
Terms: 10% 10 days/Net 30.	

Click...

- *Enter Sales* (in the Sales module).
- Ensure the *Tax Inclusive* box is ticked.
- *Customer* (select *Grace Bros*).
- *Invoice No.* (type *3310*). Press the Tab key.
- *Date* (type *2/07/17*).
- *Customer PO No.* (type *749*).
- *Ship* (insert *10*). Press the tab key four times to activate the Items List.
- *Espresso Machine*. The item price and total cost are automatically inserted.
- *Ship* (insert *5*). Press the Tab key four times to activate the Items list.
- *Coffee Plunger*.
- *Ship* (insert *2*) Press the Tab key four times to activate the Items List.
- *Cappuccino Machine*. Compare with Figure 9.10.
- *Edit* (top menu bar).
- *Recap Transaction*. See Figure 9.11.

Figure 9.10   **Sales: Grace Bros**

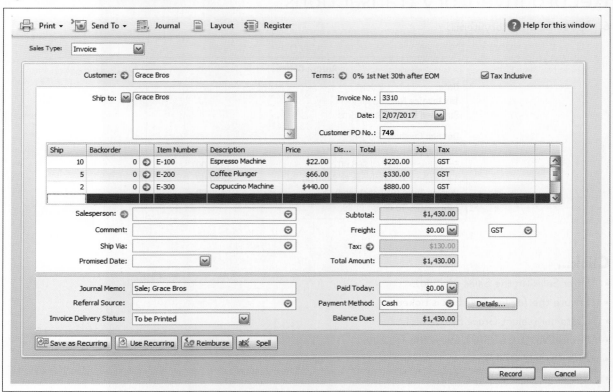

Figure 9.11   **Sales: Grace Bros Recap Transaction**

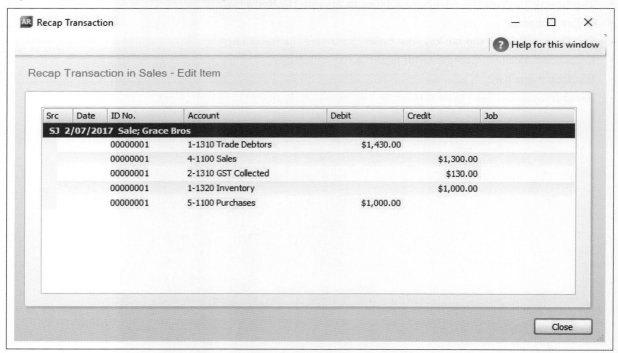

An explanation of the transaction in the general ledger:

- *1-1310 Accounts Receivable* or *Trade Debtors* (an asset) is debited (increased) by the sale price of the goods and the GST.
- *4-1100 Sales* (revenue) is credited (increased) by the sale price of the goods.
- *2-1310 GST Collected* (liability) is credited (increased) by the 10% GST on the sale.
- *5-1100 Purchases* (cost of sales, or expense) is debited (increased) with the purchase price of the goods that are being sold. This is calculated from the unit costs you entered when setting up the inventory items (see page 254). This cost price of items will update automatically in the future with their purchases recorded on item invoices.
- *1-1320 Inventory* (asset) is credited (reduced) by the purchase price of the three items being sold.

This is why

The last two lines of the journal appear because we are using a perpetual inventory system and ticked when setting up the item. In a periodic inventory system, the last two lines would *not* appear in the journal and need to be done manually at the end of the period.

Investigate the accounts

7 We will now investigate how our transactions have affected the accounts.

Click...

- *Close* (when you have understood the recap transaction).
- *Record* (to register the sale).
- *Cancel* (to return to the Command Centre).
- *Find Transactions* (at the base of the window).
- *Account* (tab at top left of the window).
- *Dated From* (type 1/07/17) and *To* (type *31/07/17*).
- *Account #* (select 1-*1320 Inventory*). See Figure 9.12.

Figure 9.12   Find Transaction: Account tab, Inventory

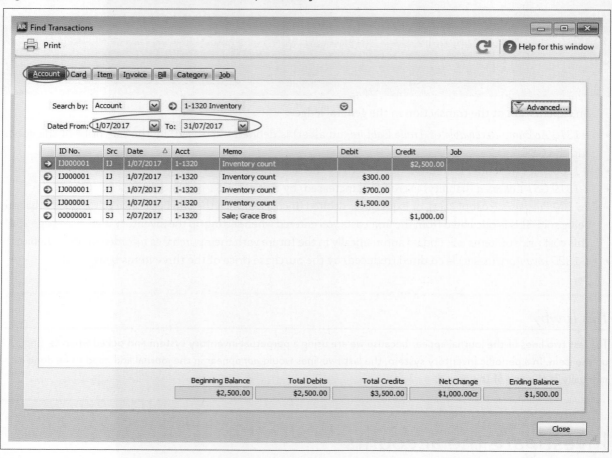

This shows your inventory count (opening balances) as debits of the cost price of the three items, increasing the account, and the sale as credits (also using the cost price) reducing the account.

Click...

- anywhere around the middle of the account name and hit the Delete key on your keyboard.
- *Drop-down arrow* (to select another account).
- *5-1100 Purchases* (scroll down and select it with a click). See Figure 9.13.

Figure 9.13   Find Transaction: Account tab, Purchases

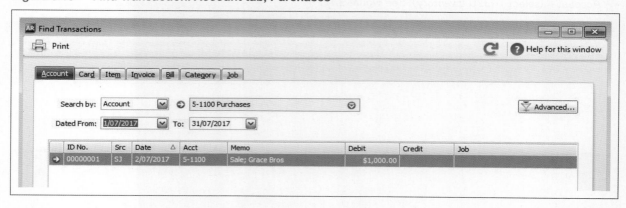

Let's look at the effect of this transaction on the Profit & Loss Statement.

Click...

- *Close* (to return to the Command Centre).
- *Reports* (at base of the window).
- *Accounts* (in the left menu).
- *Profit & Loss Statement*.
- *Dated From* (type *1/07/17*) and *To* (type *31/07/17*).
- *Display*. See Figure 9.14.

Figure 9.14   Profit & Loss statement: Aurora Coffee

Aurora Coffee Pty Ltd
21G The Market Place
Edgeworth David Avenue
Hornsby NSW 2077
Profit & Loss Statement
July 2017

Income		
Gross Receipts or Sales		
Sales	$1 300.00	
Total Income		$1 300.00
Cost of Sales		
Purchases	$1 000.00	
Total Cost of Sales		$1 000.00
Gross Profit		$300.00
Total Expenses		$0.00
Operating Profit		$300.00
Total Other Income		$0.00
Total Other Expenses		$0.00
Net Profit/(Loss)		$300.00

This shows that the gross profit on the transaction was $300.00.

Reordering inventory: Stock Alert

8   When we set up the inventory items we fixed the minimum quantities of each item that we wanted to have in stock and we also selected a *Primary Supplier* (our usual supplier for this item) and a *Default Reorder Quantity* (the quantity of the items we are most likely to order at the one time). See Figure 9.15.

Figure 9.15   Restocking information

261

To use this information and to check on current inventory levels:

Click...

- *To Do List* (bottom left of the Command Centre).
- *Stock Alert* (tab at top right of the window). See Figure 9.16.

Figure 9.16   To Do List: Stock Alert

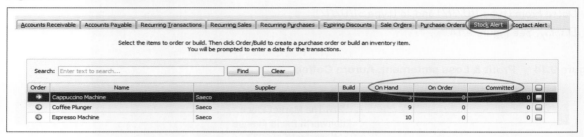

You can see that the:

- *On Hand* column shows the quantity of each item that is in stock at the moment
- *On Order* column would show if we were awaiting delivery of a previous order for any of the items
- *Committed* column would indicate if we had received firm orders for any items from customers for which we had not yet produced a sales invoice.

Click...

- *Tick* (the window at the top of right column) to select all the windows below it.
- *Order/Build* (at base of the window). See Figure 9.17.
- *Transaction Date* in the window that opens (type *3/07/17*).
- *OK.*

Figure 9.17   To Do List: Stock Alert

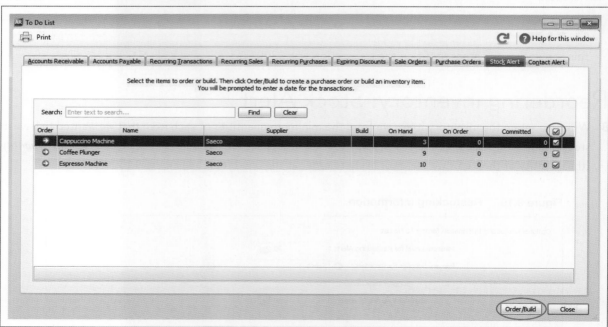

Because there is only one order to one supplier, the purchase order screen opens to show you what the order will look like. The quantities in the Order column come from the restocking information in the Inventory Cards Buying Details tab.

Click...

- *Record* (and the items vanish from the Stock Alert tab).
- *Purchase Orders* tab (and you will see the newly created purchase order). Here, you can make any changes you want to the order before sending it to the supplier by clicking on the zoom arrow next to it.
- *Close* (to return to the Command Centre).

9 Change the purchase order to a bill.

Saeco	
Date: 5 July	
Tax Invoice No.: 31185	
Supplied to: Aurora Coffee P/L	
Details: PO 0002	
50 x Espresso Machines @ $15.00	$750.00
30 Coffee Plungers @ $50.00	1 500.00
20 Cappuccino Machines @ $300.00	6 000.00
Freight:	50.00
GST:	**830.00**
Invoice Total:	$9 130.00
Terms: 10%/10 net 21	

Click...

- *Enter Purchases* (in the Purchases module).
- *Supplier* (type *Sae* and press the Tab key to accept the autofill *Saeco*). A new window pops up.
- *Use Purchase* (at the base of the window).
- *Bill* (at the base of the order window). This turns the order into a bill (as we did in Chapter 7) and the form becomes blue.
- Check the *Tax Inclusive* box is unticked.
- *Date* (change this to the date of receipt of the goods and invoice).
- *Supplier Inv. No.* (insert the invoice number).
- *Bill* (check these quantities against the invoice).
- *Price* (insert prices from the invoice).
- *Freight* (insert the amount of the freight).
- *Balance Due* (check that this is correct). Compare with **Figure 9.18**.

Figure 9.18   Bill: Saeco

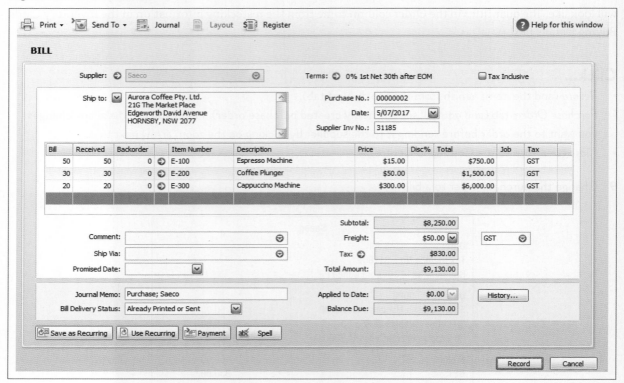

Produce reports

10 Produce an Item List [Summary] report.

 Click...

- *Inventory* (in the Reports Index).
- *Items List [Summary]*.
- *Display*. See Figure 9.19.

Figure 9.19   Item List [Summary] report: Aurora Coffee

Aurora Coffee Pty Ltd
21G The Market Place
Edgeworth David Avenue
Hornsby NSW 2077
Item List [Summary]

Item No.	Item Name	Supplier	Units On Hand	Total Value	Average Cost	Current Price
E-100	Espresso Machine	Saeco	60	$900.00	$15.00	$22.00
E-200	Coffee Plunger	Saeco	39	$1 950.00	$50.00	$66.00
E-300	Cappuccino Machine	Saeco	23	$6 900.00	$300.00	$440.00
			Grand Total:	**$9 750.00**		

The total *Current Value* of these items is $9750.00. View your Accounts List (**Figure 9.20**) and note that the value of *1-1320 Inventory* in the general ledger equals this total.

Figure 9.20   Accounts List: All Accounts, Inventory

	Account Number	Account Name	Type	Tax Code	Linked	Balance
⊙	1-1310	Trade Debtors	Accounts Receivable	N-T	✓	$1,430.00
⊙	1-1315	Less Prov'n for Doubtful Debts	Other Asset	N-T		$0.00
⊙	1-1320	Inventory	Other Asset	N-T		$9,750.00

Items: Services

11 Set up a service in the Items list.

Aurora Coffee has decided to offer a cleaning and maintenance service to purchasers of their cappuccino machines; this will be carried out in the customers' homes. To simplify the accounting, the service ($35.00 plus GST) and the associated call-out fees are to be set up as Items in MYOB.

Click...

- *Items List* (in the Inventory Command Centre).
- *New* (at base of the Items List).
- *Item Number* (insert *S-100*). Press the Tab key.
- *Name* (type *Service Fee*).
- *I Sell This Item*.
- *Income Account for Tracking Sales* (select *4-1200*). See **Figure 9.21**.

Figure 9.21   Items List: Profile tab, Service Fee

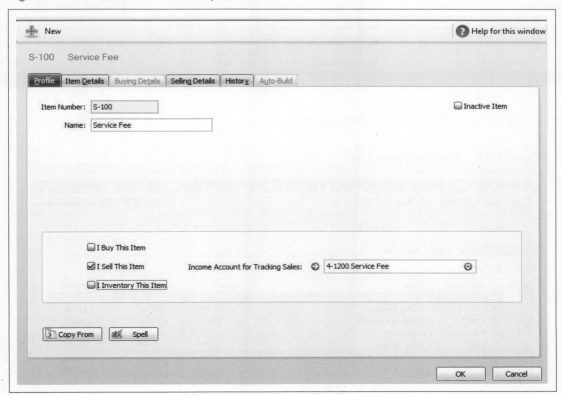

> ### This is why
>
> We don't use *I Buy This Item* because we don't buy the service to sell it later, as we would with a physical inventory item. And we don't use *I Inventory This Item* because we can't physically count it.

Click...

- *Selling Details* tab.
- *Inclusive/Exclusive* (untick as the price quoted was plus GST, which means the GST will be added on).
- *Base Selling Price* (insert 35). See Figure 9.22.

Figure 9.22   Items List: Selling tab, Service Fee

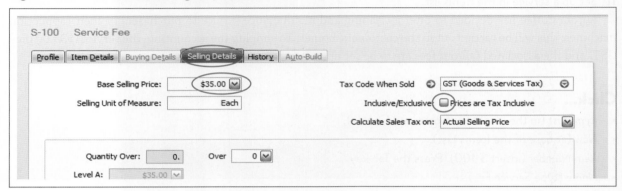

12 Set up some more service items.

Item Number	Name	Price (excluding GST)
S-200	Local Call-Out	$20.00
S-300	Metropolitan Call-Out	$60.00
S-400	Rural Call-Out	$120.00

Your Items List should now look like Figure 9.23:

Figure 9.23   Updated Items List

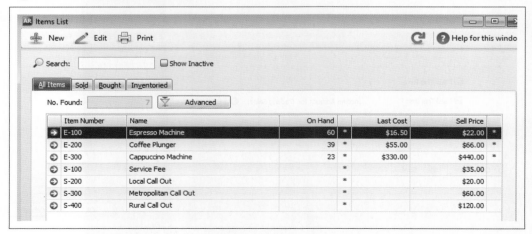

Some things to note about the list:

- The service fees just added have nothing in the *On Hand* column as there is nothing to physically count.
- The service fees *Sell Price* does not have an asterisk next to it because we unticked the **Inclusive/Exclusive** box in the Selling tab.

Click **Close** (to return to the Command Centre).

13 Create a new card in the Card File:

Card Type	Customer
Name	Cash Sales
Card ID	C 002
Terms	1-1320
Tax Code	COD

Record a sale through the Sales module:

Aurora Coffee

Date:	10 July
Tax Invoice No.:	3311
Supplied to:	Grace Bros

Details: Customer PO 756

35 x Espresso Machines @ $22.00	$770.00
26 x Coffee Plunger @ $66.00	$1 716.00
18 x Cappuccino machines @ $440.00	$7 920.00
Invoice Total (GST Included):	$10 406.00

Terms: 10% 10 days/Net 30

Record cash sales

14 A cash sale records the sale of the inventory *and* the receipt of the payment at the same time.

Aurora Coffee

Date:	10 July
Tax Invoice No.:	3312
Supplied to:	Cash Sales

Details: Weekly Cash Sales

30 x Service Fee @ $38.50:	$1 155.00
20 x Local Call Out @ $22.00	$440.00
7 x Metropolitan Call Out @ $66.00	$462.00
3 x Rural Call Out @ $132.00	$396.00
Invoice Total (GST Included):	$2 453.00

Received Cash $2 453.00

Complete the invoice part as we usually do.

Remember This

You can create a Recurring invoice.

Click...

- *Paid Today* at the bottom of the window (type in the Total Amount of the invoice). Press the Tab key.
- *Payment Method* (should say *Cash*). Compare with **Figure 9.24**.

Figure 9.24   Cash Sales: Paid Today

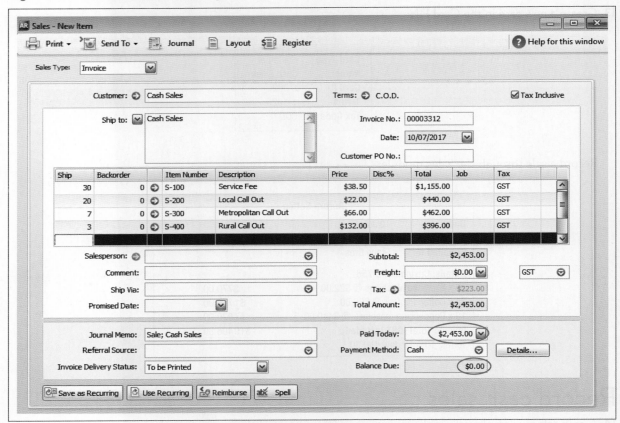

Receive items without bill

In carrying out its maintenance service for customers, Aurora Coffee often requires replacement parts for the machines. However, it does not have the facility to keep all possible parts in stock; rather, items are ordered by phone from Saeco as and when required and are delivered by courier accompanied by a delivery note (the invoice following in a few days). As all service work is carried out on a cash basis, customers are billed for parts before Saeco's invoice is even received, based on the price quoted over the phone.

15 Add in a new inventory item:

Item Number	Z-000
Item Name	Replacement parts
Cost of Sales Account	5-1300
Income Account	4-1300
Inventory Account	1-1320
Buying Tax Code	GST
Base Selling Price	$0.00
Selling Unit of Measure	Each
Price Includes GST	Yes

We deal with the new parts in two steps. First we record the purchase order as we order over the phone. Next we receive the goods into stock when they arrive or we won't be able to put them on the sales invoice.

Step 1: Record the purchase order.

Click...

- *Enter Purchases* (in the Purchases module).
- *Order* (top left of the window).
- *Supplier* (select *Saeco*).
- *Date* (insert *20/07/17*). Press the Tab key
- *Ordered* (insert *1*).
- *Item Number* (select *Z-000*) as the item received.
- *Price* (insert *33.00*, the price quoted on the phone). GST included.
- *Record*.
- *Cancel* (to return to the Command Centre).

> ### Remember This
>
> Tick the Tax Inclusive box as the price has GST included.

> ### Tip
>
> Click in the item number column again and then click on the drop-down arrow. You will see that there are only four items available – none of the service items are there. This is because we didn't tick the *I Buy This item* in their inventory card.

Step 2: Receive the goods into stock once the delivery has arrived. These sorts of deliveries typically will have a *delivery docket* as their source document.

```
Saeco
Delivery Docket
Date:                          20 July
Delivery Docket No.:           1111
Supplied to:                   Aurora Coffee P/L
Details: PO Phone Order
1 x replacement part @ $33.00  $33.00
```

Click...

- *Enter Purchases* (in the Purchases module).
- *Supplier* (select *Saeco*). A new window opens showing all the purchase orders available.
- Use *Purchase*.
- *Receive Items* (at the base of the window). See **Figure 9.25**. The screen should change to green.
- *Date* (type *20/07/17*).
- *Supplier Inv. No.* (type *DD1111*).
- *Received* (insert *1*). Compare with **Figure 9.26**.
- *Record*.
- *Cancel* (to return to the Command Centre).

Figure 9.25   Purchase Order: Receive Items

Figure 9.26   Purchases: Receive Items window

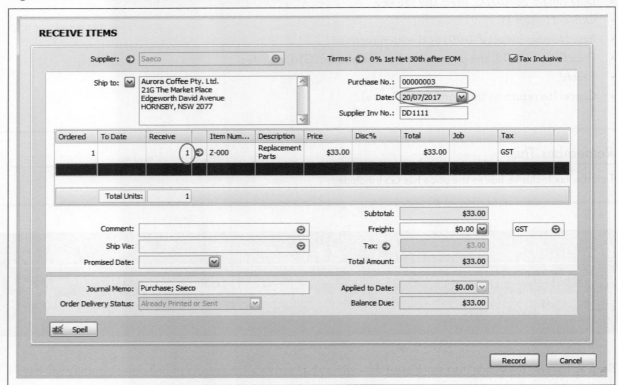

If you go to your Items List (in the Inventory module) you can see you have one replacement part in stock that you can sell. See Figure 9.27.

Figure 9.27   Items List

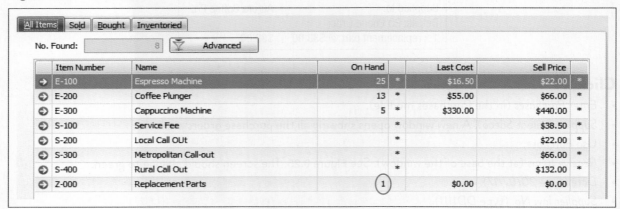

However, in the Purchases Register we can see that there isn't a bill to go with it, only an order. See Figure 9.28.

Figure 9.28 **Purchases Register**

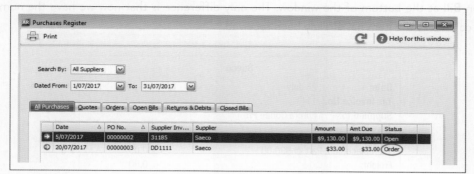

Now that the replacement parts are registered as being *On Hand*, a sales invoice can be produced to charge the customer.

16 Produce an invoice to record the following cash sale on 22 July:

	Aurora Coffee
Date:	22 July
Tax Invoice No.:	3313
Supplied to:	Cash Sale
Details:	
1 x Service Fee @ $38.50:	$38.50
1 Metropolitan Call Out @ $66.00	$66.00
1 x Replacement Part @ $44.00	$44.00
Invoice Total (GST Included):	$148.50
Received Cheque $148.50	

Remember to complete the Paid Today portion of the window. Compare your MYOB with Figure 9.29.

Figure 9.29 **Cash Sales with replacement part**

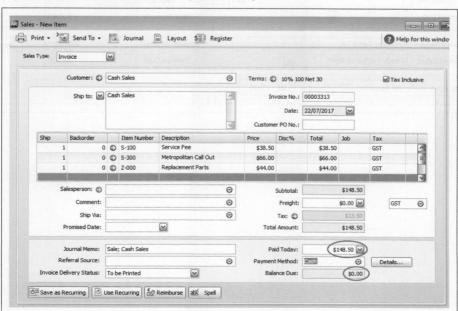

Receive bill for goods already received

17 When the bill is received from Saeco the order is changed to a bill in Enter Purchases in the usual way, by clicking on **Bill** at the bottom of the window. The only difference is that now we have the number 1 in the Received column as the item has already been received.

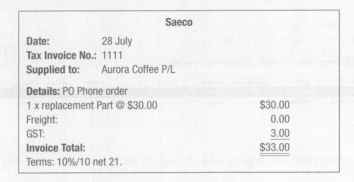

Saeco	
Date:	28 July
Tax Invoice No.:	1111
Supplied to:	Aurora Coffee P/L
Details: PO Phone order	
1 x replacement Part @ $30.00	$30.00
Freight:	0.00
GST:	3.00
Invoice Total:	$33.00
Terms: 10%/10 net 21.	

Figure 9.30   Saeco Bill for items received previously

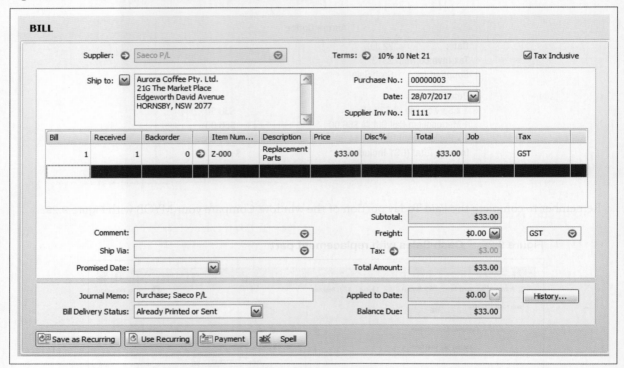

Stocktake

18 The end-of-month stocktake on 31 July reveals the following items in stock:

Stocktake on 31/07/17		
Item	**Name**	**Units Counted**
E-100	Espresso Machine	24
E-200	Coffee Plunger	12
E-300	Cappuccino Machine	5

When this is compared with the inventory items list it is found that there is a shortage of an Espresso Machine and a Coffee Plunger. This could be because a sale wasn't rung up on the till or maybe they were broken or stolen. We need to adjust MYOB to reflect these actual numbers.

Click...

- *Count Inventory* (in the Inventory module).
- *Counted Column* (Insert the numbers from you stocktake above into the appropriate line). See **Figure 9.31**.
- *Adjust Inventory* (at the base of the window).
- *Default Adjustment Account* in the window that opens (type *5-8000 Stock Adjustment*).
- *Continue*.
- *Date* (type *31/07/17*). Compare with **Figure 9.32**.
- *Record*.

Figure 9.31   Count Inventory

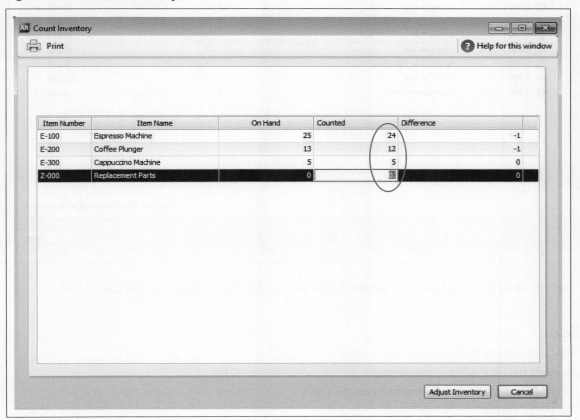

Figure 9.32   **Adjust Inventory**

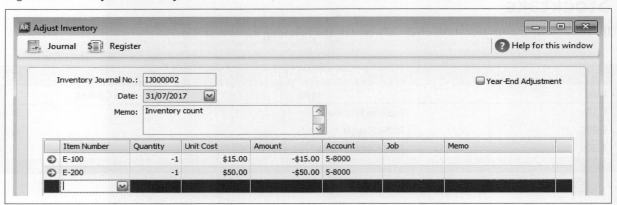

To check that the new figures have been accepted by MYOB, display your inventory items list shown in Figure 9.33.

Figure 9.33   **Items list after stocktake**

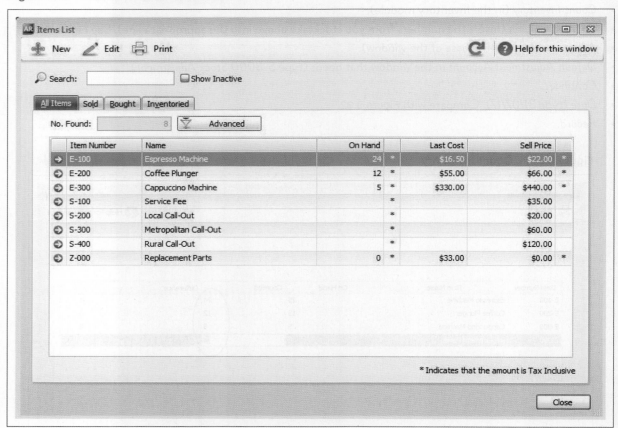

Let's check on how the Inventory general ledger account has been changed by the transactions.

Click...

- *Find Transactions* (at the base of the window).
- *Account* tab (at the top of the window).
- *Dated From* (insert *1/07/17*) and *To* (type *31/07/17*).
- *Account #* (select *1-1320 Inventory*).

From this screen (Figure 9.34) you can see that the replacement part was sold before its purchase was recorded because we used the *Receive Items* feature.

The last two entries are the inventory adjustment recording the fact that the stock count revealed a shortfall of the two items, the cost of which was transferred to the *Stock Adjustment* (Cost of Sales) account.

Figure 9.34   Find Transactions: Account tab, Inventory

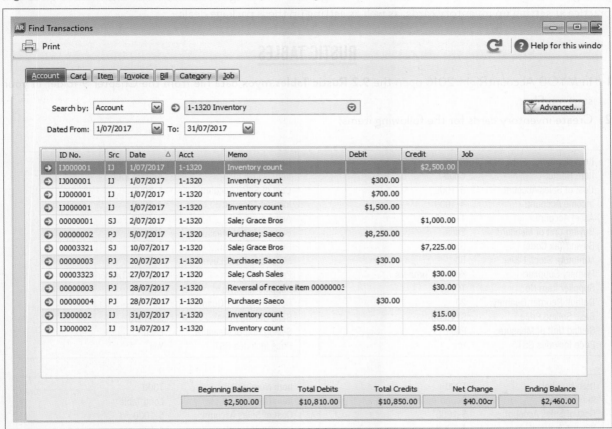

19 Produce an Items List [Summary] report for your records (Figure 9.35).

Figure 9.35   Items List [Summary] report

Aurora Coffee Pty Ltd
21G The Market Place
Edgeworth David Avenue
Hornsby NSW 2077
Item List [Summary]

Item No.	Item Name	Supplier	Units On Hand	Total Value	Average Cost	Current Price
E-100	Espresso Machine	Saeco	24	$360.00	$15.00	$22.00
E-200	Coffee Plunger	Saeco	12	$600.00	$50.00	$66.00
E-300	Cappuccino Machine	Saeco	5	$1 500.00	$300.00	$440.00
			Grand Total:	**$2 460.00**		

Auto-Build items

It is not uncommon for retailers to bundle together various individual inventory items and sell them as a package. An electronics store, for instance, selling laptops, laptop bags, monitors and mice individually may also decide to offer a package-deal featuring all of these items, often at a discounted rate. They don't buy these packages and on-sell them; they create the packages from existing stock. The following exercise gives you practice at setting up inventory cards, as well as setting up these package deals.

RUSTIC TABLES

1 In MYOB AccountRight 2016 open the **9.2 Rustic Tables.myox** data file from the Chapter 9 folder in your start-up files.

2 Create inventory cards for the following items:

Item Number:	C100
Item Name:	Chair
Cost of Sales Account:	5-1000
Income Account:	4-1000
Asset Account:	1-1320
Buying Unit of Measure:	Each
Buying Tax Code:	GST
Minimum Stock Level:	50
Primary Supplier:	Kuranda Timbers
Supplier Item No.:	TC751
Default Reorder Quantity:	20
Base Selling Price:	$110.00
Selling Unit of Measure:	Each
Price Includes GST:	Yes

Item Number:	T100
Item Name:	Square Table
Cost of Sales Account:	5-1000
Income Account:	4-1000
Asset Account:	1-1320
Buying Unit of Measure:	Each
Buying Tax Code:	GST
Minimum Stock Level:	10
Primary Supplier:	Kuranda Timbers
Supplier Item No.:	TT221
Default Reorder Quantity:	20
Base Selling Price:	$330.00
Selling Unit of Measure:	Each
Price Includes GST:	Yes

Item Number:	T200
Item Name:	Round Table
Cost of Sales Account:	5-1000
Income Account:	4-1000
Asset Account:	1-1320
Buying Unit of Measure:	Each
Buying Tax Code:	GST
Minimum Stock Level:	8
Primary Supplier:	Kuranda Timbers
Supplier Item No.:	TT284
Default Reorder Quantity:	15
Base Selling Price:	$550.00
Selling Unit of Measure:	Each
Price Includes GST:	Yes

Item Number:	T300
Item Name:	Long Table
Cost of Sales Account:	5-1000
Income Account:	4-100
Asset Account:	1-1320
Buying Unit of Measure:	Each
Buying Tax Code:	GST
Minimum Stock Level:	5
Primary Supplier:	Kuranda Timbers
Supplier Item No.:	TT578
Default Reorder Quantity:	10
Base Selling Price:	$770.00
Selling Unit of Measure:	Each
Price Includes GST:	Yes

We do not *buy* the next two items, called Patio Setting and Garden Setting. We assemble it from our other stock items when needed.

3 Set up a new Auto-Build inventory card:

Item Number:	Z500
Item Name:	Patio Setting
I Buy This Item:	[No! Do *not* click here.]
Cost of Sales Account:	5-1000
Income Account:	4-1000
Asset Account:	1-1320
Tax Code:	GST
Minimum Stock Level:	0
Default Reorder Quantity:	0
Base Selling Price:	$880.00
Selling Unit of Measure:	Each
Price Includes GST:	Yes
Auto-Build:	One T100, four C100
A Patio Setting comprises four Chairs and one Square Table.	

Click...

- *Item List* (in the Inventory module).
- *New*.
- Complete the inventory card as per the information above till you get to the Auto-Build information.
- *Auto-Build* tab. See **Figure 9.36**.
- *Item Number* (click the drop-down arrow and select *C100*).
- *Quantity* (type *4*). Press the Tab key.
- *Item Number* (click the drop-down arrow and select *T100*).
- *Quantity* (type *1*). Compare with **Figure 9.36**.
- *OK*.

Figure 9.36   Auto-Build: Patio Setting

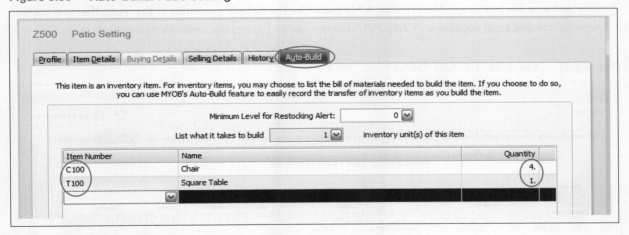

4 Set up one more Auto-Build item:

Item Number:	Z700
Item Name:	Garden Setting
I Buy This Item:	[No! Do *not* tick here.]
Cost of Sales Account:	5-1000
Income Account:	4-1000
Asset Account:	1-1320
Tax Code:	GST
Minimum Stock Level:	0
Default Reorder Quantity:	0
Base Selling Price:	$1430.00
Selling Unit of Measure:	Each
Price Includes GST:	Yes
Auto-Build:	One T300, six C100
A Garden Setting comprises six Chairs and one Long Table.	

5 Enter the quantity of each item on hand at 1 July 2017 into MYOB, using 1-1320 Inventory as the account code and the costs below for the unit costs.

Item	Name	Units On Hand	Cost (Excl GST)	Total
T100	Square Table	15	200.00	3 000.00
T200	Round Table	10	350.00	3 500.00
T300	Long Table	3	500.00	1 500.00
			TOTAL	**8 000.00**

6 Check general ledger balances to see that *3-9999 Historical Balancing* is 0.00 and *1-1320 Inventory* is $8000.00.

7 Check the To Do List Stock Alert (Figure 9.37) and order the default quantities of the items that are in short supply from the usual supplier on 1 July 2017. Remember to Record the order that pops open.

Figure 9.37 Stock Alert: Rustic Tables

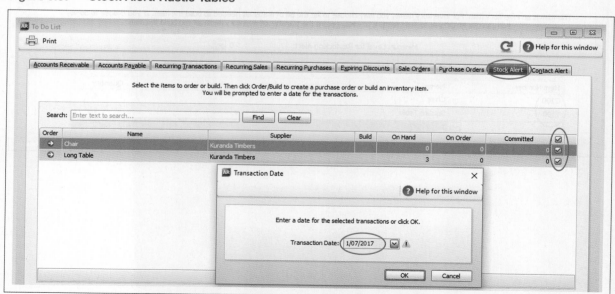

8 Change the purchase order to a bill according to the following information:

Kuranda Timbers P/L	
Date:	5 July
Tax Invoice No.:	40184
Supplied to:	Rustic Tables P/L
Details: PO 0001	
60 Chairs @ $50.00	$3 000.00
10 Long Tables @ $500.00	$5 000.00
Freight:	$300.00
GST:	$830.00
Invoice Total:	$9 130.00
Terms: Net 15.	

9 Sell the following inventory items to Home Hardware P/L:

Rustic Tables	
Date:	10 July
Tax Invoice No.:	1123
Supplied to:	Home Hardware P/L
Details:	
10 x Chairs @ $110.00:	$1 110.00
7 x Square Tables @ $330.00	$2 310.00
5 x Round Tables @ $550.00	$2 750.00
3 x Long Tables @ $770.00	$2 310.00
4 x Patio Settings @ $880.00	$3 520.00
2 x Garden Settings @ $1430.00	$2 860.00
Invoice Total (GST Included):	$14 850.00
Terms: Net 30 Days	

When you click **Record** after completing the invoice, MYOB will sense that there aren't any of the Patio or Garden Settings in stock and will give you the option to *Build*, *Buy* or *Backorder* the required items. As the Auto-Build section has been completed, MYOB will suggest (with ticks) that you build the items (see Figure 9.38).

Figure 9.38   Sales: Backorder List, Auto-Build

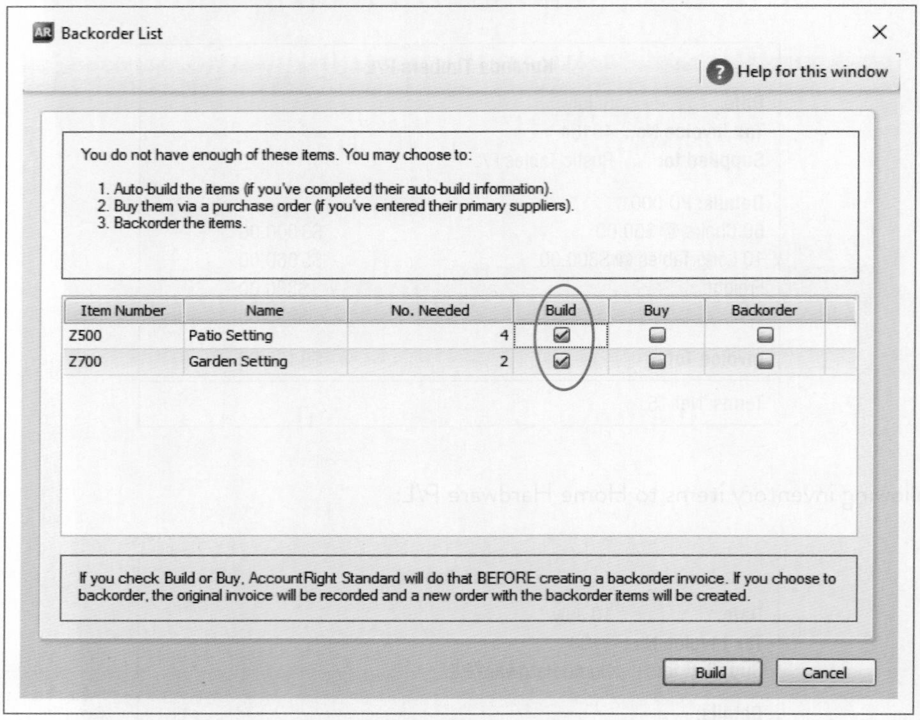

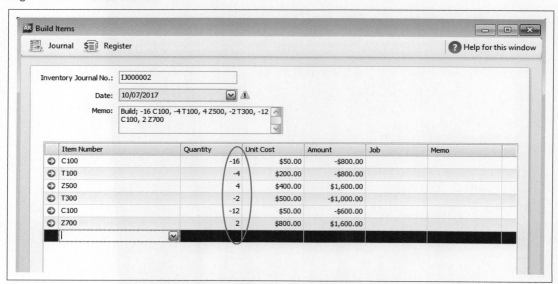

Click...

- *Build* (in the Backorder List window). A new window opens.
- *Build Items* (as the Quantity to Build has already been completed by MYOB). Another window opens.
- *Date* (type *10/07/17*). See **Figure 9.39**. It removes chairs and tables from the stock in order to build the Patio and Garden Settings.
- *Record.*
- *Cancel* (to return to the sales invoice).
- *Record.*
- *Cancel* (to return to the Command Centre).

Figure 9.39   Build Items

Produce the Item Transactions report (in the Inventory section of Reports) with a date range from 1 July to 31 July 2017. Note how the Auto-Build is recorded. See Figure 9.40.

Figure 9.40   Inventory Report: Item Transaction report

Rustic Tables
1 Lakes Street
Cairns QLD 4870
Item Transactions
1/07/2017 To 31/07/2017

ID No.	Src	Date	Memo	Debit	Credit
C100			Chair		
00000002	PJ	5/07/2017	Purchase; Kuranda Timbers	$3 000.00	
00001123	SJ	10/07/2017	Sale; Home Hardware		$500.00
IJ000002	IJ	10/07/2017	Build; −16 C100, −4 T1000, 4 Z500, −2 T300, −12 C100, 2 Z700		$1 400.00
				$3 000.00	$1 900.00
T1000			Square Table		
IJ000001	IJ	1/07/2017	Inventory count	$3 000.00	
00001123	SJ	10/07/2017	Sale; Home Hardware		$1 400.00
IJ000002	IJ	10/07/2017	Build; −16 C100, −4 T1000, 4 Z500, −2 T300, −12 C100, 2 Z700		$800.00
				$3 000.00	$2 200.00
T200			Round Table		
IJ000001	IJ	1/07/2017	Inventory count	$3 500.00	
00001123	SJ	10/07/2017	Sale; Home Hardware		$1 750.00
				$3 500.00	$1 750.00
T300			Long Table		
IJ000001	IJ	1/07/2017	Inventory count	$1 500.00	
00000002	PJ	5/07/2017	Purchase; Kuranda Timbers	$5 000.00	
00001123	SJ	10/07/2017	Sale; Home Hardware		$1 500.00
IJ000002	IJ	10/07/2017	Build; −16 C100, −4 T1000, 4 Z500, −2 T300, −12 C100, 2 Z700		$1 000.00
				$6 500.00	$2 500.00
Z500			Patio Setting		
00001123	SJ	10/07/2017	Sale; Home Hardware		$1 600.00
IJ000002	IJ	10/07/2017	Build; −16 C100, −4 T1000, 4 Z500, −2 T300, −12 C100, 2 Z700	$1 600.00	
				$1 600.00	$1 600.00
Z700			Garden Setting		
00001123	SJ	10/07/2017	Sale; Home Hardware		$1 600.00
IJ000002	IJ	10/07/2017	Build; −16 C100, −4 T1000, 4 Z500, −2 T300, −12 C100, 2 Z700	$1 600.00	
				$1 600.00	$1 600.00

10 View the Inventory Value Reconciliation report as at 31 July 2017.

Figure 9.41   Inventory Report: Inventory Value Reconciliation report

Rustic Tables
1 Lakes Street
Cairns QLD 4870
Inventory Value Reconciliation
As of 31/07/2017

Item No.	Item Name	On Hand	Current Value
1-1320 Inventory			
C100	Chair	22	$1 100.00
T1000	Square Table	4	$800.00
T200	Round Table	5	$1 750.00
T300	Long Table	8	$4 000.00
Z500	Patio Setting	0	$0.00
Z700	Garden Setting	0	$0.00
		Inventory Value:	$7 650.00
		Account Balance:	$7 650.00
		Out of Balance:	$0.00

Your instruction for this chapter is now complete.

Practice

CYCLISTS 2 GO

1 In MYOB AccountRight 2016 open the **9.3 Cyclists 2 Go.myox** data file from the Chapter 9 folder of your start-up files.

2 Create the following cards in the Card File for a Supplier and a Customer:

Card Type	Supplier	Customer
NAME	Bicycle Barn	Cash Sales
CARD ID	SUP 001	CUS 001
PURCHASE/SALE LAYOUT (in selling details tab)	Item	Item
ABN	33 007 654 414	
TERMS	Net 15	COD

3 Create inventory cards for the following items:

Item Number:	001
Item Name:	Bib Shorts
I Buy This Item:	Yes
I Sell This Item:	Yes
I Inventory This Item:	Yes
Cost of Sales Account:	5-1400
Income Account:	4-1300
Inventory Account:	1-1340
Buying Unit of Measure:	Each
Items per Buying Unit:	1
Tax Code:	GST
Minimum Stock Level:	30
Primary Supplier:	Bicycle Barn
Supplier Stock Code:	AW134
Default Reorder Quantity:	50
Base Selling Price:	$187.00
Selling Unit of Measure:	Each
Price Includes GST:	Yes

Item Number:	002
Item Name:	Helmet
I Buy This Item:	Yes
I Sell This Item:	Yes
I Inventory This Item:	Yes
Cost of Sales Account:	5-1400
Income Account:	4-1300
Inventory Account:	1-1340
Buying Unit of Measure:	Each
Items per Buying Unit:	1
Tax Code:	GST
Minimum Stock Level:	50
Primary Supplier:	Bicycle Barn
Supplier Stock Code:	AW162
Default Reorder Quantity:	50
Base Selling Price:	$99.00
Selling Unit of Measure:	Each
Price Includes GST:	Yes

Item Number:	003
Item Name:	Jersey
I Buy This Item:	Yes
I Sell This Item:	Yes
I Inventory This Item:	Yes
Cost of Sales Account:	5-1400
Income Account:	4-1300
Inventory Account:	1-1340
Buying Unit of Measure:	Each
Items per Buying Unit:	1
Tax Code:	GST
Minimum Stock Level:	30
Primary Supplier:	Bicycle Barn
Supplier Stock Code:	AW189
Default Reorder Quantity:	40
Base Selling Price:	$55.00
Selling Unit of Measure:	Each
Price Includes GST:	Yes

Item Number:	004
Item Name:	Olympic Jersey
I Buy This Item:	Yes
I Sell This Item:	Yes
I Inventory This Item:	Yes
Cost of Sales Account:	5-1400
Income Account:	4-1300
Inventory Account:	1-1340
Buying Unit of Measure:	Each
Items per Buying Unit:	1
Tax Code:	GST
Minimum Stock Level:	25
Primary Supplier:	Bicycle Barn
Supplier Stock Code:	AW168
Default Reorder Quantity:	25
Base Selling Price:	$165.00
Selling Unit of Measure:	Each
Price Includes GST:	Yes

Item Number:	005
Item Name:	Long Sleeve Jacket
I Buy This Item:	Yes
I Sell This Item:	Yes
I Inventory This Item:	Yes
Cost of Sales Account:	5-1400
Income Account:	4-1300
Inventory Account:	1-1340
Buying Unit of Measure:	Each
Items per Buying Unit:	1
Tax Code:	GST
Minimum Stock Level:	30
Primary Supplier:	Bicycle Barn
Supplier Stock Code:	AW122
Default Reorder Quantity:	20
Base Selling Price:	$110.00
Selling Unit of Measure:	Each
Price Includes GST:	Yes

Item Number:	006
Item Name:	Winter Jacket
I Buy This Item:	Yes
I Sell This Item:	Yes
I Inventory This Item:	Yes
Cost of Sales Account:	5-1400
Income Account:	4-1300
Inventory Account:	1-1340
Buying Unit of Measure:	Each
Items per Buying Unit:	1
Tax Code:	GST
Minimum Stock Level:	20
Primary Supplier:	Bicycle Barn
Supplier Stock Code:	AW118
Default Reorder Quantity:	30
Base Selling Price:	$154.00
Selling Unit of Measure:	Each
Price Includes GST:	Yes

Item Number:	007	Item Number:	008
Item Name:	Pair of Shoes	Item Name:	Budget Pack
I Buy This Item:	Yes	I Buy This Item:	No
I Sell This Item:	Yes	I Sell This Item:	Yes
I Inventory This Item:	Yes	I Inventory This Item:	Yes
Cost of Sales Account:	5-1400	Cost of Sales Account:	5-1400
Income Account:	4-1300	Income Account:	4-1300
Inventory Account:	1-1340	Inventory Account:	1-1340
Buying Unit of Measure:	Each	Buying Unit of Measure:	Each
Items per Buying Unit:	1	Items per Buying Unit:	1
Tax Code:	GST	Tax Code:	GST
Minimum Stock Level:	30	Minimum Stock Level:	0
Primary Supplier:	Bicycle Barn	Default Reorder Quantity:	0
Supplier Stock Code:	AW184	Base Selling Price:	$668.80
Default Reorder Quantity:	30	Selling Unit of Measure:	Each
Base Selling Price:	$143.00	Price Includes GST:	Yes
Selling Unit of Measure:	Each	Auto-Build:	One each of 002, 005, 007; two each of 001, 003.
Price Includes GST:	Yes		

4 Enter the quantity of each item on hand as at 1 July 2017 with their opening balances below. Use 1-1340 Inventory as the default adjustment account.

Item	Name	Units on hand	Cost (Excl GST)	Total
001	Bib Shorts	50	130.00	6 500.00
002	Helmet	75	70.00	5 250.00
003	Jersey	48	30.00	1 440.00
004	Olympic Jersey	25	120.00	3 000.00
005	Long Sleeve Jacket	60	80.00	4 800.00
006	Winter Jacket	41	110.00	4 510.00
007	Pair of Shoes	50	90.00	4 500.00
			TOTAL	**30 000.00**

5 Check general ledger balances to see that 3-9999 Historical Balancing is 0.00 and 1-1340 Clothing is $30 000.00.

6 Sell the following inventory items (cash sales) for the week ending July 10:

	Cyclists 2 Go	
Date:	10 July	
Tax Invoice No.:	6231	
Supplied to:	Cash Sales	
Details:		
21 x 001 Bib Shorts @ $187.00		$3 927.00
34 x 002 Helmet @ $99.00		$3 366.00
23 x 003 Jersey @ $55.00		$1 265.00
14 x 004 Olympic Jersey @ $165.00		$2 310.00
15 x 005 Long Sleeve Jacket @ $110.00		$1 650.00
25 x 006 Winter Jacket @ $154.00		$3 850.00
32 x 007 Pair of Shoes @ $143.00		$4 576.00
11 x 008 Budget Pack @ $668.80		$7 356.80
Invoice Total (GST Included):		$28 300.80
Received Cash $28 300.80		

7 Check the To Do List Stock Alert and order the default quantities of the item that is in short supply from the usual supplier on 12 July.

8 Change the purchase order to a bill according to the following information:

```
                    Bicycle Barn P/L

Date:              15 July
Tax Invoice No.:   10308
Supplied to:       Cyclists 2 Go P/L

Details: PO 0001
50 x Bib Shorts @ $130.00              $6 500.00
50 x Helmet @ $70.00                    3 500.00
40 x Jersey @ $30.00                    1 200.00
25 x Olympic Jersey @ $120.00           3 000.00
30 x Winter Jacket @ $110.00            3 300.00
30 x Pair of Shoes @ $90.00             2 700.00
Freight:                                  320.00
GST:                                    2 052.00

Invoice Total:                        $22 572.00

Terms: Net 15.
```

9 Sell the following inventory items (cash sales) for the week ending July 17:

```
                    Cyclists 2 Go

Date:              17 July
Tax Invoice No.:   6232
Supplied to:       Cash Sales

Details:
18 x 001 Bib Shorts @ $187.00           $3 366.00
12 x 002 Helmet @ $99.00                $1 188.00
7 x 003 Jersey @ $55.00                   $385.00
19 x 004 Olympic Jersey @ $165.00       $3 135.00
15 x 005 Long Sleeve Jacket @ $110.00   $1 650.00
10 x 006 Winter Jacket @ $154.00        $1 540.00
14 x 007 Pair of Shoes @ $143.00        $2 002.00
8 x 008 Budget Pack @ $668.80           $5 350.40

Invoice Total (GST Included):          $18 616.40

Received Cash $18 616.40
```

10 Produce the following reports from the Inventory section of the Reports Index.

- Item Transactions report (1 July to 31 July 2017). See **Figure 9.42**.
- Inventory Value Reconciliation report as at 31 July 2017. See **Figure 9.43**.
- Inventory Report: Item List [Summary] report. See **Figure 9.44**.

Figure 9.42   **Inventory Report: Item Transactions report**

Cyclists 2 Go
82 Oxford Street
Paddington NSW 2021
Item Transactions
1/07/2017 To 31/07/2017

ID No.	Src	Date	Memo	Debit	Credit
001			Bib Shorts		
IJ000001	IJ	1/07/2017	Inventory Count	$6 500.00	
00006231	SJ	10/07/2017	Sale; Cash Sales		$2 730.00
IJ000002	IJ	10/07/2017	Build; −22 001, −11 002, −22 003, −11 005, −11 007, 11 008		$2 860.00
00000002	PJ	15/07/2017	Purchase; Bicycle Barn	$6 500.00	
00006232	SJ	17/07/2017	Sale; Cash Sales		$2 340.00
IJ000003	IJ	17/07/2017	Build; −16 001, −8 002, −16 003, −8 005, −8 007, 8 008		$2 080.00
				$13 000.00	$10 010.00
002			Helmet		
IJ000001	IJ	1/07/2017	Inventory Count	$5 250.00	
00006231	SJ	10/07/2017	Sale; Cash Sales		$2 380.00
IJ000002	IJ	10/07/2017	Build; −22 001, −11 002, −22 003, −11 005, −11 007, 11 008		$770.00
00000002	PJ	15/07/2017	Purchase; Bicycle Barn	$3 500.00	
00006232	SJ	17/07/2017	Sale; Cash Sales		$840.00
IJ000003	IJ	17/07/2017	Build; −16 001, −8 002, −16 003, −8 005, −8 007, 8 008		$560.00
				$8 750.00	$4 550.00
003			Jersey		
IJ000001	IJ	1/07/2017	Inventory Count	$1 440.00	
00006231	SJ	10/07/2017	Sale; Cash Sales		$690.00
IJ000002	IJ	10/07/2017	Build; −22 001, −11 002, −22 003, −11 005, −11 007, 11 008		$660.00
00000002	PJ	15/07/2017	Purchase; Bicycle Barn	$1 200.00	
00006232	SJ	17/07/2017	Sale; Cash Sales		$210.00
IJ000003	IJ	17/07/2017	Build; −16 001, −8 002, −16 003, −8 005, −8 007, 8 008		$480.00
				$2 640.00	$2 040.00
004			Olympic Jersey		
IJ000001	IJ	1/07/2017	Inventory Count	$3 000.00	
00006231	SJ	10/07/2017	Sale; Cash Sales		$1 680.00
00000002	PJ	15/07/2017	Purchase; Bicycle Barn	$3 000.00	
00006232	SJ	17/07/2017	Sale; Cash Sales		$2 280.00
				$6 000.00	$3 960.00
005			Long Sleeve Jacket		
IJ000001	IJ	1/07/2017	Inventory Count	$4 800.00	
00006231	SJ	10/07/2017	Sale; Cash Sales		$1 200.00
IJ000002	IJ	10/07/2017	Build; −22 001, −11 002, −22 003, −11 005, −11 007, 11 008		$880.00
00006232	SJ	17/07/2017	Sale; Cash Sales		$1 200.00
IJ000003	IJ	17/07/2017	Build; −16 001, −8 002, −16 003, −8 005, −8 007, 8 008		$640.00
				$4 800.00	$3 920.00

ID No.	Src	Date	Memo	Debit	Credit
006			Winter Jacket		
IJ000001	IJ	1/07/2017	Inventory Count	$4 510.00	
00006231	SJ	10/07/2017	Sale; Cash Sales		$2 750.00
00000002	PJ	15/07/2017	Purchase; Bicycle Barn	$3 300.00	
00006232	SJ	17/07/2017	Sale; Cash Sales		$1 100.00
				$7 810.00	$3 850.00
007			Pair of Shoes		
IJ000001	IJ	1/07/2017	Inventory Count	$4 500.00	
00006231	SJ	10/07/2017	Sale; Cash Sales		$2 880.00
IJ000002	IJ	10/07/2017	Build; −22 001, −11 002, −22 003, −11 005, −11 007, 11 008		$990.00
00000002	PJ	15/07/2017	Purchase; Bicycle Barn	$2 700.00	
00006232	SJ	17/07/2017	Sale; Cash Sales		$1 260.00
IJ000003	IJ	17/07/2017	Build; −16 001, −8 002, −16 003, −8 005, −8 007, 8 008		$720.00
				$7 200.00	$5 850.00
008			Budget Pack		
00006231	SJ	10/07/2017	Sale; Cash Sales		$6 160.00
IJ000002	IJ	10/07/2017	Build; −22 001, −11 002, −22 003, −11 005, −11 007, 11 008	$6 160.00	
00006232	SJ	17/07/2017	Sale; Cash Sales		$4 480.00
IJ000003	IJ	17/07/2017	Build; −16 001, −8 002, −16 003, −8 005, −8 007, 8 008	$4 480.00	
				$10 640.00	$10 640.00

Figure 9.43   Inventory Value Reconciliation report

Cyclists 2 Go
82 Oxford Street
Paddington NSW 2021
Inventory Value Reconciliation
As of 31/07/2017

Item No.		Item Name	On Hand	Current Value
1-1340	Inventory Clothing			
001		Bib Shorts	23	$2 990.00
002		Helmet	60	$4 200.00
003		Jersey	20	$600.00
004		Olympic Jersey	17	$2 040.00
005		Long Sleeve Jacket	11	$880.00
006		Winter Jacket	36	$3 960.00
007		Pair of Shoes	15	$1 350.00
008		Budget Pack	0	$0.00
			Inventory Value:	$16 020.00
			Account Balance:	$16 020.00
			Out of Balance:	$0.00

Figure 9.44   Inventory Report: Item List [Summary]

Cyclists 2 Go
82 Oxford Street
Paddington NSW 2021
Item List [Summary]

Item No.	Item Name	Supplier	Units On Hand	Total Value	Average Cost	Current Price
001	Bib Shorts	Bicycle Barn	23	$2 990.00	$130.00	$187.00
002	Helmet	Bicycle Barn	60	$4 200.00	$70.00	$99.00
003	Jersey	Bicycle Barn	20	$600.00	$30.00	$55.00
004	Olympic Jersey	Bicycle Barn	17	$2 040.00	$120.00	$165.00
005	Long Sleeve Jacket	Bicycle Barn	11	$880.00	$80.00	$110.00
006	Winter Jacket	Bicycle Barn	36	$3 960.00	$110.00	$154.00
007	Pair of Shoes	Bicycle Barn	15	$1 350.00	$90.00	$143.00
			Grand Total:	$16 020.00		

Summary

◆ Inventory is the name given to the property that is held for sale in the normal course of business.
◆ Knowing the value of inventory on hand at the end of an accounting period is vital to being able to determine profit for that period.
◆ There are two basic ways in which to account for inventory: periodic inventory and perpetual inventory.
◆ Using periodic inventory, a physical stocktake (a count and valuation) is done on a monthly or quarterly basis. The closing value of one accounting period is the opening value of the next one.
◆ The cost of goods sold is calculated as being the value of Opening Stock plus purchases less Closing Stock.
◆ Under the perpetual inventory system an ongoing record is kept in an Inventory ledger of all the inventory items, with each item having its own card or page. Each receipt of an item is debited to its card, while each sale is credited, and the ongoing balance reflects the actual quantity and value on hand.
◆ A physical stocktake is undertaken from time to time (perhaps annually) to confirm the actual quantities on hand.
◆ This module uses the perpetual inventory system, and MYOB uses Item Purchases Invoices to increase the quantity and value of inventory, and Item Sales Invoices to decrease inventory.
◆ Restocking information can set a Minimum Level to trigger a Restocking Alert, a Primary Supplier for Reorders and a Default Reorder Quantity.
◆ Stocktake information is entered in the Count Inventory program, and it is here that MYOB is adjusted to conform to the actual quantities of inventory that are present.

Assessment

Western Scooters Pty Ltd

1   In MYOB AccountRight 2016, create a new data file based on the following information using *AccountRight Standard Australian* Version:

> **Western Scooters Pty Ltd**
> 290 Murray Street
> Perth WA 6000
> ABN 32 102 301 233
>
> **Phone:** (08) 9617 4241
> **Current Financial Year:** 2018
> **Conversion Month:** July
> **Industry:** Retail
> **Main Business Activity:** Sale of motor scooters

Click the **Easy Setup Assistant** once you have finished the company file setup. Use the third activation option – **I use this file for evaluation purposes**.

2   Create cards in the Card File for a Supplier and a Customer.

Card type	Supplier	Customer
NAME	Scooters Galore	Cash Sales
CARD ID	SUP 001	CUS 001
SALES/PURCHASE LAYOUT (in selling details tab)	Item	Item
ABN	60 206 783 046	
TERMS	Net 30	COD

3   Change the following names in the List of Accounts:

	Account Type	Account No.	New Account Name	Tax Code
Edit	Bank	1-1110	Cheque Account	N-T
Edit	Income	4-1000	Sales	GST
Edit	Cost of Sales	5-1000	Purchases	GST

4   Insert the following account opening balances:

Trial Balance as at 30/06/2017			
Account No.	**Account Name**	**Debit**	**Credit**
1-1110	Cheque Account	26 000.00	
1-1320	Inventory	41 000.00	
1-2210	Office Equipment At Cost	10 000.00	
1-2410	Store Fittings At Cost	4 000.00	
2-2100	Business Loan #1		50 000.00
3-1000	Owners/Shareholders' Capital		31 000.00
TOTALS		**81 000.00**	**81 000.00**

5   Create inventory cards for the following items:

Item Number:	S001
Item Name:	150cc Scooter
I Buy This Item:	Yes
I Sell This Item:	Yes
I Inventory This Item:	Yes
Cost of Sales Account:	5-1000
Income Account:	4-1000
Inventory Account:	1-1320
Buying Unit of Measure:	Each
Items per Buying Unit:	1
Tax Code:	GST
Minimum Stock Level:	10
Primary Supplier:	Scooters Galore
Default Reorder Quantity:	10
Base Selling Price:	$2750.00
Selling Unit of Measure:	Each
Price Includes GST:	Yes

Item Number:	S002
Item Name:	250cc Scooter
I Buy This Item:	Yes
I Sell This Item:	Yes
I Inventory This Item:	Yes
Cost of Sales Account:	5-1000
Income Account:	4-1000
Inventory Account:	1-1320
Buying Unit of Measure:	Each
Items per Buying Unit:	1
Tax Code:	GST
Minimum Stock Level:	5
Primary Supplier:	Scooters Galore
Default Reorder Quantity:	5
Base Selling Price:	$3630.00
Selling Unit of Measure:	Each
Price Includes GST:	Yes

Item Number:	C001
Item Name:	Jacket
I Buy This Item:	Yes
I Sell This Item:	Yes
I Inventory This Item:	Yes
Cost of Sales Account:	5-1000
Income Account:	4-1000
Inventory Account:	1-1320
Buying Unit of Measure:	Each
Items per Buying Unit:	1
Tax Code:	GST
Minimum Stock Level:	10
Primary Supplier:	Scooters Galore
Default Reorder Quantity:	15
Base Selling Price:	$440.00
Selling Unit of Measure:	Each
Price Includes GST:	Yes

Item Number:	C002
Item Name:	Helmet
I Buy This Item:	Yes
I Sell This Item:	Yes
I Inventory This Item:	Yes
Cost of Sales Account:	5-1000
Income Account:	4-1000
Inventory Account:	1-1320
Buying Unit of Measure:	Each
Items per Buying Unit:	1
Tax Code:	GST
Minimum Stock Level:	10
Primary Supplier:	Scooters Galore
Default Reorder Quantity:	10
Base Selling Price:	$253.00
Selling Unit of Measure:	Each
Price Includes GST:	Yes

Item Number:	Z001
Item Name:	150cc Scooter Value pack
I Buy This Item:	No
I Sell This Item:	Yes
I Inventory This Item:	Yes
Cost of Sales Account:	5-1000
Income Account:	4-1000
Inventory Account:	1-1320
Buying Unit of Measure:	Each
Items per Buying Unit:	1
Tax Code:	GST
Minimum Stock Level:	0
Default Reorder Quantity:	0
Base Selling Price:	$3003.00
Selling Unit of Measure:	Each
Price Includes GST:	Yes
Auto-Build:	One each of S001, C001 C002

Item Number:	Z002
Item Name:	250cc Scooter Value pack
I Buy This Item:	No
I Sell This Item:	Yes
I Inventory This Item:	Yes
Cost of Sales Account:	5-1000
Income Account:	4-1000
Inventory Account:	1-1320
Buying Unit of Measure:	Each
Items per Buying Unit:	1
Tax Code:	GST
Minimum Stock Level:	0
Default Reorder Quantity:	0
Base Selling Price:	$3883.00
Selling Unit of Measure:	Each
Price Includes GST:	Yes
Auto-Build:	One each of S002, C001, C002

6   Enter the quantity of each item on hand at 1 July 17 into MYOB. Adjust Inventory, using 1-1320
    Inventory as the default adjustment account, then enter the unit cost of each item as indicated.

Item	Name	Units On Hand	Cost (Excl GST)	Total
C001	Jacket	10	300.00	3 000.00
C002	Helmet	20	150.00	3 000.00
S001	150cc Scooter	10	2 000.00	20 000.00
S002	250cc Scooter	6	2 500.00	15 000.00
			TOTAL	**41 000.00**

7   Check general ledger balances to see that 3-9999 Historical Balancing is 0.00 and 1-1320 Inventory is
    $41 000.00.

8   Make the following sale:

> **Western Scooters**
>
> **Date:**   4 July
> **Tax Invoice No.:** 7194
> **Supplied to:**   Cash Sales
>
> **Details:**
> 7 x S001 150cc Scooter @ $2 750.00 $19 250.00
> 4 x S002 250cc Scooter @ $3 630.00 $14 520.00
> 3 x C001 Jacket @ $440.00 $1 320.00
> 1 x C002 Helmet @ $253.00 $253.00
> 2 x Z001 150cc Value Pack @ $3 003.00 $6 006.00
> 1 x Z002 250cc Value Pack @ $3 883.00 $3 883.00
>
> **Invoice Total (GST Included):** $45 232.00
> Cash Cheques/Cash $45 232.00

9   Check the To Do List Stock Alert and order the default quantities of the items that are in short supply
    from the usual supplier on 7 July.

10 The goods are delivered on 17 July. Change the purchase order to a bill according to the following
    information:

> **Scooters Galore**
>
> **Date:**   10 July
> **Tax Invoice No.:** 49148
> **Supplied to:**   Western Scooters P/L
>
> **Details: PO 0001**
> 10 × 150cc Scooter @ $2 000.00 $20 000.00
> 5 × 250cc Scooter @ $2 500.00 $12 500.00
> 15 × Jackets @ $300.00 $4 500.00
> **GST:** $3 700.00
> **Invoice Total:** $40 700.00
> Terms: Net 30

11 Produce the following reports from the Inventory section of the Reports Index to give to your instructor:
    –   Item Transactions report (1 July to 31 July 2017)
    –   Inventory Value Reconciliation report as at 31 July 2017
    –   Item List Summary.

10

GENERAL LEDGER

Learning outcomes

By the end of this chapter you will be competent in:
- adding new general ledger accounts
- understanding and processing balance day adjustments through the general journal
- using the general journal to buy and sell assets
- understanding the general journal links with the BAS report
- processing opening and closing stock for a periodic stock system
- filtering reports to meet your enquiry
- processing reversing journals
- producing reports
- finding balances.

There are transactions which aren't entered through the Banking, Sales or Purchases modules as they don't affect the accounts that these modules are linked to. These can be entered in through general journals. Technically you can enter every single transaction through the general journal but this is time consuming and means your customer and supplier subsidiary ledgers aren't updated. This chapter focuses mainly on balance day adjustments and the general journal.

Background information

The tax year runs from 1 July in one calendar year to 30 June of the following year, and for accounting purposes most organisations make the same period their *financial year*. The end of the financial year is the time when organisations finalise their accounts and produce the reports that indicate the performance over the past year.

Important accounting periods within the financial year are as follows:

- The month (usually aligned with the calendar month), at the end of which account statements are sent to customers who have outstanding balances. A Balance Sheet and Profit & Loss Statement (also known as a Revenue Statement) can be produced to give a comparison of performance with the previous month, with the same month in previous years, and/or with budgetary forecasts. It is also the Australian Taxation Office (ATO) reporting period for large companies to submit their Business Activity Statement (BAS) detailing income and expenditure and thus tax collected and tax paid. This BAS is due at the ATO by the 21st of the following month. This is explained in more detail in Chapters 14 and 15.

- The quarter (ending 30 September, 31 December, 31 March 31 and 30 June) is the ATO reporting period for most registered organisations and the due date for submitting the BAS is (generally) the 28th of the following month.

These accounting periods do not necessarily coincide neatly with business activity, so unless some adjustments are made between these periods, a misleading picture of the business may be presented.

These are known as balance day adjustments and company policy will dictate which adjustments are done, how often they are done and who will do them.

General journals are used to record transactions that are a little bit different from the sales and purchases described in previous chapters. The most common adjustment journals are for:

- accrued expenses
- expense prepayments
- depreciation
- bad debts
- accrued revenue
- adjusting inventory after stocktakes.

General journals

FIRE PROTECTION PTY LTD

1 In MYOB AccountRight 2016, open **10.1 Fire Protection Co.myox** data file located in the Chapter 10 folder of your start-up files.

To be able to record our general journals, we will need to update our chart of accounts with some new accounts. Make the following changes in the **Accounts List** in the Accounts module.

	Account Type	Account Number	New Account Name	Tax Code
Edit	Other Liability	2-1550	Accrued Expenses	N-T
Add	Other Asset	1-1315	Provision for Doubtful Debts	N-T
Add	Other Asset	1-1380	Accrued Revenue	N-T
Add	Cost of Goods Sold	5-0100	Opening Stock	N-T
Edit	Cost of Goods Sold	5-9000	Closing Stock	N-T

Accrued Expenses

An *accrued expense* (a liability) is a cost that has been incurred by the business but which has not yet been paid. For instance, the wages fortnight might span from 27 June to 8 July, paid on 12 July. One week of wages expense was incurred in June but not paid till July. Or the electricity bill may come every two months. So that the accounts are a true reflection of the costs incurred at the end of the month, the expense is accrued.

To do this, you:

- debit the expense account with an estimate of the cost
- credit the accrued expenses liability account with the same amount.

This increases the balance of both accounts.

2 For Fire Protection Pty Ltd, the first pay day in August 2017 is the 6th and is for pay period Monday 24 July to Friday 4 August 2017. The estimated wages for this pay period is $1000.00. This means there are six days of wages incurred between 24 and 31 July. They are highlighted in yellow in Figure 10.1.

Figure 10.1   Calendar excerpt

Monday	Tuesday	Wednesday	Thursday	Friday	Saturday	Sunday
24 July	25 July	26 July	27 July	28 July	29 July	30 July
31 July	1 August	2 August	3 August	4 August	5 August	6 August

The amount to be journaled is:

Working days in July/Working Days in Fortnight × Wages paid
6 days/10 days × $1000 = $600

Tip

As these are all monthly journals, you could set up Recurring Transactions in a real-life situation.

Click...

- *Record Journal Entry* (in the Accounts module).
- *Date* (type *31/07/17*).
- *Memo* (type *Accrue 6 days wages*).
- *Acct No.* (type *6-4100*).
- *Debit* (type *600*). Press the Tab key till you get to the next line.
- *Acct No.* (type *2-1550*).
- *Credit* (type *600*). Press the Tab key. See Figure 10.2.
- The tax codes are *N-T* because no sale or purchase was made. This is just an accounting journal.
- *Record*.

Figure 10.2   **General journal: Accrued Expenses**

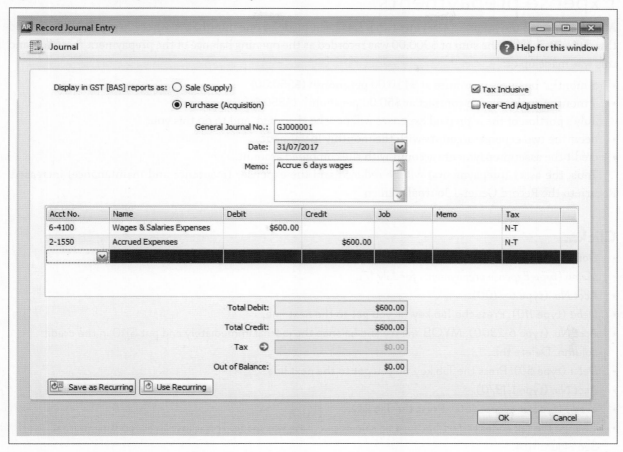

Let's see what affect this has had on the wages expense:

Click...

- *Find Transactions* (base of the Command Centre).
- *Account* (choose *6-4100*).
- *Date From* (type *1/07/17*) and *To* (type *31/0/7/17*). Figure 10.3 shows us the wages expense has increased by $600.

Figure 10.3   **Find Transactions: 6-4100 Wages & Salaries Expenses**

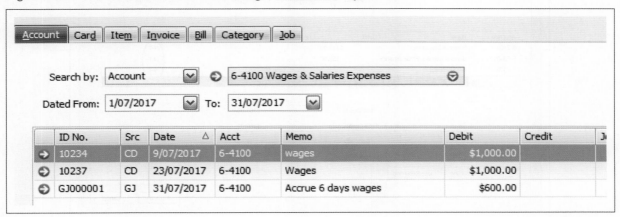

Expense prepayments

A *prepaid expense* (an asset) is a payment that has been made in one month, but whose benefit may be spread throughout the year. The sum of $900.00 was recorded as the opening balance of the prepayments account, and this was made up of:

- 5 months' business insurance at $110.00 per month ($550.00)
- 7 months' maintenance contract at $50.00 per month ($350.00).
  July's portion of these prepaid expenses will now be absorbed, and to do this you:
- debit the two expense accounts with the monthly instalment
- credit the asset prepayments account with the combined amount.

Thus, the asset (prepayments) will be reduced and the expenses (insurance and maintenance) increased. Return to the Record General Journals screen.

Click...
- *Date* (should still be *31/07/17*).
- *Memo* (type *Expense prepayments for July 17*).
- *Acct No.* (type *6-7100*).
- *Debit* (type *110*). Press the Tab key till you get to the next line.
- *Acct No.* (type *6-2300*). MYOB will try and balance the journal immediately and put $110 in the credit column. Delete this.
- *Debit* (type *50*). Press the Tab key till you get to the next line.
- *Acct No.* (type *1-1370*).
- *Credit* (type or accept *160*). Press the Tab key.
- Change the tax codes to *N-T* because no sale or purchase was made. This is just an accounting journal. See Figure 10.4.
- *Record*.

Figure 10.4   General journal: expense prepayments

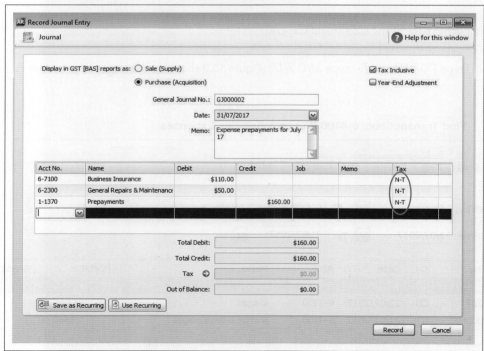

Depreciation

Depreciation is the recognition that the value of capital items (also known as non-current assets or fixed assets) decreases over time. The actual rate of depreciation differs according to the expected 'life' of the asset and can be recorded as a recurring monthly transaction or just at the end of the financial year.

There are two methods of calculating depreciation, both of which are based on the effective life of the asset:

*   *prime cost*, in which depreciation is a fixed percentage of the original price of the asset

*   *diminishing value*, in which depreciation is a fixed percentage of each period's depreciated value (or written down value) of the asset.

A business has the choice of using either method, and the choice must be made during the first year of ownership of the asset. The expected life of an asset depends on many factors and a business has the choice of self-assessing this expected life, or of adopting the commissioner's determination.

Fire Protection Pty Ltd has two types of fixed assets that are subject to depreciation, which can be seen in the Accounts List in the general ledger. (See Figure 10.5.)

Figure 10.5   Accounts List: Non-Current Assets

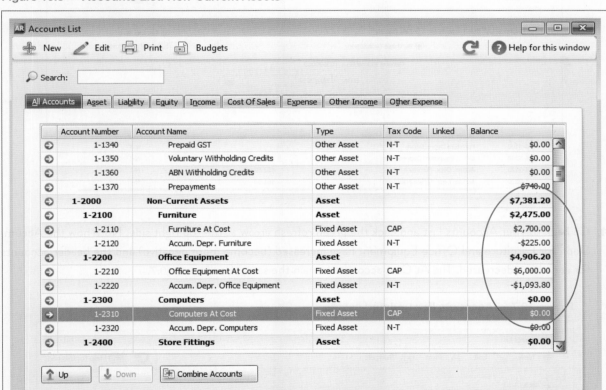

The first fixed asset is *Furniture*. The original cost was $2700.00 with **accumulated depreciation** of $225.00. These are depreciated at 10% pa (per year) using the *prime cost* method.

> **Accumulated depreciation**
> The sum of all previous depreciation instalments.

Furniture at Cost × 10% Depreciation Rate/12 months = Monthly Depreciation

2700 ×   10% / 12   = $22.50

The second fixed asset is *Office Equipment*. The original cost was $6000.00 with accumulated depreciation of $1093.80. These are to be depreciated at 15% pa (per annum) using the *diminishing value* method.

(Office Equip at Cost less Accum Depr) × 15% Depreciation Rate/12 months = Monthly Depreciation

(6000 − 1093.80) ×   15% / 12   = $61.33 (rounded)

When recording depreciation:

- debit the two depreciation expense accounts (some businesses only use one overall depreciation expense account)
- credit the asset Accum. Depr. account with their individual amount.

3 Record the monthly depreciation through the general journal and remember to save the transaction as *Recurring* so you can use the template in future. Compare with Figure 10.6 before you record. Ensure tax codes are N-T as nothing was purchased or sold.

Figure 10.6   **General journal: depreciation**

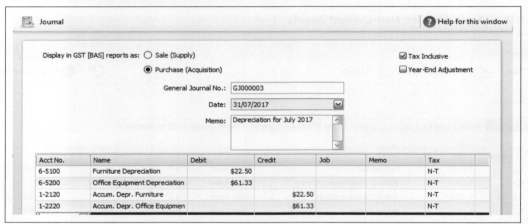

4 Go back to your Accounts List and click the green refresh arrow at the top right side. Note how the Accum. Depr. for Furniture and Office Equipment have increased (become more negative) and the header accounts for each have decreased. The At Cost accounts remain the same. See Figure 10.7.

Figure 10.7   **Accounts list: updated assets**

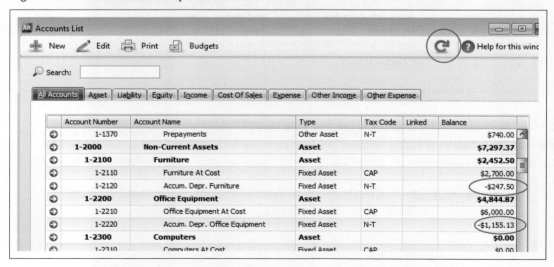

Bad debts provision

Bad debts are account customers who are unable to pay their debt. In manual bookkeeping, writing off a bad debt is a general journal entry, where a Bad Debts expense account is debited and the customer's account is credited (written off).

However, there is no access to individual customers' accounts from MYOB's Accounts module (where the general journal is located). Thus all transactions with customers are done using the Sales module, and to write off a debt as bad, a credit note (negative invoice) is posted to the customer's account.

Many business owners know that there is likely to be a small percentage of their customers whose debts cannot be collected. They believe it is prudent to make a provision in their accounts for these currently unknown defaulters, called a *Provision for Doubtful Debts*. This provision is an *internal* adjustment, often monthly, that spreads the loss associated with a bad debt over the year to avoid the appearance of profit (or loss) fluctuations. No *external* adjustment (for taxation purposes) occurs until a bad debt is actually written off.

5 Fire Protection Pty Ltd has decided to create a provision for doubtful debts of $200.00. You should have a blank general journal on screen:

- debit the bad and doubtful debt expense
- credit the *Provision for Doubtful Debt* asset account, which is a **contra account**.

> **Contra account**
> An account which has a usual balance the opposite of other accounts in its classification.

Compare with **Figure 10.8** before recording. Ensure all the tax codes are N-T.

Figure 10.8   General Journal: Provision for Doubtful Debts

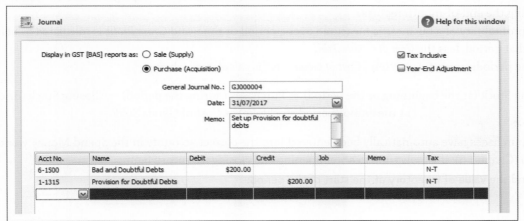

Accrued Revenue

Revenue can also be earned in one accounting period, but not invoiced until the next period as that is when the job is completed. We account for this by accruing the revenue in a similar way that we accrued the expense.

6 Fire Protection Pty Ltd installed fire extinguishers and fire blankets at Lidcome Primary School. The price quoted was $3300.00 including GST and 25% of the job was completed by 31 July. The calculation would be:

$$\text{GST Exclusive Income} \times \text{Percentage Complete} = (\$3300/1.1) \times 25\% = \$750.00$$

You are still in the **Record Journal Entry** window, so:

- debit the Accrued Revenue asset account
- credit the appropriate income account (in this case Service & Installation). Remember to change the tax code to N-T as no sale has been made yet. See **Figure 10.9**.

Figure 10.9   **General journal: Accrued Revenue**

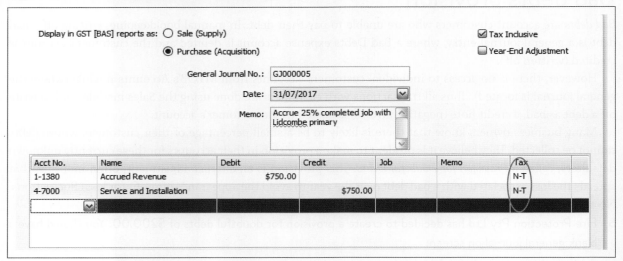

Adjusting inventory after stocktake

Fire Protection Pty Ltd uses the periodic inventory system in which *periodic* stocktakes are conducted to find the quantity (and hence the value) of inventory at specific dates.

While this is commonly done yearly (and sometimes quarterly), for the purpose of this exercise we will be doing the stocktake monthly. The general journal is used to introduce inventory figures into the computer prior to running the end-of-month reports.

The profitability of a business is measured over a period of time, and *Gross Profit* is calculated as being *Sales* during that period, less the *Cost of Goods Sold*.

In the periodic inventory system, *Cost of Goods Sold* is calculated as being:

Opening Stock (at the beginning of the period) + Purchases (during the period) − Closing Stock (discovered at the end-of-period stocktake) = Cost of Goods Sold

The purchases have automatically been entered into the correct accounts in the Spend Money work on this scenario (Chapter 5); it is now time to enter opening and closing inventory figures.

7   To find the value of inventory at the start of the period:

 Click...

- *Find Transactions* at base of the Command Centre).
- *Dated From* (type *1/07/17*) and *To* (type *30/07/17*).
- *Account* (select *1-1320 Inventory*).

We can see that the beginning balance is $30 000 (bottom of the screen). See **Figure 10.10**. Leave this screen open.

Figure 10.10   **Find Transactions: inventory beginning balance**

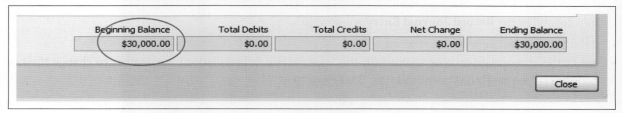

Stocktake on 31 July reveals that the stock on hand (inventory) is now valued at $35 000.00. This new valuation must be entered into the computer so it updates the inventory. We can do two separate journals or one journal in two parts. We keep the number separate (rather than doing a calculation) for the sake of clarity.

Go back to the **Record Journal Entry** window and:

- debit the Opening Stock Cost of Goods Sold account with the *opening* stock amount
- credit the Inventory asset account with the *opening* stock amount
- debit the Inventory asset account with the *closing* stock amount
- credit the Closing Stock Cost of Goods Sold account with the *closing* stock amount.

Figure 10.11   General journal: adjusting inventory

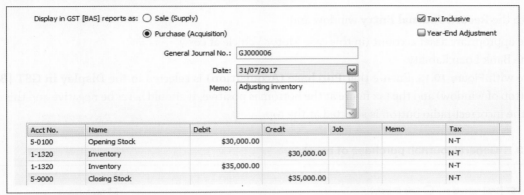

8   Go back to your Find Transactions (Account: 1-1320 Inventory) by clicking on **Window** in the top menu bar and choosing *Find Transactions*. Click the green refresh arrow at the top right side. Note the opening and closing balances at the bottom of the screen. See Figure 10.12.

Figure 10.12   Find Transactions: inventory balances after journal

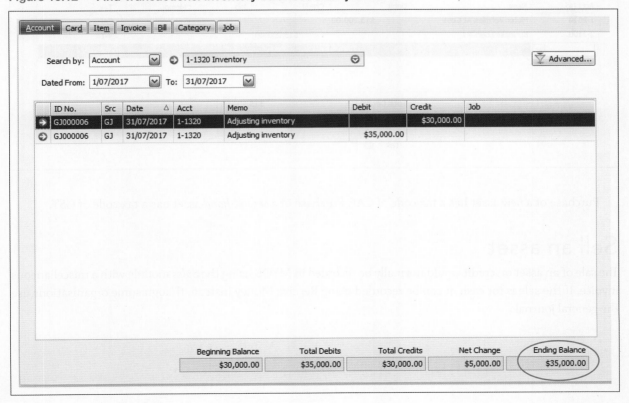

Opening stock and closing stock have now been inserted into the Cost of Goods Sold section of the general ledger. The opening stock was entered as a debit, so it will be added to the purchases (also debits) already there. Closing stock was entered as a credit, so it will be subtracted from these figures to give a net Cost of Goods Sold.

Purchase an asset

Purchase of an asset on credit would normally be recorded in MYOB using the *Purchases* module with a miscellaneous invoice. Assets paid for using a loan are recorded in the General Journal.

9 On 31 July Fire Protect Co. purchases a new Transit Van rego 1DGJ-682 for $13 200.00 and paid for it with a bank loan.

Return to the **Record Journal Entry** window and:

- debit the appropriate asset account (in this case Motor Vehicle at cost)
- credit the Bank Loan liability.

Compare with Figure 10.13. Ensure that **Purchase (Acquisition)** is selected in the **Display in GST [BAS] reports as** (top of window) and the tax figure at the bottom is positive. It should *never* be negative and this only happens if the incorrect radio button is selected at the top.

Figure 10.13   General journal: purchase of asset

Acct No.	Name	Debit	Credit	Job	Memo	Tax
1-2610	Motor Vehicles At Cost	$13,200.00				CAP
2-2100	Business Loan #1		$13,200.00			N-T

Total Debit: $13,200.00
Total Credit: $13,200.00
Tax: $1,200.00

Purchase of a *new* asset has a tax code of CAP. Purchase of a *second-hand* asset has a tax code of GST.

Sell an asset

The sale of an asset on credit would normally be recorded in MYOB using the *Sales* module with a miscellaneous invoice. If the sale is for cash, it can be recorded using Receive Money instead, though some organisations use the general journal.

10 On 1 August Fire Protection Pty Ltd sells some old bookcases for $330.00 including GST. The cash is deposited straight onto the bank account.

You are still in the **Record Journal Entry** window:

- debit the bank account
- credit the appropriate asset account (in this case Furniture At Cost).

Figure 10.14   **General journal: *incorrect* sale of asset**

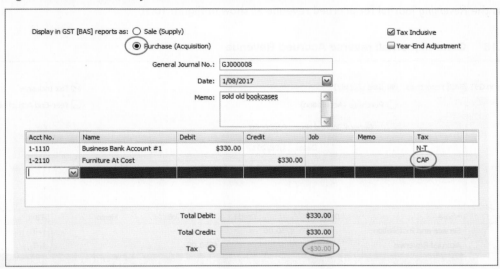

The general journal will look like Figure 10.14 (above) and it is incorrect on two counts:

- **Sales (Supply)** needs to be selected in the **Display in GST [BAS] reports as** (top of window) because a) you are selling, not buying the bookcases and b) the tax figure at the bottom is negative.
- The tax code for the sale of an asset is GST, not CAP.

  Once corrected, the general journal should look like Figure 10.15.

Figure 10.15   **General journal: *correct* sale of asset**

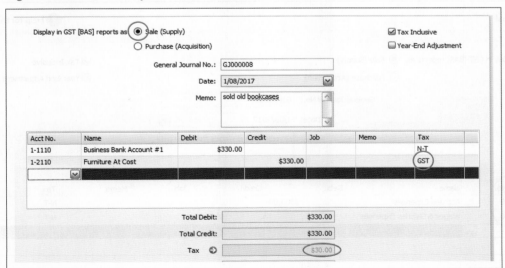

Reversing entries

In order to prepare for the new month, we need to reverse some of the accruals that we did earlier. All you need to do is identify the accruals that you made and literally record them again at the beginning of the next month but reverse the debits and credits.

Reverse Accrued Revenue

As the original journal was to debit the asset and credit the revenue, we just do the opposite.

11 Process the *Reversing* journal for accrued revenue as show in Figure 10.16.

Figure 10.16 **General journal: reverse Accrued Revenue**

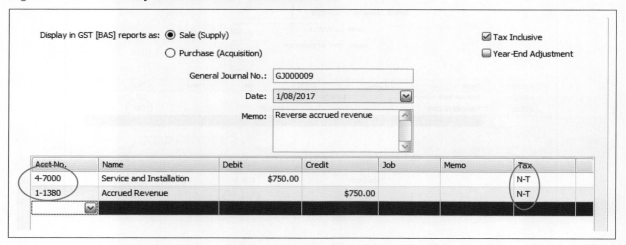

Reverse Accrued Expenses

As the original journal was to debit the expense and credit the liability, we just do the opposite.

12 Process the *Reversing* journal for wages as show in Figure 10.17.

Figure 10.17 **General journal: reverse Accrued Expenses**

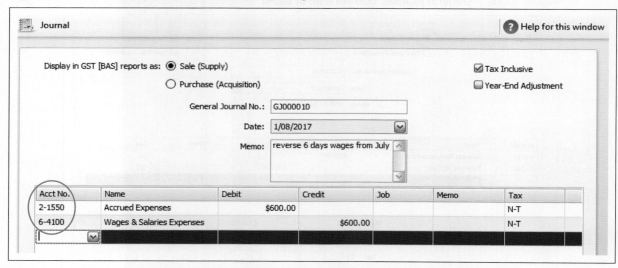

In order to show you the logic behind this accruing and reversing, let's process the first payment of wages (below) and look at some reports.

13 Pay the fortnightly wages through **Spend Money** (Banking module) using the recurring transaction. See Figure 10.18.

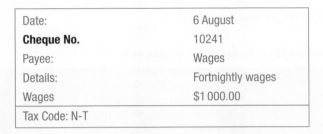

Date:	6 August
Cheque No.	10241
Payee:	Wages
Details:	Fortnightly wages
Wages	$1 000.00
Tax Code: N-T	

Figure 10.18   Spend Money: wages

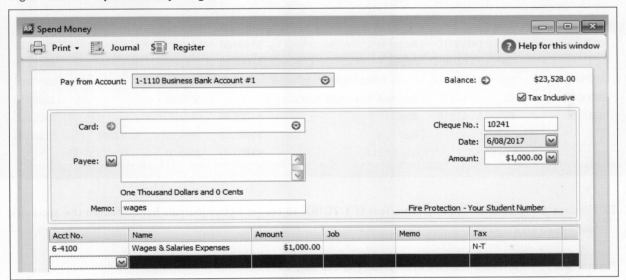

Produce reports

14 In the Reports Index, choose Accounts, then General Ledger [Detail] and filter the report from 1 July 2017 to 6 August 2017 for Account number 6-4100 by using the drop-down arrow. See Figure 10.19.

Figure 10.19   Reports Index: general ledger for wages only

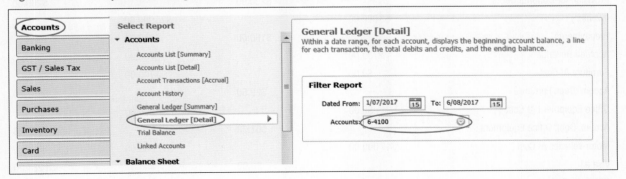

As you can see from the report in Figure 10.20 that:

- if we hadn't done the accruing of the expenses, the wages expense would have been $2000 for July
- with the addition of the accrual journal, the wages for July showed the true cost incurred (not paid) of $2600 for July
- once the accrual was reversed on 1 August 2017, effectively nulling the journal before, the Wages account only shows the amount of wages which was paid.

Figure 10.20   General Ledger [Detail] report for wages only

Fire Protection Pty Ltd
44 Boorea Street
Lidcombe NSW 2141
General Ledger [Detail]
1/07/2017 To 6/08/2017

ID No.	Src	Date	Memo	Debit	Credit	Net Activity	Ending Balance
6-4100 Wages & Salaries Expenses							
Beginning Balance: $0.00							
10234	CD	9/07/2017	Wages	$1 000.00			$1 000.00
10237	CD	23/07/2017	Wages	$1 000.00			$2 000.00
GJ000001	GJ	31/07/2017	Accrue 6 days wages	$600.00			$2 600.00
GJ000010	GJ	1/08/2017	Reverse 6 days wages from July		$600.00		$2 000.00
10241	CD	6/08/2017	Wages	$1 000.00			$3 000.00
			Total:	$3 600.00	$600.00	$3 000.00	$3 000.00
			Grand Total:	$3 600.00	$600.00		

15 Produce a trial balance for July (**This Year (FY 2018)**) to see how your journals have affected the accounts. See Figure 10.21.

Figure 10.21   Trial Balance: Fire Protection Pty Ltd July 2017

Fire Protection Pty Ltd
44 Boorea Street
Lidcombe NSW 2141
Trial Balance
July 2017

Account Name	Debit	Credit	YTD Debit	YTD Credit
Business Bank Account #1		$3 202.50	$24 297.50	
Provision for Doubtful Debts		$200.00		$200.00
Inventory	$5 000.00		$35 000.00	
Prepayments		$160.00	$740.00	
Accrued Revenue	$750.00		$750.00	
Furniture At Cost	$0.00		$2 700.00	
Accum. Depr. Furniture		$22.50		$247.50
Office Equipment At Cost	$0.00		$6 000.00	
Accum. Depr. Office Equipment		$61.33		$1 155.13
Motor Vehicles At Cost	$12 000.00		$12 000.00	
Visa #1		$0.00		$1 281.20
GST Collected		$1 088.00		$1 088.00

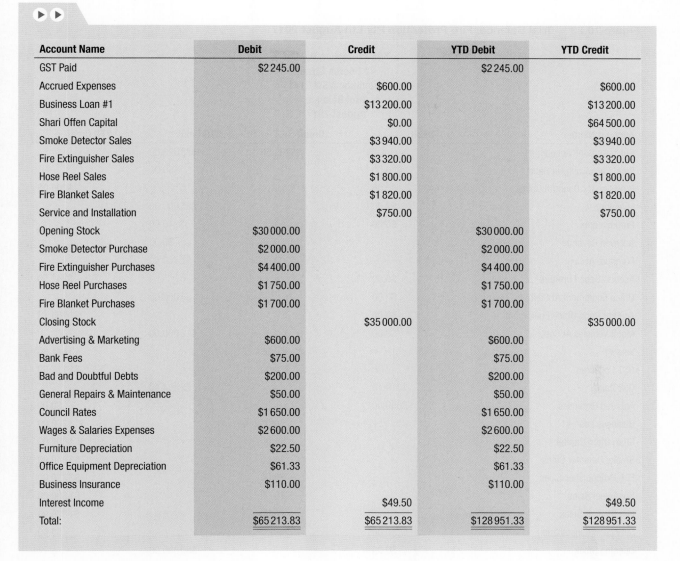

Account Name	Debit	Credit	YTD Debit	YTD Credit
GST Paid	$2 245.00		$2 245.00	
Accrued Expenses		$600.00		$600.00
Business Loan #1		$13 200.00		$13 200.00
Shari Offen Capital		$0.00		$64 500.00
Smoke Detector Sales		$3 940.00		$3 940.00
Fire Extinguisher Sales		$3 320.00		$3 320.00
Hose Reel Sales		$1 800.00		$1 800.00
Fire Blanket Sales		$1 820.00		$1 820.00
Service and Installation		$750.00		$750.00
Opening Stock	$30 000.00		$30 000.00	
Smoke Detector Purchase	$2 000.00		$2 000.00	
Fire Extinguisher Purchases	$4 400.00		$4 400.00	
Hose Reel Purchases	$1 750.00		$1 750.00	
Fire Blanket Purchases	$1 700.00		$1 700.00	
Closing Stock		$35 000.00		$35 000.00
Advertising & Marketing	$600.00		$600.00	
Bank Fees	$75.00		$75.00	
Bad and Doubtful Debts	$200.00		$200.00	
General Repairs & Maintenance	$50.00		$50.00	
Council Rates	$1 650.00		$1 650.00	
Wages & Salaries Expenses	$2 600.00		$2 600.00	
Furniture Depreciation	$22.50		$22.50	
Office Equipment Depreciation	$61.33		$61.33	
Business Insurance	$110.00		$110.00	
Interest Income		$49.50		$49.50
Total:	$65 213.83	$65 213.83	$128 951.33	$128 951.33

This is why

As financial years run from July of one year to June of next year, July 2017 forms part of the 2018 financial year. If you put in 2017 for this report, you would get July 2016 as it is part of the 2017 financial year.

16 While you are still in the Trial Balance, change to August 2017 by clicking on the drop-down arrow in the **As of** box and changing it to August, then clicking the green **Run Report** arrow. See Figures 10.22 and 10.23.

Figure 10.22   **Trial Balance: Filters**

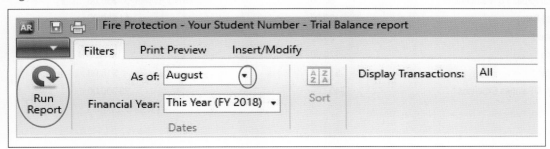

Figure 10.23   Trial Balance: Fire Protection Pty Ltd August 2017

Fire Protection Pty Ltd
44 Boorea Street
Lidcombe NSW 2141
Trial Balance
August 2017

Account Name	Debit	Credit	YTD Debit	YTD Credit
Business Bank Account #1		$769.50	$23 528.00	
Petty Cash/Cash On Hand	$50.00		$50.00	
Provision for Doubtful Debts	$0.00			$200.00
Inventory	$0.00		$35 000.00	
Prepayments	$0.00		$740.00	
Accrued Revenue		$750.00	$0.00	
Furniture At Cost		$300.00	$2 400.00	
Accum. Depr. Furniture	$0.00			$247.50
Office Equipment At Cost	$0.00		$6 000.00	
Accum. Depr. Office Equipment	$0.00			$1 155.13
Motor Vehicles At Cost	$0.00		$12 000.00	
Visa #1		$2 360.60		$3 641.80
GST Collected		$30.00		$1 118.00
GST Paid	$219.10		$2 464.10	
Accrued Expenses	$600.00			$0.00
Business Loan #1		$0.00		$13 200.00
Shari Offen Capital		$0.00		$64 500.00
Smoke Detector Sales		$0.00		$3 940.00
Fire Extinguisher Sales		$0.00		$3 320.00
Hose Reel Sales		$0.00		$1 800.00
Fire Blanket Sales		$0.00		$1 820.00
Service and Installation	$750.00			$0.00
Opening Stock	$0.00		$30 000.00	
Smoke Detector Purchase	$1 020.00		$3 020.00	
Fire Extinguisher Purchases	$0.00		$4 400.00	
Hose Reel Purchases	$0.00		$1 750.00	
Fire Blanket Purchases	$1 000.00		$2 700.00	
Closing Stock	$0.00			$35 000.00
Advertising & Marketing	$0.00		$600.00	
Bank Fees	$0.00		$75.00	
Bad and Doubtful Debts	$0.00		$200.00	
Cleaning Expenses	$18.50		$18.50	
Telephone Expenses	$56.00		$56.00	
Parking/Tolls Expenses	$6.00		$6.00	
General Repairs & Maintenance	$0.00		$50.00	
Council Rates	$0.00		$1 650.00	
Stationery	$5.50		$5.50	
Printing	$70.00		$70.00	
Postage	$15.00		$15.00	
Wages & Salaries Expenses	$400.00		$3 000.00	

Account Name	Debit	Credit	YTD Debit	YTD Credit
Office Equipment Depreciation	$0.00		$83.83	
Business Insurance	$0.00		$110.00	
Interest Income		$0.00		$49.50
Total:	$4 210.10	$4 210.10	$129 991.93	$129 991.93

17 Open the Profit & Loss Statement for July 2017 and compare with **Figure 10.24**.

Figure 10.24   **Profit & Loss Statement: Fire Protection Pty Ltd July 2017**

Fire Protection Pty Ltd
44 Boorea Street
Lidcombe NSW 2141
Profit & Loss Statement
July 2017

Income		
Smoke Detector Sales	$3 940.00	
Fire Extinguisher Sales	$3 320.00	
Hose Reel Sales	$1 800.00	
Fire Blanket Sales	$1 820.00	
Service and Installation	$750.00	
Total Income		$11 630.00
Cost Of Sales		
Opening Stock	$30 000.00	
Smoke Detector Purchase	$2 000.00	
Fire Extinguisher Purchases	$4 400.00	
Hose Reel Purchases	$1 750.00	
Fire Blanket Purchases	$1 700.00	
Closing Stock	($35 000.00)	
Total Cost of Sales		$4 850.00
Gross Profit		$6 780.00
Expenses		
General Expenses		
Advertising & Marketing	$600.00	
Bank Fees	$75.00	
Bad and Doubtful Debts	$200.00	
General Repairs & Maintenance	$50.00	
Council Rates	$1 650.00	
Payroll Expenses		
Wages & Salaries Expenses	$2 600.00	
Depreciation Expenses		
Furniture Depreciation	$22.50	
Office Equipment Depreciation	$61.33	
Insurance Expenses		
Business Insurance	$110.00	
Total Expenses		$5 368.83
Operating Profit		$1 411.17

Other Income			
Interest Income		$49.50	
Total Other Income			$49.50
Total Other Expenses			$0.00
Net Profit/(Loss)			$1 460.67

Notice in particular:

- *Service and Installation* income is included in the income, even though we haven't received any money for the work done for Lidcome Primary School. This is the money we earned in July, but have not yet invoiced for.
- *Cost of Sales* has been adjusted with the opening and closing stock. This is a true reflection of the cost of sales.
- Even though we have physically paid $2000 in wages in July, the P&L shows $2600 to reflect the actual wage expense incurred.
- Depreciation has increased the expenses (even though it hasn't physically been paid out).
- Business insurance has also increased the expenses. Both depreciation and the expensing of prepayments accounts for the portion of the asset that has been consumed.

Practice

THE BLINDS MAN

1. In MYOB AccountRight 2016, open **10.2 The Blinds Man.myox** data file located in the Chapter 10 folder of your start-up files. You will be posting general journals.
2. Make the following changes in the **Accounts List** in the Accounts module.

	Account Type	Account Number	New Account Name	Tax code
Edit	Other Liability	2-1550	Accrued Expenses	N-T
Add	Other Asset	1-1315	Provision for Doubtful Debts	N-T
Add	Other Asset	1-1370	Accrued Revenue	N-T
Add	Cost of Goods Sold	5-0100	Opening Stock	N-T
Add	Cost of Goods Sold	5-9050	Closing Stock	N-T

3. Mr Fixit Pty Ltd has done some repairs on the premises during July 2016 but won't be sending in his invoice until the middle of August when he does his monthly invoicing. He said the invoice would reflect as per the quote, which was $2200 including GST. Post the journal to accrue the expense on 31 July 2016.

Remember This

Only use the GST Exclusive amount in your journal.

4 The yearly business insurance was paid in June 16 and the Prepayments Asset account was debited at that time. Expense $75 from prepayments to the business insurance using 31 July 16 as your journal date.

5 Post the depreciation for office equipment of $100 on 31 July 16.

6 The Blinds Man management has decided it would be appropriate to set up a provision for doubtful debt of $150. Record the journal using the date 31 July 16.

7 A computer server and associated software was purchased on 31 July 16 for $16 500.00. It was paid for using a bank loan. Record this through the general journal using Business Loan #2.

8 A fax machine (Office Equipment) was sold on 31 July 16 for $132 (including GST). The cash was deposited into the Cheque Account. Record the sale in the general journal.

Remember This

Ensure your tax codes are correct for the sale and purchase of assets. Check the tax field is positive. If not, correct the *Display in GST [BAS] reports as* section at the top of the journal.

9 Accrue $1000 (excluding GST) of Installation income which was earned in July but won't be invoiced till August. Use the date of 31 July 16.

10 Stocktake reveals the closing inventory balance is $12 400. Find the opening balance and produce the Adjusting Inventory journal as at 31 July 16.

11 Reverse the accrued revenue and accrued expenses on 1 August 16.

12 Produce the following reports:

- General Ledger [Detail] for 6-2100 General Repairs & Maintenance only dated 1 July to 1 August 2016. Compare with Figure 10.25.
- Trial Balance for July 2016. Compare with Figure 10.26.
- Profit & Loss Statement for July 2016. Compare with Figure 10.27.
- Transaction Journal 1 July to 1 August 2016. General Journals only. You will need to scroll down to find this one. See Figures 10.28 and 10.29.

Figure 10.25   General Ledger [Detail]: General Repairs & Maintenance

The Blinds Man
21 Penola Rd
Mount Gambier SA 5290
General Ledger [Detail]
1/07/2016 To 1/08/2016

ID No.	Src	Date	Memo	Debit	Credit	Net Activity	Ending Balance
6-2100	General Repairs & Maintenance						
Beginning Balance:	$0.00						
GJ000001	GJ	31/07/2016	Accrue Mr Fixit Expense - Repairs to Premises	$2 000.00			$2 000.00
GJ000010	GJ	1/08/2016	Reverse Accrued Expenses		$2 000.00		$0.00
			Total:	$2 000.00	$2 000.00	$0.00	$0.00
			Grand Total:	$2 000.00	$2 000.00		

Figure 10.26   Trial Balance: The Blinds Man July 2016

The Blinds Man
21 Penola Rd
Mount Gambier SA 5290
Trial Balance
July 2016

Account Name	Debit	Credit	YTD Debit	YTD Credit
Cheque Account	$4 925.14		$15 519.14	
Accounts Receivable	$4 070.00		$8 470.00	
Provision for Doubtful debts		$150.00		$150.00
Inventory	$4 400.00		$12 400.00	
Prepayments		$75.00	$825.00	
Accrued Revenue	$1 000.00		$1 000.00	
Office Equipment At Cost		$120.00	$1 680.00	
Accum. Depr. Office Equipment		$100.00		$200.00
Computers At Cost	$15 000.00		$15 000.00	
Visa #1		$0.00		$900.00
GST Collected		$1 495.30		$1 495.30
GST Paid	$2 763.56		$2 763.56	
Accounts Payable		$6 446.00		$7 040.00
Accrued Expenses		$2 000.00		$2 000.00
Business Loan #1		$0.00		$18 000.00
Business Loan #2		$16 500.00		$16 500.00
Owner's/Shareholder's Capital		$0.00		$6 500.00
Owner's/Shareholder's Drawings		$0.00	$400.00	
Sales of Blinds		$12 600.00		$12 600.00
Installation Income		$3 900.00		$3 900.00
Freight Income		$570.00		$570.00
Discounts Received		$677.00		$677.00
Opening Stock	$8 000.00		$8 000.00	
Purchase of Blinds	$12 600.00		$12 600.00	
Discounts Given	$1 237.00		$1 237.00	
Closing Stock		$12 400.00		$12 400.00
Bad and doubtful debts	$150.00		$150.00	
Electricity Expenses	$142.60		$142.60	
General Repairs & Maintenance	$2 000.00		$2 000.00	
Freight Out	$570.00		$570.00	
Office Equipment Depreciation	$100.00		$100.00	
Business Insurance	$75.00		$75.00	
Total:	$57 033.30	$57 033.30	$82 932.30	$82 932.30

Figure 10.27   Profit & Loss Statement: The Blinds Man July 2016

The Blinds Man
21 Penola Rd
Mount Gambier SA 5290
Profit & Loss Statement
July 2016

Income		
Sales of Blinds	$12600.00	
Installation Income	$3900.00	
Freight Income	$570.00	
Discounts Received	$677.00	
Total Income		$17747.00
Cost of Sales		
Opening Stock	$8000.00	
Purchase of Blinds	$12600.00	
Discounts Given	$1237.00	
Closing Stock	($12400.00)	
Total Cost of Sales		$9437.00
Gross Profit		$8310.00
Expenses		
General Expenses		
Bad and doubtful debts	$150.00	
Electricity Expenses	$142.60	
General Repairs & Maintenance	$2000.00	
Freight Out	$570.00	
Depreciation Expenses		
Office Equipment Depreciation	$100.00	
Insurance Expenses		
Business Insurance	$75.00	
Total Expenses		$3037.60
Operating Profit		$5272.40
Total Other Income		$0.00
Total Other Expenses		$0.00
Net Profit/(Loss)		$5272.40

Figure 10.28   Reports Index: Transaction Journals

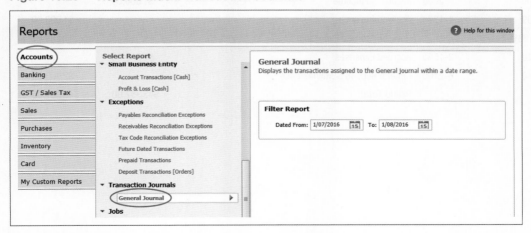

Figure 10.29   General journal: The Blinds Man

THE BLINDS MAN
21 PENOLA RD
MOUNT GAMBIER SA 5290
GENERAL JOURNAL
1/07/2016 TO 1/08/2016

ID No.	Account No.	Account Name	Debit	Credit	Job No
GJ 31/07/2016		Accrue Mr Fixit Expense - Repairs to Premises			
GJ000001	6-2100	General Repairs and Maintenance	$2 000.00		
GJ000001	2-1550	Accrued Expenses		$2 000.00	
GJ 31/07/2016		Expense Business Insurance for July 16			
GJ000002	6-7100	Business Insurance	$75.00		
GJ000002	1-1360	Prepayments		$75.00	
GJ 31/07/2016		Depreciation of Office Equipment July 16			
GJ000003	6-5200	Office Equipment Depreciation	$100.00		
GJ000003	1-2220	Accum. Depr. Office Equipment		$100.00	
GJ 31/07/2016		Set Up Provision for Doubtful Debt			
GJ000004	6-1500	Bad and Doubtful Debts	$150.00		
GJ000004	1-1315	Provision for Doubtful Debts		$150.00	
GJ 31/07/2016		Computer Server Purchased			
GJ000005	1-2310	Computers At Cost	$15 000.00		
GJ000005	2-2200	Business Loan #2		$16 500.00	
GJ000005	2-1220	GST Paid	$1 500.00		
GJ 31/07/2016		Sold Fax Machine			
GJ000006	1-1110	Cheque Account	$132.00		
GJ000006	1-2210	Office Equipment At Cost		$120.00	
GJ000006	2-1210	GST Collected		$12.00	
GJ 31/07/2016		Accrue Installation Income			
GJ000007	1-1370	Accrued Revenue	$1 000.00		
GJ000007	4-2000	Installation Income		$1 000.00	
GJ 31/07/2016		Adjusting Journal After Periodic Stocktake			
GJ000008	5-1000	Opening Stock	$8 000.00		
GJ000008	1-1320	Inventory		$8 000.00	
GJ000008	1-1320	Inventory	$12 400.00		
GJ000008	5-9050	Closing Stock		$12 400.00	
GJ 1/08/2016		Reverse Accrued Revenue from July 16			
GJ000009	4-2000	Installation Income	$1 000.00		
GJ000009	1-1370	Accrued Revenue		$1 000.00	
GJ 1/08/2016		Reverse Accrued Expenses			
GJ000010	2-1550	Accrued Expenses	$2 000.00		
GJ000010	6-2100	General Repairs & Maintenance		$2 000.00	
		Grand Total:	**$43 357.00**	**$43 357.00**	

Summary

◆ Balance day adjustments are designed to update accounts to truly reflect the income and expenses incurred in an accounting period.

◆ Balance day adjustments are done through the General Journal.

◆ Company policy dictates which adjustments are done, how often they are done and who does them.

◆ Accrued expenses and accrued income both increase their respective expense and income accounts for one month and must be reversed in the next month.

◆ GST is not recorded in most of the balance day adjustments as they are only accounting transactions. Only the actual purchase and sales have GST in them.

◆ Prepayments are expenses whose benefits last longer than one month. The original cost is debited to a Prepayments Asset account and every month a portion is expensed to the appropriate account until the benefit has been completely used up.

◆ Depreciation has a similar effect on a capital purchase. The asset is recorded at original cost and will be completely expensed by the end of its useful life. The depreciation will be recorded in a contra asset account called accumulated depreciation.

◆ Purchase of a new asset has a tax code of CAP. Purchase or sale of a used asset has a tax code of GST.

◆ Adjusting inventory after a stocktake correctly reflects the value of the inventory in the Balance Sheet and the cost of sales in the Profit and Loss.

Assessment

Magnetic Boats

1   In MYOB AccountRight 2016, open **10.3 Magnetic Boats.myox** data file located in the Chapter 10 folder of your start-up files. You will be posting journals.

2   Make the following changes in the **Accounts List** in the Accounts module.

	Account Type	Account Number	New Account Name	Tax Code
Edit	Other Liability	2-1550	Accrued Expenses	N-T
Add	Other Asset	1-1315	Provision for Doubtful Debts	N-T
Add	Other Asset	1-1380	Accrued Revenue	N-T
Add	Cost of Goods Sold	5-0100	Opening Stock	N-T
Edit	Cost of Goods Sold	5-9000	Closing Stock	N-T

3   Post the journal to accrue the wages expense of $140 on 31 July 2017.

4   The yearly business insurance was paid on 1 July 17 and the prepayments asset account was debited. Expense $55 from prepayments to the business insurance using 31 July 17 as your date.

5   Post the depreciation for July into the appropriate depreciation and accumulated depreciation account on 31 July 17:
   – Furniture $120.00
   – Boat equipment $208.33
   – Boats $1112.34.

6   Magnetic Boats management has decided it would be appropriate to set up a provision for doubtful debt of $200. Record the journal using the date 31 July 17.

7   Another Boat was purchased on 31 July 17 for $3740.00 (including GST). It was paid for using a bank loan. Record this through the general journal using Bank Loan #2.

8   Some worn boating equipment was sold on 31 July 17 for $660 including GST and the money was deposited into the Cheque Account. Record the sale in the general journal.

9   Accrue $400 (excluding GST) of Boat Hire from P. Blossom. The income was earned in July but won't be invoiced till August. Use the date of 31 July 17.

10 Stocktake reveals the closing inventory balance is $15 200. Find the opening balance and produce the Adjusting Inventory journal as at 31 July 17.

11 Reverse the accrued revenue and accrued expenses on 1 August 17.

12 Produce the following reports all from the Accounts menu in the Reports Index:
    – General Ledger [Detail] for 6-4100 Wages and Salaries only dated 1 July to 1 August 2017
    – Trial Balance for July 2017
    – Profit & Loss for July 2017
    – Transaction Journal 1 July to 1 August 2017. General journals only.

11

UNDERSTANDING AND SETTING UP PAYROLL

Learning outcomes

By the end of this chapter you will be competent in:
- understanding some payroll concepts including remuneration types, salary packaging, superannuation and taxation
- using MYOB's Easy Setup Assistant for payroll
- entering company payroll details correctly
- entering employee details correctly
- setting up MYOB's standard pay features
- generating and printing some Payroll Setup reports.

This chapter will give you an understanding of the underlying principles of payroll and the obligations that the employer and employee have towards each other. You will set up payroll in existing company files and input employee details. The files we set up for payroll in this chapter will be used in later chapters when we process the pays.

Background

Payroll is the process by which the employees of a business get remunerated (paid) for their work. This differs to paying a contractor (who is considered a supplier) in that the employer has more responsibility towards an employee than they do towards a contractor.

Fair Work Act

Australia's industrial relations system underwent a major transformation in 2006 when the Howard government introduced Work Choices legislation that was designed to bring the fragmented, largely state-based, industrial relations system into a more uniform national system. Prior to 2006, a worker in a particular industry could have different entitlements and workplace conditions depending on the industrial relation laws in the state that they were employed.

The Rudd government developed this further by asking the states to refer their Constitutional workplace powers over to the Commonwealth in 2007. This resulted in the further homogenising of employees entitlement and work conditions and became the *Fair Work Act 2009*. Most employees are now covered under the *Fair Work Act*, excluding a non-corporation entity in Western Australia or state or local government entity (except for those in Victoria).

National Employment Standards

The National Employment Standards (NES) contain the 10 minimum conditions that cannot be changed to the detriment of the employee. Together with the Modern Awards, the NES are a safety net that cannot be contracted out of. These standards, taken straight from the Fair Work Ombudsman website, are:

- A maximum standard working week of 38 hours for full-time employees, plus 'reasonable' additional hours.
- A right to request flexible working arrangements.
- Parental and adoption leave of 12 months (unpaid), with a right to request an additional 12 months.
- Four weeks paid annual leave each year (pro rata).
- Ten days paid personal/carers leave each year (pro rata), two days paid compassionate leave for each permissible occasion and two days unpaid carers leave for each permissible occasion.
- Community service leave for jury service or activities dealing with certain emergencies or natural disasters. This leave is unpaid except for jury service.
- Long service leave.
- Public holidays and the entitlement to be paid for ordinary hours on those days.
- Notice of termination and redundancy pay.
- The right of new employees to receive the Fair Work Information Statement.

More information on each condition can be found on the Fair Work Ombudsman website https://www.fairwork.gov.au NES.

No award

If there is no award covering the employees, the employer and the individual employee can mutually agree on the terms and conditions of the contract of employment, as long as they comply at least with the NES above.

In addition, employers of award-free employees are required to meet all the usual statutory employment obligations such as occupational health and safety, workers' compensation, employee pay slips and employment records.

If a contract of employment is found to be unfair, harsh, unconscionable, against the public interest or specifically designed to avoid the provisions of an award or agreement, Fair Work Australia or the Fair Work Ombudsman may declare the contract to be void or make variations to the contract.

Useful websites

Penalties for contravening the Fair Work Act can be harsh, so examples of useful websites are:

- https://www.fairwork.gov.au
- https://www.ato.gov.au
- http://www.industrialrelations.nsw.gov.au
- http://www.workplaceinfo.com.au
- http://www.employsure.com.au
- http://www.connectlegal.com.au

Rights and obligations

When a person accepts a specific offer of employment (written or oral), a *contract of employment* has been established, under which each party has certain rights and obligations towards the other.

The employer must:

- pay wages
- reimburse employees for work-related expenses
- ensure a safe working environment that is suitable for the performance of the employee's duties
- not act in a way that would seriously damage an employee's reputation, or cause humiliation or mental distress
- not act in a way likely to damage the trust and confidence necessary for a successful employment relationship
- not provide a false or misleading reference
- forward PAYG income tax deductions and SGC superannuation amounts promptly.

The employee must:

- obey the lawful and reasonable commands of the employer
- exercise due care in the performance of the work and do it competently
- account to the employer for all moneys and property received while employed
- make available to the employer any process or product invented by the employee in the course of employment
- be faithful to the employer by disclosing to the employer information received relevant to the employer's business and not pass on to a rival information likely to damage the employer.

Paying wages

All payment of remuneration (including overtime and other payments) must be made to the employee in money. Electronic funds transfer (EFT) to a bank account in the employee's name is the best-practice method as it produces an irremovable audit trail and circumvents any problems associated with the counting and distribution of cash. If the employer chooses to pay their employee with cash, they should ensure the employee counts their pay in front of them and sign a receipt stating they have received the cash. Each time an employee is paid (generally at least monthly), the employee must be provided with a pay slip.

Pay slips must contain:

- the name and **Australian Business Number (ABN)** of the employer
- the name of the employee
- the classification of the employee under any applicable industrial instrument
- the date on which payment was made
- details of the period of employment to which the payment relates
- gross amounts of remuneration including overtime and other payments
- the amount paid as overtime, or sufficient information to enable the employee to calculate the amount paid as overtime

> **Australian Business Number (ABN)**
> A unique number that identifies a business to the government and the community. It can be issued to all types of entities that run an enterprise.

- the amount deducted as taxation and all amounts deducted for other purposes
- the net amount being paid
- superannuation paid or to be paid and the superannuation fund the contribution has/is going to.

Awards and workplace agreements usually specify the interval at which an employer must pay remuneration to the employee. However, if so demanded by an employee, payment of remuneration must be at least each fortnight.

Salary packaging

Salary packaging is a method of paying the expenses of an employee using their pre-tax dollars, thus reducing their taxable income and hence their income tax. It must be agreed with your employee *before* they start earning money. In some cases, such as the purchase of electronic equipment used for work or superannuation salary sacrifice, there are no tax consequences for the employer. In other cases, such as the provision of motor vehicles that can be used privately and the payment of private expenses such as gym membership or private travel, the employer has to pay Fringe Benefits Tax.

BAS agents and payroll

On 1 June 2016, the Tax Practitioners Board officially expanded the scope of allowable BAS (Business Activity Statement) Services provided by registered BAS agents to include providing services relating to superannuation, PAYG Withholding and PAYG Instalments. However, there will be times when it would be prudent to seek advice. Salary sacrifice and Fringe Benefits can become somewhat complicated and some are matters for Human Resources, so this is the time to consult with either the government departments, such as Fair Work and the Australian Taxation Office (ATO), or get advice from independent experts.

Payroll tax

Payroll tax is a state tax on total gross payroll (above a certain threshold) and differs from state to state. For further information on rates, thresholds, registration and payments, see https://www.payrolltax.gov.au which provides information and links to the relevant websites.

Payroll components

Remuneration

It is the responsibility of the employer to ensure that employees are paid at the correct rate for all work done. There are several methods of calculating pay, the most common of which are:

- *Wages*: an agreed hourly rate multiplied by the number of hours worked. This rate usually varies with the number of hours worked in a day, and according to the day of the week on which the work is done.
- *Salary*: an agreed annual amount divided by 52 if paid weekly, or by 26 if paid every two weeks. There is usually no variation for weekend duties or for extra hours worked on a day.
- *Commission*: this is an amount calculated according to the value of the work done. It may be the sole method of payment, or it can be combined with either wages or salaries to act as an incentive.
- *Piece work*: in this method of payment the remuneration is directly related to the quantity (not value) of work done.

    Ordinary hours or *normal hours* are the employee/s normal and regular hours of work (https://www.fairwork. gov.au) and are paid at their base rate. *Wage* earners who are required to work in excess of the normal hours in a day or in a week are paid an increased hourly rate of pay called *overtime*. Overtime may also apply to hours worked before and after the usual start or finish times. For instance, the *Clerks – Private Sector Award 2010* states ordinary hours of work are from 7.00 am to 7.00 pm; so, if an employee was to work past 7.00 pm, they would be entitled to overtime even if they didn't start till, for instance, 5.00 pm. Overtime can be an actual dollar amount or the base rate multiplied by a multiplier such as time-and-a-half, double time or triple time.

Salary earners get paid the same amount each pay period, regardless of how many hours they work. They do not get paid overtime, though their leave entitlements remain the same as other part- or full-time employees.

Leave entitlements

Part- and full-time workers are entitled to paid leave as part of the minimum conditions in the NES. Leave accrues (accumulates) every pay period and, when leave is taken, it is deducted from the accrued entitlement. The types of leave include:

- *Annual leave* is for when the employee goes on holiday. (Full-time employees generally accrue four weeks a year.)
- *Personal leave* is for when the employee needs to take time off work because they or their immediate family or a household member is sick, or they have caring responsibilities or a family emergency. Legally, the employer only has to pay the personal leave that is available, though it is not uncommon for an employer to allow the personal leave to go into the negative for valued employees.
- *Long service leave* is for when employees have worked continuously for a business for a long time. Each state and territory has their own *Long Service Leave Act* which stipulate *when* an employee is eligible to receive long service leave (often after seven to 10 years continuous service) and *how much* long service leave that employee can receive.
- *Compassionate leave* is for when a member of an employee's immediate family or household dies or suffers a life-threatening illness or injury. The entitlement is two days per occasion and does not have to be consecutive days. It is paid for part- and full-time employees and unpaid for casuals.

Superannuation

Superannuation was made compulsory in 1992 to force workers to save for their retirement, thus relieving some of the tax burden of providing the Age Pension.

Superannuation guarantee is a surcharge on ordinary times earnings (OTE) for eligible employees. It is an employer expense and is paid to the superannuation fund of the employee's choice. It is a percentage calculated on specific payments, such as ordinary wages, bonuses, annual leave and sick leave. Specifically excluded from the calculation are payments such as overtime, benefits subject to Fringe Benefits Tax or reimbursements of expenses. The ATO provides a Superannuation Guarantee Contributions Calculator on its website as well as a Ruling (SGR 2009/2), which clearly defines the terms 'Salaries and Wages' and 'Ordinary Times Earnings'. For more information, go the Australian Taxation Office website (https://www.ato.gov.au).

The superannuation guarantee rate has been 9.5% since 1 July 2014. Under normal circumstances the money is not available until retirement or death. Though accounting and payroll software are generally configured to calculate superannuation on the correct payments, it is necessary for the small businesses who process their wages manually to ensure they are calculating their superannuation guarantee correctly. Penalties apply for late or under payments.

The employee may choose to pay extra superannuation to save for their retirement. The two methods are known as **additional superannuation** and **salary sacrifice**. In both circumstances, the employer organises the amounts to be deducted from the pay and remits it to the superannuation fund at the same time as the compulsory superannuation guarantee.

> **Additional superannuation**
> A voluntary deduction from wages *after* tax that is remitted to the superannuation fund.
>
> **Salary sacrifice**
> A voluntary deduction from wages *before* tax that is remitted to the superannuation fund.

SuperStream

SuperStream was introduced by the ATO to standardise the processing of superannuation payments and data. *All* employers were required to be SuperStream compliant by October 2016.

SuperStream requires that all superannuation be processed and paid electronically at the same time. Employees can request payment into the superannuation fund of their choice. Before SuperStream, this meant that payroll officers often needed to make many payments to different funds, some who insisted on being paid monthly. They also had to notify the superannuation funds by logging onto individual websites and processing the information. If company policy was to pay the superannuation quarterly, as per the ATO minimum requirements, this meant that some funds were paid monthly, some quarterly, and this could cause some administration headaches. SuperStream streamlined the process providing a one-stop electronic interface which transmitted the data to all the relevant parties, including the ATO.

Setup requires registration with an appropriate provider and then the processing of the following information:

- employee personal details such as name, address, tax file number (TFN) and date of birth
- fund information such as ABN, **USI** and member number.

After that, the process is simply to log on to the SuperStream site at appropriate times and either upload a file or fill out the manual grid with superannuation entitlements for each eligible employee. All of the superannuation will be paid in a lump sum and SuperStream will distribute it accordingly. However, in order to meet the deadline for submitting superannuation payments (generally the 28th of the month following the monthly or quarterly period), SuperStream requires you to lodge and pay by the 15th of that month. This allows enough time for the distributions to reach the appropriate superannuation funds.

> **USI (Unique Superannuation Identifier)**
> A unique number allocated to each individual Superannuation fund.

PAYG Withholding

It is a requirement that the employer apply Pay as You Go (PAYG) Withholding tax to an employee's gross wages and remit this to the Australian Taxation Office through the BAS or IAS (Instalment Activity Statement). How much tax is withheld depends on:

- how much the employees gross wage is for the pay period
- whether the employee is claiming the tax-free threshold or not
- if the employee is in a specific category, such as a Shearer or a foreign resident
- whether the employee has tax offsets such as an Overseas Force or Dependent Spouse tax offset
- whether the employee can claim a part of full Medicare deduction.

The source document, to be completed and signed by the employee, is the Tax File Number Declaration.

Deductions from wages or salary

Payment to an employee must be made in full. However, some deductions are made before the net pay is arrived at:

- deductions may be required by law, for example PAYG tax withholding and **HECS-HELP** instalments.
- courts may order deductions from an employee's pay (a garnishee order) in settlement of a debt. such an order must be in writing
- agencies, such as the Child Support Agency, can order deductions from an employee's pay. This order must also be in writing
- an employee may request an employer to deduct amounts from wages for specific purposes. Such a request must be in writing and must be for a purpose that is to the benefit of the employee.

All deductions made from an employee's pay must be itemised on their pay slip.

> **HECS-HELP**
> The Higher Education Contribution Scheme – Higher Education Loan Programme are the government-offered interest free loans that assist students undertaking higher education. These loans are repaid through the PAYG withholding system once the student has earned over the threshold, which is indexed regularly. HELP replaced HECS in 2005, but because so many people started out on the HECS programme, it is often referred to in the combined format of HECS-HELP.

Illegal deduction from wages

Unless specifically authorised by law, court order, modern award or enterprise agreement, employers are not permitted to make deductions for the following purposes:

- the cost of employee's uniform
- to make up for shortages from a till or cash float
- training courses provided to the employee
- tools or equipment provided for the employee
- the cost of mobile phones supplied to the employee for work-related purposes
- the cost of damage to the employer's assets
- the cost of breakages or accidents by the employee.

Recording payroll data

Source documents: employment pack

In order to set up the employee file correctly, the employee should receive an *employment pack*. The three forms below need to be completed by the employee and returned to the employer:

- Tax File Number Declaration form
- Superannuation Standard Choice form
- Personal Details form, which requires information such as address, phone numbers, bank account details, next of kin, medical conditions etc.
  The employer then may give the new employee:
- a copy of the NES 10 minimum conditions (compulsory)
- a copy of the signed contract and/or
- an Induction Manual, which is a way of familiarising the employee with their workplace, special procedures and the employer's expectations regarding the job.
  An example of an employment pack can be found in the Chapter 11 folder of your start-up files.

Employment records

General records to be kept include:

- the name and Australian Business Number of the employer
- the full name of each employee and whether employed full-time or part-time
- the classification of each employee under any award or enterprise agreement that applies
- whether each employee is employed on a permanent, temporary or casual basis
- the date on which each employee was first employed by the employer
- regarding apprentices and trainees, the date on which each employee first became an apprentice or trainee
- the date of termination when any employee's contract is terminated.
  Hours of pay records include:
- the number of hours to be worked per week, day or other period
- if the relevant award or agreement limits the number of daily hours of work and provides for the payment of daily overtime, then the number of hours actually worked each day and the times of starting and ceasing work
- the rate of remuneration per week, day, hour or other period depending on the basis used in calculating the pay
- if remuneration is calculated by piece work, then the number and description of the pieces completed and the rate per piece at which each employee is paid

- gross amounts of remuneration earned, deductions made and net pay.
  Leave records include:
- the accrual of annual holidays, sick leave and parental leave
- any leave taken by the employee
- each employee's entitlement regarding leave from time to time.
  Superannuation records include:
- the amount of contributions made
- the period over which the contributions were made
- the name of the fund to which the contributions were made
- the basis on which the employer became liable to make the contributions and the date on which they were made.

Setting up Payroll

MT ISA CLEANERS

1   In MYOB AccountRight 2016 open the **11.1 Mount Isa Cleaners.myox** data file from the Chapter 11 folder of your start-up files.
2   Set up Payroll:

Click...
- *Setup* (in the top menu bar).
- *Easy Setup Assistant.*
- *Payroll.* Read the introduction screen.
- *Next.*
- *Tax Tables.* Read the window that opens.
- *Load Tax Tables.* You may need to do this twice before the window opens saying the current *Tax Tables Revision Date* is *1/10/16.* Click *Yes* when it does.
- *Yes* (because you would like to continue).
- *Next* (to view the current payroll year: *2017*).
- *Next* (to move on).
- *Full Work Week Hours* (insert *36*).
- *Withholding Payer Number* (insert *00 403 048 957*).
- *Default Superannuation Fund* (select *Spectrum Super*).
- *Round Net Pay Down to a Multiple of (5) cents.* See **Figure 11.1.**

Wage categories
MYOB needs to be customised to suit your remuneration arrangements.

Click...
- *Next* (accept the linked accounts).
- *Next* (review payroll categories). We will first review the Wages Category (see **Figure 11.2**). If you scroll down to view the overtime rates, you can see there is no Overtime (1.25x). We need to set up this week-day overtime.

Figure 11.1   Payroll Easy Setup Assistant: Payroll Information

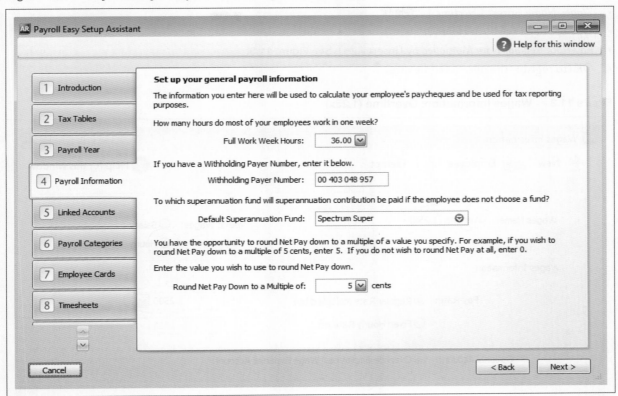

Figure 11.2   Payroll Easy Setup Assistant: Payroll Categories: Wages

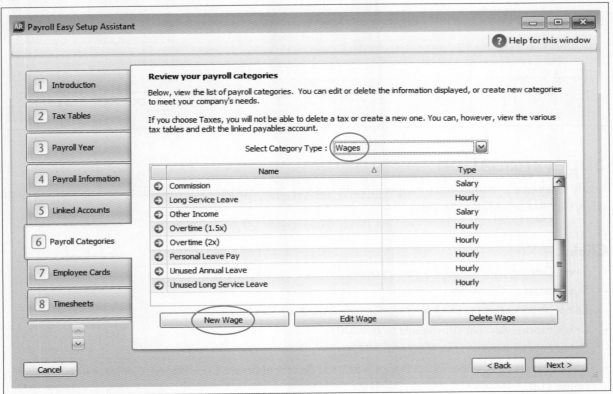

- *New Wage* (button at left of the window; also in **Figure 11.2**.) A new window opens.
- *Wages Name* (insert *Overtime 1.25x*).
- *Type of Wages* (click on *Hourly*).
- *Pay Rate Regular Rate Multiplied by* (insert *1.25*). See **Figure 11.3**.
- *OK* (to register the new overtime rate).

Figure 11.3   **Wages Information: Overtime (1.25x)**

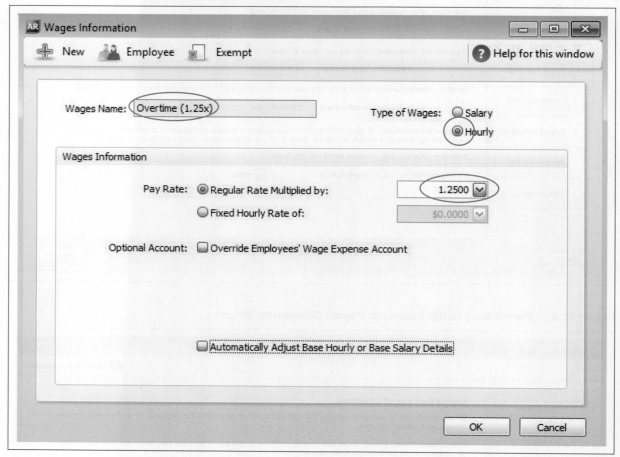

Superannuation

Nearly every employee qualifies for superannuation. Some choose to pay extra towards their retirement through salary sacrifice or additional super.

Click...

- *Select Category Type* (choose *Superannuation*).
- *Superannuation Guarantee*.
- *Edit Superannuation* (to bring up the information window). See **Figure 11.4**.
- *Linked Expense Account* (this should be *6-4300*).
- *Linked Payable Account* (this should be *2-1420*).
- At *Calculation Basis* select *Equals* (insert *9.5%*) and *Percent of* (insert *Gross Wages*). Compare with **Figure 11.5**.
- *Exempt* (in top menu bar). See **Figure 11.5**.

Figure 11.4   **Payroll Easy Setup Assistant: Payroll Categories: Superannuation**

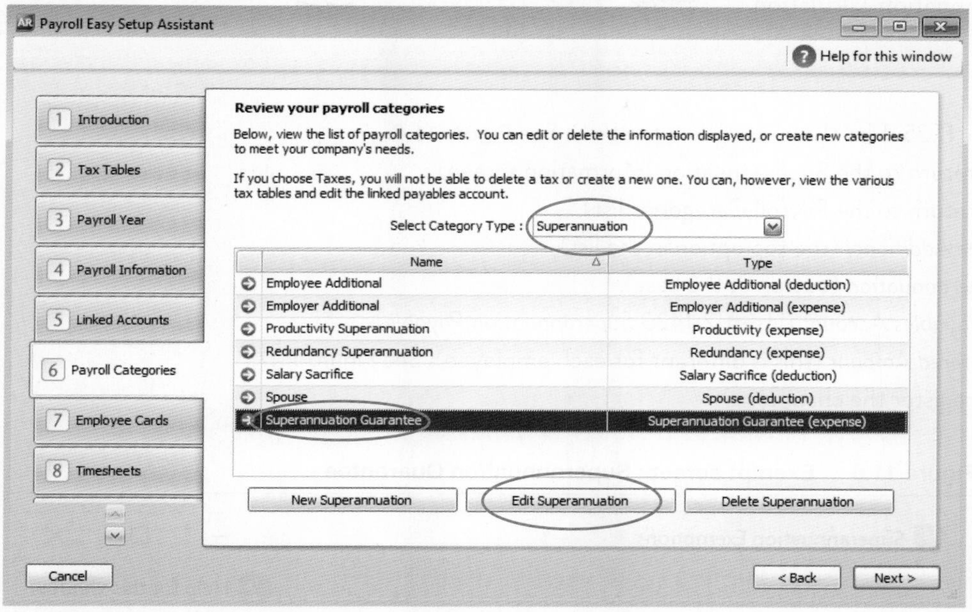

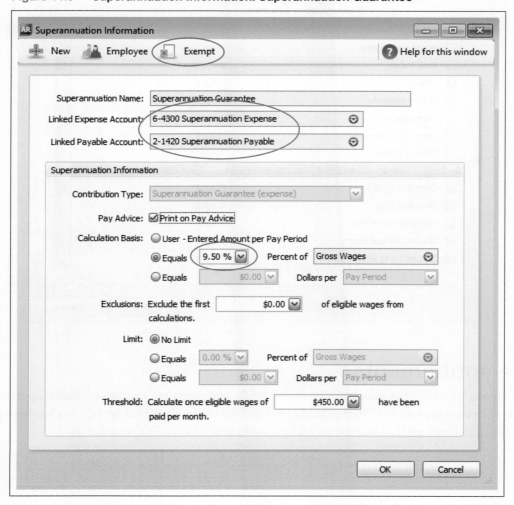

Figure 11.5   **Superannuation Information: Superannuation Guarantee**

The Exempt button may seem a little confusing. If there is a tick in the wages category, it is *not* included in the superannuation calculation.

Click...

- *Overtime (1.25x)* (so there is a tick in the box). See **Figure 11.6**.
- *OK* (to return to the Superannuation Information screen).
- *OK* (to return to the Payroll Categories list).
- *Employee Additional* (the top option in the list).
- *Edit Superannuation* (button at the base).
- *Linked Payables Account* (insert *2-1420 Superannuation Payable*).
- *User-Entered Amount* (this is different for each employee). See **Figure 11.7**.
- *OK* (to register the change).

Figure 11.6   Exempt screen: Superannuation Guarantee

Superannuation Exemptions

Help for this window

Exclude the following wages categories BEFORE calculating Superannuation Guarantee.

	Wage Categories △	Type
☐	Base Salary	Wages
☑	Bonus	Wages
☐	CDEP Payments	Wages
☐	Commission	Wages
☐	Long Service Leave	Wages
☐	Other Income	Wages
☑	Overtime (1.25x)	Wages
☑	Overtime (1.5x)	Wages
☑	Overtime (2x)	Wages
☐	Personal Leave Pay	Wages
☑	Unused Annual Leave	Wages
☑	Unused Long Service Leave	Wages

OK   Cancel

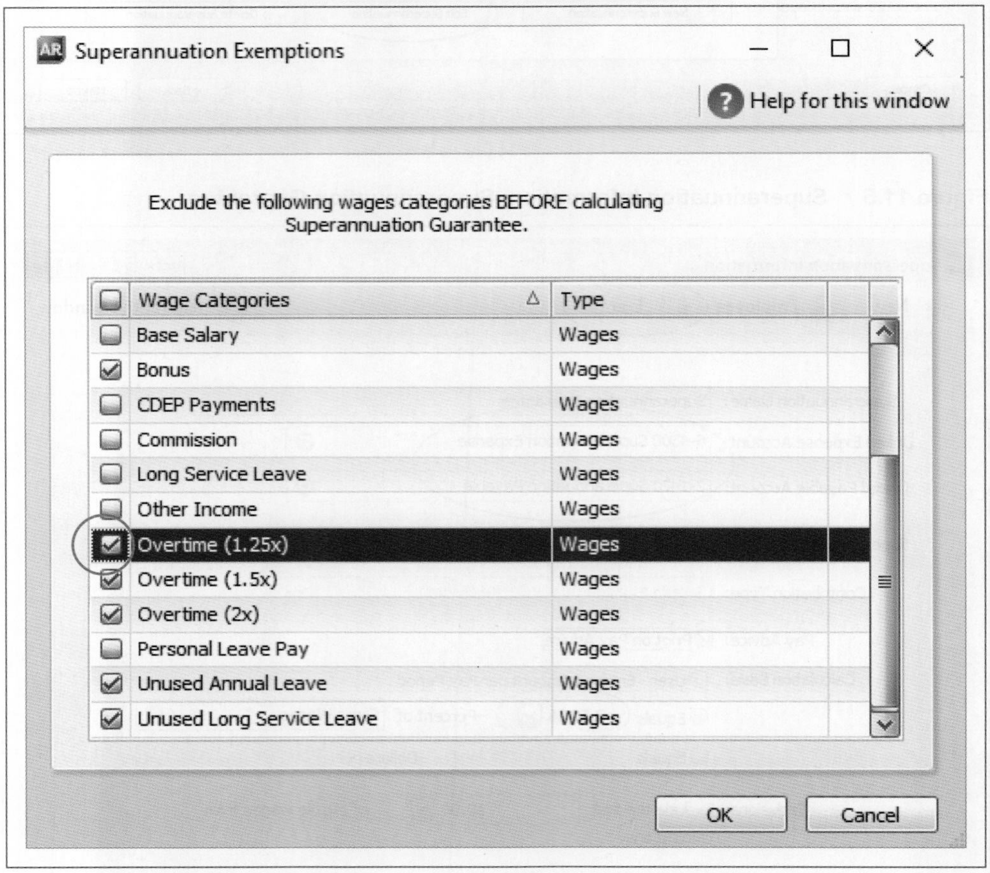

Leave entitlements

The next step is to set up the leave entitlements for full- and part-time employees. These are accumulated each week as a percentage. In MYOB, the calculation basis in the Holiday Leave Accrual box has been preset to 7.6923% of Gross hours and has been based on four weeks annual leave. The equation is:

$$\text{Annual Leave} = \frac{4 \text{ weeks} \times 36 \text{ hours}}{\text{Year } 52 \text{ weeks} \times 36 \text{ hours}} = \frac{144}{1872} = 0.076923$$

Figure 11.7   **Superannuation Information: Superannuation Additional**

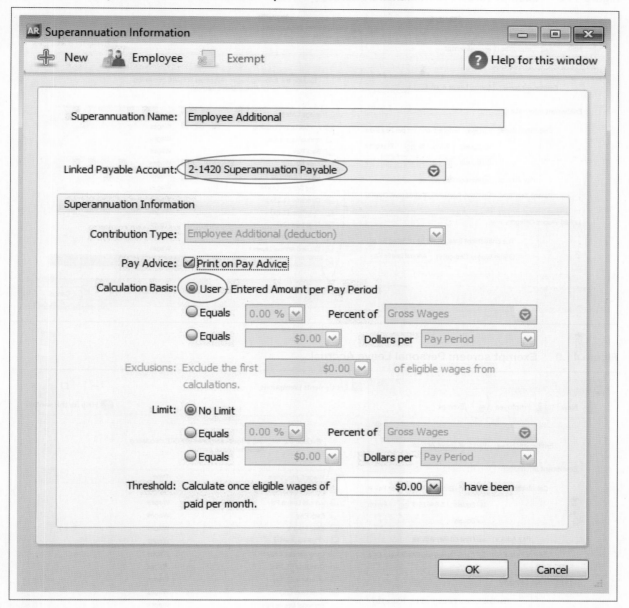

If the award or contract stipulates a different annual leave entitlement, this percentage has to be changed. The Personal Leave Accrual calculation is based on two weeks a year.

Click...

- *Select Category Type* (choose *Entitlements*).
- *Annual Leave Accrual* (the first on the list).
- *Edit Entitlement* (centre button in the window).
- *Exempt* (at the top). See Figure 11.8.
- All of the following (as Annual Leave does not accrue on these hours): *Annual leave loading, CDEP Payments,* all the *Overtime* wages, *Unused Annual Leave* and *Unused Long Service Leave*. Also in Figure 11.8.
- *OK* (to close the Exempt window).

Figure 11.8   Exempt screen: Annual Leave Accrual

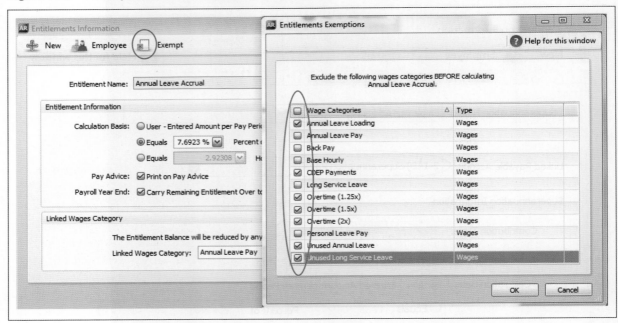

Figure 11.9   Exempt screen: Personal Leave Accrual

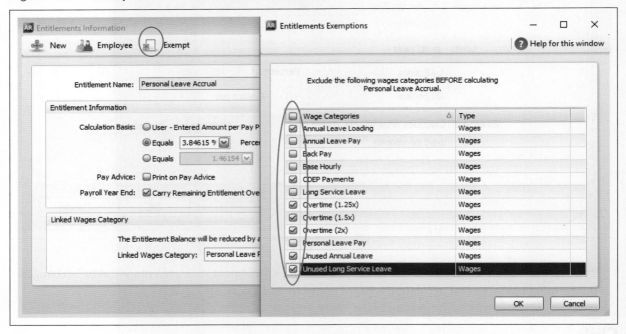

- *OK* (to return to the Payroll Categories screen).
- *Personal Leave Accrual* (follow the same process as above with the *Exempt* window). See Figure 11.9.

Deductions

Two additional wages deduction categories are needed: a *Savings Plan* of $6.00 per week and a category for *Health Fund* contributions, which vary according to the plan selected by the employee.

There are three different ways in which MYOB can handle deductions, and these are set up in the *Calculation Basis section* of the *Deduction Information* window:

- *Equals a fixed dollar amount per Pay Period* is selected when all the employees wanting this deduction have the same amount deducted, for example union fees, social club membership, lotto club.
- *User-Entered Amount per Pay Period* is selected when the employees wanting this deduction set their own individual amounts to be taken out of their pay, such as child care, health fund.
- *Equals a percentage of Gross Wages* is selected when employees want a fixed percentage of their pay to be deducted. The actual amount deducted will vary with each individual according to their gross pay.

Click...

- *Select Category Type* (choose *Deductions*).
- *New Deduction* (at the bottom of the screen).
- *Deduction Name* (insert *Savings Plan*).
- *Linked Payable Account* (choose *2-1450 Savings Plan Payable*).
- At *Calculation Basis* select *Equals* (insert *$6*) and *Dollars per* (insert *Pay Period*). Compare with **Figure 11.10**.
- *OK*.

Figure 11.10   New Deduction: Savings Plan (set amount)

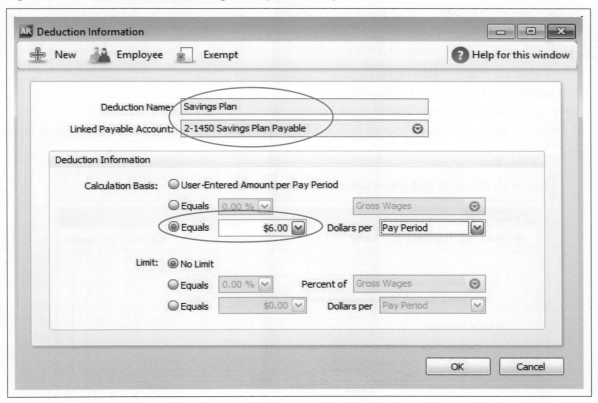

Click...

- *New Deduction*.
- *Deduction Name* (insert *Health Fund*).
- *Linked Payable Account* (choose *2-1440 Health Fund Payable*).
- At *Calculation Basis* leave as *User-Entered Amount per Pay Period*. Compare with **Figure 11.11**.
- *OK*.

Figure 11.11   **New Deduction: Health Fund (User-Entered Amount)**

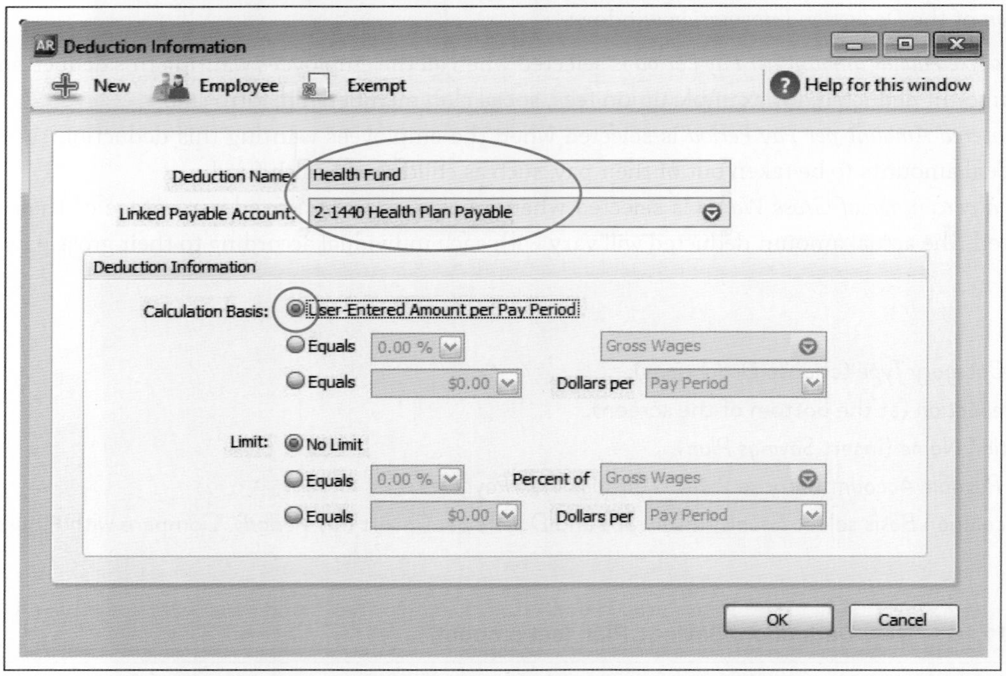

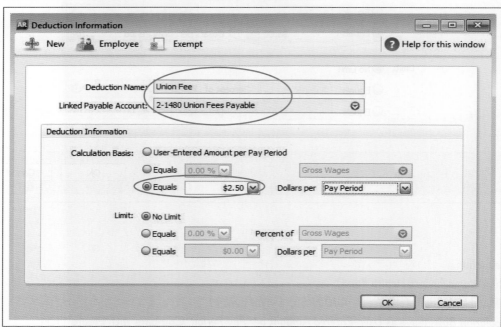

Click...

- *Union Fee* (at the bottom of the list).
- *Edit Deduction* (at the bottom of the screen).
- *Linked Payable Account* (choose *2-1480 Union Fees Payable*).
- At *Calculation Basis* select *Equals* (insert *$2.50*) and *Dollars per* (insert *Pay Period*). Compare with **Figure 11.12**.
- OK.

Figure 11.12   **Edit Deduction: Union Fee (set amount)**

WorkCover (or workers' compensation) can be set up to calculate every time a pay is processed. This is a compulsory insurance and can be paid annually or monthly.

Click...

- *Select Category Type* (choose *Expenses*). WorkCover is the only expense available.
- *Edit Expense* (at the bottom of the screen).
- *Linked Expense Account* (Choose *6-4200 WorkCover Premiums*).
- *Linked Payable Account* (choose *2-1460 WorkCover Payable*).
- At *Calculation Basis* select *Equals* (insert *2.5%*) and *Percent of* (insert *Gross Wages*). Compare with **Figure 11.13**.
- *OK*.

Figure 11.13   Expense: WorkCover (percentage)

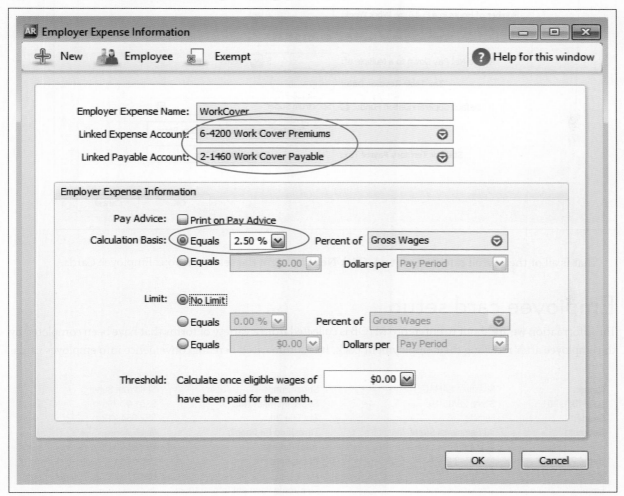

This is why

We could have left the linked expense and linked payables account as the default general ledger called Other Payroll Liabilities. However, as the superannuation, deductions and expenses all have to be paid out in full to the appropriate entities, it is often easier to reconcile by using separate general ledger accounts.

PAYG Withholding

And finally we need to check the PAYG Tax Withholding. If you can't see the PAYG Witholding, go to **Setup** and **General Payroll Information** at the bottom of the list to ensure they have been loaded properly. Check the date on the window that opens. See Figure 11.14.

Figure 11.14   **Tax: PAYG Withholding**

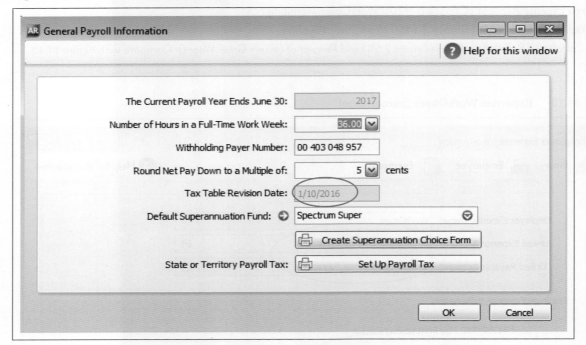

That is all of the payroll categories set up. Click **Next** to begin the set up on your Employee Cards.

Employee card setup

The information we are about to enter into MYOB is collected from a variety of forms that have been completed by the employee after receiving their employment pack. It is summarised here for convenience into employee cards.

Name:	Shashike GAMAGE
Card ID: E 001	**Start:** 28/05/16
Gender:	Female
Address:	70 Camoweal Street, Mount Isa QLD 4825
Home Phone:	(07) 7743 2377
Mobile:	0401 385 077
Email:	shagam@hotmail.com
Employment Status:	Full Time
Pay Type:	Hourly
Pay Rate:	$30.00 ph

Super Fund:	Spectrum Super
Super Member No.:	3351 0776
Tax File No.:	552 064 212
Threshold Claimed?:	Yes
Total Rebate:	$2 080.00 pa
Deductions:	Union Fee
	Health Fund: $27.90 pw
Electronic Payment Information:	
BSB Number:	580-129
Account Number:	030867
Statement Text:	MT ISA CLEANERS

Click...

- *New* (to open a new Employee Profile).
- *Yes* (to the window that opens asking whether changes should be saved).
- *Card ID* (type *E 001*). Press the Tab key.
- *Last Name* (insert *GAMAGE*) then press the Tab key.

- *First Name* (insert *Shashike*).
- Insert the contact details and compare with Figure 11.15.
- *Payroll Details* (tab at top of the window). See Figure 11.16.

Figure 11.15   Employee Card: Profile tab

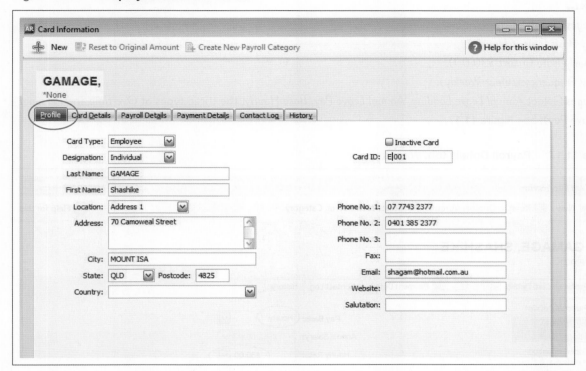

Figure 11.16   Payroll Details tab: Personal Details

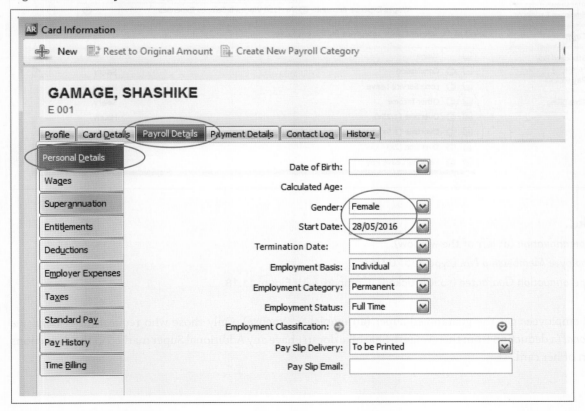

- *Gender* (select *Female*).
- *Start Date* (insert *28/05/16*).
- *Employment Status* (leave as *Full Time*).

Click...

- *Wages* (at left of the window).
- *Pay Basis* (select *Hourly*).
- *Hourly Rate* (insert *$30.00*).
- *Pay Frequency* (select *Weekly*).
- *Wages* (select *Annual Leave Loading, Annual Leave Pay, Base Hourly*, the three types of *Overtime* and *Personal Leave Pay*). See **Figure 11.17**.

Figure 11.17   Payroll Details tab: Wages

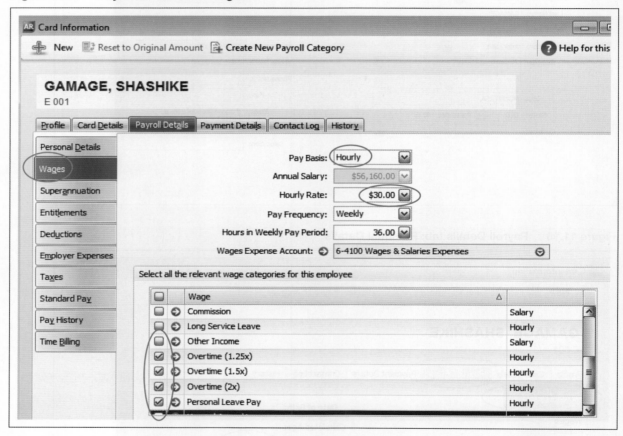

Click...

- *Superannuation* (at left of the window).
- *Employee Membership No.* (type *3351 0776*).
- *Superannuation Guarantee* (so it is ticked). Compare with **Figure 11.18**.

All employees get the guaranteed super (an employer expense). Only those who request it get *Employee Additional* (a deduction from their wages). Shashike doesn't have any Additional Super marked in the deductions section of her card.

Figure 11.18   **Payroll Details tab: Superannuation**

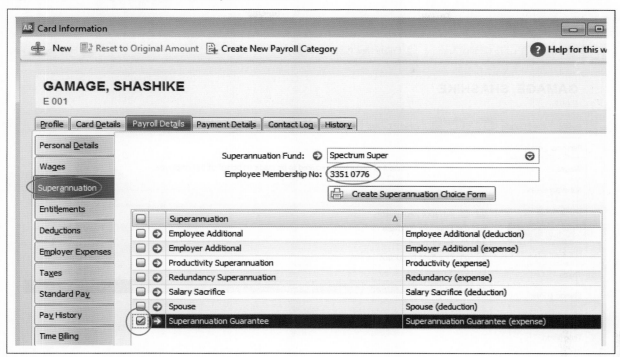

Click...

- *Entitlements* (at left of the window).
- *Entitlement* (tick both, as these apply for all employees who are not casuals). Compare with **Figure 11.19**.
- *Deductions* (at left of the window).
- *Deduction* (click all those that apply to this employee). Compare with **Figure 11.20**.
- *Employer Expenses* (at left of the window).
- *WorkCover* (tick as all employees are covered by WorkCover). Compare with **Figure 11.21**.

Figure 11.19   **Payroll Details tab: Entitlements**

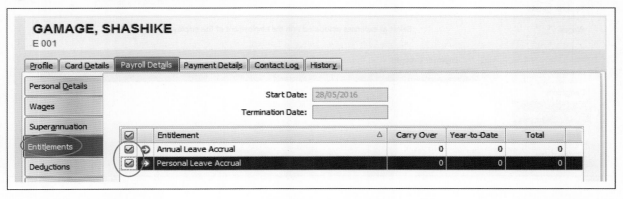

Figure 11.20   **Payroll Details tab: Deductions**

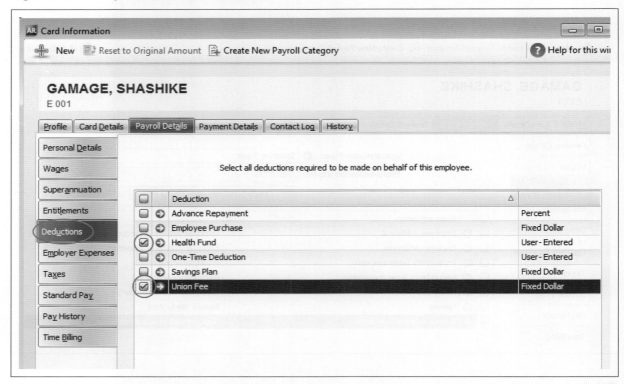

Figure 11.21   **Payroll Details tab: Employer Expenses**

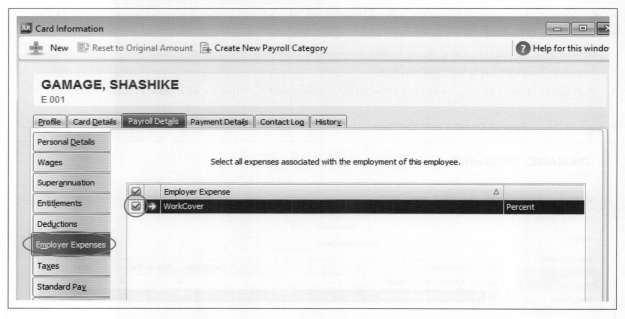

Click...

- *Taxes* (at left of the window).
- *Tax File Number* (insert the details from the employee card).
- *Tax Table* (choose *Tax Free Threshold*).
- *Total Rebates* (insert the total rebate of *$2080*). Compare with Figure 11.22.

Figure 11.22   **Payroll Details tab: Taxes**

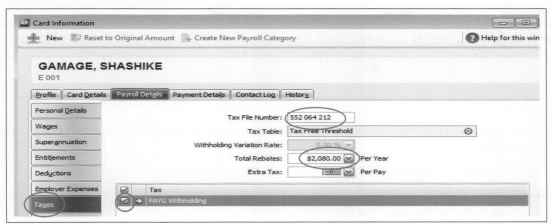

The Standard Pay section is where you set up the weekly deductions for *this* employee. See employee details on page 334.

Deductions are entered as *negative* amounts.

Click...

- *Standard Pay* (at left of the window).
- *Memo* (type *Pay S. Gamage*).
- *Amount* (insert any deductions as a minus figure). Compare with Figure 11.23.

Figure 11.23   **Payroll Details tab: Standard Pay**

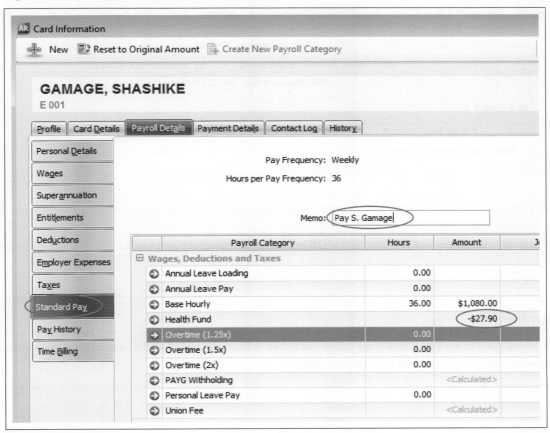

The next step is to set up the payment details. Most employees are paid by EFT and pays can be uploaded straight into the bank.

Click...

- *Payment Details* tab (at the top of the window).
- *Payment Method* (choose *Electronic*).
- *Bank Statement Text* (insert *MT ISA CLEANERS*). Press the Tab key.
- Type in the rest of the bank information into the appropriate fields. See **Figure 11.24**.

Figure 11.24   Payment Details tab

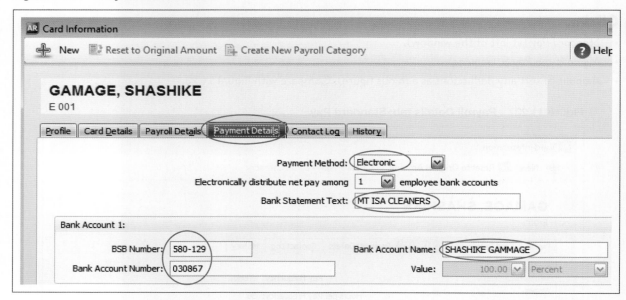

The pay could be split up into two or more different bank accounts if requested by the employee (and if allowed by the employer).

Once you have completed this card, click **OK** and enter in the other employee cards below using the same process.

Remember This

All employees need to have the same wage categories ticked as Shashike, as well as the appropriate superannuation, entitlements, WorkCover and their relevant deductions.

Name:	Ajantha BALBO	**Name:**	Federico PRELATI
Card ID: E 002	**Start:** 28/05/16	**Card ID:** E 003	**Start:** 28/05/16
Gender:	Female	**Gender:**	Male
Address:	106 Miles Street, Mount Isa QLD 4825	**Address:**	41 Doughan Terrace, Mount Isa QLD 4825
Home Phone:	(07) 7743 8017	**Home Phone:**	(07) 7743 7596
Mobile:	0472 308 551	**Mobile:**	0457 011 027
Email:	ajalbo@hotmail.com	**Email:**	fedlati@hotmail.com
Employment Status:	Full Time	**Employment Status:**	Full Time
Pay Type:	Hourly	**Pay Type:**	Hourly
Pay Rate:	$25.00 ph	**Pay Rate:**	$20.00 ph
Super Fund:	Spectrum Super	**Super Fund:**	Spectrum Super
Super Member No.:	3351 1064	**Super Member No.:**	3351 1093
Tax File No.:	450 386 937	**Tax File No.:**	302 058 914
Threshold Claimed?:	Yes	**Threshold Claimed?:**	Yes
Total Rebate:	$1300.00 pa	**Total Rebate:**	$624.00 pa
Deductions:	Union Fee Health Fund: $29.35 pw Employee Additional Super: $50.00 pw	**Deductions:**	Union Fee Savings Plan Employee Additional Super: $40.00 pw
Electronic Payment Information		**Electronic Payment Information**	
BSB Number:	580-089	**BSB Number:**	580-119
Account Number:	037168	**Account Number:**	055124
Statement Text:	MT ISA CLEANERS	**Statement Text:**	MT ISA CLEANERS

After all the employees have been entered, we can finish off the Payroll Setup.

Click...
- *Next* (bottom right corner).
- *Timesheets* (read the screen but don't do anything as we won't be using timesheets for this company).
- *Next*.
- *Close* (to get out of the Payroll Setup screen).
- *Close* (to return to the Command Centre).

Electronic file setup

As these pays will be uploaded directly to the bank electronically, some extra information has to be set up in the accounts. This allows for the smooth recording of both the upload file and the MYOB transactions.

Click...
- *Accounts List* (in the Accounts module).
- *Zoom arrow* next to *1-1110 Business Bank Account #1*. See **Figure 11.25**.
- *Banking* tab. See **Figure 11.26**.
- *BSB Number* (insert *361494*). Press the Tab key.
- *Bank Account Number* (insert *036589*). Press the Tab key.
- *Bank Account Name* (insert *MT ISA CLEANERS*). Press the Tab key.
- *Company Trading Name* (insert *MT ISA CLEANERS*). Press the Tab key.
- *Electronic Payment Type* box (so it is ticked).
- *Bank Code* (insert *WAG*). Press the Tab key.

- *Direct Entry User ID* (insert *67984*).
- *Direct Entry File* box (so it is ticked). Compare with Figure 11.26.
- *OK.*
- *Close* (to return to the Command Centre).

Figure 11.25   Accounts List: All Accounts tab

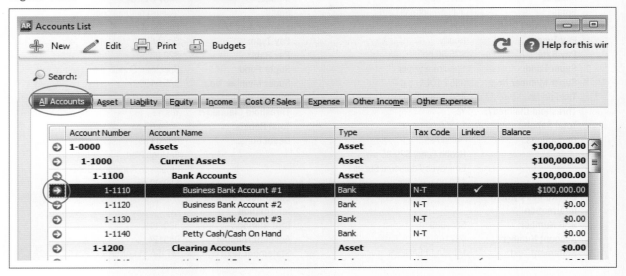

Figure 11.26   Business Bank Account #1: Banking tab

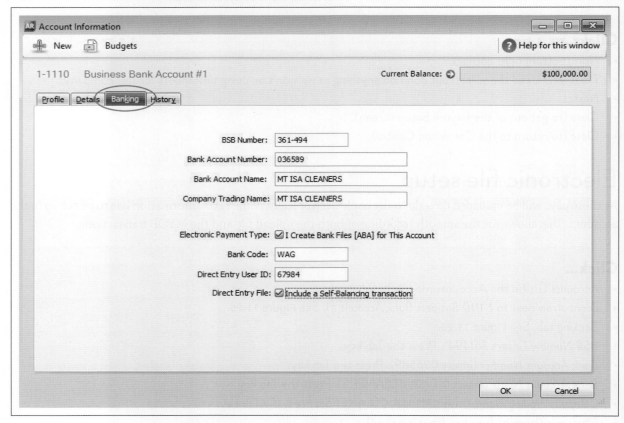

Nice work! You have just completed your first Payroll Setup.

Entitlements

As mentioned at the beginning of the chapter, part- and full-time workers are entitled to paid leave as part of the minimum conditions in the NES. Leave accrues (accumulates) every pay period and, when leave is taken, it is deducted from accrued entitlements. The following exercise gives you practice at setting up payroll, as well as setting up different categories of leave for salaried employees.

H. & K. PTY LTD

1 In MYOB AccountRight 2016 open **11.2 H & K Pty Ltd.myox** from the Chapter 11 folder of your startup files.
2 Set up Payroll for H & K Pty Ltd using the Easy Setup Assistant.
3 Load the tax tables. You may need to do this twice in order to get the screen telling you that the tax tables from 1/10/16 are being loaded.

Use the following information for the Payroll Setup:
- Current Payroll Year is 2018.
- The normal hours worked per week is 35.
- Default Superannuation fund is Spectrum Super.
- Round pay down to 0 cents.
- Linked Account for Cheque Payments (change to 1-1230 Payroll Clearing Account). See Figure 11.27.

Figure 11.27   Payroll Setup: Linked Accounts

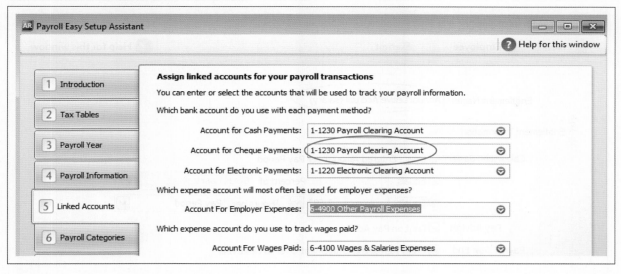

Wages:
- Add in a new Overtime rate of 1.25 times normal rate.
  Superannuation:
- Employee Additional: Linked Payable Account is 2-1420 and calculation basis is User-Entered Amount per Pay Period.
- Salary Sacrifice: Linked Payable Account is 2-1420 and calculation basis is User-Entered Amount per Pay Period.

- Superannuation guarantee: Linked Expense Account is 6-4300, Linked Payable Account is 2-1420 (both of these accounts have Superannuation in their names), the calculation basis is 9. 5%.
- Exempt the new Overtime rate of 1.25x from superannuation guarantee.

Remember This

- Salary sacrifice is when superannuation is deducted *before* calculating the tax.
- Employee additional is when superannuation is deducted *after* calculating the tax.

Entitlements:

- Both Annual and Personal Leave: Exempt the following: Annual Leave Loading, Backpay, CDEP Payments, all the Overtime wages, Unused Annual and Unused Long Service Leave.
- Create two new entitlements for salaried employees by clicking New Entitlement (no exemptions necessary, explained further in Chapter 12):
  – Annual Leave Accrual (salary): Calculation Basis equals 2.692 per pay period, tick the Print on Pay Advice box, Linked Wages Category is Annual Leave Pay. See **Figure 11.28**.
  – Personal Leave Accrual (salary): Calculation Basis equals 1.346 per pay period, Linked Wages Category is Personal Leave Pay. See **Figure 11.29**.

Figure 11.28   Annual Leave Accrual (salary) Setup

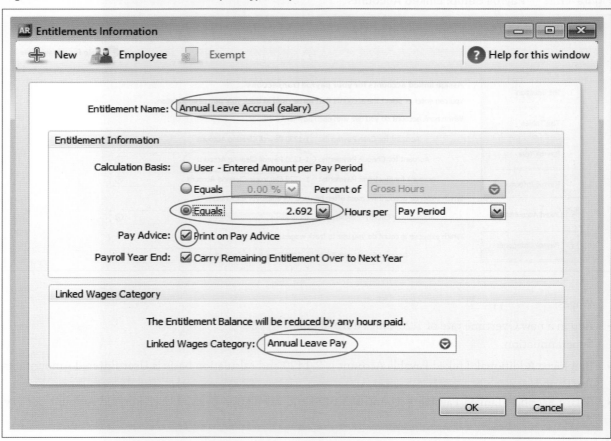

Figure 11.29   Personal Leave Accrual (salary) Setup

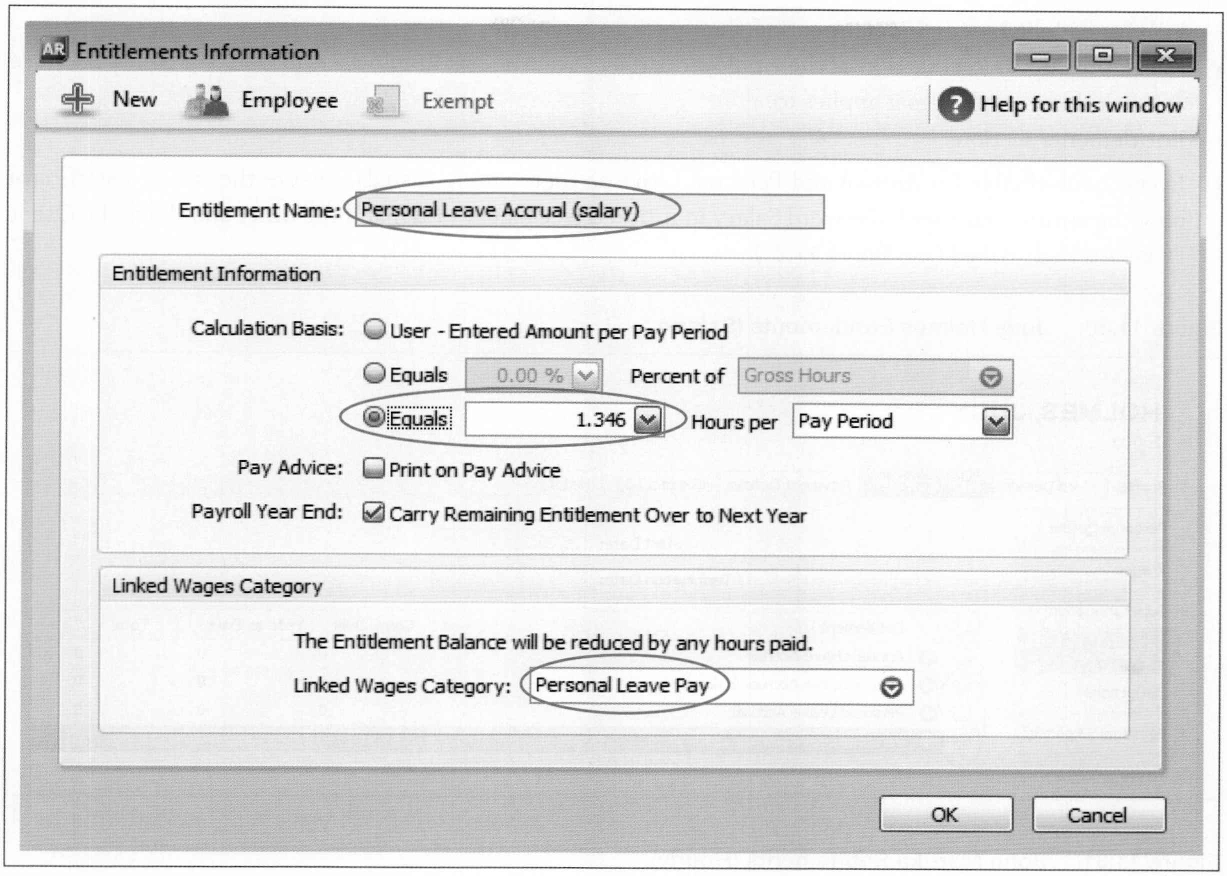

Deductions:

- Add a Health Fund: Linked Payable Account is 2-1440 and it is a (User-Entered) Deduction.
- Add a Savings Plan: Linked Payable Account is 2-1450 and $12.00 per pay period.
- Edit the Union Fee: Linked Payable Account is 2-1480 and the rate is $3.25 per pay period.

Expenses:

- WorkCover Insurance rate: Linked expense Account is 6-4200, Linked Payable Account is 2-1460 and it equals 2% of gross wages.

Taxes:

- PAYG Withholding – check the tax tables have loaded by clicking on Setup in **the top menu bar** and General Payroll Information.

4 Create cards in MYOB for the following four employees: Judy Holmes; Josephine Kelly; John Maruka and Denise Chen. Josephine Kelly has a different superannuation fund and instructions are given on how to enter this into MYOB. Use the following extra information to help you complete these employees' cards:

Wages section:

- Salaried Employees: tick Annual Leave Pay and Personal Leave Pay. Base Salary should already be ticked. As employees on salaries don't get overtime, they won't get the annual leave loading either.
- Hourly Employees: tick Annual Leave Loading, Annual Leave Pay, the three Overtime rates and the Personal Leave Pay. Base Hourly should already be ticked.

Superannuation section:

- Everyone is eligible for Superannuation Guarantee so remember to tick this.
- Check the Deductions section of the employee cards to see who has Employee Additional or Salary Sacrifice and tick those employees it applies to.

Entitlements section:

- Everyone is eligible for Annual and Personal Leave as there are no casuals. Ensure the salaried staff have only the entitlements with the word Salary in it ticked (see Figure 11.30) and the other staff have the Other Leave Accruals ticked (see Figure 11.31).

Figure 11.30   Judy Holmes Entitlements (Salary)

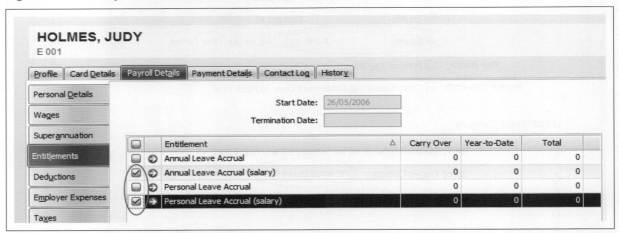

Figure 11.31   John Maruka Entitlements (Hourly)

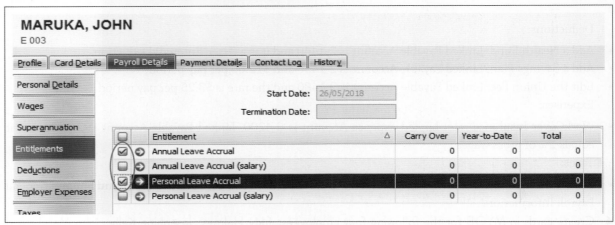

Deductions section:

- Check the employee cards to see which deductions to tick.

WorkCover section:

- Everyone is covered for WorkCover so tick this box.

Standard pay section:

- Change the memo to read Pay (then write the employee's name).
- Enter deductions in as negatives. Judy Holmes' standard pay section is shown as an example in Figure 11.32.

Figure 11.32   Standard Pay: Judy Holmes

HOLMES, JUDY E 001					

Pay Frequency: Weekly
Hours per Pay Frequency: 35

Memo: Pay J Holmes

Payroll Category	Hours	Amount	Job
Wages, Deductions and Taxes			
Annual Leave Pay	0.00		
Base Salary		$2,000.00	
Health Fund		-$32.50	
PAYG Withholding		<Calculated>	
Personal Leave Pay	0.00		
Salary Sacrifice		-$250.00	
Entitlements			
Annual Leave Accrual		<Calculated>	
Personal Leave Accrual		<Calculated>	
Employer Expenses			
Superannuation Guarantee		<Calculated>	

Name:	Judy HOLMES	**Superannuation Fund:**	Spectrum
Card ID: E 001	**Start:** 26/05/06	**Super Member No.:**	531 6582
Address:	21 Barrys Road,	**Tax File No.:**	214 037 552
	Broadmeadows VIC 3047	**Threshold Claimed?:**	Yes
Home Phone:	(03) 9309 3211	**Total Rebate:**	$1 248.00 pa
Mobile:	0417 223 214	**Deductions**	
Pay Type:	Salary	**Health Fund:**	$32.50 pw
Pay Rate:	$104 000.00 pa	**Salary Sacrifice:**	$250.00 pw

When creating the employee card for Josephine Kelly you will notice that she has Australian Super as her superannuation fund. As this is a new superannuation fund, you will need to add it in the superannuation screen. When entering information into the superannuation section, type Australian Super into the **Superannuation Fund** field and a separate screen appears. See Figure 11.33. Click on **Easy Add**.

Once Josephine's card is done, complete the cards for John Maruka and Denise Chen.

After completing the employee cards, finish the Payroll Setup by clicking through the screens. This company does not use timesheets.

5   Accrued entitlements are entitlements that have accrued prior to the establishment of this set of books. Everyone, except for John Maruka, has been working for the company for some years and has accrued the following entitlements that must be entered into MYOB:

- Judy: 141 hours' Annual Leave and 40 hours' Personal Leave.
- Josephine: 151 hours' Annual Leave and 61 hours' Personal Leave.
- Denise: 68 hours' Annual Leave and 53 hours' Personal Leave.

Figure 11.33   **Superannuation screen: adding a new super fund**

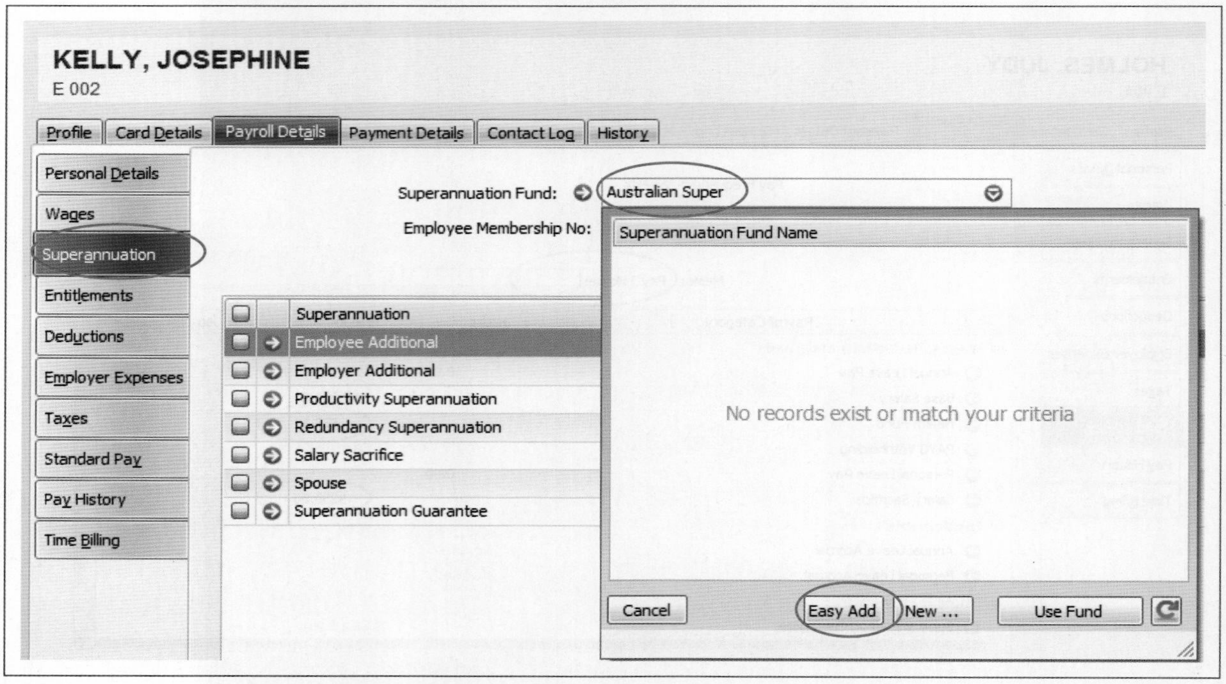

KELLY, JOSEPHINE
E 002

Profile | Card Details | Payroll Details | Payment Details | Contact Log | History

Personal Details

Wages

Superannuation

Entitlements

Deductions

Employer Expenses

Taxes

Standard Pay

Pay History

Time Billing

Superannuation Fund: ➔ Australian Super

Employee Membership No:

Superannuation Fund Name

	Superannuation
→	Employee Additional
⊙	Employer Additional
⊙	Productivity Superannuation
⊙	Redundancy Superannuation
⊙	Salary Sacrifice
⊙	Spouse
⊙	Superannuation Guarantee

No records exist or match your criteria

Cancel   Easy Add   New ...   Use Fund

Name:	Josephine KELLY
Card ID: E 002	**Start:** 26/05/06
Address:	21 Maffra Street, Broadmeadows VIC 3047
Home Phone:	(03) 9309 5104
Mobile:	0419 203 116
Pay Type:	Salary
Pay Rate:	$104 000.00 pa
Superannuation Fund:	Australian Super
Super Member No:	5668 2143
Tax File No.:	319 005 837
Threshold Claimed?:	Yes
Total Rebate:	$1248.00 pa
Deductions:	Health Fund $32.50 pw
	Employee Additional Super $250.00 pw

Name:	John MARUKA
Card ID: E 003	**Start:** 26/05/16
Address:	66 Lygon Street, Carlton VIC 3053
Home Phone:	(03) 9662 1388
Mobile:	0403 203 209
Pay Type:	Hourly
Pay Rate:	$30.00 ph
Superannuation Fund:	Spectrum
Super Member No:	523 1222
Tax File No.:	258 465 159
Threshold Claimed?:	Yes
Total Rebate:	$728.00 pa
Deductions:	Savings Plan
	Health Fund $33.25 pw
	Union Fee

Name:	Denise CHEN
Card ID: E 004	**Start:** 26/12/15
Address:	220 Lygon Street, Carlton VIC 3053
Home Phone:	(03) 9347 7033
Mobile:	0419 023 544
Pay Type:	Hourly
Pay Rate:	$20.00 ph
Superannuation Fund:	Australian Super
Super Member No:	1513 6008
Tax File No.:	402 353 914
Threshold Claimed?:	Yes
Total Rebate:	$0.00pa
Deductions:	Savings Plan
	Union Fee

Click...

- *Cards List* (in the Card File Command Centre).
- *Employee* (to reduce the number of visible cards).
- *Holmes, Judy* (double-click to access the card).
- *Payroll Details* (tab at top of the window).
- *Entitlements* (at left of the window).
- *Carry Over* (insert the details). See **Figure 11.34**.
- *OK.*

Figure 11.34   **Entitlements Carry Over: Judy Holmes**

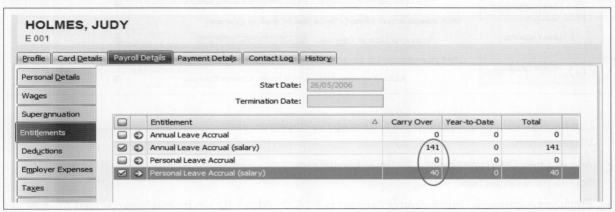

Repeat the steps above for Josephine Kelly and Denise Chen then click **Close** to return to the Command Centre.

Pay History

It is common for companies converting to MYOB to have employees already working for them. These employees will generally have a pay history, including accrued leave entitlements. These can be inserted into the Pay History section of the Payroll Details tab in the employee card. It is similar to opening balances for the accounts. In the employees' cards using Pay History in the Payroll Details window. The following exercise gives you practice at setting up payroll and employees for a company, as well as teaching you how to enter the year-to-date balances belonging to each employee.

<u>ELSMORE DEMOLITION</u>

1. In MYOB AccountRight 2016 open the **11.3 Elsmore Demolition.myox** file from the Chapter 11 folder of your startup files.
2. Set up Payroll for Elsmore Demolition using the Payroll Easy Setup Assistant.
3. Load the tax tables. You may need to do this twice in order to get the screen telling you that the tax tables from 1/10/16 are being loaded.

Use the following information for the payroll setup:

- Current Payroll year is 2018.
- The normal hours worked per week is 40.
- Default Superannuation fund is Spectrum Super.
- Round pay down to 0 cents.
- Linked Account for Cheque Payments (change to 1-1230 Payroll Clearing Account). See **Figure 11.35**.

Figure 11.35   Payroll Easy Setup Assistant: Linked Accounts

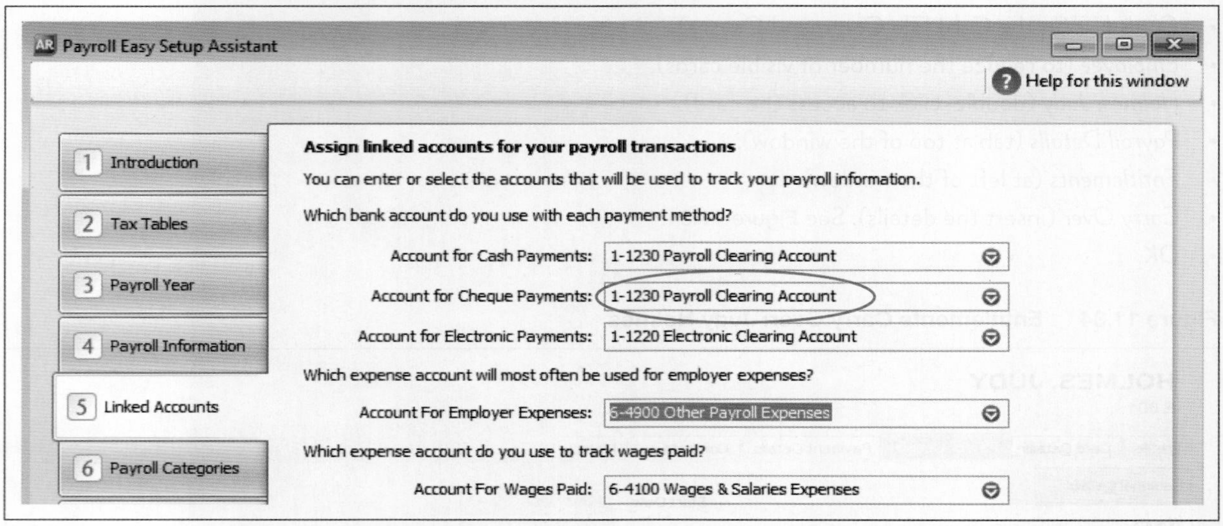

Use the following information when setting up the employee cards:

Wages section:

- Add in a new Overtime rate of 1.25 times normal rate.

  Superannuation section:

- Employee Additional: Linked Payable Account is 2-1420 and calculation basis is User-Entered Amount per Pay Period.
- Salary Sacrifice: Linked Payable Account is 2-1420 and calculation basis is User-Entered Amount per Pay Period.
- Superannuation guarantee: Linked Expense Account is 6-4300, Linked Payable Account is 2-1420, the calculation basis is 9.5%.
- Exempt the new Overtime rate of 1.25x from superannuation guarantee.

  Entitlements section:

- Both Annual and Personal Leave: Exempt the following: Annual Leave Loading, Backpay, CDEP Payments, all the Overtime wages, Unused Annual and Unused Long Service Leave.
- Personal Leave: Change the Calculation Basis to 1.3461 hours per pay period. Exempt the same as for Annual Leave.

  Deductions section:

- Add a Health Fund: Linked Payable Account is 2-1440 and it is a (User-Entered) Deduction.
- Edit the Union Fee: Linked Payable Account is 2-1480 and the rate is $3.25 per pay period.

  Expenses section:

- WorkCover Insurance rate: Linked Expense Account is 6-4200, Linked Payable Account is 2-1460 and it equals 2% of gross wages.

  Taxes section:

- PAYG Withholding: check the tax tables have loaded by clicking on Setup in **the top menu bar** and General Payroll Information.

  Standard pay section:

- Change the memo to read Pay (then write the employee's name).
- Enter deductions in as negatives.

Pay History section:

- All five employees have been working for the company prior to the establishment of this set of books and need their Pay Histories entered into their employee card. The first pay period being processed in MYOB is June, but as all of the employees have been working the entire payroll year, we need to insert the following Pay History as Year to Date figures as positives.

4 Create an employee card as usual for David Bruton and use the information in the Pay History table (below) to complete his Pay History section.

Name:	David BRUTON		Threshold Claimed?:	Yes
Card ID: E 01	Start: 01/06/14		Total Rebate:	$0.00 pa
Address:	Blakes Lane,		Deductions:	Union
	Elsmore NSW 2360			Health Fund $36.00 pw
Pay Type:	Hourly			Salary Sacrifice $250.00 pw
Pay Rate:	$28.00 ph		Bank Information	
Super Fund:	Media Super		BSB:	732-000
Super member No.:	167 352		Account No.:	801301
Tax File No.:	401 221 685		Bank Statement Text:	Elsmore Demolition

Click...

- *Pay History* (at left of the window).
- *Show Pay History for* (choose *Year-to-Date*).
- Enter David Bruton's information from the table below, except for the carry over figures in the entitlements section. See Figure 11.36.
- *Entitlements* (at left of the window).
- *Carry Over* (insert the details). See Figure 11.37.

PAY HISTORY					
Category	Bruton	Cooper	Dillon	Elliot	Wards
Base Hourly	48 160.00	46 440.00	44 720.00	43 000.00	41 280.00
Annual Leave Loading	784.00	756.00	728.00	700.00	672.00
Annual Leave Pay	4 480.00	4 320.00	4 160.00	4 000.00	3 840.00
Overtime (1.5x)	2 520.00	2 227.50	0.00	1 875.00	0.00
Overtime (2x)	1 680.00	4 860.00	0.00	0.00	288.00
Personal Leave Pay	420.00	0.00	1 664.00	0.00	0.00
Health Fund	1 692.00	1 551.00	1 410.00	1 269.00	1 175.00
Union Fee	282.00	282.00	282.00	282.00	282.00
Salary Sacrifice (Super)	11 750.00	9 400.00	7 050.00	4 700.00	2 350.00
PAYG Withholding	11 428.00	12 074.00	11 455.00	9 332.00	9 273.00
Entitlements					
Annual Leave Accrual					
– Year To Date	140.00	145.00	133.00	120.00	105.00
– Carry Over (in Entitlements)	34.00	12.00	121.00	18.00	74.00
Personal Leave Accrual					
– Year To Date	30.00	23.00	30.00	23.00	30.00
– Carry Over (in Entitlements)	18.00	72.00	16.00	34.00	18.00
Employer Expenses					
WorkCover Insurance	1 602.72	1 545.48	1 488.24	1 431.00	1 373.76
Superannuation Guarantee	4 737.60	4 568.40	4 399.20	4 230.00	4 060.80

Figure 11.36   **Pay History: David Bruton**

BRUTON, DAVID
E 01

| Profile | Card Details | Payroll Details | Payment Details | Contact Log | History |

Personal Details

Wages

Superannuation

Entitlements

Deductions

Employer Expenses

Taxes

Standard Pay

Pay History

Time Billing

Show Pay History for: Year-to-Date

Payroll Category	Activity
Wages, Deductions and Taxes	
Base Hourly	$48,160.00
Annual Leave Loading	$784.00
Annual Leave Pay	$4,480.00
Overtime (1.5x)	$2,520.00
Overtime (2x)	$1,680.00
Personal Leave Pay	$420.00
Overtime (1.25x)	$0.00
Health Fund	$1,692.00
Union Fee	$282.00
Salary Sacrifice	$11,750.00
PAYG Withholding	$11,428.00
Entitlements	
Annual Leave Accrual	140.000
Personal Leave Accrual	30.000
Employer Expenses	
WorkCover	$1,602.72
Superannuation Guarantee	$4,737.60

Figure 11.37   **Entitlements Carry Over: David Bruton**

BRUTON, |
E 01

| Profile | Card Details | Payroll Details | Payment Details | Contact Log | History |

Personal Details

Wages

Superannuation

Entitlements

Deductions

Start Date: 1/06/2014

Termination Date:

☑	Entitlement	△	Carry Over	Year-to-Date	Total
☑	Annual Leave Accrual		34	140	194
☑	Personal Leave Accrual		18	30	48

5 Complete the employee cards for Paul Cooper, Michael Dillon, Roger Elliott and Peter Wards. Use the Pay History table (from page 351) to complete their Pay History section.

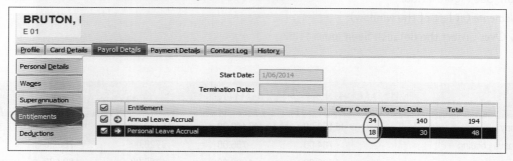

Name:	Paul COOPER	Name:	Michael DILLON
Card ID: E 02	**Start:** 01/07/12	**Card ID:** E 03	**Start:** 01/08/15
Address:	Loves Lane, Elsmore NSW 2360	**Address:**	Brodies Plains, Elsmore NSW 2360
Pay Type:	Hourly	**Pay Type:**	Hourly
Pay Rate:	$27.00 ph	**Pay Rate:**	$26.00 ph
Super Fund:	Rest	**Super Fund:**	Media Super
Super member No.:	1170 256	**Super member No.:**	167 464
Tax File No.:	388 013 978	**Tax File No.:**	509 228 476
Threshold Claimed?:	Yes	**Threshold Claimed?:**	Yes
Total Rebate:	$0.00 pa	**Total Rebate:**	$0.00 pa
Deductions:	Union Fee	**Deductions:**	Union Fee
	Health Fund: $33.00 pw		Health Fund: $30.00 pw
	Salary Sacrifice: $200.00 pw		Salary Sacrifice: $150.00 pw
Bank Information		**Bank Information:**	
BSB:	409-105	**BSB:**	732-001
Account No.:	072396	**Account No.:**	052176
Bank Statement Text:	Elsmore Demolition	**Bank Statement Text:**	Elsmore Demolition

Name:	Roger ELLIOT	**Name:**	Peter WARDS
Card ID: E 04	**Start:** 01/09/01	**Card ID:** E 05	**Start:** 01/10/12
Address:	Stannifer Road, Elsmore NSW 2360	**Address:**	Dawes Lane, Elsmore NSW 2360
Pay Type:	Hourly	**Pay Type:**	Hourly
Pay Rate:	$25.00 ph	**Pay Rate:**	$24.00 ph
Super Fund:	Australian Super	**Super Fund:**	Media Super
Super member No.:	24 68 94	**Super member No.:**	167 689
Tax File No.:	308 253 891	**Tax File No.:**	229 867 153
Threshold Claimed?	Yes	**Threshold Claimed?**	Yes
Total Rebate:	$1 664.00 pa	**Total Rebate:**	$1 092.00 pa
Deductions:	Union Fee	**Deductions:**	Union Fee
	Health Fund: $27.00 pw		Health Fund: $25.00 pw
	Salary Sacrifice: $100.00 pw		Salary Sacrifice: $50.00 pw
Bank Information:		**Bank Information**	
BSB:	831-015	**BSB:**	207-169
Account No.:	079213	**Account No.:**	128760
Bank Statement Text:	Elsmore Demolition	**Bank Statement Text:**	Elsmore Demolition

6 As this business uses timesheets, follow these instructions:

Click...

- *Next* (into the Timesheets screen).
- *I use Timesheets for* (so that the box is ticked) and use the *drop-down arrow* to choose *Payroll*.
- *My Week starts on* (choose *Saturday*). See **Figure 11.38**.
- *Next*.
- *Close* (to get out of Payroll Setup).
- *Close* (to go back to the Command Centre).

Figure 11.38   Timesheets option

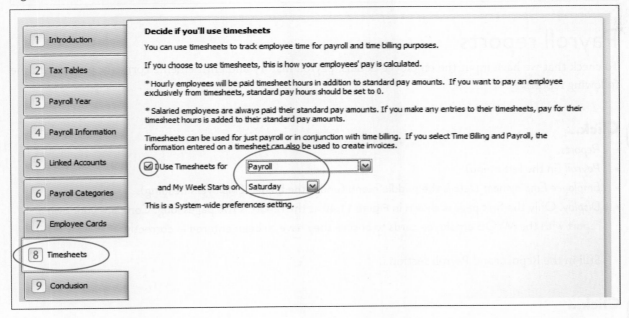

Sometimes this timesheet option doesn't 'stick' so we check that it has worked by going to our Preferences window. If the options are unticked or empty, we can complete the information again here.

Click...

- *Setup* (in the top menu).
- *Preferences.*
- *System* tab (should already be chosen).
- *I use Timesheets for* (to tick the box if it isn't already ticked) and choose *Payroll* from the drop-down menu
- *and My Week Starts on* (choose *Saturday*). See Figure 11.39.
- OK.

Figure 11.39   Preferences: System, timesheet option

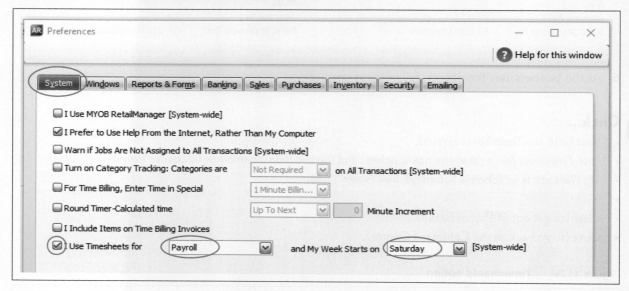

Payroll reports

To check that we have input the employee details, payroll history and entitlements correctly, we can run the following reports.

Click...

- *Reports.*
- *Payroll* (in the left menu).
- *Employee Employment Details* the middle menu (under the bolded *Employees* heading).
- *Display.* Only the first page is shown in Figure 11.40 as the report is five pages long. Compare your own report with the MYOB employee cards to ensure they have all been entered in correctly.

Still in the Reports and Payroll section...

Click...

- *Register Details* the middle menu (also under the bolded *Employees* heading).
- *Dated From* (insert *1/07/17*) and *To* (insert *30/06/18*).

- *Display*. Again, only the first page is shown in Figure 11.41 as this report is longer than five pages. Compare your own report with the year-to-date pay history to ensure it is correct.

Figure 11.40   Employee Employment Details: David Bruton

Elsmore Demolition - Your Student Number
Blakes Lane
ELSMORE NSW 2360
ABN: 31 233 312 133

Employee Employment Details

Name:	David BRUTON	Status:	Active
Card ID:	E 01	Gender:	Male
Address 1:	Blakes Lane ELSMORE NSW 2360		
Tax File Number:	401 221 685	Start Date:	1/06/2014
Employment Basis:	Individual	Payment Method:	Electronic
Employment Category:	Permanent	Pay Frequency:	Weekly
Employment Status:	FullTime	Hours in pay period:	40.000
Pay Basis:	Hourly	Hourly Rate:	$28.00
Tax Scale:	Tax Free Threshold	Annual Salary:	$58,240.00
Total Rebates:	$0.00	Extra Tax:	$0.00
Superannuation Fund:	Media Super		
Employee Membership #:	167 352		

Figure 11.41   Payroll Register Detail: David Bruton

Elsmore Demolition
Blakes Lane
Elsmore NSW 2360
Payroll Register [Detail]
July 2017 To June 2018

Category		1/07/2017 – 30/06/2018
BRUTON, David	E 01	
Wages		
Annual Leave Loading		$784.00
Hours:		0
Annual Leave Pay		$4 480.00
Hours:		0
Base Hourly		$48 160.00
Hours:		0
Overtime (1.5x)		$2 520.00
Hours:		0
Overtime (2x)		$1 680.00
Hours:		0
Personal Leave Pay		$420.00
Hours:		0
Total:		$58 044.00
Deductions		
Health Fund		$1 692.00
Union Fee		$282.00
Total:		$1 974.00

Category	1/07/2017 – 30/06/2018
Superannuation Deductions Before Tax	
Salary Sacrifice	$11 750.00
Total:	$11 750.00
Taxes	
PAYG Withholding	$11 428.00
Total:	$11 428.00
Employer Expenses	
WorkCover	$1 602.72
Total:	$1 602.72
Superannuation Expenses	
Superannuation Guarantee	$4 737.60
Total:	$4 737.60
Entitlements	
Annual Leave Accrual	
Hours:	$140.00
Personal Leave Accrual	
Hours:	$30.00
Total:	$170.00

Next report is the Entitlements Balance Summary, which is a snapshot of the annual and personal leave entitlements.

You are still in the Reports centre.

Click...

- *Balance Summary* (under the bolded *Entitlements* heading).
- *Dated From* (insert *1/07/17*) and To (insert *30/06/18*).
- *Display*. See Figure 11.42.

Figure 11.42   **Entitlements Balance [Summary]**

Elsmore Demolition
Blakes Lane
Elsmore NSW 2360
Entitlement Balance [Summary]
July 2017 To June 2018

Entitlement		Opening Hours	Hours Accrued	Hours Taken	Available Hours	Value
BRUTON, David	**E 01**					
Annual Leave Accrual		34	140	0.00	174	$4 872.00
Personal Leave Accrual		18	30	0.00	48	$1 344.00
Total:		52	170	0.00	222	$6 216.00
COOPER, Paul	E 02					
Annual Leave Accrual		12	145	0.00	157	$4 239.00
Personal Leave Accrual		72	23	0.00	95	$2 565.00
Total:		84	168	0.00	252	$6 804.00

Entitlement		Opening Hours	Hours Accrued	Hours Taken	Available Hours	Value
DILLON, Michael	E 03					
Annual Leave Accrual		121	133	0.00	254	$6 604.00
Personal Leave Accrual		16	30	0.00	46	$1 196.00
Total:		137	163	0.00	300	$7 800.00
ELLIOTT, Roger	E 04					
Annual Leave Accrual		18	120	0.00	138	$3 450.00
Personal Leave Accrual		34	23	0.00	57	$1 425.00
Total:		52	143	0.00	195	$4 875.00
WARDS, Peter	E 05					
Annual Leave Accrual		74	105	0.00	179	$4 296.00
Personal Leave Accrual		18	30	0.00	48	$1 152.00
Total:		92	135	0.00	227	$5 448.00

Summary

- ◆ Payment of wages to an employee must be made in full after allowable deductions have been taken out.
- ◆ A pay slip must be provided to each employee with each payment, detailing the period being paid, the deductions being taken out and other information.
- ◆ General records that must be kept by the employer include the full name of each employee, their classification under any award or agreement, and whether the employee is employed on a full-time or part-time basis.
- ◆ Hours and pay records that must be kept include the number of ordinary hours and overtime being worked and the rate of remuneration.
- ◆ Leave records that must be kept include annual and sick leave being accrued and any periods of leave taken.
- ◆ Superannuation records that must be kept include the amount of contributions made, the period over which they were made and the funds to which they were sent.
- ◆ MYOB uses the Payroll Easy Setup Assistant to step the user through the procedure for setting up payroll for a business.
- ◆ The PAYG Tax Tables are liable to change from year to year (usually with the new financial year on 1 July) and MYOB provides updates whenever they change.
- ◆ New wage rates are easily set up in MYOB, and these can be a multiple of the regular hourly rate (e.g. an overtime rate), a fixed rate per hour (e.g. a casual employee's rate), or a variable non-hourly rate (e.g. for a commission).
- ◆ Entitlements are easily edited to change the rate of accrual of holiday leave and sick leave to reflect the number of hours in the normal working week.
- ◆ Superannuation contributions by the employee and the employer can be allocated to the fund of the employee's choice.
- ◆ Voluntary deductions are easily edited and new ones created to cater for the needs and wishes of the staff.
- ◆ A Standard Pay feature for each employee allows each employee's requested deductions and other regular standard items to be carried forward from one week to the next, reducing the likelihood of error.

Assessment

Aurora Coffee

1   In MYOB AccountRight 2016 open the **11.4 Aurora Coffee.myox** data file from the online Chapter 11 folder of your start-up files.

2   Set up Payroll for Aurora Coffee P/L using the Payroll Easy Setup Assistant.

3   Load the tax tables. You may need to do this twice in order to get the pop up screen telling you that the tax tables from 1/10/16 are being loaded.
Use the following information for the Payroll Setup:
  – Current payroll year is 2018.
  – The normal hours worked per week is 35.
  – Spectrum Super is the default superannuation fund.
  – Round pay down to 0 cents.
Wages:
  – Add in a new overtime rate of 1.25 times normal rate.
Superannuation:
  – Employee Additional: Linked Payable Account is 2-1420 and calculation basis is User-Entered Amount Per Pay Period.
  – Superannuation guarantee: Linked Expense Account is 6-2320, Linked Payable Account is 2-1420, the calculation basis is 9. 5%.
  – Exempt the new overtime rate of 1.25x from superannuation guarantee.
Entitlements:
  – Both Annual and Personal Leave: Exempt the following: Annual Leave Loading, Backpay, CDEP Payments, all the Overtime wages, Unused Annual and Unused Long Service Leave.
Deductions:
  – Add a Health Fund: Linked Payable Account is 2-1440 and it is a (User-Entered) Deduction.
  – Add a Savings Plan: Linked Payable Account is 2-1450 and it is $6.00 per pay period.
  – Edit the Union Fee: Linked Payable Account is 2-1480 and the rate is $2.50 per pay period.
Expenses:
  – WorkCover Insurance rate: Linked Expense Account is 6-2340, Linked Payable Account is 2-1460 and it equals 2.5% of gross wages.

4   Create cards for the following four employees including their standard pays and pay history year to date using the information provided in the table below. All employees are full time.

Name:	Phil BAWEJA		Name:	Grace DE SOUSA
Card ID: E 001	**Start:** 26/05/16		**Card ID:** E 002	**Start:** 26/05/16
Address:	18 Morris Avenue,		**Address:**	150 Arthur Street,
	Wahroonga NSW 2076			Hornsby NSW 2077
Pay Type:	Salary		**Pay Type:**	Hourly
Pay Rate:	$52 000.00 pa		**Pay Rate:**	$30.00 ph
Pay Frequency:	Weekly		**Pay Frequency:**	Weekly
Super Fund:	Spectrum		**Super Fund:**	Hesta
Super Member No.:	167 589		**Super Member No.:**	178 269
Tax File No.:	711 305 074		**Tax File No.:**	302 581 601
Threshold Claimed?:	Yes		**Threshold Claimed?:**	Yes
Total Rebate:	$1 352.00 pa		**Total Rebate:**	$1 040.00 pa
Deductions:	Health Fund: $32.50 pw		**Deductions:**	Union Fee
	Employee Additional Super:			Health Fund: $29.35 pw
	$75.00 pw			Savings Plan

Name:	Harry GOLDSTEIN		Name:	Mandy STELL
Card ID: E 003	**Start:** 26/05/16		**Card ID:** E 004	**Start:** 26/05/16
Address:	70 Kendall Road,		**Address:**	41 Yaraba Avenue,
	Pymble NSW 2073			Gordon NSW 2072
Pay Type:	Hourly		**Pay Type:**	Hourly
Pay Rate:	$25.00 ph		**Pay Rate:**	$18.50
Pay Frequency:	Weekly		**Pay Frequency:**	Weekly
Super Fund:	Australian Super		**Super Fund:**	Spectrum
Super member No.:	1584 6223		**Super Member No.:**	989 657
Tax File No.:	552 064 212		**Tax File No.:**	302 058 914
Threshold Claimed?:	Yes		**Threshold Claimed?:**	Yes
Total Rebate:	$624.00 pa		**Total Rebate:**	None
Deductions:	Union Fee		**Deductions:**	Union Fee
	Health Fund: $27.90 pw			Savings Plan
	Savings Plan			

Category	Baweja	De Souza	Goldstein	Stell
Base Hourly	45 000.00	49 350.00	40 250.00	30 432.50
Annual Leave Loading		183.75	306.25	
Annual Leave Pay	2 000.00	1 050.00	1 750.00	
Overtime (1.5x)		900.00		555.00
Overtime (2x)		2 100.00		
Personal Leave Pay	1 000.00			647.50
Health Fund	1 560.00	1 408.80	1 339.20	
Union Fee	120.00	120.00	120.00	120.00
Savings Plan	288.00	288.00	288.00	288.00
Employee Additional (Super)	3 600.00			
PAYG Withholding	7 356.00	10 704.00	6 816.00	3 408.00

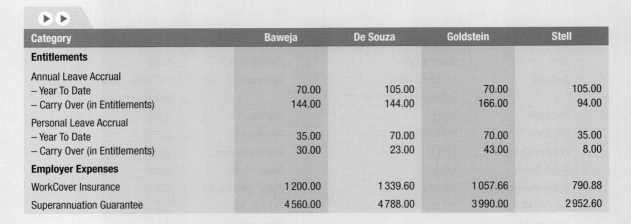

Category	Baweja	De Souza	Goldstein	Stell
Entitlements				
Annual Leave Accrual				
– Year To Date	70.00	105.00	70.00	105.00
– Carry Over (in Entitlements)	144.00	144.00	166.00	94.00
Personal Leave Accrual				
– Year To Date	35.00	70.00	70.00	35.00
– Carry Over (in Entitlements)	30.00	23.00	43.00	8.00
Employer Expenses				
WorkCover Insurance	1 200.00	1 339.60	1 057.66	790.88
Superannuation Guarantee	4 560.00	4 788.00	3 990.00	2 952.60

Print or PDF the following reports from the Payroll section of the Reports Index to give to your instructor. If dates are required, use 1 July 2017 to 30 June 2018:
- Employee Employment Detail
- Payroll Register Detail
- Entitlements Balance Summary.

12

CONDUCTING PAYROLL

Learning outcomes

By the end of this chapter you will be competent in:
- using MYOB's Payroll module
- inputting pays and understanding payroll components
- paying annual leave in advance
- paying employees with cheque or electronic transfer
- understanding leave entitlements
- producing reports relevant to payroll.

Once all the setup is complete and the timesheets calculated, the actual processing of the payroll is relatively straightforward. This chapter walks you through a variety of payroll scenarios paying full-time, salaried and casual employees as well as paying liabilities at the end of the month.

Payroll

<u>MT ISA CLEANERS</u>

1 In MYOB AccountRight 2016 open the **12.1 Mount Isa Cleaners.myox** data file from the Chapter 12 folder of your start-up files.

The following information has been extracted from this week's time cards for the pay week 28 May to 3 June 2017 (pay date 5 June 2017):

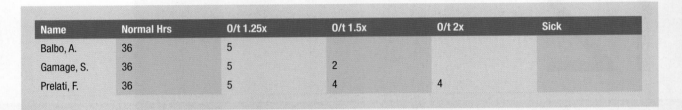

Name	Normal Hrs	O/t 1.25x	O/t 1.5x	O/t 2x	Sick
Balbo, A.	36	5			
Gamage, S.	36	5	2		
Prelati, F.	36	5	4	4	

2 Prepare the pays by entering data from the time cards summary above:

Click...

- *Process Payroll* (in the Payroll module). See Figure 12.1.
- *Process all employees paid* (select *Weekly*).
- *Payment date* (select *5/06/17*).
- *Pay period start* (select *28/05/17*).
- *Pay period end* (select *3/06/17*). See Figure 12.2.

Figure 12.1   Payroll module: Process Payroll

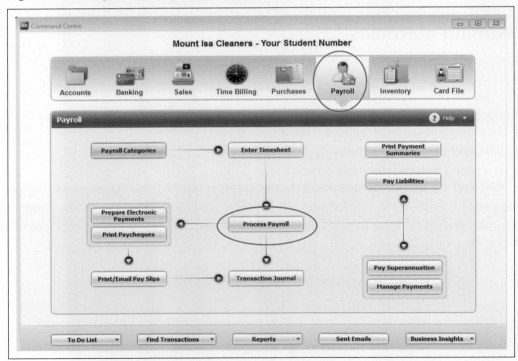

Figure 12.2   **Process Payroll: Pay Period screen**

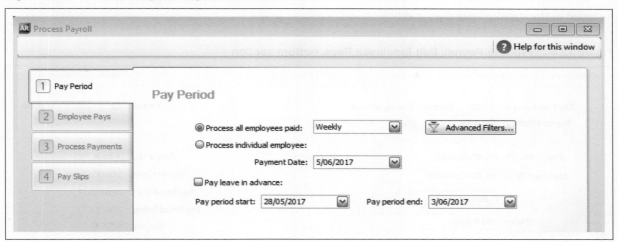

Click...

- *Next* (to get to the Employee Pays window). Note that all of the employees are ticked.
- *Zoom arrow* next to *BALBO, Ajantha*.
- *Base Hourly* (leave as *36* in the *Hours* column as per timesheet summary).
- *Overtime 1.25x* (insert 5 in the *Hours* column). Press the Tab key.
- *Health Fund* (check it shows −29.35 in the *Amount* column).
- *Union Fee* (check it shows −2.50 in the *Amount* column).
- *Employee Additional* (check it shows −50.00 in the *Amount* column). Compare with Figure 12.3.
- *Scroll down* to get to the bottom of the screen to view the *Entitlements* and *Employer Expenses*. See Figure 12.4.

Figure 12.3   **Process Payroll: Edit Employee Pays, top section**

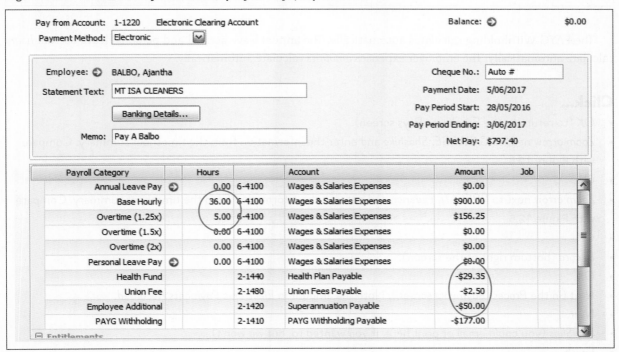

The health fund, union fee and employee additional superannuation all show up automatically as they were included in the standard pay during setup.

Figure 12.4   Process Payroll: Edit Employee Pays, bottom section

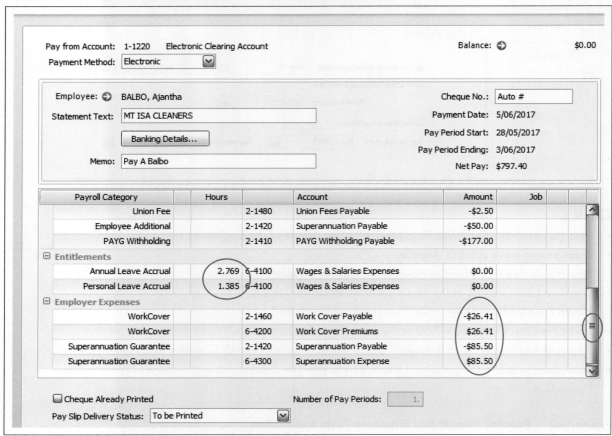

The PAYG Withholding calculates automatically. The annual leave accrual and personal leave accrual *hours* calculate automatically. The employer expenses *amounts* calculate automatically.

Click...

- *OK* (to return to the Employee Pays screen).
- *Zoom arrow* next to *GAMAGE, Shashike* and enter the information from the timesheet summary. Compare with Figure 12.5.
- *OK*.
- *Zoom arrow* next to *PRELATI, Federico* and enter in the information from the timesheet summary. Compare with Figure 12.6.
- *OK*.
- *Record* (bottom right of the screen).
- *OK*.
- *Next* (in the *Process Payments* screen). Note the amount in *Electronic Payments Recorded*.
- *Next*.
- *Pay Slips* (you could email or print here, if you wanted to, but we won't).
- *Finish*.

Figure 12.5   **Edit Employee: S. Gamage**

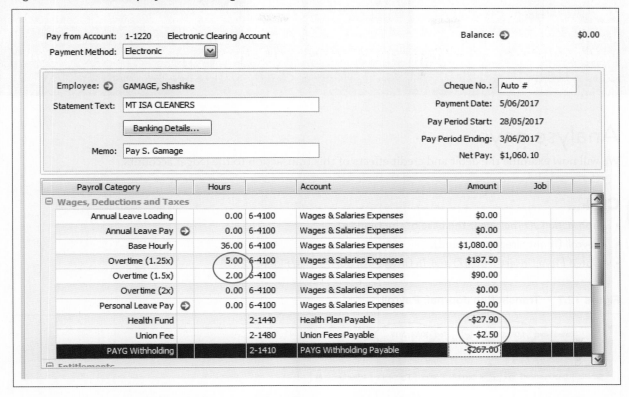

Figure 12.6   **Edit Employee: F. Prelati**

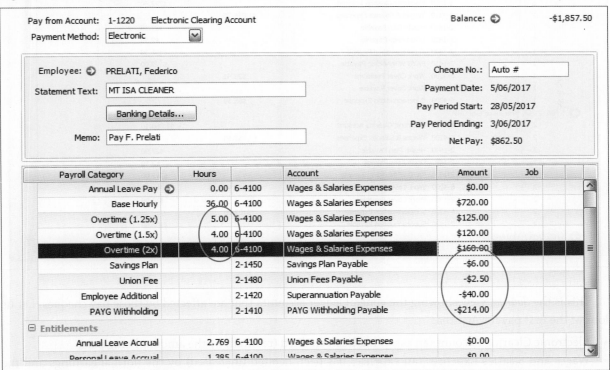

Analyse pays

We will now examine the debit and credit effects of this transaction to the ledger accounts.

Click...

- *Transaction Journal* (near the base of the window).
- *Payroll* (if not already selected).
- *Dated From* (insert *1/06/17*) and *To* (insert *30/06/17*). See Figure 12.7.

Figure 12.7   Transaction Journal: Payroll

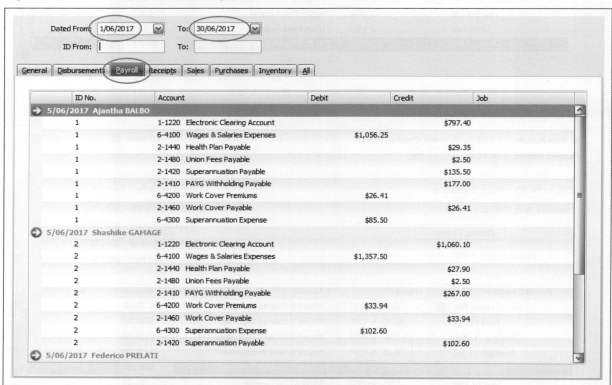

This is the *Journal* view showing the general ledger accounts that are affected by these pay cheques. Let us look at the first pay for Ajantha:

- Electronic Clearing Account (an asset) has been credited (reduced) by the amount being paid.
- Wages and Salaries Expenses (an expense) has been debited (increased) by the normal earnings and the overtime amount. It will appear in the Profit & Loss Statement.
- Health Plan Payable (a liability) has been credited (increased) by the deduction set up in the standard pay. This amount will be sent to the Health Fund at the end of the month.
- Union Fees Payable (another liability) has been credited (increased) by the deduction set up when creating the payroll categories. This amount will be sent to the union at the end of the month.

- Superannuation Payable (another liability) has been credited (increased) by both the deduction set up in the standard pay plus the superannuation guarantee (calculated at 9.5% of ordinary times earnings). This will be sent to the superannuation fund at the end of the month.
- PAYG Withholding Payable (another liability) has been credited (increased) by the amount of tax deducted. It will be forwarded to the Australian Taxation Office (ATO) with the Business Activity Statement (BAS). This will be explained in detail in Chapter 14.
- WorkCover Payable (another liability) has been credited (increased) with the amount MYOB calculated would be the insurance costs to the employer. This will be paid to the insurer at some stage.
- WorkCover Premiums (an expense) has been debited (increased) with the same amount as the WorkCover Payable. This is because the insurance is a tax deduction for the business. It will appear in the Profit & Loss Statement.
- Superannuation Expense (an expense) has been debited (increased) with the same amount calculated by MYOB as being the employer's obligation (9.5%). This is because Superannuation Guarantee is a tax deduction for the business. The Additional Super paid by the employees is not included because *that* super is being remitted by the employee and not the employer.

  Click **Close** to return to the Command Centre.

Produce reports

3 Check your work with a Payroll Activity [Summary] report.

Click...

- *Reports.*
- *Payroll* (in the left menu).
- *Activity Summary* in the middle menu (The first report).
- *Filter Report Dated From* (insert 5/06/17) and *To* (also insert 5/06/17 here).
- *Display.* See **Figure 12.8** and the resulting report in **Figure 12.9**.

Figure 12.8 Payroll Activity [Summary] report setup

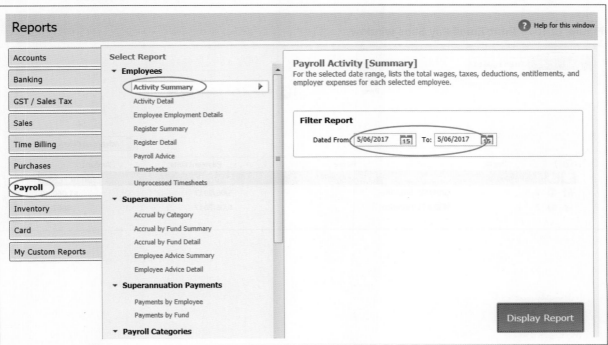

Figure 12.9   Payroll Activity [Summary] report: Mount Isa Cleaners, 5 June 2017

Mount Isa Cleaners
119 Marian Street
Mount Isa QLD 4825
Payroll Activity [Summary]
5/06/2017 To 5/06/2017

Employee	Wages	Deductions	Taxes	Net Pay	Expenses
BALBO, Ajantha	$1 056.25	$81.85	$177.00	$797.40	$111.91
GAMAGE, Shashike	$1 357.50	$30.40	$267.00	$1 060.10	$136.54
PRELATI, Federico	$1 125.00	$48.50	$214.00	$862.50	$96.53
Total:	$3 538.75	$160.75	$658.00	$2 720.00	$344.98

This is why

The report dates are based on the date the wages were paid, not the pay period.

4   Produce pay slips.

Click...

* *Print/Email Pay Slips* (in the bottom left of Payroll module). There should be three pay slips available in the *To Be Printed* tab.
* *Top box* in the left column (to select all the pay slips beneath it). See **Figure 12.10**.
* *Print.* The pay slips come out as A4 paper size. Once the pay slips are printed, they are removed from the screen and no longer available. If you need to do a reprint (or would like to do several pay slips on the one page), there is a pay slip report in the payroll section of the Reports Centre. An example of the pay slip is shown in **Figure 12.11**.

Figure 12.10   Print/Email Pay Slips window

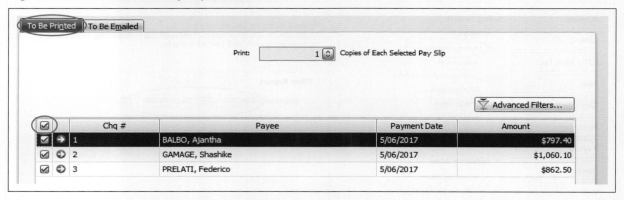

Figure 12.11   Pay Slip A. Balbo

Mount Isa Cleaners

ABN.

| Pay Slip For: | BALBO, Ajantha | | Cheque No: | 1 |
| Classification: | | | Payment Date: | 5/6/2017 |

Annual Salary: $46,800.00

Hourly Rate: $25.0000

Pay Period From: 28/5/2017   To: 3/6/2017   GROSS PAY: $1,056.25

Superannuation Fund: Spectrum Super   NET PAY: $797.40

DESCRIPTION	HOURS	CALC. RATE	AMOUNT	YTD	TYPE
Base Hourly	36.00	$25.00	$900.00	$900.00	Wages
Overtime (1.25x)	5.00	$31.25	$156.25	$156.25	Wages
Health Fund			-$29.35	-$29.35	Deduction
Union Fee			-$2.50	-$2.50	Deduction
Employee Additional			-$50.00	-$50.00	Superannuation Deductions
PAYG Withholding			-$177.00	-$177.00	Tax
Annual Leave Accrual	2.77			2.77	Entitlements
Superannuation Guarantee			$85.50	$85.50	Superannuation Expenses

Prepare electronic payments

5 The pays need to be uploaded to the bank for payment.

Click...
- *Prepare Electronic Payments* (in the Payroll module).
- *Journal Memo* (type *wages w/ending 3/06/2017*).
- *Your Bank Statement Text* (type *WAGES*).
- *Bank Processing Date* (insert 5/06/17).
- *Yes* on the pop up message. The date warning is because the date being used is older than today's date.
- *Top box* on the right column to select all the transactions below it.
- *Bank File* in the top left of the screen. See Figure 12.12.

Figure 12.12   **Preparing Electronic Payments, 5 June 2017**

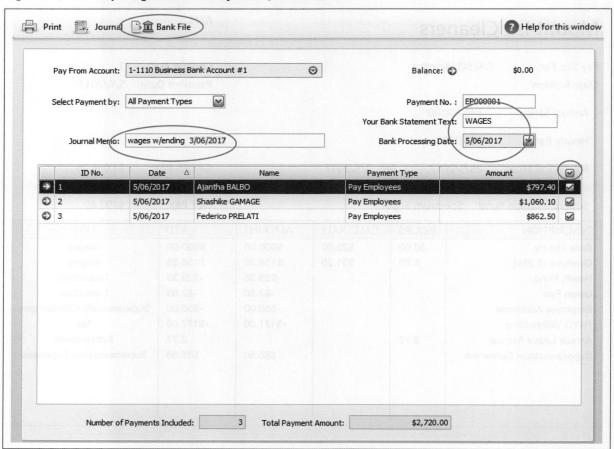

Click...

- *OK* (in the window that opens).
- *Desktop* (to save to the desktop).
- *File Name* (type *wages*). See Figure 12.13.
- *Save*. The transactions are removed from the window because MYOB assumes you will now upload the file to online banking.
- *Close* (to return to the Command Centre).

Figure 12.13   **Saving bank file for uploading**

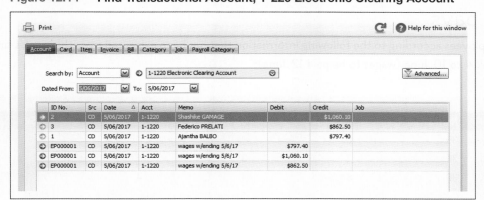

Analyse accounts

We will examine the general ledger accounts that were affected by the pay run.

Click...

- *Find Transactions* (next to *Reports*).
- *Account* (tab at top of the window).
- *Search By* (select *Account*) and select *1-1220 Electronic Clearing Account*.
- *Dated From* (insert *5/06/17*) and *To* (also insert *5/06/17* here). See Figure 12.14.

Figure 12.14   **Find Transactions: Account, 1-220 Electronic Clearing Account**

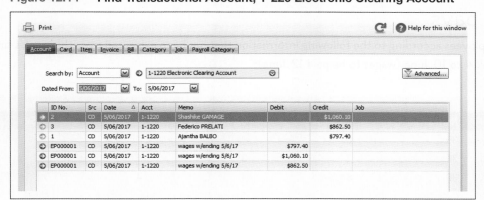

This shows that:

- the net amount of the three pays were credited to this account (wages were recorded)
- the same amounts were debited when the bank file was created (wages were paid out)
- the end result is zero, which is appropriate as this is a clearing account.

See Figure 12.15.

Click...

- *Search By* (select *Account*) and select or type *6-4100 Wages & Salaries Expense*. See Figure 12.15.

Figure 12.15   **Find Transactions: Account, 6-4100 Wages & Salaries Expense**

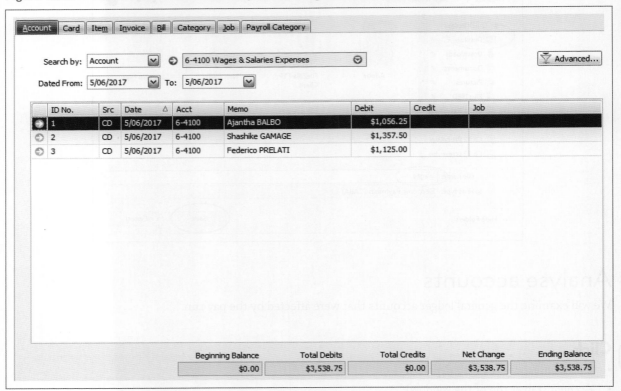

This shows that each payment amount (normal rate and overtime) has been debited to this expense account. To the Beginning Balance of zero has been added a total of $3538.75 and the Ending Balance is $3538.75 Dr.

More pays

6 Pay employees according to the following information that has been extracted from this week's time cards for the week 4 to 10 June (wages to be paid 12 June):

Name	Normal Hrs	O/t 1.25x	O/t 1.5x	O/t 2x	Sick
Balbo, A.	36	8			
Gamage, S.	36	8	3		
Prelati, F.	36	8	4	4	

7 Check your work with a Payroll Activity [Summary] for 12 June. Compare with Figure 12.16.

Figure 12.16 **Payroll Activity [Summary] report: Mount Isa Cleaners, 12 June 17**

<table>
<tr><td colspan="6" align="center">**Mount Isa Cleaners**
119 Marian Street
Mount Isa QLD 4825
Payroll Activity [Summary]
12/06/2017 To 12/06/2017</td></tr>
<tr><th>Employee</th><th>Wages</th><th>Deductions</th><th>Taxes</th><th>Net Pay</th><th>Expenses</th></tr>
<tr><td>BALBO, Ajantha</td><td>$1 150.00</td><td>$81.85</td><td>$210.00</td><td>$858.15</td><td>$114.25</td></tr>
<tr><td>GAMAGE, Shashike</td><td>$1 515.00</td><td>$30.40</td><td>$321.00</td><td>$1 163.60</td><td>$140.47</td></tr>
<tr><td>PRELATI, Federico</td><td>$1 200.00</td><td>$48.50</td><td>$240.00</td><td>$911.50</td><td>$98.40</td></tr>
<tr><td>Total:</td><td>$3 865.00</td><td>$160.75</td><td>$771.00</td><td>$2 933.25</td><td>$353.12</td></tr>
</table>

8 Prepare the Electronic Payments file and save to desktop as *Wages10June*.

9 Pay employees according to the following information that has been extracted from this week's time cards for the week 11 to 17 June (wages to be paid on 19 June).

Name	Normal Hrs	O/t 1.25x	O/t 1.5x	O/t 2x	Sick
Balbo, A.	36	6			
Gamage, S.	36	6	2		
Prelati, F.	36	6	4	4	

10 Check your work with a Payroll Activity [Summary] for 19 June. Compare with Figure 12.17.

Figure 12.17 **Payroll Activity [Summary] report: Mount Isa Cleaners, 19 June 17**

<table>
<tr><td colspan="6" align="center">**Mount Isa Cleaners**
119 Marian Street
Mount Isa QLD 4825
Payroll Activity [Summary]
19/06/2017 To 19/06/2017</td></tr>
<tr><th>Employee</th><th>Wages</th><th>Deductions</th><th>Taxes</th><th>Net Pay</th><th>Expenses</th></tr>
<tr><td>BALBO, Ajantha</td><td>$1 087.50</td><td>$81.85</td><td>$188.00</td><td>$817.65</td><td>$112.68</td></tr>
<tr><td>GAMAGE, Shashike</td><td>$1 395.00</td><td>$30.40</td><td>$280.00</td><td>$1 084.60</td><td>$137.48</td></tr>
<tr><td>PRELATI, Federico</td><td>$1 150.00</td><td>$48.50</td><td>$223.00</td><td>$878.50</td><td>$97.15</td></tr>
<tr><td>Total:</td><td>$3 632.50</td><td>$160.75</td><td>$691.00</td><td>$2 780.75</td><td>$347.31</td></tr>
</table>

11 Prepare the Electronic Payments file and save to desktop as *Wages19June*.

12 Pay employees according to the following information that has been extracted from this week's time cards for the week 18 to 24 June (wages to be paid on 26 June):

Name	Normal Hrs	O/t 1.25x	O/t 1.5x	O/t 2x	Sick
Balbo, A.	36	5			
Gamage, S.	36	5	2		
Prelati, F.	36	5	4	4	

13 Check your work with a Payroll Activity [Summary] for 26 June. Compare with Figure 12.18.

Figure 12.18 **Payroll Activity [Summary] report: Mount Isa Cleaners, 26 June 17**

Mount Isa Cleaners
119 Marian Street
Mount Isa QLD 4825
Payroll Activity [Summary]
26/06/2017 To 26/06/2017

Employee	Wages	Deductions	Taxes	Net Pay	Expenses
BALBO, Ajantha	$1 056.25	$81.85	$177.00	$797.40	$111.91
GAMAGE, Shashike	$1 357.50	$30.40	$267.00	$1 060.10	$136.54
PRELATI, Federico	$1 125.00	$48.50	$214.00	$862.50	$96.52
Total:	$3 538.75	$160.75	$658.00	$2 720.00	$344.97

14 Prepare the Electronic Payments file and save to desktop as *Wages26June*.

15 Produce a Payroll Register [Summary] for 1 to 30 June 17 (fourth report in the Reports Centre). Compare with Figure 12.19.

Figure 12.19 **Payroll Activity [Summary] report: Mount Isa Cleaners, June 17**

Mount Isa Cleaners
119 Marian Street
Mount Isa QLD 4825
Payroll Register [Summary]
June 2017

Employee	Wages	Deductions	Taxes	Net Pay	Expenses
BALBO, Ajantha	$4 350.00	$327.40	$752.00	$3 270.60	$450.75
GAMAGE, Shashike	$5 625.00	$121.60	$1 135.00	$4 368.40	$551.03
PRELATI, Federico	$4 600.00	$194.00	$891.00	$3 515.00	$388.60
Total:	$14 575.00	$643.00	$2 778.00	$11 154.00	$1 390.38

Pay liabilities

The payroll liabilities periodically need to be paid to the appropriate entities. Some companies do this every month, others every quarter, depending on the agreement made with those entities and company policy.

16 Produce a Superannuation Accrual by Fund [Summary] report for the June (fourth) quarter to confirm numbers for paying the superannuation.

Click...

- *Reports*.
- *Payroll* (in the left menu).
- *Accrual by Fund Summary* in the middle menu (under the bolded *Superannuation* heading).
- *Filter Report Dated From* (insert *1/06/17*) and *To* (insert *30/06/17*).
- *Display*. See Figure 12.20.

Figure 12.20   Accrual by Fund Summary report setup

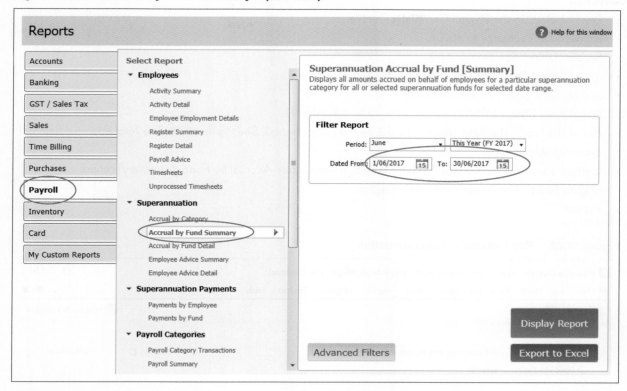

Figure 12.21   Supperanuation Accrual by Fund [Summary]: Mount Isa Cleaners, June 2017

Mount Isa Cleaners
119 Marian Street
Mount Isa QLD 4825
Superannuation Accrual by Fund [Summary]
June 2017

Superannuation Category	Amount	
Superannuation Fund:	Spectrum Super	
Employer Membership No.:		
BALBO, Ajantha	Employee Membership No.: 3351 1064	
Employee Additional		$200.00
Superannuation Guarantee		$342.00
Employee Total:		$542.00
GAMAGE, Shashike	Employee Membership No.: 3351 0776	
Superannuation Guarantee		$410.40
Employee Total:		$410.40
PRELATI, Federico	Employee Membership No.: 3351 1093	
Employee Additional		$160.00
Superannuation Guarantee		$273.60
Employee Total:		$433.60
Fund Total:		$1 386.00

17 Write a cheque to Spectrum Super for the total superannuation that is due for payment.

Click...

- *Pay Liabilities* (in the Payroll Command Centre).
- *Payment Date* (change to *30/06/17*).
- *Supplier* (select *Spectrum Super*).
- *Memo* (insert *Spectrum Super for June 17*).
- *Liability Type* (select *Superannuation*).
- *Dated From* (insert *1/06/17*) and *Dated To* (insert *30/06/17*).
- *Box* at the top of the right column (to tick all the components). See **Figure 12.22**. The *Total Payment* field will automatically update.
- Compare with the amounts and totals in the Superannuation Accrual by Fund [Summary] report (Figure 12.21). The amount should correspond.
- *Record*.

Figure 12.22   Pay Liabilities: Superannuation

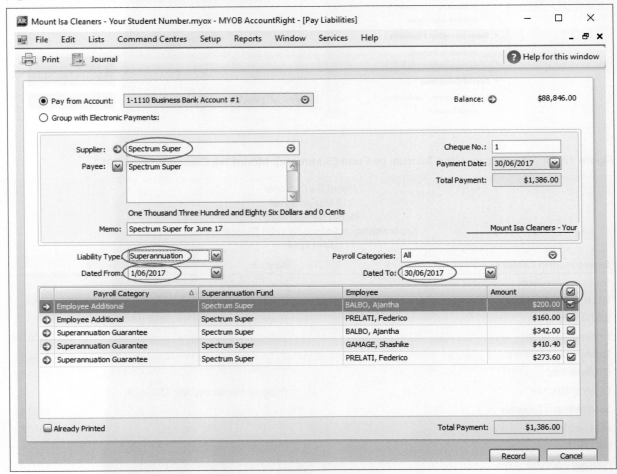

18 Still in the Pay Liabilities screen, change the **Liability Type** to *Expenses* and pay the WorkCover Insurance liability to Total Insurance Pty Ltd. See Figure 12.23. All the memos from now on should state that they are for June 2017.

Figure 12.23   **Pay Liabilities: WorkCover**

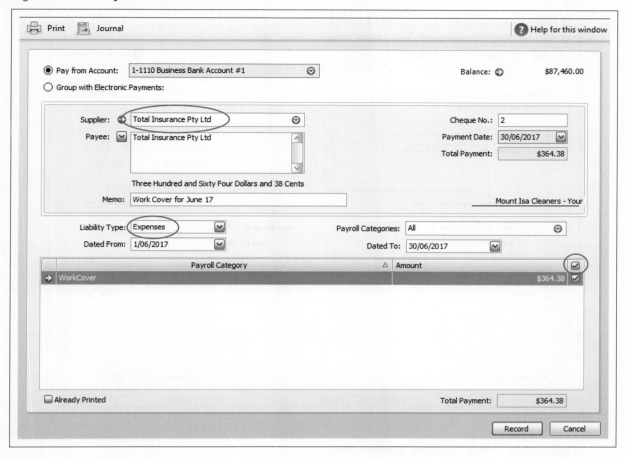

19 We next need to pay all the employee deductions individually.

Click...

- *Liability Type* (select *Deductions*).
- *Box* to the right of the Health Fund (to select it).
- *Supplier* (select *Spritely Health Fund Pty Ltd*).
- *Memo* (insert *Health Fund for June 17*).
- *Dated From* (leave as *1/06/17*) and *Dated To* (leave as *30/6/17*). Compare with Figure 12.24.
- *Record.*
- *Box* to the right of the *Savings Plan* (to select it).
- *Supplier* (select *Which Special Savers*).
- *Memo* (insert *Savings Plan for June 17*). Compare with Figure 12.25.
- *Record.*
- *Box* to the right of the *Union Fee* (to select it).
- *Supplier* (select *Australian Workers Union*).
- *Memo* (insert *Union fee for June 17*). Compare with Figure 12.26.
- *Record.*
- *Cancel* (to return to the Command Centre).

Figure 12.24   **Pay Liabilities: Health Fund**

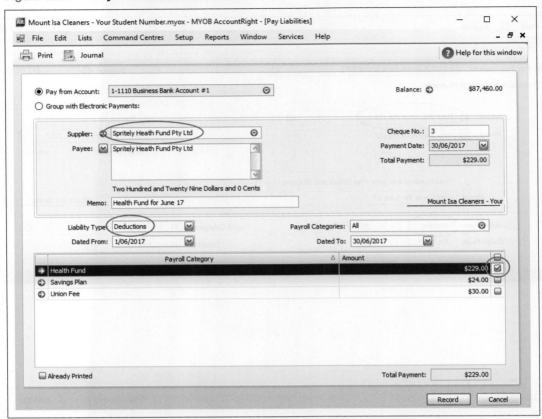

Figure 12.25   **Pay Liabilities: Savings Plan**

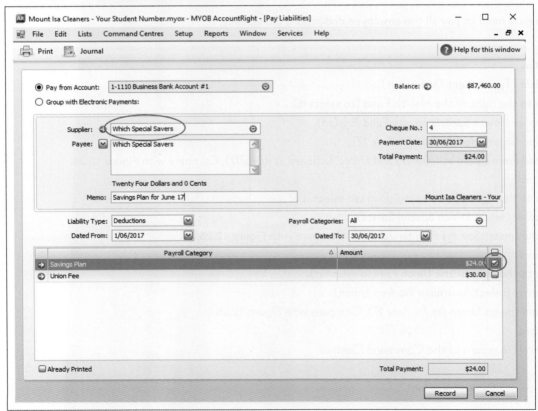

Figure 12.26   **Pay Liabilities: Union Fee**

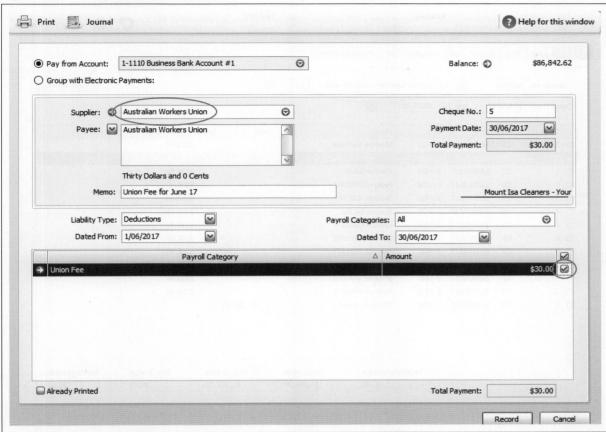

This is why

The PAYG Withholding tax is not paid through Pay Liabilities as it is lodged and paid along with the BAS.
(See Chapter 14.)

Analyse accounts: liabilities

We will now analyse some of the accounts. Note that the value of the cheques allocated to the liability accounts exactly match the amounts withheld from employees' pays.

Click...

- *Find Transactions* (next to *Reports*).
- *Account* (tab at top of the window).
- *Search By* (select *Account*) and select *2-1420 Superannuation Payable*.
- *Dated From* (insert *1/06/17*) and *To* (insert *30/06/17*). Press the Tab key. See Figure 12.27.

Figure 12.27   Find Transactions: Account, 2-1420 Superannuation Payable

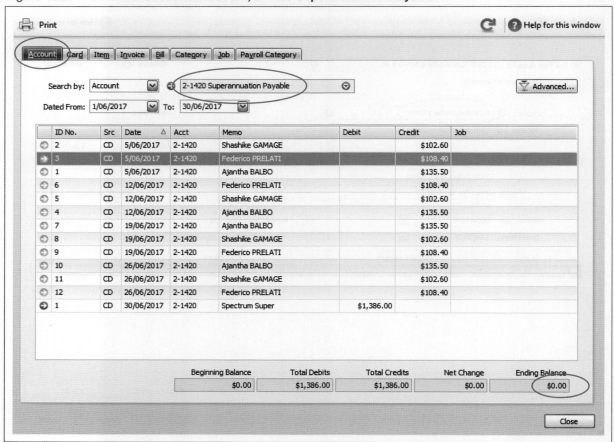

This shows that:

- the superannuation liability recorded for each pay is debited. This includes the Employee Additional or Salary Sacrifice superannuation requested by the employee
- at the end of the month, payment to Spectrum Super is credited to the account
- the end result is zero, which is appropriate as all current liabilities have been paid, so nothing is owing.

Click...

- *Search By* (select *Account*) and select *6-4300 Superannuation Expense*.
- *Dated From* (leave as 1/6/17) and *To* (leave as 30/06/17). Press the Tab key. See Figure 12.28.

Figure 12.28   Find Transactions: Account, 6-4300 Superannuation Expense

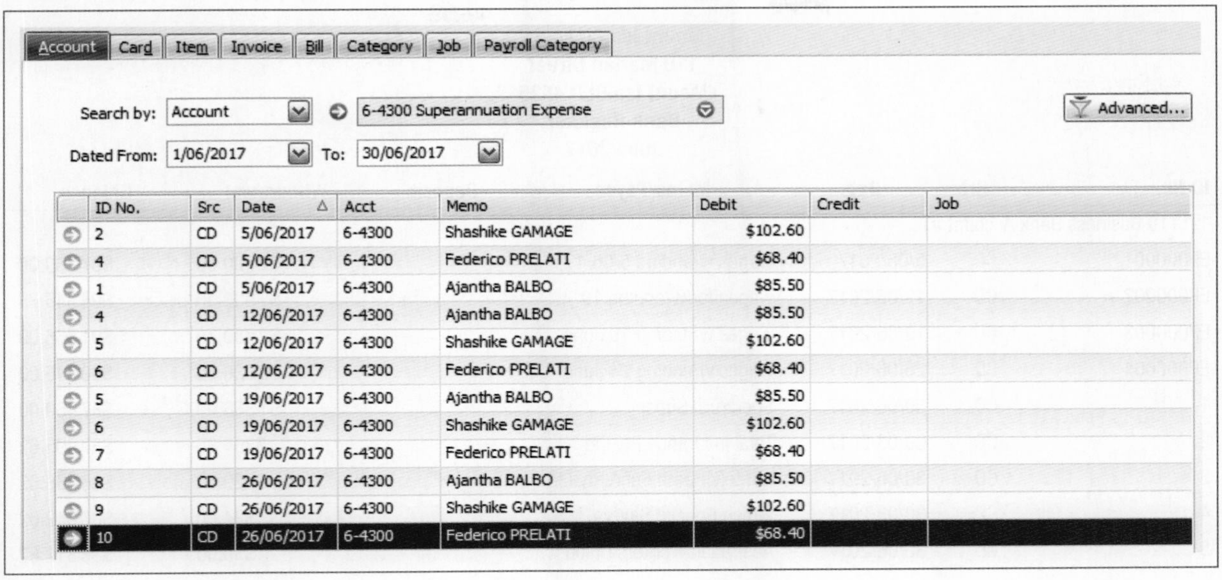

	ID No.	Src	Date △	Acct	Memo	Debit	Credit	Job
	2	CD	5/06/2017	6-4300	Shashike GAMAGE	$102.60		
	4	CD	5/06/2017	6-4300	Federico PRELATI	$68.40		
	1	CD	5/06/2017	6-4300	Ajantha BALBO	$85.50		
	4	CD	12/06/2017	6-4300	Ajantha BALBO	$85.50		
	5	CD	12/06/2017	6-4300	Shashike GAMAGE	$102.60		
	6	CD	12/06/2017	6-4300	Federico PRELATI	$68.40		
	5	CD	19/06/2017	6-4300	Ajantha BALBO	$85.50		
	6	CD	19/06/2017	6-4300	Shashike GAMAGE	$102.60		
	7	CD	19/06/2017	6-4300	Federico PRELATI	$68.40		
	8	CD	26/06/2017	6-4300	Ajantha BALBO	$85.50		
	9	CD	26/06/2017	6-4300	Shashike GAMAGE	$102.60		
	10	CD	26/06/2017	6-4300	Federico PRELATI	$68.40		

This show the superannuation expense *for the employer* recorded for each pay is debited. This does not include the Employee Additional or Salary Sacrifice superannuation requested by the employee as that is *not* a tax deduction for the business.

Click...

- *Search By* (select *Account*) and select *2-1440 Heath Fund Payable*. This should also have a zero ending balance.
- *Search By* (select *Account*) and select *2-1450 Savings Plan Payable*. This should also have a zero ending balance.
- *Search By* (select *Account*) and select *2-1460 WorkCover Payable*. This should also have a zero ending balance.
- *Search By* (select *Account*) and select *6-4200 WorkCover Premiums*. This is a deduction for the business (like the superannuation expense).

If further transactions had taken place before the cheques were drawn (as might well be the case in real life) the balances remaining would be reconciled with the new transactions.

20 Display the Bank Register report for June 2017 quarter. See Figure 12.29.

Figure 12.29 Bank Register report: Mount Isa Cleaners, June 2017

Mount Isa Cleaners
119 Marian Street
Mount Isa QLD 4825
Bank Register
June 2017

ID No.	Src	Date	Memo/Payee	Deposit	Withdrawal	Balance
1-1110 Business Bank Account #1						
EP000001	CD	5/06/2017	wages w/ending 5/06/17		$2720.00	$97280.00
EP000002	CD	12/06/2017	wages for w/ending 10		$2933.25	$94346.75
EP000003	CD	19/06/2017	wages w/ending 19 June		$2780.75	$91566.00
EP000004	CD	26/06/2017	wages w/ending 24 June		$2720.00	$88846.00
1	CD	30/06/2017	Spectrum Super		$1386.00	$87460.00
2	CD	30/06/2017	Total Insurance Pty Ltd		$364.38	$87095.62
3	CD	30/06/2017	Spritely Heath Fund Pty Ltd		$229.00	$86866.62
4	CD	30/06/2017	Which Special Savers		$24.00	$86842.62
5	CD	30/06/2017	Australian Workers Union		$30.00	$86812.62
				$0.00	$13187.38	
1-1220 Electronic Clearing Account						
1	CD	5/06/2017	BALBO, Ajantha		$797.40	($797.40)
2	CD	5/06/2017	GAMAGE, Shashike		$1060.10	($1857.50)
3	CD	5/06/2017	PRELATI, Federico		$862.50	($2720.00)
EP000001	CD	5/06/2017	wages w/ending 5/06/17	$797.40		($1922.60)
EP000001	CD	5/06/2017	wages w/ending 5/06/17	$1060.10		($862.50)
EP000001	CD	5/06/2017	wages w/ending 5/06/17	$862.50		$0.00
4	CD	12/06/2017	BALBO, Ajantha		$858.15	($858.15)
5	CD	12/06/2017	GAMAGE, Shashike		$1163.60	($2021.75)
6	CD	12/06/2017	PRELATI, Federico		$911.50	($2933.25)
EP000002	CD	12/06/2017	wages for w/ending 10	$858.15		($2075.10)
EP000002	CD	12/06/2017	wages for w/ending 10	$1163.60		($911.50)
EP000002	CD	12/06/2017	wages for w/ending 10	$911.50		$0.00
7	CD	19/06/2017	BALBO, Ajantha		$817.65	($817.65)
8	CD	19/06/2017	GAMAGE, Shashike		$1084.60	($1902.25)
9	CD	19/06/2017	PRELATI, Federico		$878.50	($2780.75)
EP000003	CD	19/06/2017	wages w/ending 19 June	$817.65		($1963.10)
EP000003	CD	19/06/2017	wages w/ending 19 June	$1084.60		($878.50)
EP000003	CD	19/06/2017	wages w/ending 19 June	$878.50		$0.00
10	CD	26/06/2017	BALBO, Ajantha		$797.40	($797.40)
11	CD	26/06/2017	GAMAGE, Shashike		$1060.10	($1857.50)
12	CD	26/06/2017	PRELATI, Federico		$862.50	($2720.00)
EP000004	CD	26/06/2017	wages w/ending 24 June	$797.40		($1922.60)
EP000004	CD	26/06/2017	wages w/ending 24 June	$1060.10		($862.50)
EP000004	CD	26/06/2017	wages w/ending 24 June	$862.50		$0.00
				$11154.00	$11154.00	

Congratulations! You have completed your first month's worth of paying employees and liabilities.

Annual and personal leave

<u>H & K PTY LTD</u>

1 In MYOB AccountRight 2016, open **12.2 H & K Pty Ltd.myox** from the Chapter 12 folder of your start-up file or use the file you set up in Chapter 11.

H & K Pty Ltd have four employees. Holmes and Kelly are on salary and so do not get overtime. Chen and Maruka are on an hourly rate.

2 Pay employees according to the following information for the week 28 May 2018 to 3 June 2018 (paid on 5 June 2018) through Process Payroll in the Payroll module:

Name	Normal Hrs	O/t 1.25x	O/t 1.5x	O/t 2x	Personal
Chen, D.	28	3			7
Holmes, J.	Salary				
Kelly, J.	Salary				
Maruka, J.	35	4	3		

- Denise was sick and took a personal day, so instead of working her standard 35-hour week, she only worked 28 hours (excluding overtime). See Figure 12.30.

Figure 12.30 Pay Employee: Denise Chen

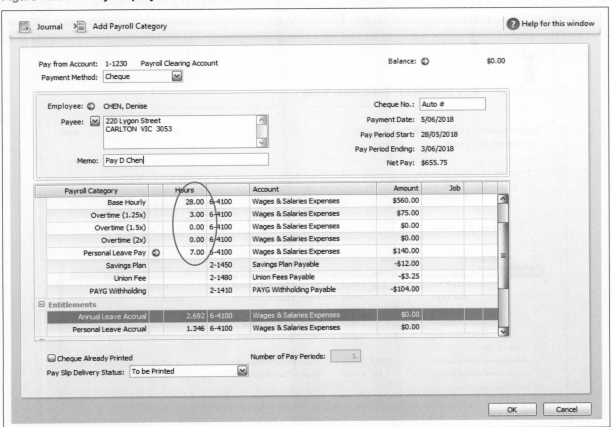

- Nothing needs to be done with Judy Holmes' pay as she is on salary. **Figure 12.31** shows Judys' Pay screen – note that her Base Salary is $2000 and that no changes can be made in the Hours column. She has Salary Sacrifice (superannuation deducted *before* tax is calculated) so her tax is $422 and her net pay is $1295.50. This is because she is being taxed on $1750 per week ($2000 minus $250) rather than the full $2000.

Figure 12.31   Pay Employee: Judy Holmes

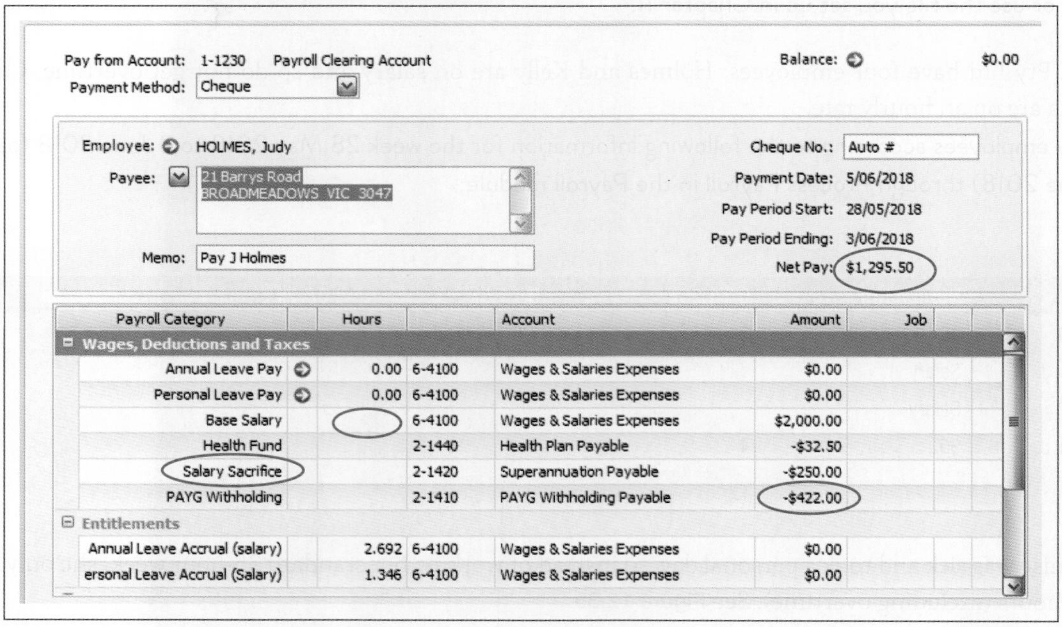

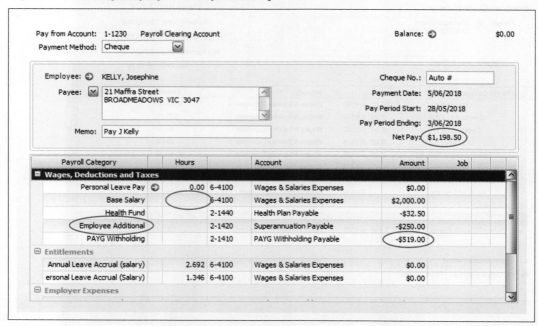

- Nothing needs to be done with Josephine Kelly's pay as she is also on salary. **Figure 12.32** shows Josephine's Pay screen – note that her Base Salary is also $2000. She has Employee Additional (superannuation deducted *after* tax is calculated) so her tax is $519 and her net pay is $1198.50. This is because she is being taxed on the full $2000 per week.

Figure 12.32   Pay Employee: Josephine Kelly

- John's pay is straightforward – just the Hourly rate and Overtime. See Figure 12.33.

Figure 12.33   Pay Employee: John Maruka

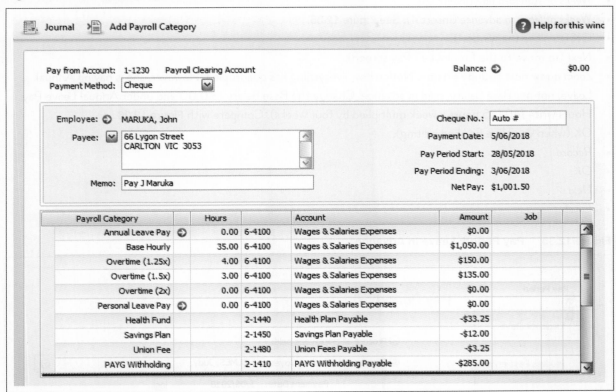

3   Produce an Employee Activity [Summary] report for 5 June 2018 to check your work. Compare with Figure 12.34. If correct, then Record and move through the screens.

Figure 12.34   Employee Activity [Summary] report: H & K Pty Ltd, 5 June 2018

H & K Pty Ltd
Payroll Activity [Summary]
5/06/2018 To 5/06/2018

Employee	Wages	Deductions	Taxes	Net Pay	Expenses
CHEN, Denise	$775.00	$15.25	$104.00	$655.75	$82.00
HOLMES, Judy	$2 000.00	$282.50	$422.00	$1 295.50	$230.00
KELLY, Josephine	$2 000.00	$282.50	$519.00	$1 198.50	$230.00
MARUKA, John	$1 335.00	$48.50	$285.00	$1 001.50	$126.45
Total:	$6 110.00	$628.75	$1 330.00	$4 151.25	$668.45

Judy Holmes is taking her four weeks' annual leave commencing on 4 June and has asked to be paid her holiday pay in advance on 5 June 2018:

Click...

- *Process Payroll.*
- *Process individual employee (select HOLMES, Judy).*
- *Payment Date (insert 5/06/18).*

- *Pay period start* (insert *4/06/18*) and *Pay period end* (insert *2/07/18*).
- *Pay leave in advance* (a new screen opens).
- *Weeks of standard pay* (insert *0*).
- *Weeks of leave in advance* (insert *4*). See **Figure 12.35**.
- OK (to close the window).
- *Next* (to move to the Employee's Pay screen).
- *Zoom arrow* next to Judy's name. Notice how everything has quadrupled. However, she is having Annual Leave, not her Base Salary, paid in advance. Change the Base Salary to 0.00 and under Annual Leave Pay Hours write *140* (35 hours a week multiplied by four weeks). Compare with **Figure 12.36**.
- OK (when you have finished editing).
- *Record.*
- *OK.*
- *Next.*
- *Finish.*

Figure 12.35   Pay Period: Leave In Advance

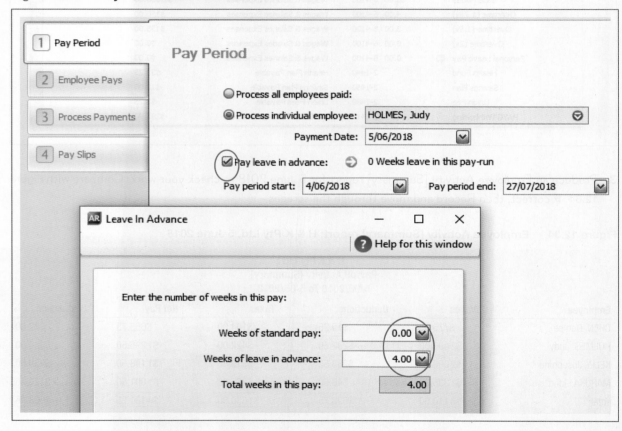

Figure 12.36   **Pay Employee: Judy Holmes four weeks annual leave**

Pay from Account:	1-1230	Payroll Clearing Account		Balance:	-$4,151.25

Payment Method: Cheque

Employee: HOLMES, Judy

Payee: 21 Barrys Road
BROADMEADOWS VIC 3047

Memo: Pay J Holmes

Cheque No.: Auto #
Payment Date: 5/06/2018
Pay Period Start: 4/06/2018
Pay Period Ending: 2/07/2018
Net Pay: $5,182.00

Payroll Category	Hours		Account	Amount	Job
Wages, Deductions and Taxes					
Annual Leave Pay	140.00	6-4100	Wages & Salaries Expenses	$8,000.00	
Personal Leave Pay	0.00	6-4100	Wages & Salaries Expenses	$0.00	
Base Salary		6-4100	Wages & Salaries Expenses	$0.00	
Health Fund		2-1440	Health Plan Payable	-$130.00	
Salary Sacrifice		2-1420	Superannuation Payable	-$1,000.00	
PAYG Withholding		2-1410	PAYG Withholding Payable	-$1,688.00	
Entitlements					
Annual Leave Accrual (salary)	10.768	6-4100	Wages & Salaries Expenses	$0.00	
ersonal Leave Accrual (Salary)	5.384	6-4100	Wages & Salaries Expenses	$0.00	
Employer Expenses					

4   Produce a new Payroll Activity [Summary] report to check your work for accuracy. See Figure 12.37.

Figure 12.37   **Employee Activity [Summary] report: H & K Pty Ltd, 5 June 2018 after annual leave in advance**

H & K Pty Ltd
Payroll Activity [Summary]
5/06/2018 To 5/06/2018

Employee	Wages	Deductions	Taxes	Net Pay	Expenses
CHEN, Denise	$775.00	$15.25	$104.00	$655.75	$82.00
HOLMES, Judy	$10 000.00	$1 412.50	$2 110.00	$6 447.50	$1 150.00
KELLY, Josephine	$2 000.00	$282.50	$519.00	$1 198.50	$230.00
MARUKA, John	$1 335.00	$48.50	$285.00	$1 001.50	$126.45
Total:	$14 110.00	$1 758.75	$3 018.00	$9 333.25	$1 588.45

5   Pay employees according to the following information for the week 4 to 10 June (pay day is 12 June 18):

Name	Normal Hrs	O/t 1.25x	O/t 1.5x	O/t 2x	Sick
Chen, D.	35	5	4	4	
Holmes, J.	On Leave				
Kelly, J.	Salary				7
Maruka, J.	35	5	3		

When you are in the Edit Employees window, you should *deselect* Judy Holmes from the selected list to be paid (by deleting the tick), then edit Denise Chen and John Maruka as usual. Josephine Kelly was sick and had a personal leave day, which is processed like this:

Click...

- *Process Individual Employee* (select *KELLY, Josephine*).
- *Personal Leave Pay* (insert *7* in the *Hours* column). MYOB calculates the leave as $400.
- *Base Salary* (deduct the $400 of Personal Leave Pay amount from the Base Salary). The total is still $2000, but it is now made up of normal hours and sick leave. See Figure 12.38.
- *OK* (when you have finished editing).

Figure 12.38   Pay Employee: Josephine Kelly with sick leave

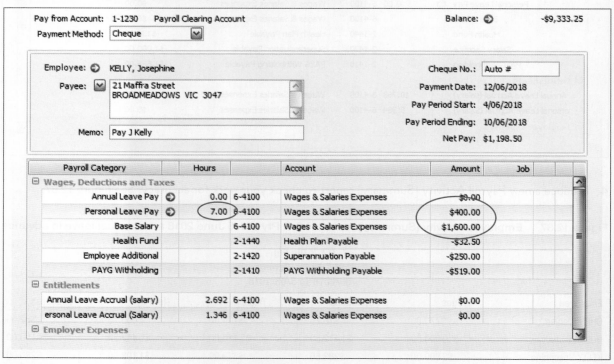

Compare your final screen (after all the employee edits) with Figure 12.39.

Figure 12.39   Employee Pays: payment date 12 June 2018

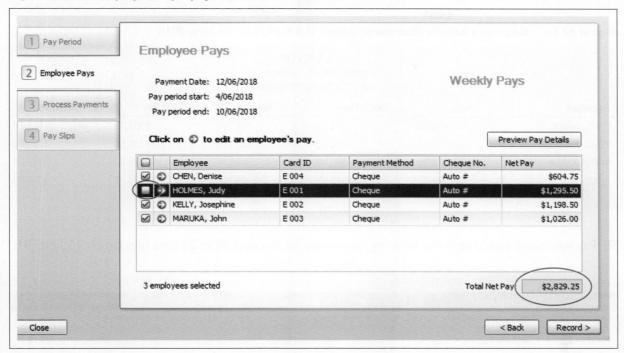

6   Produce a Payroll Activity [Summary] report for 12 June to check your work. See Figure 12.40.

Figure 12.40   Employee Activity [Summary] report: H & K Pty Ltd, 12 June 2018

H & K Pty Ltd
Payroll Activity [Summary]
12/06/2018 To 12/06/2018

Employee	Wages	Deductions	Taxes	Net Pay	Expenses
CHEN, Denise	$1 105.00	$15.25	$219.00	$870.75	$88.60
KELLY, Josephine	$2 000.00	$282.50	$519.00	$1 198.50	$230.00
MARUKA, John	$1 372.50	$48.50	$298.00	$1 026.00	$127.20
Total:	$4 477.50	$346.25	$1 036.00	$3 095.25	$445.80

7   Pay employees according to the following information for the week 11 to 17 June (pay day is 19 June 18):

Name	Normal Hrs	O/t 1.25x	O/t 1.5x	O/t 2x	Sick
Chen, D.	35	10	4	4	
Holmes, J.	On Leave				
Kelly, J.	Salary				
Maruka, J.	35	5	3		

8 Produce a Payroll Activity [Summary] report for 19 June to check your work. See Figure 12.41.

Figure 12.41   **Employee Activity [Summary] report: H & K Pty Ltd, 19 June 2018**

H & K Pty Ltd
Payroll Activity [Summary]
19/06/2018 To 19/08/2018

Employee	Wages	Deductions	Taxes	Net Pay	Expenses
CHEN, Denise	$1 230.00	$15.25	$263.00	$951.75	$91.10
KELLY, Josephine	$2 000.00	$282.50	$519.00	$1 198.50	$230.00
MARUKA, John	$1 372.50	$48.50	$298.00	$1 026.00	$127.20
Total:	$4 602.50	$346.25	$1 080.00	$3 176.25	$448.30

9 Pay employees according to the following information for the week 18 to 24 June (pay date is 26 June 18):

Name	Normal Hrs	O/t 1.25x	O/t 1.5x	O/t 2x	Sick
Chen, D.	35	10	4	4	
Holmes, J.	On Leave				
Kelly, J.	Salary				14
Maruka, J.	35	10	4		

10 Produce a Payroll Activity [Summary] report for 26 June to check your work. See Figure 12.42.

Figure 12.42   **Employee Activity [Summary] report: H & K Pty Ltd, 26 June 2018**

H & K Pty Ltd
Payroll Activity [Summary]
26/06/2018 To 26/06/2018

Employee	Wages	Deductions	Taxes	Net Pay	Expenses
CHEN, Denise	$1 230.00	$15.25	$263.00	$951.75	$91.10
KELLY, Josephine	$2 000.00	$282.50	$519.00	$1 198.50	$230.00
MARUKA, John	$1 605.00	$48.50	$378.00	$1 178.50	$131.85
Total:	$4 835.00	$346.25	$1 160.00	$3 328.75	$452.95

11 Produce a Payroll Register [Summary] for 1 to 30 June 2018. See Figure 12.43.

Figure 12.43 **Payroll Register [Summary] report: H & K Pty Ltd, June 2018**

H & K Pty Ltd
Payroll Register [Summary]
June 2018

Employee	Wages	Deductions	Taxes	Net Pay	Expenses
CHEN, Denise	$4 340.00	$61.00	$849.00	$3 430.00	$352.80
HOLMES, Judy	$10 000.00	$1 412.50	$2 110.00	$6 447.50	$1 150.00
KELLY, Josephine	$8 000.00	$1 130.00	$2 076.00	$4 794.00	$920.00
MARUKA, John	$5 685.00	$194.00	$1 259.00	$4 232.00	$512.70
Total:	$28 025.00	$2 797.50	$6 294.00	$18 933.50	$2 935.50

12 Create the following supplier cards in the Cards module:
- Australian Taxation Office (S 01)
- Australian Workers' Union (S 02)
- Medibank Private Pty Ltd (S 03)
- Prudent Insurance (S 04)
- Spectrum Super. (S 05)
- *Which?* Savings Bank (S 06)
- Australian Super (S 07).

13 Produce your Superannuation Accrual by Fund [Summary] report for June 18. See Figure 12.44.

Figure 12.44 **Superannuation Accrual by Fund [Summary] report: H & K Pty Ltd, June 2018**

H & K Pty Ltd
Superannuation Accrual by Fund [Summary]
June 2018

Superannuation Category	Amount
Superannuation Fund:	Australian Super
Employer Membership No.:	
CHEN, Denise	Employee Membership No.: 1513 6008
Superannuation Guarantee	$266.00
Employee Total:	$266.00
KELLY, Josephine	Employee Membership No.: 5668 2143
Employee Additional	$1 000.00
Superannuation Guarantee	$760.00
Employee Total:	$1 760.00
Fund Total:	$2 026.00
Superannuation Fund:	Spectrum Super
Employer Membership No.:	
HOLMES, Judy	Employee Membership No.: 531 6582
Salary Sacrifice	$1 250.00
Superannuation Guarantee	$950.00
Employee Total:	$2 200.00

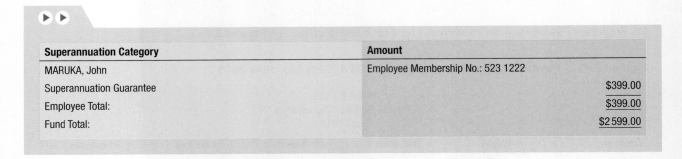

Superannuation Category	Amount
MARUKA, John	Employee Membership No.: 523 1222
Superannuation Guarantee	$399.00
Employee Total:	$399.00
Fund Total:	$2 599.00

14 We need to pay all our liabilities for June. Write cheques (dated 30 June 2018) to the appropriate recipients for the payroll deductions that are due for payment using **Pay Liabilities** in the Payroll module. Pay from the Business Bank Account #1.

- Australian Workers' Union (Union Fees)
- Medibank Private Pty. Ltd. (Health Fund)
- *Which?* Savings Bank (Savings)
- Prudent Insurance (Workcover)
- Spectrum Super (Super). Make sure you only select the lines with Spectrum super in it. See **Figure 12.45**. You can compare this cheque to your Superannuation Accrual by Fund [Summary] report (**Figure 12.44**) to ensure the cheque totals are correct
- Australian Super (Super).

Figure 12.45   Pay Liabilities, Spectrum Super only

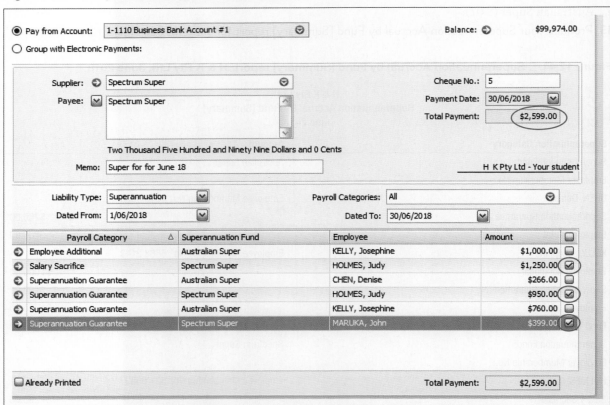

15 Go to the **Accounts List** in the Accounts module and view the Liability Tab, scrolling down to the Payroll Liabilities section. All of the payroll liabilities (with the exception of PAYG Withholding Payable) should be zero. See **Figure 12.46**.

Figure 12.46   Accounts List: Liability tab, Payroll Liabilities

Account Number	Account Name	Type	Tax Code	Linked	Balance
2-0000	Liabilities	Liability			$6,294.00
2-1000	Current Liabilities	Liability			$6,294.00
2-1100	Credit Cards	Liability			$0.00
2-1110	Visa #1	Credit Card	N-T		$0.00
2-1120	Mastercard #1	Credit Card	N-T		$0.00
2-1130	AMEX #1	Credit Card	N-T		$0.00
2-1140	Visa #2	Credit Card	N-T		$0.00
2-1150	Mastercard #2	Credit Card	N-T		$0.00
2-1160	AMEX #2	Credit Card	N-T		$0.00
2-1200	GST Liabilities	Liability			$0.00
2-1210	GST Collected	Other Liability	N-T		$0.00
2-1220	GST Paid	Other Liability	N-T		$0.00
2-1300	Other Tax/Withholding Liab.	Liability			$0.00
2-1310	Voluntary Withholdings Payable	Other Liability	N-T		$0.00
2-1320	ABN Withholdings Payable	Other Liability	N-T		$0.00

16 Produce an Entitlements Balance [Summary] report for June 2018. Compare with Figure 12.47. The Hours Accrued column contains the hours of leave accrued every pay. The Hours Taken column shows the hours of leave taken which reduces the available balance. The value column shows the value of the various leave liabilities.

Figure 12.47   Entitlements Balance [Summary] report for June 2018

H & K Pty Ltd
Entitlement Balance [Summary]
June 2018

Entitlement		Opening Hours	Hours Accrued	Hours Taken	Available Hours	Value
CHEN, Denise	E 004					
Annual Leave Accrual		68	10.77	0.00	78.77	$1 575.36
Personal Leave Accrual		53	5.12	7.00	51.12	$1 022.30
Total:		121	15.88	7.00	129.88	$2 597.66
HOLMES, Judy	E 001					
Annual Leave Accrual (salary)		141	13.46	140.00	14.46	$826.29
Personal Leave Accrual (Salary)		40	6.73	0.00	46.73	$2 670.29
Total:		181	20.19	140.00	61.19	$3 496.57
KELLY, Josephine	E 002					
Annual Leave Accrual (salary)		151	10.77	0.00	161.77	$9 243.89
Personal Leave Accrual (Salary)		61	5.38	21.00	45.38	$2 593.37
Total:		212	16.15	21.00	207.15	$11 837.27
MARUKA, John	E 003					
Annual Leave Accrual		0.00	10.77	0.00	10.77	$323.04
Personal Leave Accrual		0.00	5.38	0.00	5.38	$161.52
Total:		0.00	16.15	0.00	16.15	$484.56

Practice

AURORA COFFEE PTY LTD

1 In MYOB AccountRight 2016, open **12.3 Aurora Coffee.myox** from the Chapter 12 folder of your start-up files or use the file you set up in Chapter 11.

Aurora Coffee Pty Ltd have four employees. Phil Baweja is on salary and so does not get overtime. The others are full time and have an hourly rate. The hourly employees get overtime.

2 Pay employees according to the following information for the week 28 May 2018 to 3 June 2018 (paid on 5 June 2018) through Process Payroll in the Payroll module:

Name	Normal Hrs	O/t 1.25x	O/t 1.5x	O/t 2x	Sick
Baweja, P.	Salary				
De Sousa, G.	35	5			
Goldstein, H.	35	5			
Stell, M.	35		4	4	

3 Produce a Payroll Activity [Summary] report for 5 June to check your work and compare with Figure 12.48.

Figure 12.48   **Payroll Activity [Summary] report: Aurora Coffee Pty Ltd, 5 June 18**

Aurora Coffee Pty Ltd
21G The Market Place
Edgeworth David Avenue
Hornsby NSW 2077
Payroll Activity [Summary]
5/06/2018 To 5/06/2018

Employee	Wages	Deductions	Taxes	Net Pay	Expenses
BAWEJA, Phil	$1 000.00	$116.00	$157.00	$727.00	$120.00
DE SOUSA, Grace	$1 237.50	$37.85	$245.00	$954.65	$130.69
GOLDSTEIN, Harry	$1 031.25	$36.40	$181.00	$813.85	$108.91
STELL, Mandy	$851.00	$8.50	$131.00	$711.50	$82.79
Total:	$4 119.75	$198.75	$714.00	$3 207.00	$442.39

4 Phil Baweja started four weeks' annual leave on 4 June. Process the holiday pay, then check your work with another Payroll Activity [Summary] report as shown in Figure 12.49.

Figure 12.49   Payroll Activity [Summary] report: Aurora Coffee Pty Ltd, 5 June 18, after annual leave in advance

Aurora Coffee Pty Ltd
21G The Market Place
Edgeworth David Avenue
Hornsby NSW 2077
Payroll Activity [Summary]
5/06/2018 To 5/06/2018

Employee	Wages	Deductions	Taxes	Net Pay	Expenses
BAWEJA, Phil	$5 000.00	$580.00	$785.00	$3 635.00	$600.00
DE SOUSA, Grace	$1 237.50	$37.85	$245.00	$954.65	$130.69
GOLDSTEIN, Harry	$1 031.25	$36.40	$181.00	$813.85	$108.91
STELL, Mandy	$851.00	$8.50	$131.00	$711.50	$82.79
Total:	$8 119.75	$662.75	$1 342.00	$6 115.00	$922.39

5 Pay employees according to the following information for the pay week 4 June 2018 to 10 June 2018 (pay date 12 June 2018):

Name	Normal Hrs	O/t 1.25x	O/t 1.5x	O/t 2x	Sick
Baweja, P.	On Leave				
De Sousa, G.	35	2	2		
Goldstein, H.	35	5			
Stell, M.	35	5	4	4	

6 Produce a Payroll Activity [Summary] report for 12 June to check your work and compare with Figure 12.50.

Figure 12.50   Payroll Activity [Summary] report: Aurora Coffee Pty Ltd, 12 June 18

Aurora Coffee Pty Ltd
21G The Market Place
Edgeworth David Avenue
Hornsby NSW 2077
Payroll Activity [Summary]
12/06/2018 To 12/06/2018

Employee	Wages	Deductions	Taxes	Net Pay	Expenses
DE SOUSA, Grace	$1 215.00	$37.85	$237.00	$940.15	$130.12
GOLDSTEIN, Harry	$1 031.25	$36.40	$181.00	$813.85	$108.90
STELL, Mandy	$1 022.13	$8.50	$190.00	$823.63	$87.07
Total:	$3 268.38	$82.75	$608.00	$2 577.63	$326.09

7 Pay employees according to the following information for the pay week 11 June 2018 to 17 June 2018 (pay date 19 June 2018):

Name	Normal Hrs	O/t 1.25x	O/t 1.5x	O/t 2x	Sick
Baweja, P.	On Leave				
De Sousa, G.	35	5	4	4	
Goldstein, H.	35	5	1		
Stell, M.	35	2	2		

8 Produce a Payroll Activity [Summary] report for 19 June to check your work and compare with Figure 12.51.

Figure 12.51 **Payroll Activity [Summary] report: Aurora Coffee Pty Ltd, 19 June 18**

Aurora Coffee Pty Ltd
21G The Market Place
Edgeworth David Avenue
Hornsby NSW 2077
Payroll Activity [Summary]
19/06/2018 To 19/06/2018

Employee	Wages	Deductions	Taxes	Net Pay	Expenses
DE SOUSA, Grace	$1 657.50	$37.85	$390.00	$1 229.65	$141.19
GOLDSTEIN, Harry	$1 068.75	$36.40	$194.00	$838.35	$109.85
STELL, Mandy	$749.25	$8.50	$95.00	$645.75	$80.24
Total:	$3 475.50	$82.75	$679.00	$2 713.75	$331.28

9 Pay employees according to the following information for the pay week 18 June 2018 to 24 June 2018 (pay date 26 June 2018):

Name	Normal Hrs	O/t 1.25x	O/t 1.5x	O/t 2x	Sick
Baweja, P.	On Leave				
De Sousa, G.	32	3	2		3
Goldstein, H.	35	5	2		
Stell, M.	35	5	4	4	

10 Produce a Payroll Activity [Summary] report for 26 June to check your work and compare with Figure 12.52.

Figure 12.52   Payroll Activity [Summary] report: Aurora Coffee Pty Ltd, 26 June 18

Aurora Coffee Pty Ltd
21G The Market Place
Edgeworth David Avenue
Hornsby NSW 2077
Payroll Activity [Summary]
26/06/2018 To 26/06/2018

Employee	Wages	Deductions	Taxes	Net Pay	Expenses
DE SOUSA, Grace	$1 252.50	$37.85	$250.00	$964.65	$131.06
GOLDSTEIN, Harry	$1 106.25	$36.40	$207.00	$862.85	$110.78
STELL, Mandy	$1 022.13	$8.50	$190.00	$823.63	$87.06
Total:	$3 380.88	$82.75	$647.00	$2 651.13	$328.90

11 Produce a Payroll Activity [Summary] report for all of June and compare with Figure 12.53.

Figure 12.53   Payroll Activity [Summary] report: Aurora Coffee Pty Ltd, June 18

Aurora Coffee Pty Ltd
21G The Market Place
Edgeworth David Avenue
Hornsby NSW 2077
Payroll Activity [Summary]
1/06/2018 To 30/06/2018

Employee	Wages	Deductions	Taxes	Net Pay	Expenses
BAWEJA, Phil	$5 000.00	$580.00	$785.00	$3 635.00	$600.00
DE SOUSA, Grace	$5 362.50	$151.40	$1 122.00	$4 089.10	$533.06
GOLDSTEIN, Harry	$4 237.50	$145.60	$763.00	$3 328.90	$438.44
STELL, Mandy	$3 644.51	$34.00	$606.00	$3 004.51	$337.16
Total:	$18 244.51	$911.00	$3 276.00	$14 057.51	$1 908.66

12 Produce a Superannuation Accrual by Fund [Summary] report for June 2018. Compare with Figure 12.54.

Figure 12.54   Superannuation Accrual by Fund [Summary] report: Aurora Coffee Pty Ltd, June 18

Aurora Coffee Pty Ltd
21G The Market Place
Edgeworth David Avenue
Hornsby NSW 2077
Superannuation Accrual by Fund [Summary]
June 2018

Superannuation Category	Amount
Superannuation Fund:	Australian Super
Employer Membership No.:	
GOLDSTEIN, Harry	Employee Membership No.: 1584 6223
Superannuation Guarantee	$332.50
Employee Total:	$332.50
Fund Total:	$332.50

Superannuation Category	Amount
Superannuation Fund:	Hesta
Employer Membership No.:	
DE SOUSA, Grace	Employee Membership No.: 178 269
Superannuation Guarantee	$399.00
Employee Total:	$399.00
Fund Total:	$399.00
Superannuation Fund:	Spectrum Super
Employer Membership No.:	
BAWEJA, Phil	Employee Membership No.: 167 589
Employee Additional	$375.00
Superannuation Guarantee	$475.00
Employee Total:	$850.00
STELL, Mandy	Employee Membership No.:
Superannuation Guarantee	$246.05
Employee Total:	$246.05
Fund Total:	$1 096.05

13 Create brief profile cards for the following:
- Australian Taxation Office (PAYG Withholding)
- Australian Workers' Union (Union)
- Medibank Private Pty Ltd (Health Fund)
- Prudent Insurance Pty Ltd (WorkCover).
- Spectrum Assurance Pty Ltd (Superannuation)
- Which? Savings Bank Pty Ltd (Savings)
- HESTA (Superannuation)
- Australian Super (Superannuation).

14 Write cheques to the appropriate recipients for the payroll deductions that are due for payment. Go through the Pay Liabilities screen in the Payroll module. The cheques are dated 30 June 2018 and come from the Business Bank Account #1. Compare the superannuation cheques with the Super Accrual report in Figure 12.53 before recording.

15 Display the Payroll Liabilities section of the general ledger and make certain all the accounts have a zero balance after you have written the cheques.

Summary

◆ Setting up the standard pay details in the employee's card with deductions can save a lot of time.

◆ A payroll electronic payment file can be produced that can be uploaded to the online banking to save input errors and time.

◆ Liabilities can be paid easily through the Pay Liabilities function in the Payroll module.

◆ Superannuation liabilities need to be paid to the individual superannuation funds.

◆ Salaried employees do not get overtime.

◆ Annual and sick leave taken are entered in hours so that the accrual can be reduced.

◆ Casual employees do not get annual or sick leave.

◆ Annual or personal leave can be taken in advance and will be taxed at the normal rate as long as you correctly fill the Pay in Advance field.

◆ Payroll mistakes cannot be corrected. The pay needs to be deleted and re-entered.

Assessment

Quick Aid Relief Staff

1   Create the following data file in MYOB *AccountRight Plus 2016 Australian* version. Only very brief company details are required.

> **Quick-Aid Relief Staff**
> 261 Grange Road
> Findon SA 5023
> ABN 67 505 337 385
>
> **Financial year:** 2018
> **Last Month of Financial Year:** June
> **Conversion Month:** July
> **Industry Classification:** Service

2   Make the following changes to the chart of accounts:

	Account type	Account number	New account name	Tax code
Edit	Liability	2-1420	Superannuation Payable	N-T
Edit	Liability	2-1430	Health fund Payable	N-T
Edit	Liability	2-1440	WorkCover Payable	N-T
Edit	Liability	2-1450	Union Fee Payable	N-T
Edit	Expense	6-4300	Superannuation Expense	N-T

> ### Remember This
>
> Make sure you change the tax code in superannuation expense to N-T.

3   Enter account opening balances:
   –   1-1110 Business Bank Account #1 $30 000.00
   –   3-1100 Owner's/Shareholders Capital $30 000.00.

4   Change the Preferences (Security Tab) in MYOB *not* to warn before recording post-dated transactions (i.e. untick it).

5 Set up Payroll for Quick-Aid Relief Staff through Payroll Easy Setup Assistant.
- Load the tax tables. You may need to do this twice in order to get the screen telling you that the tax tables from 1/10/16 are being loaded.

Use the following information for the payroll setup:
- Current Payroll year is 2018.
- The normal hours worked per week is 35.
- Withholder Payer number is 00 505 337 385.
- Spectrum Super is the default superannuation fund.
- Round pay down to 0 cents.

Wages:
- Create *Casual Rate A* (fixed rate of $18.00).
- Create *Casual Rate B* (fixed rate of $22.00).
- Create *Casual Rate C* (fixed rate of $25.00).

Superannuation:
- Superannuation Guarantee: Linked Expense Account is 6-4300, Linked Payable Account is 2-1420, the calculation basis is 9. 5%.

Entitlements:
- Deductions: check the employees card
- No entitlements apply; these are casual employees.

Deductions:
- Add a Health Fund: Linked Payable Account is 2-1430 and it is a (User-Entered) Deduction.
- Edit the Union Fee: Linked Payable Account is 2-1480 and the rate is $3.25 per pay period.

Expenses:
- WorkCover Insurance rate: Linked Expense Account is 6-4200, Linked Payable Account is 2-1440 and it equals 2% of gross wages.

Taxes:
- PAYG Withholding (Linked Payables Account is 2-1410).

6 Create cards for the following six employees. As casuals they do not get annual or personal leave.
- Wages: tick all three casual rates A, B and C.
- Entitlements: do not tick.
- Everyone gets superannuation guarantee and WorkCover.
- Deductions: check the employee's card.
- Taxes: ensure the correct tax table is used per individual. See Figure 12.55.

Figure 12.55   **Employee Card: Taxes**

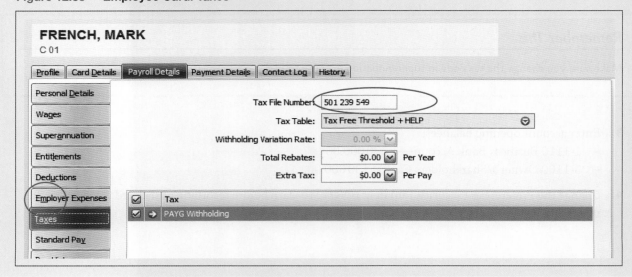

Name:	Mark FRENCH		**Name:**	Lisa MATHISON
Card ID:	C-01		**Card ID:**	S-01
Position:	Casual Chef		**Position:**	Customer Service
Address:	13 Colley Terrace, Glenelg SA 5045		**Address:**	406 Bird Road, Brooklyn Park SA 5032
Mobile:	0429 101 206		**Mobile:**	0412 397 115
Pay Type:	Hourly		**Pay Type:**	Hourly
Pay Frequency:	Fortnightly		**Pay Frequency:**	Fortnightly
Pay Rate:	$14.00		**Pay Rate:**	$12.00
Super:	Spectrum		**Super:**	Spectrum
Super Member No.:	134 568		**Super Member No.:**	134 823
Tax File No.:	501 239 549		**Tax File No.:**	348 155 937
Tax:	Tax Free Threshold + HELP		**Tax:**	No Tax Free Threshold
Total Rebate:	N/A		**Total Rebate:**	$1040.00 pa
Deductions:	Union Fee Health Fund: $18.50		**Deductions:**	Union Fee Health Fund: $15.40

Name:	Sean EADIE		**Name:**	Sara CARRIGAN
Card ID:	C-02		**Card ID:**	S-02
Position:	Casual Chef		**Position:**	Customer Service
Address:	204 Greenhill Road, Eastwood SA 5063		**Address:**	54 Gulf View Road, Christies Beach SA 5165
Mobile:	0404 298 142		**Mobile:**	0487 291 433
Pay Type:	Hourly		**Pay Type:**	Hourly
Pay Frequency:	Fortnightly		**Pay Frequency:**	Fortnightly
Pay Rate:	$14.00		**Pay Rate:**	$12.00
Super:	Spectrum		**Super:**	Spectrum
Super Member No.:	134 314		**Super Member No.:**	134 007
Tax File No.:	238 092 355		**Tax File No.:**	636 514 227
Tax:	Tax Free Threshold		**Tax:**	Tax Free Threshold + HELP
Total Rebate:	$0.00 pa		**Total Rebate:**	$520.00 pa
Deductions:	Union Fee Health Fund: $21.45		**Deductions:**	Union fee Health Fund: $13.85

Name:	Ben KERSTEN		Name:	Baden COOKE
Card ID:	K-01		Card ID:	K-02
Position:	Kitchen Hand		Position:	Kitchen Hand
Address:	516 Glynburn Road, Burnside SA 5066		Address:	337 Torrens Road, Croydon SA 5008
Mobile:	0415 227 597		Mobile:	0402 555 291
Pay Type:	Hourly		Pay Type:	Hourly
Pay Frequency:	Fortnightly		Pay Frequency:	Fortnightly
Pay Rate:	$10.00		Pay Rate:	$10.00
Super:	Spectrum		Super:	Spectrum
Super Member No.:	134 258		Super Member No.:	134 114
Tax File No.:	Not provided		Tax File No.:	305 113 782
Tax:	No TFN Resident		Tax:	No Tax Free Threshold
Total Rebate:	N/A		Deductions:	Union Fee
Deductions:	Union Fee			Health Fund: $17.70
	Health Fund: $15.40			

Timesheets are not used.

7 Pay the employees according to the following information for the pay *fortnight* 28 May to 10 June (pay date 12 June 2018):

Name	Normal	Rate A	Rate B	Rate C
Carrigan, S.	10	5	7	18
Cooke, B.	10	5	2	25
Eadie, S.	10		28	4
French, M.	12		35	
Kersten, B.	10	18	6	2
Mathison, L.	10	15		2

8 Pay the employees according to the following information for the *fortnight* 11 June to 24 June (pay date 26 June):

Name	Normal	Rate A	Rate B	Rate C
Carrigan, S.	5	5		
Cooke, B.	7	5	8	
Eadie, S.	5	5		
French, M.	8			16
Kersten, B.	6			24
Mathison, L.	8	5		

Produce the following reports to give to your instructor:
- Payroll Activity [Summary] report for 12 June 2018
- Payroll Activity [Summary] report for 26 June 2018.

Timesheets, terminations and payment summaries

13

TIMESHEETS AND PAYROLL OBLIGATIONS

Learning outcomes

By the end of this chapter you will be competent in:

- accurately entering timesheet information and process payroll over a two-month period
- producing payment summaries and balancing with MYOB reports
- calculating entitlements and terminating employment
- understanding the difference between an allowance and a reimbursement
- backing up and rolling over payroll year.

  Entering timesheets into MYOB is a handy way to keep track of daily hours of employees.
We will also learn how to terminate employment and correctly pay out annual leave accrual. The processing of payment summaries (formerly known as group certificates) and rolling over the end of payroll year in preparation for the new year is also explained in full.

Timesheets, terminations and payment summaries

ELSMORE DEMOLITION

Timesheets

Some businesses enter their timesheets straight into MYOB or use the timesheets function in conjunction with the normal hours. Elsmore Demolition uses the timesheets function to enter in the overtime hours only.

1 In MYOB AccountRight 2016 open the **13.1 Elsmore Demolition.myox** file from the Chapter 13 folder of your start-up files.

2 Check the timesheets option is selected in Setup/Preferences/Systems window. The field *I use Timesheets* should be ticked and the *and My Week Starts on* field should be set to Saturday. See Figure 13.1.

Figure 13.1   Preferences: timesheet option

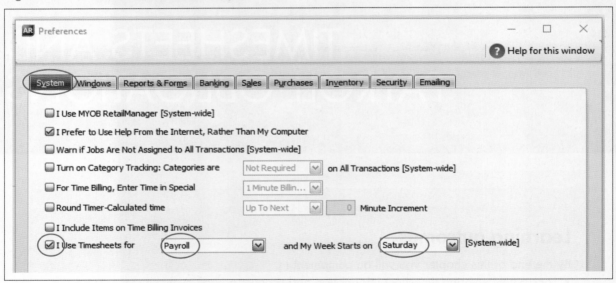

3 Enter timesheet information for the pay week 26 May to 1 June (payment made 4 June 18) ready for processing.

Employee	Rate	S	S	M	T	W	T	F
Bruton, D.	1.25x				2	2	2	2
	1.5x	4						
	2x	4						
Cooper, P.	1.25x			2	2	2		2
	1.5	4			4			
	2x	4			4			
Dillon, M.	1.25x			2	2		2	2
	1.5	4						
	2x	4						
Elliot, R.	1.25x			2		2	2	2
	1.5	4						
	2x	4						
Wards, P.	1.25x				2	2	2	2
	1.5	4						
	2x		8					

Click...

- *Enter Timesheet* (in the Payroll module).
- *Employee* (choose *BRUTON, David*).
- *Calendar* (in the top right-hand corner) and select *26 May 2018*. This is the first day of the pay period. See Figure 13.2. This shows you the weekly pay period.
- *Payroll Category* (select *Overtime (1.25x)*).
- *Column T 29* (type *2*). This is because Tuesday is the first day David has worked 1.25x Overtime hours. Press the Tab key. Insert the rest of the overtime (1.25x) hours in the appropriate days as per the timesheet above.
- *Payroll Category* (select *Overtime (1.5x)*).
- *Column S 26* (type *4*).
- *Payroll Category* (select *Overtime (2x)*).
- *Column S 26* (type *4*). Compare with Figure 13.3.
- *New Timesheet*. Also in Figure 13.3.
- *Yes* (to the window that pops up as you wish to save the changes).
- *Employee* (choose *COOPER, Paul*). Follow the same process until all the overtime has been recorded in the timesheets.
- *OK*.

Figure 13.2 Enter Timesheet: first steps

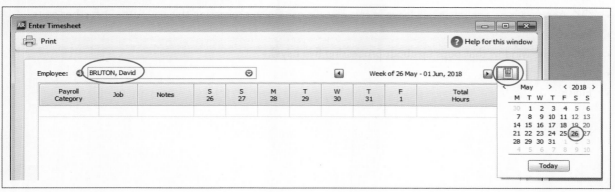

Figure 13.3   Enter Timesheet: David Bruton

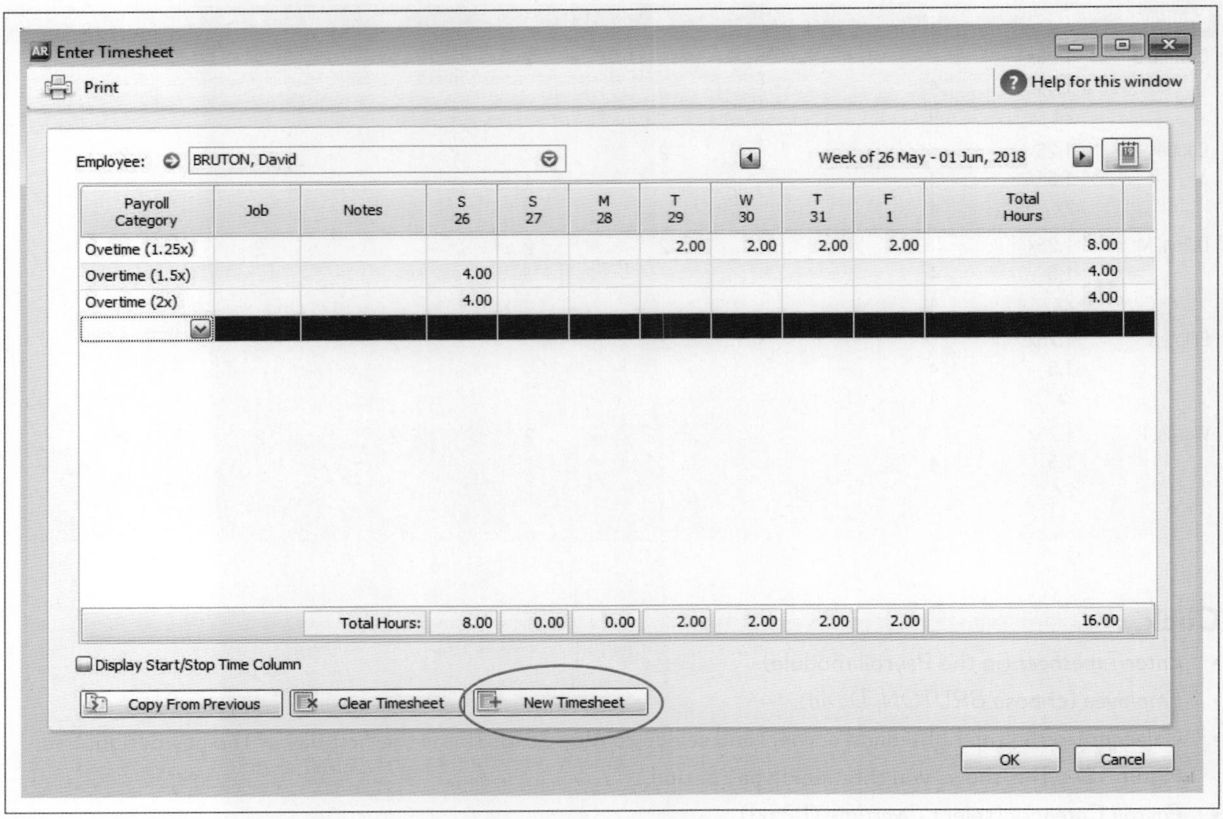

The next step is to process the actual payroll.

Click...

- *Process Payroll* (in the Payroll module).
- *Process all employees paid* (should have *Weekly* already selected).
- *Payment Date* (select *4/06/18*).
- *Pay period start* (select *26/05/18*).
- *Pay period end* (select *1/06/18*). Press the Tab key. A summary of the payroll is produced with both the normal hours and the overtime hours from the timesheet. See Figure 13.4.
- *Next*.
- *Zoom arrow* next to *BRUTON, David*. The overtime hours have been added automatically into the pay. We could make any adjustments, such as annual or personal leave, in this window if needed. See Figure 13.5.
- *OK*. As there is no annual or sick leave in this pay, we can finish processing this pay without further edits.
- *Record*.
- *OK* (to the window that pops up about processing five pays).
- *Next*.
- *Finish*.

Figure 13.4 Process Payroll: Pay Period

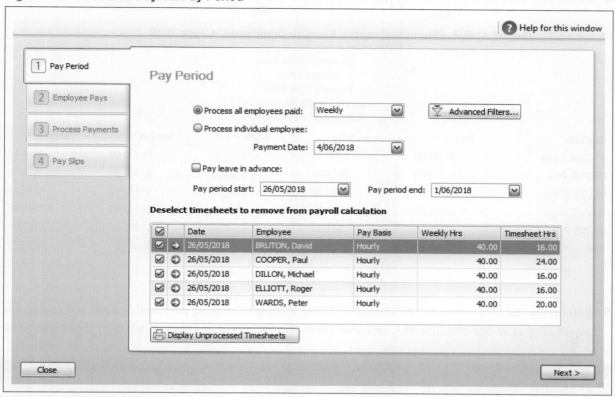

Figure 13.5 Edit Payroll: David Bruton

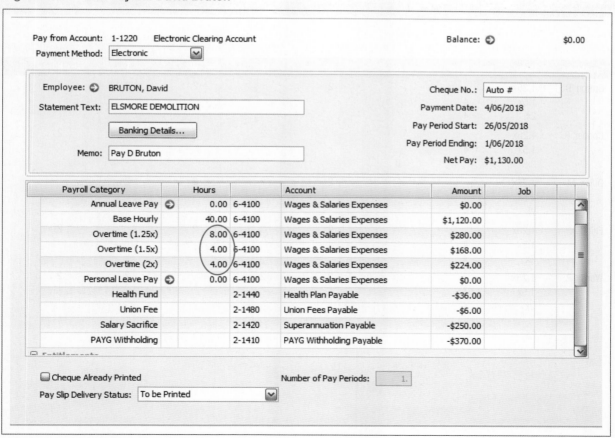

4 Check your work against an Activity [Summary] report. Compare with Figure 13.6

Figure 13.6   **Payroll Activity [Summary] report: Elsmore Demolition, 4 June 2018**

**Elsmore Demolition
Blakes Lane
Elsmore NSW 2360
Payroll Activity [Summary]
4/06/2018 To 4/06/2018**

Employee	Wages	Deductions	Taxes	Net Pay	Expenses
BRUTON, David	$1 792.00	$292.00	$370.00	$1 130.00	$160.16
COOPER, Paul	$2 106.00	$239.00	$506.00	$1 361.00	$165.78
DILLON, Michael	$1 664.00	$186.00	$361.00	$1 117.00	$148.72
ELLIOTT, Roger	$1 600.00	$133.00	$324.00	$1 143.00	$143.00
WARDS, Peter	$1 728.00	$81.00	$397.00	$1 250.00	$143.04
Total:	$8 890.00	$931.00	$1 958.00	$6 001.00	$760.70

5 Enter timesheet information for the week 2 to 8 June 2018 (payroll being processed 11 June) and process the payroll using a pay date of 11 June 18. Check your work with a Payroll Activity [Summary] report (See Figure 13.7).

Tip

When processing the next week's timesheets, you can click the arrow on the top right-hand side of the Enter Timesheet screen. This moves your pay period to the next week instead of having to click on the calendar.

Employee	Rate	S	S	M	T	W	T	F
Bruton, D.	1.25x			2		2	2	2
	1.5x	4						
	2x	4						
Cooper, P.	1.25x				2	2	2	2
	1.5x	4			4			
	2x		8					
Dillon, M.	1.25x			2	2	2	2	
	1.5x	4						
	2x	4						
Elliot, R.	1.25x			2	2	2		2
	1.5x	4						
	2x	4						
Wards, P.	1.25x			2	2		2	2
	1.5x	4						
	2x	4						

Figure 13.7   Payroll Activity [Summary] report: Elsmore Demolition, 11 June 2018

Elsmore Demolition Blakes Lane Elsmore NSW 2360 Payroll Activity [Summary] 11/06/2018 To 11/06/2018					
Employee	**Wages**	**Deductions**	**Taxes**	**Net Pay**	**Expenses**
BRUTON, David	$1 792.00	$292.00	$370.00	$1 130.00	$160.16
COOPER, Paul	$2 106.00	$239.00	$506.00	$1 361.00	$165.78
DILLON, Michael	$1 664.00	$186.00	$361.00	$1 117.00	$148.72
ELLIOTT, Roger	$1 600.00	$133.00	$324.00	$1 143.00	$143.00
WARDS, Peter	$1 536.00	$81.00	$330.00	$1 125.00	$137.28
Total:	$8 698.00	$931.00	$1 891.00	$5 876.00	$754.94

Terminating employment

6 Peter Wards has terminated his employment with the company and has given the required notice. He has finished on Wednesday 13 June and his pay will be process on 14 June 2018. He has worked his normal 24 hours and no overtime. He will be paid any outstanding annual leave only. These two pays will be processed separately.

Click...

- *Process Payroll* (in the Command Centre).
- *Process individual employee* (select *WARDS, Peter*).
- *Payment Date* (insert *14/06/18*).
- *Pay Period Start* (insert *9/06/18*).
- *Pay Period Ending* (insert *13/06/18*).
- *Next*.
- *Base Hourly* (insert *24*). See Figure 13.8.
- *Record*.
- *OK*.
- *Next*.
- *Finish*.

Figure 13.8   **Edit Payroll: Peter Ward**

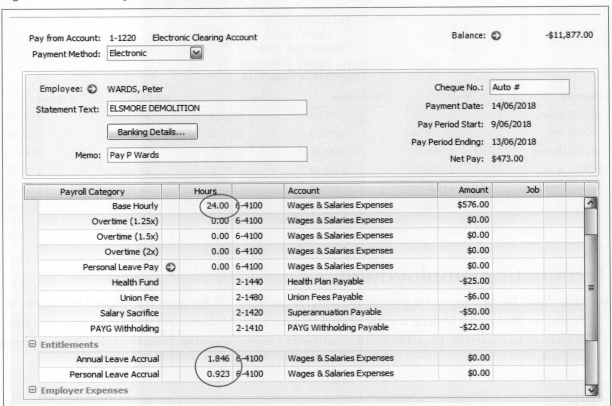

| Pay from Account: | 1-1220 | Electronic Clearing Account | | Balance: | | -$11,877.00 |

Payment Method: Electronic

Employee: WARDS, Peter		Cheque No.: Auto #
Statement Text: ELSMORE DEMOLITION		Payment Date: 14/06/2018
Banking Details...		Pay Period Start: 9/06/2018
		Pay Period Ending: 13/06/2018
Memo: Pay P Wards		Net Pay: $473.00

Payroll Category	Hours		Account	Amount	Job	
Base Hourly	24.00	6-4100	Wages & Salaries Expenses	$576.00		
Overtime (1.25x)	0.00	6-4100	Wages & Salaries Expenses	$0.00		
Overtime (1.5x)	0.00	6-4100	Wages & Salaries Expenses	$0.00		
Overtime (2x)	0.00	6-4100	Wages & Salaries Expenses	$0.00		
Personal Leave Pay	0.00	6-4100	Wages & Salaries Expenses	$0.00		
Health Fund		2-1440	Health Plan Payable	-$25.00		
Union Fee		2-1480	Union Fees Payable	-$6.00		
Salary Sacrifice		2-1420	Superannuation Payable	-$50.00		
PAYG Withholding		2-1410	PAYG Withholding Payable	-$22.00		
⊟ Entitlements						
Annual Leave Accrual	1.846	6-4100	Wages & Salaries Expenses	$0.00		
Personal Leave Accrual	0.923	6-4100	Wages & Salaries Expenses	$0.00		
⊟ Employer Expenses						

This is why

We process the pay with Peter's last working hours separately as he accrues annual leave and superannuation on this pay. His termination pay will not accrue either.

Click...

- *Payroll Categories* (in the Command Centre).
- *Zoom arrow* next to *Unused Annual Leave* (in the *Wages* tab).
- *Employee* (top left side). See Figure 13.9.
- Box next to *WARDS, Peter*. Also in Figure 13.9.
- *OK* twice (to return to payroll category list).
- *Close*.

Figure 13.9   **Payroll categories: Unused Annual Leave**

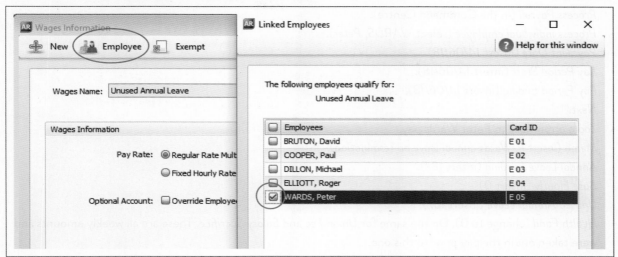

Unused Annual Leave and Unused Long Service leave is only used in termination pays. Some extra things to note with termination pays:

- Annual Leave and Personal Leave do not accrue when paying out Unused Annual Leave.

- Superannuation Guarantee is not paid out on a termination pay as it is not considered ordinary times earnings.

- The total amount of the termination pay is taxed at the employees' **marginal tax rate**. The calculation is a little complicated, and the formula can be found by entering 52074 in the search field at www.ato.gov.au.

> **Marginal tax rate**
> The term used for the highest tax rate applied to an employee. This rate varies depending on their annual income.

7 Produce an Entitlements Balance [Summary] report dated 1 June to 30 June 2018. Once the report is open, you can filter for Peter Wards by choosing his name in the Employees field at the top of the screen and Run Report. Compare you report with Figure 13.10. We need to pay out the available hours of annual leave only.

Figure 13.10   **Entitlements Balance [Summary]: Peter Wards, June 2018**

Elsmore Demolition
Blakes Lane
Elsmore NSW 2360
Entitlement Balance [Summary]
June 2018

Entitlement		Opening Hours	Hours Accrued	Hours Taken	Available Hours	Value
WARDS, Peter	E 05					
Annual Leave Accrual		179	8	0.00	187	$4 488.00
Personal Leave Accrual		48	4	0.00	52	$1 247.98
Total:		227	12	0.00	239	$5 735.98

8 Process the termination pay.

⌖ Click...

- *Process Payroll* (in the Command Centre).
- *Process individual employee* (select *WARDS, Peter*).
- *Payment Date* (insert *14/06/18*).
- *Pay Period Start* (insert *14/06/18*).
- *Pay Period Ending* (insert *14/06/18*).
- *Next.*
- *Zoom arrow* next to Peter Wards pay.
- *Memo* (insert *P. Wards annual leave on termination*).
- *Annual Leave Loading* (insert *187*).
- *Base Hourly* (insert *0*).
- *Unused Annual Leave* (insert *187*).
- *Health Fund* (change to *0*). Do the same for *Union Fee* and *Salary Sacrifice*. These are all weekly amounts and were taken out in the pay prior to this one.
- *PAYG Withholding* (insert *0*). Press the Tab key. You can see now the net pay at the top right side is the gross (before tax) pay of $5273.40. Multiply this by 32.5% (Peter's marginal rate) and insert this number ($1713.85) as a negative in the PAYG Withholding field. Net pay is now $3559.55. See **Figure 13.11**. Notice that entitlements and superannuation are not calculated, but WorkCover is.
- *OK.*
- *Record.*
- *OK.*
- *Next.*
- *Finish.*

Figure 13.11   Edit Payroll: Peter Wards' Termination Payment

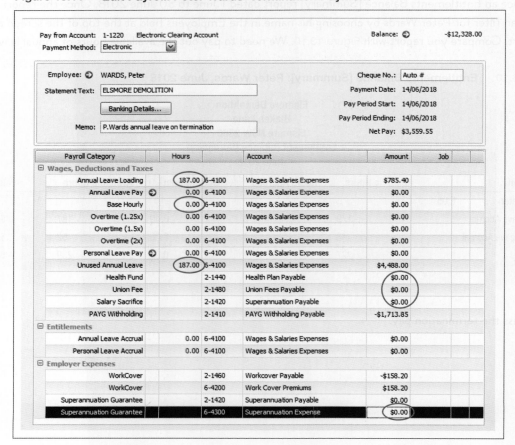

9 Produce payroll advices for Peter Wards only (by changing the **Employee** field at the top of the report once it has been generated, then clicking **Run Report**) dated 14 June 2018. Compare with Figure 13.12.

Figure 13.12   **Payroll Advice: Peter Wards, 14 June 2018**

Elsmore Demolition
Blakes Lane
Elsmore NSW 2360
Payroll Advice
14/06/2018 To 14/06/2018

Elsmore Demolition

ABN: 31 233 312 133

Peter WARDS   Card ID: E 05

Pay Frequency: Weekly

Pay Period: 14/06/2018 to
              14/06/2018

Annual Salary: $49 920.00

Hourly Rate: $24.00

Employment Classification:

Superannuation Fund: Media Super

Cheque No: 12

Payment Date: 14/06/2018

Gross Pay: $5 273.40

Net Pay: $3 559.55

Description	Hours	Calc. Rate	Amount	YTD	Type
Annual Leave Loading	187	$4.20	$785.40	$1 457.40	Wages
Unused Annual Leave	187	$24.00	$4 488.00	$4 488.00	Wages
Base Hourly				$43 776.00	Wages
Health Fund				($1 250.00)	Deductions
Union Fee				($300.00)	Deductions
Annual Leave Accrual				$187.00	Entitlements
PAYG Withholding			($1 713.85)	($11 735.85)	Tax
Salary Sacrifice				($2 500.00)	Superannuation Deductions
Superannuation Guarantee				$4 297.92	Superannuation Expenses

Elsmore Demolition

ABN: 14 347 475 637

Peter WARDS   Card ID: E 05

Pay Frequency: Weekly

Pay Period: 9/06/2018 to
              13/06/2018

Annual Salary: $49 920.00

Hourly Rate: $24.00

Employment Classification:

Superannuation Fund: Media Super

Cheque No: 11

Payment Date: 14/06/2018

Gross Pay: $576.00

Net Pay: $473.00

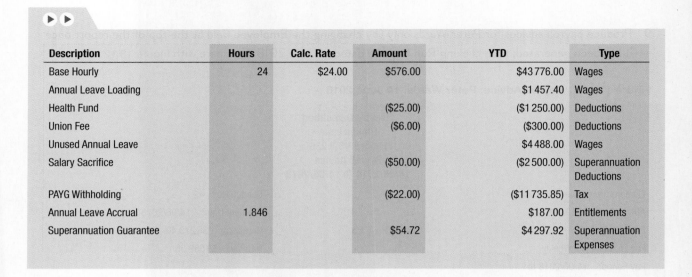

Description	Hours	Calc. Rate	Amount	YTD	Type
Base Hourly	24	$24.00	$576.00	$43 776.00	Wages
Annual Leave Loading				$1 457.40	Wages
Health Fund			($25.00)	($1 250.00)	Deductions
Union Fee			($6.00)	($300.00)	Deductions
Unused Annual Leave				$4 488.00	Wages
Salary Sacrifice			($50.00)	($2 500.00)	Superannuation Deductions
PAYG Withholding			($22.00)	($11 735.85)	Tax
Annual Leave Accrual	1.846			$187.00	Entitlements
Superannuation Guarantee			$54.72	$4 297.92	Superannuation Expenses

10 Put Peter's termination date of 13 June 18 in his card.

Click...

- *Card List* (in the Card File module).
- *Zoom arrow* next to *WARDS, PETER*.
- *Payroll Details* tab.
- *Personal Details* (at left of window).
- *Termination Date* (type or select *13/06/18*). See Figure 13.13.
- *Yes* (to the screen that opens).
- *OK*.
- *Close*.

Figure 13.13   **Employee Card: Peter Wards' Termination Date**

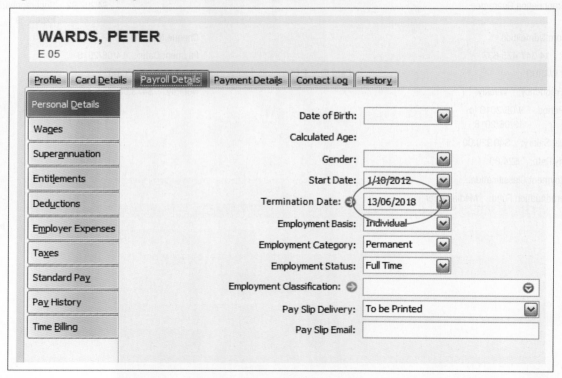

Timesheets continued

11 Enter timesheet information for the week 9 to 15 June 2018 (payment date 18 June) and process the payroll. Paul's annual leave and annual leave loading is processed in the Process Payroll section, not the timesheets. Check your work with a Payroll Activity [Summary] report.

> **Tip**
>
> If the employee works similar overtime hours or days, you can copy their timesheet from the previous week. Change the pay week first, select their name then click on *Copy from Previous* at the bottom left side of the Enter Timesheets window.

Employee	Rate	S	S	M	T	W	T	F
Bruton, D.	1.25x			3	3	3	3	3
	1.5x	4						
	2x	4						
Cooper, P.	1.25x				3	3	3	3
	1.5x	4						
	2x	4						
	Annual			8				
Dillon, M.	1.25x			3	3	3	3	3
	1.5x	4						
	2x	4	8					
Elliot, R.	1.25x			3	3	3	3	3
	1.5x	4						
	2x	4						

Figure 13.14   Payroll Activity [Summary] report: Elsmore Demolition, 18 June 2018

Elsmore Demolition
Blakes Lane
Elsmore NSW 2360
Payroll Activity [Summary]
18/06/2018 To 18/06/2018

Employee	Wages	Deductions	Taxes	Net Pay	Expenses
BRUTON, David	$2 037.00	$292.00	$460.00	$1 285.00	$167.51
COOPER, Paul	$1 900.80	$239.00	$426.00	$1 235.80	$159.62
DILLON, Michael	$2 307.50	$186.00	$604.00	$1 517.50	$168.03
ELLIOTT, Roger	$1 818.75	$133.00	$401.00	$1 284.75	$149.56
Total:	$8 064.05	$850.00	$1 891.00	$5 323.05	$644.72

12 Enter timesheet information for the week 16 to 22 June (pay date 25 June) and process the payroll. Check your work with a Payroll Activity [Summary] report.

Employee	Rate	S	S	M	T	W	T	F
Bruton, D.	1.25x			3	3	3	3	3
	1.5x	4						
	2x	4						
Cooper, P.	1.25x			3	3	3	3	3
	1.5x	4						
	2x	4						
Dillon, M.	1.25x			3	3	3	3	
	1.5x	4						
	2x	4						
	Personal							8
Elliot, R.	1.25x			3	3	3	3	3
	1.5x	4						
	2x	4	8					

Remember This

Michael Dillon's personal leave is entered in the process payroll section, not the timesheets section.

Figure 13.15   Payroll Activity [Summary] report: Elsmore Demolition, 25 June 2018

Elsmore Demolition
Blakes Lane
Elsmore NSW 2360
Payroll Activity [Summary]
25/06/2018 To 25/06/2018

Employee	Wages	Deductions	Taxes	Net Pay	Expenses
BRUTON, David	$2 037.00	$292.00	$460.00	$1 285.00	$167.51
COOPER, Paul	$1 964.25	$239.00	$451.00	$1 274.25	$161.53
DILLON, Michael	$1 794.00	$186.00	$406.00	$1 202.00	$152.62
ELLIOTT, Roger	$2 218.75	$133.00	$557.00	$1 528.75	$161.57
Total:	$8 014.00	$850.00	$1 874.00	$5 290.00	$643.23

13 Produce an Entitlement Balance [Summary] report for June 2018. Note that even though the employees have had different overtime hours throughout June, their Hours Accrued are the same. This is because annual leave and sick leave only accrue on their normal hours (hourly, annual and personal leave) not on overtime hours.

Figure 13.16   Payroll Register [Summary] report: Elsmore Demolition, June 2018

Elsmore Demolition
Blakes Lane
Elsmore NSW 2360
Entitlement Balance [Summary]
June 2018

Entitlement		Opening Hours	Hours Accrued	Hours Taken	Available Hours	Value
BRUTON, David	E 01					
Annual Leave Accrual		174	12.31	0.00	186.31	$5 216.62
Personal Leave Accrual		48	6.15	0.00	54.15	$1 516.26
Total:		222	18.46	0.00	240.46	$6 732.88
COOPER, Paul	E 02					
Annual Leave Accrual		157	12.31	8.00	161.31	$4 355.32
Personal Leave Accrual		95	6.15	0.00	101.15	$2 731.10
Total:		252	18.46	8.00	262.46	$7 086.42
DILLON, Michael	E 03					
Annual Leave Accrual		254	12.31	0.00	266.31	$6 924.01
Personal Leave Accrual		46	6.15	8.00	44.15	$1 147.95
Total:		300	18.46	8.00	310.46	$8 071.96
ELLIOTT, Roger	E 04					
Annual Leave Accrual		138	12.31	0.00	150.31	$3 757.70
Personal Leave Accrual		57	6.15	0.00	63.15	$1 578.80
Total:		195	18.46	0.00	213.46	$5 336.50

Payment summaries

At the end of the payroll year, employees must be provided with a Payment Summary which is a statement summarising their gross income, amount of tax withheld and any **reportable employer superannuation** and fringe benefits. The payment summary is used by the employee to complete their income tax return. The information is also sent to the ATO for data matching purposes.

> **Reportable employer super**
> The extra super contributions an employer makes above what is required by law or an industrial agreement.

14 Using AccountRight 2016, open the file called **13.2 Elsmore Demolition.myox** from Chapter 13 of your online supplementary material or continue using the file you have been using so far.

15 Produce a Payroll Register [Summary] Report for the payroll year 1 July 2017 to 30 June 2018. Compare with Figure 13.17.

Figure 13.17   **Payroll Register [Summary] report: Elsmore Demolition, 1 July 17 to 30 June 18**

Elsmore Demolition
Blakes Lane
Elsmore NSW 2360
Payroll Register [Summary]
July 2017 To June 2018

Employee	Wages	Deductions	Taxes	Net Pay	Expenses
BRUTON, David	$65 702.00	$14 892.00	$13 088.00	$37 722.00	$6 995.66
COOPER, Paul	$66 680.55	$12 189.00	$13 963.00	$40 528.55	$6 766.59
DILLON, Michael	$58 701.50	$9 486.00	$13 187.00	$36 028.50	$6 505.53
ELLIOTT, Roger	$56 812.50	$6 783.00	$10 938.00	$39 091.50	$6 348.13
WARDS, Peter	$55 193.40	$4 050.00	$11 735.86	$39 407.54	$5 945.08
Total:	$303 089.95	$47 400.00	$62 911.86	$192 778.09	$32 560.99

16 Prepare payment summaries.

Click...

- *Prepare Payment Summaries* (in the Payroll module). Read the Introduction screen.
- *Next*.
- *State* and *Postcode* fields (ensure they are completed).
- *Contact Details Name* (insert your own).
- *Phone* (insert a fictitious phone number). This field is compulsory.
- *Authorised Signatory* (insert your own name). This would generally be the name of the Chief Financial Officer (CFO).
- *I use a third-party service provider...* box should be left *unticked*. You would only tick this if you use a BAS agent or accountant to lodge your payment summaries.
- *Next*.
- *Gross Payments* (in the left column).
- *Tick* all the following boxes in the right column: *Annual Leave Loading*, *Annual Leave Pay*, *Base Hourly*, the three *Overtime* options, *Personal Leave*, *Unused Annual Leave*. If your payroll included other payroll categories, such as backpays and salaries, these would need to be ticked too. Compare with **Figure 13.18**.
- *Deduction 1 – Union Fees* (in the left column) and type *Union Fees* in the *Description* field).
- Box for *Union Fee* (in the right column, under the *Deductions* heading (you will have to scroll down to find it). See Figure 13.19. This is the only one of the voluntary deductions which is tax deductible to the employee. If there were others, we would list them individually.

Figure 13.18   **Payment Summary Fields: Gross Payments**

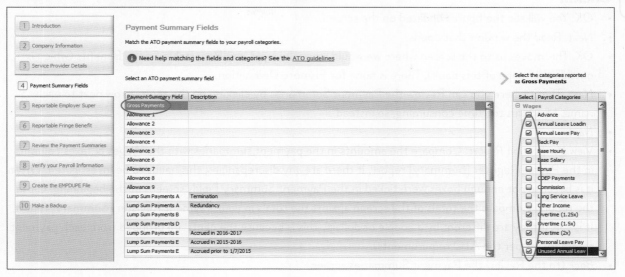

Figure 13.19   **Payment Summary Fields: Deduction – Union Fee**

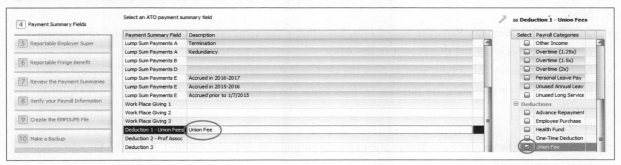

Click...

- *Next.* This is where we manually input any Reportable Employer Superannuation, which includes salary sacrifice but not employee additional super.
- *Link Superannuation Categories.*
- *Salary Sacrifice* (in the window that opens). See Figure 13.20.

Figure 13.20   **Payment Summaries: Reportable Employer Super screen**

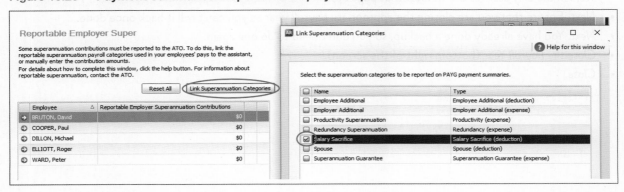

Click...

- *OK.* You will see the figures updated on the screen.
- *Next.* Read the window that opens.
- *OK.* This moves us to the screen where we would manually input any Reportable Fringe Benefits (which is outside the scope of this book). There is none for Elsmore Demolition.
- *Next.* This is where you can Review the Payment Summaries by clicking on the zoom arrow next to each name. I find this too time consuming, so instead...
- *Next.*
- *View Verification Report.* Compare the amounts in the payment summaries with the Wages & Taxes columns in the Payroll Register [Summary] report. If there are any discrepancies, this needs to be investigated. Often it is because not enough boxes were ticked in the Payment Summary Fields screens at the beginning. Close the report. Compare the totals of the screen against the totals in your Payment Register [Summary] report. It is OK if they are different by a couple of dollars. This is because the cents are dropped from each payment summary (as per the ATO requirements).
- *Back* (to the Review the Payment Summaries screen).
- *Save to PDF* (save to a location given to you by your instructor).
- *Next.* We have already verified the payment summaries.
- *Next.*
- *Save Payment Summary Report (empdupe) file.* Save this in the same location that you saved your payment summaries. This is the file that is sent to the ATO.
- *No* (to the question of *Do you want to print the electronic storage media information form?*) You only need to print this if you are sending in a physical USB or copy. The preferred format is an upload from a business tax portal.
- *Next.*
- *Backup* (to the same place you stored the payment summaries and emdupe file). After the file name type *before payroll 2018 rollover.*
- Click *Save*, then Click *Close.*

17 Rollover to a new Payroll Year so you can create pays in July.

Click...

- *File* (in the top menu bar).
- Hover over *Close a Year* and click on *Close a Payroll Year.* See **Figure 13.21.**
- *Yes, I'm the only user* (in the window that pops up).
- *Next.* Ensure that you are closing the appropriate payroll year as you can't roll it back once done.
- *Next.* You have already done a backup, so you don't need to do one again.
- *Close the Payroll Year* (bottom right of the screen).
- *Close.*

Figure 13.21   **Closing a Payroll Year**

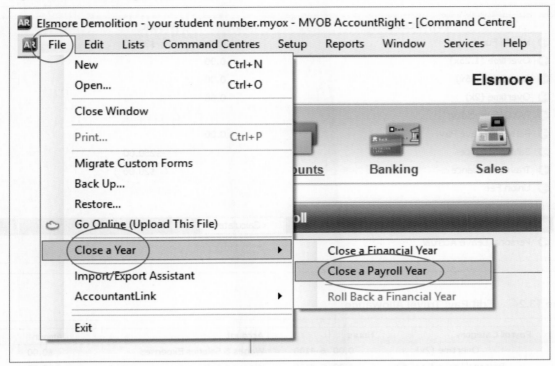

Allowances

Allowances are defined by the ATO as amounts that are paid to cover anticipated costs (such as tool allowance or travel allowance) or as compensation for conditions of employment (for example meal allowance if having to work overtime or under certain conditions). Allowances are assessable income and are generally included as income in their tax return. They are often recorded separately in the payment summaries. These allowances are paid whether the employee incurs the cost or not and the employee is often entitled to claim a deduction for the actual expense. So if the employee receives a tool allowance of $2600 a year and spends $2000 on tools, they will ultimately have extra assessable income of $600 in their tax return.

Allowances are set up as a salary item. See **Figure 13.22**. They can either be paid through standard pay if they are the same recurring amount such as a tool allowance (**Figure 13.23**) or edited in the payroll if they apply after certain conditions such as a travel allowance (**Figure 13.24**).

Figure 13.22   **Wages Setup: Allowance**

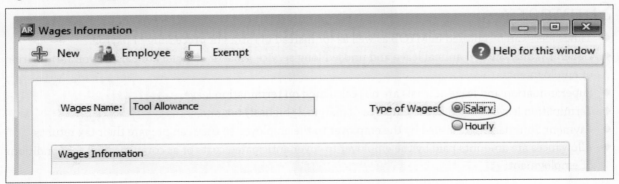

Figure 13.23   **Standard Pay: Tool Allowance**

Payroll Category	Hours	Amount	Job	
Health Fund		-$36.00		
Overtime (1.25x)	0.00			
Overtime (1.5x)	0.00			
Overtime (2x)	0.00			
PAYG Withholding		\<Calculated\>		
Personal Leave Pay	0.00			
Salary Sacrifice		-$250.00		
Travel Allowance		$20.00		
Union Fee		\<Calculated\>		
Entitlements				
Annual Leave Accrual	\<Calculated\>			
Personal Leave Accrual	\<Calculated\>			

Figure 13.24   **Edit Pay: Travel Allowance**

Payroll Category	Hours		Account	Amount	
Overtime (2x)	0.00	6-4100	Wages & Salaries Expenses	$0.00	
Personal Leave Pay	0.00	6-4100	Wages & Salaries Expenses	$0.00	
Travel Allowance		6-4100	Wages & Salaries Expenses	$15.00	
Health Fund		2-1440	Health Plan Payable	-$36.00	
Union Fee		2-1480	Union Fees Payable	-$6.00	
Salary Sacrifice		2-1420	Superannuation Payable	-$250.00	

Either way they are entered in as *positive* amounts as they are extra money received, not deductions being subtracted, from the normal pay.

Allowances shouldn't be confused with reimbursements. An example of a reimbursement is when an employee presents a receipt to their employer for an expense he has incurred and the employer pays them the exact amount on that receipt. It is not assessable income and does not get processed through the payroll system.

Summary

◆ Timesheets can be entered in MYOB as well as (or instead of) straight processing of payroll.

◆ Generally, only unused annual leave and unused long service leave (if eligible) are paid out on termination of employment.

◆ Superannuation and leave accruals are not calculated on termination leave.

◆ Termination leave is taxed at the employee's marginal (highest) tax rate.

◆ Payment Summaries are issued by the employer to the employee so they can prepare their tax returns.

◆ Allowances are amounts paid by the employer to cover anticipated costs or as compensation for conditions of employment.

Assessment

<u>CAPITAL PLUMBERS</u>

1   In MYOB AccountRight 2016 open the **13.3 Capital Plumbers.myox** data file from the Chapter 13 folder of your start-up files.

2   Set up Payroll for Capital Plumbers by using the Payroll Easy Setup Assistant:
  −   Load the tax tables. You may need to do this twice in order to get the screen telling you that the tax tables from 1/10/16 are being loaded.

The Company:
  −   Current Payroll year is 2017.
  −   The normal hours worked per week is 37.5.
  −   Default superannuation fund is Australian Super (Easy Add).
  −   Round pay down to 0 cents.

Wages:
  −   Create an Overtime (1.25x) Rate (Hourly. Regular Rate times 1.25).
  −   Create Casual Rate A (a Fixed Rate of $25.00 per hour).
  −   Create Casual Rate B (a Fixed Rate of $35.00 per hour).
  −   Create Casual Rate C (a Fixed Rate of $45.00 per hour).
  −   Create Meal Allowance (type of wage: salary).
  −   Create Travel Allowance (type of wage: salary).

Superannuation:
  −   Employee Additional: Linked Payable Account is 2-1420 and calculation basis is User-Entered Amount Per Pay Period.
  −   Salary Sacrifice: Linked Payable Account is 2-1420 and calculation basis is User-Entered Amount Per Pay Period.
  −   Superannuation guarantee: Linked Expense Account is 6-4300, Linked Payable Account is 2-1420, the calculation basis is 9.5%.
  −   Exempt the following from superannuation guarantee in addition to those already ticked: Overtime (1.25x), Tool Allowance, Travel Allowance.

Entitlements (full-time employees only):
  −   Both Annual and Personal Leave Accrual: exempt the following: Annual Leave Loading, Backpay, CDEP Payments, all the Overtime wages, Unused Annual and Unused Long Service Leave.
  −   Create two new entitlements by clicking New Entitlement (no exemptions necessary).
      •   Annual Leave Accrual (salary): Calculation Basis equals 5.7692 per pay period, tick the Print On Pay Advice box, Linked Wages Category is Annual Leave Pay.
      •   Personal Leave Accrual (salary): Calculation Basis equals 2.8846 per pay period, Linked Wages Category is Personal Leave Pay.

Deductions:
  −   Add a Health Fund: Linked Payable Account is 2-1440 and it is a (User-Entered) Deduction.
  −   Edit the Union Fee: Linked Payable Account is 2-1480 and the rate is $4.00 per pay period.

Expenses:
  −   WorkCover Insurance rate: Linked Expense Account is 6-4200, Linked Payable Account is 2-1450 and it equals 3% of gross wages.

Taxes:
  −   Check the tax tables have loaded correctly by clicking on **Setup** and **General Payroll Information**.

3   Create cards for the following 5 employees, and note:
  – All employees are entitled to Superannuation Guarantee and WorkCover Insurance.
  – Only the *hourly* full-time employees are entitled to:
    • Wages: Base Hourly, Annual Leave Loading, Annual Leave, all the Overtime options and Personal Leave (and whatever their allowances are on their employee card).
    • Entitlements: Annual Leave Accrual and Personal Leave Accrual.
  – Only the *salary* employees are entitled to:
    • Wages: Base Salary, Annual Leave and Personal Leave (and whatever their allowances are on their Employee Card).
    • Entitlements: Annual Leave Accrual (salary) and Personal Leave Accrual (salary).
  – The details of the allowances for each employee can be found in their employee cards. Tick the applicable allowances in the wages area and enter the amounts in standard pay as a positive.
  – The year to date histories after the employee cards need to be entered into the appropriate section.

Name:	Greg SCLIPPA
Card ID: E 001	**Start:** 26/05/06
Address:	35 Aspinal Street,
	Watson ACT 2602
Pay Type:	Salary
Pay Rate:	$80 000.00 pa
Pay Frequency:	Fortnightly
Allowances:	Travel: $100.00 pf
Super Fund:	Australian Super
Member No.:	165 348
Tax File No.:	311 050 122
Threshold Claimed?	Yes
Total Rebate:	$1 248.00 pa
Deductions:	Health Fund: $25.00 pf
	Employee Additional: $200.00 pf

Name:	Enzo BINOTTO
Card ID: E 001	**Start:** 26/05/06
Address:	47 Stirling Avenue,
	Watson ACT 2602
Pay Type:	Hourly (Full time)
Pay Rate:	$24.00 ph
Pay Frequency:	Fortnightly
Allowances:	Travel: $50.00 pf
	Meals: $40.00 pf
Super Fund:	Media Super
Member No.:	324681
Tax File No.:	202 142 331
Threshold Claimed?	Yes
Total Rebate:	$572.00 pa
Deductions:	Union Fee
	Health Fund: $23.00 pf

Name:	Frank TOSONI
Card ID: E 003	**Start:** 01/07/06
Address:	523 Northbourne Ave,
	Downer ACT 2602
Pay Type:	Hourly (Full time)
Pay Rate:	$20.00 ph
Pay Frequency:	Fortnightly
Allowances:	Travel: $25.00 pf
	Meals: $30.00 pf
Super Fund:	Australian Super
Member No.:	132 348
Tax File No.:	442 206 530
Threshold Claimed?	Yes
Total Rebate:	$1 248.00
Deductions:	Union Fee
	Health Fund: $25.00 pf

Name:	Loris GATTO
Card ID: E 004	**Start:** 15/03/16
Address:	30 National Circuit,
	Forrest ACT 2603
Pay Type:	Hourly (Casual)
Pay Rate:	$22.00
Pay Frequency:	Fortnightly
Pay Rate:	Casual A, B, C
Super Fund:	Australian Super
Member No.:	523 457
Tax File No.:	606 210 153
Tax:	Tax Free Threshold
Threshold Claimed?	Yes
Total Rebate:	$1 300.00 pa
Deductions:	Health Fund: $18.50 pf

Name:	Sylvano PINESE
Card ID: E 005	**Start:** 1/07/15
Address:	45 Heard Street,
	Mawson ACT 2607
Pay Type:	Hourly (Casual)
Pay Rate:	$22.00
Pay Frequency:	Fortnightly
Pay Rate:	Casual A, B, C
Super Fund:	Rest
Member No.:	437 162
Tax File No.:	000 000 000
Tax:	No TFN Resident
Threshold Claimed?	N/A
Total Rebate:	N/A
Deductions:	Union Fee

This is why

Even though Sylvano has declined to provide his Tax File Number (TFN), we still need to enter a number into MYOB or we won't be able to process the payment summaries. That is why we use nine zeros – it indicates to the ATO that the employee hasn't quoted a TFN.

4   Enter the Year-to-Date histories from the two tables below into the employee's Pay History screen, ensuring you change *Show Pay History for* to *Year-to-Date*:

CATEGORY: FULL TIME		
	Binotto	Sclippa	Tosoni
Salary		70 769.23	
Base Hourly	41 400.00	0.00	34 500.00
Annual Leave Loading	472.50	0.00	0.00
Annual Leave Pay	2 700.00	9 230.77	0.00
Allowances Travel	1 200.00	2 400.00	575.00
Meal	1 760.00	0.00	690.00
Overtime (1.25x)	2 400.00	0.00	3 300.00
Overtime (1.5x)	2 160.00	0.00	2 700.00
Overtime (2x)	768.00	0.00	3 920.00
Personal Leave Pay	900.00	0.00	1 500.00
Health Fund	552.00	650.00	600.00
Union Fee	96.00	0.00	96.00
Employee Additional	0.00	4 800.00	0.00
Salary Sacrifice (Super)	0.00	0.00	0.00
PAYG Withholding	10 224.00	19 584.00	7 344.00

Entitlements			
Annual Leave Accrual			
– Year To Date	75.00	105.00	120.00
– Carry Over (in Entitlements)	65.00	15.00	45.00
Personal Leave Accrual			
– Year To Date	45.00	52.50	22.50
– Carry Over (in Entitlements)	15.00	0.00	7.50
Employer Expenses			
WorkCover Insurance	1612.81	2472.00	1415.55
Superannuation Guarantee	4319.89	7600.00	3420.00

CATEGORY: CASUAL		
	Gatto	Pinese
Base Hourly	13200.00	7450.00
Casual Rate A	3600.00	4225.00
Casual Rate B	6125.00	3045.00
Casual Rate C	3420.00	3937.50
Health Fund	630.00	
Union Fee		70.00
PAYG Withholding	1960.00	10318.00
Employer Expenses		
WorkCover Insurance	809.25	619.73
Superannuation Guarantee	2562.63	1962.46

5. Pay the employees according to the following information for the *fortnightly* pay period 31 May to 13 June 2017 (pay date 14 June 2017). We *will not* be using timesheets to record the overtime as there are no fortnightly timesheets to work from:

Name	Normal Hrs	O/t 1.25x	O/t 1.5x	O/t 2x	Casual Rates A	B	C	Sick
Binotto, E.	75	4	3					
Gatto, L.	11				20	4		
Pinese, S.	17				15	7.5	4	
Sclippa, G.	Salary							
Tosoni, F.	75	5	4	4				

6. Enzo Binotto started his four weeks' annual leave on 14 June to 11 July. Process his holiday pay (with loading) in advance as a separate pay on 14 June 2017. Delete any allowances as they are not paid during holidays.

7. Pay the employees according to the following information for pay period 14 June to 27 June 2017 (pay date 28 June):

Name	Normal Hrs	O/t 1.25x	O/t 1.5x	O/t 2x	Casual Rates A	B	C	Sick
Binotto, E.	On Leave							
Gatto, L.	6l				20	4		
Pinese, S.	48				15	7.5	4	
Sclippa, G.	Salary							
Tosoni, F.	75	5	4	4				

8 Create the following supplier cards and pay the liabilities for June 17. Date of payment is 30 June 17:
   – Australian Workers' Union (Union)
   – Medibank Private Pty Ltd (Health Fund)
   – Prudent Insurance (WorkCover)
   – Media Super (Superannuation)
   – Rest (Superannuation)
   – Australian Super (Superannuation).

9 Produce an Employee Register Summary report for 1 July 2016 to 30 June 2017. Prepare the payment summaries:
   – Show the allowances separately on the payment summaries by allocating them in the same way that we allocate the union deduction.
   – Show the union deduction separately.
   – Check the Payment Summaries Verification report against the Employee Register Summary report. In this case, Gross Wages *plus* the allowances (on the payment summary) should equal the Wages on the Employer Register Summary report. Check this for each person and for the totals at the bottom of the report.
   – PDF the payment summaries to submit to your instructor.

10 Make a backup and rollover the payroll year.

11 Pay the employees according to the following information for pay period 28 June to 11 July 2017 (pay date 12 July):

Name	Normal Hrs	O/t 1.25x	O/t 1.5x	O/t 2x	Casual Rates A	B	C	Sick
Binotto, E.	On Leave							
Gatto, L.	42				15	4	4	
Pinese, S.	On Leave							
Sclippa, G.	Salary							7.5
Tosoni, F.	75	8	4	4				

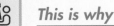

This is why

Sylvano Pinese is a casual and does not get any annual or sick leave. Just untick him so he doesn't get paid at all.

12 Enzo Binotto is retiring and finished work on 14 July (three days' work: 12 to 14 July).
   – On 15 July, process his final pay (removing all deductions or allowances).
   – Pay him his Unused Annual Leave using 32.5% tax rate. Produce a Payslip report for the two pays to give to your instructor.
   – Put the termination date in his employee card.

13 Pay the employees according to the following information for pay period 12 July to 25 July 2017 (pay date 26 July):

Name	Normal Hrs	O/t 1.25x	O/t 1.5x	O/t 2x	Casual Rates			Sick
					A	B	C	
Gatto, L.	22				15	4	4	
Pinese, S.	36				15	7.5	4	
Sclippa, G.	Salary							
Tosoni, F.	75	5	4	4				

14 Produce an Employee Activity [Summary] report for 1 July 2017 to 31 July 2017.

14

BUSINESS ACTIVITY STATEMENTS: INTRODUCTION

Learning outcomes

By the end of this chapter you will be competent in:
- identifying individual compliance and other requirements for Business Activity Statement (BAS)
- recognising and applying goods and services tax (GST) implications and code transactions
- reporting on payroll activities
- reporting on GST, Pay As You Go Withholding (PAYGW) and Pay As You Go Instalments (PAYGI)
- completing and reconciling the activity statement.

The BAS is used to report a variety of taxes. Lodgement can be monthly, quarterly or annually, depending on the size and nature of the enterprise. This chapter introduces you to the BAS principles and the most common items reported on a BAS.

Background

Businesses use a Business Activity Statement (BAS) to report, calculate and pay several of their tax obligations, including:

- Goods and services tax (GST): a tax on many sales and purchases
- Pay As You Go Withholding (PAYGW): the income tax you have withheld from your employees' gross wages, directors' and office holders' fees and contractors under a voluntary agreement to meet their future tax liabilities
- No ABN Withholding: if a supplier doesn't give you an ABN, you are required to withhold tax at their marginal rate (49% in 2016) and submit it to the ATO
- Other amounts withheld: from certain interest, dividends, unit trusts and other investment distributions you are making where the recipient hasn't provided a tax file number declaration or is a non-resident, and certain other payments made to foreign residents and any DASP Payments
- Pay As You Go Instalment (PAYGI): the income tax you have been asked to pay up front in order to meet your future tax liabilities
- Luxury Car Tax (LCT): on the import of luxury cars over a certain threshold
- Wine Equalisation Tax (WET): for wholesalers or importers of wine
- Fuel Tax Credits: credits on the tax component of fuel for eligible tax payers
- Fringe Benefits Tax (FBT): a tax on Fringe Benefits provided to your employees or their associates.

The BAS will also report for the period:

- Total sales, broken down into components
- Total capital expenditure (purchase of assets)
- Total non-capital expenditure
- Total payments made to employees, company directors, office holders, workers under a labour hire agreement or voluntary agreements.

The Income Activity Statement (IAS) is used to report and pay:

- Pay As You Go Withholding (PAYGW)
- No ABN Withholding
- Other amounts withheld.

The IAS also reports for the period:

- Total payments made to employees, company directors, office holders, workers under a labour hire agreement or voluntary agreements.

The IAS is often used when an organisation is not registered for GST, but has employees. The Instalment Notice (IN) is used if you report and pay your GST and/or PAYGI quarterly using the amounts advised by the ATO and have no other reporting requirements.

We will concentrate on the BAS and IAS as these are the forms that you will become the most exposed to as a bookkeeper. Your reporting and payment period can be monthly, quarterly or yearly depending on the size of your business and your preference.

A monthly BAS:

- is compulsory for organisations who have a GST turnover of $20 million or more
- can be requested if you earn less than $20 million

- is a great way for businesses with poor cashflow to keep on top of their compliance as it means there are smaller amounts being paid out each month instead of a larger sum every quarter
- is required to be lodged by the 21st of the following month.
A quarterly BAS:
- is the default for organisations with a GST turnover of less than $20 million
- is generally required to be lodged on the 28th of the month following the end of the quarter, except for December BAS which is due on 28 February instead of January.

It is not uncommon for a business to lodge both a quarterly BAS and monthly IAS.

BAS and IAS can either be lodged online or by completing and returning a paper form issued by the ATO. The ATO is pushing for more online reporting for the obvious reasons that it decreases processing time on their end and is more efficient. Online lodgement options are expanded upon later in this chapter.

Each activity statement is personalised to the taxpayer's situation and the options that have been chosen previously. They are issued by the ATO a few weeks prior to the end of each reporting period.

The paper BAS we use in this chapter contains five sections:

- Goods and services tax (GST): reports the sales and purchases figures
- PAYG tax withheld: reports the payments and amounts withheld from others such as employees, certain contractors, directors and officeholders etc,
- PAYG income tax instalment: reports the PAYG to be withheld for *your* future tax liabilities,
- Summary: reports amounts you owe the ATO and credits available to you
- Payment or refund?: the end result of the summary – do you need to pay or do you receive a refund?

Labels are the sections or fields of the activity statement where information is required. Each label has its own title and requires specific information. Only those labels that apply to a particular business or individual will appear on their statement.

Terms used in activity statements are sometimes different from those used in the GST legislation:

- *GST Credit* means the GST term input tax credit.
- *Payment (made or received)* means the GST term consideration.
- *Purchases* means the GST term acquisitions, and includes the purchase of goods and services and the payment of business expenses.
- *Sales* means the GST term supplies.

Accrual vs cash basis

The BAS can be calculated on either a cash or accrual basis.

Cash basis

An organisation can only use the *cash* basis if one of the following applies:

- Annual turnover (current or projected) is $2 million or less
- Income tax is calculated on the cash basis
- The entity is a charity
- You apply and receive permission from the ATO commissioner.

Cash basis means the GST is reported when payments have been:

- received from customers, and
- made to suppliers.

Just like with our cash accounting method in Chapter 5, the date of the invoice is irrelevant. The reporting is done as money flows in and out of the business. So if a customer invoice is sent in March and the payment is received in April, the GST collected will be reported and paid to the ATO in the June quarterly BAS (or April BAS if it is reported monthly).

The benefit of using the cash basis is that you don't have to pay the GST collected on a customer invoice until it has actually been paid to you. You aren't out of pocket waiting for your customer to pay.

Accrual basis

An organisation will use the *accrual* basis:

- compulsorily if the annual turnover current or projected is over $2 million
- voluntarily if it works in their favour. For instance, their suppliers may give generous credit payment terms (such as 30 days after EOM) and their customers may be required to pay within a shorter time (such as a 14 days).

Accrual basis means the GST is reported at the time of the invoice. Whether payments have been received or made is irrelevant. Using the same scenario as above, if a customer invoice is sent out in March and the payment is received in April, the GST collected will be reported and paid to the ATO in the March monthly or quarterly BAS.

The benefit of using the accrual basis is that you get the tax credits from the GST you have paid before you have even paid the supplier invoice by the time of lodging the BAS.

Either way, the GST collected and paid will at some stage make its way through the ATO. It is just a matter of timing.

The decision to go with cash or accrual reporting is an important one as it affects cashflow. Many smaller businesses prefer the cash accounting method as it means that they aren't paying the GST collected before they have actually been paid it by the customer.

Penalties

Penalties may apply for failure to lodge on time. A general interest charge may apply to any amount not paid by the due date in addition to a penalty for late lodgement, should that also be late. Note that the penalty is for late lodgement, not late payment. However, the ATO acknowledges that there may be occasions where businesses may need to pay their liabilities through a payment plan and they are often accommodating towards this.

Payments, refunds and offsets

- *Payment* is due to the ATO on the same date as lodgement of the BAS.
- *Refunds* are paid directly into the taxpayer's nominated account at a bank or other financial institution in Australia when the *GST Paid* is greater than the sum of *GST Collected* and any of the other reportable taxes such as PAYGI, PAYGW and FBT in the reporting period.
- *Offsets* occur when the ATO applies any refund due to offset any other taxation debt or an Australian Government debt such as a Child Support Agency debt or previous income tax debt.

Record keeping

- A copy of each BAS should be kept for five years after the date of its preparation, together with the records used to prepare it.
- The records should be in writing and in English.
- If the information is stored in electronic form it must be readily accessible and easily converted into English. Pre-printed details on the BAS are show in **Figure 14.1**.

Figure 14.1 **Paper BAS header for OneCo Pty Ltd**

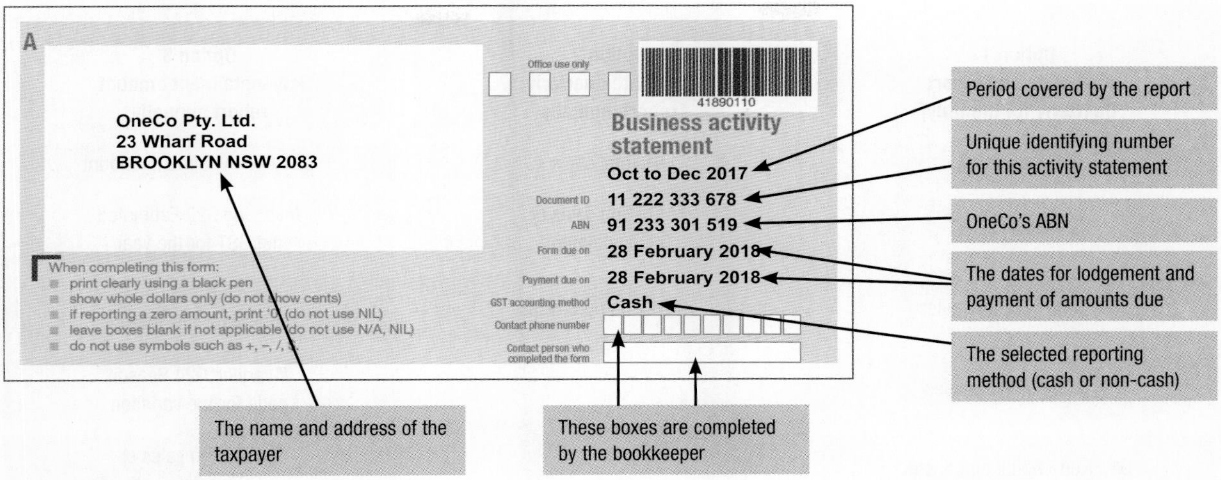

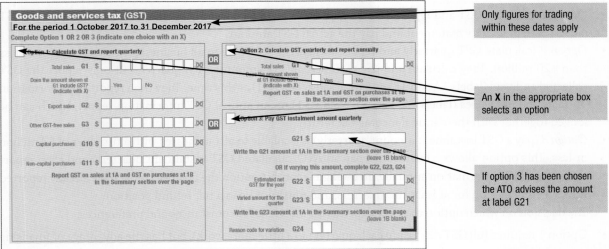

Goods and services tax (GST)

Reporting choices are made in the first activity statement after registering for the GST with the ATO. **Figure 14.2** shows the options available for reporting GST in a paper BAS.

Figure 14.2 **Paper BAS GST reporting choices for OneCo Pty Ltd**

Most small businesses report and pay their GST quarterly and have a choice each year of how they do this. If a paper activity statement shows that more than one option is available, one must be chosen. If any option is not available to a business for the current paper activity statement, the message *Not eligible for this option* will be printed over that option.

Figure 14.3 shows the GST labels that apply depending upon the option that has been chosen.

Figure 14.3 **Paper BAS GST reporting options**

Option 1 Calculate and report Quarterly (or monthly)	Option 2 Calculate quarterly, report annually	Option 3 Pay instalment amount, report annually
G1 Total sales	G1 Total sales	G21 ATO instalment amount
G2 Export sales	1A GST on sales or GST instalment	*If varying* G22 Estimated net GST for the year
G3 Other GST-free sales	1B GST on purchases	*If varying* G23 Varied amount for this quarter
G10 Capital purchases		*If varying* G24 Reason code for the variation
G11 Non-capital purchases		1A GST on sales or GST instalment
1A GST on sales or GST instalment		
1B GST on purchases		

Choosing a GST option (quarterly payers):

- *Option 1* (calculate GST and report quarterly) is available to all quarterly businesses. They report at all GST labels on their activity statement and pay the actual GST amount.
- *Option 2* (calculate GST quarterly and report annually) is available to all businesses with a turnover of less than $20 million. They calculate and pay their actual GST amounts each quarter, but only report the GST collected and paid (labels 1A and 1B) and total sales (label G1) at this time. They then report full information on sales and purchases (labels G2, G3, G10 and G11) on an annual GST information report, which can be lodged together with their annual income tax return.
- *Option 3* (pay a GST instalment amount quarterly) is available to all businesses with a turnover of $2 million or less. This option allows a business to pay an ATO-calculated GST instalment quarterly and then report their actual GST information annually. To be eligible for this option the business must have already reported full GST information for at least two quarters, and must not be in a net refund position.

The decision on which option to select depends on individual circumstances and preferences:

- Option 1 requires full GST disclosure each quarter (so a little more work), but has the advantage of finalising the period, with no annual GST return being required.
- Option 1 with monthly (rather than quarterly) activity statements can be requested and are a great way of staying on top of your ATO obligations if cashflow is tight. Smaller monthly payments may be easier that paying larger amounts of money each quarter.
- Option 2 involves a little less disclosure each quarter, but additional work at the end of each financial year with an annual GST return being required. A refund from the ATO is available using Options 1 and 2 should GST Paid exceed GST Collected in that quarter.

- Option 3 involves the least quarterly work as the business need only pay the ATO's calculated amount. The amount actually paid can be varied by the business (up or down as circumstances change), but the varied instalment cannot fall below zero. A refund is only possible with the lodgement of the annual GST return. A penalty may be imposed if the *varied instalments actually paid* during the year add up to less than 85% of the total GST liability for the year (as disclosed in the annual GST return).

Regardless of which option is selected, a business has the choice of two methods of calculating its GST liability:

- A calculation worksheet method is available using material supplied by the ATO. This method uses GST Inclusive figures to report on sales and purchases.
- The accounts method may be used, where figures are transcribed from the business accounts into the activity statement. GST Inclusive or GST Exclusive figures may be used, but an indication must be given in the box provided as to which has been chosen.

ONECO PTY LTD

OneCo Pty Ltd is a small business that is operated by its owner. It has no paid employees and all purchases and sales are paid for at the time of the transaction. Records are kept on MYOB AccountRight 2016 using the Banking module, with the computer being updated monthly with summaries of business activity.

Print a copy of their Business Activity Statement (BAS) for use in this exercise. It is located in the Chapter 14 folder of your start-up files, entitled *14.1 OneCo BAS*.

In this exercise we will be completing the activity statement for GST only:

- for Option 1 (calculate and report quarterly)
- on a cash basis
- using the business accounts method.

1 In MYOB AccountRight 2016, open the **14.1 OneCo.myox** data file from the Chapter 14 folder of your start-up files.

2 Print the following reports for the period 1 October 2017 to 31 December 2017:

- Bank Register (Banking section of the Reports Centre). See Figure 14.4.
- GST [Summary – Cash] (GST/Sales Tax section of the Reports Centre). See Figure 14.5.
- Transaction Tax Codes (GST/Sales Tax section of the Reports Centre). See Figure 14.6

Figure 14.4   Bank Register report: OneCo Pty Ltd

OneCo Pty Ltd
23 Wharf Road
Brooklyn NSW 2083
Bank Register
October 2017 To December 2017

ID No.	Src	Date	Memo/Payee	Deposit	Withdrawal	Balance
1-1110	Business Bank Account #1					
1	CD	1/10/2017	Purchases		$605.00	$99 395.00
2	CD	1/10/2017	EquipCo		$1 100.00	$98 295.00
3	CD	3/10/2017	Purchases		$10 900.00	$87 395.00
4	CD	28/10/2017	Expenses		$1 100.00	$86 295.00
CR000001	CR	31/10/2017	Sales	$21 935.00		$108 230.00
5	CD	7/11/2017	Purchases		$6 330.00	$101 900.00

▶ ▶

ID No.	Src	Date	Memo/Payee	Deposit	Withdrawal	Balance
6	CD	25/11/2017	Expenses		$1 100.00	$100 800.00
CR000002	CR	30/11/2017	Sales	$10 655.00		$111 455.00
7	CD	5/12/2017	Purchases		$9 695.00	$101 760.00
8	CD	30/12/2017	Expenses		$1 100.00	$100 660.00
9	CD	30/12/2017	Expenses		$770.00	$99 890.00
10	CD	31/12/2017	bank fees		$35.00	$99 855.00
CR000003	CR	31/12/2017	Sales	$16 075.00		$115 930.00
CR000004	CR	31/12/2017	interest income	$745.00		$116 675.00
				$49 410.00	$32 735.00	

Figure 14.5   GST [Summary – Cash] report: OneCo Pty Ltd

OneCo Pty Ltd
23 Wharf Road
Brooklyn NSW 2083
ABN: 91233 301 519
GST [Summary – Cash]
October 2017 To December 2017

Code	Description	Rate	Sale Value	Purchase Value	Tax Collected	Tax Paid
CAP	Capital Acquisitions	10.00%		$1 705.00		$155.00
FRE	GST Free	0.00%	$7 668.00	$4 300.00		
GST	Goods & Services Tax	10.00%	$40 997.00	$26 730.00	$3 727.00	$2 430.00
ITS	Input Taxed Sales	0.00%	$745.00			
				Total:	$3 727.00	$2 585.00

Figure 14.6   Transaction Tax Codes report: OneCo Pty Ltd

OneCo Pty Ltd
23 Wharf Road
Brooklyn NSW 2083
Transaction Tax Codes
October 2017 To December 2017

Src	Date	Memo	ID No.	Debit	Credit	Account Tax	Entered Tax	Default Tax
1-2210	Office Equipment At Cost							
CD	1/10/2017	Purchases	1	$550.00		CAP	CAP	CAP
CD	1/10/2017	EquipCo	2	$1 000.00		CAP	CAP	CAP
4-1000	Sales							
CR	31/10/2017	Sales	CR000001		$18 000.00	GST	GST	GST
CR	30/11/2017	Sales	CR000002		$8 450.00	GST	GST	GST
CR	31/12/2017	Sales	CR000003		$10 820.00	GST	GST	GST
4-2000	GST Free Sales							
CR	31/10/2017	Sales	CR000001		$2 135.00	FRE	FRE	FRE
CR	30/11/2017	Sales	CR000002		$1 360.00	FRE	FRE	FRE
CR	31/12/2017	Sales	CR000003		$4 173.00	FRE	FRE	FRE

▶ ▶

Src	Date	Memo	ID No.	Debit	Credit	Account Tax	Entered Tax	Default Tax
5-1000	Purchases							
CD	3/10/2017	Purchases	3	$9 000.00		GST	GST	GST
CD	7/11/2017	Purchases	5	$5 000.00		GST	GST	GST
CD	5/12/2017	Purchases	7	$6 600.00		GST	GST	GST
5-2000	GST Free Purchases							
CD	3/10/2017	Purchases	3	$1 000.00		FRE	FRE	FRE
CD	7/11/2017	Purchases	5	$830.00		FRE	FRE	FRE
CD	5/12/2017	Purchases	7	$2 435.00		FRE	FRE	FRE
6-1100	Accounting/Bookkeeping Fees							
CD	28/10/2017	Expenses	4	$1 000.00		GST	GST	GST
CD	25/11/2017	Expenses	6	$1 000.00		GST	GST	GST
CD	30/12/2017	Expenses	8	$1 000.00		GST	GST	GST
6-1300	Bank Fees							
CD	31/12/2017	bank fees	10	$35.00		FRE	FRE	FRE
6-1700	Electricity Expenses							
CD	30/12/2017	Expenses	9	$700.00		GST	GST	GST
8-1000	Interest Income							
CR	31/12/2017	interest income	CR000004		$745.00	ITS	ITS	ITS

Label G1: Total sales

The BAS term *sales* has the same meaning as the GST term *supplies*. The items to include at G1 are:

- GST-free sales
- input-taxed sales
- taxable sales.
  Examples of sales include:
- Sales of goods and services (including or excluding GST)
- Sales of business assets
- Government grants and certain private sector grants
- Interest earned
- Sale, lease or rental of buildings or land
- Contributions received from employees for fringe benefits you have provided.
  It excludes:
- Salary and wages received by the owner
- Pension and annuities
- Dividends
- Loans received
- Proceeds from sale of shares
- Hobby activities
- Gifts
- Trust or partnership distributions.

3 Check that all the receipts recorded in the Bank Register deposit column appear in the Transaction Tax Codes report as credits and have an appropriate tax code (GST for taxable sales; EXP for export sales; FRE for GST-free sales; ITS for interest received).

Check also that the *Entered Tax* code is the same as the *Default Tax* code in all credit entries. Any difference here would indicate that the tax code had been altered manually for that transaction, and would be investigated. It doesn't mean that it is wrong. It just needs to be checked.

All is correct, so the sum of the Sale Value from the GST [Summary – Cash] report (**Figure 14.7**) can be used as the *Total Sales* figure at label G1.

Figure 14.7   Extract GST [Summary – Cash] report: OneCo Pty Ltd

Code	Description	Rate	Sale Value
FRE	GST Free	0.00%	$7 668.00
GST	Goods & Services Tax	10.00%	$40 997.00
ITS	Input Taxed Sales	0.00%	$745.00
		Total Sales	$49 410.00

This total figure is GST Inclusive and is transferred to OneCo's activity statement Option 1 section. Cross the box next to **Option 1: Calculate GST and report quarterly** and the box next to **Does the amount shown at G1 include GST?** See Figure 14.8.

Figure 14.8   Paper BAS OneCo Pty Ltd, label G1

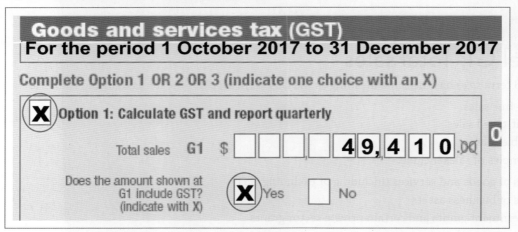

Label G2: Export sales

Export sales are sales made to an overseas customer for consumption overseas and so G2 includes:

- the free on-board value (the value declared at Customs) of exported goods that meet the GST-free export rules
- payments for the repair of goods from overseas that are to be exported
- payments for goods used in the repair of goods from overseas that are to be exported.
  It excludes:
- amounts for GST-free services unless they relate to the repair or modification of goods from overseas whose destination is outside Australia
- amounts for freight and insurance for freight of the goods outside Australia included in the free on-board value
- amounts for international transport of goods or passengers.

MYOB AccountRight identifies all sales to be reported at label G2 by using the tax code EXP (which has a tax rate of zero) on exports. Such sales would be shown as a separate amount in the GST [Summary – Cash] report and itemised in the Transaction Tax Codes report.

4 MYOB AccountRight 2016 reports zero export sales, but do not write anything in the activity statement at label G2. Leave it blank. See Figure 14.9.

Figure 14.9   Paper BAS OneCo Pty Ltd, label G2

Label G3: Other GST-free sales

GST-free sales within Australia include:

- most basic food
- health and education services
- some childcare facilities.

They exclude:

- processed food (such as biscuits, cakes, prepared meals and soft drinks) as they have GST
- foods consumed on premises or taken away (such as food from cafes) as they have GST.

MYOB AccountRight 2016 identifies all sales to be reported at label G3 by using the tax codes FRE and ITS (which both have a tax rate of zero). A total of $8413.00 is calculated from the GST [Summary – Cash] report in Figure 14.10, so this total is entered at G3 in the activity statement.

Figure 14.10   Extract GST [Summary – Cash] report: OneCo Pty Ltd, tax rate 0%

Code	Description	Rate	Sale Value
FRE	GST Free	0.00%	$7 668.00
ITS	Input Taxed Sales	0.00%	$745.00
		Total Sales	$8 413.00

5 Complete G3 in your activity statement. See Figure 14.11.

Figure 14.11   **Paper BAS OneCo Pty Ltd, label G3**

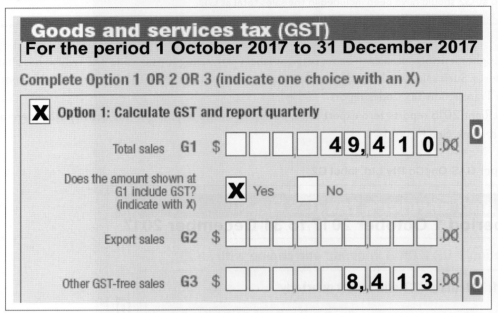

Remember This

All amounts reported at G3 should also have been included in the sales total at G1.

Label G10: Capital purchases

Capital purchases include:

- land and buildings
- machinery and equipment
- cash registers
- computers
- furniture and fixtures
- motor vehicles.

MYOB AccountRight 2016 identifies capital purchases using the tax code *CAP*. They are reported separately in the totals in the GST [Summary – Cash] report and show $1705.00 (including GST) has to be entered at G10.

6 Complete G10 in your activity statement and compare to Figure 14.12.

Figure 14.12   **Paper BAS OneCo Pty Ltd, label G10**

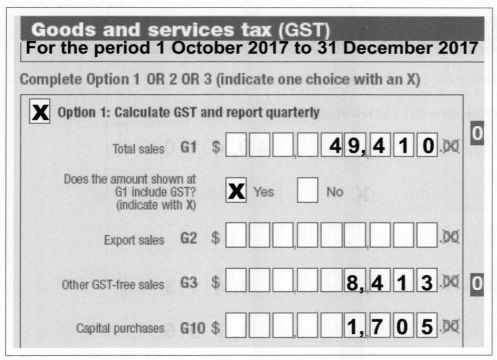

Note: If the accounting system does not separate capital purchases from non-capital ones it is acceptable to include non-capital purchases below $1000.00 at label G11.

Label G11: Non-capital purchases

Non-capital purchases are, as the name suggests, any purchases of a non-capital nature. A business would normally expect to consume the purchase within a year. These include:

- trading stock
- stationery
- maintenance and repairs
- equipment rental and leases
- business operating expenses.

The GST [Summary – Cash] report extract (Figure 14.13) shows total non-capital purchases for the period as two amounts: those that are subject to GST and those that are GST-free. These amounts are combined for entry at G11 on the activity statement as shown in Figure 14.14.

Figure 14.13   **Extract GST [Summary – Cash] report: OneCo Pty Ltd, purchases**

Code	Description	Rate	Purchase Value
FRE	GST Free	0.00%	$4 300.00
GST	Goods & Services Tax	10.00%	$26 730.00
		Total Purchases	$31 030.00

7 Complete G11 in your activity statement and compare with Figure 14.14.

Figure 14.14 **Paper BAS OneCo Pty Ltd, label G11**

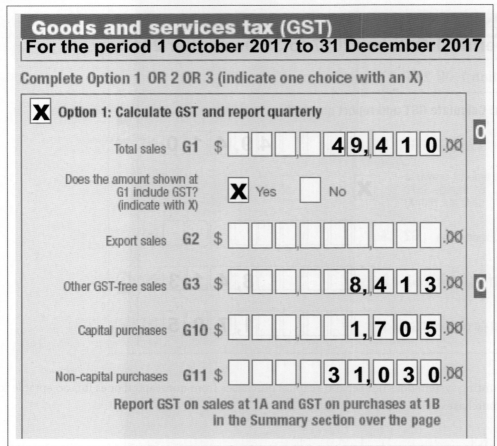

Labels 1A and 1B: Summary of GST on sales and purchases

Label 1A, on the reverse side of the paper activity statement, records the total GST collected on sales during the quarter, after any adjustments. Label 1B records GST credits (after adjustments) obtained from purchases.

The figures can be obtained directly from the GST [Summary – Cash] report as seen in Figure 14.15.

Figure 14.15   **Extract GST (Summary – Cash) report: OneCo Pty Ltd, Tax Collected and Paid**

Code	Description	Rate	Tax Collected	Tax Paid
CAP	Capital Acquisitions	10.00%		$155.00
FRE	GST Free	0.00%		
GST	Goods & Services Tax	10.00%	$3 727.00	$2 430.00
ITS	Input Taxed Sales	0.00%		
		Totals	$3 727.00	$2 585.00

8 Insert these numbers into the activity statement and, as there is nothing more to add to this statement, these figures are copied to 8A and 8B respectively as seen in Figure 14.16.

Figure 14.16   **Paper BAS OneCo Pty Ltd, Summary section**

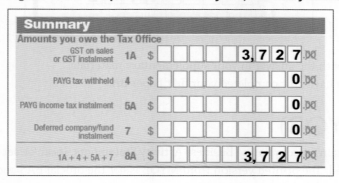

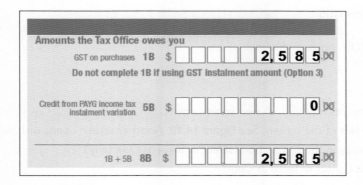

9 The *Payment or refund?* section can now be completed by putting a cross in the appropriate box as in Figure 14.17.

Figure 14.17   **Paper BAS OneCo Pty Ltd, Payment or refund?**

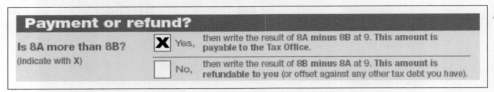

10 And finally, the amount due to the ATO is calculated and entered at label 9, as shown in Figure 14.18.

Figure 14.18   **Paper BAS OneCo Pty Ltd, label 9**

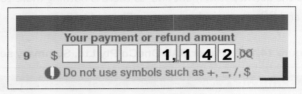

Compare your copy with the answer in your supplementary materials.
Congratulations! You have now completed your first paper BAS.

BASlink (MYOB)

BASlink is MYOB's program for completing Business Activity Statements. It can be set up so that a draft version of the BAS can be printed. The printed version from MYOB is *not* the official BAS and should *not* be sent into the ATO.

1 Set up the BAS information.

Return to your MYOB company file and....

Click...

- *BASlink* (in the Accounts module). A new screen opens.
- *BAS Info* at the top left of the screen. See Figure 14.19. Another screen opens with reporting options.
- *GST reporting frequency* in the top section (select or leave as *Quarterly*).
- *GST accounting basis* (select or leave as *Cash*).
- *GST option* (select or leave as *Option 1*).
- *Calculation method* (select or leave as *Calculation worksheet*). Note the other options available in the top section, but leave them unticked.
- *Instalment reporting frequency* in the middle section (select *Not registered*).
- *Withholding reporting frequency* in the bottom section (select *Not Registered*). Compare with Figure 14.20.

Figure 14.19   **BASlink info screen**

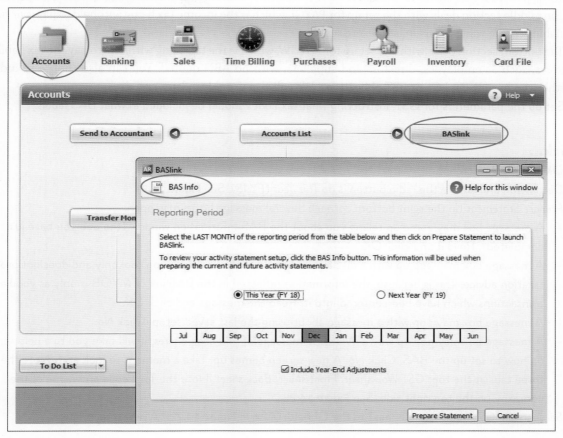

Figure 14.20   **Set Up Activity Statement screen**

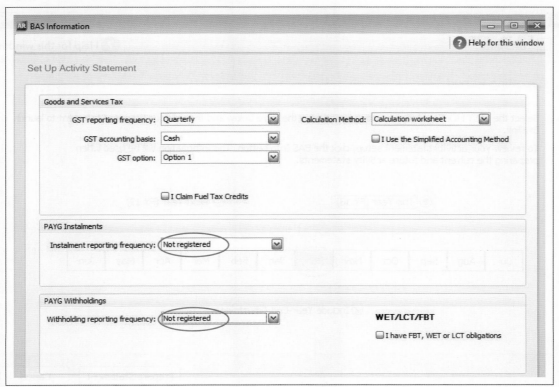

The top section deals with the set up for GST. You can also indicate here whether you claim Fuel Tax Credits. The middle section deals with the set up for PAYGI, which is the income tax being withheld to pay *your* future tax liabilities. We will use this in later exercises.

The bottom section deals with the set up for PAYGW, which is the tax being withheld to pay the tax liabilities of *others*, such as employees, directors and suppliers, with no ABN quoted. You can also choose to indicate whether you have WET, LCT or FBT obligations. We will also use this in later exercises.

2 Set up the parameters for GST, instructing what tax codes should be included in what BAS labels.

Click...

- *OK* (to exit the screen).
- *Dec* button and ensure the radio button is on *This Year (FY 18)*. See **Figure 14.21**.
- *Prepare Statement* (in the right bottom corner). Several message boxes may open:
  - A message box may come up telling you about the BAS Information window (the one you have just completed). Read it and click *OK*.
  - A message box may pop up with a disclaimer that BASlink is a calculation tool only and does not provide taxation advice. This is because the information reflected in the BASlink of MYOB is only as good as the transactions which have been entered into it. Read the message and click *OK*.
  - A message box may pop with a message about using the last saved setup. Click *No*.
  - A message box *may* pop up with a Welcome message. If you click on *Yes*, it will take you to a help screen on how to set up the BAS. Click *No*. A new screen comes up. Take a moment to look at it. Note the three tabs at the top: *GST Worksheet, Front sheet, Back sheet*. Note the *Tax Period* and name of the company on the top right side. See **Figure 14.22**.
- *Setup* in the *GST worksheet* tab, next to the G1 field. (Also in **Figure 14.22**.) A new screen opens.

Figure 14.21   BASlink Reporting Period screen

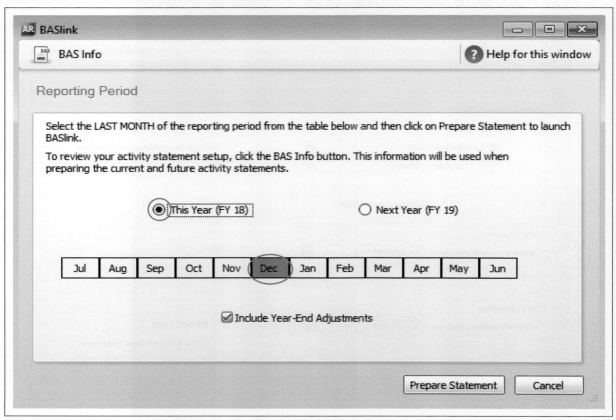

Figure 14.22   Calculation worksheet: G1 Setup

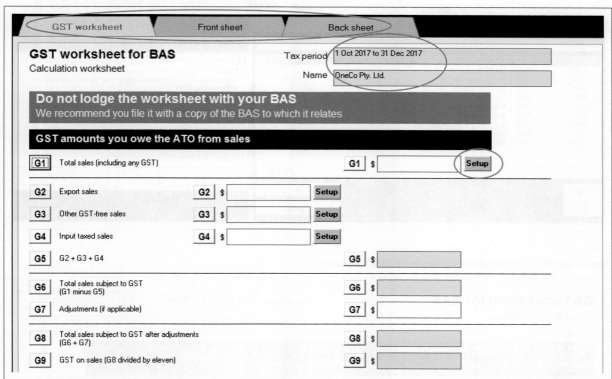

Click...

- *Cell in left column* to place an *X* next to *GST* and *FRE*. A new window pops up letting you know that any GST-free sales will also record in G3. See Figure 14.23. Read it and click *OK*.
- *Cell in left column* to place an *X* next to *ITS*. The same window pops up.
- *Radio button next to G4 Input taxed sales*. Compare with Figure 14.24.
- *OK* to close the window. Compare the amounts in the fields Setup (Figure 14.25) against your GST [Summary – Cash] report that you printed earlier (recreated in Figure 14.26).
- *OK* (to close the window).

Figure 14.23   BASlink G1 setup: GST-free tax code window

Figure 14.24   BASlink G1 setup: ITS tax code window

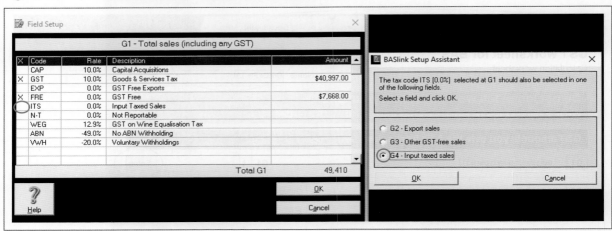

Figure 14.25   Calculation worksheet: GST on sales

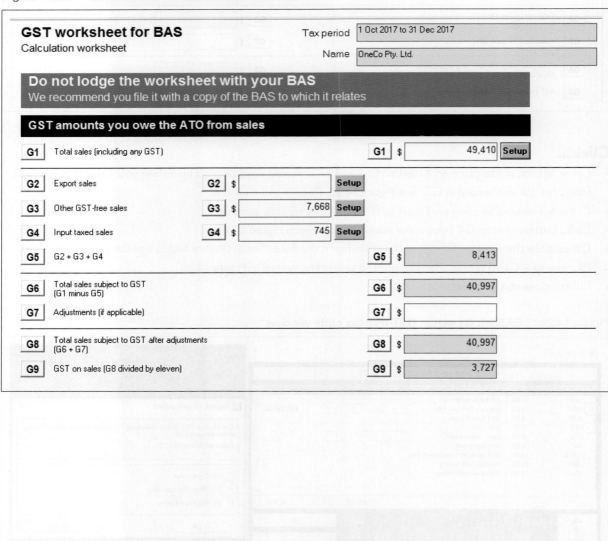

Figure 14.26   GST [Summary – Cash] report: OneCo Pty Ltd

OneCo Pty Ltd						
23 Wharf Road						
Brooklyn NSW 2083						
ABN: 91233 301 519						
GST [Summary – Cash]						
October 2017 To December 2017						
Code	**Description**	**Rate**	**Sale Value**	**Purchase Value**	**Tax Collected**	**Tax Paid**
CAP	Capital Acquisitions	10.00%		$1 705.00		$155.00
FRE	GST Free	0.00%	$7 668.00	$4 300.00		
GST	Goods & Services Tax	10.00%	$40 997.00	$26 730.00	$3 727.00	$2 430.00
ITS	Input Taxed Sales	0.00%	$745.00			
				Total:	$3 727.00	$2 585.00

We can compare Figure 14.25 to our manual calculations and also to Figure 14.26 and see that:

- G1 is the sum of all of the Sale Values in Figure 14.26.
- G3 is the Sale Value for the FRE tax code in Figure 14.26.
- G4 is the Sale Value for the ITS tax code in Figure 14.26.
  In Figure 14.25, we can see that:
- G5 is the total of G2 + G3 + G4.
- G6 is the total sales subject to GST (G1 minus G5).
- G9 is calculated by dividing G6 by 11 = 40 997/11 = 3.27. This matches the Tax Collected in Figure 14.26. We know that we have done our GST on sales setup correctly.

3 Set up the Purchase tax codes. Scroll down to the bottom half of the Calculation worksheet.

Click...

- *Setup* next to the G10 field. A new screen opens.
- *Cell in left column* to place an *X* next to *CAP*. Compare with Figure 14.27.
- *OK*.
- *Setup* next to the G11 field. A new screen opens.
- *Cells in left column* to place an *X* next to *GST* and *FRE*. A new window opens with G14 selected. Compare with Figure 14.28 and click *OK*.
- *Cell in left column* to place an *X* next to *GNR*, which means the supplier has an ABN but is not registered for GST. A new window opens with G14 selected. Read it, compare with Figure 14.29 and click *OK*.
- *Cell in left column* to place an *X* next to *INP*. A new window opens. Select *G13* as that is the correct corresponding field. See Figure 14.30. Click *OK* to exit the window. Even though these two windows have *$0* in the amount column, it is important to set them up correctly in the first place in case there are transactions using these tax codes in later BAS periods.
- *OK* to exit the fields setup.

Figure 14.27   **BASlink G10 Setup: Capital purchases**

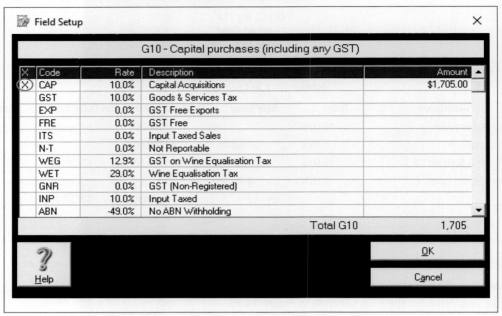

Figure 14.28   **BASlink G11 Setup: Non-capital purchases**

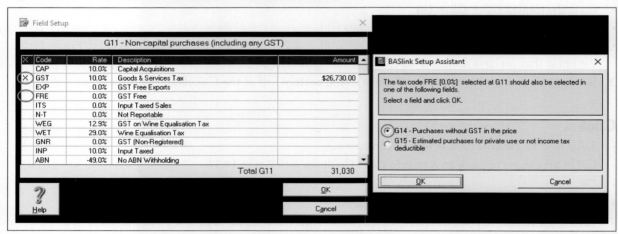

Figure 14.29   **BASlink G14 Setup: GNR tax code**

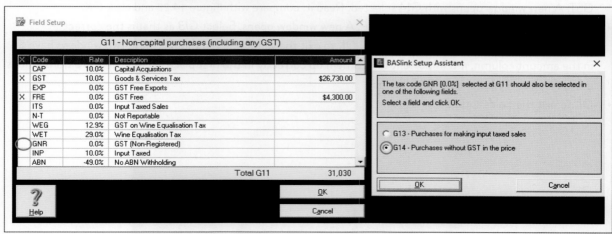

Figure 14.30   BASlink G13 Setup: INP tax code

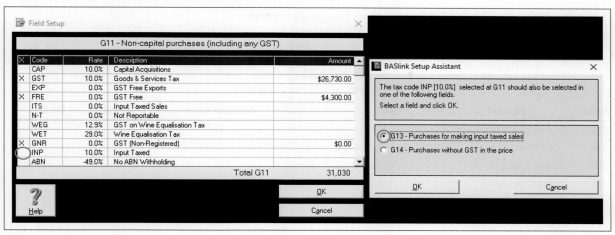

Let's analyse the now completed GST on purchases section of the Calculation worksheet, shown in Figure 14.31 and compare it to the GST [Summary – Cash] report recreated in Figure 14.32.

Figure 14.31   Calculation worksheet: GST on Purchases

GST amounts the ATO owes you from purchases

G10	Capital purchases (including any GST)	G10 $	1,705	Setup
G11	Non-capital purchases (including any GST)	G11 $	31,030	Setup
G12	G10 + G11	G12 $	32,735	
G13	Puchases for making input taxed sales	G13 $	0	Setup
G14	Purchases without GST in the price	G14 $	4,300	Setup
G15	Estimated purchases for private use or not income tax deductible	G15 $		Setup
G16	G13 + G14 + G15	G16 $	4,300	
G17	Total purchases subject to GST (G12 minus G16)	G17 $	28,435	
G18	Adjustments (if applicable)	G18 $		
G19	Total purchases subject to GST after adjustments (G17 + G18)	G19 $	28,435	
G20	GST on purchases (G19 divided by eleven)	G20 $	2,585	

Figure 14.32   GST [Summary – Cash] report: OneCo Pty Ltd

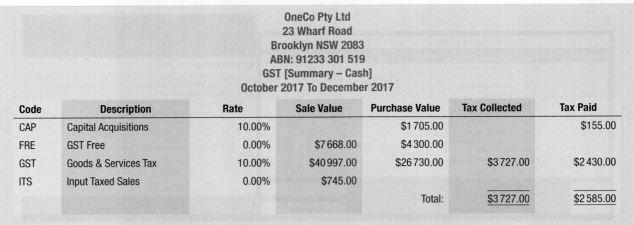

OneCo Pty Ltd
23 Wharf Road
Brooklyn NSW 2083
ABN: 91233 301 519
GST [Summary – Cash]
October 2017 To December 2017

Code	Description	Rate	Sale Value	Purchase Value	Tax Collected	Tax Paid
CAP	Capital Acquisitions	10.00%		$1 705.00		$155.00
FRE	GST Free	0.00%	$7 668.00	$4 300.00		
GST	Goods & Services Tax	10.00%	$40 997.00	$26 730.00	$3 727.00	$2 430.00
ITS	Input Taxed Sales	0.00%	$745.00			
				Total:	$3 727.00	$2 585.00

We can see that:

- G10 in MYOB is the Purchase Value of the CAP code in Figure 14.32.
- G11 in MYOB is sum of the Purchase Value for the FRE and GST tax codes in Figure 14.32.
- G14 in MYOB is the Purchase Value for the FRE tax code in Figure 14.32.

In Figure 14.31, we can see that:

- G17 and G19 is All Purchases minus Purchases without GST (G12 minus G16).
- G20 is calculated by dividing G19 by 11 = 28 435/11 = 2585. This matches the total Tax Paid in Figure 14.32.

We know that we have set up our GST on purchases correctly. We can now look at the other two tabs: Front sheet and Back sheet. The information from the Calculation worksheet has flowed through to complete the fields of our draft BAS. This can be printed off and used to complete the paper BAS rather than do the manual calculations. Compare your own screens with your manual calculations and Figures 14.33 and 14.34.

Figure 14.33   Front sheet: GST section

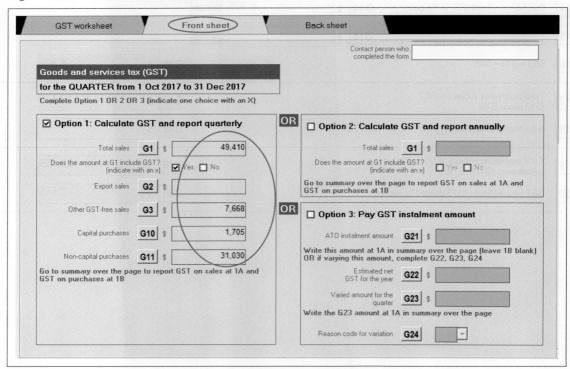

Figure 14.34   Back sheet: Summary and Payment or refund?

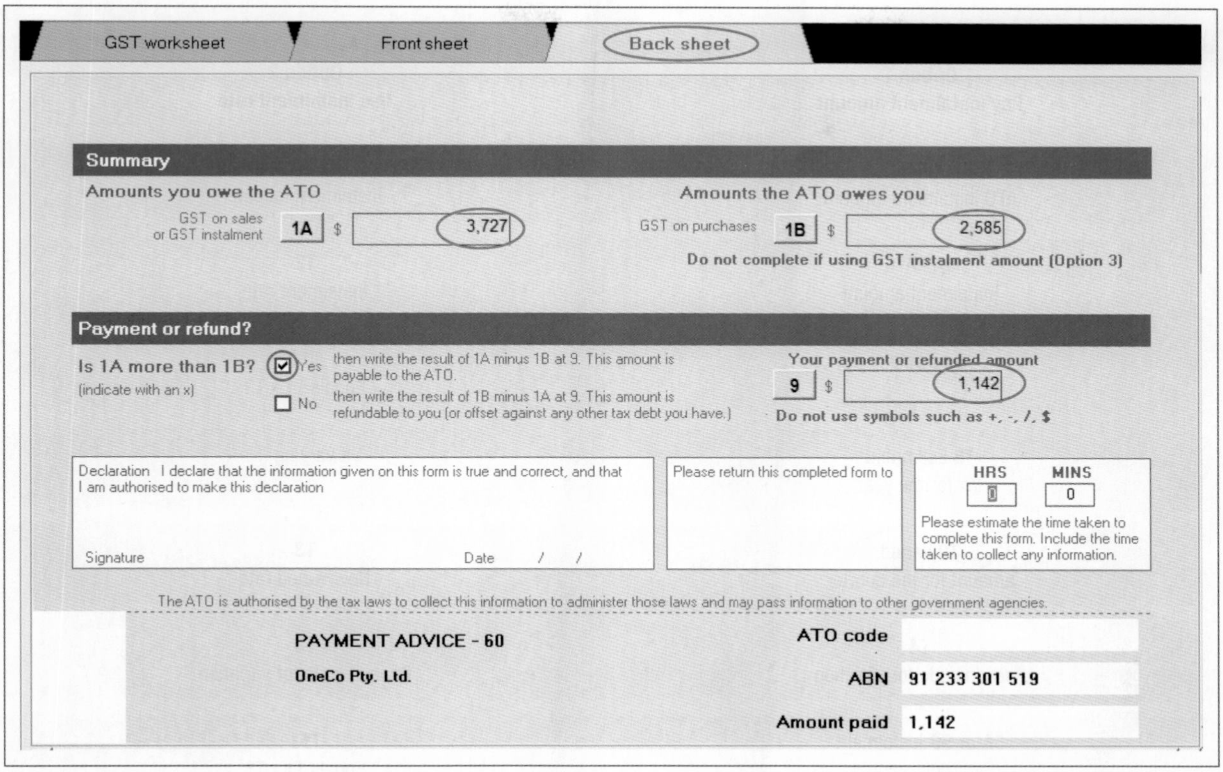

Click...

- *Save Setup* and *Exit* (bottom right corner).
- *No* (as we do not need to save for this exercise).

PAYG income tax instalments

Pay As You Go (PAYG) income tax instalments are used by the ATO as a way to charge taxpayers with business and/or investment income a quarterly portion of their expected annual income tax bill.

Two PAYG income tax instalment options are usually available to taxpayers for calculating and paying the instalments. Once an option has been chosen it remains active until it is changed, and a change can only take place in the first quarter of any financial year. An activity statement will indicate if an option is not currently available to the taxpayer.

The options are:

- *Option 1: instalment amount.* The ATO works out an instalment amount based on the previous year's assessed income tax return, taking into account business and investment income. The benefit of selecting this method is that the taxpayer knows the amount to be paid in each quarter, which may assist with budgeting.
- *Option 2: instalment rate.* The taxpayer works out the instalment amount based on the actual income for the quarter multiplied by a rate provided by the ATO. The rate by which income must be multiplied is pre-printed on the activity statement when this option has been chosen. The advantage of using this method is that the instalment reflects the actual income for the quarter, and may be preferable in situations where there are fluctuations in income.

Variations to either the instalment amount or the multiplication rate supplied by the ATO are permitted if their use will result in the payment of significantly more (or less) than the anticipated tax for the year.

The PAYG labels that apply depend upon the option that has been chosen and whether or not the ATO figures are being varied. See **Figure 14.35**.

Figure 14.35   **PAYG income tax instalment options**

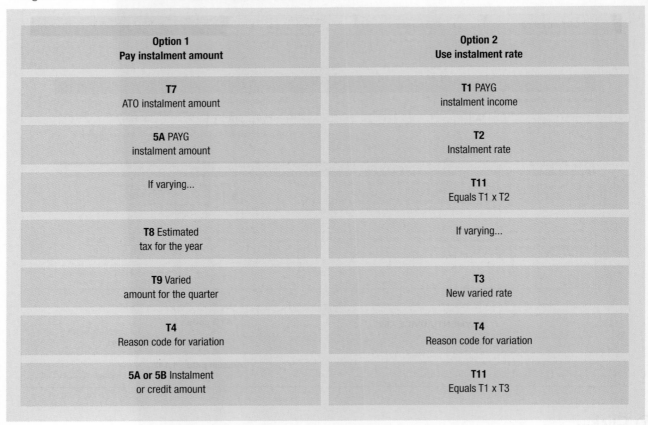

The section of the paper BAS that needs to be completed for PAYG income tax instalment is shown in Figure 14.36.

Figure 14.36   **Paper BAS: PAYG income tax instalment section**

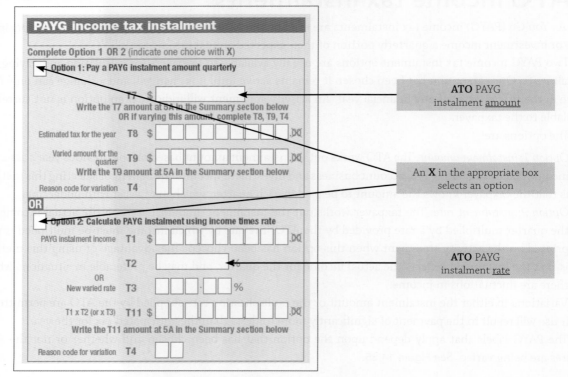

T. W. ONSLOW

T. W. Onslow is in business as a sole proprietor, buying and selling items from a small shop in the Robina CBD. Export sales form a significant part of the business income. Trading is on a cash basis, with records being kept on MYOB AccountRight 2016 using the Banking module.

In this exercise we will be completing T. W. Onslow's activity statement for GST and PAYG income tax instalments:

- for GST: Option 1 (calculate and report quarterly)
- for PAYGI: Option 1 (instalment method)
- on a cash basis
- using the business accounts method.

4 Print T. W. Onslow's paper activity statement for use in this exercise. It is located in the Chapter 14 folder of your start-up files, entitled *14.2 TWOnslow BAS*.

5 In MYOB AccountRight 2016, open *14.2 TWOnslow.myox* data file from the Chapter 14 folder of your start-up files.

6 Print the following reports for the period 1 January 2018 to 31 March 2018:

- Bank Register
- GST [Summary – Cash]
- Transaction Tax Codes.

7 Check the reports for accuracy and consistency in GST recording. There are three transactions that need to have their tax codes corrected. Correct these and refresh the report. Complete the following BAS labels on the paper BAS:

- G1: Total sales
- G2: Export sales
- G3: Other GST-free sales
- G10: Capital purchases
- G11: Non-capital purchases
- 1A: GST on sales
- 1B: GST on purchases.

> **Tip**
>
> Click on the *incorrect transactions tax code* in the Entered Tax column of your Transaction Tax Codes report. This will open the transaction that you want to fix. Click *Run Report* after you have finished your corrections to refresh the report.

T. W. Onslow has selected Option 1 in previous activity statements, so the ATO has indicated their required PAYG income tax instalment at label T7 (**Figure 14.37**).

Figure 14.37   Paper BAS: label T7

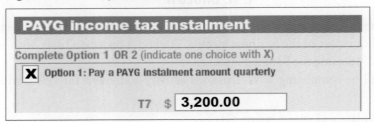

Label T8: Estimated tax for the year

In previous BAS for this year, the business has paid the instalment amount at T7. However, the business has suffered a downturn in income this quarter, and it is now expected that the tax for the year will amount to $10 500.00. It is decided to reduce the instalment according to the ATO's rules:

PAYG variation rules are:

- First Quarter: 25% of the estimated tax at T8 for the income year.
- Second Quarter: 50% of the estimated tax at T8 for the income year, *less* the amount paid in the first quarter instalment.
- Third Quarter: 75% of the estimated tax at T8 for the income year, *less* the amount paid in the first and second quarter instalments, plus any credit claimed at 5B on a previous statement.
- Fourth Quarter: 100% of the estimated tax at T8 for the income year, *less* amounts paid in previous instalments, and *plus* any credits previously claimed at 5B.

Note: If, as the result of varying instalments, the total paid is less than 85% of the actual tax liability at the end of the year, an interest charge may be payable.

The calculation for the March BAS is:

Estimated tax for the year	$10 500.00
3rd Quarter requirement	= 75%
75% of $10 500.00	= $7 875.00
less previous *two* instalments paid ($3200.00 × 2)	$6 400.00
equals varied tax for the quarter	$1 475.00

The paper BAS will be completed as per Figure 14.38.

Figure 14.38   Paper BAS: labels T8 and T9

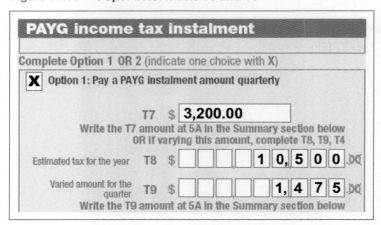

8 Insert the varied instalment amounts in T. W. Onslow's activity statement.

Label T4: Reason code for variation

The ATO must be informed of the reason for the reduction in an instalment, and the codes for various acceptable reasons are shown in Figure 14.39:

Figure 14.39 ATO instalment variation codes

Reason	Code
Change in investments	21
Current business structure not continuing	22
Significant change in trading conditions	23
Internal business restructure	24
Change in legislation or product mix	25
Financial market changes	26
Use of income tax losses	27
Consolidations	28

Code 23 is the most appropriate for T. W. Onslow's situation and is inserted into T4. See Figure 14.40.

Figure 14.40 Paper BAS: labels T4

PAYG income tax instalment

Complete Option 1 OR 2 (indicate one choice with X)

[X] **Option 1: Pay a PAYG instalment amount quarterly**

T7 $ 3,200.00

Write the T7 amount at 5A in the Summary section below
OR if varying this amount, complete T8, T9, T4

Estimated tax for the year T8 $ 10,500 .00

Varied amount for the quarter T9 $ 1,475 .00

Write the T9 amount at 5A in the Summary section below

Reason code for variation T4 23

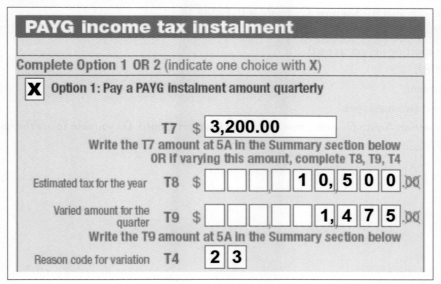

9 Insert the reason code for the instalment variation at T4 in T W Onslow's activity statement.

Label 5A: PAYG income tax instalment

Carry the varied instalment amount at T9 down to the summary section and insert it at 5A.

Figure 14.41   Paper BAS: label 5A

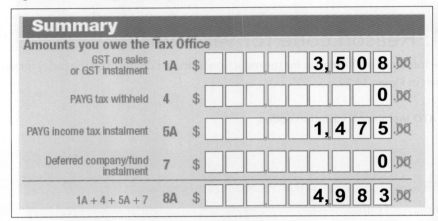

10 Insert the varied PAYG income tax instalment at 5A in T. W. Onslow's activity statement, perform the calculations, complete the Payment or Refund? section, and the payment amount at label 9.

BASlink (MYOB)

11 Use MYOB's BASlink program to set up the activity statement for the March 2018 quarter. Usually the setup would have been saved from the previous BAS but they have been deleted for this exercise so you can practise.

Click...

- *BASlink* (in the Accounts module).
- *BAS Info* (top left side). Note that the PAYG Instalments of *$3200* and *Option 1* have already been selected as part of the previous BAS setups. Compare with **Figure 14.42**.
- *OK.*
- *Mar* (in the reporting period screen).
- *This Year (FY18).*
- *Prepare Statement.*
- *OK* to the next two messages.
- *No* (to the question *A data file with a new ABN/TFN has been opened. Do you wish to use the last saved setup?*).
- *No* (to the Welcome screen).

Figure 14.42   Set Up Activity Statement: T. W. Onslow BASlink

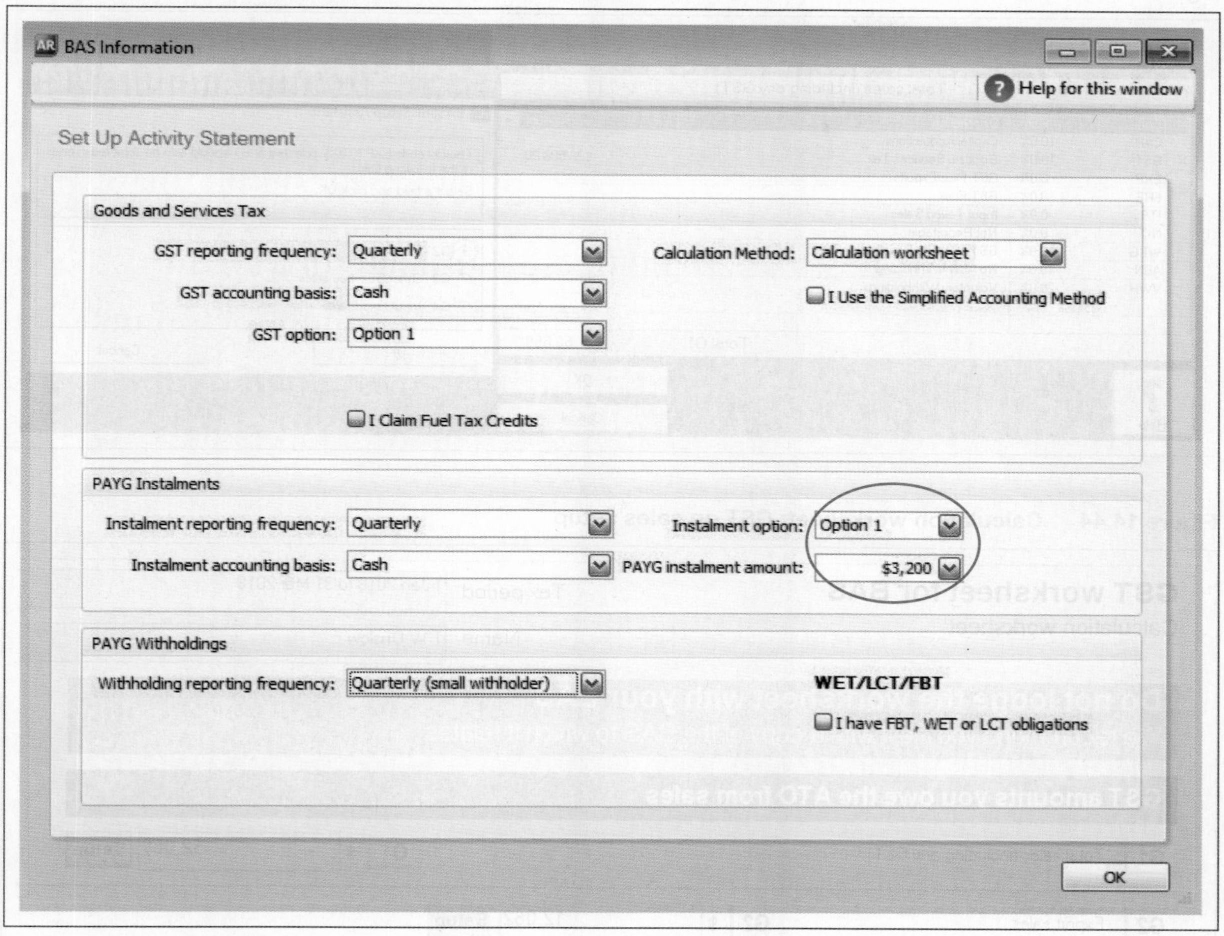

12 Set up the GST on sales in the usual way. We know (from our Transaction Tax Codes report) that we need to include Export items in our G1 sum.

Click...

- *Setup* next to the G1 field.
- *Cell in left column* to place and *X* next to *GST* and *EXP*. A new screen opens.
- *G2 – Export Sales*. Compare with Figure 14.43 and click *OK*.
- *Cell in left column* to place and *X* next to *FRE*. A new window opens with G3 selected. Click *OK*.
- *Cell in left column* to place and *X* next to *ITS*. Select *G4*. Click *OK*.
- *OK* (to return to the Calculation worksheet). Compare with Figure 14.44.

Figure 14.43   BASlink G1 setup: EXP tax code

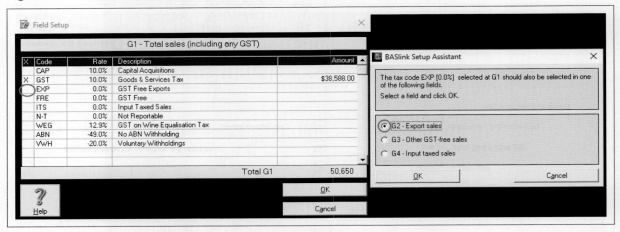

Figure 14.44   Calculation worksheet: GST on sales setup

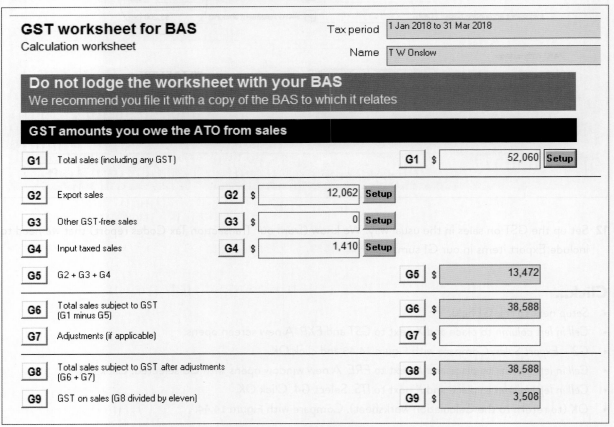

This is why

Is nothing showing in your G4 Input Taxed Sales? Maybe you didn't correct the tax code that was applied to the interest. Exit BASlink, correct the transaction, then open up BASlink once more.

13 Set up the GST on Purchases section of the worksheet the same as we did for OneCo.

Click...

- *Setup* next to the G10 field. A new screen opens.
- *Cell in left column* to place and *X* next to *CAP*. Click *OK*.
- *Setup* next to the G11 field. A new screen opens.
- *Cell in left column* to place and *X* next to *GST* and *FRE*. A new window opens with G14 selected. Click *OK*.
- *Cell in left column* to place and *X* next to *GNR*. A new window opens with G14 selected. Click *OK*.
- *Cell in left column* to place and *X* next to *INP*. A new window opens. Select *G13*.
- *OK* to exit the fields setup. Compare with Figure 14.45.
- *Front sheet* tab at the top of the screen and compare with Figure 14.46.

Figure 14.45   Calculation worksheet: GST on purchases set up

GST amounts the ATO owes you from purchases

G10	Capital purchases (including any GST)	G10 $ 0 Setup	
G11	Non-capital purchases (including any GST)	G11 $ 31,749 Setup	
G12	G10 + G11		G12 $ 31,749
G13	Purchases for making input taxed sales	G13 $ 0 Setup	
G14	Purchases without GST in the price	G14 $ 135 Setup	
G15	Estimated purchases for private use or not income tax deductible	G15 $ Setup	
G16	G13 + G14 + G15		G16 $ 135
G17	Total purchases subject to GST (G12 minus G16)		G17 $ 31,614
G18	Adjustments (if applicable)		G18 $
G19	Total purchases subject to GST after adjustments (G17 + G18)		G19 $ 31,614
G20	GST on purchases (G19 divided by eleven)		G20 $ 2,874

Figure 14.46   Front sheet: GST section

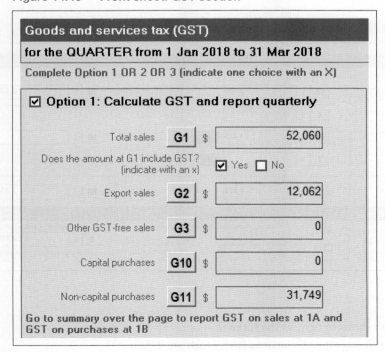

Goods and services tax (GST)

for the QUARTER from 1 Jan 2018 to 31 Mar 2018

Complete Option 1 OR 2 OR 3 (indicate one choice with an X)

☑ **Option 1: Calculate GST and report quarterly**

Total sales	G1	$	52,060
Does the amount at G1 include GST? (indicate with an x)		☑ Yes ☐ No	
Export sales	G2	$	12,062
Other GST-free sales	G3	$	0
Capital purchases	G10	$	0
Non-capital purchases	G11	$	31,749

Go to summary over the page to report GST on sales at 1A and GST on purchases at 1B

14 Complete the PAYG income tax instalment and apply the variation. These numbers are from the calculation you made on page 450.

Click...

- *Back sheet* (tab at the top).
- in the field next to T8 (type *10500*)
- in the field next to T9 (type *1475*)
- in the field next to T4 (select *23* – the code for *Significant change in trading conditions*). Compare with Figure 14.47.
- to scroll down to the *Summary* and *Payment or refund?* sections. Compare with your manual BAS and Figure 14.48. If it is different from either, investigate why.

Figure 14.47   Back sheet: PAYG income tax instalment section

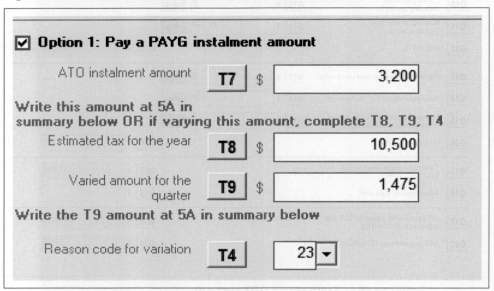

Figure 14.48   Back sheet: Summary and Payment or refund? sections

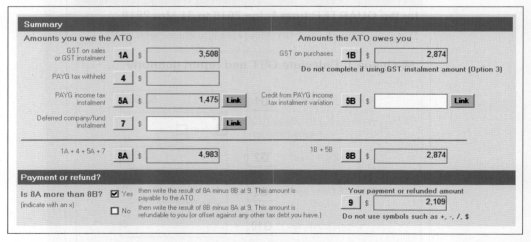

Click...

- *Save Setup* and *Exit* (bottom right of the screen)
- *No* (as we will be running other companies BAS which are different)
- *Cancel* (to close the BASlink screen).

PAYG Withholding

PAYG Withholding are amounts withheld from payments to an individual in the following circumstances to meet *their* future tax liabilities:

- *Employees*: gross income such as salary, wages or commission
- *Company Directors*: payment for their services
- *Contractors*: under a voluntary agreement
- *Contractors*: subject to withholding (currently 49%) if they do not supply their Australian Business Number (ABN)
- *Other amounts withheld*: from certain interest, dividends, unit trusts and other investment distributions you are making where the recipient hasn't provided a tax file number declaration or is a non-resident and certain other payments made to foreign residents.

THREEWAYS BOOKS

ThreeWays Books is a business that buys and sells rare books, magazines and antique memorabilia. Export sales form a significant part of the business income and the only other GST-free income is bank interest. Accounting is on a cash basis. The proprietor is registered for GST, PAYGW from employees, and is liable for PAYGI.

In this exercise we will be completing the activity statement for GST, PAYGI and PAYGW:

- for GST: Option 1 (calculate and report quarterly)
- for PAYGI: Option 1 (instalment method)
- for PAYGW (quarterly)
- on a cash basis
- using the business accounts method.

1 Print ThreeWays Books' paper activity statement for use in this exercise. It is located in the Chapter 14 folder of your start-up files, entitled *14.3 ThreeWays BAS*.

2 In MYOB AccountRight 2016, open **14.3 ThreeWays Books.myox** data file from the Chapter 14 folder of your start-up files.

3 Print or display the following reports for the period 1 July 2017 to 30 September 2017:

- Bank Register
- GST [Summary – Cash]
- Transaction Tax Codes
- Payroll Register [Summary].

4 Check the first three reports for accuracy and consistency in GST recording, then complete the following BAS labels:

- G1: Total sales
- G2: Export sales
- G3: Other GST-free sales
- G10: Capital purchases
- G11: Non-capital purchases
- 1A: GST on sales
- 1B: GST on purchases.

Remember This

If there are anomalies in the Transaction Tax Codes report, there may be a mistake that needs to be corrected.

5 Calculate the varied amount for this quarter using the information below and insert into the appropriate labels. Use the previous exercise instructions to guide you.

- Label T7. Amount of $10 200.00 is too high. The ATO's calculation was based on last year's tax return and trading conditions have changed considerably since then.
- Label T8. Estimated tax for the year is $29 400.00.

Label W1: Total wages, salaries and other payments

Include the sum of the following in label W1:

- salary, wages, allowances and leave loading paid to employees
- director fees
- salary and allowances paid to office holders (including Members of Parliament, statutory office holders, defence-force members and police officers)
- payments to religious practitioners
- Commonwealth education and training payments

Note: Include all payments of types that are *subject to withholding*, even if no amount was actually withheld (because of a tax-free threshold, for instance).

Label W1 excludes:

- superannuation contributions
- departing Australia superannuation payments
- payments from which an amount was withheld because an ABN was not quoted
- an investment distribution from which an amount was withheld because no tax file number was quoted
- interest, dividends and royalty payments from which an amount was withheld for payment to a non-resident
- payments to foreign residents for entertainment, sports or construction activities.

Reporting and payment options differ according to the size of the withholder:

- A *Large Withholder* is an enterprise (or part of a company group) that withheld amounts of over one million dollars in the previous tax year. They must report and pay electronically, usually weekly.
- A *Medium Withholder* is an enterprise that withheld between $25 000.00 and one million dollars in the previous tax year. They report and pay monthly.
- A *Small Withholder* is an enterprise that withheld less than $25 000.00 in the previous tax year. They usually report and pay quarterly, but can choose to do so monthly if they wish.

6 Insert the total of the Wages column in the Payroll Register report (Figure 14.49) you displayed/printed earlier into label W1 of the ThreeWays Books' paper activity statement (Figure 14.50).

Figure 14.49 Payroll Register [Summary], 1 July to 30 September 2017

		ThreeWays Books ThreeWays Arcade Melbourne VIC 3000 Payroll Register [Summary] July 2017 To September 2017			
Employee	**Wages**	**Deductions**	**Taxes**	**Net Pay**	**Expenses**
Wolenski, Barek	$11 999.97	$0.00	$2 028.00	$9 971.97	$1 140.00
Yelavich, Branko	$9 000.00	$0.00	$1 014.00	$7 986.00	$855.00
Zamprogno, Sergio	$9 000.00	$0.00	$1 014.00	$7 986.00	$855.00
Total:	$29 999.97	$0.00	$4 056.00	$25 943.97	$2 850.00

Figure 14.50 **Paper BAS: label W1**

PAYG tax withheld

| Total salary, wages and other payments | W1 | $ | | | | | 2 | 9, | 9 | 9 | 9 | .00 |

Label W2: Amounts withheld from the payments at W1

Label W2 includes the total PAYG amount withheld from employees' pay during the period of the activity statement.

7 Insert the total of the Taxes column from the Payroll Activity Summary at W2 in your activity statement.

Figure 14.51 **Paper BAS: label W2**

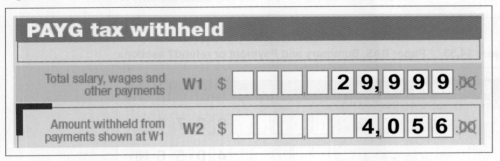

Label W4: Amounts withheld because no ABN quoted

Payments made by the business to suppliers or contactors who do not quote their ABN must have 49% of the payment withheld for onward transmission to the ATO. Such payments would have the Tax Code *ABN* and would appear in the GST [Summary – Cash] report. No such payments appear, so W4 is left blank.

Label W3: Other amounts withheld

Any other amounts withheld would be identified at the same time as the amounts for Label W4, having the Tax Code *ABN*. If any amount had appeared with this tax code, the transaction would be investigated in the Transaction Tax Codes report to see which label applied. As the code does not appear, W3 is left blank.

Label W5: Total amounts withheld

This is the total of all amounts withheld (W2 + W4 + W3). Do not include W1 in the W5 total!

8 Calculate and insert your W5 total, then copy this figure to label 4 in the Summary section.

Then complete the rest of your activity statement. Compare your BAS with **Figures 14.52** and **14.53**.

Figure 14.52   **Paper BAS: PAYG tax withheld section**

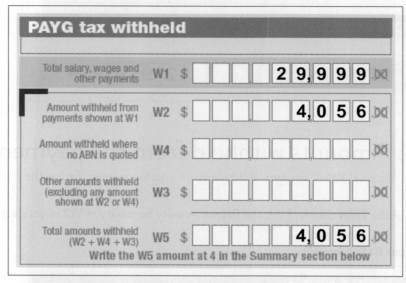

PAYG tax withheld		
Total salary, wages and other payments	W1 $	2 9 , 9 9 9 .00
Amount withheld from payments shown at W1	W2 $	4 , 0 5 6 .00
Amount withheld where no ABN is quoted	W4 $	.00
Other amounts withheld (excluding any amount shown at W2 or W4)	W3 $	.00
Total amounts withheld (W2 + W4 + W3)	W5 $	4 , 0 5 6 .00

Write the W5 amount at 4 in the Summary section below

Figure 14.53   **Paper BAS: Summary and Payment or refund? sections**

Summary		
Amounts you owe the Tax Office		
GST on sales or GST instalment	1A $	9 , 2 7 0 .00
PAYG tax withheld	4 $	4 , 0 5 6 .00
PAYG income tax instalment	5A $	7 , 3 5 0 .00
Deferred company/fund instalment	7 $	.00
1A + 4 + 5A + 7	8A $	2 0 , 6 7 6 .00

Amounts the Tax Office owes you		
GST on purchases	1B $	7 , 2 7 5 .00

Do not complete 1B if using GST instalment amount (Option 3)

Credit from PAYG income tax instalment variation	5B $	.00
1B + 5B	8B $	7 , 2 7 5 .00

Your payment or refund amount

$,   1 3 , 4 0 1 .00

⚠ Do not use symbols such as +, −, /, $

BASlink (MYOB)

9 Use MYOB's BASlink program to produce an activity statement for the September quarter. Use the *BAS Info* button after selecting September as the quarter, and set up your activity statement according to the following screen (Figure 14.54).

Figure 14.54 **Set Up Activity Statement**

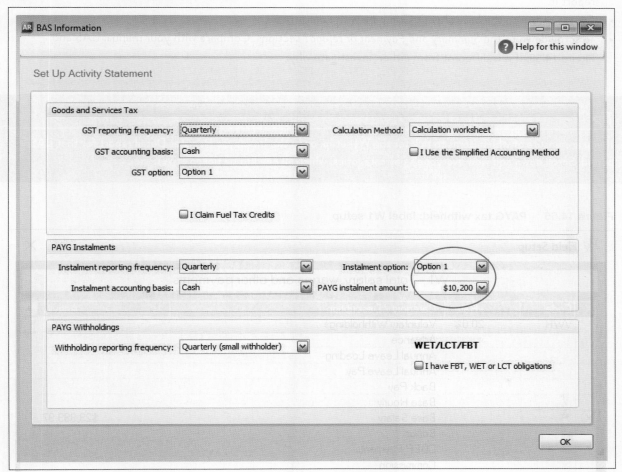

10 Complete the steps to set up the system for GST.

11 Complete the steps to set up the system for PAYG Instalment. The details are:

- Label T7. Amount of $10 200.00 is too high. The ATO's calculation was based on last year's tax return and trading conditions have changed considerably since then.
- Label T8. Estimated tax for the year is $29 400.00.

12 Complete the following steps to set up the system for PAYG tax withheld. You should still be in the Back sheet after setting up your PAYGI section.

Click...

- *Setup* next to the W1 field. A new screen opens.
- To add an *X* in the left column for *Base Salary* as this is the only wage category that was used. See Figure 14.55. It should match the total for Wages in the Payroll Register [Summary] report. If it doesn't, you need to select the appropriate categories.

- *Setup* next to the W2 field. A new screen opens.
- To add an *X* in the left column for *PAYG Withholding* as this is the only category that was used. See Figure 14.56. It should match the total for Tax in the Payroll Register [Summary] report.
- *Setup* next to the W4 field. A new screen opens.
- To add an *X* in the left column for *No ABN withholding*. See Figure 14.57. Even though there was none of this sort of withholding, we still need to set it up in case such a transaction occurs in the future and we need to report it.
- *OK* (to return to the back sheet). Compare with Figure 14.58.
- To scroll down to the *Summary* and *Payment or refund?* sections. Compare with your manual BAS and Figure 14.59. If it is different from either, investigate why.

Tip

If you are unsure of which items to tick for the W1 setup, open the Employee Register Detail report for that BAS period. Scroll down and view everyone's pay categories, which all need to be ticked at W1.

Figure 14.55   **PAYG tax withheld: label W1 setup**

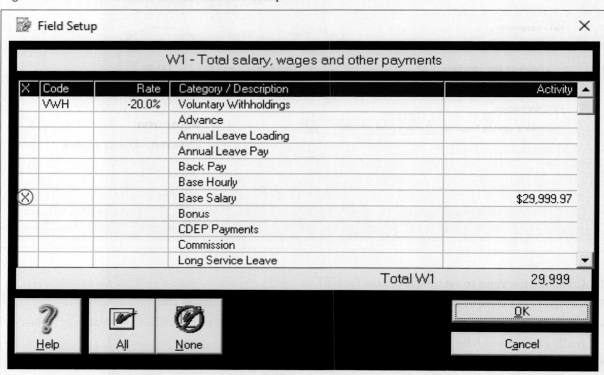

Figure 14.56 **PAYG tax withheld: label W2 setup**

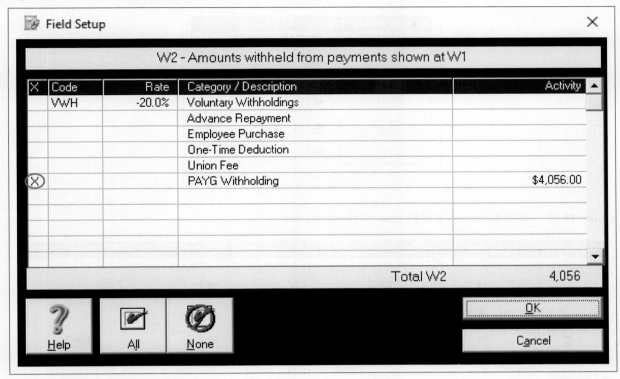

Figure 14.57 **PAYG tax withheld: label W4 setup**

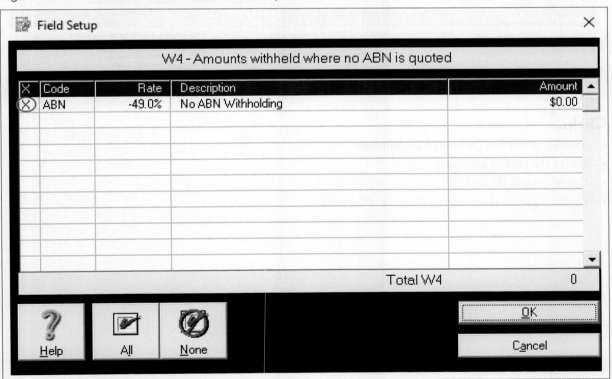

Figure 14.58   PAYG tax withheld section

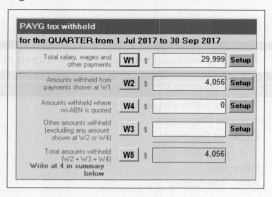

Figure 14.59   BAS Summary and Payment/refund section

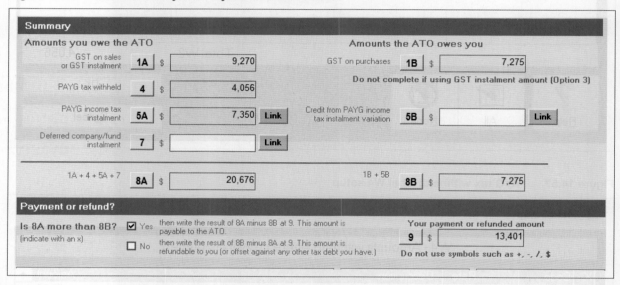

Click...

- *Save Setup* and *Exit* (at base of the window).
- *No* (to the backup question).
- *Cancel* (to exit BASlink).
- *Cancel* (again to return to the Command Centre).

Summary

- The Business Activity Statement (BAS) is used to report a variety of taxes.
- BAS can to be lodged monthly, quarterly or yearly depending on the size of the organisation.
- Each BAS is customised for that particular business.
- The Transaction Tax Codes report can be used to check the transactions tax types. Individual transactions can be opened by clicking in the Entered Tax column.
- BASlink is MYOB's program for setting up and completing BAS.
- PAYG Instalments are prepayments towards the businesses expected income tax bill. The ATO will offer an amount or percentage of income to be paid based on the most recent tax return. These can be varied by amounts or percentages if the business situation has changed.
- PAYG Withholdings are amounts withheld from wages during the BAS period to assist employees to meet their income tax obligations.

Assessment

FourSeasons restaurant

FourSeasons Restaurant buys mostly GST-free fresh food and converts it into fine dining products which are taxable.

Complete the activity statement for GST, PAYGI and PAYGW using the following information:

- GST: Option 1 (calculate and report quarterly).
- PAYGI: Option 2 (PAYG percentage). The taxpayer works out the instalment amount based on the actual income for the quarter multiplied by a rate provided by the ATO. The rate by which income must be multiplied is pre-printed on the activity statement when this option has been chosen.
- PAYGW (quarterly).
- On a cash basis.
- Using the business accounts method.

In MYOB AccountRight 2016, open the *14.4 FourSeasons restaurant BAS* data file from the Chapter 14 folder of your start-up files.

1   Print the personalised activity statement for use in this exercise. It is located in the Chapter 14 folder of your start-up files, entitled *14.4 Four Seasons Restaurant BAS*.

2   In MYOB AccountRight Plus 2016, open the data file **14.4 Four Seasons Restaurant.myox** from the Chapter 14 folder of your start-up files.

3   Display the following reports for the period 1 July to 30 September 2017:
    - GST [Summary – Cash]
    - Transaction Tax Codes
    - Payroll Register [Summary].

4   Examine the GST reports for accuracy and consistency in GST recording, then complete the following BAS labels in your paper BAS:
    - G1: Total sales
    - G2: Export sales
    - G3: Other GST-free sales
    - G10: Capital purchases
    - G11: Non-capital purchases
    - 1A: GST on sales
    - 1B: GST on purchases.

5 Use the Payroll report to complete the following labels in the PAYG Withholding section:
   - W1: Total salary, wages and other payments
   - W2: Amount withheld from payments at W1
   - W5: Total amounts withheld.
   -    4: PAYG tax withheld (in the Summary section).

6 PAYG instalment Option 2 is used and the following information is supplied:
   - Label T1: Insert total sales and other income ($159 791). This *excludes* GST.
   - Label T2: The ATO's suggested percentage is too high as it is based on last year's trading and would result in paying too high an instalment.
   - Label T3: A percentage of 1.1% is thought to better reflect current trading. Insert this percentage at T3.
   - Label T11: Multiply your entry at T1 by the varied percentage at T3 to find the revised instalment amount and insert this at label T11.
   - Label T4: The instalment variation codes for Option 2 are the same as those for Option 1. Insert *23* here.
   - Label 5A: Copy the instalment at T11 to Label 5A in the summary section.

7 Complete the Summary section of the activity statement and calculate the amount due to the ATO.

BASlink (MYOB)

8 Access BASlink and after selecting September as the last month of the reporting period, click *BAS Info* in the top left corner then apply the following:
   - Goods and services tax section: Quarterly, Cash, Option 1, Calculation Method (select *Calculation worksheet*).
   - PAYG Instalments section: Quarterly, Cash, Option 2, PAYG Instalment Rate (insert *1.9%*, the ATO's suggestion).
   - PAYG Withholdings section (select *Quarterly (small withholder)*).

9 Click *Prepare Statement* and complete the steps to set up the system for GST in the GST Worksheet tab.

10 Complete the steps to set up the system for PAYG Withholding and PAYG income tax instalments on the Back sheet tab.

11 Set up the system for PAYG income tax instalment by setting up T1 as you did in previous exercises, inserting *1.1%* in T3 and choosing a reason in T4.

12 Scroll down to the Summary section and compare your manual work with MYOB's calculation.
    The results should be the same. If they aren't, investigate! If they are, print your BAS and give it to your instructor.

Remember This

Compare your W1 total wages with the total wages in the Payroll Register [Summary] report. If it doesn't match, you need to tick more boxes in the setup window. You can use the Payroll Register Detail report to show what wages categories were used in the pays. These should all be selected in the W1 label.

15

BUSINESS ACTIVITY STATEMENTS: ALTERNATIVE APPROACHES AND PAYMENT

Learning outcomes

By the end of this chapter you will be competent in:

- understanding the eligibility requirements for each of the five Simplified Accounting System methods
- understanding and calculating the Stock Purchases, Business Norms and Snapshot methods of accounting for GST
- understanding some Fringe Benefits basics
- calculating and reporting Fringe Benefits Tax (FBT)
- calculating and reporting Fuel Tax Credits
- understanding the transaction that needs to be processed when paying the BAS.

This chapter introduces you to Fringe Benefits Tax and Fuel Tax Credits, which are available to all businesses meeting certain criteria. It also introduces you to - other possible methods of calculating the BAS using the Simplified Accounting System, which are only available to certain types of small businesses.

Simplified Accounting System: an overview

The Simplified Accounting System was introduced by the ATO as a way for small business to account for their GST liability without having to keep a detailed breakdown of the GST-free and taxable portions of their activities.

It is particularly suitable for small food retailers or mixed businesses and, for those who qualify, there are five accounting methods to choose from. Each method is governed by its own set of regulations (full details can be obtained by searching the ATO website https://www.ato.gov.au) and have their own document ID, starting with NAT.

The methods are:

- *Business Norms*: no detailed records are kept concerning the GST-free and taxable portions of their transactions. Rather, a *set percentage* is applied to total purchases and total sales for the period and this is used to estimate the GST liability. The fixed percentage varies from one type of business to another. (NAT 16013.)
- *Stock Purchases*: using this method, it is assumed that the percentage of GST-free sales is the same as GST-free purchases. Only *purchases* are accurately identified as GST-free or taxable, and the same proportions are then applied to sales. (NAT 16015.)
- *Snapshot*: a snapshot is taken of both *sales and purchases* over a two-week period twice a year, during which transactions are accurately recorded as being GST-free or taxable. The same proportion is applied to the rest of the year. (NAT 16014.)
- *Sales Percentage*: using accurate *sales* data for the whole accounting period, the same proportions of GST-free and taxable sales is applied to purchases. (NAT 16016.)
- *Purchases Snapshot*: a snapshot is taken of *purchases* made in two four-week periods in each financial year and the proportion of GST-free acquisitions is calculated. This proportion is then applied in each activity statement for the whole year. (NAT 15978.)

To be eligible to use a simplified GST accounting method, a business must be:

- registered for GST
- a retailer that sells both GST-free and taxable food from the same premises, and
- have a relevant turnover of not more than $2 million, either:
  - Simplified Accounting Method (SAM) turnover of $2 million or less for the Snapshot, Business Norms and Stock Purchases method, or
  - GST turnover of $2 million or less for the Sales Percentage or Purchases Snapshot method.

GST turnover and SAM turnover for a business should be quite similar; however, they are calculated differently:

- GST turnover is the actual gross income (sales) of the business:
  - not including GST
  - not including any input taxed sales
  - not including export sales, and
  - not including private sales by the proprietor.
- SAM turnover is the total sales as calculated by one of the simplified accounting method formulae:
  - not including GST, or
  - not including the sale of capital items.

Additional eligibility criteria to be able to use the different simplified accounting methods may further narrow the choices available to a business:

- Resellers can choose any of the simplified accounting methods.
- Converters whose conversions account for less than 5% of their sales can use any of the methods *except* the Stock Purchases method.
- Converters whose conversions account for 5% or more of their sales can use any method *except* the Stock Purchases and Sales Percentage methods.

Remember This

Resellers only resell goods without changing their taxable status, either GST-free or taxable (e.g. greengrocers). *Converters* change the taxable status of all or part of their stock between the time of purchase and the time of sale (e.g. bakers).

A further limitation is that to be able to use any simplified accounting method (except the Purchases Snapshot method) the business must *not* have an adequate point-of-sale accounting system. The ATO considers point-of-sale equipment to be adequate if it can:

- identify and record each separate sale as either GST-free or taxable, and
- identify and record separately the amount of your GST-free and total sales.

Electronic scanning systems, touch-screen registers and product-specific registers are considered adequate by the ATO. A cash register requiring operator decisions on each sale as to its taxable status is not considered adequate.

Further considerations include:

- When a business chooses to use one of the simplified accounting methods, it must notify the ATO using their form *Election to use a simplified GST accounting method* (NAT 4370), obtainable from their website.
- Having made the decision to use a simplified accounting method and notified the ATO, the decision cannot be changed within 12 months.
- Having elected to use one of the simplified accounting methods the business is not permitted to switch to a different one.
- Having decided not to continue using a simplified accounting method, the business needs to notify the ATO by using their form *Notice to revoke an election to use a simplified GST accounting method* (NAT 4371). The business is not permitted to elect to use another one within 12 months of revoking the decision.

Stock Purchases method

The Stock Purchases method is available to resellers:

- without adequate point-of-sale equipment, and
- with a SAM turnover of less than $2 million.

There are three ways the Stock Purchases method can be used:

- For the whole of every tax period an accurate record is kept of GST-free *purchases* and this percentage is used to estimate the GST-free value of *sales*.
- Two four-week sample periods per year are used to estimate the value of both *GST-free sales and GST-free purchases* for the whole of the year.
- The 5% GST-free stock estimation basis is where *only the GST-free purchases that are sold GST-free are tracked*. This can be used where GST-free purchases are not more than 5% of total purchases.

<u>FIVESTAR MILK BAR</u>

FiveStar Milk Bar is a small business in Broome. It is registered for the GST, has PAYG Withholding (PAYGW) and PAYG income tax instalment (PAYGI) obligations, and has elected to use the Stock Purchases method of the simplified accounting system to identify their GST obligations. They have chosen to keep an accurate record of all purchases for the entire year. Although the SAM regulations state that a daily worksheet must be kept detailing the calculations, the purchase records in MYOB AccountRight are quite sufficient.

Every tax period, the business calculates their GST credits on purchases and estimates their GST collected on their sales. There are four steps:

Step 1: The business records its total stock purchases for that period. Note that it is *only purchases of trading stock* that apply; operating expenses such as rent, power and wages have no place in this calculation.

Step 2: The business records its total GST-free purchases for the period.

Step 3: The GST-free purchases for that period are divided by the total stock purchases for the period and multiplied by 100 to obtain the percentage of GST-free purchases.

Step 4: The same percentage is applied to sales to estimate the GST-free sales for the period, and thus (by subtraction) the GST collected.

This calculation is done *independently* for each tax period to calculate the percentage of purchases that are GST-free.

In this exercise we will be completing the activity statement for GST, PAYGI and PAYGW:

* for GST: Option 1 (calculate and report quarterly)
* for PAYGI: Option 2 (PAYG percentage)
* for PAYGW (quarterly)
* on a cash basis
* using the worksheet method.

1 In MYOB AccountRight 2016, open the **15.1 FiveStar Milk Bar.myox** data file from the Chapter 15 folder of your start-up files.

2 Print or display the following reports for the period 1 July 2017 to 30 September 2017:

* GST [Summary – Cash] (GST/Sales Tax section of the Reports Centre). See **Figure 15.1**.
* Transaction Tax Codes (GST/Sales Tax section of the Reports Centre). See **Figure 15.2**.
* Payroll Register [Summary] (Payroll section of the Reports Centre). See **Figure 15.3**.
* Profit and Loss [Cash] (Accounts section of the Reports Centre under the bolded heading Small Business Entity). See **Figure 15.4**.

Figure 15.1   GST Summary [Cash] report: FiveStar Milk Bar

FiveStar Milk Bar
1 Weld Street
Broome WA 6725
ABN: 72 338 947 661
GST [Summary – Cash]
July 2017 To September 2017

Code	Description	Rate	Sale Value	Purchase Value	Tax Collected	Tax Paid
CAP	Capital Acquisitions	10.00%		$2 200.00		$200.00
FRE	GST Free	0.00%		$29 452.00		
GST	Goods & Services Tax	10.00%	$130 823.00	$30 997.00	$11 893.00	$2 817.91
				Total:	$11 893.00	$3 017.91

Figure 15.2   **Transaction Tax Codes report: FiveStar Milk Bar**

FiveStar Milk Bar
1 Weld Street
Broome WA 6725
ABN: 72 338 947 661
Transaction Tax Codes
July 2017 To September 2017

Src	Date	Memo	ID No.	Debit	Credit	Account Tax	Entered Tax	Default Tax
1-2310	Equipment At Cost							
CD	30/09/2017	EquipCo	37	$2 000.00		CAP	CAP	CAP
4-1000	Sales							
CR	6/07/2017	Sales	CR000001		$9 120.00	GST	GST	GST
CR	13/07/2017	Sales	CR000002		$8 770.00	GST	GST	GST
CR	20/07/2017	Sales	CR000003		$11 205.00	GST	GST	GST
CR	27/07/2017	Sales	CR000004		$13 500.00	GST	GST	GST
CR	3/08/2017	Sales	CR000005		$7 945.00	GST	GST	GST
CR	10/08/2017	Sales	CR000006		$9 950.00	GST	GST	GST
CR	17/08/2017	Sales	CR000007		$8 760.00	GST	GST	GST
CR	24/08/2017	Sales	CR000008		$11 320.00	GST	GST	GST
CR	31/08/2017	Sales	CR000009		$7 960.00	GST	GST	GST
CR	7/09/2017	Sales	CR000010		$1 220.00	GST	GST	GST
CR	14/09/2017	Sales	CR000011		$7 925.00	GST	GST	GST
CR	21/09/2017	Sales	CR000012		$11 870.00	GST	GST	GST
CR	28/09/2017	Sales	CR000013		$9 385.00	GST	GST	GST
5-1000	Taxable Purchases							
CD	5/07/2017	Cash	3	$2 500.00		GST	GST	GST
CD	19/07/2017	Cash	7	$4 000.00		GST	GST	GST
CD	2/08/2017	Cash	14	$4 109.09		GST	GST	GST
CD	16/08/2017	Cash	19	$3 520.00		GST	GST	GST
CD	30/08/2017	Cash	24	$3 000.00		GST	GST	GST
CD	13/09/2017	Cash	30	$4 400.00		GST	GST	GST
CD	27/09/2017	Cash	35	$3 000.00		GST	GST	GST
5-2000	GST Free Purchases							
CD	2/07/2017	Cash	2	$1 500.00		FRE	FRE	FRE
CD	5/07/2017	Cash	3	$400.00		FRE	FRE	FRE
CD	9/07/2017	Cash	5	$2 015.00		FRE	FRE	FRE
CD	16/07/2017	Cash	8	$1 290.00		FRE	FRE	FRE
CD	19/07/2017	Cash	7	$1 725.00		FRE	FRE	FRE
CD	23/07/2017	Cash	10	$1 745.00		FRE	FRE	FRE
CD	30/07/2017	Cash	12	$1 927.00		FRE	FRE	FRE
CD	2/08/2017	Cash	14	$290.00		FRE	FRE	FRE
CD	6/08/2017	Cash	16	$1 760.00		FRE	FRE	FRE
CD	13/08/2017	Cash	18	$2 010.00		FRE	FRE	FRE
CD	16/08/2017	Cash	19	$1 380.00		FRE	FRE	FRE

Src	Date	Memo	ID No.	Debit	Credit	Account Tax	Entered Tax	Default Tax
CD	20/08/2017	Cash	21	$1 785.00		FRE	FRE	FRE
CD	24/08/2017	Cash	23	$1 785.00		FRE	FRE	FRE
CD	30/08/2017	Cash	24	$640.00		FRE	FRE	FRE
CD	3/09/2017	Cash	27	$2 050.00		FRE	FRE	FRE
CD	10/09/2017	Cash	29	$1 645.00		FRE	FRE	FRE
CD	13/09/2017	Cash	30	$480.00		FRE	FRE	FRE
CD	17/09/2017	Cash	32	$1 920.00		FRE	FRE	FRE
CD	24/09/2017	Cash	34	$2 345.00		FRE	FRE	FRE
CD	27/09/2017	Cash	35	$760.00		FRE	FRE	FRE

6-1600   Laundry

Src	Date	Memo	ID No.	Debit	Credit	Account Tax	Entered Tax	Default Tax
CD	6/07/2017	Cash	4	$50.00		GST	GST	GST
CD	13/07/2017	Cash	6	$50.00		GST	GST	GST
CD	20/07/2017	Cash	9	$50.00		GST	GST	GST
CD	27/07/2017	Cash	11	$50.00		GST	GST	GST
CD	3/08/2017	Cash	15	$50.00		GST	GST	GST
CD	10/08/2017	Cash	17	$50.00		GST	GST	GST
CD	17/08/2017	Cash	20	$50.00		GST	GST	GST
CD	24/08/2017	Cash	22	$50.00		GST	GST	GST
CD	31/08/2017	Cash	25	$50.00		GST	GST	GST
CD	7/09/2017	Cash	28	$50.00		GST	GST	GST
CD	14/09/2017	Cash	31	$50.00		GST	GST	GST
CD	21/09/2017	Cash	33	$50.00		GST	GST	GST
CD	28/09/2017	Cash	36	$50.00		GST	GST	GST

6-1700   Rent

Src	Date	Memo	ID No.	Debit	Credit	Account Tax	Entered Tax	Default Tax
CD	1/07/2017	Estate Agent	1	$1 000.00		GST	GST	GST
CD	1/08/2017	Estate Agent	13	$1 000.00		GST	GST	GST
CD	1/09/2017	Estate Agent	26	$1 000.00		GST	GST	GST

Figure 15.3   **Payroll Register report: FiveStar Milk Bar**

FiveStar Milk Bar
1 Weld Street
Broome WA 6725
ABN: 72 338 947 661
Payroll Register [Summary]
July 2017 To September 2017

Employee	Wages	Deductions	Taxes	Net Pay	Expenses
Chong, Della	$12 000.00	$0.00	$2 196.00	$9 804.00	$1 140.00
Li, Lilly	$9 600.00	$0.00	$1 356.00	$8 244.00	$912.00
Tung, Devina	$9 600.00	$0.00	$1 356.00	$8 244.00	$912.00
Total:	$31 200.00	$0.00	$4 908.00	$26 292.00	$2 964.00

Figure 15.4   Profit & Loss [Cash] report: FiveStar Milk Bar

FiveStar Milk Bar
1 Weld Street
Broome WA 6725
ABN: 72 338 947 661
Profit & Loss [Cash]
July 2017 To September 2017

Income		
Sales	$118 930.00	
Total Income		$118 930.00
Cost Of Sales		
Taxable Purchases	$24 529.09	
GST Free Purchases	$29 452.00	
Total Cost Of Sales		$53 981.09
Gross Profit		$64 948.91
Expenses		
General Expenses		
Laundry	$650.00	
Rent	$3 000.00	
Total General Expenses	$3 650.00	
Payroll Expenses		
Wages & Salaries Expenses	$31 200.00	
Other Payroll Expenses	$2 964.00	
Total Payroll Expenses	$34 164.00	
Total Expenses		$37 814.00
Operating Profit		$27 134.91
Total Other Income		$0.00
Total Other Expenses		$0.00
Net Profit/(Loss)		$27 134.91

3 Examine the GST and transaction reports for accuracy and consistency in GST recording. Then examine the Profit & Loss [Cash] report and note the sales and stock purchases amounts.

> **Remember This**
>
> Financial reports such as the Balance Sheet and Profit & Loss are always GST Exclusive.

4 Calculating GST-free sales is done using the figures from the Profit & Loss [Cash] report. Using the steps given on page 476:

Total stock purchases:	53 981.09
GST-free stock purchases:	29 452.00
GST-free divided by total purchases and multiplied by 100:	$\frac{29\,452}{53\,981} \times 100 = 54.56\%$
Apply this percentage to total sales to arrive at your GST-free sales:	$\frac{118\,930 \times 54.56}{100} = 64\,888$

Thus it is estimated (calculated) that FiveStar Milk Bar's income was:

Total Sales (GST Exclusive)		$118 930.00
GST-Free Sales (from the calculation above)		$64 888.00
Taxable Sales	$118 930 − 64 888 =	$54 042.00
GST Collected	54 042 × 10% =	$5 404.20
Total Sales *Including GST* (ignoring cents)	64 888 + 54 042 + 5 404 =	$124 334.00

You are now able to insert the figures at labels G1, G3, G5, G6, G8 and G9.

Figure 15.5   GST calculation worksheet: sales

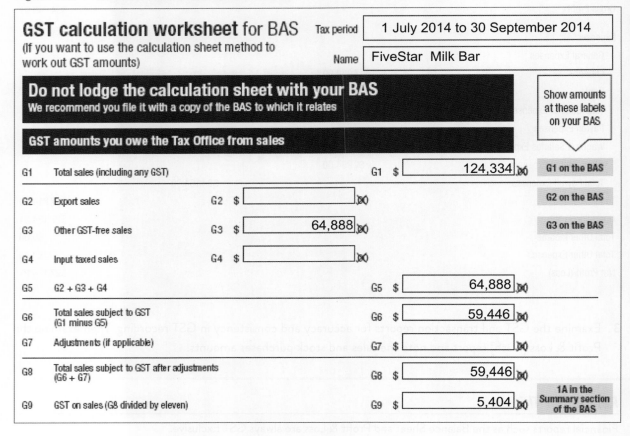

5 Use the figures from the GST [Summary – Cash] report to complete the Purchases section of the worksheet, and note that here the amounts include expenses (rent, wages, etc.).

6 Transfer the amounts from your GST worksheet to the appropriate labels in the BAS (Business Activity Statement) to complete the GST information.

7 Use your Payroll Register [Summary] report to complete the PAYGW labels W1, W2 and W5. Copy the W5 (total amounts withheld) to item 4 in the Summary section of the BAS.

8 PAYGI Option 2 is used and the ATO's suggested rate percentage is too high for current trading conditions. Use the revised rate of 1.6% to complete this section.

9 Complete the Summary section of the activity statement and calculate the amount due to the ATO. See Figure 15.6.

Figure 15.6 **Summary and Payment or refund? sections:
FiveStar Milk Bar**

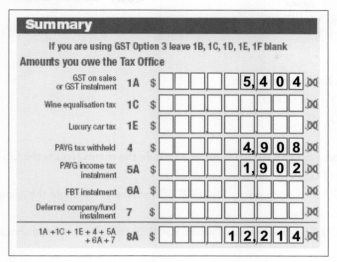

MYOB Setup

10 In MYOB AccountRight 2016:

 Click...

- *Receive Money* (in the Banking module).
- *Tax Exclusive* (ensure it is not ticked).
- *Date* (insert *30/09/17*).
- *Payor* (insert *Sales*).
- *Amount Received* (insert −$6488.80). Ensure you include the minus. This is the GST component.
- *Memo* (insert *Transfer of GST Free Sales*).
- *Account* (select *4-1000 Sales* and insert −$64 888.00 [ensure you include the minus]). The tax code should be GST. This is the actual sales.
- *Account* (select *4-2000 GST Free Sales* and insert $64 888.00). The tax code should be FRE. Compare with Figure 15.7.
- *Record*.
- *Cancel* (to return to the Command Centre).

Figure 15.7   Receive Money: Transfer of GST-free sales

Acct No.	Name	Amount	Job	Memo	Tax
4-1000	Sales	-$64,888.00			GST
4-2000	GST Free Sales	$64,888.00			FRE

Deposit to Account: 1-1110 Business Bank Account #1   Balance: $131,882.00

Payor: Sales   ID No. : CR000001
Amount Received: -$6,488.80   Date: 30/09/2017
Payment Method: Details..
Memo: Transfer of GST Free Sales

Total Allocated: $0.00
Tax: -$6,488.80
Total Received: -$6,488.80
Out of Balance: $0.00

Save as Recurring   Use Recurring

Record   Cancel

This is why

The Total Allocated field in Figure 15.7 is zero. The sales value is unchanged. The tax is a negative. This means the GST has been removed.

11 Access BASlink in the Accounts module and after selecting September as the last month of the reporting period, click the **BAS Info** button, then:

Click...

- the following in the Goods and Services tax section:
  - *GST reporting frequency* (select *Quarterly*).
  - *GST accounting basis* (select *Cash*).
  - *GST option* (select *Option 1*).
  - *Calculation Method* (select *Calculation worksheet*).
  - *I use the Simplified Accounting Method* (to ensure it's ticked).
  - *GST-free Sales* field (insert 54.56%).
  - *GST-free Purchases* (select 0%).
- the following in the PAYGI section:
  - *Instalment reporting frequency* (select *Quarterly*).
  - *Instalment accounting basis* (select *Cash*).
  - *Instalment option* (select *Option 2*).
  - *PAYGI Rate* (insert 2.2%, the ATO's suggestion).
- the following in the PAYGW section:
  - *Withholding reporting frequency* (select *Quarterly (small withholder)*).
- Compare with Figure 15.8.

Figure 15.8   **Set Up Activity Statement: FiveStar Milk Bar**

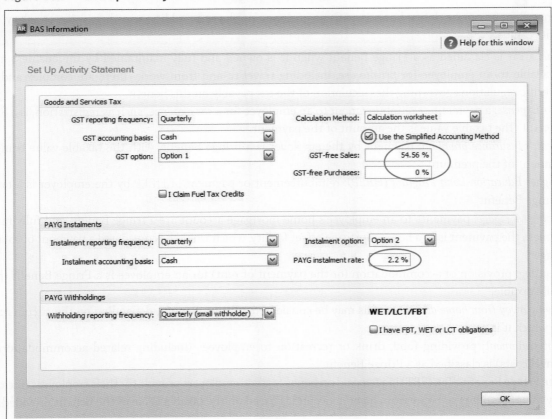

12 Complete the steps described in Chapter 14 to set up MYOB for GST, PAYGW and PAYGI Option 2. Use the revised rate of 1.6% for the PAYGI as trading conditions have changed. Compare MYOB's results with your manual work and investigate any differences. (There should be none!)

Figure 15.9   MYOB BAS Summary and Payment or refund? sections: FiveStar Milk Bar

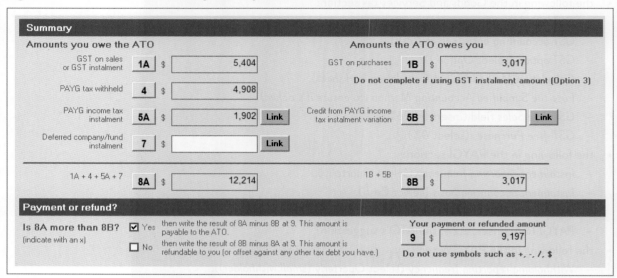

Fringe Benefits Tax

A Fringe Benefit can be defined as a benefit given to an employee in addition to their wage or salary. Such benefits can be:

- *Car*: a car is classified as a Fringe Benefit when it is owned and fully maintained by the business and is available to an employee for *private use*, including travel to and from work. There are complex and very specific regulations governing the calculation of the tax payable on this benefit.
- *Car Expense*: a payment or reimbursement to an employee for a car expense, such as registration, is a Fringe Benefit. The taxable value is the amount of the payment.
- *Health Insurance premium*: payment by the employer is a Fringe Benefit, with the taxable value being the amount of the premium.
- *Higher Education Loan Program (HELP)*: reimbursement or payment of HELP by the employer is a taxable Fringe Benefit.
- *Home Mortgage*: payments to an employee's home mortgage account are a fringe Benefit and fully taxable (unless the payment is to a home mortgage offset facility, which would be considered a payment of salary or wages).
- *Housing*: provision of accommodation (or the payment of rent) for an employee is a Fringe Benefit that is fully taxable.
- *Living away from home allowance*: this may be considered a Fringe Benefit, depending on the circumstances in which it is paid.
- *Entertainment*: providing food, drink or recreation to employees (including related accommodation and travel costs) is classified as a Fringe Benefit.

The Fringe Benefits Tax (FBT) is a tax paid on benefits some employers provide for their employees (including family members). It is separate from income tax and is based on the taxable value of the benefit provided.

In deciding whether or not an employee is receiving a Fringe Benefit in relation to employment, the *acid test* suggested by the ATO is for the business to ask itself if they would provide the benefit if the recipient was not an employee. If the answer is no, then the benefit is a Fringe Benefit. An *employee* can be a current, future or former employee.

The FBT varies from year to year and is payable by employers on the grossed-up value of the benefit (explained later in this chapter). The FBT Year runs from 1 April of one year to 31 March of the next. The FBT rate for FBT year ending March 2015 was 47%, for the FBT years ending March 2016 and March 2017 it was 49%. The FBT rate for the FBT year ending March 2018, and the rate we will be using for our calculations, is 47%.

The status of the employer makes no difference: a sole trader, partnership, trust, incorporated or unincorporated body etc., are all liable to pay the FBT. The cost of providing a Fringe Benefit and its associated tax are classified as business expenses, which may reduce income tax payable.

Having decided that the business is paying Fringe Benefits, the steps involved in complying with the FBT regulations are as follows:

Step 1: Calculate how much FBT is payable by:
- identifying what types of Fringe Benefits are being provided
- calculating the taxable value of each benefit to each employee
- calculating the taxable values by grossing up the value of all the Fringe Benefits. This is done using the Type 1 gross-up rate where Fringe Benefits being provided have a GST content that can be reclaimed as a credit (for 2018 this is 2.0802) and using the Type 2 gross-up rate where Fringe Benefits being provided *don't* have a GST content (for 2018 this is 1.8868)
- adding the two grossed-up amounts to find the total FBT amount
- multiplying the total taxable amount by the 2018 rate of 47.0% to find the FBT payable.

Step 2: Keep records and receipts that show exactly what the Fringe Benefits cost and when they were paid for. These records must be kept for five years.

Step 3: Register for FBT by completing form NAT 1055 (available from the ATO website https://www.ato.gov.au or by phoning 13 28 66) and sending it to the ATO. The FBT registration number is the same as the Tax File Number.

Step 4: Report Fringe Benefits on the employee's annual payment summary. If the taxable value of those benefits exceeds $2000.00 in an FBT year (1 April to 31 March) it is reported in the payment summary for the tax year ending 30 June. The value to report is the actual cost of the benefits multiplied by the lower of the two grossing-up rates, regardless of whether or not GST formed a part of the calculation.

If this is the first year the business has to pay FBT, or if the amount they had to pay in the previous year was less than the instalment threshold (currently $3000.00), payment must be made to the ATO with an annual return lodged no later than 21 May.

If the business had to pay FBT of $3000.00 or more in the previous year, then the tax must be paid quarterly with other taxes in the activity statement. This rule applies even if it is estimated that the FBT will amount to less than $3000.00 in the current year. However, if the ATO's instalment amount is too high for Fringe Benefits being given in the current year, it can be varied similarly to other instalment suggestions.

Business Norms method

The Business Norms method is available to enterprises that:
- have a SAM turnover of $2 million or less
- do not have adequate point-of-sale equipment, and
- are of a type mentioned in the following table (**Figure 15.10**).

Figure 15.10   Business Norms percentages

Type of retailer	Percentage of sales that are GST-free	Percentage of purchases that are GST-free
Cake shops	2%	95%
Continental delicatessens	85%	90%
Convenience stores that prepare takeaway food, but not fuel or alcohol	22.5%	30%
Convenience stores that do not prepare takeaway food, and don't sell fuel or alcohol	30%	30%
Fresh-fish retailers	35%	98%
Health-food shops	35%	35%
Hot-bread shops	50%	75%
Pharmacies that also sell food	Dispensary: non-claimable 98% Over the counter: 47.55%	Nil% 2%
Rural convenience stores	Converters: 22.5% Non-converters: 30%	30%

Each of the business types above has a standard percentage that is considered normal for their activities. It has been developed in consultation with industry and using information collected from retailers.

Note that *only* the business types listed above are currently able to use this method to calculate their GST liability.

Every tax period, the business uses its standard percentages to calculate its GST-free sales and purchases. There are four steps:

Step 1: The business calculates out its total stock sales for the period.

Step 2: The business multiplies its total stock sales by the percentage from the table that applies to its business type. The result is the dollar value of its GST-free sales.

Step 3: Similarly, the business works out its total purchases of trading stock for the period.

Step 4: The total stock purchases figure is multiplied by the business norms percentage from the table. The result identifies GST-free purchases for the period.

SIX-TIL-SIX HOT BREAD SHOP

Six-til-Six Hot Bread Shop is a small business in Inverell NSW. It is registered for the GST, has PAYGW, PAYGI and FBT obligations, and has elected to use the Business Norms method of the simplified accounting system to identify their GST obligations.

In this exercise we will be completing the activity statement for GST, PAYGI and PAYGW:

- for GST: Option 1 (calculate and report quarterly)
- for PAYGI: Option 1 (PAYG instalment)
- for PAYGW (quarterly)
- on a cash basis
- using the worksheet method.

1 Print the personalised activity statement and worksheet for use in this exercise. It is in the Chapter 15 folder, entitled *15.2 Six-til-Six BAS*.

2 In MYOB AccountRight Plus 2016, open the data file **15.2 Six-til-Six Hot Bread.myox** from the Chapter 15 folder of your start-up files.

3 Print or view the following reports for the period 1 July 2017 to 30 September 2017:

- Account Transactions [Cash]. (Accounts section of the Reports Centre under the bolded heading Small Business Entity). See Figure 15.11.
- Payroll Register [Summary]. (Payroll section of the Reports Centre). See Figure 15.12.
- GST [Summary – Cash]. (GST/Sales Tax section of the Reports Centre). See Figure 15.13.
- Bank Register (Banking section of the Reports Centre). See Figure 15.14.

Figure 15.11   Account Transactions [Cash] report: Six-til-Six Hot Bread Shop

Six-til-Six Hot Bread Shop
Evans Street
Inverell NSW
ABN: 63 228 576 921
Account Transactions [Cash]
July 2017 To September 2017

ID No.	Src	Date	Memo	Debit	Credit
4-1000 Sales					
CR000001	CR	6/07/2017	Sales		$10 400.00
CR000002	CR	13/07/2017	Sales		$12 000.00
CR000003	CR	20/07/2017	Sales		$15 000.00
CR000004	CR	27/07/2017	Sales		$12 500.00
CR000005	CR	3/08/2017	Sales		$11 700.00
CR000006	CR	10/08/2017	Sales		$10 200.00
CR000007	CR	17/08/2017	Sales		$13 400.00
CR000008	CR	24/08/2017	Sales		$15 500.00
CR000009	CR	31/08/2017	Sales		$12 100.00
CR000010	CR	7/09/2017	Sales		$11 300.00
CR000011	CR	14/09/2017	Sales		$15 400.00
CR000012	CR	21/09/2017	Sales		$10 700.00
CR000013	CR	28/09/2017	Sales		$13 400.00
				$0.00	$163 600.00
5-1000 Purchases					
1	CD	2/07/2017	Cash	$2 000.00	
2	CD	9/07/2017	Cash	$1 980.00	
3	CD	16/07/2017	Cash	$3 000.00	
4	CD	23/07/2017	Cash	$1 900.00	
5	CD	30/07/2017	Cash	$3 100.00	
6	CD	6/08/2017	Cash	$1 500.00	
7	CD	13/08/2017	Cash	$1 750.00	
8	CD	20/08/2017	Cash	$3 000.00	
9	CD	27/08/2017	Cash	$2 000.00	
10	CD	3/09/2017	Cash	$3 100.00	

ID No.	Src	Date	Memo	Debit	Credit
11	CD	10/09/2017	Cash	$2 100.00	
12	CD	17/09/2017	Cash	$2 450.00	
13	CD	24/09/2017	Cash	$2 080.00	
				$29 960.00	$0.00

6-1700   Electricity Expenses

ID No.	Src	Date	Memo	Debit	Credit
4	CD	31/07/2017	PowerCo	$380.00	
9	CD	31/08/2017	PowerCo	$380.00	
14	CD	30/09/2017	PowerCo	$380.00	
				$1 140.00	$0.00

6-2000   Telephone Expenses

ID No.	Src	Date	Memo	Debit	Credit
5	CD	31/07/2017	Optus	$56.00	
10	CD	31/08/2017	Optus	$56.00	
15	CD	30/09/2017	Optus	$56.00	
				$168.00	$0.00

6-2100   Rent

ID No.	Src	Date	Memo	Debit	Credit
1	CD	1/07/2017	Estate Agent	$1 454.55	
7	CD	1/08/2017	Estate Agent	$1 454.55	
11	CD	1/09/2017	Estate Agent	$1 454.55	
				$4 363.65	$0.00

6-2110   Jackie Hardwick's Rent

ID No.	Src	Date	Memo	Debit	Credit
3	CD	31/07/2017	Cash	$700.00	
8	CD	31/08/2017	Cash	$700.00	
16	CD	30/09/2017	Cash	$700.00	
				$2 100.00	$0.00

6-4100   Wages & Salaries Expenses

ID No.	Src	Date	Memo	Debit	Credit
14	CD	31/07/2017	Pay Employee	$6 933.34	
15	CD	31/07/2017	Pay Employee	$5 200.01	
16	CD	31/07/2017	Pay Employee	$4 166.67	
17	CD	31/08/2017	Pay Employee	$6 933.34	
18	CD	31/08/2017	Pay Employee	$5 200.01	
19	CD	31/08/2017	Pay Employee	$4 166.67	
20	CD	30/09/2017	Pay Employee	$6 933.34	
21	CD	30/09/2017	Pay Employee	$5 200.01	
22	CD	30/09/2017	Pay Employee	$4 166.67	
				$48 900.06	$0.00

6-4700   Other Payroll Expenses

ID No.	Src	Date	Memo	Debit	Credit
14	CD	31/07/2017	Pay Employee	$658.67	
15	CD	31/07/2017	Pay Employee	$494.00	
16	CD	31/07/2017	Pay Employee	$395.83	
17	CD	31/08/2017	Pay Employee	$658.67	

ID No.	Src	Date	Memo	Debit	Credit
18	CD	31/08/2017	Pay Employee	$494.00	
19	CD	31/08/2017	Pay Employee	$395.83	
20	CD	30/09/2017	Pay Employee	$658.67	
21	CD	30/09/2017	Pay Employee	$494.00	
22	CD	30/09/2017	Pay Employee	$395.83	
				$4 645.50	$0.00
6-7100	Business Insurance				
2	CD	1/07/2017	Cash	$400.00	
6	CD	1/08/2017	Cash	$400.00	
12	CD	1/09/2017	Cash	$400.00	
				$1 200.00	$0.00

Figure 15.12 Payroll register report: Six-til-Six Hot Bread Shop

Six-til-Six Hot Bread Shop
Evans Street
Inverell NSW
ABN: 63 228 576 921
Payroll Register [Summary]
July 2017 To September 2017

Employee	Wages	Deductions	Taxes	Net Pay	Expenses
Fielder, Chris	$20 800.02	$0.00	$5 070.00	$15 730.02	$1 976.01
Forbes, Glen	$15 600.03	$0.00	$3 276.00	$12 324.03	$1 482.00
Hardwick, Jackie	$12 500.01	$0.00	$2 196.00	$10 304.01	$1 187.49
Total:	$48 900.06	$0.00	$10 542.00	$38 358.06	$4 645.50

Figure 15.13 GST Summary [Cash] report: Six-til-Six Hot Bread Shop

Six-til-Six Hot Bread Shop
Evans Street
Inverell NSW
ABN: 63 228 576 921
GST [Summary – Cash]
July 2017 To September 2017

Code	Description	Rate	Sale Value	Purchase Value	Tax Collected	Tax Paid
CAP	Capital Acquisitions	10.00%		$1 980.00		$180.00
FRE	GST Free	0.00%		$2 100.00		
GST	Goods and Services Tax	10.00%	$179 960.00	$40 514.80	$16 360.00	$3 683.15
				Total:	$16 360.00	$3 863.15

Figure 15.14   Bank Register report: : Six-til-Six Hot Bread Shop

Six-til-Six Hot Bread Shop
Evans Street
Inverell NSW
ABN: 63 228 576 921
Bank Register
July 2017 To September 2017

ID No.	Src	Date	Memo/Payee	Deposit	Withdrawal	Balance
1-1110	Business Bank Account #1					
1	CD	2/07/2017	Cash		$2 200.00	$72 800.00
CR000001	CR	6/07/2017	Sales	$11 440.00		$84 240.00
2	CD	9/07/2017	Cash		$2 178.00	$82 062.00
CR000002	CR	13/07/2017	Sales	$13 200.00		$95 262.00
3	CD	16/07/2017	Cash		$3 300.00	$91 962.00
CR000003	CR	20/07/2017	Sales	$16 500.00		$108 462.00
4	CD	23/07/2017	Cash		$2 090.00	$106 372.00
CR000004	CR	27/07/2017	Sales	$13 750.00		$120 122.00
5	CD	30/07/2017	Cash		$3 410.00	$116 712.00
CR000005	CR	3/08/2017	Sales	$12 870.00		$129 582.00
6	CD	6/08/2017	Cash		$1 650.00	$127 932.00
CR000006	CR	10/08/2017	Sales	$11 220.00		$139 152.00
7	CD	13/08/2017	Cash		$1 925.00	$137 227.00
CR000007	CR	17/08/2017	Sales	$14 740.00		$151 967.00
8	CD	20/08/2017	Cash		$3 300.00	$148 667.00
CR000008	CR	24/08/2017	Sales	$17 050.00		$165 717.00
9	CD	27/08/2017	Cash		$2 200.00	$163 517.00
CR000009	CR	31/08/2017	Sales	$13 310.00		$176 827.00
10	CD	3/09/2017	Cash		$3 410.00	$173 417.00
CR000010	CR	7/09/2017	Sales	$12 430.00		$185 847.00
11	CD	10/09/2017	Cash		$2 310.00	$183 537.00
CR000011	CR	14/09/2017	Sales	$16 940.00		$200 477.00
12	CD	17/09/2017	Cash		$2 695.00	$197 782.00
CR000012	CR	21/09/2017	Sales	$11 770.00		$209 552.00
13	CD	24/09/2017	Cash		$2 288.00	$207 264.00
CR000013	CR	28/09/2017	Sales	$14 740.00		$222 004.00
				$179 960.00	$32 956.00	
1-1120	Business Bank Account #2					
1	CD	1/07/2017	Estate Agent		$1 600.00	$48 400.00
2	CD	1/07/2017	Cash		$440.00	$47 960.00
14	CD	31/07/2017	Fielder, Chris		$5 243.34	$42 716.66
15	CD	31/07/2017	Forbes, Glen		$4 108.01	$38 608.65
16	CD	31/07/2017	Hardwick, Jackie		$3 434.67	$35 173.98
3	CD	31/07/2017	Cash		$700.00	$34 473.98
4	CD	31/07/2017	PowerCo		$418.00	$34 055.98
5	CD	31/07/2017	Optus		$61.60	$33 994.38
6	CD	1/08/2017	Cash		$440.00	$33 554.38
7	CD	1/08/2017	Estate Agent		$1 600.00	$31 954.38

ID No.	Src	Date	Memo/Payee	Deposit	Withdrawal	Balance
10	CD	31/08/2017	Optus		$61.60	$31 892.78
17	CD	31/08/2017	Fielder, Chris		$5 243.34	$26 649.44
18	CD	31/08/2017	Forbes, Glen		$4 108.01	$22 541.43
19	CD	31/08/2017	Hardwick, Jackie		$3 434.67	$19 106.76
8	CD	31/08/2017	Cash		$700.00	$18 406.76
9	CD	31/08/2017	PowerCo		$418.00	$17 988.76
11	CD	1/09/2017	Estate Agent		$1 600.00	$16 388.76
12	CD	1/09/2017	Cash		$440.00	$15 948.76
13	CD	28/09/2017	EquipCo		$1 980.00	$13 968.76
14	CD	30/09/2017	PowerCo		$418.00	$13 550.76
15	CD	30/09/2017	Optus		$61.60	$13 489.16
16	CD	30/09/2017	Cash		$700.00	$12 789.16
20	CD	30/09/2017	Fielder, Chris		$5 243.34	$7 545.82
21	CD	30/09/2017	Forbes, Glen		$4 108.01	$3 437.81
22	CD	30/09/2017	Hardwick, Jackie		$3 434.67	$3.14
				$0.00	$49 996.86	

4   Examine the Bank Register and note that two accounts have been used. Cheque Account #1 is used *exclusively* for purchases and sales of trading stock. The numbers are *GST Inclusive*, so that the figures represent the actual cash movement, regardless of their tax content.

5   Calculating GST-free sales and purchases is done using the figures from the Bank Register report (Business Bank Account #1) and the percentages given in the Business Norms table:

1. Total sales (Deposits):	179 960.00	
2. GST-free sales (50% in table):	$\dfrac{179\,960 \times 50}{100}$	= $89 980.00
3. Total purchases (Withdrawals):	32 956.00	
4. GST-free purchases (75% in table):	$\dfrac{32\,956 \times 75}{100}$	= $24 717.00

Thus it is estimated (calculated) that Six-til-Six Hot Bread Shop's GST on sales and purchases is:

GST-free sales (from calculation above)	$89 980.00
Taxable sales (inclusive) $179 960 − 89 980 =	[1] 89 980.00
Total sales including GST =	$179 960.00
GST collected on taxable sales [1] 89 980/11 =	8 180.00
GST-free purchases (from calculation above)	24 717.00
Taxable purchases (GST Inclusive) $32 956 − 24 717 =	[2] 8 239.00
Total stock purchases (including GST) =	$32 956.00
Including GST paid [2] 8239/11 =	749.00

You are now able to insert the figures at labels G1, G3, G5, G6, G8 and G9 in the printed worksheet.

6 The amount of capital purchases for label G10 can be taken from the GST [Summary – Cash] report.

7 Label G11 (non-capital purchases) includes stock purchases from above, plus the expenses *only* from the Bank Register listing of the Business Bank Account #2. This account is used for purchases not connected with trading stock and payroll. As we don't want to include the Capital amount (already recorded in G10) or the wages (which is recorded in a separate section) we need to make the following calculation:

Total Stock Purchases including GST (from the calculation above)	32 956.00
Plus Total Withdrawals from Business Bank Account #2	49 996.00
Less Capital Purchase on 28/9/17	(1 980.00)
Less Net Pay from Payroll register	(38 358.00)
Total Non Capital Purchases (incl GST)	$42 614.00

8 Label G14 (Purchases without GST in the price) requires a small calculation as well as the GST [Summary – Cash] shows a figure of $2100.00 which would have been from the operating expenses in business Bank Account #2. This needs to be added to the $24 417 GST-free purchases from the very first calculation on page 491. Thus, the total for G14 becomes $26 817.

9 Complete the Purchases section of the worksheet (labels G10 to G20), then transfer the figures to the front of the activity statement and complete the GST labels in the Summary section.

10 Use your Payroll Register [Summary] report to complete the PAYGW labels W1, W2 and W5. Copy W5 (total amounts withheld) to item 4 in the Summary section of the BAS.

11 PAYGI option 1 is used and the ATO's suggested instalment amount of $1472.00 is thought to be about right. Complete this section by transferring the $1472.00 to the Summary section.

12 Six-til-Six Hot Bread Shop provides a Fringe Benefit for one of its employees (Jackie Hardwick) in that it pays the rent on the Hardwick family home of $700.00 per month. This is a domestic rental, so no GST is involved.

The taxable grossed-up value of this Fringe Benefit and the FBT payable is:

$$700 \text{ per month} \times 12 \text{ months} = \$8400.00 \text{ per year.}$$
$$8400 \text{ annual benefit} \times 1.8868 \text{ grossing-up rate} = \$15\,849.12.$$
$$15\,849 \text{ taxable benefit} \times 47\% \text{ FBT} = \$7449 \text{ annual FBT.}$$
$$7449 \text{ annual FBT divided by four} = \$1862 \text{ per quarter.}$$

The ATO's nominal FBT instalment of $4518.00 at F1 was based on the previous year's return when a former employee was also receiving a similar benefit.

You should insert the estimated FBT for the year at label F2, and this quarter's FBT at label F3 on the activity statement.

You should also insert the reason code for this variation at label F4, then copy your F3 figure to label 6A in the Summary section of the activity statement.

Figure 15.15   **Codes for varying FBT instalment**

Reason	Code
Current business structure not continuing	22
Change in Fringe Benefits for employees	30
Change in employees with Fringe Benefits	31
Fringe Benefits rebate now claimed	32

13 Complete the Summary section of the activity statement and calculate the amount due to the ATO.

Figure 15.16   **Paper BAS Summary section: Six-til-six Bread shop**

Summary

If you are using GST Option 3 leave 1B, 1C, 1D, 1E, 1F blank

Amounts you owe the Tax Office

GST on sales or GST instalment	1A	$ 8,180.00
Wine equalisation tax	1C	$ .00
Luxury car tax	1E	$ .00
PAYG tax withheld	4	$ 10,542.00
PAYG income tax instalment	5A	$ 1,472.00
FBT instalment	6A	$ 1,862.00
Deferred company/fund instalment	7	$ .00
1A +1C + 1E + 4 + 5A +6A +7	8A	$ 22,056.00

Amounts the Tax Office owes you

GST on purchases	1B	$ 1,616.00
Wine equalisation tax refundable	1D	$ .00
Luxury car tax refundable	1F	$ .00
Credit from PAYG income tax instalment variation	5B	$ .00
Credit from FBT instalment variation	6B	$ .00
1B + 1D +1F + 5B + 6B	8B	$ 1,616.00

Your payment or refund amount

9 $ 20,440.00

● Do not use symbols such as +, −, /, $

MYOB Setup

14 All the stock purchases and sales for the period have been recorded GST-inclusive, using the tax code GST. Now that trading has ended, it is possible to register the correct percentage of transactions that are GST-free according to the Business Norms table.

In the Banking module, use **Receive Money** to change the tax code on $89 980.00 worth of sales from GST to FRE as shown in Figure 15.17. Use the last day of the BAS quarter, in this case 30 September 2017. Note the **Tax Inclusive** box is ticked; note also the negative number in the first line.

Figure 15.17   **Receive Money: converting GST sales to FRE sales**

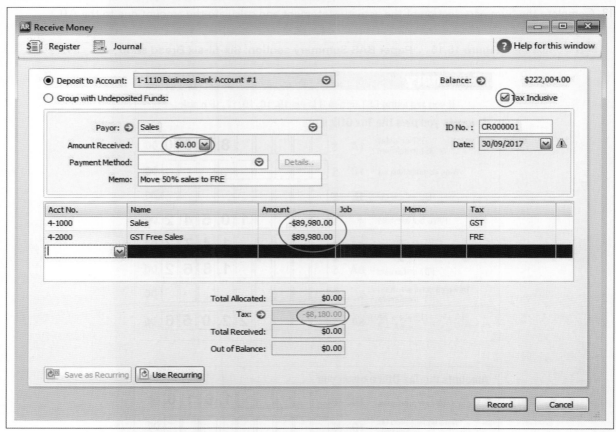

Click **Record**, then **OK** to void the entry. This transaction is considered void as there is a zero in the amount received. However, there will be an impact on the GST sales and FRE sales as well as the GST collected.

15 Perform a similar action in **Spend Money** to register the GST-free proportion of stock purchases. Again, use the last day of the BAS quarter. Compare with Figure 15.18.

Figure 15.18   Spend Money: converting GST purchases to FRE purchases

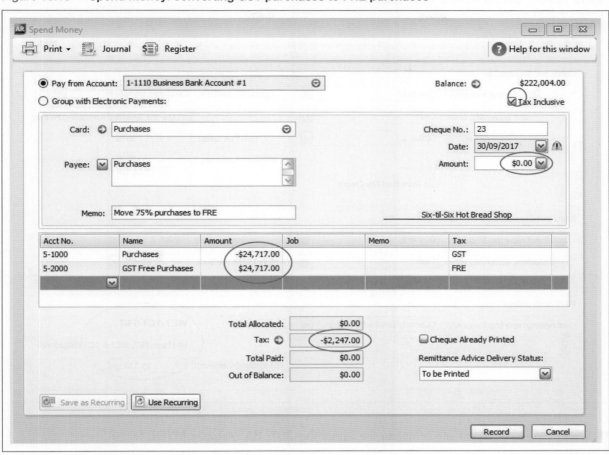

16 Re-run the GST [Summary – Cash] report from 1 July 2017 to 30 September 2017 (Figure 15.19) and note how it has changed compared with the original report in Figure 15.13.

Figure 15.19   GST [Summary – Cash] report: Six-til-Six Hot Bread Shop after Business Norms transactions

Six-til-Six Hot Bread Shop
Evans Street
Inverell NSW
ABN: 63 228 576 921
GST [Summary – Cash]
July 2017 To September 2017

Code	Description	Rate	Sale Value	Purchase Value	Tax Collected	Tax Paid
CAP	Capital Acquisitions	10.00%		$1 980.00		$180.00
FRE	GST Free	0.00%	$89 980.00	$26 817.00		
GST	Goods and Services Tax	10.00%	$89 980.00	$15 797.80	$8 180.00	$1 436.15
				Total:	$8 180.00	$1 616.15

17 Use MYOB's BASlink program to produce an activity statement for the September quarter. Use the **BAS Info** button after selecting September as the quarter and set up your activity statement according to the following screen. Note the tick next to *I use the Simplified Accounting Method* when setting up the parameters and the percentages. Note also the tick next to *I have FBT, WET or LCT obligations*.

Figure 15.20   **Set Up Activity Statement: Six-til-Six Hot Bread Shop**

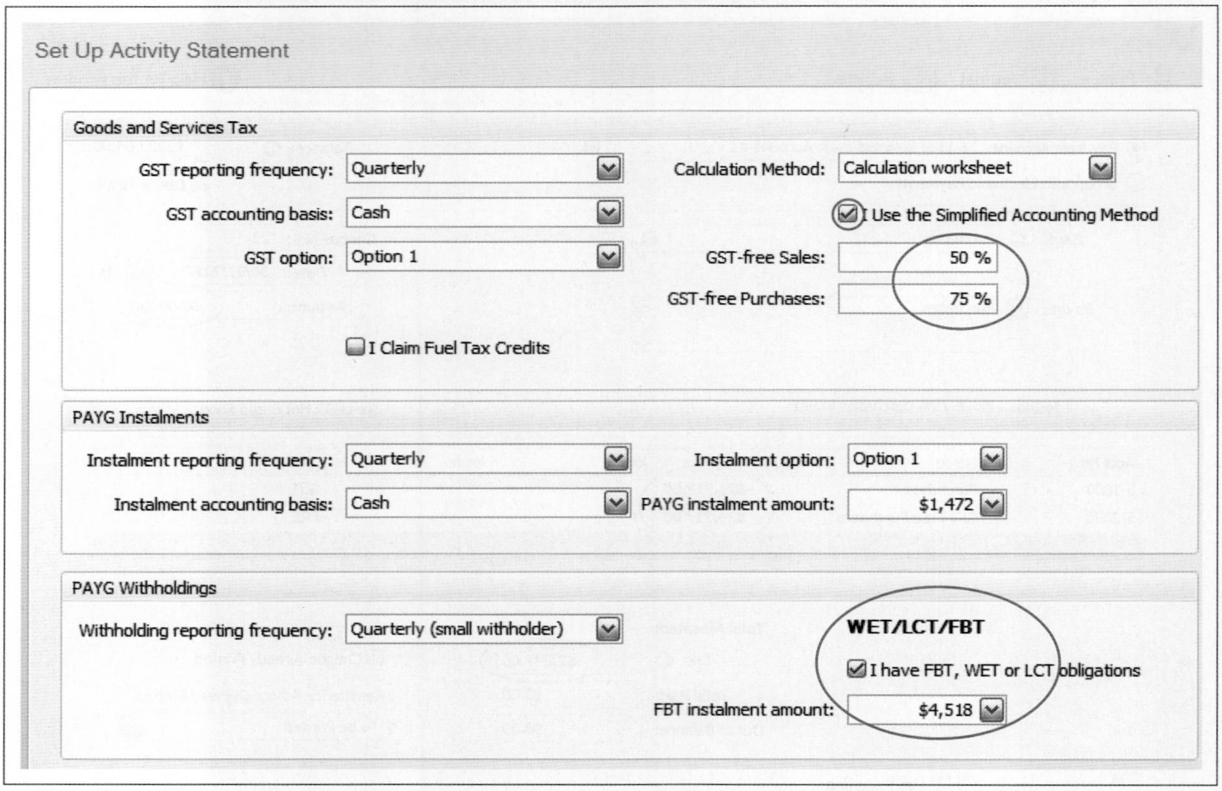

18 Click prepare statement and complete the September 2017 BAS setup in MYOB for:

- GST
- PAYGW (on the Front sheet tab this time)
- PAYG tax withheld
- FBT.

Compare with your manual calculations and investigate any discrepancies.

Fuel Tax Credits

Fuel Tax Credits were introduced at the start of the 2007 tax year for fuel used in heavy vehicles and some other business activities. It has since been expanded to cover most taxable fuel used in other business activities, plant and machinery. The credits allow a business to reclaim the fuel tax (customs duty or excise) included in the fuel price they purchase for approved use.

Approved use includes:

- heavy vehicles (> 4.5 tonnes GVM) used on a public road
- households using fuel to generate electricity
- vehicles and machinery used off-road in eligible business activity.

Eligible business activity includes:

- agriculture, forestry, fishing and mining
- construction and manufacture
- landscaping and garden maintenance
- marine transport
- non-fuel use such as cleaning plant and equipment

- fuel used as an ingredient in the manufacture of another product (e.g. paint, plastics and adhesives).
  To be able to claim Fuel Tax Credits, a business must:

- be registered for the GST
- be registered for Fuel Tax Credits by submitting a form to the Tax Office.
  The only fuels currently *not* eligible are:

- alternative fuels (e.g. biodiesel, ethanol, LPG and natural gas)
- aviation fuels
- fuels purchased but not used because they were lost or stolen
- fuels used in light (< 4.5 tonnes GVM) vehicles on public roads.

All other taxable fuels are eligible. However, the rate changes regularly and should be reviewed before every BAS calculation. The rates are indexed in February and August of every year in line with the consumer price index. Businesses claiming less than $10 000 worth of Fuel Tax Credits may use the simplified Fuel Tax Credits, which allows for the use of only one rate in the BAS period where the rates change. The rate to use in that scenario is the one that applies at the end of the period.

So for a March BAS, a business claiming *over* $10 000 in Fuel Tax Credits in a year would need to claim tax credits on eligible fuel purchased in January at one rate and tax credits for eligible fuel purchased in February and March at another rate. A business claiming *under* $10 000 in Fuel Tax Credits in a year would use just the latter rate to claim tax credits for eligible fuel purchased for January to March.

Rates also differ depending on the use of the fuel and whether it is liquid, gaseous or blended.

Fuel Tax Credit claims are self-assessed and form part of the BAS return. Where fuel purchased is used for both eligible and non-eligible purposes, only the proportion used for eligible activity can be claimed, and records must be kept detailing how this was arrived at.

Fuel Tax Credits calculations can be made by using a form, using the fuel tax calculator on the ATO website (https://www.ato.gov.au> search for Fuel Tax Credit) or by using the ATO deductions App.

Snapshot method

When using the Snapshot method, you measure GST-free sales and GST-free purchases. You will be eligible for this method if you are a food retailer, such as grocery shop, convenience store, bakery or kiosk.

There are three ways the Snapshot method can be used:

- Two sample periods: where you accurately record your *sales* for a continuous two-week period and your *purchases* for a continuous four-week period twice a year. These results are used to estimate your GST-free sales and GST-free purchases.
- Every tax period: GST-free *purchases* are recorded accurately but the *sales* are estimated.
- The 5% GST-free stock estimation: you only track the GST-free goods that you purchase and resell without converting.

HAWKESBURY FARM

Hawkesbury Farm is situated at Gronos Point, near Wilberforce NSW, where it has two distinct enterprises:

- *The Farm*, which sells its produce GST-free, but pays GST on all its purchases. These purchases attract GST credits which will be claimed on activity statements.
- *The Kiosk*, which buys and sells a mixture of taxable and GST-free goods, and uses the Simplified Accounting System for its records. It uses the Snapshot method for working out its GST liability.

The Snapshot method of the Simplified Accounting System used by the Kiosk involves keeping an accurate record of taxable and GST-free sales over a two-week period (to obtain a percentage of each), and then applying this percentage to sales for the whole quarter.

The percentages arrived at for *sales* in the September quarter are:

- 60% taxable
- 40% GST-free.

Purchases are always accurately recorded directly from Supplier invoices, so there is no further calculation required for their GST reporting.

The business has the following activity statement obligations:

- GST: Option 1 (calculate and report quarterly)
- PAYGI: Option 2 (PAYG percentage)
- PAYGW (quarterly)
- Fuel Tax Credits claim
- on a cash basis.

1   Print the personalised activity statement and worksheet for use in this exercise. They are located in the Chapter 15 folder and are entitled **15.3 Fuel Tax Credit worksheet** and **15.3 Hawkesbury Farm BAS**.

2   In MYOB AccountRight 2016, open the data file **15.3 Hawkesbury Farm.myox** from your Chapter 15 folder.

3   All of the fuel was used on the farm and is eligible for the Fuel Tax Credits. The farm claims less than $10 000 Fuel Tax Credits a year so can used the simpled Fuel Tax Credits which uses a rate of 39.6 cents per litre. Use the Fuel Tax Credits worksheet to calculate the credits to be claimed. The litres can be found in MYOB by using the following steps:

Click...

- *Find Transactions.*
- *Account* (tab at the top) and select *6-6300 Motor vehicle Petrol/Diesel.*
- *Dated From* (type *1/07/17* and *To* (type *30/09/17*). Compare with Figure 15.21.

Figure 15.21   Find Transactions: Account 6-6300

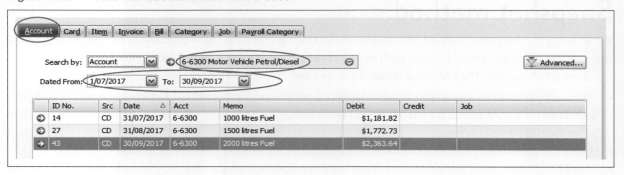

The Memo column in Figure 15.21 reveals how much fuel was purchased: a total of 4500 litres for that BAS period. Multiply this by the applicable rate (use 39.6 cents) to calculate the total Fuel Tax Credit for this BAS period:

$$4500 \text{ litres} \times 0.396 = \$1782.00$$

The Fuel Tax Credits Calculation worksheet needs to be completed with the appropriate information. Compare it with the answer sheet in your supplementary materials.

MYOB Setup

4 In MYOB, use your *Record Journal Entry* to post the Fuel Tax Credits being claimed by debiting 2-1350 and crediting 4-6000 with the value you calculated. See Figure 15.22.

Figure 15.22   General Journal: recording Fuel Tax Credits

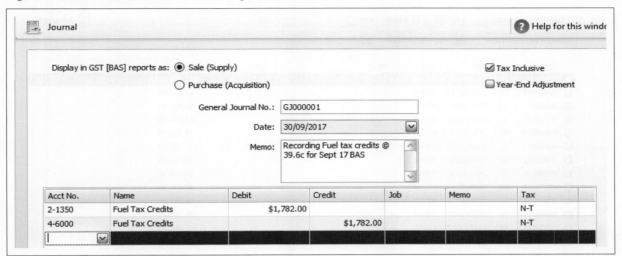

5 Produce the following reports for the period 1 July to 30 September 2017 and perform the following checks:
- Transaction Tax Codes report. Investigate any anomalies in the last three tax column. Check that the tax on farm income transactions is FRE.
- Sales [Customer Summary] report. Check that all sales invoices are closed (have been paid).
- Purchases [Supplier Summary] report. Check that all purchases invoices are closed (have been paid).

6 All Kiosk sales have been credited to account 4-5100 Sales using the tax code GST. The FRE portion of these sales was calculated as 40% using the Snapshot method and needs to be altered in MYOB.

Click...
- *Find Transactions*.
- *Account* (tab at the top) and select *4-5100 Kiosk Sales*.
- *Dated From* (type 1/7/17 and *To* (type 30/9/17). See Figure 15.23. Note that all of the invoices are credits in this account. Look at the total credits at the bottom of the screen (Figure 15.23) and multiply by 40% to work out the GST-free portion in dollar terms. $115 654.55 × 40% = $46 261.82.
- *Close* (to return to the Command Centre).
- *Record Journal Entry* (in the Accounts module). Complete the General Journal as per Figure 15.24. Note the tax codes.

Figure 15.23   Find Transactions: 4-5100 Kiosk Sales

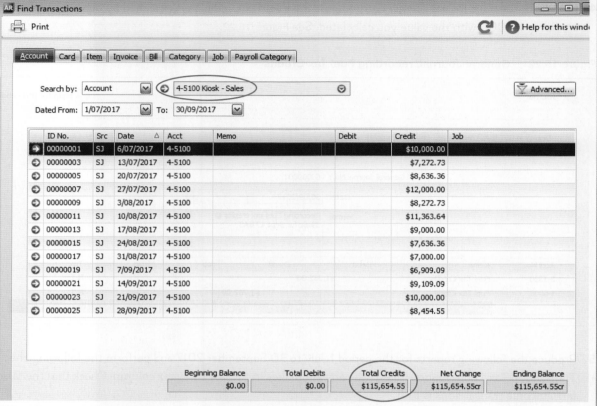

Figure 15.24   General Journal: Move GST sales to FRE sales, Hawkesbury Farm

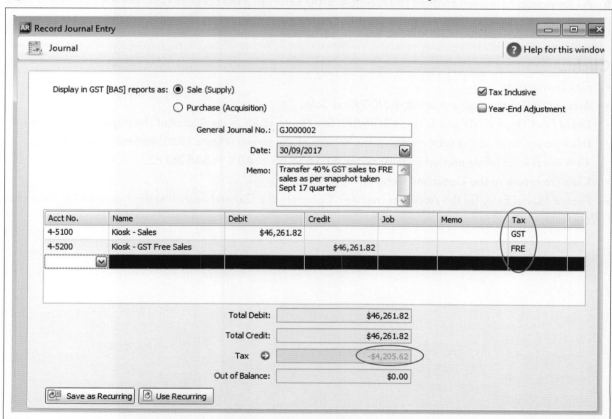

This is why

The tax is negative in this journal because the *Sales (Supply)* radio button is selected at *Display in GST [BAS] reports as* (at the top of the journal). This is correct as we are converting GST sales to FRE sales and are thus reducing the GST collected.

7 Produce the GST [Summary – Cash] report for 1 July to 30 September 2017 Figure 15.25). Note the top line with the **No ABN Withholding**.

• When calculating G11, the tax paid component of the ABN Withholding needs to be *added* to the total purchase value. In this case, G11 would be 6375 + 6125 + 225130 + 59726 = 297356.

• The tax paid component of $6125 will also be entered as a positive at label W4 in our PAYG tax withheld section because it has not been paid to the supplier: it was withheld as he hasn't given an ABN.

Use the rest of the figures to complete the GST worksheet, then transfer the amounts to the activity statement.

Figure 15.25   GST [Summary – Cash]: Hawkesbury Farm

		Hawkesbury Farm				
		Gronos Point				
		via Wilberforce NSW 2756				
		GST [Summary – Cash]				
		July 2017 To September 2017				
Code	**Description**	**Rate**	**Sale Value**	**Purchase Value**	**Tax Collected**	**Tax Paid**
ABN	No ABN Withholding	−49.00%		$6 375.00		($6 125.00)
CAP	Capital Acquisitions	10.00%		$55 000.00		$5 000.00
FRE	GST Free	0.00%	$315 891.82	$225 130.00		
GST	Goods and Services Tax	10.00%	$80 958.18	$59 726.00	$7 359.83	$5 429.63
				Total:	$7 359.83	$4 304.63

8 Display the Profit & Loss [Cash] report for 1 July to 30 September 2017. Use your Total Income figure to complete PAYGI option 2 using the ATO's percentage of 2.1%.

This is why

The Fuel Tax Credit is considered income to the business and forms part of the PAYGI calculation.

9 Transfer your figures to the Summary section of the activity statement. The Fuel Tax Credits are entered into 7D. Calculate the liability. Compare it with the answer in your supplementary materials.

10 Use MYOB's BASlink to set up and then process the September 2017 activity statement. In the BASlink setup screen, insert the ATO's PAYGI rate of 2.1% and tick the appropriate boxes. See Figure 15.26.

Figure 15.26   **BASlink Setup: Hawkesbury Farm**

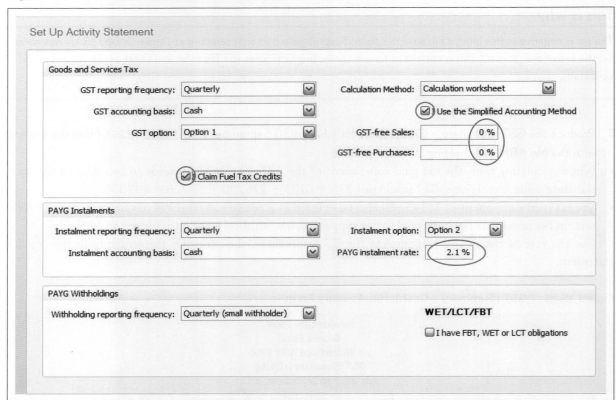

11 Display the Payroll Activity Summary report for July to September 2017. Set up W1, W2 and W4 in your PAYG tax withheld section, using the report to balance, as you have done for all the previous BAS. However, in this instance you will see W4 actually has a number in it for the supplier without an ABN.

12 Set up T1 in your PAYG income tax instalment section. Ensure T1 balances with your total income in your Profit & Loss [Cash].

13 Set up label 7D in your Summary section by clicking on the setup button and linking it to 4-6000 Fuel Tax Credits. See Figure 15.27.

Figure 15.27   **BAS Setup: label 7D, Hawkesbury Farm**

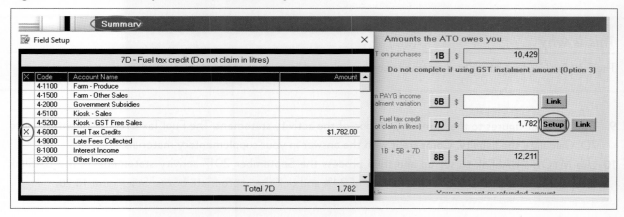

14 Compare the result with your manual work. Investigate and correct any difference.

Processing and recording payments or refunds

The BAS payment or refund will, of course, have to be processed through MYOB once the payment is made or received. Before closing down the BASlink BAS you have just prepared, click on **Transaction** at the bottom of the screen. See Figure 15.28.

Figure 15.28 **BASlink BAS: Transaction button**

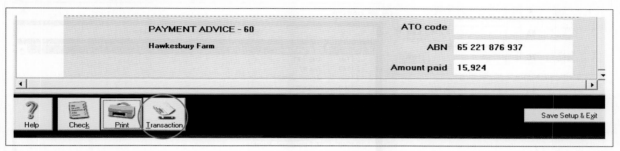

Click...

- *No* (to the message asking if you want to view the error list).
- *No* (to the message asking if you will use the Pay Liabilities function).

A Spend Money screen will open with the transaction that you need to process when paying the BAS. See Figure 15.29.

Figure 15.29 **BASlink Spend Money screen**

Spend Money

Card :	Australian Taxation Office	Cheque No :	1
Payee :	Australian Taxation Office	Date :	23/01/2017
		Amount :	$15,924.00

Fifteen Thousand Nine Hundred and Twenty Four Dollars and 0 Cents

Memo : BAS July 2017 to 30 September 2017   *Hawkesbury Farm*

	Allocation Account	Amount	Job	Tax
2-1210	GST Collected	$7,359.83	———	———
2-1220	GST Paid	-$10,429.63	———	———
2-1320	ABN Withholdings Payable	$6,125.00	———	———
2-1410	PAYG Withholding Payable	$6,435.00	———	———
	Adj - 5A - PAYG Instalment	$8,216.00	———	———
	Adj - 7D - Fuel tax credit	-$1,782.00	———	———
	Rounding, various Adjustments and data entry error	-$0.20	———	———
	Total Allocated	$15,924.00		Tax : $0.00

Notice how the second- and third-to-last transactions haven't been allocated an account code. These two need to be linked to their appropriate account codes so click **Close** to exit the transaction.

Click...

- *Link* (next to the 5A field in the Summary section).
- *Cell in left column* to place an *X* next *to 2-1330 Company Tax Instal.* Payable . See Figure 15.30.
- *OK.*

Figure 15.30   Linking PAYG income tax instalment

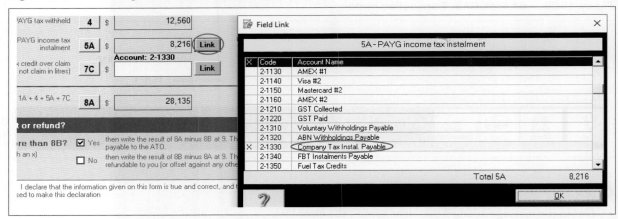

Click...

- *Link* (next to the 7D field in the Summary section).
- *2-1350 Fuel Tax Credits* (an *X* appears in the column to the left). See Figure 15.31.
- *OK.*

Figure 15.31   Linking Fuel Tax Credits

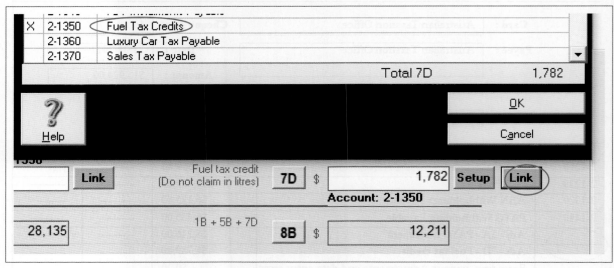

Open your Spend Money by clicking **Transaction** again and note how now the transactions shows account codes for all of the taxes. Also notice that some of these are *negative* and need to be entered as such when processing through Spend Money.

Figure 15.32   **Spend Money screen**

Spend Money					
Card : Australian Taxation Office			**Cheque No :** 1		
Payee : Australian Taxation Office			**Date :** 23/01/2017		
			Amount : $15,924.00		
Fifteen Thousand Nine Hundred and Twenty Four Dollars and 0 Cents					
Memo : BAS July 2017 to 30 September 2017			*Hawkesbury Farm*		

	Allocation Account	Amount	Job	Tax
2-1210	GST Collected	$7,359.83	——	——
2-1220	GST Paid	-$10,429.63	——	——
2-1320	ABN Withholdings Payable	$6,125.00	——	——
2-1330	Company Tax Instal. Payable	$8,216.00	——	——
2-1350	Fuel Tax Credits	-$1,782.00	——	——
2-1410	PAYG Withholding Payable	$6,435.00	——	——
	Rounding, various Adjustments and data entry error	-$0.20	——	——
	Total Allocated	$15,924.00		Tax : $0.00

This completes your instruction for this chapter.

Summary

- ◆ The Simplified Accounting System for BAS was designed to assist certain small retail businesses (those with a SAM or GST turnover of less than $2 million) to account for their GST without having to keep detailed records. Eligibility requirements vary depending on the Simplified Accounting System method chosen.
- ◆ Reports from MYOB provide the information for the basis of the calculations and the results are then entered into MYOB to reflect the changes.
- ◆ Fuel Tax Credits are available to businesses who use fuel for an approved use, such as heavy vehicles used on a public road, households using fuel to generate electricity, and vehicles and machinery used off-road in eligible business activities. Eligible business activities for Fuel Tax Credits include, among others, agriculture, construction, manufacture, marine transport and farm activities.
- ◆ Some fuels are not eligible for the Fuel Tax Credits and there is a different rate for liquid, gas and blended fuels. The rates are updated every February and August.
- ◆ Fringe Benefits are a benefit given to an employee (or their associate) in addition to their wage or salary. An example is the business providing a car where the employee has private use of the vehicle.
- ◆ Fringe Benefits are first grossed up using a different rate for benefits with GST and those without. Then the applicable tax rate is applied against them.
- ◆ If a supplier doesn't provide an ABN, you are required to withhold 49% of their invoice and submit it to the ATO through the BAS. The full amount of their invoice is still deductible for tax purposes.

Assessment

Stock Purchases method

Four Siblings Vietnamese Deli has elected to use the Stock Purchases method of calculating their GST and have been keeping accurate records of their taxable and GST-free stock. Using their Profit & Loss [Cash] extract below, complete the steps that follow.

Four Siblings Vietnamese Deli 29 Oxford Street Leederville WA 6007 Profit & Loss [Cash] July 2017 To September 2017		
Income		
Sales	$63 000.00	
Total Income		$63 000.00
Cost Of Sales		
Taxable Purchases	$4 204.30	
GST Free Purchases	$24 529.00	
Total Cost Of Sales		$28 733.30
Gross Profit		$34 266.70

1 Calculate the purchases percentage that will be applied to the total sales:

Total stock purchases:	
GST-free stock purchases:	
GST-free divided by total purchases and multiplied by 100:	
Apply this percentage to total sales to arrive at your GST Free Percentage	

2 Split up the total sales into GST-free sales and taxable sales:

Total Sales (GST Exclusive)	
GST-free sales (from the calculation above)	
Taxable sales	
GST collected	
Total sales including GST (ignoring cents) =	

3 Record the figures against the appropriate labels:

G1	Total Sales (incl GST)	
G3	GST Free Sales	
1A	GST on Sales	

All Hours Convenience Store

All Hours convenience store sells some basic food and toiletry items as well as preparing takeaway food. It does not sell fuel or alcohol. It uses the Business Norms method of identifying and reporting their GST obligations.

Their spreadsheet has the following information for the BAS period:

Total deposits for sales:	$385 240
Total stock purchases paid:	$100 231

Ignoring cents throughout your calculations, complete the following four steps.

1   Calculate their GST-free sales and purchases according to the Business Norms table:

Total sales:
GST-free sales (% in table):
Total purchases:
GST-free purchases (% in table):

2   Calculate the taxable sales and purchases; then calculate the GST on sales and GST on purchases:

GST-free sales (from calculation above)
Taxable sales (inclusive) $385 240 − 86 679 =
Total sales including GST =
GST collected on taxable sales =
GST-free purchases (from calculation above)
Taxable purchases =
Total stock purchases (including GST) =
Including GST paid

3   Record the figures against the appropriate labels:

Sales		
G1	Total Sales (incl GST)	
G3	GST Free Sales	
1A	GST on Sales	
Purchases		
G11	Total Purchases (incl GST)	
1B	GST on Purchases	

Troy Electrical Services

Troy Electrical Services pays for a gym and tennis membership for one of their employees. Total cost for the year is $2200.00 (including GST). Calculate the Fringe Benefits Tax using the Type 1 gross-up rate of 2.0802 and the 2018 tax rate of 47%.

Annual benefit
Multiplied by grossing-up rate of 2.0802
Multiplied by 47% FBT

A Bit of Everything

A Bit of Everything is a shop that sells a mixture of GST-free and taxable food. They use the Snapshot method of accounting for GST. They kept an accurate record of taxable and GST-free sales over a two-week period and have calculated that the percentages for sales for this BAS period is 45% GST-free.

Their sales account shows $261 000 for the quarter. Calculate the GST-free portion and complete the numbers in the General Journal below:

Code	Account Name	Debit	Credit
4-1000	Sales		
2-1210	GST Collected		
4-2000	GST Free Sales		

INTEGRATED ACTIVITY 1

HOLISTIC REVIEW

Learning outcomes

By the end of this activity you will have demonstrated your competency in:
- creating a new MYOB file
- customising a chart of accounts
- using all of the MYOB modules except payroll and time billing
- understanding the command centres
- processing general journals
- completing bank reconciliations
- producing reports.

This integrated activity incorporates several of the modules and culminates in a bank reconciliation, which assists you in checking your work.

1   In MYOB AccountRight 2016, create a new data file based on the following information, using the AccountRight Plus, Australian version:

The Sports Warehouse Pty. Ltd.
Gap Road
Alice Springs, NT 0870
ABN 32 233 312 123

Phone: (08) 8950 5177
Financial year: 2017
Conversion Month: July
Industry Classification: Wholesale and Export/Import

The main business activity of The Sports Warehouse is the wholesale supply of sporting goods.

2   Make the following changes in the List of Accounts:

	Account type	Account number	New account name	Tax code
Edit	Bank	1-1110	Cheque Account	N-T
Add	Other Asset	1-1315	Provision for Doubtful Debts	N-T
Add	Other Asset	1-1360	Prepayments	N-T
Edit	Equity	3-1000	Owners Capital	N-T
Edit	Income	4-1000	Sales of Apparel	GST
Edit	Income	4-2000	Sales of Equipment	GST
Add	Income	4-9000	Discounts Received	GST
Edit	Cost of Sales	5-1000	Purchases of Apparel	GST
Edit	Cost of Sales	5-2000	Purchases of Equipment	GST
Edit	Cost of Sales	5-9000	Discounts Given	GST
Edit	Expense	6-2800	Machinery & Equipment Lease	GST
Edit	Expense	6-2900	Motor Vehicle Lease	GST

Change the linked accounts:

Type	Terms	From	To
Sales	I give discounts for early payment	6-3400 Discounts Given	5-9000 Discounts Given
Purchases	I take discounts for early payment	5-6000 Discounts Received	4-9000 Discounts Received

Then make the following changes:

	Account type	Account number	New account name
Delete	Expense	6-3400	Discounts Given
Delete	Cost of Sales	5-6000	Discounts Received

3   Insert the following account opening balances:

Account no.	Account name	Debit	Credit
1-1110	Cheque	67 000.00	
1-1310	Trade Debtors	11 000.00	
1-1320	Inventory	30 000.00	
1-2110	Plant & Equipment at cost	5 000.00	
1-2310	Office Equipment at cost	3 000.00	
2-1210	GST Collected		1 000.00
2-1220	GST Paid	1 500.00	
2-1510	Trade Creditors		16 500.00
2-2100	Business Loan #1		50 000.00
3-1000	Owners Capital		50 000.00
		$117 500.00	**$117 500.00**

4 Create cards for the following suppliers using Easy Setup Assistant/Purchases. Use an Items purchase layout:

Name:	Adidas Pty. Ltd.
Card ID:	Sup 001
Address:	10 South Street
	Rydalmere, NSW 2116
Terms:	5% 15 days/Net 30
Expense Account:	5-1000
Credit Limit:	$20 000.00
ABN:	18 103 083 318

Name:	Nike Australia P/L
Card ID:	Sup 002
Address:	483 Parramatta Rd
	Leichhardt, NSW 2040
Terms:	5% 15 days/Net 30
Expense Account:	5-1000
Credit Limit:	$20 000.00
ABN:	23 404 204 332

Name:	Sports Medical Aids Co.
Card ID:	Sup 003
Address:	6 Goobarah Rd
	Cronulla, NSW 2230
Terms:	5% 15 days/Net 30
Expense Account:	5-2000
Credit Limit:	$20 000.00
ABN:	66 151 053 356

Name:	VIP Sports Pty. Ltd.
Card ID:	Sup 004
Address:	30 Johns Rd
	Heidelberg West, Vic 3081
Terms:	5% 15 days/Net 30
Expense Account:	5-2000
Credit Limit:	$20 000.00
ABN:	35 135 535 153

5 Record the outstanding supplier balances in the Historical Purchases section in June 2016:

Date:	30 June
Tax Invoice No.:	101551
Supplier:	Adidas Pty. Ltd.
Details:	
50 pr Sports Shorts @ $30.00	$1 500.00
20 pr Adidas Shoes @ $110.00	$2 200.00
15 Track Suits @ $250.00	$3 750.00
Sales Total:	$7 450.00
Freight:	$50.00
GST:	$750.00
Invoice Total:	$8 250.00
5% 15 days/Net 30	

Date:	30 June
Tax Invoice No.:	550987
Supplier:	Nike Australia Pty. Ltd.
Details:	
500 Baseball Caps @ $10.00	$500.00
15 pr Nike Sports Shoes @ $210.00	$3 150.00
Sales Total:	$3 650.00
Freight:	$100.00
GST:	$375.00
Invoice Total:	$4 1250.00
5% 15 days/Net 30	

Date:	10 July
Tax Invoice No.:	339021
Supplier:	Sports Medical Aids Co. Pty. Ltd.
Details:	
2 First Aid Kits @ $100.00	$200.00
10 Massage Kits @ $170.00	$1 700.00
Sales Total:	$1 900.00
Freight:	$100.00
GST:	$200.00
Invoice Total:	$2 200.00
5% 15 days/Net 30	

Date:	30 June
Tax Invoice No.:	002501
Supplier:	VIP Sports Pty. Ltd.
Details:	
10 Footballs @ $40.00	$400.00
40 Soccer Balls @ $30.00	$1 200.00
Sales Total:	$1 600.00
Freight:	$150.00
GST:	$175.00
Invoice Total:	$1 925.00
5% 15 days/Net 30	

6 Create cards for the following customers through Easy Setup Assistant/Sales. Use the Item invoice layout:

Name:	Dept. of Education
Card ID:	Cus 001
Address:	93 Mitchell Street
	Darwin, NT 0800
Phone:	(08) 9813 3901
Contact:	Cherry Small
Credit Limit:	$50 000.00
Terms:	10% 10 days/Net 30

Name:	Katherine Sports Store
Card ID:	Cus 002
Address:	47 Giles Street
	Katherine, NT 0850
Phone:	(08) 9722 7272
Contact:	David Cheng
Credit Limit:	$20 000.00
Terms:	10% 10 days/Net 30

Name:	Tennant Creek Sports
Card ID:	Cus 003
Address:	101 Paterson Street
	Tennant Creek, NT 0860
Phone:	(08) 9622 2402
Contact:	Clive Martin
Credit Limit:	$20 000.00
Terms:	10% 10 days/Net 30

Name:	Todd Sports Store
Card ID:	Cus 004
Address:	Todd Mall
	Alice Springs, NT 0870
Phone:	(08) 9850 5128
Contact:	Jenny Millington
Credit Limit:	$20 000.00
Terms:	10% 10 days/Net 30

7 Record the following historical sales:

The Sports Warehouse
ABN 32 233 312 123

Tax Invoice Number: 1015
Date: 30 April
Customer: Dept. of Education

No.	Item	Price
10	Tracksuits	$3 850.00
10	Adidas sports shoes	$1 650.00
Delivery:		0.00
Invoice Total:		$5 500.00

(Invoice includes $500.00 GST)
10%/10 Net 30

The Sports Warehouse
ABN 32 233 312 123

Tax Invoice Number: 1083
Date: 31 May
Customer: Katherine Sports

No.	Item	Price
25	T-Shirts	$2 475.00
10	Track Suits	3 850.00
5	First Aid Kits	770.00
Delivery:		55.00
Invoice Total:		$2 750.00

(Invoice includes $250.00 GST)
10%/10 Net 30

The Sports Warehouse
ABN 32 233 312 123

Tax Invoice Number: 1101
Date: 11 June
Customer: Tennant Creek Sports

No.	Item	Price
10	Footballs	$660.00
5	Soccer Balls	275.00
30	Baseball Caps	495.00
3	Massage Kits	676.50
Delivery:		132.00
Invoice Total:		$1 650.00

(Invoice includes $150.00 GST)
10%/10 Net 30

The Sports Warehouse
ABN 32 233 312 123

Tax Invoice Number: 1102
Date: 30 June
Customer: Todd Sports Store

No.	Item	Price
20	T-Shirts	$1 980.00
10	pr Adidas Shoes	1 650.00
10	pr Nike Shoes	3 080.00
20	Baseball Caps	330.00
Delivery:		0.00
Invoice Total:		$1 100.00

(Invoice includes $100.00 GST)
10%/10 Net 30

8 Set up the following inventory items:

Item Number:	A-101
Item Name:	T-Shirt
Cost of Sales Account:	5-1000
Income Account:	4-1000
Inventory Account:	1-1320
Buying Unit of Measure:	Each
Items per Buying Unit:	1
Tax Code:	GST
Minimum Stock Level:	20
Primary Supplier:	Adidas Pty. Ltd.
Default Reorder Quantity:	100
Base Selling Price:	$99.00 incl GST
Selling Unit of Measure:	Each

Item Number:	A-111
Item Name:	Sports Shorts
Cost of Sales Account:	5-1000
Income Account:	4-1000
Inventory Account:	1-1320
Buying Unit of Measure:	Pair
Items per Buying Unit:	1
Tax Code:	GST
Minimum Stock Level:	20
Primary Supplier:	Adidas Pty. Ltd.
Default Reorder Quantity:	100
Base Selling Price:	$55.00 incl GST
Selling Unit of Measure:	Pair

Item Number:	A-121
Item Name:	Track Suit
Cost of Sales Account:	5-1000
Income Account:	4-1000
Inventory Account:	1-1320
Buying Unit of Measure:	Each
Items per Buying Unit:	1
Tax Code:	GST
Minimum Stock Level:	20
Primary Supplier:	Adidas Pty. Ltd.
Default Reorder Quantity:	100
Base Selling Price:	$385.00 incl GST
Selling Unit of Measure:	Each

Item Number:	A-131
Item Name:	Adidas Sports Shoes
Cost of Sales Account:	5-1000
Income Account:	4-1000
Inventory Account:	1-1320
Buying Unit of Measure:	Pair
Items per Buying Unit:	1
Tax Code:	GST
Minimum Stock Level:	20
Primary Supplier:	Adidas Pty. Ltd.
Default Reorder Quantity:	100
Base Selling Price:	$165.00 incl GST
Selling Unit of Measure:	Pair

Item Number:	A-201
Item Name:	Baseball Cap
Cost of Sales Account:	5-1000
Income Account:	4-1000
Inventory Account:	1-1320
Buying Unit of Measure:	Each
Items per Buying Unit:	1
Tax Code:	GST
Minimum Stock Level:	20
Primary Supplier:	Nike Australia P/L
Default Reorder Quantity:	100
Base Selling Price:	$16.50 incl GST
Selling Unit of Measure:	Each

Item Number:	A-231
Item Name:	Nike Sports Shoes
Cost of Sales Account:	5-1000
Income Account:	4-1000
Inventory Account:	1-1320
Buying Unit of Measure:	Pair
Items per Buying Unit:	1
Tax Code:	GST
Minimum Stock Level:	20
Primary Supplier:	Nike Australia
Default Reorder Quantity:	100
Base Selling Price:	$308.00 incl GST
Selling Unit of Measure:	Pair

Item Number:	E-501
Item Name:	Football
Cost of Sales Account:	5-2000
Income Account:	4-2000
Inventory Account:	1-1320
Buying Unit of Measure:	Each
Items per Buying Unit:	1
Tax Code:	GST
Minimum Stock Level:	10
Primary Supplier:	VIP Sports P/L
Default Reorder Quantity:	50
Base Selling Price:	$66.00 incl GST
Selling Unit of Measure:	Each

Item Number:	E-511
Item Name:	Soccer Ball
Cost of Sales Account:	5-2000
Income Account:	4-2000
Inventory Account:	1-1320
Buying Unit of Measure:	Each
Items per Buying Unit:	1
Tax Code:	GST
Minimum Stock Level:	10
Primary Supplier:	VIP Sports P/L
Default Reorder Quantity:	20
Base Selling Price:	$55.00 incl GST
Selling Unit of Measure:	Each

Item Number:	E-521		Item Number:	E-531
Item Name:	First Aid Kit		Item Name:	Massage Kit
Cost of Sales Account:	5-2000		Cost of Sales Account:	5-2000
Income Account:	4-2000		Income Account:	4-2000
Inventory Account:	1-1320		Inventory Account:	1-1320
Buying Unit of Measure:	Each		Buying Unit of Measure:	Each
Items per Buying Unit:	1		Items per Buying Unit:	1
Tax Code:	GST		Tax Code:	GST
Minimum Stock Level:	10		Minimum Stock Level:	10
Primary Supplier:	Sports Medical Aids		Primary Supplier:	Sports Medical Aids
Default Reorder Quantity:	50		Default Reorder Quantity:	40
Base Selling Price:	$154.00 incl GST		Base Selling Price:	$225.50 incl GST
Selling Unit of Measure:	Each		Selling Unit of Measure:	Each

9   Enter the quantity of each item on hand as at 1/7/16 with their opening balances below. Use 1-1320 Inventory as the default adjustment account.

Item	Name	Units on hand	Cost (Excl GST)	Total
A-101	T Shirt	100	50.00	5 000.00
A-111	Sports Shorts	65	30.00	1 950.00
A-121	Track Suit	35	250.00	8 750.00
A-131	Adidas Sports Shoes	17	110.00	1 870.00
A-201	Baseball Cap	75	10.00	750.00
A-231	Nike Sports Shoes	32	210.00	6 720.00
E-501	Football	35	40.00	1 400.00
E-511	Soccer Ball	12	30.00	360.00
E-521	First Aid Kit	15	100.00	1 500.00
E-531	Massage Kit	10	170.00	1 700.00
			TOTAL	**30 000.00**

10 Use Spend Money in the Banking module to process the cheque below for 12 months' business insurance. Create a supplier card called *Global Insurance* and post to the prepayments asset account.

Date:	1/7/16
Cheque No:	00135
Payee:	Global Insurance
Details:	
12 months' business insurance	
Amount:	$2 640.00
Dissection	
Prepayments	2 400.00
GST Component:	240.00
Total:	2 640.00

11 Record the following July transactions

Receipts

(Use Undeposited Funds/Bank Deposits for receipts with the same date).

Date:	06/7/16
Receipt No:	025
Received from:	Dept. of Education
Details:	
All invoices	
Cash Received:	$5 500.00
Dissection	
Discount:	
GST Component:	
Discount Total:	0.00

Date:	06/7/16
Receipt No:	026
Received from:	Katherine Sports Store
Details:	
All invoices	
Cash Received:	$2 750.00
Dissection	
Discount:	
GST Component:	
Discount Total:	0.00

Date:	08/7/16
Receipt No:	027
Received from:	Tennant Creek Sports
Details:	
All invoices after prompt payment discount	
Cash Received:	$1 485.00
Dissection	
Discount:	150.00
GST Component:	15.00
Discount Total:	165.00

Date:	09/7/CY
Receipt No:	028
Received from:	Todd Sports Store
Details:	
All invoices after prompt payment discount	
Cash Received:	$990.00
Dissection	
Discount:	100.00
GST Component:	10.00
Discount Total:	110.00

Cheques

Date:	6/7/16
Cheque No:	00136
Payee:	Adidas
Details:	
Payment of all invoices with prompt payment discount	
Amount:	$7 837.50
Dissection	
Discount:	375.00
GST Component:	37.50
Discount Total:	412.50

Date:	6/7/16
Cheque No:	00137
Payee:	Nike
Details:	
Payment of all invoices with prompt payment discount	
Amount:	$3 918.75
Dissection	
Discount:	187.50
GST Component:	18.75
Discount Total:	206.25

Date:	6/7/16
Cheque No:	00138
Payee:	Sports Medical Aids
Details:	
Payment of all invoices with prompt payment discount	
Amount:	$2 090.00

Dissection	
Discount:	100.00
GST Component:	10.00
Discount Total:	110.00

Date:	6/7/16
Cheque No:	00139
Payee:	VIP Sports
Details:	
Payment of all invoices with prompt payment discount	
Amount:	$1 828.50

Dissection	
Discount:	87.50
GST Component:	8.75
Discount Total:	96.25

Credit Purchases

Date:	10 July 16
Tax Invoice No.:	101632
Supplier:	Adidas Pty. Ltd.
Details:	
60 pr Sports Shorts @ $30.00	$1 800.00
20 pr Adidas Shoes @ $110.00	$2 200.00
10 Track Suits @ $250.00	$2 500.00
Sales Total:	$6 500.00
Freight:	$125.00
GST:	$662.50
Invoice Total:	$7 287.50
5% 15 days/Net 30	

Date:	10 July 16
Tax Invoice No.:	551285
Supplier:	Nike Australia Pty. Ltd.
Details:	
100 Baseball Caps @ $10.00	$1 000.00
20 pr Nike Sports Shoes @ $210.00	$4 200.00
Sales Total:	$5 200.00
Freight:	$55.00
GST:	$525.50
	$5 780.50
5% 15 days/Net 30	

Date:	11 July 16
Tax Invoice No.:	339021
Supplier:	Sports Medical Aids Co. Pty. Ltd.
Details:	
30 First Aid Kits @ $100.00	$3 000.00
20 Massage Kits @ $170.00	$3 400.00
Sales Total:	$6 400.00
Freight:	$145.00
GST:	$654.50
Invoice Total:	$7 199.50
5% 15 days/Net 30	

Date:	12 July
Tax Invoice No.:	002647
Supplier:	VIP Sports Pty. Ltd.
Details:	
60 Footballs @ $40.00	$2 400.00
50 Soccer Balls @ $30.00	$1 500.00
Sales Total:	$3 900.00
Freight:	$62.00
GST:	$396.20
Invoice Total:	$4 358.20
5% 15 days/Net 30	

Credit Sales

<table>
<tr><td colspan="3" align="center">**The Sports Warehouse**
ABN 32 233 312 123</td></tr>
<tr><td>**Tax Invoice Number:** 1105</td><td></td><td></td></tr>
<tr><td>**Date:**</td><td>14 July 16</td><td></td></tr>
<tr><td>**Customer:**</td><td>Dept. of Education</td><td></td></tr>
<tr><td>No.</td><td>Item</td><td>Price</td></tr>
<tr><td>25</td><td>Footballs</td><td>$1 650.00</td></tr>
<tr><td>10</td><td>Soccer Balls</td><td>550.00</td></tr>
<tr><td>**Delivery:**</td><td></td><td>28.00</td></tr>
<tr><td>**Invoice Total:**</td><td></td><td>$2 228.00</td></tr>
<tr><td colspan="3">(Invoice includes $202.55 GST)</td></tr>
<tr><td colspan="3">10%/10 Net 30</td></tr>
</table>

<table>
<tr><td colspan="3" align="center">**The Sports Warehouse**
ABN 32 233 312 123</td></tr>
<tr><td>**Tax Invoice Number:** 1106</td><td></td><td></td></tr>
<tr><td>**Date:**</td><td>14 July 16</td><td></td></tr>
<tr><td>**Customer:**</td><td>Katherine Sports</td><td></td></tr>
<tr><td>No.</td><td>Item</td><td>Price</td></tr>
<tr><td>25</td><td>T-Shirts</td><td>$2 475.00</td></tr>
<tr><td>10</td><td>Track Suits</td><td>3 850.00</td></tr>
<tr><td>5</td><td>First Aid Kits</td><td>770.00</td></tr>
<tr><td>**Delivery:**</td><td></td><td>55.00</td></tr>
<tr><td>**Invoice Total:**</td><td></td><td>$7 150.00</td></tr>
<tr><td colspan="3">(Invoice includes $650.00 GST)</td></tr>
<tr><td colspan="3">10%/10 Net 30</td></tr>
</table>

<table>
<tr><td colspan="3" align="center">**The Sports Warehouse**
ABN 32 233 312 123</td></tr>
<tr><td>**Tax Invoice Number:** 1107</td><td></td><td></td></tr>
<tr><td>**Date:**</td><td>15 July 16</td><td></td></tr>
<tr><td>**Customer:**</td><td>Tennant Creek Sports</td><td></td></tr>
<tr><td>No.</td><td>Item</td><td>Price</td></tr>
<tr><td>10</td><td>Footballs</td><td>$660.00</td></tr>
<tr><td>5</td><td>Soccer Balls</td><td>275.00</td></tr>
<tr><td>30</td><td>Baseball Caps</td><td>495.00</td></tr>
<tr><td>3</td><td>Massage Kits</td><td>676.50</td></tr>
<tr><td>**Delivery:**</td><td></td><td>132.00</td></tr>
<tr><td>**Invoice Total:**</td><td></td><td>$2 238.50</td></tr>
<tr><td colspan="3">(Invoice includes $203.50 GST)</td></tr>
<tr><td colspan="3">10%/10 Net 30</td></tr>
</table>

<table>
<tr><td colspan="3" align="center">**The Sports Warehouse**
ABN 32 233 312 123</td></tr>
<tr><td>**Tax Invoice Number:** 1108</td><td></td><td></td></tr>
<tr><td>**Date:**</td><td>17 July 16</td><td></td></tr>
<tr><td>**Customer:**</td><td>Todd Sports Store</td><td></td></tr>
<tr><td>No.</td><td>Item</td><td>Price</td></tr>
<tr><td>20</td><td>T-Shirts</td><td>$1 980.00</td></tr>
<tr><td>10</td><td>pr Adidas Shoes</td><td>1 650.00</td></tr>
<tr><td>10</td><td>pr Nike Shoes</td><td>3 080.00</td></tr>
<tr><td>20</td><td>Baseball Caps</td><td>330.00</td></tr>
<tr><td>**Delivery:**</td><td></td><td>0.00</td></tr>
<tr><td>**Invoice Total:**</td><td></td><td>$7 040.00</td></tr>
<tr><td colspan="3">(Invoice includes $640.00 GST)</td></tr>
<tr><td colspan="3">10%/10 Net 30</td></tr>
</table>

Cheques

<table>
<tr><td>Date:</td><td>13/7/16</td></tr>
<tr><td>**Cheque No:**</td><td>00140</td></tr>
<tr><td>Payee:</td><td>Adidas</td></tr>
<tr><td>Details:</td><td></td></tr>
<tr><td colspan="2">*Payment of all invoices with prompt payment discount*</td></tr>
<tr><td>Amount:</td><td>$6 923.12</td></tr>
<tr><td>**Dissection**</td><td></td></tr>
<tr><td>Discount:</td><td>331.25</td></tr>
<tr><td>GST Component:</td><td>33.13</td></tr>
<tr><td>Discount Total:</td><td>364.38</td></tr>
</table>

<table>
<tr><td>Date:</td><td>13/7/16</td></tr>
<tr><td>**Cheque No:**</td><td>00141</td></tr>
<tr><td>Payee:</td><td>Nike</td></tr>
<tr><td>Details:</td><td></td></tr>
<tr><td colspan="2">*Payment of all invoices with prompt payment discount*</td></tr>
<tr><td>Amount:</td><td>$5 491.47</td></tr>
<tr><td>**Dissection**</td><td></td></tr>
<tr><td>Discount:</td><td>262.75</td></tr>
<tr><td>GST Component:</td><td>26.28</td></tr>
<tr><td>Discount Total:</td><td>289.03</td></tr>
</table>

Date:	13/7/16
Cheque No:	00142
Payee:	VIP Sports
Details:	
Payment of all invoices with prompt payment discount	
Amount:	$4 140.29

Dissection	
Discount:	198.10
GST Component:	19.81
Discount Total:	217.91

Receipts

(Use Undeposited Funds/Bank Deposits for receipts with the same date).

Date:	21/7/16
Receipt No:	028
Received from:	Dept. of Education
Details:	
All invoices with prompt payment discount	
Cash Received:	$2 005.20

Dissection	
Discount:	208.00
GST Component:	20.80
Discount Total:	222.80

Date:	22/7/16
Receipt No:	029
Received from:	Katherine Sports Store
Details:	
All invoices with prompt payment discount	
Cash Received:	$6 435.00

Dissection	
Discount:	650.00
GST Component:	65.00
Discount Total:	715.00

Date:	22/7/16
Receipt No:	030
Received from:	Tennant Creek Sports
Details:	
All invoices after prompt payment discount	
Cash Received:	$2 014.65

Dissection	
Discount:	203.50
GST Component:	20.35
Discount Total:	223.85

Date:	26/7/16
Receipt No:	031
Received from:	Todd Sports Store
Details:	
All invoices after prompt payment discount	
Cash Received:	$6 336.00

Dissection	
Discount:	640.00
GST Component:	64.00
Discount Total:	704.00

Cash Purchases

Using Enter Purchases and the Paid Today field.

Date:	26 July 16	
Tax Invoice No.:	551358	
Supplier:	Nike Australia Pty. Ltd.	
Details:	50% Discount taken on these *Cash Specials*.	
200 Baseball Caps @ $5.00		$1 000.00
20 pr Nike Sports Shoes @ $105.00		$2 100.00
Sales Total:		$3 100.00
Freight:		$60.00
GST:		$316.00
Total Sales:		$3 476.00
Paid Today by Cheque:		$3 476.00
Balance Owing:		$0.00
Cash Specials		

Date:	31 July 16	
Tax Invoice No.:	339156	
Supplier:	Sports Medical Aids Co. Pty. Ltd.	
Details:	25% Discount taken on these *Cash Specials*.	
20 First Aid Kits @ $75.00		$1 500.00
20 Massage Kits @ $127.50		$2 550.00
Sales Total:		$4 050.00
Freight:		$105.00
GST:		$415.50
Total Sales:		$4 570.50
Paid Today by Cheque:		$4 570.50
Balance Owing:		$0.00
Cash Specials		

Cash Sales

Using Enter Sales and the Paid Today field (insert the discount % in the discount column).

The Sports Warehouse
ABN. 32 233 312 123

Tax Invoice Number:	1113	
Date:	29 July 16	
Customer:	Dept. of Education	
	25% Off *Cash Specials*	

No.	Item	Price
40	T-Shirts	$2 970.00
40	Sports Shorts	1 650.00
40	Baseball Caps	495.00
Delivery:		0.00
Total Sales:		$5 115.00
Paid Today:		$5 115.00
Balance Owing:		$0.00
(Invoice includes $465.00 GST)		
Cash Specials		

The Sports Warehouse
ABN. 32 233 312 123

Tax Invoice Number:	1114	
Date:	31 July	
Customer:	Katherine Sports	
	25% Off *Cash Specials*	

No.	Item	Price
10	Massage Kits	$1 691.25
30	Sports Shorts	1 237.50
20	Soccer Balls	825.00
Delivery:		0.00
Total Sales:		$3 753.75
Paid Today:		$3 753.75
Balance Owing:		$0.00
(Invoice includes $341.25 GST)		
Cash Specials		

12 Record the following General Journals on 31 July.
- Depreciation: Plant & Equipment $104.00, Office Equipment $43.75.
- Expense the monthly prepayment: Business Insurance $200
- Provision for doubtful debts: increase by $100.00

13 Reconcile your records with the following bank statement:

Which? Bank
Gap Road, Alice Springs NT 0800
Statement of Account for The Sports Warehouse Pty. Ltd.
July

Date	Details	Withdrawals	Deposits	Balance
01	Balance b/f			$67 000.00 Cr
01	Cheque book fee	15.00		66 985.00 Cr
03	Cheque 00135	2 640.00		64 345.00 Cr
06	Deposit		8 250.00	72 595.00 Cr
08	Deposit		1 485.00	74 080.00 Cr
	Cheque 00136	7 837.50		66 242.50 Cr
09	Cheque 00139	1 828.75		64 413.75 Cr
	Cheque 00138	2 090.00		62 323.75 Cr
10	Deposit		990.00	63 313.75 Cr
	Cheque 00137	3 918.75		59 395.00 Cr
14	Cheque 00142	4 140.29		55 254.71 Cr
	Cheque 00140	6 923.12		48 331.59 Cr
21	Deposit		2 005.20	50 336.79 Cr
22	Deposit		8 449.65	58 786.44 Cr
26	Deposit		6 336.00	65 122.44 Cr
	Cheque 00143	3 476.00		61 646.44 Cr
29	Deposit		5 115.00	66 761.44 Cr
31	Interest		30.24	66 791.68 Cr
30	**Statement Closing Balance**			**$66 791.68 Cr**

15 Set up BASlink, reporting the GST on a monthly cash basis. Prepare a BAS for July 16. Print the BAS by clicking on the Print button, bottom right hand side.

16 Produce the following reports:
  - Bank Reconciliation Report for Cheque Account for July
  - Trial Balance for July
  - All Transaction Journals for July
  - GST [Summary – Cash], 1 to 31 July.

  Suggested solutions are in the Instructor's support material.

INTEGRATED ACTIVITY 2

PAYROLL

Learning outcomes

By the end of this activity you will have demonstrated your competency in:

- using MYOBs Easy Setup Assistant for Payroll
- entering company payroll details correctly
- entering employee details correctly
- accurately entering timesheet information and process payroll.

This activity uses a mixture of concepts learned in the payroll Chapters 12 and 13. Particular attention needs to be given to the interpretation of the timesheets, as some payroll hours are entered through Enter Timesheets and some through Process Payroll.

1 In MYOB AccountRight 2016 open the The Stylish Stalk.myox data file from the Integrated Exercise folder of your startup files.
2 Set up Payroll for The Stylish Stalk by using the Easy Setup Assistant for payroll:
   – Load the tax tables. You may need to do this twice in order to get the screen telling you that the tax tables from 1/10/16 are being loaded.

The company

• Current Payroll year is 2017.
• The normal hours worked per week is 37.5.
• Default superannuation fund is Australian Super (Easy Add).
• Round pay down to 0 cents.

Wages

• Create an Overtime (1.25x) Rate (Hourly. Regular Rate times 1.25).
• Create Casual Rate A (a Fixed Rate of $35.00 per hour).
• Create Casual Rate B (a Fixed Rate of $45.00 per hour).
• Create Laundry Allowance (type of wage: salary).

Superannuation

• Salary Sacrifice: Linked payable account is 2-1420 and calculation basis is User-Entered amount per pay period.
• Superannuation guarantee: Linked Expense Account is 6-4300, Linked Payable about is 2-1420, the calculation basis is 9.5%.
• Exempt the following from superannuation guarantee in addition to those already ticked: Overtime (1.25x), laundry allowance.

Entitlements (full-time employees only)

• Both Annual and Personal leave accrual: exempt the following: Annual Leave Loading, Backpay, CDEP Payments, all the Overtime wages, Unused Annual and Unused Long Service Leave.
• Create two new entitlements by clicking New Entitlement (no exemptions necessary):
   – Annual Leave Accrual (salary): Calculation Basis equals 5.7692 per pay period, tick the print on pay advice box, Linked Wages Category is Annual Leave Pay.
   – Personal Leave Accrual (salary): Calculation Basis equals 2.8846 per pay period, Linked Wages Category is Personal Leave Pay.

Deductions

• Add a Health Fund: Linked Payable account is 2-1440 and it is a (user-entered) deduction.
• Edit the Union Fee: Linked Payable account is 2-1480 and the rate is $6.00 per pay period.

Expenses

- WorkCover Insurance rate: Linked expense account is 6-4200, Linked Payable account is 2-1450 and it equals 2% of gross wages.

Taxes

- Check the tax tables have loaded correctly by clicking on *Setup* and *General Payroll Information*.
3 Create cards for the following four employees, and note:
  - All employees are entitled to Superannuation Guarantee and WorkCover Insurance.
  - Only the *hourly* full-time employees are entitled to:
    - Wages: Base Hourly, Annual Leave Loading, Annual Leave, all the overtimes and Personal Leave (and whatever their allowances are on their Employee Card).
    - Entitlements: Annual Leave Accrual, and Personal Leave Accrual.
  - Only the *salary* employees are entitled to:
    - Wages: Base Salary, Annual Leave and Personal Leave (and whatever their allowances are on their Employee Card).
    - Entitlements: Annual Leave Accrual (salary), and Personal Leave Accrual (salary).
  - The details of the allowances and deductions for each employee can be found in their employee cards. Tick the applicable allowances in the wages area and the applicable deductions in the deductions area. Enter the amounts in the standard pay area.
  - The year-to-date histories after the employee cards need to be entered into the appropriate section.
  - Timesheets are used for Payroll and are *only* used for overtime and casual rates. The rest of the information from the timesheets is entered through Process Payroll. The week starts on Monday.

Name:	Beau MICHAELS
Card ID:	E 001
Start:	23/02/12
Address:	35 Rokeby Street, BURNLEY, VIC 3121
Pay Type:	Salary
Pay Rate:	$80 000.00 pa
Pay Frequency:	fortnightly
Allowances:	
Super Fund:	Australian Super
Member No.:	165 348
Tax File No.:	311 050 122
Threshold Claimed?:	Yes
Total Rebate:	$624.00 pa
Deductions:	Health Fund $34.00 pf
	Salary Sacrifice $150.00 pf

Name:	Gus POULOS
Card ID:	E 001
Start:	26/05/13
Address:	21 Stock Avenue, BURNLEY, VIC 3121
Pay Type:	Hourly (Full time)
Pay Rate:	$35.00 ph
Pay Frequency:	fortnightly
Allowances:	Laundry $50.00 pf
Super Fund:	Media Super
Member No.:	324681
Tax File No.:	202 142 331
Threshold Claimed?:	Yes
Total Rebate:	$572.00 pa
Deductions:	Union Fee
	Health Fund $18.00 pf

Name:	Milton BRELLIM		Name:	Gael MATTHEWS
Card ID:	E 004		Card ID:	E 005
Start:	15/3/14		Start:	1/7/15
Address:	18 Churchill Ave, FAIRFIELD VIC 3078		Address:	12A Notting Street, FAIRFIELD, VIC 3708
Pay Type:	Hourly (Casual)		Pay Type:	Hourly (Casual)
Pay Rate:	$30.00		Pay Rate:	$28.00
Pay Frequency:	fortnightly		Pay Frequency:	fortnightly
Extra Pay Rates:	Both Casual rates, Overtime (1.25x)		Extra Pay Rates:	Both Casual rates, Overtime (1.25x)
Super Fund:	Australian Super		Super Fund:	Media Super
Member No.:	523 457		Member No.:	437162
Tax File No.:	606 210 153		Tax File No.:	213 564 771
Tax:	Tax Free Threshold		Tax:	Tax Free Threshold
Threshold Claimed?:	Yes		Threshold Claimed?:	Yes
Total Rebate:	$1300.00 pa		Total Rebate:	N/A
Deductions:	Union Health Fund $12.00 pf		Deductions:	Union Fee

Year-to-date histories

Category	Brellim (Casual)	Matthews (Casual)	Michaels (Salary)	Poulos (Fulltime)
Salary			15384.65	
Base Hourly	9840.00	10640.00		15750.00
Annual Leave Loading				459.38
Annual Leave Pay			4918.29	2625.00
Casual Rate A	420.00	700.00		
Casual Rate B	2160.00	1800.00		
Laundry Allowance				300.00
Overtime (1.25x)	525.00	420.00		
Overtime (1.5x)				2800.00
Overtime (2x)				1960.00
Personal Leave Pay			1229.57	
Health Fund	84.00		238.00	126.00
Union Fee	42.00	42.00		42.00
Salary Sacrifice (Super)			1050.00	
PAYG Withholding	1558.00	1722.00	4998.00	4378.00
Entitlements				
Annual Leave Accrual – Year To Date			40.38	35.72
– Carry Over (in Entitlements)			15.00	45.00
Personal Leave Accrual – Year To Date			20.19	7.85
– Carry Over (in Entitlements)			75.00	825.00
Employer Expenses				
WorkCover Insurance	258.90	271.20	430.65	477.89
Superannuation Guarantee	1229.78	1288.20	2045.59	2269.96

3 Pay the employees according to the following information for the *fortnightly* pay period 19 September to 2 October (pay date 4 October 2016). Use Enter Timesheets to record the overtime, casual rate A and casual rate B. Use Process Payroll to record any normal hours, annual leave or personal leave:

Employee	Rate	M 19/09	T 20/09	W 21/09	T 22/09	F 23/09	S 24/09	S 25/09	Total
Brellim, M (Casual)	Norm	5	5	5	4	6			25
	Rate A						4		4
	Rate B							4	4
	1.25x					2			2
Matthews, G (Casual)	Norm	5	5	6	4	3			23
	Rate A						4		4
	1.25x					2			2
Michaels, B (Salary)	Salary								
	Sick			7.5					7.5
Poulos, G (Full time)	Full time								
	1.5x						4		4
	2x							4	4

Employee	Rate	M 26/09	T 27/09	W 28/09	T 29/09	F 30/09	S 01/10	S 02/10	Total
Brellim, M (Casual)	Norm	5	5	5	4	6			25
	Rate B							4	4
	1.25x					2			2
Matthews, G (Casual)	Norm	5	5	6	4	3			23
	Rate B							4	4
	1.25x					2			2
Michaels, B (Salary)	Salary								
Poulos, G (Full time)	Full time								
	Sick	7.5							7.5
	1.5x						4		4

4 Gus Poulos is having an operation and will be on personal leave from 3 October to 13 November. Process his personal leave (6 weeks) in advance as a separate pay on 4 October. Delete any allowances as they are not paid during leave.

5 Pay the employees according to the following information for pay period 3 to 16 October (pay date 18 October 2016). Use Enter Timesheets to record the overtime, casual rate A and casual rate B. Use Process Payroll to record any normal hours, annual leave or personal leave:

Employee	Rate	M 03/10	T 14/10	W 05/10	T 06/10	F 07/10	S 08/10	S 09/10	Total
Brellim, M (Casual)	Norm	5	5	5	4	6			25
	Rate A						4		4
	Rate B							4	4
	1.25x					2			2
Matthews, G (Casual)	Norm	5	5	6	4	3			23
	Rate A						4		4
	1.25x					2			2
Michaels, B (Salary)	Salary								
	Annual Leave	7.5	7.5	7.5					22.5

Employee	Rate	M 10/10	T 11/10	W 12/10	T 13/10	F 14/10	S 15/10	S 16/10	Total
Brellim, M (Casual)	Norm	5	5		4	6			20
	Rate B							4	4
	1.25x					2			2
Matthews, G (Casual)	Norm	5	5	6	4	3			23
	Rate A						4		4
	1.25x					2			2
Michaels, B (Salary)	Salary								

6 Create the following supplier cards and pay the liabilities for October 16. Date of payment is 31 October 16:
 – Australian Workers' Union (Union)
 – Medibank Private Pty. Ltd. (Health Fund)
 – Prudent Insurance (WorkCover)
 – Media Super (Superannuation)
 – Australian Super (Superannuation).
7 Produce the following reports for your instructor:
 – Employees/Register Detail (01/07/16 to 31/10/16)
 – Entitlements/Balance Detail (01/10/2016 to 31/10/2016)
 – Employees/Activity Summary (01/10/2016 to 31/10/2016).

INDEX